To Luke, computer expert, pool partner and best friend.
Derek Bosworth

To my wife Sue, for her encouragement.
Peter Dawkins

To Elizabeth, Elvira, Eva and Emma.
Thorsten Stromback

The Economics of the Labour Market

DEREK BOSWORTH, PETER DAWKINS AND
THORSTEN STROMBACK

FINANCIAL TIMES
Prentice Hall

An imprint of Pearson Education
Harlow, England · London · New York · Reading, Massachusetts · San Francisco
Toronto · Don Mills, Ontario · Sydney · Tokyo · Singapore · Hong Kong · Seoul
Taipei · Cape Town · Madrid · Mexico City · Amsterdam · Munich · Paris · Milan

Pearson Education Limited
Edinburgh Gate
Harlow
Essex CM20 2JE
England

and Associated Companies throughout the world

Visit us on the World Wide Web at:
http://www.pearsoneduc.com

First published 1996

British Cataloguing in Publication Data
A catalogue entry for this title is available from the British Library

ISBN: 0582-44377-6

Library of Congress Cataloging-in-Publication Data
A catalog entry for this title is available from the Library of Congress

Set by 30 in 9/11 pt Times
Produced by Pearson Education Asia (Pte) Ltd.
Printed in Singapore (B & Jo)

10 9 8 7 6 5 4 3
04 03 02 01 00

Contents

List of tables

Acknowledgements

During the preparation of the manuscript, many people provided helpful comments. Special thanks go to Rob Wilson for extensive suggestions on a number of chapters. David Bailey and Jackie Lewis also gave constructive criticisms of earlier drafts of the manuscript, and Mark Wooden has been a constant source of useful information.

PART I Introduction

CHAPTER 1 Introduction to labour economics

1 Introduction

Labour economics is concerned with understanding the underlying economic behaviour of individuals, households and firms involved in the supply of and demand for labour services. We will not burden the reader by worrying too much about what is meant by a 'labour market' this early in the book. For the time being it is sufficient to regard it as the 'place' where labour supply and labour demand come together, to determine the prices and quantities of labour services exchanged. We will see, however, that the 'labour market' is quite distinctive, essentially because it is a market for 'human' resources. Much of the rapid development in the economic analysis of labour markets over the last 30 or 40 years is the result of attempts to incorporate the special features of the labour market arising from its 'human' dimensions.

This book adopts a supply and demand framework, which was first formalized by Alfred Marshall and dates back to Adam Smith. In so doing it presents material that has formed the basis of labour economics for a long time. As the book progresses, however, the more modern developments that have greatly influenced and changed traditional analysis are incorporated. In particular, the discussion includes coverage of search theory, internal labour markets, efficiency wages, implicit contracts, segmentation and discrimination.

The framework is also extended to reflect the importance of institutions for the operation of the labour market. In particular, the role of trade unions receives attention at relevant stages in the discussion throughout the book. In addition, the material on trade unions is brought together in a chapter devoted to this topic. The role of government is referred to continually as the book progresses, and as particular policy issues arise. Examples include the effects of taxes and subsidies on labour supply, the role of government in the provision of education and training, and the control of wages as part of macroeconomic policy. Again, the material is brought together in a chapter devoted to this topic, at the end of the book.

2 Some peculiarities of labour as a factor of production

It is useful to start by asking what it is about labour, as opposed to other factors of production, that has led to the development of labour economics as a subject in its own right, with a great deal of quite distinct analysis. There are a number of major peculiarities of labour which help to distinguish it from other factors of production.

1 'The worker sells his work but retains capital in himself' (Marshall, 1890).
2 Each seller of labour possesses subjective preferences about the use to which that labour is put, the location of employment and working conditions.
3 Employers may possess subjective preferences about who they wish to employ.
4 The decisions to supply labour and consume goods are strongly interdependent.
5 The labour supply decisions of persons within the same household are strongly interdependent.
6 The suppliers of labour often form interdependent labour unions, and take collective action in pursuit of their goals. (Buyers of labour services can also band together.)

7 Psychological factors can have an important influence on the relationship between employers and employees. Concepts such as trust, loyalty, fairness and motivation are very important.

Peculiarity 1 was used by Alfred Marshall in order to justify distinguishing labour from other factors of production. What it means is that workers have the ability to provide labour services by virtue of the productive skills they possess. However, while they can sell these services, they cannot sell the human being in which they are embodied. Thus workers and their skills, which can be regarded as 'human capital', cannot be sold in the same way as physical capital. Marshall also stressed a further peculiarity of labour, that the 'seller of labour must deliver it himself'. Both of these characteristics arise out of the preclusion of slavery.

Quite apart from the aptitudes and abilities of different workers, which make them more or less suitable for different types of work (a characteristic which labour has in common with other factors of production), peculiarity 2 points out that a worker will be greatly influenced in the labour supply decision by **perceived**, non-pecuniary advantages and disadvantages of different sorts of work. That is to say that each worker is interested in the total net advantages of a job, which, as Adam Smith (1776) pointed out, will include such things as the 'ease', 'cleanliness' and 'honourableness' of the employment concerned.

Subjective preference may also affect the nature of an employer's demand for labour (peculiarity 3). There may be circumstances in which an employer's choice of who to employ for what wage, is influenced not only by the productive capacity of that worker but by certain other characteristics such as sex or race. Thus employers may subjectively discriminate between units of labour in a way that is quite peculiar to labour as a factor of production.

Peculiarity 4 points out that workers who supply labour services are also consumers who purchase the fruits of labour effort. What is more, the consumption of goods requires both money and time, the availability of which depends on both the quantity and quality of the labour which the worker supplies, and the income derived from that work. Consumption and labour supply decisions are thus simultaneously determined. To complicate matters further, peculiarity 5 indicates that the individual is often part of a wider social unit, such as the family or the household. Thus, the supply and consumption decisions of one person can affect the corresponding decisions of other members of the group. For example, if a husband is made unemployed, this may affect the willingness of the wife to supply her labour services, or vice versa.

The fact that the suppliers of labour often form collective labour unions and take collective action in pursuit of their goals (peculiarity 6), has formed the basis for a large body of theoretical and empirical literature. This work is concerned with the interface between labour economics and industrial relations. In this case, workers form a group that acts as a single seller (i.e. a monopolist). Those who hire labour can also band together and act as if they are a single buyer (i.e. monopsony). Indeed, the existence of monopoly power may encourage the development of monopsony (or vice versa), leading to a situation of 'countervailing power'. With a bilateral monopoly (i.e. a single buyer and single seller of labour services), theories of bargaining become important. The role of unions in the allocation of resources, in particular their potential for raising wages above their competitive market level in the unionized sector and for creating unemployment, became a major issue in the economic and political debate that took place during the 1970s and at the beginning of the 1980s. More recently, attention has switched to the role of unions in encouraging investment in training and in new technology.

The final peculiarity highlighted above, 7, concerned psychological influences on the relationship between employers and employees. Economists had been rather slow to recognize the influence of concepts such as trust, loyalty, fairness and motivation. In part, these factors remain implicit in the underlying utility functions of the individuals making their supply decisions. However, a number of developments in the literature in the 1970s and 1980s (i.e. implicit contract theory and efficiency wage theory) not only recognized the relevance of these concepts, but also tried to explain the economic forces that accompany them.

All of these, in some way, relate to the subjective values and preferences of human beings. This immediately suggests that a range of disciplines and methodological approaches will be relevant. The study of labour markets is not the sole domain of economists; sociologists, geographers, psychologists, etc., all have something important to contribute. The emphasis of this text is primarily the contribution of economic analysis to the understanding of labour markets. Labour economics, however, is more influenced by other disciplines than most other branches of economic analysis.

3 Structure and content of the book

Labour economics contains an analysis of many important economic and social issues. Some of these are of great interest to the population at large, such as the causes of unemployment and the distribution of earnings. Some are of interest in the area of the economics of human resource management, such as the incentive effects of wages and wage payment systems and the determinants of absenteeism. Some relate to important social issues such as sex discrimination in the labour market and the incidence of long-term unemployment.

In an era in which governments are increasingly concerned about productivity and competitiveness, the role of human resources in the process of economic growth is another important aspect of labour economics. Related to this is the value of training and education, not only to individual persons but to society in general, and the role of government in education and training. An allied concern is about the employment implications of technological change. The role of industrial relations structures, especially trade unions, in the labour market, and their effects on wages and productivity, is another important topic.

This book includes material on these and many other economic and social issues, which pertain to the labour market. In order to be able to analyse such issues, labour economics has developed an analytical framework that is built around the supply of and demand for labour.

Parts II and III of the book, therefore, establish the foundations of labour economics by considering labour supply and labour demand, respectively. The starting point for analysing labour supply is the individual choice of whether to participate in the labour market, job choice, how many hours to work and how much effort to impart. In the long run there are also decisions about how much investment to undertake in education and training. Extensions of labour supply theory consider the relationship between household production and labour supply to the market, the household as a decision-making unit and the labour supply decision over the life-cycle.

Labour demand is a derived demand, in that in turn it depends upon product demand. The price that employers are prepared to pay for labour depends upon the price they can get for the product and the productivity of labour. Thus it is necessary to bring together the production function and the product demand curve to derive the firm's demand for labour. Having isolated the firm's labour demand curve, attention turns to the market demand curve and thus to the implications of aggregating across firms to the level of the market. Alternative market structures are also considered. Extensions of labour demand analysis include: a consideration of the distinction between persons and hours and time patterns of work; the distinction between production and non-production workers; multi-period models; and the implications of technological change.

In Part IV of the book, on equilibrium, disequilibrium and adjustment, we bring the supply of and demand for labour services curves together to study the operation of labour markets. We first consider equilibrium wage and employment outcomes under different market structures. We then go on to look at disequilibrium models and finally at adjustment. Adjustment can occur at different speeds and in different ways, with wages not necessarily the primary mechanism which secures the observed labour market outcome. The analytical frameworks developed in this part of the book enable us to consider such issues as the effect of minimum wages on employment.

Part V of the book focuses on a very important aspect of labour economics, which is concerned with human capital investment in education and training. First, we look at this issue from the point of view of the individual. We then go on to look at the market for training and for trained individuals. Finally, we consider the concept of the social rate of return and the role of government in education and training. This enables us to consider some important education and training policy issues associated with imperfections in the 'market for training', and the evaluation of training programmes.

The importance of training is one reason why firms tend to employ many workers for long periods. Thus the conventional spot market analysis that is applied to many transactions and exchanges may not be appropriate for the analysis of many labour market issues. Further, a great deal of labour mobility may be within firms rather than between firms. That is to say that internal labour markets may operate as well as external labour markets.

The employment relationship is very often an 'idiosyncratic exchange' in which it is very difficult, if not impossible, to write down the expectations of employers and employees and not easy to measure the output of employees on a continuous basis. These information imperfections can lead to incentive problems and those of risk bearing which need to be confronted in the employment relationship. Implicit contract theory, efficiency wage theory and the principal–agent models, have been developed to analyse these issues, in addition to the concept of internal labour markets. These aspects of labour economics are considered under the title of the 'employment relationship' in Part VI.

Traditional, mainstream labour economics tends to assume that labour is mobile and competitive forces work to equalize 'net advantages' of alternative forms of employment. Some labour market analysts, however, have been dissatisfied with the mainstream market paradigm and have emphasized the fragmentation of labour markets, the immobility of labour and the tendency for certain groups to get trapped in 'bad jobs'. In Part VII we outline the propositions that have been developed by the 'segmentationists' and review the evidence that has been put forward to support this perspective. An important aspect of the segmentation literature is concerned with discrimination in labour markets, which is therefore also covered in this part of the book. Part VII also examines the very important labour market institution of trade unions. The origin, structure and membership of trade unions, and the industrial relations systems they operate within, are considered. We then extend the discussion to look at the economic theory of unions and bargaining, and the economic effects of unions. The last chapter of Part VII examines the factors that determine the structure of wages and earnings, paying regard to the extent to which competitive forces and non-competitive forces are important. This allows the discussion to examine the importance of discrimination as an influence on earnings and the magnitude of the union mark-up, amongst other things.

Part VIII focuses on what we describe as economic performance and the labour market. These chapters are concerned with such topics as unemployment, inflation, productivity and growth. There is a greater coverage of the macroeconomics of the labour market in Part VIII than elsewhere but microeconomic analysis drawn from earlier parts of the book remains an important ingredient in the analysis. This final part 'closes the system'. While the earlier chapters often focus on the factors impacting on the labour market, the discussion in Part VIII places more emphasis on the impact of labour on various aspects of economic performance.

4 Conclusions

It should be stressed that, throughout the book, we have sought to present a suitable blend of theoretical and empirical content. The analytical framework is provided by the economic theory of labour markets which therefore governs the structure of the book. We believe, however, that it is very important to keep a close eye on the empirical evidence relevant to each topic. To this end we have a number of empirical contributions, such as Chapters 5 and 11, but in many other chapters we seek to provide a blend of theoretical and empirical content. Sometimes our discussion of empirical evidence involves a review of the empirical literature on a particular topic and sometimes it involves particular case studies to bring to life certain aspects of the book. The empirical content of the book is international in its coverage without seeking to be comprehensive, and refers to evidence from many industrialized economies such as the UK, the USA, Australia, Sweden, Germany and Japan, to name but a few. Since the book is published in the UK, a slight bias towards British evidence and British labour market policies is to be found, and since two of the authors are from Australia, there are also quite a few references to that country.

References

Marshall, A. (1948). *Principles of Economics*. 8th Edition. New York: Macmillan. (Reprinted from 1890.)

Smith, A. (1932). *An Inquiry into the Nature and Causes of the Wealth of Nations*. New York: Modern Library, Random House. (Reprinted from 1776.)

PART II Labour Supply

CHAPTER 2 Introduction to labour supply

1 Introduction

This part of the book is concerned with both the theory and evidence of the supply of labour and its various dimensions. These include the supply of persons and hours to the labour market, the intensity of effort associated with these person hours, the nature of the supplier's job choice, the quality of the labour supplied and the associated question of skill acquisition. This chapter introduces some important concepts and distinctions, identifying the various dimensions of labour supply (i.e. the short run and the long run, and the various levels of aggregation at which labour supply can be considered). Chapter 3 considers the basic theory of the individual labour supply decision, including participation in the labour market, and the number of hours of work and how much effort to impart, as well as how much training or education to undertake. Chapter 4 focuses upon household production and considers labour supply decisions in a family context as well as dynamic (or life-cycle) models of labour supply. Finally, Chapter 5 concentrates on providing an overview of the empirical evidence on labour supply.

2 Dimensions of labour supply

2.1 Taxonomy

There are essentially three dimensions to variations in the volume of labour supply in the short run, in particular:

1. the number of persons who supply labour from a population of given size (participation in the labour market);
2. the number of hours supplied by each person to the labour market (the timing of working hours is also an important dimension as is the supply of hours of work to household production);
3. the intensity of effort associated with each 'person hour'.

In the long run there are the issues of the size and structure of the population and the quality of the labour force, which therefore give us two more dimensions to consider, in particular:

4. the number of persons who are available to supply labour, associated with the size and structure of the population due to demographic factors (i.e. births, ageing, deaths, immigration and emigration);
5. the amount of education, training and experience, including learning by doing (which affect the level and nature of skills offered by each individual).

2.2 Participation

The participation decision concerns the willingness of the individual to supply labour at the going (net) wage (we return to this again early in Chapter 3). At any given wage, w, the individual participates if their desired hours of work, H^*, are greater than zero, $H^* > 0$. In general the number of people willing to supply some positive value of hours ($H^* > 0$) is expected to increase with the wage rate offered, as shown in Figure 2.1.

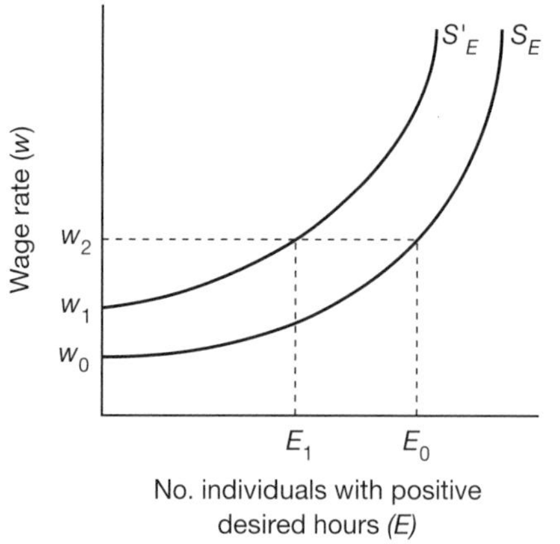

Fig 2.1 Participation: number of individuals with positive desired hours.

We use E to denote the number of individuals and S_E denotes the supply of persons (i.e. the number of persons with positive hours) at different wage rates. Below a wage rate w_0, no one is willing to supply themselves to paid work. As the wage rate rises supply increases, but approaches an upper limit (which may be below the 'technical' maximum formed by a participation rate of 100 per cent).

Various comparative static issues can be dealt with via shifts in the underlying curves. A change in any factor which influences the supply curve other than wage will cause a shift in the curve. An example would be where, say, all jobs become dirtier or riskier, or the individuals' tastes for work or leisure change. If the change has an adverse affect on labour supply, a smaller number of individuals are forthcoming at each wage and the supply curve shifts from S_E to S_E' in Figure 2.1. The minimum wage necessary to produce a positive labour supply rises from w_0 to w_1, and at wage w_2, the number of workers who offer their services falls from E_0 to E_1.

2.3 Hours of (paid) market work

As well as deciding whether to participate in the labour market at all, individuals must also decide how many hours of work they wish to supply, H^*. The choice of the supply of hours, S_H, is likely to be affected by the wage rate. However, an increase in the wage rate may either raise or lower the individual's preferred hours of work. One may be induced to supply more and more hours as the wage rate rises, while another individual might use the increased wage to 'buy' more leisure. For yet other individuals, the supply schedule S_H might be upward sloping for some distance at low wages, but backward sloping at higher wages. It is not immediately clear whether the aggregate supply schedule (i.e. aggregated across individuals) will be positively or negatively sloped. This is an empirical question, which depends on the proportions of individuals with upward- and backward-sloping supply schedules at each wage and the slopes of the individual schedules. The causes of the forward- and backward-sloping supply schedules at the individual level are discussed in detail in Chapter 3.

2.4 Hours of (unpaid) domestic work

The main focus of interest in the labour economics literature has been on the supply of labour to (paid) market work, as opposed to leisure. However, the dichotomy between market work and leisure is simplistic and, in some models, a distinction is made between market (paid) and domestic (unpaid) work. Such models emphasize the fact that a significant proportion of time spent in the home is devoted to domestic chores and household production activities, and that the outputs of these processes are often close substitutes for market-produced goods. We return to this issue in Chapter 4 below.

2.5 Effort

A number of factors are expected to affect the intensity of effort, or the pace of work, including both the basic wage rate and special incentive payments, such as piecework rates. The wage rate can affect effort independently of the existence of an incentive scheme. In particular, when real wages are very low, a wage increase may induce a rise in the intensity of effort, simply because it enables workers to afford a better diet and improved medical care, which allows them to work harder (Liebenstein, 1956). This type of 'efficiency–wage' effect is likely to be particularly important in less developed countries. In developed countries 'efficiency–wage' mechanisms are likely to be somewhat different. A 'pure wage–effort' relationship was enunciated as long ago as 1928 by Lionel Robbins. Robbins' backward- bending supply curve of labour related income to effort and implied that when income reaches a certain level an increase in the wage may result in reduced effort, as the individual trades off extra income against extra effort. A variety of mechanisms have been suggested in the employment contract literature. For example, a wage increase might improve the morale of workers and thereby work intensity (particularly if, prior to this, there was widespread dissatisfaction and disillusionment with the level of wages). In addition higher wages raise the cost of labour to the firm and the cost of job loss to the individual. Under such circumstances, higher wages increase the returns to 'policing' individual effort by the firm and reduce the benefits of 'shirking' to the individual. The various mechanisms linking wages to effort are discussed in more detail in Part VI of the book.

The method of payment may also influence the intensity of effort. Where the individual works alone or independently of other employees, individual piece rates are sometimes used. Where the work is done in teams, group incentives are sometimes used. There are possible social limits to the magnitude of the effect that piece rates might have on productivity. Individuals who are inclined to work at a very rapid pace may be restricted by their fellow workers, who might impose an unofficial quota, which no one is to exceed. Likewise, individuals who put in less effort than the collective norm may also be subjected to social pressure for change as the group rewards are affected.

2.6 Life-cycle aspects of labour supply

The theory of labour supply discussed so far views the supply decision in a static, one-period, or comparative static, two-period framework. Since the 1970s, however, there has developed a major literature focusing on labour supply decisions in a dynamic or life-cycle framework. People have a tendency to supply less labour to the labour market in their early years, more in middle age, and less again later in their lives. Such decisions are affected by their productivity over the life-cycle, by the interest rate and by their rate of 'time preference' (the premium they place on enjoyment of consumption goods immediately rather than in the future).

Another important aspect of decision making in a life-cycle context is how much training and education to undertake, which in turn affects the individual's earning capacity at different ages. In models of life-cycle labour supply in which wages are endogenized, labour supply, investment in education and training, and the lifetime wage path are jointly determined.

2.7 Long-run labour supply

In the short run no allowance is made for decisions which change the size and skills of the population, such as immigration, birth control or education. In this instance, attention focuses on the supply of hours and intensity of effort by a population whose size and skills are given. In the long run the determination of the size and structure of the population provides an added quantitative dimension, and the determination of the capacity or skill of the resultant labour force, which depends upon such things as training and education, adds an extra qualitative dimension. Such training and education decisions are the focus of human capital theory which forms the subject of Part V of the book, but is introduced in Chapter 3.

3 Decision-making units

Chapter 1 suggested that a major distinguishing feature of labour as a factor of production is that it has control over its own supply. Thus, the bulk of labour supply theory treats the individual (person) as the decision-making unit, attempting to choose between hours of work and leisure time to optimize personal utility. However, while recognizing the importance of the individual there are a number of alternative developments in the literature that focus on the individual within some larger decision-making unit. Perhaps the most obvious of these is the issue of the individual in the context of the family or household unit.

The household is seen as a composite of individuals, held together by some common bond (family ties, friendship, economic considerations, etc.). Thus, family units are a sub-set of all households. It is worth adding that we might expect labour supply behaviour to differ depending on the rationale which binds the household unit together. However, for the moment at least we will continue to use the two terms, household and family, interchangeably. The economic theories can be categorized into four types (see Chapters 3 and 4) in particular:

1 The 'individual utility' maximization model (i.e. the single-person household);

2 The 'chauvinistic model', in which one partner (normally assumed to be the male) decides on his labour supply independently of the female. The

latter treats the male income as if it were given exogenously (i.e. as if it were property income), and then makes her own labour supply decision.

3 The 'family utility/family budget constraint' model, which specifies some overall family utility function containing the leisure of each family member. The earnings from family members are pooled and the family maximizes the overall utility function.

4 The 'individual utility/family budget constraint' models. In this case, individuals have their own goals which they pursue within the various constraints set by the family unit.

In each of the true family models (i.e. examples 2–4 above), the individual, single-person household outcome appears as a special case. A number of elements of the composition of the family have been incorporated in the economic theories of labour supply. Single-parent families, for example, have been a special focus in the empirical literature. In addition, there is increasing interest in the influences on the optimal size and structure of the family and household unit. This is touched on briefly in Chapter 4.

4 Search and labour supply

Traditional labour supply theory tends to ignore the time and effort required to locate a job. In practice it is clearly unrealistic to assume that search is instantaneous and that there are no problems or costs associated with obtaining information about job opportunities. Thus, there has been considerable interest in the economics of search in recent years, especially in the context of theories of labour supply (although we note that firms also undertake a search process in order to fill vacancies). Search can be shown to be closely related to labour supply, as those participating in the labour market are defined as the employed plus those not in employment but searching for work and able to take up a job offer within a reasonable period. However, not everyone searching for a new job is necessarily unemployed. Data from the *UK Labour Force Survey* in the mid-1980s, for example, showed that approximately 50 per cent of job seekers were employed and 50 per cent were unemployed (Bosworth and Westaway, 1987; Bosworth and Ebrahimi, 1989). Around three-quarters of individuals start searching for a new job at the time they quit. However, just under one-quarter of the unemployed quit before beginning their job search (some might have been housewives, individuals living off redundancy payments or other non-wage income). Finally, about 5 per cent of the unemployed started searching for work while they were still in their previous job, before entering unemployment. In addition there are a significant proportion of newcomers to the labour market (i.e. school leavers); the precise numbers vary with the time of year and demographic trends.

Accepting the first available job opportunity is unlikely to be the worker's optimal solution. The individual is likely to investigate a range of possibilities and may refuse a number of offers before settling on a job. This process of search necessitates the individual incurring search costs. There are the direct costs of travel, postage, etc., and the indirect costs of foregone earnings (less any social security payments received from the state). On the other hand, it is sometimes argued that there are compensating benefits, including increased leisure for those searching from unemployment and the higher future pecuniary and non-pecuniary rewards of locating a better job offer. The employed searcher still receives earnings (although search time can eat into both potential work and leisure time).

A variety of different search theories have been developed, which are discussed in greater depth in Chapter 3. However, they generally include some form of rational optimizing behaviour in the face of imperfect information. For example, insofar as potential job opportunities can be ranked, the search process will generally begin with the most promising possibilities, such as firms close to home who are thought to be 'good payers', and will move towards less promising possibilities the longer the search goes on. Optimal search implies the existence of some form of 'stopping' rule, for example that the individual continues to search until the expected benefits of further search are less than the expected costs, at which point the best available offer is accepted.

Search theory has made a number of important contributions to our understanding of labour supply. One concept we will find extremely useful in later chapters is that of the 'reservation wage'. Holt and David (1966) developed an account of labour market search in which the worker enters the search process with a 'reservation price', which represents the lowest wage that a worker will consider to be acceptable. This reservation price may be revised during the period of search, in the light of experience, until the worker is willing to accept an offer. It should be added, however, that while Holt and David refer to the reservation wage and labour supply theory uses the wage rate as the crucial independent variable, the worker can be expected to have wider considerations in their search process. Job security, fringe benefits, work patterns and the nature of the work will all be relevant considerations. Additionally, workers may set higher reservation wages for jobs which involve geographical relocation, higher commuting costs, more responsibility, etc.

5 Aggregate labour supply

5.1 Introduction

If all labour were homogeneous, perfectly mobile, possessed perfect information about job opportunities, were indifferent between all possible forms of employment and had identical labour–leisure preferences then all individuals would possess identical labour supply curves and there would be a single labour market incorporating one aggregate labour supply curve which would be the horizontal summation of all the individuals' supply curves. These theoretically convenient assumptions, however, do not hold and it is much more realistic to conceive of a number of different labour markets delineated by the sources of immobility such as occupational categories and geographical regions. If these sources of immobility were in fact rigid barriers, then there would be a number of non-competing groups supplying labour in compartmentalized labour markets, each compartment being quite distinct and separate. In practice, barriers are rarely totally rigid and it is more realistic to think of the strength of the boundaries between markets as being determined by the degree of immobility.

5.2 Occupational labour supply

In the short run the skills of individuals are given and thus there are a limited number of occupations to which an individual can supply labour. Assuming away all other types of immobility (such as geographical sources), then each individual will possess a short-run labour supply function for each occupation for which they possess the required skills (see Chapter 3). The aggregate occupational supply curve will be the summation across individuals who possess a supply function for that particular occupation. This is demonstrated in Figure 2.2. Other things being equal, individual 1 requires a wage of $w_0(1)$ in order for them to supply their labour at all, while individual 2 requires a wage of $w_0(2)$, and so on for each individual with the required qualifications. Thus, at some wage, such as w_1, individual 1 will supply H_1 hours to this occupational labour market, individual 2 will supply H_2, and so on for all individuals who have a minimum wage less than w_1. By implication, total labour supply will be $H_1 + H_2 + H_3 + \ldots$, as shown in the final quadrant on the right hand side of Figure 2.2. This is the total number of person hours supplied to the market. The average hours supplied

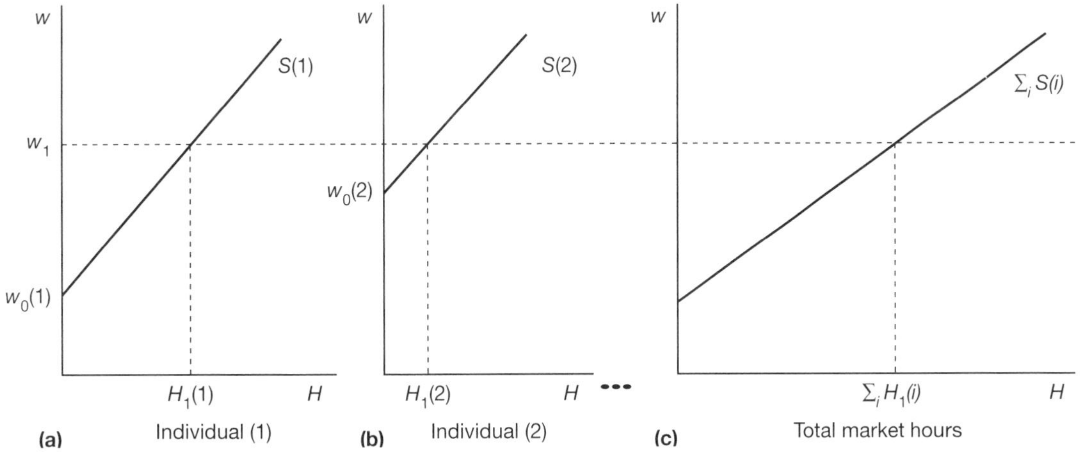

Fig 2.2 Individual and market supply of hours.

per person is derived by dividing the total person hours by the number of individuals participating in the market at the going wage rate.

As in the case of the individual supply functions, an aggregate occupational supply curve is derived assuming every explanatory variable except the wage rate of the relevant occupation to be constant. If effort is assumed to be constant there will be two dimensions to this supply: persons and hours. An increase in the relative wage of a given occupation can be expected to attract workers from other occupations. That is to say that the supply of persons curve is positively sloped. However, an increase in the wage will also influence the supply of hours by those persons in the occupation. If individuals' supply of hours curves are backward sloping, then there is a negative effect counteracting the increased supply of persons. The slope of the supply of person hours would then depend upon the net effect of these two forces. If the supply of hours curves are upward sloping, an increase in the wage influences both participation and hours in the same direction and the supply of the person hours curve is also upward sloping.

In the long run, human capital theory suggests that skilled workers will be supplied at that wage which compensates them for the costs of attaining those skills. That is to say, to induce an unskilled worker to invest in human capital, the discounted sum of the difference between the wage offered for the skilled and unskilled jobs must be at least as great as the discounted cost of the investment. Assuming a perfectly competitive labour market with homogeneous and perfectly mobile labour (in the long run) then there would be a perfectly elastic supply curve of labour at the wage which just compensates for the costs of human capital investment. There would thus be a series of horizontal supply curves, one for each occupation, with the vertical distance between each being explained by the costs of the associated human capital investment.

Under these assumptions human capital theory can explain wage differentials in the long run. However, contrary to the assumptions of perfect competition, labour is not homogeneous in two major senses. First, labour differs in the skills derived from training and education and in terms of the innate abilities and aptitudes possessed. Some people, however hard they train, would never be able to supply themselves as professional footballers or ballet dancers. There are other occupations, such as accountancy, for which there may be more people with the potential skills required, but the size of the human capital investment necessary for each individual may differ. Those for whom more investment is required than others will require a higher wage, other things being equal, to induce them to make the relevant long-run supply decision. This gives the long-run supply curve a positive slope.

An additional factor contributing to the heterogeneity of labour is that people possess different evaluations of the non-pecuniary advantages and disadvantages associated with different forms of employment. The fact that evaluations differ across workers adds a further complication when aggregation is undertaken to the level of the occupation. Those who are less attracted by the non-pecuniary aspects of a particular occupation will require a higher monetary reward. This also then leads to a degree of inelasticity in the long-run supply of labour to an occupation. However, we can be confident that the long-run supply of employees to a given occupation is more elastic than the short-run supply. In the short run an increase in the wage paid can only induce the supply of labour of those who do not have to invest in human capital in order to obtain the skill.

5.3 Local labour supply

The geographical immobility of labour constitutes a potentially significant source of labour market segmentation. Consequently it might be more useful to consider occupational labour supply to be divided between a number of local labour markets. An individual may wish to supply labour at £5 per hour in a given locality, whilst requiring, say, £10 to induce labour supply in the same occupation in a different locality. Consequently, employers may be faced with different supply curves depending on which locality they decide to operate in. It may, therefore, be more realistic to aggregate individual labour supplies to an occupational level within each locality. Recent work has clustered these localities according to certain common characteristics, to form coherent groupings, such as high-status growth areas, high unemployment problem areas, etc. (Green and Owen, 1988; Green *et al.* 1991). Thus, there is one supply curve of labour for each of the $n \times m$ local occupational labour markets, where n = number of occupations and m = number of localities. As one might expect there are considerable empirical problems in defining the local labour market (we return to this issue in Chapter 12 below).

5.4 Labour supply to the firm

Under the assumptions of perfect competition no individual firm which employs labour can affect the price at which that labour is bought and sold. The interaction of the market supply and demand curves determines the wage rate, as in Figure 2.3(a), and that is the wage that the perfectly competitive firm must pay. Consequently the firm faces a perfectly elastic supply curve, as in Figure 2.3(b). If the firm employs labour from a number of occupational labour markets, each of which is characterized by perfect competition, then it faces a number of perfectly elastic supply curves of labour. However, when a firm has an influence on the wage rate when changing its demand for labour, the supply curve facing it ceases to be perfectly elastic. In the extreme case of a monopsonistic firm (which is the case of a single buyer of labour in the relevant market) the firm itself faces the market supply curve. These issues are taken up in Part IV of the book.

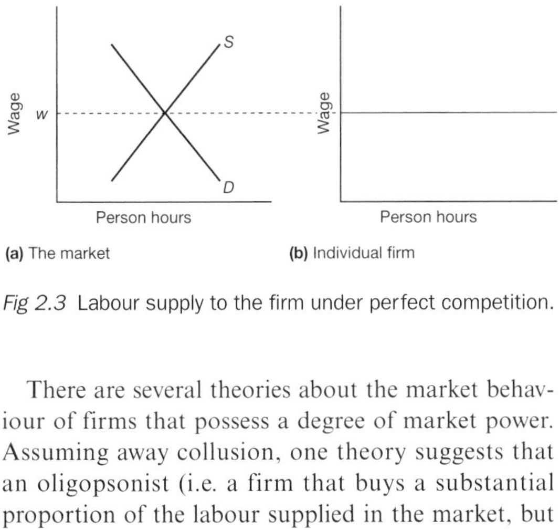

Fig 2.3 Labour supply to the firm under perfect competition.

There are several theories about the market behaviour of firms that possess a degree of market power. Assuming away collusion, one theory suggests that an oligopsonist (i.e. a firm that buys a substantial proportion of the labour supplied in the market, but which exists alongside a few other comparable firms in the market) faces a kinked supply curve (see Coyne, 1975). Maintaining the other, perfectly competitive assumptions (homogeneous and unorganized labour, perfect mobility and perfect information), the supply of labour curve facing the oligopsonist is shown in Figure 2.4.

If w_0 is the existing wage rate, then S_1 is the supply curve facing the oligopsonist on the assumption that none of its competitors react to any changes it makes to its wage. S_2, in contrast, is the supply curve which the oligopsonist would face if its competitors copy any wage change which it undertakes. Thus S_2 is more inelastic than S_1. The theory giving rise to a kinked supply curve suggests that competitors would not follow a wage reduction but accept the more favourable supply conditions that would result from their higher wage, but they would follow a wage increase since they could not accept the loss of workers that might result. Thus, above the existing wage rate, S_2 is relevant, but below w_0, S_1 is relevant. The result is a kinked labour supply curve, *abc*, with a kink at the existing wage. Some evidence of this type of supply curve is reported in surveys of graduate shortages in science and engineering in the UK (Tarsh, 1985, p. 13). However, while the theory provides an intuitive explanation for the stickiness of wages downwards, we demonstrate later that it is a far from complete explanation of oligopolistic behaviour.

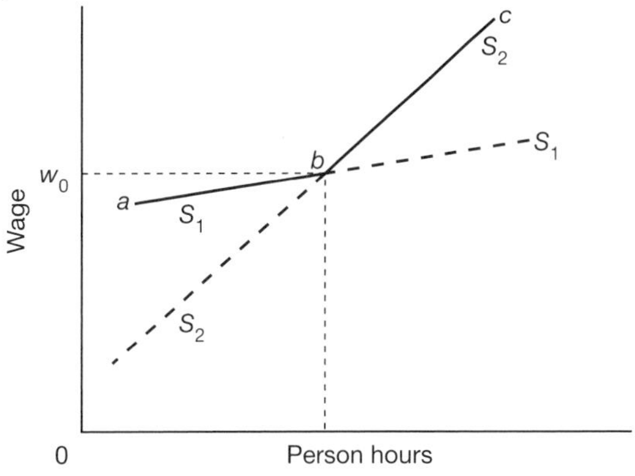

Fig 2.4 Supply of labour to an oligopsonist.

5.5 Supply of labour to an industry

Industries are defined according to the type of output that they produce and not according to the factors of production that they employ. Firms are allocated to industries according to their principal products. Consequently, in many instances, the concept of an industrial labour market may be inappropriate. That is to say that, in some instances, industrial boundaries do not represent a significant source of immobility of labour. There are some industries, such as mining or health care, which are more likely to employ labour that is specific to that industry. However, many occupations such as secretaries, drivers and computer operators are employed across a wide range of industries. Indeed, if the proportion of the occupational group employed in a given industry was sufficiently small, then the industry faces a perfectly elastic supply curve of the relevant labour, in the same way as a perfectly competitive firm.

5.6 Aggregate labour supply

As noted in Section 5.1, if all labour were homogeneous, perfectly mobile, possessed perfect information about job opportunities and were indifferent between all possible forms of employment, then each individual would possess one labour supply curve and there would be one labour market incorporating one aggregate labour supply curve which would be the horizontal summation of all the individuals' supply curves at a given wage. It has been shown how dropping certain of these assumptions makes it more realistic to conceive of a number of different supply curves at a lower level of aggregation than the whole economy. Economists interested in macro issues have developed models of the aggregate economy which have incorporated an aggregate supply curve which implicitly assumes away such problems as heterogeneity and immobility. The aggregate supply is clearly a very important part of these macro models.

Up to this point in the discussion, labour supply has been considered as a function of the money wage. However, under the *ceteris paribus* assumption, the labour supply functions have been drawn assuming the price of goods to be constant. If the price level were to rise the real value of a given money wage would fall. When representing the supply of labour as a function of the money wage, the effect of a price change is to shift the supply function. In the case of a positively sloped labour supply curve in relation to the money wage, an increase in the price level causes the curve to shift to the left. In other words, at a given money wage, fewer hours are supplied. In the case of a negatively sloped supply curve, in relation to the money wage, the curve shifts to the right if the price level increased. We demonstrate in the next chapter that the direction of the outcome depends on the relative values of the income and substitution effects. A rise in the price level at a given wage reduces the real income level and one reaction of the individual is to increase their hours to compensate (i.e. the income effect). On the other hand, the price rise at a given wage reduces the benefit of work relative to leisure and the individual reacts by substituting away from work and towards leisure by reducing their hours of paid work (i.e. the substitution effect).

Assuming aggregation to be legitimate, the aggregate supply curve is the sum of all the individual supply curves and would shift accordingly following a price change. Macroeconomists have generally assumed the aggregate supply curve to be positively sloped. In that case one would expect the supply curve, in relation to the money wage, to shift to the left following an increase in the price level. The possibility that individuals suffer from money illusion, however, is a further complication (Leijonhufvud, 1969). Keynes argued that, 'although a reduction in the existing money-wage would lead to a withdrawal of labour, it does not follow that a fall in the value of the existing money-wage in terms of wage-goods would do so, if it were due to a rise in the price of the latter,' (Keynes, 1936, p. 8). The implication of this would seem to be that a reduction in the real wage may not lead to a reduction in labour supply if it is caused by an increase in prices, because of money illusion. If suppliers of labour exhibited perfect money illusion and thus did not respond at all to changes in prices, then the labour supply curve representing supply as a function of the money wage would not shift in the way implied by the discussion above. In practice, the real world appears likely to be characterized by some, though not complete, money illusion.

Assume that the aggregate labour market is initially in equilibrium at money wage w_1 and price level p_1, at point a on supply curve S_1 in Figure 2.5. The real wage is thus $w_1/p_1 = (w/p)_1$. Let us consider the effect of a reduction in the real wage to $(w/p)_2$, first,

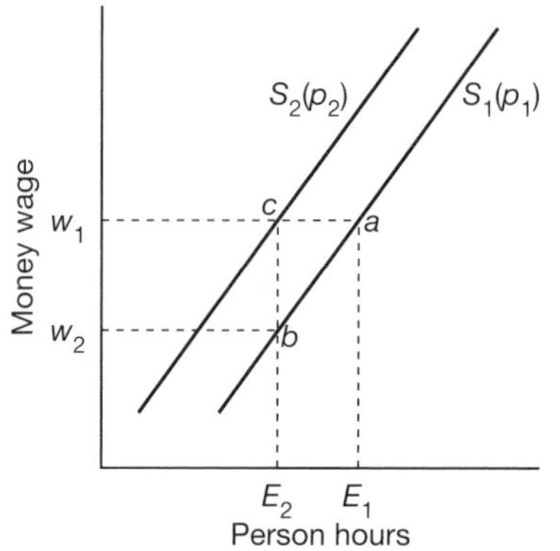

Fig 2.5 Money illusion and labour supply.

as the result of a money wage cut and, second, as the result of an increase in the price level. If the money wage is reduced to w_2, wage falls to $w_2/p_1 = (w/p)_2$, there is a movement along supply curve S_1 to point *b* and the supply of labour falls from E_1 to E_2. However, if reduction in the real wage from $(w/p)_1$ to $(w/p)_2$ results from an increase in the price level from p_1 to p_2 such that $w_1/p_2 = (w/p)_2$, the labour supply response depends on the degree of money illusion. If there is no money illusion then market supply moves from *a* to *c*, and the supply of labour at the new real wage will be equal to E_2 as in the case when the money wage was reduced to w_2 with the price level staying at p_1. If there is perfect money illusion, however, an increase in the price level from p_1 to p_2 would have no effect on the labour supply curve and the supply of labour would remain at E_1. A degree of money illusion would involve shifts in the labour supply curve to positions between S_1 and S_2 dependent on the degree of money illusion present. The response of labour supply to changes in prices as opposed to changes in wages has been an important issue in the debate about unemployment and wage inflation, which we focus on in Chapter 29.

Some authors have also suggested that the aggregate labour supply curve implied by Keynes in the *General Theory* incorporates one further important complication: the contention that there is a resistance on the part of employees to reductions in money wages. According to Keynes, this resistance arises out of the rigid structure of wage differentials, which implies that it 'may be extremely sensible' for any given group of workers 'to resist a fall in money wages' which would lead to a fall in real wages, but not to 'resist a fall in real wages which comes about through a rise in prices which is the natural resultant of the operation of the other forces of the economic system', since the latter 'will not disturb their relative real wage and is, moreover, the inevitable accompaniment of increased employment on the whole'. That is to say, 'since there is, as a rule, no means of securing a simultaneous and equal reduction of money wages in all industries, it is in the interest of workers to resist a reduction in their own particular case. In fact, a movement by employers to revise money wage bargains downwards will be much more strongly resisted than a gradual and automatic lowering of real wages as a result of rising prices.' (Keynes, 1936; Trevithick, 1976.)

Trevithick interprets this as implying 'the familiar reverse Keynesian L-function in which employment is infinitely elastic with respect to the money wage rate below full employment.' This is represented in Figure 2.6 by the supply curve *SS*, where E_1 is full employment. The resistance of employees to cuts in money wages because of the desire to maintain differentials gives rise to the horizontal section (*ab*) of the supply curve. This resistance would not exist if the money wages of all groups of workers could be reduced uniformly. In that case, the supply curve would be S_1S and there need not be an excess supply of labour if the demand curve intersected the supply curve at a level of employment below E_1. However, in the presence of downward wage rigidity (i.e. with the reverse Keynesian L-function), if the demand curve intersects the supply curve at a level of employment less than E_1, such as at point *a*, there is an excess supply of labour equal in this case to E_1E_2.

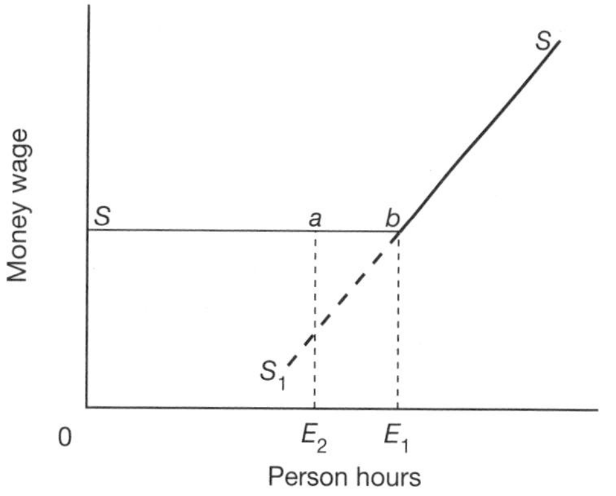

Fig 2.6 Reverse Keynesian L-function.

6 Aggregate labour supply in the long run

The long run is assumed to be a period of time during which both the skill level and the size of the population can change. When considering labour supply in aggregate, the size of the population and its age structure are very important. It was this aspect of labour supply that was of prime interest to the early classical economists. In particular, Malthus (1826) developed the subsistence theory of wages in which the long-run labour supply curve was infinitely elastic at the subsistence level. Any increase in real wages above that level would induce population growth and consequently increase the pressure on agricultural land which would tend to reduce wages back to the subsistence level. Such analysis is still relevant for some less developed economies, but since the Industrial Revolution in the Western world the rate of growth of the population, although very substantial, has not prevented a secular increase in real wages let alone reduced them to the subsistence level.

In more recent times, labour economists have shown increasing interest in the economic influences on demographic trends (Becker, 1981 and 1985), although the area remains one which is dominated by sociologists. Early econometric evidence suggested that, while major changes in fertility do not appear to be a function of business cycles, 'deviations from trend fertility rates seem to move in the same direction as the trend deviations of economic indicators' (Kirk, 1960). Becker (1960) attempted to move the debate beyond a simple correlation of fertility with economic variables. In his model, the 'quality of children' is seen as a decision variable as well as the number of children. 'Higher quality children' does not mean that they are morally better, but more expensive in the sense of sending them to nursery school, private colleges and giving them music lessons.

Becker's framework, therefore, can be viewed as a generalization of the Malthusian model. Parents' income elasticity of demand for children may show up in greater expenditure on a given number of children, as well as in a greater number of children, which was the Malthusian prediction. Furthermore, Becker suggests that the responsiveness of the quality variable is greater than that of the quantity. He goes on to point out that although it is difficult to separate expenditure on children from general family expenditures, wealthier families and countries spend much more per child than do poorer families and countries. As far as the responsiveness of quantity to income is concerned he admits that cross-sectional data on income and fertility tend to show a negative relationship. However, he goes on to suggest that this is because contraceptive knowledge has been positively related with income and supports this contention with data on family size and income for those couples who have planned the size of their families. These data suggest that there is a positive income elasticity of family size for those who plan the size of their families (Becker, 1981 and 1985).

Fertility rates are of course only one of the determinants of population size. Death rates and net migration are also important and both may be influenced by economic variables. Better housing, diets, working conditions, etc., are associated with higher income levels and improved life expectancy. Thus as income has increased, so greater proportions of people have entered the labour force and indeed remained in the labour force until retiring age. The decision to migrate can also be influenced by the relative levels of wages in different locations. While regulation often severely constrains the magnitude and nature of these flows, the flows are still subject to the influence of economic variables. It is also interesting to note that in Europe the European Union has done much to remove barriers to the flow of labour between Member countries.

Many studies have demonstrated how migration flows and the choice of destination, and the 'quality' of migrant, are influenced by economic and other variables, including immigration policies of destination countries. In some countries immigrants are an important source of labour supply. Borjas (1988) has studied immigration in the USA, Canada and Australia, which have been the three most important destinations of migrants in the last 30 years. The framework of analysis is one in which potential migrants assess the costs and benefits of international immigration (including both 'push' and 'pull' factors) and the relative advantages of migrating to different countries. Thus, the 'quality' of immigrants entering Australia and the USA, for example, depends partly on the relative returns to migrating to these respective countries. These flows are also subject to substantial influence by immigration policy changes in host countries. The quality of immigrants entering Australia (measured in terms of their earnings disadvantage) was found to have increased over the last 20 to 30 years, while the quality has decreased in the USA and Canada. These changes in quality are shown to be heavily influenced by economic variables and by changes in immigration policy (especially in the USA).

7 Conclusions

This chapter introduced the concept of labour supply and outlined the important distinctions between participation, hours of work, effort and skill. However, the discussion also noted that, while the decision-making 'unit' is sometimes an individual, it might equally be a group of individuals within a family or household. In addition, the labour supply decision frequently involves a distinction between paid (market) work and unpaid (domestic) work. While the traditional analysis is static, this has been extended to a multi-period, dynamic context in order to focus on life-cycle patterns and, in particular, the causes and consequences of individual investments in human capital (i.e. health, education and training). The discussion has also dealt with a number of issues of aggregation and the distinction between short- and long-run labour supply. In Chapter 3 we cover the basic theory of individual labour supply including the decision to participate, the hours decision, the effort decision, job search and the education and training decision. In Chapter 4 we move on to consider household production, family models and the life-cycle. In Chapter 5 we provide a brief overview of empirical evidence on labour supply.

References

Becker, G. (1960). 'An Economic Analysis of Fertility'. In *Demographic Change in Developed Countries*. A Conference of the Universities. New York National Bureau of Economic Research.

Becker, G.S. (1981). A *Treatise on the Family*. Cambridge, MA: Harvard University Press.

Becker, G.S. (1985). *An Economic Analysis of the Family*. Dublin: Economic and Social Research Institute.

Borjas, G.J. (1988). 'International Differences in the Labour Market Performance of Immigrants'. W.E. Upjohn Institute for Employment Research. Kalamazoo, Michigan.

Bosworth, D. and A. Ebrahimi (1989). *Characteristics of the Unemployed and the Duration of Unemployment, Methods and Intensity of Job Search*. Project Report. Institute for Employment Research. Coventry: University of Warwick.

Bosworth, D. and A. Westaway (1987). *Determinants of Long Term Unemployment: A Review of the Literature.* Project Report. Institute for Employment Research. Coventry: University of Warwick.

Coyne, J. (1975). 'Kinked Supply Curves and the Labour Market'. *Journal of Economic Studies*, Vol. 2, No. 2, 139–151.

Green, A. and D. Owen (1988). *The Development of a Classification of Travel to Work Areas*. Project Report. Institute for Employment Research. Coventry: University of Warwick.

Green, A., D. Owen and C. Hasluck (1991). *The Development of Local Labour Market Typologies: Classifications of Travel to Work Areas*. Project Report. Institute for Employment Research. Coventry: University of Warwick.

Holt, C.C. and M.H. David (1966). 'The Concept of Job Vacancies in a Dynamic Theory of the Labour Market'. In *The Measurement and Interpretation of Job Vacancies*. New York: National Bureau of Economic Research.

Keynes, J.M. (1936). *The General Theory of Employment, Interest and Money*. London: Macmillan.

Kirk, D. (1960). 'The Influence of Business Cycles on Marriage and Birth Rates'. In *Demographic and Economic Change in Developed Countries*. A Conference of the Universities. New York: National Bureau of Economic Research.

Leijonhufvud, A. (1969). *Keynes and the Classics.* Occasional Paper No. 3. London: Institute of Economic Affairs.

Liebenstein, H. (1956). 'The Theory of Underemployment in Densely Populated Backward Areas'. In G. Akerlof and J. Yellen (eds) *Efficiency Wage Models of the Labour Market*. Cambridge: Cambridge University Press, pp. 22–40.

Malthus, T. (1826). *An Essay on the Principle of Population*. London. 6th edition. [See E.A. Wrigley and D. Souden (eds) (1986). *The Works of Thomas Robert Malthus.* Eight volumes. London: Pickering and Chatto.]

Tarsh, J. (1985). *Graduate Shortages in Science and Engineering: A Survey of Employers in 1983 and 1984*, Research Paper Number 50, Department of Employment, London.

Trevithick, J.A. (1976). 'Money Wage Inflexibility in Keynesian Theory'. *Economic Journal*, 86, 327–332.

CHAPTER 3 Individual labour supply

1 Introduction

This chapter develops the microeconomic foundations of labour supply theory. It focuses on the individual's decision although individuals are often part of a larger decision-making unit. The implications of this are postponed until Chapter 4, as is the issue of the role of household production and the choice between paid (market) work, unpaid (domestic) work and leisure. In Section 2 we develop the basic choice theoretic framework within which the short-run theory of labour supply is to be developed. In Sections 3, 4 and 5 we go on to develop the standard short-run labour supply theory. Section 3 is concerned with the decision to participate in the labour market. Section 4 is about job choice. Section 5 deals with the decision about how many hours of work to supply. In Section 6 we use this standard framework to consider the effect of taxes and transfers on the supply of labour. In Section 7 we deal with the question of how much effort an individual will offer. In Section 8 we move on to introduce the long-run theory of labour supply, in which the individual can vary their skill level by investing in education or training. This chapter also includes two case studies: the first is about the effect of income tax on labour supply in Sweden; the second is about the choice between full-time work, part-time work and retirement in the UK.

2 Short-run labour supply: theoretical framework

2.1 Graphical exposition

Chapter 2 defined the short-run supply of labour as the quantity of labour services supplied by a population of given size and skill level. It is possible to consider the short-run supply of labour at different levels of aggregation: at the level of the individual, the household, the firm, the market or the economy. It is logical, however, to begin at the level of the labour supply decision-making unit, which will be either the individual or the household. For the moment, assume that an individual's labour supply decision is independent of other people. The easiest way to proceed is to divide 'commodities' into two distinct groups: goods and leisure. Here leisure, L, is defined as the total time available, T, which is not devoted to market activity, H (i.e. $L = T - H$). It is assumed that all goods consumed must be purchased by money derived from income which may be earned by supplying labour, or in the form of rent, dividends, interest, etc. (i.e. non-labour or property income).

The individual's utility function is then defined on the consumption of goods, G, and leisure, L,

$$u = \mathbf{u}(G,L) \tag{1}$$

where: u denotes total utility; G refers to the amount of goods; and L the number of hours of leisure. This utility function can then be represented diagrammatically by an indifference map. Any given indifference curve, such as I^1 in Figure 3.1, represents all combinations of goods and leisure which yield a given level of utility. In this instance, the indifference curve I^1 is assumed to be associated with a level of utility u^1. The individual is similarly indifferent between all combinations of goods and leisure on indifference curves I^2 or I^3 and so on.

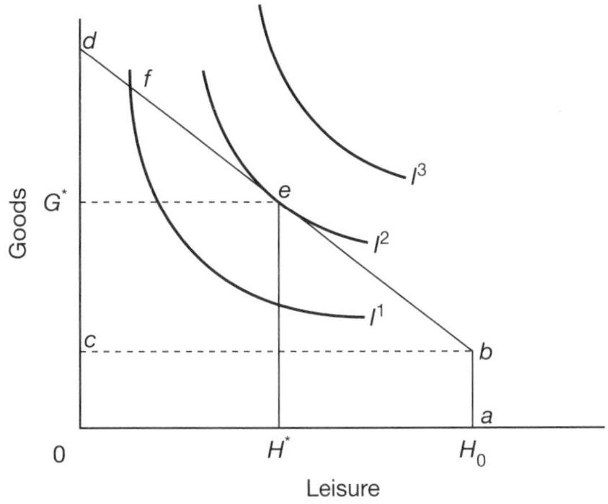

Fig 3.1 Maximization of utility subject to the consumption opportunities constraint.

It is assumed that the indifference curves are characterized by the usual properties.

1 Indifference curves further from the origin represent higher levels of utility. This follows from the assumption of non-satiation (i.e. an individual always prefers more goods to fewer and more leisure to less, $u^3 > u^2 > u^1$).

2 Indifference curves slope down from left to right. This also follows from the assumption of non-satiation. If an individual gives up a certain amount of leisure, they must gain a certain amount of goods in order to maintain the same level of satisfaction.

3 Indifference curves cannot cross. This follows from the assumption of transitive preferences (i.e. if bundle of goods A is preferred to bundle B, and B is preferred to C, then A is preferred to C).

4 Indifference curves are convex to the origin. The marginal rate of substitution of leisure for goods (MRS_{LG}), falls as leisure increases (i.e. the rate at which an individual is prepared to substitute leisure for goods, while maintaining the same level of utility, falls as leisure increases and vice versa). Note that,

$$MRS_{LG} = \frac{\text{marginal utility of leisure}}{\text{marginal utility of goods}} = \frac{\partial u/\partial L}{\partial u/\partial G} \quad (2)$$

where the marginal utility of leisure is the change in utility caused by a small change in leisure, other things held constant, $\partial u/\partial L$, and the marginal utility of goods is the change in utility brought about by a small change in the quantity of goods, $\partial u/\partial G$, other things being equal.

If there were no restrictions on an individual's choice of goods and leisure, they would choose to consume an infinite amount of both. However, there are several constraints preventing this. First, the amount of non-labour income (i.e. not earned through paid work in the current period) is limited. The individual's non-labour income is represented by an amount equivalent to goods, *ab* in Figure 3.1. Second, the number of hours which can be devoted to work or leisure is limited to a maximum of 24 hours a day. Finally, the wage rate constrains the amount of labour income an individual can earn from any given number of hours of work in a day. Labour income is represented by the line *bd*, where cd/cb (the negative of the slope of the constraint) represents the wage rate in a single time period. The wage rate is assumed to be constant and, therefore, the constraint *bd* is linear. Thus, every hour of leisure the individual gives up, moving from H_0 towards 0, results in a further increment of income of $w = cd/cb$. The constraint *abd* represents the individual's 'consumption opportunities'. Operating at any point on that constraint, the individual cannot increase their leisure without a reduction in income (and thus their consumption of goods) and vice versa.

Denoting the price per unit of goods p, and the volume of goods purchased G, the wage rate w, non-labour (or property) income V and the number of hours worked H, then the budget constraint is described by the equation,

$$pG \leq V + wH = V + w(T - L) \qquad (3)$$

where T is total time available and L hours are devoted to leisure activities. This assumes no saving; all income is spent on goods, such that total income, $V + wH$, equals total expenditure, pG. The slope of the consumption opportunities constraint is

$$-\frac{cd}{cb} = \frac{(w/p)T}{T} = -\frac{w}{p} \qquad (4)$$

where wT (the maximum earned income) would buy wT/p of goods, giving a value of goods per hour or real income of wT/pT. Put another way, the real wage rate can be written

$$w/p = cd/cb \qquad (5)$$

Having determined the nature of the indifference map and the budget constraint it is now possible to establish what the maximization of utility implies for an individual's supply of labour. The individual attempting to maximize utility subject to the constraint imposed by the size of non-labour income, the availability of time and the wage rate, will operate on the indifference curve furthest from the origin which satisfies the budget constraint, represented by *abd*. That indifference curve will be tangential to the budget constraint on the line segment *bd*, or at one of the corners *b* or *d*.

As shown in Figure 3.1 the individual's optimum is at point e on indifference curve I^2. Point e is termed an interior solution, one associated with an outcome between b and d, rather than a corner point. At point e, the individual takes OH^* of leisure per period, works for H^*H_0 hours per period and consumes G^* of goods. Other combinations of goods and leisure, such as at point f, are associated with lower levels of utility. The individual does not have sufficient resources to reach higher levels of utility such as I^3.

2.2 Mathematical exposition

The problem for the individual is to maximize utility (represented by equation (1)) subject to the budget constraint (represented by equation (3)). There are many discussions of this problem in the literature: see, for example, Layard and Walters (1978) and Silberberg (1978) This can be written as the Lagrangian expression

$$\text{Max } \mathscr{L} = \mathbf{u}(G,L) + \lambda\,[(w/p)(T - L) + (V/p) - G] \qquad (6)$$

and the first-order conditions can be written,

$$\partial\mathscr{L}/\partial G = \partial u/\partial G - \lambda = 0 \qquad (7)$$

$$\partial\mathscr{L}/\partial L = \partial u/\partial L - \lambda\,(w/p) = 0 \qquad (8)$$

$$\partial\mathscr{L}/\partial\lambda = (w/p)\,(T - L) + (V/p) - G = 0 \qquad (9)$$

Equations (7) and (8) yield

$$\frac{\partial u/\partial L}{\partial u/\partial G} = \frac{w}{p} \qquad (10)$$

Equation (10) indicates that the slope of the indifference curve equals the slope of the consumption opportunities constraint (see Figure 3.1 for confirmation of this result). The form of the equation shows that, in equilibrium, the marginal rate of substitution of leisure for goods (MRS_{LG}) is equal to the real wage rate (see equation (2) above).

The first-order conditions form three equations in three unknowns (L, G and λ). The implicit function theorem indicates that explicit solutions for L, G and λ should exist:

$$L^* = \mathbf{L}^*(w, p, v, T) = L^*(w/p, v/p, \ldots) \qquad (11)$$

and $H = T - L$,

$$H^* = \mathbf{H}^*(w, p, v, T) = H^*(w/p, v/p, \ldots) \qquad (12)$$

Thus, in terms of the supply curve of labour, interest centres on the relationship between L^*, H^* and w/p. It is easy to demonstrate, for example, that, if the utility function is loglinear,

$$u = aG^{\alpha}L^{\beta} \qquad (13)$$

then the optimal hours of leisure can be written

$$L^* = \left(\frac{\beta}{\alpha + \beta}\right)\left(T + \frac{V}{w}\right) \qquad (14)$$

It can be seen that, with this very simple utility function, optimal leisure is always inversely related to the wage rate (and, by implication, hours of market work are positively related). More general functions give more complex relationships between L^* or H^* and w/p. Changes in labour supply can be decomposed into income and substitution effects.

This analysis is developed in detail in Section 5.2 below. Figure 3.1 indicates that $H > 0$, which implies that the individual will participate in the labour market. This is not always the case and this forms the focus of attention in Section 3 below.

3 Participation

3.1 Introduction

The utility-maximizing solution derived in Section 2 corresponds to an interior solution and must be considered against the possibility of a 'corner solution', which is not a point of tangency. The distinction between the interior and corner solutions lies at the heart of the debate concerning first- and second-generation models of labour supply (see Chapter 5 for a discussion of the empirical results of the labour supply literature).

The traditional goods/leisure analysis, outlined in Section 2 above, concludes that an individual will choose to participate, if their utility-maximizing exercise leads to a point which entails less than 24 hours 'leisure' per day. In Figure 3.2(a) person A maximizes their utility on indifference curve I'_A at point *b*, choosing 24 hours leisure (zero work) at the going wage rate *cd*/*cb*, given a non-labour income *ab*. Figure 3.2(b) shows that at the same wage rate with the same non-labour income, person B maximizes their utility at point *e*, where I'_B is tangential to the constraint *db*. Thus, person A does not wish to participate in the labour market, whereas person B chooses to work H_0H_1, hours per day. The difference between person A and person B is their relative preference for goods and leisure, as represented by the different shapes and slopes of their indifference curves.

3.2 Reservation wage

In the simplest of neoclassical models used to underpin labour supply theory, the individual is assumed to maximize their utility subject to a budget constraint. In this model, the individual compares the wage offer with their reservation wage, w^r The concept of a reservation wage runs through much of the supply literature and, for the moment, can be defined as the minimum wage necessary to induce the individual to work (for a discussion see Mortensen, 1986; Devine and Keifer, 1988). If the going wage, w, is higher than the reservation wage, the individual would prefer hours of work, H^* that maximize their utility,

$$H^* > 0 \text{ if } w > w^r \quad (15)$$

However, if the wage offer is lower than the reservation wage, the individual decides not to participate, and hours are set to zero,

$$H^* = 0 \text{ if } w \leq w^r \quad (16)$$

In summary, therefore, preferred hours $H^* > 0$ implies that the individual participates, while preferred hours $H^* = 0$ implies that the individual is not in the labour force.

Figure 3.3 illustrates the derivation of the individual's reservation wage. The reservation wage is discussed again in the context of search theory in Section 9 of this chapter. At the going wage, w_1, the individual chooses a corner solution at point *e*, using all the time available, *T*, for leisure. This is true for all wage rates up to and including w_2, but, at any higher wages, $w > w_2$, the individual would choose some

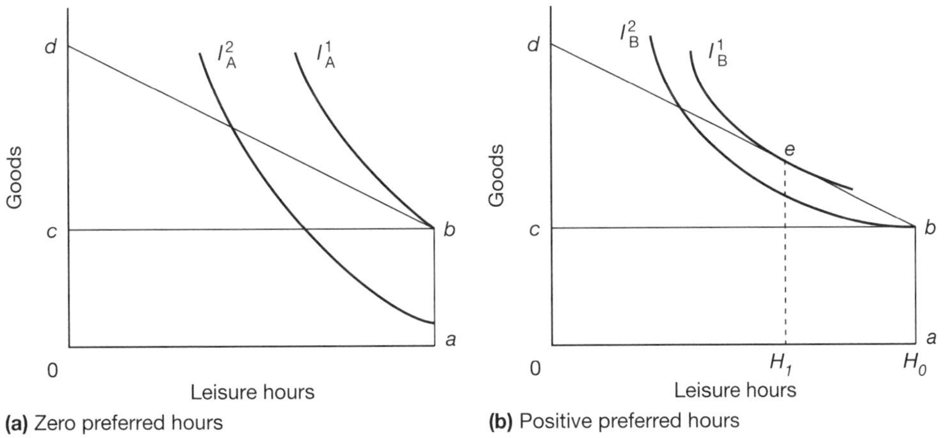

(a) Zero preferred hours

(b) Positive preferred hours

Fig 3.2 Participation.

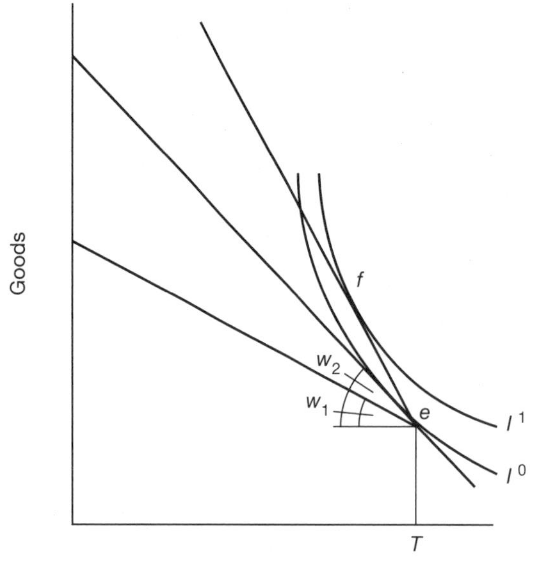

Fig 3.3 Derivation of the individual's reservation wage.

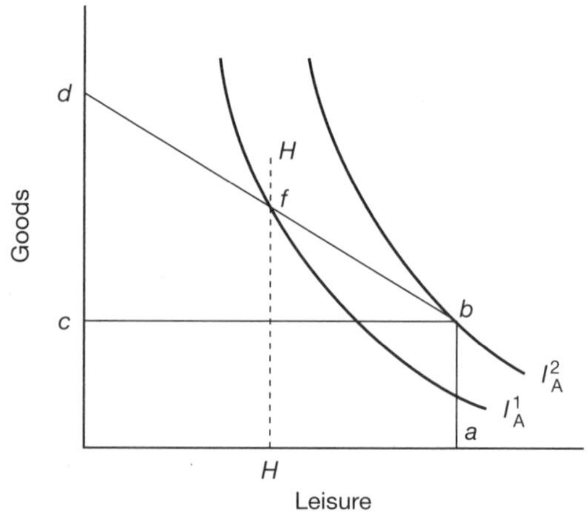

Fig 3.4 Hours of work constrained.

positive value of hours of work. At some wage w_3, for example, the individual would choose point *f*. Thus, the reservation wage $w^r = w_2$, such that

$$H^* > 0 \text{ if } w > w^r = w_2 \quad (17)$$

$$H^* = 0 \text{ if } w \leq w^r = w_2 \quad (18)$$

Participation is not the same as employment. For the individual to be employed, they require a job to be offered where $w \geq w^r$. Under certain market conditions, therefore, it is possible for the individual to have preferred hours $H^* > 0$ but observed hours of $H = 0$ $(H^* > H)$ because the individual is currently unemployed. Normally, we would expect such an individual to be actively searching for work (and the participation rule and the job search definition of unemployment both indicate that the individual is currently in the labour force).

3.3 Hours of work constraint

One criticism that can be levelled at this analysis is that an individual in the real world does not have complete choice over the number of hours that they can work. Individuals are often faced with a limited number of choices. For example, an individual may be faced with a choice of working eight hours a day or not at all. In terms of Figure 3.4 *abd* again represents the budget constraint; *HH* represents the hours constraint. The individual must choose to work eight hours on the constraint represented by line *HH*, or not at all. It is for this reason that this is referred to as a 'take it or leave it' labour supply decision.

In effect, the decision simplifies to a choice between points *f* and *b*. Participation will occur if the individual can achieve a higher level of utility at the going wage rate by working, say, eight hours per day than by not working at all. In Figure 3.4 individual A achieves a higher level of utility at point *b* than at point *f*, and chooses not to work ($I_A^2 > I_A^1$. Another individual B might prefer point *f* to *b*, working *H* hours per week, while yet other persons might be indifferent between zero hours at work, at *b*, and, say, eight hours work at point *f* (on *HH*), when the wage rate is *cd*/*cb*.

When the hours constraint is binding then, at any given wage rate, some workers participate at less hours than they would wish, some at more hours. There are, however, a number of ways in which individuals can achieve an optimal number of hours, even when only standard hours are on offer. For example, multiple job holding, overtime working, part-time working, etc., all provide opportunities.

The part-time case is shown in Figure 3.5. Individual A is faced with a choice between no work, part-time work (H_{PT} hours) and full-time work (H_{FT} hours), with the same wage rate *cd*/*cb* whichever choice they make. In other words the individual can choose between points *b*, *e* or *f*. This particular indifference map would lead the individual to choose part-time employment on I_A^3 in preference to full-time employment on I_A^1. If part-time employment

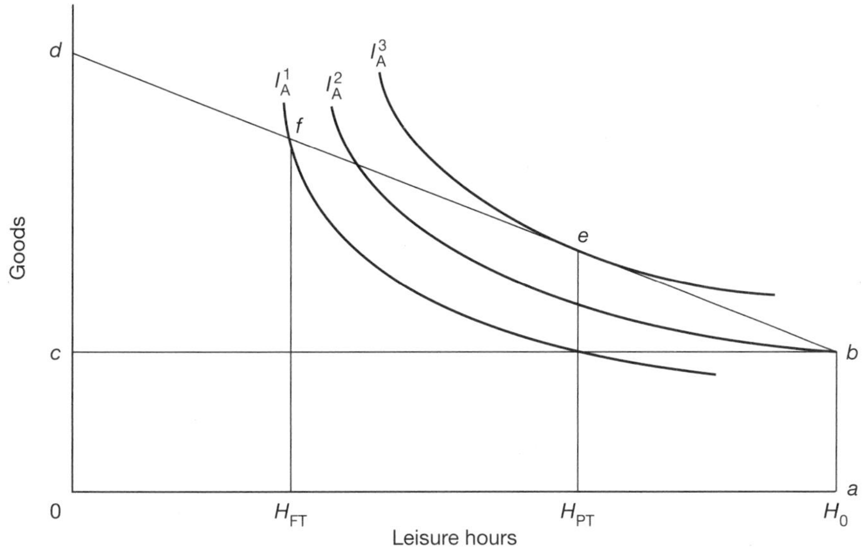

Fig 3.5 No work, part-time or full-time employment.

were not available the individual would actually prefer not to work on I_A^2 rather than to work full-time on I_A^1.

4 Short-run occupational choice

Up to now, it has been assumed that an individual possesses a utility function defined in terms of goods and leisure. It is unreasonable, however, to assume that utility is the same regardless of the nature of the employment concerned. Adopting the traditional approach, the individual's relative evaluation of leisure and work is likely to vary between different jobs. In the short run, since skill stays fixed, there are a limited number of jobs open to the individual. In the long run, the individual has the option of investing in education and training, altering, within certain constraints, their qualifications, skills and occupation. The topic of long-run occupational choice (sometimes called 'dynamic' or 'life-cycle' labour supply theory) is considered in Chapter 4.

For the moment, the analysis is wholly static; the individual's skills are assumed to be fixed and problems associated with the costs of moving between jobs and of obtaining information about jobs are ignored. The individual is assumed to choose a job that maximizes their utility. For the sake of argument, there are only two jobs which an individual can undertake, say teaching or selling insurance. For every indifference curve representing a certain level of utility derived from combinations of goods and leisure as a teacher, there is a comparable indifference curve giving the same level of utility from combinations of goods and leisure if the individual is, instead, an insurance salesman. For purposes of comparison, the indifference curves are both drawn in Figure 3.6

I_B^1 is taken from a map of indifference curves representing an individual's utility function when the relevant employment is selling insurance, while I_A^1 represents combinations of goods and leisure necessary to achieve the same level of utility as a teacher (i.e. the indifference curves are drawn in such a way that the level of utility on indifference curve I_B^1 is equal to that on I_A^1) They appear as two distinct curves in the figure because 'everything else' is not equal: the non-pecuniary disadvantages of teaching are greater at every level of hours. Notice that, as they are drawn in Figure 3.6, the individual associates a degree of disutility with teaching at all hours of work, but more so as the number of hours of work increases; when zero hours are supplied the utility curves meet. That is to say that the indifference curves which the individual associates with teaching lie 'above' (i.e. the individual requires a higher wage at every level of hours) the comparable curves for selling insurance at every point except where they

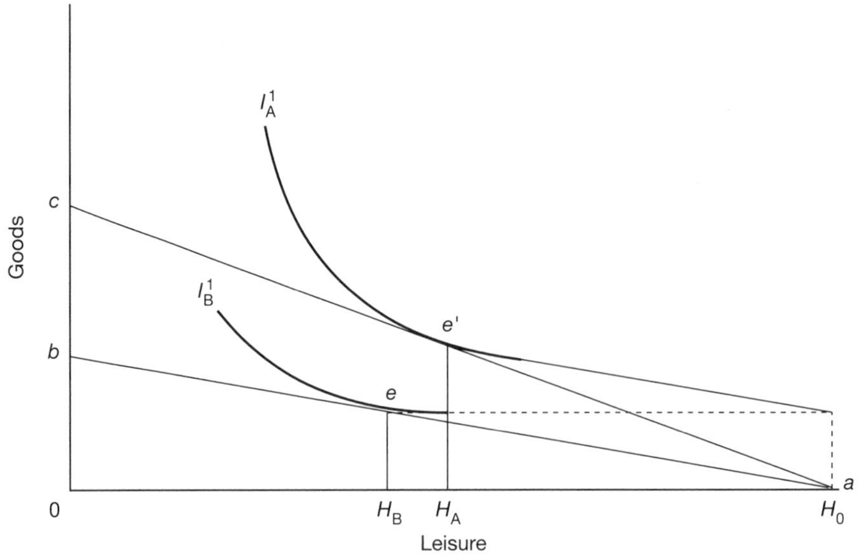

Fig 3.6 Occupational choice.

intersect with the time constraint, and they have a steeper slope (i.e. $MRS_{LG}(A) > MRS_{LG}(B)$).

Clearly, if the same wage rates were offered for selling insurance and teaching, the individual would choose the former. This preference reflects the individual's relative evaluation of the non-pecuniary advantages of selling insurance and teaching. The figure shows the extra amount of pay required to induce the individual to teach rather than to sell insurance, which is a monetary estimate of the non-pecuniary differences between the two jobs. If the wage rate for selling insurance is $0b/0a$, such that the individual would choose point e if there is no alternative employment, then a wage rate of at least $0c/0a$ is required to induce the individual to choose teaching. At these wage rates the individual is indifferent between the two occupations. In other words, assuming that there is complete choice over the number of hours worked, at the wage rates shown in Figure 3.6 the 'net advantages' (to use Adam Smith's term) of both forms of employment are identical. Thus, the premium $cb/0b$ represents the individual's evaluation of the mark-up necessary to compensate for the non-pecuniary disadvantages of teaching, *vis-à-vis* selling insurance as the ratio of the wages is $(0c/0a)/(0b/0a) = 1+bc/0b$.

5 Hours of work

5.1 Introduction

The simplest way of explaining an individual's decision about the number of hours of work is to use the traditional income/leisure trade-off model developed above. In this section it is assumed that there are no demand-side constraints on the number of hours that the individual can work. The aim here is to derive the individual's supply of hours curve, where desired hours are a function of the real wage rate. In order to do so, it is necessary to establish how many hours the individual would prefer to work at each possible wage rate.

Figure 3.7 shows that a change in the wage rate causes a rotation of the budget constraint about point b. If the wage rate increases then the constraint rotates clockwise, if it falls the constraint rotates anti-clockwise. If the wage rate increases from cd/cb to cj/cb, then the new constraint is represented by the line bj, and the number of hours that the individual wishes to work is reduced from H_0H to H_0H_1. The income earned at the higher

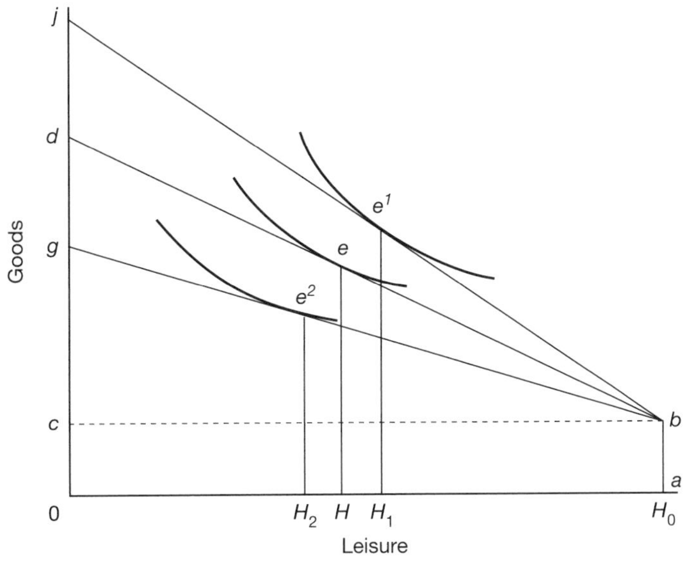

Fig 3.7 Changes in the wage rate and maximization of utility.

wage equals $(cj/cb)H_1$. If the individual worked all of the hours available (i.e. *cb* hours) this would generate an income of $cj = (cj/cb)cb$. This income, *cj*, is denoted the individual's 'full income' (Becker, 1965, pp. 497–498), because it represents the overall value of earned income and leisure time (where leisure is valued at the marginal cost of forgone work time – the wage rate). If the real wage rate falls to *cg*/*cb*, then the new constraint is represented by the line *bg*.

Ignoring corner solutions, at each wage, the utility-maximizing individual chooses a point on the indifference curve which is tangential to the budget constraint. The individual is in 'equilibrium' at points e, e^1 and e^2 in Figure 3.7 when the wage rate is *cd*/*cb*, *cj*/*cb* and *cg*/*cb* respectively, working H_0H, H_0H_1 and H_0H_2 hours respectively. In this particular example, as the wage rate increases, the individual's supply of labour falls. This is because the income effect of a change in the real wage rate outweighs the substitution effect (these concepts are discussed at length in Section 5.2 below). There is no reason to expect this result a priori: if the substitution effect outweighs the income effect, the supply curve exhibits a positive slope.

5.2 Income and substitution effects

The labour supply response to a change in the wage rate can be decomposed into income and substitution effects as shown in Figures 3.8 and 3.9. The substitution effect is caused by the change in the price of

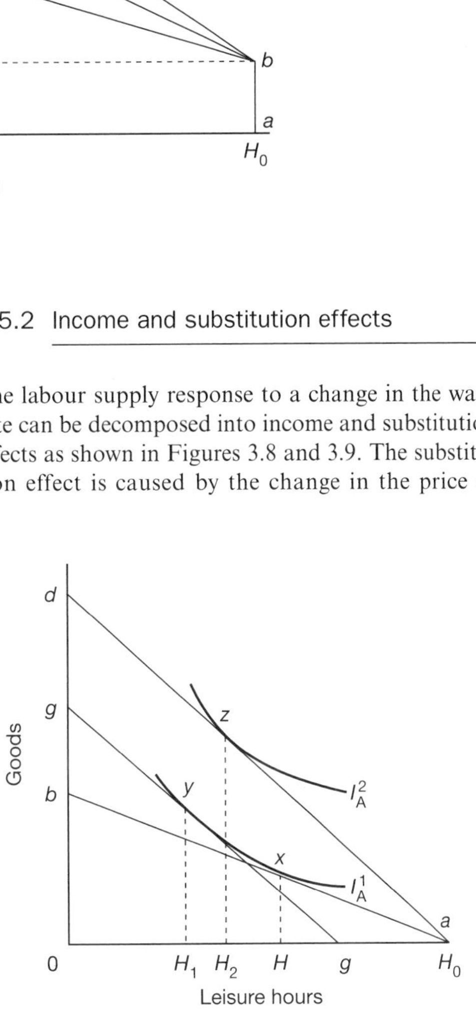

Fig 3.8 Substitution effect outweighs income effect.

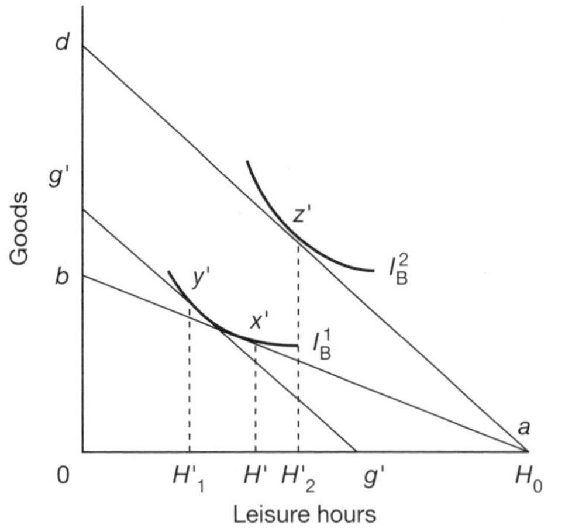

Fig 3.9 Income effect outweighs substitution effect.

leisure relative to goods following a change in the wage rate. One unit of leisure costs more in terms of goods after a wage increase. The effect of this is for an individual to substitute goods for leisure, by working more. The substitution effect is represented by the change in the slope of the budget constraint. The income effect is caused by the fact that an increase in the wage rate allows an individual to achieve a given level of utility by working less hours than originally. By implication, the substitution effect tends to induce the individual to work longer as the wage rises, while the income effect works in the opposite direction (if leisure and goods are 'normal goods').

Separation of the substitution effect from the income effect can be undertaken using the method suggested either by Hicks, or by Slutsky. Both require the introduction of an imaginary budget constraint. In the Hicks method the 'imaginary' budget constraint takes the individual back to their old level of utility; in the Slutsky method it forces them back to a level of income which just enables them to 'buy' their original bundle of goods and leisure. The distinction between the two approaches is dealt with at length in most standard microeconomics texts and is not considered further here. The principal features of the results remain the same.

Consider the substitution effects for persons A and B, when the wage rate increases from $0b/0a$ to $0d/0a$. To isolate the substitution effect (i.e. the relative price effect), it is important to establish how many hours an individual would choose to work at the new relative price of leisure in terms of goods, but at the old level of utility, so as to eliminate the effect of income on this decision. To do this we draw an imaginary budget constraint parallel to the new constraint *ad*, but tangential to the old indifference curve (i.e. *gg* tangential to I_A^1 and $g'g'$ tangential to I_B^1 for persons A and B respectively). Given such constraints, persons A and B would choose to operate at *y* and *y'* respectively. Both would increase their hours of work, person A from H_0H to H_0H_1 and person B from H_0H' to $H_0H'_1$. The substitution effect of an increase in the price of leisure (an increase in the wage rate) always has a negative effect on the amount of leisure 'consumed' and thus a positive influence on the number of hours worked.

The income effect depends crucially on the position of the various indifference curves. In Figures 3.8 and 3.9 both income effects are positive (i.e. leisure and goods are both 'normal goods'), with the growth in real income caused by the wage change increasing the amount of leisure by H_1H_2 for individual A and $H'H'_2$ for individual B. This is the general result obtained when both income (goods) and leisure are normal goods. Notice, however, the relative sizes of the income and substitution effects for the two individuals. In the case of person A, the small negative income effect H_1H_2 is outweighed by the major substitution effect HH_1 and this corresponds to a positively sloped supply of hours of work curve. In the case of person B, however, the small substitution effect $H'H'_1$ is substantially outweighed by the major income effect $H'_1H'_2$, and this results in a negatively sloped supply of hours curve.

5.2.1 Mathematical exposition

The Slutsky equation for the decomposition of hours of labour supply can be written (Layard and Walters, 1978, pp. 138–139 and 304–306)

$$\frac{\partial H}{\partial w} = \left(\frac{\partial H}{\partial w}\right)_{u\,=\,\text{const}} + H\left(\frac{\partial H}{\partial G}\right) \tag{19}$$

The effect of a per unit change in wages on hours with utility constant, $(\partial H/\partial w)_{u\,=\,const} > 0$ is ensured by the convexity of the indifference curve. The effect of a per unit change of income on hours $\partial H/\partial G < 0$ (because $\partial L > \partial G > 0$ if leisure is a normal good). Thus, the overall impact of a change in wages on hours depends on the relative magnitudes of the substitution effect (i.e. the first expression on the right-hand side of equation (19) and the income effect (i.e.

the second expression on the right-hand side of the equation). By implication,

$$\frac{\partial H}{\partial w} \gtreqless 0 \text{ as } \left(\frac{\partial H}{\partial w}\right)_{u = \text{const}} \gtreqless H\left|\frac{\partial H}{\partial G}\right| \quad (20)$$

According to Layard and Walters,

> The size of the substitution effect in labour supply is one of the oldest issues in political economy. Those who worry about incentives tend to imply that the effect is large, while people on the Left tend to imply that it is small. (Layard and Walters, 1978, p.306)

This debate obviously assumes central importance in the context of (optimal) tax rates. In general, the interior solution for hours is a function of take-home pay, rather than gross pay. This might be illustrated by

$$\mathbf{H}^* = \mathbf{H}^*(w(1-t), p, V, T) \quad (21)$$

where t is the tax rate. In the real world, however, the tax structure can be very complicated and its effects on the supply of labour can be extremely difficult to disentangle. The discussion returns to these issues below.

5.3 Overtime

Employees who work more hours in the day than is regarded as 'normal' typically receive a higher wage rate (i.e. a rate that will include an overtime premium) for those extra hours. Figure 3.10 shows a situation where, after normal hours of work of H_0H_N, a 'double time' overtime premium is paid. This has the effect of increasing the slope of the consumption opportunities constraint beyond H_0H_N hours of work by 100 per cent. Thus, the budget constraint line is modified from *abd* to *abe*, where *de* is equal to *cd*. Prior to the introduction of overtime, the individual was initially in equilibrium on budget line *ad* at point *b* (working normal hours). The availability of overtime at a premium *ed*/*cd* increases the marginal wage rate beyond H_0H_N hours, resulting in a new equilibrium at point *f*. The higher marginal wage above H_N has induced the individual to work a total of H_0H_V hours, including H_NH_V hours of overtime. The individual's income is $(0d/0a)H_0H_N + (ce/cb)\,H_NH_V$. Finally, it is fairly straightforward to show that, for most individuals, offering an overtime premium is a more efficient option for the employer than changing the basic wage rate. Figure 3.10 shows that, in order to induce the employee to work H_V by changing basic wages, the wage rate would have needed to rise to $0h/0a$, and this would have been paid on all H_0H_V hours of work.

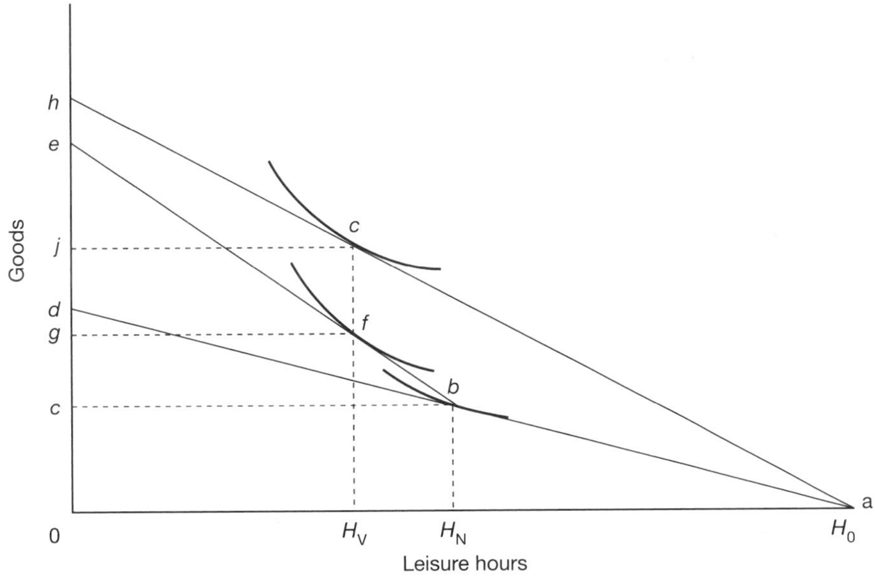

Fig 3.10 Overtime and labour supply.

CASE STUDY 1 Taxes and labour supply in Sweden

The tax rates in Sweden are amongst the highest in the world. It is natural, therefore, that the effect of taxes of hours of work has been a major economic and political issue in Sweden. In 1988, tax revenue was about 56 per cent of GDP and with an average tax rate this high, marginal tax rates were also very high. For a typical worker who consumes all labour income, the total marginal tax was about 70 per cent (of which income tax contributed 37 per cent, payroll taxes 27 per cent and value-added tax 6 per cent). A study by Blomquist and Hansson-Brusewitz (1990) provides a range of estimates of how such high tax rates affect labour supply. The methodological issues in estimating labour supply functions are discussed in greater detail in Chapter 5. Their sample consisted of persons aged between 25 and 55 years for whom they had data on annual hours of work in 1980, the wage rate and range of socioeconomic characteristics. The data also contained very detailed information about the income and tax position of each individual and their spouses, their total income, the actual deductions for income tax purposes and the assessed income. This enabled the researchers to calculate the precise budget constraint faced by each individual in the sample.

For males they estimated that the uncompensated wage elasticity was in the range 0.081 to 0.127, depending on the precise specification of the model and the estimation technique. The income elasticity was estimated to be very close to zero, between 0.0017 and –0.0077 when evaluated at the mean values of hours and wage rates. For females the corresponding elasticities for the full sample (including females who worked zero hours) was a wage elasticity of between 0.386 and 0.773, and an income elasticity of between –0.030 –0.243.

These findings suggest that the high marginal taxes had only a small effect on the labour supply of males. In order to predict the effect of taxes on labour supply the authors simulated the effect of a tax change by calculating the predicted effect of the change in hours of work for each individual. They found that replacing the existing highly progressive tax system with a proportional tax yielding the same revenue would increase male hours of work by 6.6 per cent. These simulations highlight that while a wage elasticity of around 0.1 may seem small, changes in marginal tax rates can have quite a large effect on hours of work. For example, a reduction of the marginal tax rate from 60 to 40 per cent effectively increases the net wage by 50 per cent and would lead to a 5 per cent increase in hours of work for the average male.

As in most other studies, female labour supply is estimated to be more responsive to both wages and income than male labour supply. However, the difference is exaggerated by comparing the elasticities evaluated at the respective means. When the female wage elasticity is evaluated at the mean values of wages and hours the estimates are much lower. This is also reflected in the simulations. Replacing the progressive with a proportional tax system was estimated to increase female hours of work by 10.3 per cent.

Source: Blomquist and Hansson-Brusewitz (1990)

CASE STUDY 2 Full-time work, part-time work and retirement

In most developed economies, individuals above a certain age can choose not to participate in the labour market by retiring and obtaining a pension. The choice between full-time work and retirement has been analysed by Zabalza *et al.* (1980). The example is based on the system which prevailed at the time of the study. In the UK state retirement pensions become available for men at the age of 65 and for women at the age of 60 and over.

The income/leisure constraint faced by men in the 65–69 and women in the 60–64 age group is represented by the line *acdef* in Figure 3.11. The retirement pension is indicated by the distance *cb*. An implicit tax on this pension applied if earnings exceeded certain limits, causing kinks in the income/hours trade-off at points *d* and *e*,

continues

CASE STUDY 2 continued

with the individual effectively forfeiting pension rights if operating on the segment *ef*. The system offers the opportunity for individuals to defer their pension for a higher one in the future giving a current budget line *abf*. However, in these circumstances, such an individual's income from work should be adjusted upwards by the present value of the higher future income resulting from the deferment (i.e. from whenever the pension is claimed until their death). Finally men aged 70 and over and women aged 65 and over could claim a retirement pension irrespective of their labour market status giving a budget constraint *acg*.

Analysing the decision of a person of retirement age, Zabalza *et al.* (1980) characterized the decision as a choice between three states: part-time work, full-time work and retirement, represented by the three points *c*, *d* and *e* in the figure. Clearly the decision depended on the shape of the individual's indifference curves, in particular on the MRS_{LG}. The authors undertook an empirical analysis of this decision to find out what characteristics influenced the marginal rates of substitution of individuals and, thereby, their choice between part-time, full-time work and retirement.

Based on data for Great Britain in 1977, they found that women's supply elasticities were higher than men's at all ages. The usual backward-bending labour supply curve for prime-age males became upward sloping when pensionable age was reached. For women, the supply curve was upward sloping both before and after pensionable age. In estimating the effect of non-economic variables on the retirement decision they found poor health to be the most important inducement to retirement before pensionable age. Age also had a very significant impact independently of the pensionable age effect. It was also found that individuals who had left their main lifetime job involuntarily due to mandatory retirement or other factors were much more likely to retire than other workers. Finally, the disincentive effects of the earnings rule were found to be very small and it was estimated that its abolition would increase the labour supply of those affected by less than 2 per cent.

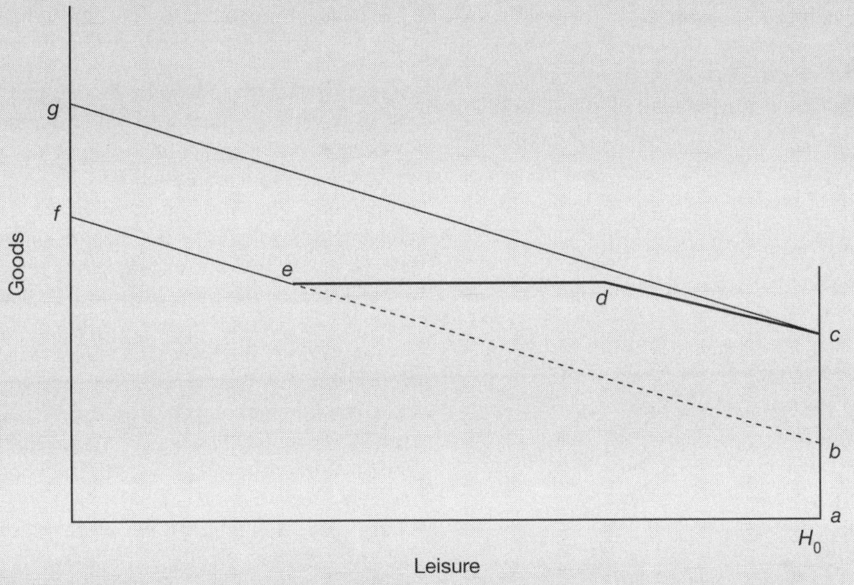

Fig 3.11 The budget line for persons of retirement age.

5.4 Absenteeism

Just as some workers may choose to work more than standard hours, some may choose to work less. One way of doing this is to take days off every now and again. This is referred to as absenteeism when the individual takes time away from work for reasons other than illness or injury. Figure 3.12 shows normal (or standard) hours of H_0H_N. The individual's preferences are represented by the indifference curves I^1 and I^2 and equilibrium would on indifference curve I^1 at point *c* when working normal hours. However, a higher level of satisfaction can be obtained on indifference curve I_2 at point *d*, by absenteeism of H_1H_N. In many countries there are provisions for sick pay (10 days per year has been the norm in Australia), such that an individual can take days off without losing income, ostensibly due to illness. If paid leave entitlement was equal to H_1H_N hours per week, at the standard rate of pay, this would enable the absenteeism to take place without any loss of income, allowing the individual to reach indifference curve I^3 at point *g*.

This analysis assumes that one day of absence gives equal utility to any other day of leisure and, thus, that there is no stigma or guilt associated with absenteeism. Further it assumes that employers are unable to impose penalties for absenteeism, for example, in the form of reduced promotion opportunities. An alternative way in which employers are potentially able to control absenteeism is by paying a bonus for those who attend for 100 per cent of standard hours. In Figure 3.12, a bonus of *ch* would just compensate

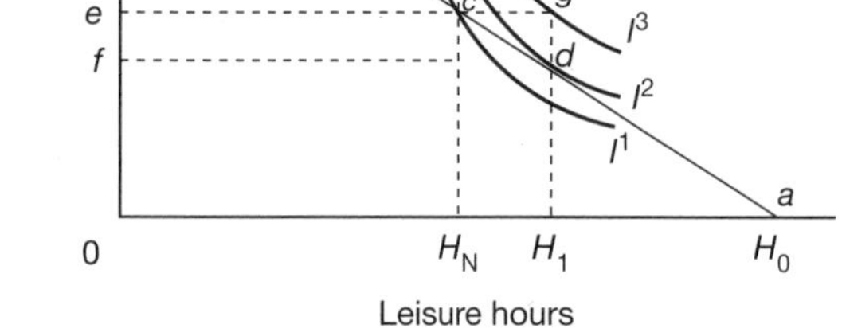

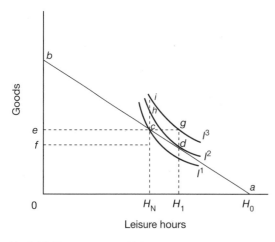

Fig 3.12 Absenteeism and labour supply.

the worker enough to induce full attendance when there is no sick pay, but *ci* would be the required compensation where the individual is entitled to sick pay. More details of this model of absenteeism and econometric tests for the USA and Australia can be found in Allen (1981) and Kenyon and Dawkins (1989).

6 Taxation, transfers and labour supply

6.1 Introduction

In the earlier analysis of the supply of hours of work it was assumed that the individual received gross labour income. Typically, however, in most societies governments impose taxes on labour incomes. As a consequence, an extra hour of work does not increase take home pay by the full amount of the wage rate, as some income is taken away in the form of taxes. The supply of labour should be seen as a function of the net wage rather than the gross wage. The effect on the supply of hours of work depends on the level and progressiveness of the income tax, and on the nature of the individual's preferences with regard to work and leisure.

6.2 A proportional tax on labour income

Assuming that an individual faces a given wage rate for all possible hours of work and can adjust hours of work at will, a proportional income tax reduces the gradient of the leisure income trade-off by a given proportion. The effect on hours of work depends on the relative strengths of the income and substitution effects. The substitution effect tends to reduce hours of work (i.e. as the net wage rate falls because of the increases in tax rate, the price of leisure falls, causing a substitution effect towards leisure and away from work). Whether the overall effect on hours of work is negative, however, depends on the size of the offsetting income effect (assuming leisure to be a normal good). Where the substitution effect outweighs the income effect, there is a positively sloping supply of hours curve, but where the income effect outweighs the substitution effect there is a backward-sloping supply of hours curve. The two cases are shown in Figures 3.13(a) and 3.13(b).

In Figure 3.13(a) the effect of a lower wage rate is to reduce hours of work (i.e. the substitution effect

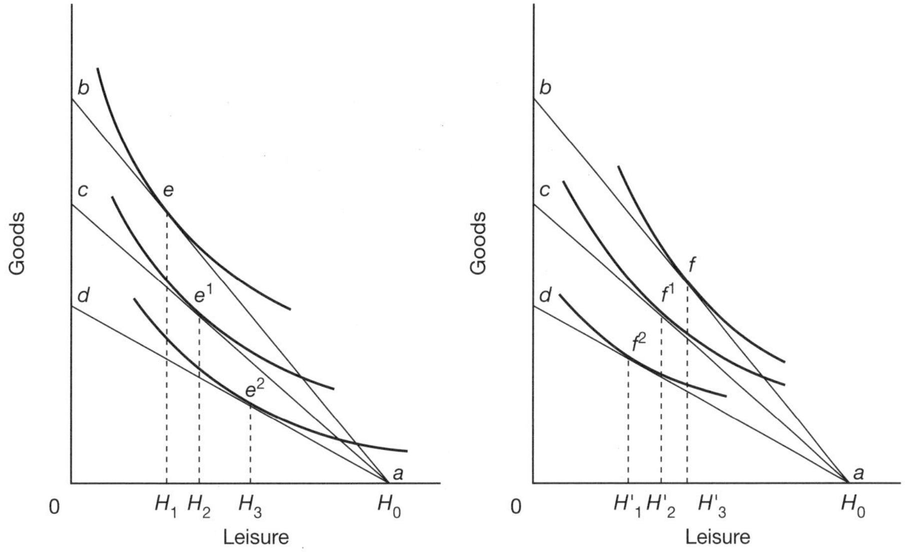

(a) Increased taxes reduce hours of work

(b) Increased taxes raise hours of work

Fig 3.13 Labour supply and a proportional income tax.

outweighs the income effect to produce a positively sloped supply of hours curve). In Figure 3.13(b), the income effect outweighs the substitution effect to produce a negative relationship between the wage rate and hours of work. Thus, imagine that, initially, the wage rate is *0b/0a* and there are no taxes on earned income. The introduction of a proportional income tax at the rate of *cb/0b* reduces a gross wage rate of *0b/0a* to a net wage rate of *0c/0a*. With a positively sloping supply curve (Figure 3.13(a)) this reduces hours of work from H_0H_1 to H_0H_2, but with a negatively sloped supply curve (Figure 3.13(b)) the effect is to increase hours of work from H_0H_3' to H_0H_2'.

6.3 A progressive tax on labour income

This section considers the effect of a tax rate which increases with the size of labour income (i.e. a progressive tax). In order to make a comparison with the effect of a proportional income tax, compare the effect on an individual of a progressive rather than a proportional rate of tax which yields the same amount of revenue. At wage rate *0b/0a*, Figure 3.14 shows that the individual's pre-tax equilibrium is at point *e*. If a proportional income tax is now imposed at the rate *cb/0b*, the new income/leisure trade-off is represented by the line *ac*, and the new equilibrium is at point *f*. For H_0H_1 hours of work, the individual receives a pre-tax income of $0Y_1$, which, after tax, becomes $0Y_2$, with $(Y_1 - Y_2)$ paid as tax to the government.

Consider a progressive income tax which yields the same revenue to the government from the worker.

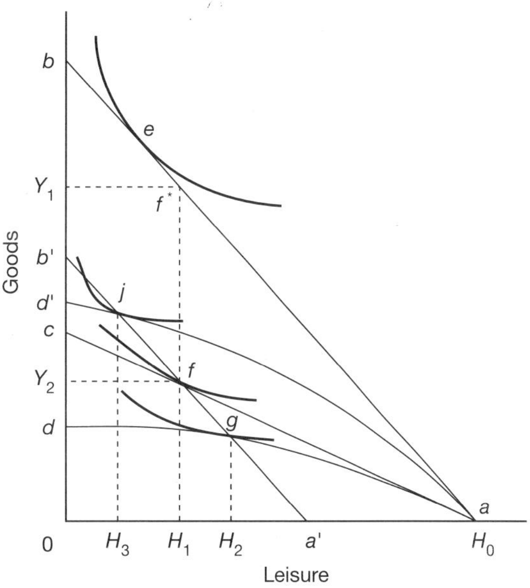

Fig 3.14 Labour supply and a progressive income tax regime.

Any such system must give an equilibrium on a line parallel to *ab*, passing through *f*, such that the tax yield is equal to *ff** (or $Y_1 - Y_2$). Thus, the solution must be on *a′b′*, as this line is equidistant below *ab* throughout (i.e. *ff** below *ab* throughout). A progressive income tax system gives rise to an income/leisure trade-off such as *ad* in Figure 3.13. The slope of the budget constraint diminishes with hours of work, reflecting the increasing rate of tax as income rises. The new point of tangency at *g* is on the line *a′b′* such that the new tax yield is equal to the previous yield under the proportional tax system. However, the individual's hours of work have fallen from $H_0 H_1$ to H_0H_2.

This progressive tax regime is only one of a number of possible systems yielding the same revenue and the effect on hours of work could be quite different under an alternative regime. A progressive tax system producing an income/leisure trade-off *ad′* in Figure 3.14 yields an equilibrium at *j*, also on the line *a′b′*. The tax revenue is the same as before, but the individual now works H_0H_3 hours (more hours than under the proportional tax system). So the effect of a progressive income tax system on hours of work is indeterminate. It depends on the nature of the system, the rates and progressiveness of the tax involved, and on the shape of the individual's indifference map. Note that the individual at point *j* is not only working more hours than under the two other systems, but also achieving a higher level of utility. It is very difficult to predict the impact of different systems of income tax on an individual's supply of labour.

6.4 Expenditure taxes and the supply of labour

A tax on expenditure may also affect the supply of hours of work. If a general flat rate tax is introduced on all expenditure, the price of goods increases and this reduces the real wage rate. Ignoring saving, future consumption and money illusion, a flat rate expenditure tax, with the same yield as a flat rate income tax, can be expected to have the same effect on hours of work. If, however, expenditure taxes are imposed on some goods but not others, the effect on hours of work depends on the nature of those goods. Here Becker's theory of the allocation of time can provide some useful insights (Becker, 1965; see Chapter 5 for a more detailed discussion). If the incidence of taxes falls disproportionately on time-intensive commodities (as opposed to goods-intensive commodities), the effect on labour supply will be less. If luxury goods are relatively time-intensive, then this suggests that expenditure taxes on luxury goods will prove less of a disincentive to work.

6.5 Social benefits and the supply of labour

Governments affect labour supply not only by means of taxes, but also in the way that they provide individuals with non-labour income, for example in the form of unemployment benefits and other social security payments.

The effects of social benefits, like taxes, depend critically on the precise rules governing their entitlement. The principal issue is evident from Figure 3.2 which showed how the individual's decision to participate depends on their work–leisure preferences and the amount of non-labour income. In Figure 3.2 individual A chooses not to participate because the utility of not working is higher than the utility of working positive hours. Now if we assume that the non-labour income in Figure 3.2 is a social benefit, had this benefit not been available the budget constraint would be parallel to *bd* but originate from point *a*, and the individual would maximize utility by working positive hours.

In reality social benefit systems are more complex than this example suggests. Unemployment benefit, for example, is often conditional on the individual engaging in active job search, and other forms of income support are contingent on income from work being below a certain level. This means that individuals can face quite a complex budget constraint and it is difficult to predict how labour supply is affected by social benefits.

7 Long-run occupational choice and human capital investment

7.1 Present values

In the long run individuals can 'invest in human capital' in the form of education and training to increase their earnings potential. For ease of exposition and in order to arrive at a testable theory, human capital theory is normally outlined on the assumption, explicit or implicit, that non-pecuniary advantages and disadvantages are identical across different jobs. This allows the discussion to concentrate on the pecuniary costs and benefits whilst recognizing that individuals will take non-pecuniary factors into account. The individual is assumed to maximize the present value of future expected lifetime net earnings, where net earnings are take-home pay (adjusted, where possible, by the pecuniary value of fringe benefits) minus any direct human capital investment costs incurred, such as the costs of training.

Note that it is the present value of net earnings which is considered to be maximized, and not the crude aggregate of lifetime net earnings. These two measures generally differ because £1000 this year is not regarded as equivalent to £1000 next year. It is clear, for example that £1000 this year could be invested at a rate of interest, r, to provide a total of £1000$(1 + r)$ next year. Similarly the present value of £1000 to be paid one year hence is £1000/$(1 + r)$, while £1000 two years hence has a present value of £1000/$(1 + r)^2$, since a second year's compound interest has to be allowed for, and so on.

Thus, in comparing different labour market supply decisions in the long run, it is assumed that the individual will compare the present value of the different possible income streams. The following formula represents the present value of future expected income from a particular long-run decision:

$$\text{PV} = \sum_{t=1}^{n} \frac{Y_t}{(1 + i)^t} = \frac{Y_1}{(1 + i)^1} + \ldots + \frac{Y_n}{(1 + i)^n} \qquad (22)$$

where: PV denotes present value; n = the number of years for which the net income is considered; Y_t = the expected net income in year t; and i = the rate of interest.

7.2 Internal rate of return

An alternative way of viewing the human capital investment decision is in terms of the internal rate of return. Consider an 18 year old who has just successfully completed school and is considering studying for a degree. According to human capital theory, the decision to undertake a degree or not depends upon the rate of return to that higher qualification. If the age of retirement is 65, and differences in pensions are ignored, then the rate of return to the degree can be computed as r in the following equation:

$$0 = \sum_{t=18}^{65} \frac{Y_t - W_t}{(1 + r)^t} \qquad (23)$$

where: Y_t is the net income in year t if the individual undertakes the degree; W_t is the net income in year t if the individual chooses not to undertake the degree; r denotes the internal rate of return (i.e. the discount rate that sets the weighted sum of $Y - W$ equal to zero). Thus, during the period of higher education $(Y_t - W_t)$ will enter as a negative sum. During this early period the student also takes into account the direct costs of education (i.e. expenditures minus grants). To take this into account, either Y can be reduced or W can be increased by the net costs to the student of the education. In the early years of graduate employment $Y - W$ may remain negative, but the individual expects it to become positive in later years. If the expected net 'age–earnings profile' of a graduate was like YY' in Figure 3.15 and that of a non-graduate was like WW', then clearly $(Y_t - W_t)$ becomes positive at point b.

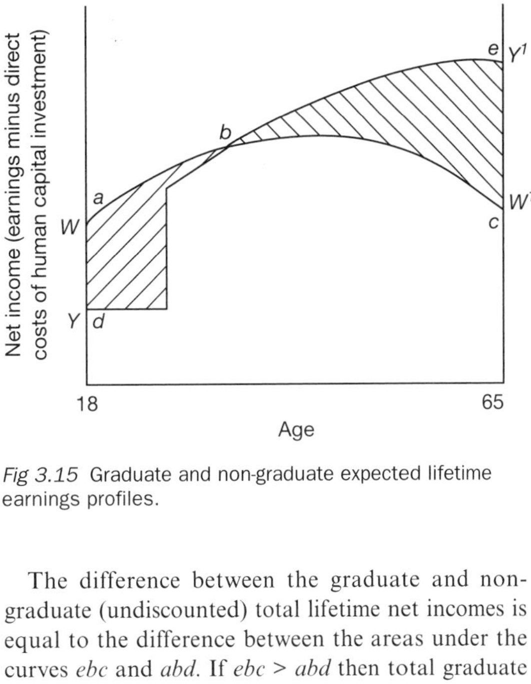

Fig 3.15 Graduate and non-graduate expected lifetime earnings profiles.

The difference between the graduate and non-graduate (undiscounted) total lifetime net incomes is equal to the difference between the areas under the curves *ebc* and *abd*. If *ebc* > *abd* then total graduate lifetime net earnings exceed total non-graduate lifetime net earnings. However, as has been pointed out, it is not the crude aggregate lifetime figure that is relevant. Bearing in mind the discounting procedure, if *ebc* = *abd* the individual would, according to theory, definitely not invest in a university education because the present value of *ebc* is less than the present value of *abd* (for positive rates of interest, i). What is required if the individual is to undertake the university education is that the present value of *ebc* is greater than the present value of *abd*.

The internal rate of return, r, is, therefore, the rate at which the expected net earnings should be discounted such that the graduate discounted net lifetime earnings equal the discounted net earnings from non-graduate employment. The internal rate of return is then, in theory, compared with the private discount rate which, given a perfect capital market, would be the rate of interest at which every individual could borrow funds. If the internal rate of return exceeds the rate of interest ($r > i$) then the individual will invest.

This exposition has been oversimplified in that it has implicitly assumed that there are two possible courses of action: undertaking a degree or no human capital investment at all. There are of course a range of possible forms of human capital investment, each of which has its own rate of return. Furthermore different subjects of degree yield different employment opportunities and different rates of return (we return to this in Chapter 15 below). Of course, what counts is the *ex ante* or perceived rates of return at the time the individual undertakes the investment, rather than the *ex post* rates actually experienced. The individual will in theory choose the 'route' with the highest rate of return.

7.3 On-the-job training

There are of course other ways of investing in human capital apart from undertaking full-time education. Becker (1965), for example, specifically considered investment in on-the-job training. He suggested that the implications of on-the-job training for the age–earnings profile of the individuals concerned would depend on whether the training in question was specific or general. Specific training increases the productivity of the individual in the firm which employs the individual. In contrast, general training has the effect of increasing the individual's productivity by an equivalent amount in other firms, if they were to employ the individual concerned.

The more specific the training to the employing firm, the more inclined the employer is to pay for the training. This is because the training raises the productivity of the individual in that company alone and will not raise the potential wage of the individual in other companies (where their productivity remains at its old, lower level). Clearly, for the same reasons, the more general the training, the less inclined the employer is to pay for it. If the employer in a competitive industry chose to pay for general training, this would increase their costs even if they did not raise the trained individual's wage. Other firms in the industry, however, which did not finance general training could afford to offer higher wages and 'poach' the trained individuals away. In the case of general training, the individual rather than the company would be willing to pay the costs, as these can be recouped in future years in the form of higher earnings received as a result of their increased skill independent of which company they work for. Again, the expenditures include the direct costs of training (tuition fees, etc.) and the difference between the wage the trainee receives and the going market wage the individual would have received in the absence of training.

In the real world, wage differentials reflect more than just differences in human capital investment. If the individual associates non-pecuniary advantages with the skilled occupation as against the occupation chosen without training, they would be prepared to accept a lower wage (or incur a higher training cost than suggested above). Similarly the education or training itself could be regarded as a consumption good such that the value of the benefits derived from the education is included in the investment decision and would imply the necessity of a lower monetary rate of return than if it were ignored. A more detailed consideration of education and training can be found in Chapter 15.

8 Job search and labour supply

8.1 Introduction

The discussion of labour supply outlined above regards the individual as deciding whether to participate in the labour market or not based upon the prevailing wages. Even in the long run, the individual was deciding whether to participate now or to leave the labour market for a period in order to undertake education or training with a view to participating once qualified. In our discussions to date, if the individual participates, they are assumed to be employed; if they undertake an educational course, they obtain employment at the end of it. Equally importantly, we have, up to now, assumed that the individual not only can obtain employment but knows also the wage and other conditions of employment.

These assumptions are clearly unrealistic for a number of reasons. First, participation does not automatically imply employment; the individuals may be unemployed. Second, obtaining a job involves the individual in a process of search, sifting through the alternative employment opportunities. Third, as employment is a contractual relationship between the employer and employee, just because the individual finds a job they want does not mean they will be offered it. Fourth, the nature of the contract is rarely if ever fully specified (or, at least, known to the job seeker) until the time of the job offer. Fifth, search is a dynamic process, which takes time. Finally search is a form of investment. Costs are incurred during the period of search which are expected to be covered when an appropriate job is found.

Imperfections in information about the key labour market variables lie at the heart of search theory. With perfect information individuals might have some important calculations to undertake, but search would not be necessary. The sort of information the individual needs concerns all of those variables that we have been discussing in the context of labour markets: vacancies, wages, non-pecuniary conditions of employment, etc. Most search models, however, assume that the job offer can be represented simply by the wage rate, w. Search models require there to be a dispersion of wages (i.e. competitive forces do not equalize wages across all firms). In the real world, a variety of wages have often been observed, even in fairly tightly defined markets for a given skill. Search models often assume that individuals know about the distribution of wage offers (or, in more complicated models, are assumed to learn about this distribution during the process of searching). However, even if the individual knows the wage distribution, most of the theories assume that individuals are uncertain as to which firms are offering which wages. By implication, in order to make an optimal decision about the choice of employment, the individual becomes involved in a search process, gathering information.

8.2 Central features of search theory

When different firms pay different wages accepting the first available job opportunity is unlikely to be in a worker's best interests; the individual is likely to search for some time and to investigate a number of employment possibilities, refusing a number of offers before settling on a job. The earlier discussion suggested that, given that there are costs and benefits attached to further search, it should be possible to isolate an optimal amount of search for the individual (i.e. the 'optimum stopping rule' might involve the individual in continuing to search until the expected gain from further search is less than the expected cost, at which point the best available offer is accepted). In general, such models are explicitly dynamic, specifying the optimization problem as the maximization of the present value of expected lifetime income.

Holt and David (1966) developed an account of labour market search in which the worker enters the search process with a 'reservation price', which represents the lowest wage that a worker will consider accepting. This concept has become central to many search models. In these models search continues until the wage offer exceeds some minimum acceptable wage (see, for example, Burdett and Vishwanath, 1988). The reservation wage, however, is endogenously determined, dependent on the 'market opportunities' which are summarized by the distribution of wage offers and the rate at which offers arrive. This reservation price is revised during the period of search, in the light of experience, until the worker is willing to accept an offer. This concept of the reservation wage is distinct from that developed in deterministic models of labour force participation (for a discussion, see Section 3 above), where the reservation wage was determined by the individual's tastes, fixed costs of working, the shadow price of time, etc. – the individual faces a given wage and the reservation wage does not depend on its level (for a discussion see Devine and Keifer, 1988, p.13). Nevertheless, the reservation wage is not entirely endogenous in the more realistic models, because it will be influenced by various exogenously determined factors, the most important of which are probably the conditions for and level of unemployment benefits.

8.3 Optimal number sampled

The pioneering work on search focused on the optimal number of firms to be sampled (Stigler, 1961 and 1962). For a discussion see Mortensen (1986, p. 853) and McKenna (1990). It is assumed that there are a very large number of potential employers offering jobs in the market and the distribution of wage offers is known (i.e. the number or proportion of firms likely to be willing to offer each wage), but the individual does not know which employer will offer a particular wage rate. This is a non-sequential type of search in which the individual decides the optimal number of firms to sample, n^*, within a given period, and accepts the highest resulting wage offer. As the number of firms sampled, n, increases, the costs of search rise and the expected returns from search change. The relationship between the costs and expected returns determines the optimal sample size of the search. In general, not all firms will be searched because the marginal cost of search rises with n, while, eventually, the marginal returns to search in terms of improved wage offers begin to fall. The expected wage of size $E(w)_1$ from a single, random search is simply the weighted mean of the wage distribution,

$$E(w)_1 = \sum_{j=1}^{n_1} Pr_j w_j \qquad (24)$$

where Pr_j denotes the relative frequency that a wage w_j is offered, $j = 1, ..., n_1$.

McKenna (1990) demonstrates that, for an approximately normal distribution of wage offers, as shown in Figure 3.16, the probable maximum wage offer, $E(w|n)$, rises as the number of firms sampled increases, as shown in Figure 3.17. Intuitively, this is fairly obvious. If only one firm is selected at random, this has a high probability of lying close to the mode and there is a very low probability of selecting a wage offer associated with one of the small number of firms in the upper tail of the distribution. However, as n is increased, there is an increasing chance that some will be drawn from the extremes of the distribution. Clearly, if search were costless, the individual would simply sample all firms and choose the highest payer. In practice, as search is costly, this is an uneconomic strategy. With a linear cost function (i.e. a constant marginal cost of search), total costs rapidly overhaul the total benefits of search, as at point f. Optimal search occurs where the slope of the expected maximum wage curve is equal to the marginal cost of search (i.e. at point e with a total number of firms sampled equal to n^*). It can be seen that a rise in the per unit cost of search reduces the optimal number of searches below n^* and a rise in the wage offer distribution (i.e. each firm offers a higher wage rate), produces an increase in the optimal amount of search above n^*.

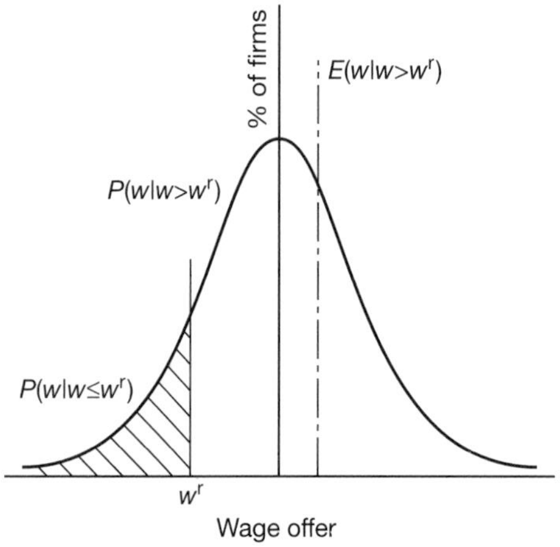

Fig 3.16 Wage offer distribution.

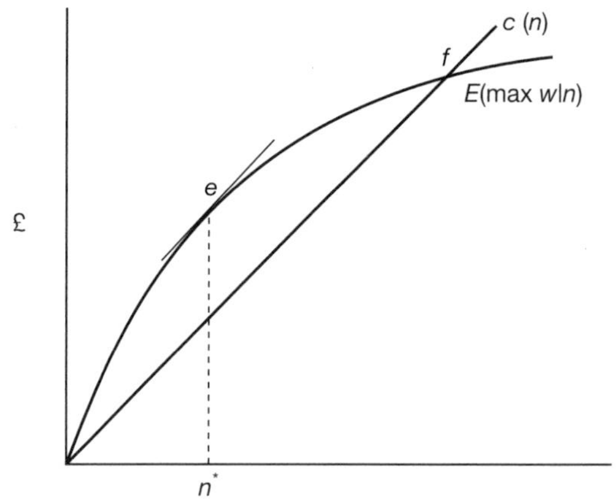

Fig 3.17 Expected wage and the number of offers samples.

8.4 Reservation wages and search

A search rule based on taking the maximum wage from a predetermined sample of size n seems likely to be an imperfect description of how search is conducted in the real world. Search theories have therefore made use of the reservation wage concept, introduced in Section 3. Thus, the individual uses information about the (known) wage distribution of job offers to construct a reservation wage, w^r (again, for detailed discussion see McKenna, 1990). The individual would therefore accept an offer prior to completing n searches if that offer were 'sufficiently high' (i.e. above the reservation wage),

$$\begin{aligned} w^0 &\geq w^r \leftrightarrow \text{accept} \\ w^0 &< w^r \leftrightarrow \text{reject} \end{aligned} \qquad (25)$$

where w^0 is the wage offered and w^r is the reservation wage.

If any job is accepted by the individual for an 'indefinitely long period', at a wage w, then the return to the individual, R, can be defined as

$$R(w) = R = w/i \quad (26)$$

where i is the rate of interest.[1] The reservation wage, w^r, therefore yields a return, R^r,

$$R^r = w^r/i = R(w^r) \quad (27)$$

Thus, the search rule based on the idea of a reservation wage implies that the individual should continue looking until an offer is found which yields $R \geq R^r$. The search is assumed to be sequential: the individual searches the first wage offer, comparing R with R^r and, if the current offer is unacceptable (i.e. $R < R^r$), continues searching as long as the individual can expect an offer greater than the reservation wage. The sequential nature of the search simplifies the analysis, allowing the model to focus on the decision to undertake the first search, the second search, etc.

To make life simple we adopt some fairly heroic assumptions. Again, it is assumed that there are a very large number of employers in the market and a fixed distribution of wage offers known to the individual (McKenna, 1990). In addition, although search is essentially sequential, we ignore discounting. The first question concerns the probability of receiving a wage offer which is greater than or equal to the reservation wage, $w \geq w^r$. Assume, for the moment, that w^r is given exogenously (although the discussion below shows that the model generates an optimal value of w^r for the individual, based on the distribution of wage offers shown in Figure 3.16. If the reservation wage is set at w^r, the expected wage offer from those which would be acceptable to the individual is given by $E(w|w \geq w^r)$, which is the weighted average of the wages above the w^r line. The probability of receiving an offer in this range is shown by the area under the distribution to the right of w^r, $Pr(w \mid w \geq w^r)$. However, the individual has a $1 - Pr(w \mid w \geq w^r)$ chance of not being made an acceptable wage offer on the first search (shown by the area to the left of w^r in Figure 3.15). If this happens, then the expected return to searching again is R_2. Thus, the expected return to the first search can be written

$$R(w)_1 = E(w \mid w \geq w^r)Pr(w \mid w \geq w^r) + R(w)_2[1 - Pr(w \mid w \geq w^r)] - c \quad (28)$$

where $R_1 = R_2$, and c denotes the per unit costs of search. An intuitive interpretation of this equation is that the expected wage is calculated from the distribution of wages which would be acceptable to the individual, multiplied by the probability of receiving that wage, plus the returns from continuing the search if the wage offer at time 1 turned out to be unacceptable, multiplied by the probability that the individual does not receive an acceptable wage offer at time 1.

Equation (28) can be used to derive the reservation wage. Thus, setting $R_1 = R_2 = R$ and solving,[2] yields

$$R(w) = E(w \mid w \geq w^r) - [c/Pr(w \mid w \geq w^r)] \quad (29)$$

which, given some explicit distribution for wage offers, can be solved for w given some w^r. By implication, it is possible to set different w^r in order to establish w^{r*}, which yields the highest $R(w)$. Again, based on an approximately normal distribution of wage offers (similar to Figure 3.16, McKenna (1990) derives the result illustrated in Figure 3.18. Thus, the optimal reservation wage in this model is determined endogenously by the shape of the search cost curve

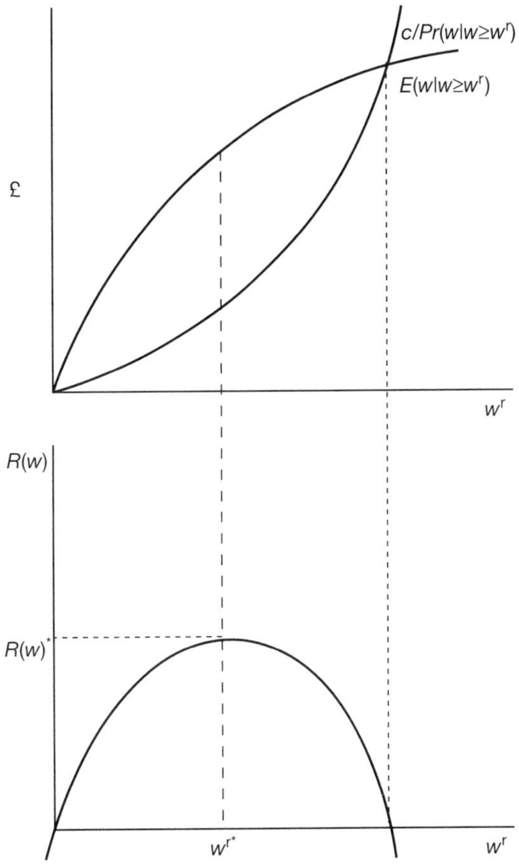

Fig 3.18 Derivation of optimal reservation wage.

and the nature of the wage offer distribution. The reservation wage is determined at a level that equates the expected present value of income from employment to the expected present value of continued (optimal) search.

8.5 Further results of search models

The models outlined above are useful in illuminating the main principles of search theory. They omit a number of key dimensions, however, such as the existence of unemployment benefits, which affect the individual's decision. Nevertheless they lead naturally to the basic job search model found widely in the literature (Mortensen, 1984 and 1986; Lippman and McCall, 1976; Devine and Keifer, 1988). In these more general models it is usually assumed that the individual is unemployed, attempts to maximize the present value of expected lifetime income, receives income in the form of unemployment benefit and/or the value of alternative activities net of search costs, during the spell of unemployment, and experiences job offers (at a certain arrival rate) and, if accepted, the wage is paid over an indefinitely long period. These job offers are independent of each other and drawn from a known wage distribution. Once an offer is rejected, it is lost to the individual.

Relaxation of the heroic simplifying assumptions adopted above leads to a more general equation for the reservation wage:

$$\begin{aligned} w^r &= b + \frac{\gamma}{i} E(w \mid w \geq w^r - w^r)[1 - F(w^r)] \\ &= b + \frac{\gamma}{i} \int_A (w - w^r)\, dF(w) \end{aligned} \tag{30}$$

Where: b is the income per period net of (constant) search costs during unemployment; γ is the (constant) arrival rate of job offers; and A is the acceptance wage set $[w^r, \infty]$ (Devine and Keifer, 1988, pp. 11–12). It can be seen that the reservation wage is positively related to unemployment income, b, and to the arrival rate of job offers, γ.

From assumptions of this type Mortensen (1986), for example, derives a reservation wage at which the imputed income from further search is just equal to the imputed income from accepting the wage offer. Thus the marginal benefits from further search are equal to the marginal costs. Mortensen shows that the reservation wage increases with the value the individual attaches to leisure and decreases with the cost of search and with the interest rate. The reservation wage is also positively related to the mean of the wage offer distribution, other things being equal. However, the increase in the reservation wage is less than the increase in the mean of the wage offer distribution. This implies that a marginal rise in the mean raises the 'hazard rate' (the escape probability) because the reservation wage rises by a smaller amount. Also the reservation wage is positively related to the degree of dispersion of the wage offer distribution, holding the mean constant. Mortensen (1986, p. 864) explains this in the following way: 'Shoppers love bargains, and bargains are only possible where prices are dispersed.' The reservation wage is also positively related to the offer arrival rate. The impact on the hazard rate depends on the balance of two separate effects. On the one hand, an increase in arrival rate gives rise to a greater number of potentially acceptable job offers which tends to increase the hazard rate (probability of accepting a job). On the other hand, the increase also has the effect of raising the reservation wage which tends to reduce the hazard rate. The model developed by Devine and Keifer (1988) adopts the same basic framework, but focuses particularly on the effects of unemployment benefits. Such benefits enter the analysis in an identical way to the value of leisure forgone in the Mortensen (1986) model. In this model the existence of benefits raises the reservation wage but not by as much as the value of the benefits.

The literature has tended to focus on the duration of the spell of search given some rate at which offers are forthcoming. While the literature has moved away from the restrictive assumption of one offer per period (Mortensen, 1986, p. 855), the offer rate is still largely treated as exogenous, when, in fact, the offer and thereby the probability of leaving unemployment is related to the intensity of job search. We return to the issue of search at a number of places in the book, but especially in Chapter 28 on unemployment. An important issue in the unemployment literature concerns whether the reservation wage declines with the duration of unemployment. Various explanations have been put forward, which include a further category of models which build learning into the job search process. To date, less attention has been paid to the determinates of the intensity of job search: if the same number of offers is sampled, more intensive search will reduce the duration of the spell in real time. In addition, the idea that the 'productivity of search' will differ between individuals has also received less attention. Job search tends to be treated as a homogeneous process, but, in the real world, it can take a variety of forms, ranging from glancing through the situations vacant columns, using information and contacts of friends and relatives, to the use of government and private job centres. Finally we note that some doubt has been cast on the hypothesis that unemployed individuals form a consistent idea of a reservation wage.

9 Conclusions

This chapter has developed the basic theory of individual labour supply, including the decision to participate, the hours decision, job choice and skills acquisition or human capital investment. In the next chapter we will see how the theory can be generalized to allow for household production, decision making in a family or household environment, and decision making in a life-cycle context.

References

Allen, S.G. (1981). 'An Empirical Model of Work Attendance'. *Review of Economics and Statistics*, 63, 77–87.

Barron, J.M. and O. Gilley (1981) 'Job Search and Vacancy Contacts: Note'. *American Economic Review*, 71, September, 747–752.

Becker, G. (1965). 'A Theory of the Allocation of Time'. *Economic Journal*, 75, 493–517.

Blomquist, N.S. and U. Hansson-Brusewitz (1990). 'The Effect of Taxes on Male and Female Labour Supply in Sweden'. *Journal of Human Resources*. 25, 3, 317–348.

Burdett, K. and T. Vishwanath (1988). 'Declining Reservation Wages and Learning'. *Review of Economic Studies*, LV, 655–666.

Devine, T.J. and N.M. Keifer (1988). *Empirical Labour Economics in the Search Framework*. Second Draft, January. Department of Economics. Pennsylvania: Pennsylvania State University.

Holt, C. C. and M. H. David (1966). 'The Concept of Job Vacancies in a Dynamic Theory of the Labour Market'. In *The Measurement and Interpretation of Job Vacancies*. New York: National Bureau of Economic Research.

Keeley, M. and P. Robbins (1985). 'Government Programs, Job Search Requirements, and the Duration of Unemployment'. *Journal of Labour Economics*, 3, 337–362.

Kenyon, P.D. and P.J. Dawkins (1987). 'Explaining Labour Absence in Australia' . Murdoch University Economic Programme Working Papers, No. 1.

Kenyon, P.D. and P.J. Dawkins (1989). 'A Time Series Analysis of Labour Absence in Australia'. *Review of Economics and Statistics*, LXXI, 2, 232–239.

Keifer, N.M. and G.R. Neumann (1989). *Search Models and Applied Labour Economics*, Cambridge: Cambridge University Press.

Layard, P.R.G. and A.A. Walters (1978). *Microeconomic Theory*. New York: McGraw-Hill.

Lippman, S.A. and J.J. McCall (1976). 'The Economics of Job Search: a Survey'. *Economic Enquiry*, 14, 155–189 and 347–368.

McKenna, V. (1990). 'The Theory of Search in Labour Markets'. In D. Sapsford and Z. Tzannatos (eds) *Current Issues in Labour Economics*. London: Macmillan, pp. 33–62.

Mortensen, D. T. (1984). 'Job Search and Labour Market Analysis'. Northwestern University. Discussion Paper No. 594.

Mortensen, D.T. (1986). 'Job Search and Labour Market Analysis'. In O. Ashenfelter and R. Layard (eds) *Handbook of Labour Economics*. Vol. II. Amsterdam: Elsevier, pp. 848–919.

Silberberg, E. (1978). *The Structure of Economics: A Mathematical Analysis*, New York: McGraw-Hill.

Stigler, G.J. (1961). 'The Economics of Information'. *Journal of Political Economy*, 69, 213–225.

Stigler, G.J. (1962). 'Information in the Labour Market'. *Journal of Political Economy*, 70. 94–104.

Zabalza, A., C.A. Pissarides and M. Barton (1980). 'Social Security and the Choice Between Full Time Work, Part Time Work and Retirement'. *Journal of Political Economy*, 14, 245–276.

Footnotes

1 This is a standard result for a job which begins in period 2, as the discounted income stream can be written

$$\frac{w}{(1+i)} + \frac{w}{(1+i)^2} + \dots = \frac{w}{(1+i)}\left(1 + \frac{1}{(1+i)} + \frac{1}{(1+i)^2} + \dots\right)$$

which for an infinite series can be written

$$\frac{w}{1+i} \cdot \frac{1}{1-[1/(1+i)]} = \frac{w}{(1+i)} \cdot \frac{(1+i)}{i} = \frac{w}{i}$$

2 Alternatively, consider the sequential substitution for R_2, R_3, ... in equation (28). Substituting for R_2 in terms of R_3 yields

$$R(\,)_1 = E(\,)\,Pr(\,) + R(\,)_2\,[1 - Pr(\,)] - c$$
$$= E(\,)\,Pr(\,) - c + [1 - Pr(\,)]\,\{E(\,)\,Pr(\,) + R_3(\,)\,[1 - Pr(\,)] - c\}$$

and further substitution yields the infinite series,

$$R(\,)_1 = [E(\,)\,Pr(\,) - c]\,\{\,1 + [1 - Pr(\,)] + [1 - Pr(\,)]^2 + \ldots$$

From footnote 1, we see that

$$R(\,)_1 \frac{E(\,)Pr(\,)}{Pr(\,)} - \frac{c}{Pr(\,)} = E(\,) - \frac{c}{Pr(\,)}$$

CHAPTER 4 Extensions to the theory of labour supply

1 Introduction

Chapter 3 developed the theory of individual labour supply ignoring the possibility of household production. It provided a static or comparatively static analysis, ignoring life-cycle effects. In the present chapter we consider three strands of the literature which have attempted to relax different aspects of the assumptions associated with the basic theory of individual labour supply. First we look at theories that have attempted to incorporate the effect to household production. Second, we examine theories that have broadened the decision-making unit to the family and allow for interdependencies between family members. Third, we explore life-cycle effects, which form the focus of dynamic theories of labour supply.

2 Household production and labour supply

2.1 Introduction

This section focuses on issues of the allocation of time and household production. Allocation of time models date back to the 1960s (Mincer, 1962; Becker, 1965) and have given rise to a rich and diverse literature, within which household production has formed an increasingly important topic, making up ground on the theories of market production. The household is seen as a production unit which combines intermediate goods (which it purchases using income earned in market work) with the time of household members to produce basic commodities (Becker, 1965; Gronau, 1977 and 1986). Household members are faced with a choice between market (paid) work, domestic/home (unpaid) work and leisure. For a review of the overall development of the literature, see Juster and Stafford (1991), and for a discussion of models of home production, see Cigno (1990). The basic theory, which is generally attributed to Becker, has certain similarities with Lancaster's theory of goods (Lancaster, 1966).

The theory is one in which households attempt to maximize utility from the consumption of commodities, which are produced by combining goods and leisure. The production of these commodities takes time, and the model therefore generates a value (shadow price) of time. While the models are more sophisticated in their treatment of time than the traditional labour/leisure trade-off models outlined in Chapter 3, the interaction between household members is generally less well developed than the family decision models described in Section 3 below. In this chapter, the household is more often treated as a single (composite) decision-making unit, rather than as a collection of individuals, each with their own desires and goals.

The discussion in this section also addresses the thorny issue of the time of day (week or year) at which labour services are delivered. This is clearly not entirely a supply side phenomenon. For certain, often non-storable, goods and services, the timing of demand is crucial in establishing the times at which labour services will be required. On the other hand, the timing of market (and domestic) production activities are also driven by the preferences of household members. The extent of shiftwork and other forms of non-standard hours, and their remuneration, have been significant issues in Europe and Australia, although less so in the UK and USA (European Foundation, 1991; Bosworth, 1995).

2.2 Home production

The home production function lies at the heart of the allocation of time models. It specifies the way in which market-produced goods, G, purchased with income from market work, are combined with time, D, within the home, to produce commodities, Z. Thus, the home production function can be written

$$Z = \mathbf{Z}(D,G) \tag{1}$$

where $\mathbf{Z}(.)$ is well behaved, with D and G imperfect substitutes in the production process. D does not correspond in any precise way with hours of work, H, or leisure, L, from the earlier models. In this instance, all activities, including leisure-time pursuits, involve both time and goods. Home production takes place subject to various constraints,

$$0 \leq D \leq T \tag{2}$$

where T denotes the total time available. The goods input must be funded by income,

$$G \leq wH + V \tag{3}$$

where: w is the market wage; H are hours of work; and V is property (unearned) income. Hours of market work and domestic activities sum to the total available,

$$\mathrm{H = T - D} \tag{4}$$

In the simplest of home production models, the individual household may be assumed to maximize the output of commodities (see Cigno, 1990),

$$\text{Max } \mathcal{L} = \mathbf{Z}(T,G) + \lambda\,(wH + V - G) \tag{5}$$

where $H = T - D$. This yields the first-order conditions for a maximum:

$$\frac{\partial \mathcal{L}}{\partial D} = \frac{\partial Z}{\partial D} - \lambda\, w = 0 \tag{6}$$

$$\frac{\partial \mathcal{L}}{\partial G} = \frac{\partial Z}{\partial G} - \lambda = 0 \tag{7}$$

$$\frac{\partial \mathcal{L}}{\partial \lambda} = w\,(T\text{–}D) + V - G = 0 \tag{8}$$

$$z = \frac{\partial Z/\partial D}{\partial Z/\partial G} = w \tag{9}$$

Dividing equation (6) by (7) yields the interior solution illustration in Figure 4.1. The slope of the isoquant, z, can be rationalized as the 'shadow wage' of non-market work. Thus, the household maximizes its production of commodities at the point where the rate

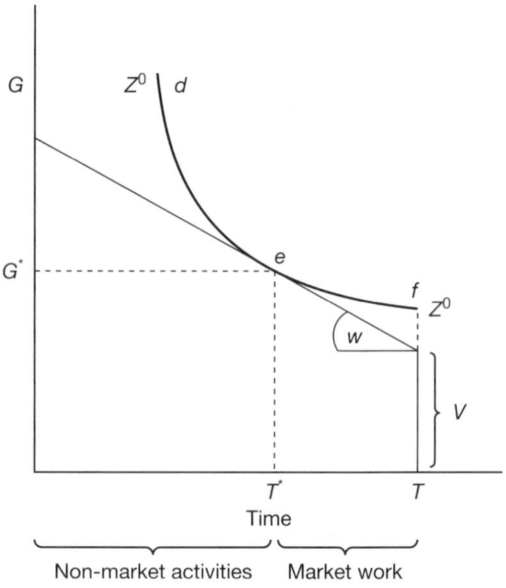

Fig 4.1 Output-maximizing single-person household.

it trades off goods for time is equal to the market wage. It can be seen that, to the left of e, $z > w$ and it pays the household to undertake (more) non-market work; on the other hand, to the right of e, $z < w$ and it pays the household to undertake (more) market work.

Although only the interior solution is illustrated the analysis appears to admit the possibility of corner solutions: for some households, their marginal productivity at home can exceed the wage they can earn in the market for all hours; for other households, the market wage may exceed their marginal productivity in domestic work for all hours. In practice, these corner solutions are more difficult to imagine in the more general, Becker, allocation of time framework described below. In this framework, market goods are inputs to the production process and home 'production' time is required in order to produce leisure-time activities.

The results of this analysis suggest that the production possibility frontier for the household can be represented by a line such as *abc* in Figure 4.2. The slope of the curve *abd* represents the marginal productivity of home work, while the slope of the line *bc* denotes the marginal return from working in the market (i.e. the wage). Thus, imagine the household begins from T and decides how to allocate its first hour. As the return to domestic work exceeds the return in the market, the household works at home. This is true for all subsequent hours until $T = T^{**}$ is

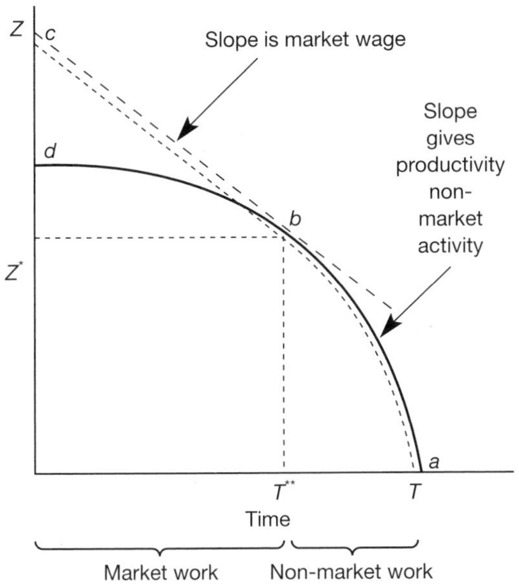

Fig 4.2 Household production possibility frontier.

reached, at which the return in the market exceeds the return from any further activity at home. Given the assumed constant wage, this is true for all remaining hours. Thus, *abc* effectively forms the production possibility frontier for the household (Gronau, 1977).

The household production function is only part of the overall picture; in general, for example, the household is not expected to attempt to maximize its production of commodities, but to maximize the utility of its constituent members (this forms the subject of subsequent sections). On the other hand, focusing on the production function helps to address a number of crucial issues in the formation and operation of the household. First, there may be economies of scale in various types of household production. Second, there may be economies in utilization of various types of durable goods (i.e. a household only requires one washing machine, whether there is only one individual or 10 in the household). Such factors can influence optimal family or household size (Cigno, 1990, pp. 27–31). Other influences may include housing prices (Borsch-Supan, 1986; Ermisch, 1987) and the increasing disutility from a lack of privacy as membership grows. In addition, the focus on the production function raises the issue of technical change in the household context, with many goods saving time (i.e. washing machines, electric razors, etc.) and others relaxing time constraints (i.e. time switches, video recorders, etc.).

2.3 Leisure, household production or market work

Traditional labour/leisure analysis does not make any allowance for the different ways in which non-market time is used, or the inter-relationship between time spent on consumption and on work. Allocation of time models, on the other hand, not only incorporate the concept of home production of commodities, but also distinguish between three different types of time allocation: leisure, home production and work (Gronau, 1977).

The choice between home and market production is represented by a production possibility frontier of the type shown in Figure 4.2. However, for the moment, it is assumed that domestic and market work both produce goods, G_D and G_M, which can be combined with leisure time to produce utility. Assuming a single-person household, the person obtains utility from combining goods G and leisure time L. Goods can be obtained from home production G_D, or from the market G_M. The home production function is represented by the function *abc* in Figure 4.3. The more time the individual spends working at home (shown by the horizontal distance from point T_0) the greater the amount of home goods produced. If the individual spends all available time working at home, they can produce G_0 units of goods. The changing slope of the function represents the diminishing marginal productivity of home production. The fact that the individual can work in the market expands this opportunity to the left of point *b*, where the goods that can be purchased

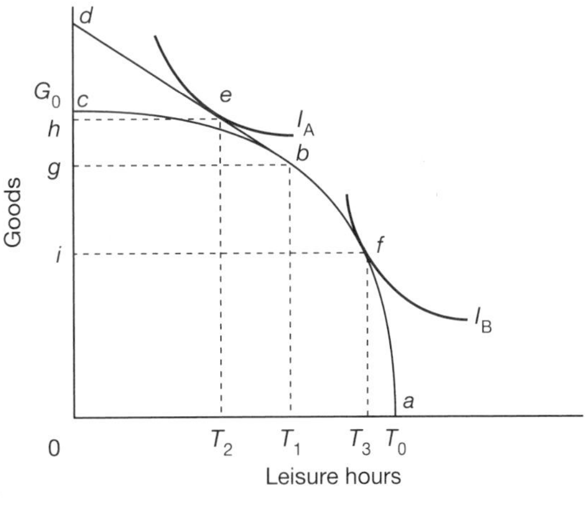

Fig 4.3 Home production, market work and leisure.

from the market as a result of working for an extra hour (the real wage rate) exceed the additional amount of goods that can be produced at home. By implication, the consumption opportunities constraint is now represented by the line *abd*.

The individual's indifference map, representing their work/leisure preferences, is superimposed on the consumption opportunities constraint in Figure 4.3. The indifference map implicitly assumes that the net disutilities of home and domestic work are identical. An individual with indifference curve I_A shows a relatively high preference for goods (or a goods-intensive combination of G and L). This person chooses point e, maximizing utility subject to the consumption opportunities constraint. This involves $0T_2$ consumption time, T_1T_2 units of time working in the market, and T_0T_1 units of domestic work. The individual consumes $0g$ of home goods and gh of market goods. On the other hand, an individual with an indifference curve I_B shows a relatively high preference for leisure (or a leisure-intensive combination of G and L), choosing point f. Person B does not work in the market, dividing time between leisure ($0T_3$) and work at home (T_0T_3), consuming $0i$ of home goods and no market goods.

The effect of an increase in the real wage rate is illustrated in Figure 4.4. Clearly the tangency between the wage rate line and the household production function will now occur at a lower level of domestic activity, b′, compared with b. The consumption opportunities constraint is modified to *ab′d′*, rather than *abd*, and it is more efficient to work in the market home after T_0T_1' of domestic work, compared with the previous value, T_0T_1. Individual B maintains their allocation of time, but individual A is affected. The increase in the wage rate lowers the price of goods in terms of time, making production less profitable for A. Work at home is therefore cut from T_0T_1 to T_0T_1'. However, the effect on leisure is indeterminate: the substitution effect towards goods reduces leisure, but the income effect tends to increase it. In Figure 4.4, the net effect on A's leisure is positive (i.e. from $0T_2$ to $0T_2'$). The effect on market work is complex: it depends on the extent of the reduction of work at home and on the change in leisure. If the reduction in work at home exceeds the increase in leisure, as in Figure 4.4, the supply to the market increases, from T_1T_2 to $T_1'T_2'$. As Gronau (1977) points out, the supply curve tends to be positively sloped, 'the greater the rate of substitution between goods and consumption time, the less sensitive the marginal productivity in home production to changes in the amount of work, and the smaller the income elasticity of leisure'.

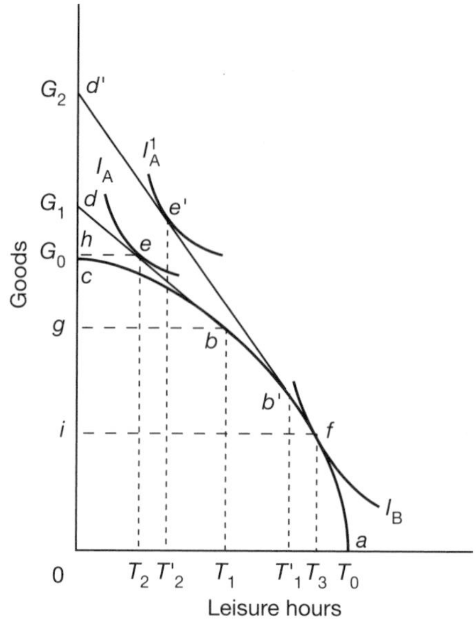

Fig 4.4 Effect of a change in the wage rate on home production, market work and leisure.

2.4 Optimal allocation of time: Becker's model

2.4.1 Introduction

An alternative approach to the theory of labour supply has been developed on the basis of Becker's theory of consumption (Becker, 1965). This approach assumes that any consumption activity not only involves an input of goods but also of time. Obtaining utility not only involves a cost in terms of goods, but also a cost in terms of the time used in consuming these goods (time which could have been devoted to earning income). Becker assumes that households combine market goods (G_j) and time (T_j) to produce 'basic commodities' (Z_j),

$$Z_j = \mathbf{Z}_j(G_j, T_j) \quad j=1, 2, \ldots, m \tag{10}$$

which enter the consumer's utility function,

$$u = \mathbf{u}(Z_1, Z_2, \ldots, Z_m) \tag{11}$$

The consumer is then faced with the choice between basic commodities or consumption activities, each of which has a goods and a time component. The balance between goods and time varies between different 'basic commodities'. Some are relatively time and others relatively goods intensive (i.e. squash has a relatively low input of time, compared with, say, golf).

2.4.2 Budget and time constraints

Household utility maximization is assumed to take place subject to two types of constraint: a time constraint and a budget constraint (equations (2) and (3)). These two constraints appear directly if hours of paid work are fixed exogenously (Gronau, 1986), but the two constraints decompose to a single 'basic constraint', that of time, where hours of market work are determined endogenously (Becker, 1965, p. 109). Distinguishing m different goods (rather than a single good or a composite commodity) and, in equilibrium, representing the expressions by equalities (rather than inequalities), substitution of equation (2) into (4) and then into equation (3) yields

$$\sum_{i=1}^{m} p_i G_i + \sum_{i=1}^{m} w D_i = V + wT \tag{12}$$

where i denotes the ith market-produced good (and, by implication, the use of the ith good in the production of some basic commodity). Note that $V+wT$ is Becker's concept of 'full income' (see Chapter 3 above); this is equal to the expenditure on goods (i.e. the first term on the left hand side) and the value of the time devoted to home activities (i.e. the second term on the left hand side); this is, in turn, equal to property income plus the total time available multiplied by the going market wage.

Becker (1965, p. 109) assumes fixed-coefficient production technologies in household production,

$$D_i = d_i Z_i \tag{13}$$

$$G_i = g_i Z_i \tag{14}$$

where d_i and g_i are the inputs of time and goods respectively per unit of the 'basic commodity'. Substitution of (13) and (14) into equation (12) yields

$$\sum_{i=1}^{m} (p_i g_i + w d_i) Z_i = V + wT \tag{15}$$

Thus, the 'full price' of a unit of Z_i can be defined as π_i,

$$\pi_i = p_i g_i + w d_i \tag{16}$$

where the first term on the right hand side is the goods input element and the second term is the time element, valued at the going market wage.

2.4.3 Optimization: hours of work fixed exogenously

Where hours are determined exogenously (i.e. on the demand side), the household is faced by a 'take it or leave it' labour supply decision of the type discussed in Chapter 3. Under these circumstances, the household is faced by two constraints: a budget constraint and a time constraint (Gronau, 1986, pp. 276–277). The problem, therefore, is to maximize utility represented by equation (11), subject to the budget constraint

$$\sum_{i=1}^{m} p_i G_i = Y \tag{17}$$

and the time constraint

$$\sum_{i=1}^{m} D_i = T \tag{18}$$

which is defined to exclude labour time (i.e. T denotes total, non-labour time). Thus, the household problem is to maximize the Lagrangian,

$$\text{Max } \mathcal{L} = \mathbf{u}(Z_1,\ldots,Z_m) + \lambda(Y - \Sigma_i p_i G_i) + \mu(T - \Sigma_i D_i) \tag{19}$$

and the first-order conditions imply

$$\frac{\partial u}{\partial Z_i} = \lambda \pi_i \tag{20}$$

where

$$\pi_i = p_i g_i + s d_i \tag{21}$$

and s is the shadow price of time ($= \mu/\lambda$ = marginal utility of time divided by the marginal utility of income). The optimal combination of inputs in the production of Z_i is given by

$$\frac{\partial Z_i/\partial D_i}{\partial Z_i/\partial G_i} = \frac{g_i}{d_i} = \frac{s}{p_i} \tag{22}$$

which indicates that the marginal rate of substitution in production is the same as the input price ratio.

In this model, the demand for goods, G_i, is a derived demand. It depends on: the demand for the 'basic commodity', Z_i, determined by the utility maximization problem; the share of the market input costs in the total costs of producing the commodity; the elasticity of substitution between the two home production inputs (i.e. goods and time). The demand for Z_i depends on: the underlying shape of the utility map and its price (i.e. its marginal cost of production, determined by the amount of goods and time it requires). While the assumption that working time given is very restrictive, it does allow the crucial role of the value of time to be highlighted. The larger the exogenously determined value of the labour supply, the higher is income and the less time is available for home activities. As a result, time is more scarce and the shadow price of time is higher. Thus, an exogenous increase in hours of market work raises the shadow price of time, making time-intensive activities more expensive to the household (i.e. those activities associated with high d_i/g_i). The result is a substitution of goods for time and a movement away from time-intensive activities.

2.4.4 Optimization: hours of work determined endogenously

While the model described in Section 2.4.3 is a useful starting point, the assumption that hours of market work are exogenously determined implies that nothing can be said about the nature of the labour supply function (i.e. about the relationship between market wages and desired hours of market work). In the present section, the household is left free to determine its hours of market work. Under these circumstances, time is the only constraint, as hours of market work and therefore household income are endogenous. In the general Becker model, therefore, the aim is to maximize utility, as shown in equation (11), subject to the single (consolidated) budget constraint, given as equation (12).

Gronau (1986, pp. 277–279) argues that, under these circumstances, market work can be treated as any other activity, requiring inputs of time and goods. Market work is assumed to be the *m*th activity, Z_m, requiring G_m of goods and D_m of time (i.e. where G_m and D_m are now to be determined endogenously). Earnings in the market are therefore a function of the amount of time and goods devoted to this activity,

$$W = \mathbf{W}(Z_m) \qquad (23)$$

where $\partial W(Z_m)/\partial Z_m$ is the marginal market wage. The household budget constraint (formerly equation (3)) can be rewritten

$$\sum_{i=1}^{m} p_i G_i = \mathbf{W}(Z_m) + V \qquad (24)$$

and the time constraint represented by equation (18) now incorporates market work activities (i.e. T is total time available).

The optimum for Z_m derived from the first-order conditions can be written

$$\frac{\partial u}{\partial Z_m} = \lambda\,[(p_m G + sd_m) - \partial \mathbf{W}(Z_m)/\partial Z_m] \qquad (25)$$

where s is again the shadow price of time. Normalizing the units of measurement such that d_m=1, equation (25) can be rearranged, so that the shadow price of time can be written

$$s = \frac{\partial \mathbf{W}(Z_m)}{\partial Z_m} - p_m G_m - \frac{\partial(u/\partial Z_m)}{\lambda} \qquad (26)$$

Gronau (1986, p. 277) concludes that the shadow price of time will only equal the market wage if: the wage rate is constant (i.e. independent of the number of paid hours worked); no market goods are used in the supply of labour services to the market (G_m=0); work in the market involves no marginal utility or disutility ($\partial u/\partial Z_m = 0$). In general, not all of these conditions will be met and the traditional assumption, that the value the household puts on its time at the margin is equal to the market wage, will not be valid.

Attention now turns to the way in which changes in wages affect labour supply. Becker (1965, p. 112) notes that an exogenous increase in property income, V, would tend to increase the consumption of most commodities and, if this was the case, then hours of work must, by definition, fall. Under these circumstances, hours worked could only increase if a sufficient number of relatively time-intensive commodities were 'sufficiently inferior'. Becker goes on to argue that, if the market wage rises, then the income-compensated result (i.e. the substitution effect) would tend to be away from time-intensive commodities, reducing the time spent in consumption activities and increasing the time available for market work. As in traditional labour supply theory, the uncompensated increase in earnings will affect the supply of labour to the market through the substitution and income effects; the former will tend to increase hours of paid work and the latter to reduce them, with the final outcome unknown a priori.

2.4.5 Becker's model: graphical exposition

The previous two sections have set out the main features of the allocation of time model formally. This section attempts to illustrate the operation of the model graphically. To simplify the analysis, assume there are just two basic classes of commodities: Z_1 is the class of commodities with a relatively high time input, T_1, and low goods input, G_1; on the other hand, Z_2 has a relatively high goods input, G_2, and low time input, T_2.

$$Z_1 = \mathbf{Z}_1(G_1, T_1) \tag{27}$$

$$Z_2 = \mathbf{Z}_2(G_2, T_2) \tag{28}$$

The individual's utility function is defined on Z_1 and Z_2:

$$u = \mathbf{u}(Z_1, Z_2) \tag{29}$$

Assume that the time-intensive commodity, Z_1, requires four hours per £10 worth of goods, whereas the goods-intensive commodity Z_2 requires one hour per £10 worth of goods. If this is combined with information about the wage rate, it is possible to derive the consumption opportunities curve, which forms the budget constraint against which the consumer attempts to maximize utility. If the wage rate is £10 per hour then one unit of Z_1 has a total price of £10 + (£10 × 4) = £50, since each unit of Z_1 requires £10 worth of G_1 and incurs four hours of forgone earnings in its consumption. In contrast one unit of Z_2 has a total price of £10 + (£10 × 1) = £20 (again comprised of £10 of goods, but, only one hour of time at a cost of £10 per hour). Thus, the relative price of Z_2 in terms of Z_1 is 2/5.

To simplify the example further, assume that one week contains 100 hours. If the worker spent all of the available time working, this would provide a maximum possible income of £1000 per week at the wage rate of £10 per hour. Becker calls this the individual's 'full income' (see Section 2.4.2 above). Any of these 100 hours not spent undertaking market work are spent on consumption activities Z_1 and Z_2. To find out how many units of Z_1 can be consumed, divide the full income of £1000 by the 'total price' per unit of Z_1, £50, which equals 20. Consuming 20 units of Z_1 would take up 20 × 4 hours = 80 hours, leaving 20 hours for market work. This would yield an income of £200 to pay for the 20 units of G_1 consumed. Similarly, the consumer could consume 1000/20 = 50 units of Z_2. Consumption time would then equal 50 × 1 = 50 hours. This would release 50 hours for market work yielding an income of 50 × £10 = £500, enabling the consumer to purchase the required 50 units of G_2.

Figure 4.5 shows the consumption of Z_1 (time-intensive commodities) on the vertical axis, and Z_2 (goods-intensive commodities) on the horizontal axis. The consumption opportunities constraint intersects the vertical axis at 20 (the maximum consumption of Z_1) and the horizontal axis at 50 (the maximum consumption of Z_2). Assuming the prices of G_1 and G_2 and the amount of time T_1 and T_2 required to consume G_1 and G_2 are constant, then the feasible consumption opportunities which the individual can choose lie in the region *abc* in Figure 4.5.

Introducing the indifference map, showing an individual's set of preferences over bundles of Z_1 and Z_2, reveals how much Z_1 and Z_2 the individual consumes when maximising utility. In Figure 4.5 the individual maximizes utility subject to the consumption opportunities constraint at point *e* on indifference curve I_1, consuming 10 units of Z_1 and 25 units of Z_2. Thus, consumption time equals (10 × 4) + (25 × 1) = 65 hours, and the amount spent on consumption equals

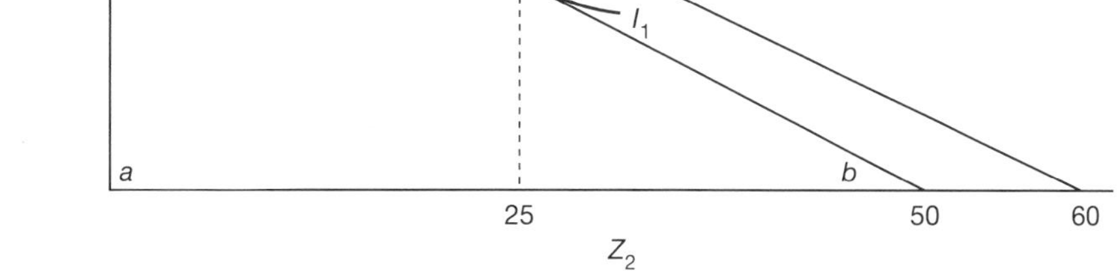

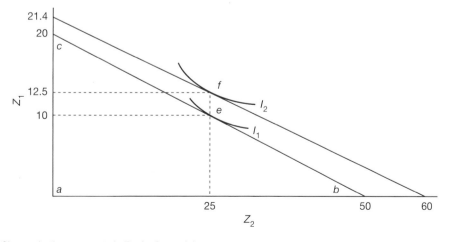

Fig 4.5 Change in the wage rate in Becker's model.

£10 × 35 = £350. Since the amount of time spent on consumption is 65 hours, the individual undertakes 35 hours of market work, yielding income of £350, which is spent on consumption goods.

To derive the individual's supply of labour curve, it is necessary to consider what happens to the amount of time devoted to market work when the real wage rate changes. If the wage rate increases to £15 per hour, the individual's 'full income' becomes £1500 per week. The total price of one unit of Z_2 is now £10 + (£15 × 1) = £25, and the total price of one unit of Z_1 is £10 + (£15 × 4) = £70. Thus, the maximum amount of Z_2 which can be consumed is £1500/£25 = 60, and the maximum amount of Z_1 which can be consumed is £1500/£70 = 21.4 units. There is now a new budget constraint and a new equilibrium position, point *f*, in Figure 4.5. Both the position and the slope of the constraint have changed, because the price of Z_1 (time-intensive commodities) has risen relative to Z_2 (goods-intensive commodities), as commodity 1 embodies more forgone earnings.

In this example, at the new equilibrium position the individual continues to consume 25 units of Z_2, but now consumes 12.5 units of Z_1. The time spent on consuming Z_2 stays at 25 hours, but consumption time on Z_1 increases to (12.5 × 4) = 50 hours. Thus, total consumption time equals 75 hours and total market work time is 25 hours. Twenty-five hours of market work yield £375 income at the new wage rate of £15 per hour, and this pays for the 37.5 units of consumption. In this example, increasing the wage rate from £10 to £15 per hour reduces market work by 10 hours. The analysis has established two points on the individual's supply of work hours curve. In this example, the supply curve is backward sloping (i.e. increases in the wage rate reduce hours of market work).

The move from *e* to *f* in Figure 4.5 incorporates both an income and a substitution effect. The substitution effect is caused by the fall in the relative price of Z_2 (goods-intensive commodities), which tends to increase hours of work. The income effect has the effect of increasing consumption time and thus reducing the number of hours of work. In this example, the negative income effect outweighs the positive substitution effect on hours of work similar to the traditional labour–leisure analysis (see Chapter 3). The only real difference is that the substitution effect is now between goods with different degrees of time-intensiveness rather than between goods and leisure.

Becker's theory, however, gives other interesting insights into hours of work, in terms of the effect of changes in the productivity of consumption time. Empirical analysis has shown that there has been a secular decline in the number of hours worked in a week, and some have suggested that this is evidence of a backward-bending supply curve. Traditional labour–leisure analysis would explain this in terms of the income effect. However, Becker's theory of the allocation of time suggests that this is only part of the story: the productivity of consumption time has also increased, as well as the productivity of working time which led to the increase in wage rates. In other words, there has been a decline in the T_j required to produce the units of Z_j as improvements in the technology of consumption have taken place. Such improvements include the development of telephones, supermarkets, sleeping pills, electric razors and videos.

A uniform increase in the productivity of consumption time (a decline in all T_j required to produce a unit of Z_j) is analogous to Hicks neutral technological change (for a discussion, see Chapter 10). The relative prices of commodities with large forgone earnings would fall, and substitution would be induced towards these and away from other commodities, causing hours of work to fall. The income effect of this increased productivity of time would induce an increase in the demand for goods, but since the productivity of working time is assumed not to change, more goods could be obtained only by an increase in work. So, an emphasis on the secular increase in the productivity of consumption time would lead to a very different interpretation of the secular decline in hours of work. Instead of claiming that a powerful income effect swamped a weaker substitution effect, the claim would have to be that a powerful substitution effect swamped a weaker income effect.

Of course, both the productivity of working and consumption time have increased secularly, and the true interpretation is somewhere between these extremes. If both increased at the same rate there would be no change in relative prices, and thus no substitution effect. The income effects would also tend to offset each other. Becker states that they would do so completely only if the income elasticity of demand for time-intensive commodities was equal to unity. Hours worked would decline if it was above and increase if it was below unity. Since these commodities have, on the whole, been luxuries, an increase in income can generally be expected to reduce hours of work.

2.5 Time-dependent activities, unsocial hours and shiftworking

2.5.1 Valuation of time

The previous sections introduced the idea of a cost of time which influenced the individual's allocation of time between different activities. This section is concerned with the idea that the returns to various activities may vary with the time of day (week or year). This may arise because of time-varying utility or time-varying prices. Becker (1965) indicates that units of time are valued differently depending on when in the day, week or year they occur. In principle, the allocation of time theories can accommodate this because the costs of producing each commodity and the utility derived from consuming a unit of each commodity can be 'time dated'. However, this is too general to give any major insights about how individuals or households will actually allocate their time.

The literature on the supply of individuals to unsocial hours and shiftworking begins from the premise that there are physiological, psychological, social and economic influences governing this decision. Perhaps the most fundamental of these are the physiological influences associated with natural body rhythms, which reflect the 24 hour day and the seasons of the year. The human body has its own technology of production; it requires a variety of inputs (food, drink, rest, etc.) and produces a variety of outputs (hours of effort). The human physiology, however, is driven by the circadian cycle, which is a natural, inbuilt 'clock', roughly 24 hours in length (and regularly 'corrected' by outside stimuli, such as light and dark, and other fixed time references). Individuals whose 'clocks' are out of step with the 24 hour day often experience a number of physiological and psychological side-effects. In addition, individuals whose natural body rhythms are disturbed, find some difficulty in adjusting to changes of times they are expected to sleep, work, etc. The larger the change, the longer and more difficult the adjustment.

Shiftwork is sometimes simply defined as work which lies outside of the 'normal day' (i.e. 09.00–17.00) (Walker, 1978). While this is too simplistic, it nevertheless emphasizes that shiftwork will involve some form of 'unsocial hours' of work, which, in turn, may have knock-on effects for the times at which the shiftworker can undertake other domestic activities. If, in addition, the system involves 'alternation' or 'rotation' of shifts (i.e. the individual works 06.00 to 14.00 one week, 14.00 to 22.00 the next and 22.00 to 06.00 in the third week), the individual is faced by periods of change which may involve considerable adjustment not only physiologically, but also socially.

This raises the possibility that the individual may be differently productive at different times of the day. Thus, their productivity in market work and in domestic activities might depend on which they do first (or which they do when they are most fatigued). Figure 4.6 illustrates this possibility, using the framework developed above. If the individual worked in the market during their most productive period, they would earn a higher wage, w_1, but they would be less productive in the home, as indicated by the relatively shallowly sloped *ab'd'*. On the other hand, if they reversed their allocation of time and spent their most productive time in home production, this would result in a fairly steeply sloped line *abd*. As a consequence, however, they would be less productive in paid market work, gaining a lower wage, w_2. The optimal way of allocating time depends on the underlying indifference map. If the individual's indifference map includes u_1, they would be best to allocate their most productive time to market work; if, however, their map included u_0, they would do better to put non-market activities first and undertake a small amount of lower-paid work in the market. This analysis yields some insights about the allocation of

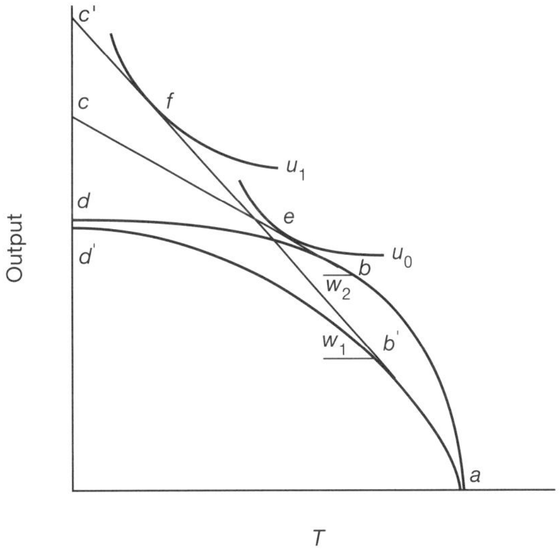

Fig 4.6 Productivity and the timing of domestic and market work.

time and the consumption opportunities constraint. However, it says little or nothing about the case where the individual prefers to undertake certain activities at certain times of the day, week or year (i.e. where their indifference map is itself time dependent).

Most individuals, for a variety of reasons, prefer to undertake their market work during the 'normal working day period' (09.00 to 17.00), and few individuals prefer to work during the night. Figure 4.7 shows that, as a consequence, the supply curve of labour is further to the right during the daytime period than during the night. The position of the demand curve for labour is assumed to be fixed, independent of the time of day (i.e. in other words, if the going wage was w_M at every instant during the day, firms would employ E_M workers at every point during the day). In practice, however, because the supply curve shifts over the 24 hour period, the instantaneous, time of day wage varies between w_N and w_M (which is assumed to be, approximately, mid-day and mid-night). Thus, the maximum time of day premium is w_M/w_N. Figure 4.8 shows the resulting premium: as the supply curve in Figure 4.7 treks from right to left after mid-day, the premium rises, continuing to increase until around mid-night – tracing out the instantaneous time of day wage curve in Figure 4.8; after mid-night, the supply curve begins to shift back outwards, and the associated premium falls until it becomes zero at w_N (Sergean *et al.*, 1969; Bosworth and Dawkins, 1980 and 1981). Winston and McCoy (1974) adopt a rhythmical, time-varying, instantaneous wage of this type in a theoretical model explaining the extent of capital utilization; the optimal length of operating day for the firm is related, in part, to the shape of this cyclical pattern.

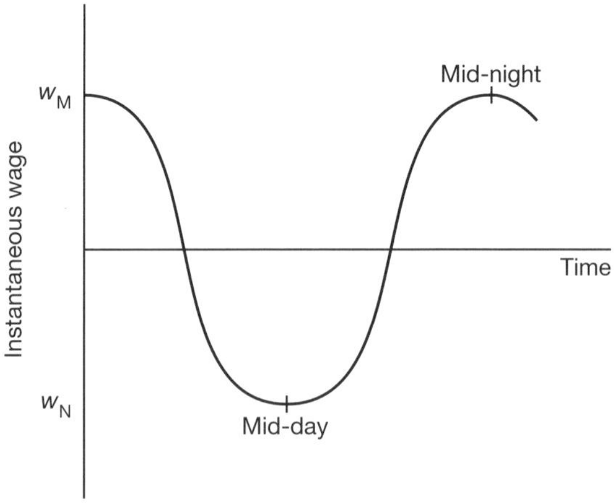

Fig 4.8 Instantaneous time of day wage.

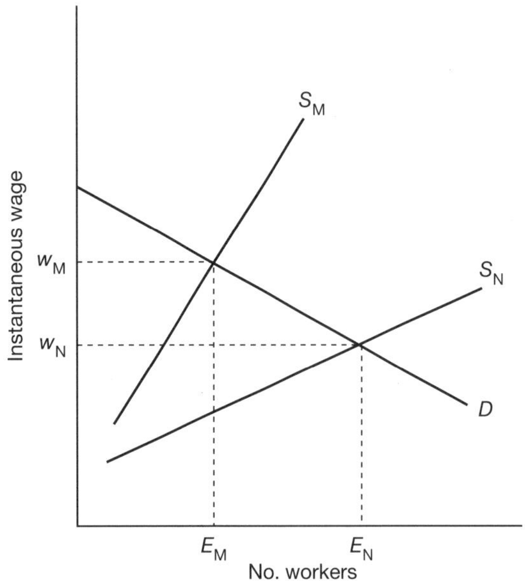

Fig 4.7 Shifts in the supply of labour over 24 hours.

2.5.2 When to work

The time of day is a further important dimension of labour supply. Workers may have to be paid a premium to work overtime, and also to work at unsocial times of the day (week or year). Hence, particular levels of shift premiums are associated with particular types of shift patterns because they involve different numbers of unsocial hours. If working at night is less desirable than working during the day, the amount of goods (income) required to give the same level of utility is higher for night work. Thus, the individual will require a shift premium to induce night work. Notice the similarity between the work pattern and job choice decisions.

Chapter 3 discussed the way in which employees associate different levels of disutility with different lengths of working day. In addition, for any given length of working day, a worker will associate different levels of disutility with various types of shifts. Note also that, if normal hours are worked during the relatively social times of the day, overtime hours will generally spill over in relatively unsocial hours, and the overtime premium may incorporate an 'unsocial time of work' payment. There are, in fact, an enormous number of length of day and time of day combinations which could constitute one shift.

The remainder of this section develops a theoretical framework which disentangles the time of day and length of day influences on the wage paid for a particular work pattern (Bosworth and Dawkins, 1980). It is possible to identify three components associated with compensation for the disutility of: (i) a minimum payment to induce labour to supply themselves at all; (ii) a length of day mark-up, and (iii) a 'time of day' mark-up. The total compensation curve is an aggregate of these three elements. For a given length of day, the aggregate compensation curve will vary depending on the time at which the day starts. Assuming that different sorts of shifts involve the same fixed costs (i.e. travel to work and length of work), it is the time of day which explains the different shift premiums.

First we begin by illustrating the 'time of day mark-up', holding the length of shift constant. Figure 4.9 illustrates the wage path from 6.00 a.m. to 6.00 p.m. Comparing two shifts of equal length (eight hours), one starting at 6.00 a.m. and the other at 8.00 a.m., the 'instantaneous' wage curve is *ab* for the former and *cd* for the latter. The employer, however, pays a fixed wage over the whole shift by averaging out the instantaneous wage. Thus, the employer pays a wage w_1 for the 6.00 a.m. to 2.00 p.m. shift (such that the area under *ab* is equal to the area under *a'b'*) and w_0 for the 8.00 a.m. to 4.00 p.m. shift (such that the area under *cd* is equal to the area under *c'd'*). The wages w_1 and w_0 can be viewed as the average remunerations necessary to induce a given desired size of workforce to work the respective shifts.

Next we turn to the effects of the length of the shift, holding the time of day constant (conceptually, this is quite difficult, as it involves imagining, for example, that all hours, whatever the length of shift, are supplied at the least cost/least unsocial time of day). It is assumed that workers experience rising marginal disutility as hours of work increase. In addition, there are certain fixed costs to be borne by the workers in getting to their place of employment. The underlying instantaneous wage rate curve associated with various lengths of shift is therefore likely to decrease initially as hours increase, before turning up again. The curve w_{LM} in Figure 4.10 denotes the perceived marginal cost of each hour, given the length of shift already worked. The minimum point of the curve is associated with the lowest wage, w_M, required to induce labour to supply itself for any of the hours of work. If H_N represents normal hours, the average hourly wage for the day is w_0. The area under the curve w_0 between 0 and H_N is equal to the corresponding area under the w_{LM} curve between 0 and H_N. If the employee works more hours than this, an overtime premium can be earned. In the real world, the steepness of the w_{LM} curve beyond normal hours is reflected in the overtime premiums which are paid in a number of stages. Negotiated premiums are generally constructed as the ratio of the two average rates, w_1/w_0. The premium $(w_1 - w_0)/w_0$, however, is

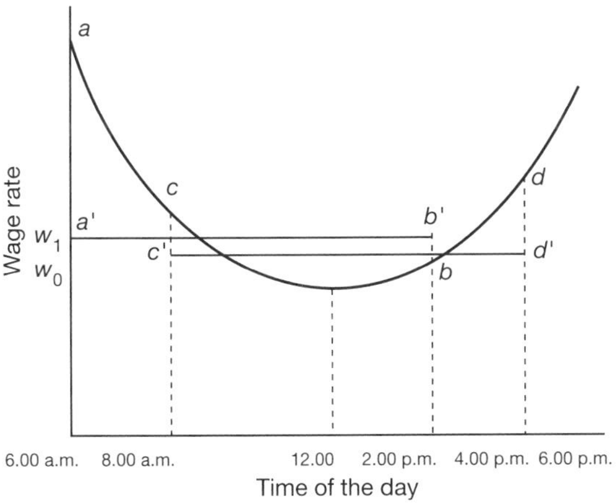

Fig 4.9 Effect of the time of day on the wage rate.

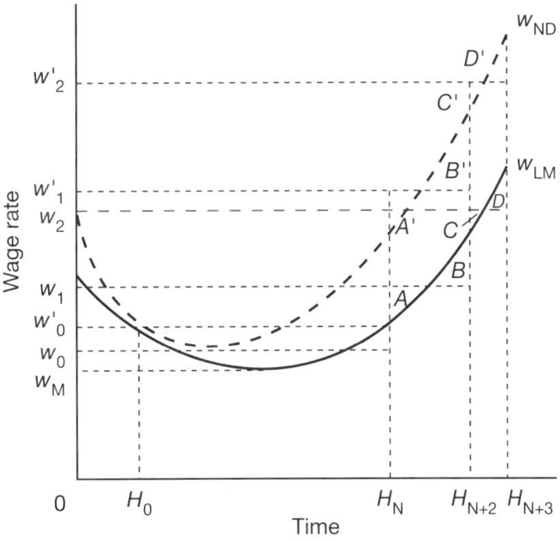

Fig 4.10 Integration of time of day and length of day payment

not the one we observe in the real world as, by assumption, our w_{LM} curve is devoid of any time of day effects. The average wage rate for the two hours of overtime is constructed such that the area A is equal to the area B (i.e. w_1 is the average wage rate for the two overtime hours, where the marginal rate increases from the beginning of hour 1 to the end of hour 2). The second jump is from w_1 to w_2 for the third and subsequent hours, such that the area C is equal to the area D, and the pure length of day mark-up is $(w_2 - w_0)/w_0$.

Figure 4.10 illustrates the total compensation curve, w_{ND}, constructed for a system of normal day plus overtime, by adding the appropriate time of day mark-up to the length of day curve w_{LM}. The distance between the two curves (w_{ND} and w_{LM}) represents the instantaneous time of day premium. The precise relationship will depend on what time of day we set the shift off. In this case, the shift starts just before 12.00 mid-day and the curves are tangential at H_0 hours, when the time of day premium falls to zero. In this particular case, the gap between the two curves increases to the right of H_0, as hours of work become more and more unsocial. The average wage rate we would observe for normal hours of work H_N for this particular shift is w_0'. Thus, $(w_0' - w_0)/w_0$ is the unsocial hours premium component of the observed normal wage and $(w_0 - w_m)/w_m$ is some measure of the length of day mark-up. The observed 'overtime' premium for the first few additional hours (often a jump from 1 to 1.33) is represented by w_1'/w_0'. It is immediately clear that the overtime premium as traditionally measured is a composite of both time of day and length of day effects. The best way of measuring the decomposition is in the difference between w_{ND}, w_{LM} and w_M for any given length of working day. At the first overtime threshold, however, the two effects can be approximately measured as: (i) the time of day effect w_1'/w_1; (ii) the length of day effect, w_1/w_0.

Thus, it would be inaccurate to think of premiums as being purely compensation for long hours. Given certain typical start and finish times for each type of shift system, overtime tends to be worked at particular times of day (i.e. in this case, at the end of the normal day period). Overtime work on a double-day shift might be worked prior to the morning shift or at the end of the afternoon shift. Equally, it would be wrong to think of shift premiums as purely compensation for time of day effects insofar as different shift patterns involve different lengths of working day. In general, therefore, both the negotiated wage for the shift and the overtime premium will reflect a time of day element as well as a length of day element.

3 Family models

3.1 Introduction

In Chapter 3 we assumed that labour supply decisions were taken by individuals. This section considers the extensions of the traditional labour supply model to account for household or family decisions. The discussion treats the family and household as interchangeable terms, although, in the real world, they can be quite different and a given theory may be more appropriate to one than the other. However, both the family and the household can be viewed as a composite of individuals, held together by common bonds (i.e. genetic, social, psychological and economic ties). At first sight, it seems natural to consider family or household issues as following on naturally from the discussion of the allocation of time. In practice, given our current state of knowledge, the linkages remain fairly weak.

The literature breaks down into three broad categories of models (for a review see Killingsworth, 1983, Chapter 2):

1 'chauvinist models' in which (normally) the male decides his supply independently and the female treats male income as if it were property income;

2 'family utility/family budget constraint models', in which the household maximizes an overall utility function;

3 'individual utility/family budget constraint models', in which individuals have their own interests and, even, potentially competing goals; each individual attempts to maximize their utility subject to the overall household budget constraint.

In some theories, the household maximizes an overall welfare function, in others it recognizes the separate utilities of each individual member. Some theories emphasize the cooperative nature of the household environment, while others see the goals of each member as potentially competitive. In this more complex world, the simplifying dichotomy between paid work and leisure is maintained.

3.2 Chauvinistic model

There are a large number of examples of the chauvinistic model in the literature (Barth, 1967; Bowen and Finegan, 1965, 1966 and 1969; Parker and Shaw, 1968; Tella *et al.*, 1971). Again, for a review see Killingsworth (1983). In essence, the model assumes that one of the partners (typically the male) maximizes their utility independent of the choices of the other partner. Thus, the outcome is essentially the same as the individual optimization described in Chapter 3,

$$\mathrm{H}_{\mathrm{m}}^{*} = \mathbf{H}_{\mathbf{m}}^{*}(w_{\mathrm{m}}/p, V_{\mathrm{m}}/p) \qquad (30)$$

which yields male income from market work, Y_{m}, of

$$Y_{\mathrm{m}}^{*} = (w_{\mathrm{m}}/p)H_{\mathrm{m}}^{*} \qquad (31)$$

Once H_{m}^{*} and Y_{m}^{*} are determined, the other partner maximizes their utility, u_{f},

$$u_{\mathrm{f}} = \mathbf{u}_{\mathrm{f}}(G, L_{\mathrm{f}}) \qquad (32)$$

subject to a budget constraint which includes male earnings as if it were property income,

$$(w_{\mathrm{f}}/p)H_{\mathrm{f}} + [(V_{\mathrm{f}}/p) + Y_{\mathrm{m}}] \geq G_{\mathrm{f}} \qquad (33)$$

Despite the simplicity of the model, it results in a number of predictions consistent with female labour supply in the real world. One result is that historically, at least, females were less likely to participate than males, other things being equal. On the other hand, given the increases in real male income which occurred over a significant period of time, the model required significant shifts in the female utility function in order to explain the increased participation of women in the workforce over time that characterized many industrial countries. It is possible, however, that these trends reflect the growing insecurity of male employment or the experience of particular groups (such as spouses of somewhat older males in manual jobs in manufacturing industries). However, the model has little to say about changing attitudes and culture which have tended to increase the participation of women and effectively to undermine the realism of the chauvinistic model. A further limitation of the model is that the male and the household utility outcome might be suboptimal *vis-à-vis* some non-chauvinistic goal.

3.3 Family utility/family budget constraint

This class of family labour supply models (which can be traced to Samuelson, 1956, and Kosters, 1966) has, to date, proved to be the most commonly used in empirical analysis (see, for example, MacRae and Yezer, 1976; Abbott and Ashenfelter, 1976; Ashenfelter and Heckman, 1974; Bognanno *et al.*, 1974; Gramm, 1974; Olsen, 1977). Again, for a review, see Killingsworth (1983).

In general, the family utility function can be written

$$u_{\mathrm{h}} = \mathbf{u}_{\mathrm{h}}(G_1, G_2, \ldots, G_m, L_1, L_2, \ldots, L_n) \qquad (34)$$

where u_{h} denotes household utility, there are m different goods consumed and there are n family members, $i = 1, \ldots, n$. The family budget constraint is written

$$\sum_{j=1}^{m} p_j G_j = \sum_{i=1}^{n} w_i H_i + V_{\mathrm{f}} \qquad (35)$$

where V_{f} denotes family property income. If the prices of goods (i.e. the p_j) stay in the same proportion, the G_j can be aggregated into a composite commodity, G; likewise, if all family wage rates change in the same proportion, family leisure time can also be aggregated (using the Hicks composite commodity theorem). If the aggregation of both goods and leisure is valid, the family labour supply problem is identical in all important respects to that of the individual, discussed in Chapter 3. Thus, an income-compensated equiproportional increase in the wage rates of all family members (i.e. the pure substitution effect) will always reduce (composite) leisure, L, and increase the consumption of the (composite) commodity, G. Again, as before, the overall outcome with regard to labour supply depends on the relative sizes of income and substitution effects.

This form of aggregation, however, hides the potential richness of family decision models. If only goods are aggregated into a composite, G, equation (34) simplifies to

$$u_{\mathrm{h}} = \mathbf{u}_{\mathrm{h}}(G_{\mathrm{h}}, L_1, \ldots, L_n) \qquad (36)$$

but leisure is separately distinguished for each of the n family members. This enables the treatment of consumption activities to be simplified while allowing the analysis to focus on two types of substitution effects: own substitution and cross-substitution. Own substitution is concerned with what happens to individual *i*'s labour supply as their own wage rate changes; cross-substitution is concerned with what happens to individual *i*'s labour supply as *j*'s wage changes, where *i* and *j* belong to the same family.

Equation (36) is maximized subject to the family budget constraint,

$$\sum_{i=1}^{n} (w_i/p)H_i + (V_f/p) \geq G \tag{37}$$

where $H_i = T - L_i$. Thus, the Lagrangian expression can be written

$$\text{Max } \mathcal{Y} = \mathbf{u}(G, L_1, ..., L_n) + \lambda \,(\sum_{i=1}^{n} (w_i/p)H_i + (v_f/p) - G) \tag{38}$$

The first-order conditions are,

$$\frac{\partial \mathcal{Y}}{\partial G} = \frac{\partial u}{\partial G} - 1 = 0 \tag{39}$$

$$\frac{\partial \mathcal{Y}}{\partial L_1} = \frac{\partial u}{\partial L_1} - \lambda \left(\frac{w_1}{p}\right) = 0 \tag{40}$$

$$\frac{\partial \mathcal{Y}}{\partial L_n} = \frac{\partial u}{\partial L_n} - \lambda \left(\frac{w_n}{p}\right) = 0 \tag{41}$$

$$\frac{\partial \mathcal{Y}}{\partial \lambda} = (V_f/p) + \sum (w_i/p)H_i = 0 \tag{42}$$

In the same way as the individual optimization problem described in Chapter (3), the solution of equations (39)–(42) yields a labour supply function for each family member,

$$H_i^* = \mathbf{H}_i^*(w_1/p, w_2/p, ..., w_n/p, V_f/p) \tag{43}$$

The hours of work of each household member depend on the real wage rates of the others, on the price of consumption goods and non-labour income. If, for example, the real wage rate of either the husband or the wife goes up, this will generally affect both partners' labour supply decisions. Again, a priori, there is no single expected outcome in terms of labour supply of such a change in the real wage. The relative preferences of the household members for goods and leisure as well as the relative real wage rates and the level of any household non-labour income will all affect the outcome.

As far as the participation decision is concerned, we are interested in determining what leads H_i to be positive. Let us consider for example the female's decision to participate. The higher the wage of the male relative to the female the less inclined she is to participate because he has a comparative advantage at income earning. However, her decision also depends on the nature of the utility function. The less satisfaction she associates with non-market activity the more inclined she will be to work. Empirical evidence shows that the participation of married women has risen significantly in the post-war period in most industrialized countries. This trend can be explained, in part, in terms of rising female wage rates, changes in the household utility function and changes in societal attitudes to women working. At the same time, there have been significant changes in the technology of household production, reducing the labour time required for any given level of household production. On average, however, married women still spend less time in the labour market than their husbands and are often referred to in the literature as 'secondary' members of the labour market, as opposed to 'primary workers', although this position varies enormously across countries (compare Sweden, where female participation is extremely high, and Japan, where it is low) and over time (with a general shift towards the increased participation of women).

If intra-family (i.e. cross-substitution) effects are zero (i.e. if one person's supply is not influenced by the wage of another family member), then equation (43) simplifies to

$$H_i^* = \mathbf{H}_i^* \left(w_i/p, V_f/p + \sum_{g \neq i} (w_g/p)\, H_g\right) \tag{44}$$

Thus, the only effect of other family members on individual *i*'s decision is via family income, which is now formed from V_f and the sum of the incomes of other family members ($g = 1, ..., n$; $g \neq i$). Thus, the model again collapses to a form similar to the one shown in Chapter 3, which has proved popular in the literature (Bognanno *et al.*, 1974; Cohen *et al.*, 1970; Fisher, 1971).

3.4 Individual utility/family budget constraint models

There are a variety of family models which emphasize the individual within the household context which can be traced back through Leuthold (1968) and Ashworth and Ulph (1981) (see Killingsworth, 1983, pp. 34–38). They focus on individual utility maximization (where individual utility is a function of individual leisure and family consumption), subject to a family budget constraint. Such models raise interesting questions about the gains to be made from living within a household, and the optimal size and mix of the household (see Section 3.5 below).

Some theories treat husbands and wives as duopolists (for a discussion, see Killingsworth, 1983, pp. 34–35). These models analyse the reaction curves of family members and derive their competitive (and cooperative) labour supply decisions. The reaction curves of the husband (m) and wife (f) in a two-person household are shown in Figure 4.11. Each reaction curve shows the optimal (utility-maximizing) choice of hours for that partner, given the hours worked by the other partner. Notice that, if the wife is supplying H_f^1 of hours to the labour market, then the husband maximises his utility by supplying H_m^1. However, these levels of supply by the two individuals are inconsistent (i.e. both in terms of the two family members and with regard to family consumption). Once the wife realizes that the husband is supplying H_m^1, she revises her own supply to H_f^2. Then H_m^1 is no longer the utility-maximizing hours for the husband; in maximizing his utility he revises his decision to H_m^2. Given the two reaction curves shown in Figure 4.11, this process continues until the two partners reach point *e*, where the decisions are consistent and there is no further pressure for change. A similar movement towards equilibrium would ensue if the initial positions were to the right of point *e*.

Figure 4.11 represents a convergent process, and point *e* is a stable equilibrium for both partners. If the slopes of the reaction curves are reversed, the result would be a divergent process and any 'equilibrium' point such as *e* would be unstable (i.e. if the process started at *e*, any minute disturbance would move the partners away from *e*, towards increasingly inconsistent hours decisions). Killingsworth (1983, pp. 35–36) reports that,

> A sufficient condition for this [a stable equilibrium] to be true is that consumer goods are normal goods for both spouses.

While point *e* is the only point at which the family maximizes utility in a 'competitive environment' (i.e. where household partners compete to maximize their utility), there is usually a cooperative solution which yields at least as high utility. Clearly, some mechanism is required in order to allocate the additional utility generated (i.e. the difference between the 'competitive' and 'cooperative' solutions). However, even where the reaction curves have the necessary slopes to ensure a 'stable equilibrium' it is interesting to ask whether a partnership based on a 'competitive' solution is in anyway potentially inherently unstable, when a 'cooperative' solution exists which yields a higher utility for one or both partners, and this superior solution is ignored.

The outcome of a 'duopoly'-type model is quite distinct from the more conventional family utility/family budget constraint models. Even where there is some similarity in the outcome, it tends to occur for quite different reasons (Killingsworth, 1983, p. 36). The cross-substitution effects of the family utility model are generated by the assumption of a common utility function. In the individual utility/family budget constraint models, cross-effects are generated by 'indirect income effects': a change in one partner's behaviour alters the family income and feeds back to the supply decisions of other family members. If, for example, the husband's wage rises, there are the normal income and substitution effects on the male. The income effect experienced by the husband raises household income and this has a 'direct income effect' on the other partner. In addition, the substitution effect for the husband induces the male to work more, raising household income further, and this causes an 'indirect income effect' on the female, increasing her leisure and reducing her labour supply (as long as leisure is a normal good).

Other authors have adopted a different approach, based more on an analogy with bilateral monopoly models (for a discussion of household 'bargaining' models, see Horney and McElroy 1978; Manser and Brown, 1979; McElroy and Horney, 1981). Such models still fall within the category of individual util-

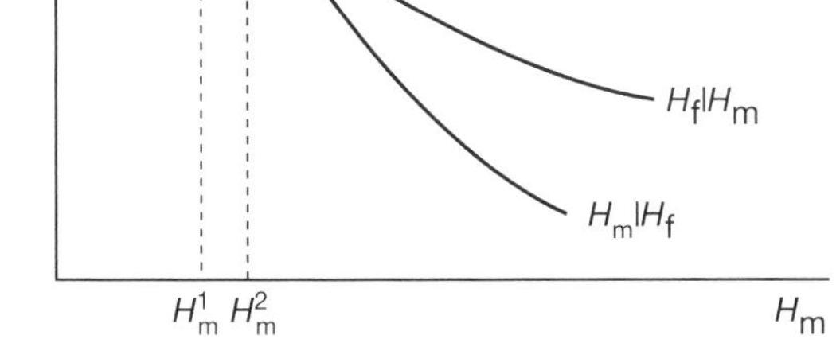

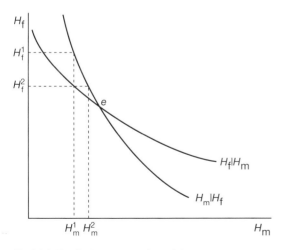

Fig 4.11 Family duopoly supply model.

ity/family budget constraint theories: each partner is still attempting to maximize their own utility. In the more conventional models discussed in earlier chapters, it makes no difference who receives earned income because all income is in some sense pooled. In a bargaining model context, however, this may be crucial because the bargaining strength of the partners may depend on their earning power. Killingsworth (1983, p. 37) comments that

> What was once the basis of dozens of Victorian novels may form the basis for new economic models of household behaviour!

3.5 Broader family issues

The economic literature appears to have glossed over the important distinction between the household (i.e. a group of individuals living at a given address) and the family (i.e. a group of individuals related by birth or through marriage). It seems likely that the goals of the household and the extent to which various, potentially 'public goods' are shared, differ between these two groupings. Some variation can also be expected even within family units. There appears to be an important distinction between the nuclear family units of industrialized countries and the extended family units more commonly found in less developed countries. Social and cultural mores will play a crucial part in determining the goals, division of labour, and extent to which various goods are shared between family members.

In the models developed above, the family pools resources and consumption. This is clearly an interesting approach where some purchases (such as heating, lighting and certain durable goods) exhibit the characteristics of 'public goods' (Cigno, 1990), but not all goods exhibit characteristics that lead to 'pooling' (Pfouts, 1955). This raises the question of the optimal size and mix of the family (and household) unit (Cigno, 1990, pp. 27–31). This essentially reverses the direction of causation, suggesting that various economic influences, including the nature of the employment available to individuals, will affect the size and composition of the family/household unit. Comparative UK and French research, for example, has investigated the relationship between unemployment, 'precarious' paid employment and the composition of the household (Lagree *et al.*, 1990). For example, one hypothesis is that where the primary 'bread-winner' of the household is in temporary or fixed contract work, this results in the eldest sibling remaining in the household for longer, in order to supplement family income.

However, there are many other possible influences. In particular, there may be economies of scale in various types of household production, for example arising from the division of tasks and labour specialization. In addition, there may be economies in utilization of various types of durable goods (i.e. a household only requires one washing machine, whether there is only one individual or 10 in the household). The relative importance and role of these factors are likely to differ considerably between one society and another, particularly between developed and less developed countries. Other influences suggested in the literature to date include housing prices and the increasing disutility from a lack of privacy as membership grows (Borsch-Supan, 1986; Ermisch, 1987). In addition, the focus on the production function raises the issue of technical change in the household context, with many new labour-saving goods (such as washing machines, electric razors, etc.) and others which free the household from fixed time constraints (i.e. time switches, video recorders, etc.).

These issues suggest that it may be important to consider the specification of the underlying production function with some care in the context of a household production/allocation of time model. Cigno (1990, pp. 27–31) illustrates the concept by specifying the household expenditure function as

$$G = n^{\Gamma} Y \quad 0 \le \Gamma \le 1 \tag{45}$$

where n is the number of household members and Y is household income. Γ is a congestion parameter: if Γ takes a value of zero, all goods in the household are pure public goods; a Γ of unity implies that there is no scope for joint consumption (all commodities are private goods). Denoting $C(w,n,X)$ as the minimum cost of producing some level of household output, X, it is possible to show that

$$C_n = -(1 - \Gamma) Y n^{\Gamma - 2} \tag{46}$$

and the minimum cost of X falls as n rises. However, other economic factors, such as transaction costs, tend to rise disproportionately with household size. The result is a finite optimal household size of n^*. Lower transaction costs and higher market wages both have the effect of increasing optimal household size.

A variety of topics linked to the structure of the family unit have attracted a considerable degree of interest. These include the economics of marriage and divorce (Kirk, 1970; Becker *et al.*, 1977; Peters, 1986; Sprague, 1990; Weiss and Willis, 1985); the decision to leave home (European Foundation, 1991); household social and information networks (Lagree *et al.*, 1990). The role of economic factors as influences on such variables suggests that marital status and labour supply may be jointly determined through a much more general optimization process (Becker, 1960, 1974 and 1981). The possible reversal in causality or jointness of labour supply and marital status raises important question marks over many of the empirical estimates where marital status is included as an explanatory variable.

4 Life-cycle models

4.1 Introduction

The models outlined in the previous chapters have viewed the labour supply decision in a static, or comparative static, framework. Since the 1970s, however, a major literature has developed focusing on the labour supply decisions about participation and hours of work (as well as job choice) in a dynamic or life-cycle framework. Dynamic labour supply models have basically extended the static framework into a multi-period model. There are essentially two variants: models in which wages are either exogenous or endogenous. The former primarily attempt to explain how much labour the individual supplies now rather than in the future (i.e. the pattern of labour supply over time) and, thereby, the total volume of labour supply over the life-cycle. The second group of models, which assume that wages are determined endogenously, focus on the individual's education and training activity.

In models in which wages are exogenous, the behaviour of labour supply over time in dynamic equilibrium is the net result of three forces (Weiss, 1972): an 'efficiency' effect (which makes individuals work more during periods in which the wage is higher); an 'interest rate' effect, which makes individuals work more at first and less later on (effectively 'banking' some part of their earnings to earn high rates of compound interest); and a 'time preference rate' effect, which tends to make individuals work less at first and more later (i.e. arising from a natural desire to take leisure now and put off work to a later date).

In the short run the individual's labour supply choice is constrained by the skills possessed. In the long run the individual can choose to extend their skills or capacity to work by investing in activities such as training or education. Such human capital investments are now embedded in the second branch of dynamic labour supply models in which wages are endogenous. Thus the supply decision is further complicated by the possibility of influencing the lifetime wage path by various forms of human capital investment (i.e. investment in health, education and/or training).

4.2 Life-cycle labour supply: stylized facts

Killingsworth (1983, pp. 207–209) outlined a number of stylized empirical facts about the life-cycle behaviour of men and women that appear with surprising regularity in a variety of different kinds of data, although there is some evidence that these patterns are changing (or even breaking down in some countries) in more recent years. First, the data for men suggest that time profiles of labour supply or market time, wage rates and earnings per year are all concave. Annual hours of work and annual earnings actually decline for the typical man as retirement approaches, although hourly wage rates do not appear to decline, or, if they do fall, they do so only slightly towards the end of the individual's working life. Hence, the decline in annual earnings towards the end of the individual's working life would appear to be mainly due to a decline in hours worked per year. Second, the typical man spends the first part of his life in full-time education or training (sometimes starting to work while still at school or college, but more usually after the school-leaving age), and works more or less continuously until retirement. Having retired he usually remains out of the labour force until death.

The average woman, on the other hand, at least in earlier years, did not follow these patterns but, rather, moved in and out of the labour market after leaving school. For some women, the interrupted career pattern of individual B, illustrated in Figure 4.12, is more typical. However, the average across women is an amalgamation of both A and B, produced by the fact that some women work more or less continuously until retirement, while others have interrupted

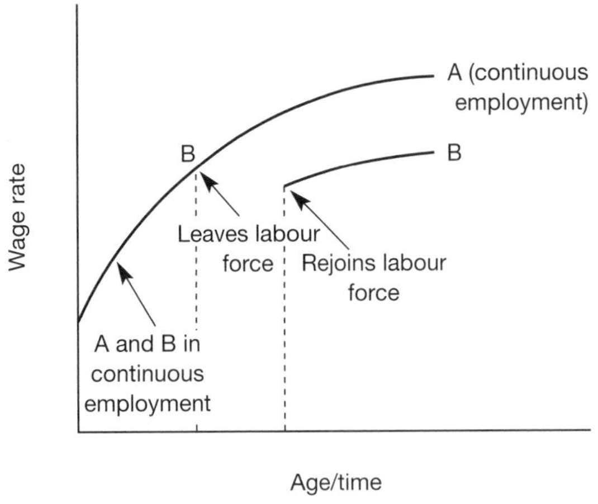

Fig 4.12 Wage profiles: continuous and interrupted careers.

patterns (and some spend little or no time in the labour force). The former type is becoming more prevalent at the expense of the latter.

The 'stylized facts' can be extended to include a discussion about what happens to training over the life-cycle. Early in life, because the individual's current earning potential is low, so are the earnings they forgo while undertaking training. On the other hand, wages are typically higher later in life, the opportunity cost of training is therefore higher and the payback period is shorter. Eventually, the payback period becomes so short that the net present value of training becomes negative (i.e. the rate of return to training is less than the rate of interest), and no further training is undertaken.

The pattern of market productivity, over time, however, is determined by both gross additions to human capital, $k(t)$, and depreciation and obsolescence, $\delta K(t)$. The likely paths of these two elements of the stock–flow expressions are illustrated in Figure 4.13(a). Total human capital depreciation (i.e. the rate of depreciation, δ, multiplied by the stock of human capital) initially increases with time, even though δ is constant, as the stock of human capital is growing ($k(t) > \delta K(t)$). However, given declining additions to the stock of human capital over time as investment in training falls away, eventually $\delta K(t) > k(t)$, and the stock of human capital begins to decline. This, in turn, reduces the total size of the individual's human capital depreciation, as shown in Figure 4.13(a).

By implication, the market productivity of the individual (and, therefore, the potential wage) tracks the stock of human capital, $K(t)$. It will, therefore, have a broadly inverse 'U' shape, as shown in Figure 4.13(b). The individual's wage rate at time t is positively related to their productivity and negatively related to the extent of their investment in education $k(t)$. Thus, the individual's wage follows broadly the same pattern, but peaks after the maximum productivity is attained. In addition, it may have a discontinuity at A^{**}, the time at which the individual ceases to invest in training, and a steeper slope thereafter.

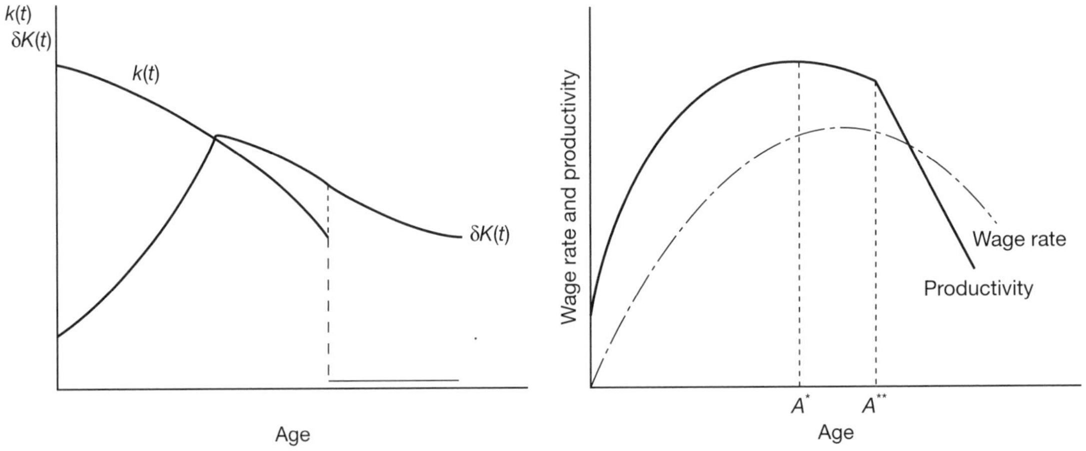

Fig 4.13 (a) Investments in and depreciation of human capital over the life-cycle. (b) Productivity and the wage rate over the life-cycle.

4.3 Dynamic labour supply with exogenous wages

This section summarizes the principal features of dynamic labour supply theory, with exogenous wages. In a multi-period, dynamic model, the assumption that all income is consumed in every period is no longer tenable. Even when assuming that the path of wages is exogenous, in dynamic models, savings and thereby the individual's stock of financial assets must be endogenous. The initial wealth of the individual plus their accumulated income minus expenditure forms the budget constraint in this theory. An assumption needs to be made about the individual's planned wealth when they die, although, for simplicity, it is often assumed to be zero.

The individual is then assumed to maximize lifetime utility, subject to the budget constraint. The utility-maximizing decision in each time period is assumed to be independent of the decision in each other time period, so that lifetime utility is simply the sum of the utilities from each individual period.

Constrained maximization yields three important effects on the labour supply decision. First, there is the 'efficiency effect', second the 'interest rate', and third the 'time preference rate effect'.

Killingsworth (1983, pp. 228–229) shows that, under the further simplifying assumption

$$\dot{\mathbf{p}}(t)/p(t) = 0 \quad \text{for all } t \tag{47}$$

(note • indicates a change over time) then the path of H over time is determined by

$$\dot{H}(t) = a\dot{w}(t)/w(t) + b(\phi - r) \tag{48}$$

where

$$a = \mathbf{u}_{\mathrm{L}}(t)\mathbf{u}_{\mathrm{GG}}(t)/D(t) > 0 \tag{49}$$

and,

$$b = [\mathbf{u}_{\mathrm{L}}(t)\mathbf{u}_{\mathrm{GG}}(t) - \mathbf{u}_{\mathrm{G}}(t)\mathbf{u}_{\mathrm{LG}}(t)]/D(t) > 0 \tag{50}$$

The first term on the right-hand side of equation (48) forms the 'efficiency effect' and the second term the 'time effect'. The 'efficiency effect' induces individuals to work when the wage rate is higher and to take their leisure when it is lower. This is analogous to the traditional substitution effect in static models of supply. Time effects, on the other hand, are divided into an 'interest rate' effect (associated with r) and a 'time preference rate' effect (associated with ϕ, the individual's rate of time preference). The interest rate effect persuades individuals to work earlier, 'banking' their earnings to earn the going rate of interest. The time preference rate effect tends to make individuals work less now and more later, simply because there is a natural tendency to postpone less pleasurable activities. Note that the sign of the time effect changes depending on whether r is greater than, equal to or less than ϕ. Further discussion can be found in Weiss (1972) and Killingsworth (1983, p. 216).

The effect of changes in exogenous variables is quite complicated and depends upon whether the changes are anticipated or unanticipated. Figure 4.14 illustrates an example of an anticipated change in the wage rate between time periods t_1 and t_2. The effect

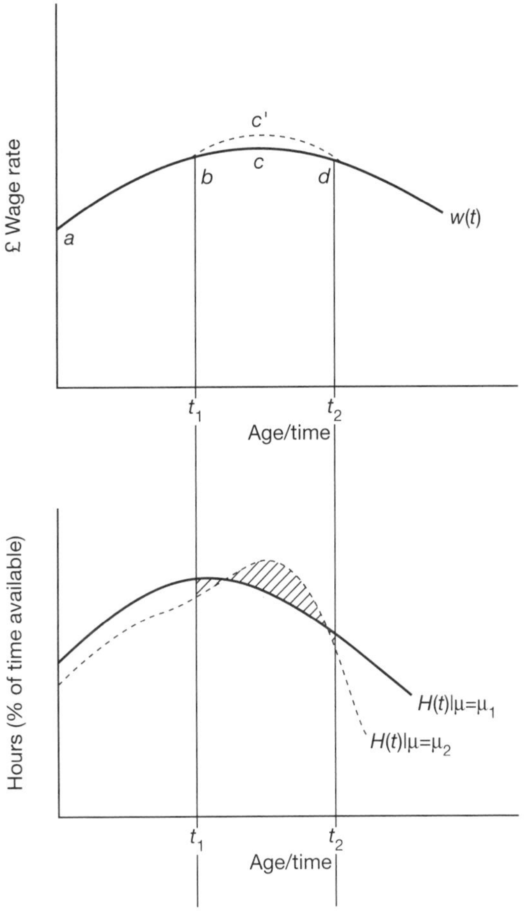

Fig 4.14 Anticipated changes in wage rates and labour supply.

on the individual can be decomposed into a wage effect and a wealth effect. The wage effect causes the individual to increase their labour supply between t_1 and t_2. Changes in labour supply outside of that time period are the result of effects on imputed wealth which has risen from μ_1 to μ_2. In the case of unanticipated changes in the wage rate, the individual decides what they would choose to supply if the wage profile is *abcd* but this expectation proves to be inaccurate. The individual then undertakes some 'replanning' in the light of unanticipated changes. For a discussion of 'replanning' see MaCurdy (1981 and 1985) and Bover (1989).

Dynamic labour supply models can produce corner solutions, at which hours of work are zero in one or more time periods (Killingsworth, 1983, p. 217). In the simplest of all worlds this just requires the wage offer to fall below the reservation wage in that period. This gives rise, however, to a number of issues about the dynamics of employment. First, wage rates depend on the continuity of employment (i.e. a state dependence effect). There is clear evidence, for example, of the effects of absence from the labour force on female wage profiles, as illustrated in Figure 4.12. One explanation may be the continuing depreciation of human capital, with females unable to make any compensating investments in human capital while they are intensively involved in a caring role. Second, there are quasi-fixed costs of job search which must be taken into account in any decision to leave employment or rejoin the labour force. Third, the probability of being made a job offer as soon as the perceived market wage exceeds the reservation wage may depend on a variety of factors acting on the demand side of the market, including length of the individual's spell out of the workforce.

4.4 Dynamic labour supply with endogenous wages

This section summarizes the principal features of dynamic labour supply theory with endogenous wages. In dynamic models with endogenous wages, the wage is a function of the individual's productivity in employment, which is assumed to be determined by their stock of human capital. Thus wages are endogenized because the individual can influence them through their investment in human capital. Three broad types of models are distinguished in the literature: 'training models'; 'experience models', based on 'learning-by-doing' formulations; models which contain the main features of both of the first two.

Training models emphasize the trade-off between current and future earnings; the individual gives up some proportion of current earnings in order to achieve higher levels of future wages. Experience models focus on the impact of learning by doing. Individuals who spend more time in market work learn more, and this raises their productivity and their wages. The trade-off here is between valuable leisure time that they give up (as they spend longer at work than they would have done without any learning effects), and the higher future income that the additional learning brings.

Given that the training and experience models can coexist, it is possible to produce a formulation that contains the main features of both (Killingsworth, 1983). Killingsworth (1983, pp. 309–310), for example, outlines a 'general model' that combines aspects of the allocation of time and learning-by-doing formulations. In this model, additions to human capital are defined by the production function

$$k(t) = \mathbf{k}(I(t), H(t), K(t)) \tag{51}$$

$k_i > 0$ for $i = I(t), H(t), K(t)$; $k(t) > 0$ if $H(t) > I(t) > 0$ where individuals have positive hours and some of these are spent training. If $H(t) > I(t) = 0$, individuals undertake no training but still learn by doing during the hours they spend in market work. However, if neither of these situations applies, $k(t) = 0$ otherwise.

The wage rate is determined by

$$w(t) = w(I(t), PR(t)) \tag{52}$$

where $w_I < 0$ and $w_{PR} > 0$; such that $w(t) = 0$ if $I(t) = H(t)$ (i.e. individuals are not paid by the firm if they are effectively full-time students) and $w(t) = PR(t)$ if $I(t) = 0$ (i.e. individuals are paid their full market productivity in the current period if they spend no time training). Finally, the individual's earnings are defined by

$$W(t) = w(t)H(t) \tag{53}$$

The pattern of hours over the life-cycle is again determined by efficiency, interest rate (r) and time preference rate (ϕ) effects. Thus, the expression for the change in hours in the training model is almost identical to equation (48) above (which was developed on the assumption that wages were exogenous). In this instance,

$$\dot{H}(t) = a(t)\left(\frac{\dot{PR}(t)}{PR(t)}\right) + b\,(\phi - r) \tag{54}$$

where the sign on the second term on the right changes depending on whether ϕ is greater than, equal to or less than r. Thus, if $r > \phi$, then the peak in hours of work occurs earlier, rather than later (the individual 'banks' their income at a compound rate of interest. On the other hand, if $r < \phi$, then the individual puts off work until later. Whatever the outcome from the interest and time preference rate effects, the efficiency effect tends to dominate time preference effects as long as PR grows sufficiently rapidly. Hence, H rises early in life, but, later on, as PR grows more slowly, the efficiency effect which raises hours gets weaker and, eventually, the time effect outweighs the ever weaker efficiency effect and hours tend to fall. By implication, the earnings profile will also be an inverted 'U' shape.

5 Conclusions

In this chapter we have considered three inter-related extensions of labour supply theory: household production theory, family models and the life-cycle. Each has provided interesting insights that the basic model of individual labour supply does not incorporate. It remains a challenge, for the theory of labour supply, to integrate all three of these areas into one model! So far in this part of the book we have been mainly concerned with the theory of labour supply but, in the next chapter, we turn to the corresponding empirical evidence on labour supply.

References

Abbott, M. and O. Ashenfelter (1976). 'Labour Supply, Commodity Demand and the Allocation of Time'. *Review of Economic Studies*, 43, 389–411.

Ashenfelter, O. and J.J. Heckman (1974). 'The Estimation of Income and Substitution Effects in a Model of Family Labour Supply'. *Econometrica*, 42, 73–85.

Ashworth, J. and D. Ulph (1981). 'Household Models'. In C. Brown (ed.) *Taxation and Labour Supply*. London: Allen and Unwin.

Barth, P.S. (1967). 'A Cross-Sectional Analysis of Labour Force Participation Rates in Michigan'. *Industrial and Labour Relations Review*, 20, 234–249.

Becker, G. (1960). 'An Economic Analysis of Fertility'. In *Demographic Change in Developed Countries*. A Conference of the Universities. New York: National Bureau of Economic Research.

Becker, G. (1965). 'A Theory of the Allocation of Time'. *Economic Journal*, September, 493–517 (reprinted in (1971) J. Burton, L. Benham, W. Vaughn and R. Flanagan (eds) *Readings in Labour Market Analysis*. New York: Holt, Rinehart and Winston).

Becker, G. (1974). 'A Theory of Marriage'. In T.W. Schultz, (ed.) *Economics of the Family*. Chicago: Chicago University Press. 293–344.

Becker, G. (1981). *A Treatise on the Family*. Cambridge, MA: Harvard University Press.

Becker, G.S., E.M. Landes and R.T. Michael (1977). 'An Economic Analysis of Marital Instability'. *Journal of Political Economy*, 85, 6, 1141–1187.

Bognanno, M.F., J.S. Hixson and I.R. Jeffers (1974). 'The Short Run Supply of Nurses' Time'. *Journal of Human Resources*, 9, 80–94.

Borsch-Supan, A. (1986). 'Household Formation, Housing Prices and Public Policy Impact'. *Journal of Public Economics*, 30, 145–64.

Bosworth, D.L. (1995). 'Shiftwork and Capital Operating Hours: the UK'. In D. Anxo, D. Bosworth, T. Sterner, D. Taddei and G. Cette (eds) *Shiftwork and Capital Operating Hours in Europe*. New York: Kluwer.

Bosworth, D.L. and P.J. Dawkins (1980). 'Compensation for Workers Disutility: Time of Day, Length of Shift and Other Features of Work Patterns'. *Scottish Journal of Political Economy*, 27, 1, 80–96.

Bosworth, D.L. and P.J. Dawkins (1981). *Work Patterns: An Economic Analysis*. Gower Press: Aldershot.

Bover, O. (1989). 'Estimating Intertemporal Labour Supply Elasticities Using Structural Models'. *Economic Journal*, 99, 398, 1026–1040.

Bowen, W.G. and T.A. Finegan (1965). 'Labour Force Participation and Unemployment'. In A.M. Ross (ed.) *Employment Policy and the Labour Market*. Berkeley: University of California Press, pp. 115–161.

Bowen, W.G. and T.A. Finegan (1966). 'Comment (on Mincer, 1966)'. In R. Gordon and M. Gordon (eds) *Prosperity and Unemployment*. New York: Wiley, pp. 113–131.

Bowen, W.G. and T.A. Finegan (1969). *The Economics of Labour Force Participation*. Princeton, NJ: Princeton University Press.

Cigno, A. (1990). 'Home Production and the Allocation of Time'. In D. Sapsford and Z. Tzoannos (eds) *Current Issues in Labour Economics*. London: Macmillan.

Cohen, M.S., S.A. Rea and R.I. Lerman (1970). 'A Micro Model of Labour Supply'. BLS Staff Paper No. 4. US Department of Labor. Washington, DC: Government Printing Office.

Ermisch, J. (1981). 'An Economic Analysis of Household Formation: Theory and Evidence from the General Household Survey'. *Scottish Journal of Political Economy*, 28, 1, 1–19.

Ermisch, J. (1987). 'Impacts of Policy Actions on the Family'. *Journal of Public Policy*, 6, 297–318.

European Foundation (1991). 'Working Time in the Member States'. *News From the Foundation*, 28, 3. Dublin: European Foundation for the Improvement of Living and Working Conditions.

Fisher, M.R. (1971). *The Economic Analysis of Labour*. London: Weidenfeld and Nicolson.

Gramm, W.L. (1974). 'The Demand for the Wife's Nonmarket Time'. *Southern Economic Journal*, 41, 124–133.

Gramm, W.L. (1975). 'Household Utility Maximisation and the Working Wife'. *American Economic Review*, 65, 90–100.

Gronau, R. (1977). 'Leisure, Home Production and Work – the Theory of The Allocation of Time Revisited'. *Journal of Political Economy*, 84, 4, S201–220.

Gronau, R. (1986). 'Home Production – A Survey'. In O. Ashenfelter and R. Layard (eds). *Handbook of Labour Economics*. Amsterdam: North-Holland.

Horney, M. and M. McElroy (1978). 'A Nash Bargained Linear Expenditure System'. Mimeo. Department of Economics, Duke University.

Juster, F.T. and F.P. Stafford (1991). 'The Allocation of Time: Empirical Findings, Behavioural Models, and Problems of Measurement'. *Journal of Economic Literature*, 29, 2, 471–522.

Killingsworth, M. (1983). *Labour Supply*. Cambridge, MA: Cambridge University Press.

Kirk, D. (1970). 'The Influence of Business Cycles on Marriage and Birth Rates'. In *Demographic and Economic Change in Developed Countries*. A Conference of the Universities. New York: National Bureau for Economic Research.

Kosters, M. (1966). 'Income and Substitution Effects in a Family Labour Supply Model'. Report No. P-3339. Rand Corporation.

Lagree, J-C., P. Lew Fai, D.L. Bosworth, D.L. and S. Dex (1990). *Les Amortisseurs de la Crise Economique. (Re)entrées sur le marché de l'emploi, précarisation et liens de solidarité. Etude en France et au Royaume Uni.* Final Report. Commission des Communautés Européennes. Brussels.

Lancaster, K. (1966). 'A New Approach to Consumer Theory'. *Journal of Political Economy*, 74, 132–157.

Leuthold, J. (1968). 'An Empirical Study of Formula Income Transfers and the Work Decision of the Poor'. *Journal of Human Resources*, 3, 312–323.

MaCurdy, T.E. (1981). 'An Empirical Model of Labour Supply in a Life-Cycle Setting'. *Journal of Political Economy*, 89, 1059–1085.

MaCurdy, T.E. (1985). 'Interpreting Empirical Models of Labour Supply in an Intertemporal Framework with Uncertainty'. In J.J. Heckman and B. Singer (eds.) *Longitudinal Analysis of Labour Market Data*. Cambridge, MA: Cambridge University Press.

MacRae, C. and A. Yezer (1976). 'The Personal Income Tax and Family Supply'. *Southern Economic Journal*, 43, 783–792.

McElroy, M. and J. Horney (1981). 'Nash Bargained Household Decisions: Towards a Generalisation of the Theory of Demand'. *International Economic Review*, 22, 333–349.

Manser, M. and M. Brown (1979). 'Bargaining Analyses of Household Decisions'. In C. Lloyd, E. Andrews and C. Gilroy (eds) *Women in the Labour Market*. New York: Columbia University Press, pp. 3–26.

Manser, M. and M. Brown (1980). 'Marriage and Household Decision Making: a Bargaining Analysis'. *International Economic Review*, 21, 31–44.

Mincer, J. (1962). 'Labour Force Participation of Married Women'. In *Aspects of Labour Economics Universities*. National Bureau Conference Series No. 14. New York: National Bureau of Economic Research.

Morris, L. (1988). 'Employment in the Household and Social Networks'. In D. Gallie (ed.) *Employment in Britain*. Oxford: Basil Blackwell.

Olsen, R.J. (1977). *An Econometric Model of Family Labour Supply*. Unpublished PhD Dissertation. Department of Economics, University of Chicago.

Parker, J. and L. Shaw (1968). 'Labour Force Participation in Metropolitan Areas'. *Southern Economic Journal*, 34, 538–547.

Peters, H.E. (1986). 'Marriage and Divorce: Informational Constraints and Private Contracting'. *American Economic Review*, June, 76, 3, 437–454.

Pfouts, R.W. (1955). 'Some Difficulties in a Certain Concept of Community Indifference'. *Metroeconomica*, 7, 16–26.

Samuelson, P.A. (1956). 'Social Indifference Curves'. *Quarterly Journal of Economics*, 70, 1–22.

Sergean, R., D. Howell, P. Taylor and S. Pocock (1969). 'Compensation for Inconvenience: An Analysis of Shift Payments in Collective Agreements in the U.K.'. *Occupational Psychology*, 43, 183–192.

Sprague, A. (1990). 'The Duration to Marriage: An Empirical Analysis'. Discussion Paper No. 104. Institute of Economics and Statistics. Oxford University.

Tella, A., D. Tella and C. Green (1971). *The Hours of Work and Family Income Response to Negative Income Tax Plans*. Kalamazoo, MI: Upjohn Institute.

Walker, J. (1978). *Human Aspects of Shiftwork*. London: Institute of Personnel Management.

Weiss, Y. (1972). 'On the Optimal Pattern of Labour Supply'. *Economic Journal*, 82, 1293–1315.

Weiss, Y. and R.J. Willis (1985). 'Children as Collective Goods and Divorce Settlements'. *Journal of Labour Economcs*, 3, 3, 268–292.

Winston, G.C. and T.O. McCoy (1974). 'Investment and the Optimal Idleness of Capital'. *Review of Economics and Statistics*, 127, 419–428.

CHAPTER 5 Empirical evidence on labour supply

1 Introduction

The previous chapters in this part of the book have been mainly theoretical. Labour economics does, however, have a very strong empirical orientation. All the dimensions of labour supply brought up in Chapter 2 have been the subject of quite extensive empirical analysis. Labour economists are fortunate in that they can draw on an extensive range of sources to support empirical analysis. Most countries have regular population surveys recording the labour force status, hours, earnings and other information relevant to understanding the labour supply decisions. Employer surveys form another source of data about hours and earnings. The population censuses undertaken in most countries are generally less frequent, but they record the labour force status and hours of work of each and every individual. The frequency and scope of such surveys and censuses means that, taken as a whole, there is a vast amount of factual material about the supply of labour.

The empirical evidence in this chapter is concerned with two dimensions of labour supply: participation and hours of work. In the first instance we look at some broad historical trends in participation and hours which are common to most developed countries. Taking a long perspective, the changes in participation and hours have been very substantial. The rising participation of females in paid market work has perhaps been the most significant change, but the labour supply behaviour of males has also undergone large changes. The theory of the supply of labour has much to contribute to our understanding of these trends, although changes over long periods of time reflect the net result of a number of other influences in addition to economic forces. Key examples of non-economic factors include demographic changes, such as an ageing population whose skills are becoming less relevant and whose health is deteriorating.

Time series data reflecting the average behaviour of large groups of individuals are difficult to interpret using a framework based on individual optimization with given preferences. In such databases, the separation of cause and effect is also often problematic. Is women's increasing participation due to the lower opportunity cost of home time associated with having fewer children, or do women have fewer children because of the higher family income arising from the participation of women in paid work? For these reasons most analytical research on labour supply, certainly in recent years, has relied on cross-section rather than time series data. The cross-section data sets often consist of very large samples of individuals for which data on hours, earnings and a wide range of individual characteristics are recorded. More recently still, panel data sets, which follow a cross-section of individuals over time, have increasingly become widely used in modelling labour supply behaviour. These have the combined advantage of the large number of individual-level, cross-sectional series to allow at least some exploration of the dynamic processes.

2 Historical trends in labour supply

Since there are so many differences in the supply behaviour of males and females we discuss each group in turn.

2.1 Males

The most striking fact about male labour supply is the decreasing proportion of time that males spend at work. This decline has taken mainly four forms. First, young persons have stayed at school longer and increasingly continued their education after leaving school. Second, males have been retiring, either wholly or partially, at younger ages. Third, weekly hours of work have declined and, fourth, so have the number of weeks worked per year.

The first two factors are reflected in the participation rate. For all males, participation rates have declined from over 90 per cent in the beginning of this century to about 75 per cent. In view of the main reasons for this, later entry and earlier exits from the labour force, the decline in participation has been highest for the youngest and the oldest age groups. However, participation rates have also declined among the so-called prime age (25–44 years old) males. At the turn of the century virtually all males in the 24–45 age group were working. By the early 1990s, participation rates had fallen to around 90–95 per cent in most developed countries.

Amongst males participating in the labour force, most of the reduction in hours can be traced to a reduction in weekly hours of work. These reductions are closely aligned to reductions in standard working hours as regulated by legislation or collective agreements. A century ago, a 10 hours a day, six-day working week was the norm. With industrialization and increasing prosperity the working week was reduced and in the early post-war period a 40 or 45 hour week became the standard in a number of countries. The past 40 years have seen some further reductions to below 40 hours. However, during the post-war period, the reduction in working hours has been more modest in comparison with the first half of this century. Instead, increased paid vacation has contributed to the decline in hours worked. In the UK, for example, two weeks' paid vacation was the norm in collective agreements in 1951, but by the late 1980s four or five weeks had become standard. Actual hours worked by males usually exceed the standard owing to overtime and other factors, but until the 1980s, at least, they generally followed the reduction in the standard hours.

During the 1980s the trend of decline in weekly hours was halted or even reversed in many countries There is a popular conception that most male workers work an approximately 40 hour week for 48 weeks per year, i.e. about 2000 hours per year. This is, however, a very incomplete characterization. In fact only about a third of prime-aged males fit the stereotype description of working about 2000 hours per year. The remaining two-thirds are spread over quite a large range of hours due to variations in weekly hours and weeks worked per year. A large group of males have yearly hours in the 2300–2400 range due to overtime. At the other end of the distribution part-time work among males has been increasing and some 10–20 per cent of males work less than 1000 hours per year. Part of the explanation for this lies in the 'flexibilization' of labour markets, which we return to in later chapters.

2.2 Females

The increasing participation of women in market work has been one of the most significant changes in the labour markets of developed economies. The trend has been evident since early this century but began to accelerate markedly in the 1950–1960 period. The female participation rate was around 30 per cent during the early post-war period, but by the early 1990s it had reached 60 per cent. Interestingly, in the UK, the increased participation of females has been almost exactly offset by the declining male participation, leaving the overall participation rate roughly constant for almost a century.

Given that, in terms of their labour market behaviour, younger females look more like their male counterparts, most of the increase in participation has come from married females. Early this century, less than 10 per cent of married females in the UK undertook market work. By 1951 the participation rate had gone up to 21.5 per cent and by the early 1990s to over 50 per cent. The increase has been even more striking in other countries. In Sweden, the participation rate of married women reached 70 per cent in the late 1980s. These changes, having taken place over a long period of time, can be decomposed into two components. First, more recent cohorts have shown a greater tendency to participate than previous cohorts. Second, within a given cohort of women there has been a tendency for participation to increase over time.

In contrast to the rising participation, weekly hours worked by females have shown a downward trend. One reason is the decline in the full-time working week which of course has affected females as well. Another reason is the compositional effect of the large proportion of females who work part time. Thus, as the proportion of part-time workers increased average hours of work have tended to fall. The increase in part-time workers is a fairly recent phenomenon and very closely related to the rapid growth of the participation of married females, but further encouraged by the 'flexibilization' of labour markets. In a number of countries about 20 per cent of female employment is part time. Given that part-time work is so important for females the distribution of their weekly hours is much more dispersed than for males. The female hours distribution has two peaks: one at 'full-time' (30–35) hours and one at 'half-time' (15–20) hours but significant proportions can be found over the whole range of hours. The exceptions are perhaps at the tails of the hours distribution: compared with males, the proportion of females who have very long weekly hours (45 or more per week) appears to be quite small. In addition, there is a tendency for standard surveys to under-record the very lowest numbers of hours of (paid) work, which are often carried out by female home-workers.

Cross-section analysis of female participation has uncovered a number of empirical regularities. Being married lowers the probability of participation as does the presence of children, and pre-school-age children in particular. Educational attainment has the opposite effect. The same regularities can be observed for hours of work. Many of these regularities can be given an economic interpretation. More educated persons have a higher prospective wage, so their higher participation and longer hours can be interpreted as a wage effect on labour supply. Similarly, the effect of being married may represent the income effect of a higher household income. These interpretations are, however, somewhat speculative. Direct estimation of models of labour supply based on the theory outlined in the previous chapters is clearly preferable and this is the route that the majority of empirical research has taken.

3 From theory to empirical models

According to the theoretical development of individual labour supply in Chapter 3, the hours of work decision is an interior solution to a utility maximization problem. This solution implies that an individual's hours of work (H) is a function of the wage rate (w), the price of a basket of consumption goods (p) and non-labour income (V). That is,

$$H = H(w,p,V) \tag{1}$$

When viewed in isolation from the consumption decision the theory has only two implications for the form of (1). First, equation (1) is homogeneous of degree zero. Second, although the sign of dH/dw is indeterminate, depending as it does on the relative magnitude of the income and substitution effect, the theory implies that the substitution effect is positive. In view of the limited implications of the theory, it is not surprising that empirical research has tended to focus on the magnitude of these effects rather than being directed towards testing the theory. Of course the magnitudes are themselves very important in the context of the debate about taxes and transfer payments.

As explained above, since individual data became more widely available labour supply models have been estimated from data sets which record hours worked and other variables for each individual in the sample. This in principle allows the empirical work to avoid the aggregation problem inherent in the use of time series averages, which do not represent the decisions and environment of any one person but sample averages taken from a changing heterogeneous population. On the other hand, it means that individual differences in hours worked must be accounted for in the empirical model. Two individuals facing the same values of w, p and V would in general choose to work different numbers of hours since their work/leisure preferences would differ. The most common way to account for this is to augment the hours equation with a vector of individual characteristics (X_i) and a random error (ε_i). The first set of variables capture the observable differences between individuals and normally include age, marital status and level of education. Even for individuals who are observationally identical, however, hours of work generally differ because of unobservables and the random error is a natural way to allow for these remaining differences.

Finally, in order to operationalize the empirical analysis, an explicit functional form must be adopted for equation (1). One method has been to assume a particular form of the underlying utility function and then to derive the resulting hours of work function. However, a more common approach has been simply to choose a convenient function. Linear or log-linear functions have often been chosen as the basis for estimation:

$$\ln H_i = a_0 + a_1 \ln(w/p)_i + a_2 \ln(V/p)_i + a_3 X_i + \varepsilon_i. \tag{2}$$

where i denotes the ith individual and a_0, a_1, a_2 and a_3 are constant coefficients to be estimated from the data. The zero homogeneity is imposed by the implied constraint on the coefficient of p, but when the model is estimated from a cross-section sample, p is generally assumed to be the same to all individuals and effectively drops out of the model. Given observations of all the relevant variables for all individuals in the sample, the parameters can be estimated by ordinary least squares.

To interpret the parameters in (2) we return to the Slutsky decomposition of the wage effect into a substitution and income effects. In Chapter 3 the decomposition was given as

$$dH/dw = s + H(dH/dV) \quad (3)$$

In making comparisons between estimates from different models, it is convenient to state all the results as elasticities rather than in terms of the effect of a unit change of a variable. Reformulating the Slutsky identity in terms of elasticities we multiply through by w/H to obtain

$$(dH/dw)(w/H) = s(w/H) + w(dH/dV) \quad (4)$$

The left hand side is normally referred to as the uncompensated (for income changes) wage elasticity. Like the derivative dH/dw, the uncompensated wage elasticity can be broken down into two components. The first, reflecting the substitution effect, is now also expressed as an elasticity and is usually referred to as the compensated wage elasticity. The second component, reflecting the income effect, indicates how earnings (the wage rate times the change in hours) respond to changes in non-labour income. This term is often referred to as the marginal propensity to earn.

Returning to equation (2), the log-linear specification, we see that a_1 yields a direct estimate of the uncompensated wage elasticity. From a_2 we also get a direct estimate of the income elasticity. However, the compensated wage elasticity must be derived from the other two parameters using the Slutsky identity. Thus given that $a_1 = (dH/dw)(w/H)$, the compensated wage elasticity is given by $a_1 - (wH/V)\, a_2$. Presenting the results of estimated models in terms of the uncompensated and compensated wage elasticities is now common practice. There is, however, less agreement when it comes to the income effect. Some authors give the income elasticity, while others prefer to give the marginal propensity to earn. The income elasticity is easier to interpret but the disadvantage is that the income and substitution elasticities do not add to the uncompensated wage elasticity.

3.1 Early empirical findings

The first published study to estimate hours of work functions from individual data is due to Kosters (1966, 1969). He drew his sample of married men aged 50–64 years from the 1 in 1000 sample of the 1960 US Census of Population. A typical equation estimated by Kosters was

$$\underset{}{\ln H_i = \underset{(0.0044)}{-0.094} \ln w_i - \underset{(0.0015)}{0.0073} \ln V_i + \dots + \varepsilon_i} \quad (5)$$

The standard errors, given in brackets beneath the coefficients, reveal that the key parameters are significantly different from zero and the equation had an R^2 of 0.10. Only the key estimates are presented. The equation also included 15 variables representing individual differences in tastes (the X_i vector in equation (2) above).

As explained above the first coefficient (–0.094) is a direct estimate of the uncompensated wage elasticity. The negative sign means that the supply curve is backward bending, i.e. that the negative income effect exceeds the positive substitution effect. To calculate the compensated wage elasticity we use the formula above which gives 0.041 evaluated at the geometric mean of the observations. Thus the only refutable implication of the theory, a positive substitution effect, cannot be rejected. The negative estimate of the income elasticity (–0.0073) confirms what has typically been thought to be the case – that leisure is a normal good and thus that hours of work are declining in non-labour income.

These early estimates stood the test of time fairly well even though subsequent studies along the same lines varied substantially in the measurement of variables, functional form and many other matters. Summarizing in Table 5.1 the results from what Killingsworth (1983) called first-generation models, most of the estimates of the male uncompensated wage elasticity fall in the range 0.0 to –0.4. Thus these early studies were fairly unanimous in finding a backward-bending supply curve for males. They also concurred that the male income elasticity is negative but fairly small.

In the case of females, the range of the estimates of the wage elasticity is much larger. This is an issue which we return to later. For the moment we note that although the greater range makes it difficult to make strong statements it is generally agreed that the estimates obtained indicate that female labour supply is much more responsive to wages, but not to income, than male labour supply. This accords with simple intuition. Generally speaking, females have two alternatives to market work – leisure and work at home.

To most males non-market alternatives tend to be more limited. However, more recent research questions such sweeping generalizations.

Table 5.1 Ranges of estimated wage and income elasticities in first-generation studies of labour supply

	Uncompensated	Compensated	Income
Males	0.0 to –0.4	0.00 to 0.36	0.00 to –0.16
Females	0.2 to 0.9	0.1 to 2.0	–0.1 to –0.2

Source: Killingsworth (1983)

4 Methodological issues in the estimation of labour supply functions

Following the early studies based on individual cross-section data there have been numerous developments in the econometric techniques used to estimate supply functions. Many of these developments have been at the forefront of the development of applied econometrics generally. To understand how empirical research has progressed it is important to have a basic idea about the methodological problems and how they have been resolved. In this section we take up three of the most important issues, measurement errors, exogeneity and sample selection.

4.1 Measurement errors

In theory the concept of an hourly wage rate is straightforward but in practice it is not. In many cases there is no single rate but a multitude of rates of different hours of work (overtime, shiftwork, etc.). In other cases, there are numerous additions to pay over and above the hourly rate, such as holiday pay, supplements and bonuses. In the case of salaried employees, the rate is implied by the salary and the 'expected' hours of work. For these reasons, most of the data sets used to estimate labour supply equations do not include a direct measure of the hourly wage rate, but an estimate based upon earnings divided by an estimate of the number of hours worked. The effect of this is to introduce a common measurement error in hours and the estimated wage rate, as hours worked are regressed on the implied wage rate (earnings divided by hours). Any measurement error in the latter results in an error of the opposite sign in the implied wage rate and a spurious negative correlation between hours worked and the wage rate. In a least-squares regression this would impart a downward bias on the wage rate coefficient. In principle, the bias can be corrected through the use of an instrumental variable estimator (see Section 4.2 below). However, the application of an instrumental variable method is far from straightforward in cross-section data and a range of approaches have been used. This takes us to the exogeneity problem.

4.2 Exogeneity

The common measurement error which arises in the calculation of the hourly wage provides a strong case for instrumental variable estimation of the labour supply. This usually entails instrumenting the observed average earnings with age, education, previous work experience and other variables which are thought to determine a person's wage. However, the consistency of the instrumental variable estimator depends on the instruments being exogenous. This assumption is often questionable. Consider, for example, the case of previous work experience by females. Women who have worked many years in the past tend to have both higher wages and to work more in the present. This is because previous work experience reflects a woman's tastes for work – implying that experience is endogenous to the labour supply decision. The notional experiment for measuring an uncompensated wage effect requires an exogenous change in the wage holding all other things, including tastes, constant. However, if the predicted wage is based on previous experience, the requisite *ceteris paribus* assumption may not be met. The exogeneity of other variables can also be questioned for similar reasons. The presence of children and non-wage income are partly a result of previous labour supply decisions. As such they reflect the influence of a person's tastes. For example, having few or no children may reflect a strong taste for work. If that is the case, observing that women with fewer children work more hours may not be due to the influence of children but simply reflect the tastes for work.

Whether the variables in the female labour supply equation are exogenous, and, if not, finding a valid set of instruments, is not a trivial matter. This has been a very important issue in empirical research and the results obtained appear sensitive to how this issue is handled.

4.3 Sample selection

The source of the sample selection problem is that many persons and, historically, at least many females, do not work. This simple fact has surprisingly far-reaching implications for the empirical estimation of labour supply functions. First, non-participants whose prospective wage is well below the wage they would require to supply positive hours (the reservation wage) will be completely insensitive to small variations in wages and non-labour income. Thus the regression models of the type outlined above, which seek to estimate how small changes in wages and non-labour income affect hours worked, are inappropriate in the case of non-participants. At best, these models estimate the wage and income responses of those who are working. Second, we do not in general observe the wages of non-participants. Obviously, there is no way in which the actual wage of somebody who is not working can be observed, and often it is not possible to observe the wages offered, but rejected by non-participants as being too low. Some surveys (such as the Youth Cohort Study in the UK) do collect information about reservation wages, which can be of use in modelling participation decisions.

The easiest way seemingly to avoid both of these problems, however, is to fit the labour supply function only to those who are working. This is precisely what early research in this field did. Unfortunately, this solution gives rise to an econometric problem known as the sample selection or selectivity bias. Individuals who work are not representative of the population of working age as a whole and a failure to take this into account will, in general, lead to biased estimates of the 'true' wage and income responses. Such estimation methods may also lead to biased estimates of the parameters relating to the working population.

The non-representativeness of participants can be explained with reference to reservation wages. An individual's decision to participate is based on a comparison of their reservation wage, w^r, with the market wage, w. Consider now individuals faced by the same market wage w. Those who work at this wage do so because their reservation wage is below w, and those who do not work have a higher reservation wage $w^r > w$. In other words, those who work have relatively low reservation wages. Next, consider the individuals with the same reservation wage w^r. The workers in this group will have a market wage larger than w^r while non-workers have $w < w^r$. Whichever way we look at it, the conclusion is the same: that workers are atypical of the population as a whole, because they have either low reservation wages or high market wages or both.

This argument only establishes that the workers are unrepresentative of the population as a whole. To see how this may bias the estimated responses we have to consider the stochastic part of the regression model. This is an econometric issue, and rigorous explanations of how selectivity bias arises can be found in most econometric texts. At an intuitive level an example is helpful – how the selection may bias the coefficient on the non-labour income. In the population as a whole there may be no correlation between the random error and non-labour income – there is no particular reason why those with high(low) non-labour income should also have a strong(weak) preference for leisure. But this independence does not necessarily hold in a selected sample if, as is highly likely, there is a positive relationship between the reservation wage and non-labour income.

According to the previous argument, those included in the sample tend to have low reservation wages. But inclusion also depends on the stochastic term in the hours equation. For a given reservation wage (or non-labour income) those observed to be working would have a weaker preference for leisure. Thus, there are two factors which influence the selection: low reservation wages and/or a weak preference for leisure. Those with a high reservation wage and high non-labour income would tend to be excluded owing to the first consideration, but not if ε is positive and large. Thus in the sample there would be a tendency for large values of ε to be associated with large values of non-labour income. Those with high non-labour income and a strong preference for leisure (negative ε) would tend to be excluded. The effect of this is to induce a positive correlation between the error term and non-labour income in the sample leading to an upward bias in the estimate of the non-labour income effect. By a similar line of reasoning we would conclude that the selection imparts a negative bias to the wage effect, i.e. the coefficient on the wage variable is underestimated. The selection would exclude those with a strong preference for leisure (negative values of ε) at low values of w but not those with high values of w. This exclusion imparts a negative correlation between ε and w. Hence, the coefficient of w is underestimated.

The selection bias is commonly regarded as more serious in the case of females, and married females in particular. For married females the participation rates in many data sets are around 50 per cent. Restricting the analysis to those who work positive hours excludes half of the population of interest. On the other hand, in the case of males the participation rate in the prime-age group is often close to 100 per cent, and the exclusion of a small proportion should not impart a large bias. The empirical evidence tends to concur with this intuition, but it would be going too far to suggest that the sample selection problem can be ignored in estimating male labour supply functions. First, the participation rate has been falling for quite some time and in many recent data sets the male prime-age participation rate can be as low as 80 per cent. Second, it is not just the proportion with zero hours that matters for the selectivity bias. How the selection interacts with other specification and estimation issues also matters.

5 Recent empirical findings

There have been important advances in econometric techniques used to estimate labour supply functions which have yielded new insights. Nevertheless, the new econometric techniques developed and applied to particular data sets have not succeeded in pinning down the parameters any more precisely than earlier studies. If anything, the opposite has been the case: the more complex the estimators used the more sensitive they have tended to become to specific auxiliary assumptions. The range of estimates of the wage and income elasticities for females is still very large. Table 5.2 shows the range of the elasticity estimates of most studies published during the 1976–1983 period. Killingsworth (1983) referred to these studies as 'second-generation models', in order to distinguish them from the first-generation models which did not address the econometric issues discussed above. The table understates the ranges by omitting 'outliers' in which the estimates are very different. While most estimates of the uncompensated wage elasticity of females are in the range 0.6 to 1.1, much larger estimates have been reported in several important and influential studies.

Table 5.2 Ranges of estimated wage and income elasticities in second-generation studies published during the 1976–1983 period

	Uncompensated	Compensated	Income
Males	–0.23 to –0.05	0.13 to 0.23	–0.1 to –0.4
Females	0.6 to 1.1	0.7 to 1.2	–0.1 to –0.2

Source: Killingsworth (1983)

Although the ranges of estimates are quite wide, some conclusions can still be drawn. With respect to males, the second-generation research finds a negative, but small, uncompensated wage elasticity. Thus, in line with the early findings, it appears that the male labour supply is backward bending. Second, the substitution effect is positive (as required by the theory) but fairly small. Third, and this applies to both males and females, the income elasticity is negative, indicating that leisure is a normal good. Fourth, female labour supply is much more responsive to wages than male labour supply. For females the substitution effect is quite large. In conjunction with a smaller negative income elasticity, this implies a large, positive, uncompensated wage elasticity (i.e. a positively sloped labour supply curve).

These estimates, obtained from cross-sectional data sets dating from the 1970s and 1980s, offer a plausible explanation for long-run trends in aggregate labour supply. They suggest that the fall in male labour supply can be attributed to the rise in real wages and non-labour income. Conversely, the increased labour supply by women is explained by the strong positive effect of rising real wages dominating the tendency to reduce labour supply because of rising non-labour income (including the rise in husband's real income). This fit, between cross-section evidence and long-run historical trends, may be fortuitous – there is, after all, no compelling reason for believing that tastes have remained the same. Also, for some particular time periods it is difficult to reconcile the cross-section estimates with trends in labour supply. For example, since the mid-1970s real wage growth has been fairly moderate in a number of countries, but female labour supply continued to increase. Nevertheless, the compatibility of the results with long-run trends does lend some credibility to the econometric estimates.

The very wide range of estimates of the key parameters have been of long-standing concern to researchers in this field. However, very few have actually tried to answer the obvious question: Why are the estimates of the key parameters so different? A notable exception is Mroz (1988) who investigated the sensitivity of the estimates to a number of economic and statistical assumptions. Mroz found that the three most important methodological issues were: the assumption that the wage is exogenous, the use of previous labour market experience as an instrument to control for the endogeneity of the wage, and the technique to control for self-selection. The two exogeneity assumptions induce a very large upward bias in the estimated wage effect but the upward bias is much smaller once sample selection is taken into account. The answer to the question of why estimates differ is thus, that different studies have addressed these issues in different ways, but once these three specification problems have been controlled for, the estimates are invariant to a number of other assumptions.

An important by-product of this type of research is that Mroz was able to reject a number of specifications in favour of alternatives which were more compatible with the data. Most importantly, while some specifications result in large wage and income elasticities, the economic and statistical assumptions needed to obtain these large estimates can be rejected by the appropriate statistical tests. Thus we are left with a much smaller range of estimates. The largest estimate of the uncompensated wage elasticity reported by Mroz was 0.22, which is considerably below the upper end of the range in Table 5.2. Based on these findings the author concludes that the labour supply behaviour of working married women matches the estimated behaviour of prime-aged males. This is clearly a very important conclusion as it overturns the conventional wisdom that has emerged from a very extensive range of research programmes. Further comparative research will eventually reveal whether this conclusion stands the test of time. There is much to suggest, however, that as female participation and hours of work continue to increase and accompanying social changes take place, the wage and income responses of males and females will converge. It should be noted, though, that relatively small elasticities in the mean values of the relevant variables do not imply weak wage and income responses at the extensive margin – at the margin of entry and exit from the labour force.

6 Taxes and labour supply

As discussed in Chapter 3, a progressive tax system has the effect of making the budget constraint non-linear – the marginal rate of tax depends on income and the more hours an individual works the higher is the tax rate and the lower is the marginal wage. To avoid having to work with non-linear budget constraints an early solution to this problem was to linearize the budget constraint. This approach is based on the fact that an individual with a budget constraint *ad'* in Figure 3.14, whose optimum is at *j*, behaves exactly as if they faced a budget constraint given by the tangent to the indifference curve at point *j* and a non-labour income given by the intersection of this line with a vertical line from point *a*. For the purpose of the empirical analysis each individual is imputed a certain non-labour income (usually called the virtual income) while the marginal wage is taken to be the gross wage times one minus the marginal tax rate at the individual's income level. Having linearized the budget constraint in this way an empirical model can be derived on the assumption that the budget constraint is linear, even though this is not really the case. This solution is both elegant and simple, but it does create an econometric problem – both the marginal wage and virtual income will in general be correlated with the error term. Other things equal, individuals with high values of ε will have a low marginal wage and high virtual income.

Of course, the budget constraint is really piecewise linear. It consists of linear segments with kinks at the points where the marginal tax rate changes. One very obvious consequence of this is that for individuals located at the kinks there is no unique marginal wage – an increase in hours of work would be associated with a different (lower) marginal wage than a decrease in hours. Several methods have been used to deal with this issue. The most sophisticated method developed by Burtless and Hauseman (1978) is a model with two random errors instead of one. One represents the unobserved heterogeneity of preferences and the other 'optimization errors' – it allows for individuals with the same observable and unobservable characteristics to choose different hours of work. The main reason they would do so is because of constraints on the hours they can work. An individual might wish to locate at a kink but it may be impossible to fine-tune hours to obtain this outcome. The estimation of this model entails locating each individual's optimum by checking the entire budget constraint of every person in the sample. For this reason it is sometimes referred to as the complete budget constraint approach.

The effect of taxes on labour supply is usually summarized by comparing the hours of work under an existing progressive tax system with the predicted hours under a proportional tax yielding the same revenue. There is, however, no consensus or consistency in the presentation of research findings. Some researchers prefer to state the effect of existing tax systems relative to a lump sum tax or a no-tax situation. In the event this does not matter much because the predictions of hours work tend to be very similar.

Hauseman (1985) developed a method which used the complete budget line approach to estimate the effect of taxes. For males he found a zero uncompensated wage elasticity, but his estimate of the income elasticity was fairly large relative to that found in many other studies (–0.17). The net effect of those estimates is a compensated wage elasticity of 0.17 and it is this estimate which drives the predictions in Table 5.3. Even though the USA does not have a sharply progressive tax system, male hours of work are 8 per cent lower than they would have been in the absence of income tax. In the case of a high-tax country like Sweden the effect of progressive taxes is even larger, though the estimated reduction in hours, 13.4 per cent, was based on a smaller compensated wage elasticity of 0.08.

Table 5.3 Predicted effects of progressive income tax systems on hours worked

		Per cent decrease in hours worked of the existing progressive system relative to:		
Author(s) (and country)	Gender	Proportional tax	No tax	Lump sum tax
Hauseman (1981) (US)	Males		–8.2	
	Females		–18.2	
Blomquist and Hansson-Bruzewitz (1990) (Sweden)	Males	–6.2	–13.4	–13.6
	Females	–9.3	–23.0	–23.3
Bourguignon and Magnac (1990) (France)	Females	–16.6	–19.3	
Columbino and del Boca (1990) (Italy)	Females	–7.1		
van Soest *et al.* (1990) (Netherlands)	Males		–14.1	
	Females		–16.0	
Triest (1990) (US)	Males		–2.6	
	Females		–30.3	
			–9.8	

The greater responsiveness of female labour supply wage and income changes is also reflected in the estimates of how female hours of work are affected by income taxes. The Hauseman study estimated that female hours of work were reduced by 18.1 per cent by income taxes. Estimates of the same order of magnitude have also been obtained in a number of other studies relating to other countries. In percentage terms, the effect on female hours of work is about twice that for males. In absolute terms, however, the effect is more similar. The average male is estimated to reduce hours from about 2200 to 2000 hours per year owing to income taxes. The typical figures for females would be a reduction from 1500 to 1200 hours.

All calculations in Table 5.3 are the predicted effect on hours of work for each individual in the sample based upon the labour supply parameters estimated by the authors of the respective studies. However, the precise assumptions and methods used by various authors do vary. But even allowing for such problems of comparability it is evident that progressive taxes have a much larger effect on female labour supply than on males. This is primarily due to the estimates of the compensated wage elasticity being greater, but this effect is partially offset by females' lower earnings, and thus lower marginal tax rates, than males'. A move to a proportional tax would increase female hours of work by 10–20 per cent while a lump sum tax or no tax at all would lead to increases of the order of 20–30 per cent.

Like all the empirical results reviewed in this chapter the estimates or predictions are very sensitive to the precise specification and method of estimation. Triest (1990), in replicating Hauseman's work with a later wave of the data set, found that the male income elasticity was essentially zero but that the uncompensated wage elasticity was positive – that is, the exact opposite of Hauseman's results. Such divergent results which appear to arise simply from the use of data pertaining to a different year are of course disconcerting. The concern is magnified by the effect of taxes being so different. According to the Triest results, US income taxes have only a small effect on male labour supply. This difference in the predicted effect can only be understood with reference to the specific features of a progressive tax system. In the case of a proportional tax there are two effects on labour supply. The substitution effect would reduce hours as the tax decreases the net marginal wage, while the income effect of the tax, due to the effective reduction in income, would tend to increase hours – the overall outcome determined by the net impact of these two effects. In a progressive system, however, there is an additional consideration. Moving from a no-tax to a progressive system leads to an increase in virtual income – an effective increase in non-labour income. The virtual income is higher the higher the marginal rate of tax and for high marginal rate tax payers the increase in virtual income can more than compensate for the real income reduction of the tax. These tax payers would then respond as if the tax increased their income and the income effect of the tax would decrease hours of work. As Triest (1990, p. 492) puts it, 'progressive taxation combines reductions in the net wage with implicit subsidies for upper bracket tax payers', with the result that studies which find a large income elasticity will yield a large estimate of the effect of an income tax on hours. This explains why Hauseman, who found a large income elasticity, found a much larger effect of taxes than Triest, whose estimate of the income effect was close to zero. At the same time it illustrates the complicated relationship between the estimated parameters and the predicted effects of changing the tax system. The simple theory would suggest that the magnitude of the uncompensated wage elasticity would be the primary determinant of how taxes affect labour supply. According to the argument above, the effect of the estimated income elasticity is just as large.

Since taking account of taxes substantially complicates the empirical analysis one might ask whether the gain from doing so is really worth it. Comparisons of the range of estimates obtained in studies which do account for taxes with those that do not reveal one major difference: accounting for taxes seems to result in a larger estimate of the uncompensated wage elasticity. In studies which do not take account of taxes the uncompensated elasticity is generally negative. Taking account of taxes yields either a positive elasticity or a negative estimate close to zero. This is important because the finding of a backward-bending supply curve for males can easily be interpreted to imply that the effect of income taxes is to increase labour supply. As we have seen, the studies which do take account of taxes reach the opposite conclusion. Being such an important policy issue it is clearly important to have reliable evidence. Another view which the empirical evidence also refutes is the idea that income taxes have reached such a high level that a reduction in income tax would actually increase tax revenue. However, for this to be the case, labour supply has to be much more responsive to tax changes than the evidence above indicates. For example, according to the Ashworth and Ulph (1981) results, the rise in labour supply from a tax cut would offset only about 10 per cent of the fall in tax revenue from a tax cut.

While the complete budget line approach represents a major advance in the estimation of labour supply functions it is not without its problems. As explained by MaCurdy *et al.* (1990), maximum likelihood estimation of this model imposes the Slutsky condition (positive substitution effect) on all the observations on the non-linear segment of the budget constraint. This explains why studies which use this method invariably find a positive compensated wage elasticity – the estimation technique constrains the elasticity to be non-negative. The constraint is more likely to be satisfied the larger is the uncompensated wage elasticity and the smaller (i.e. the more negative) is the income elasticity. As we have noted, studies which use this method do tend to produce a larger uncompensated elasticity, but it is less clear that the estimate of the income elasticity is smaller.

7 Dynamic models

As we have seen, most empirical models of labour supply have been estimated using annual hours of work. Clearly, one reason for this is the availability of data, but, in addition, a year seems a reasonable time frame for analysing the labour supply decision. The static model fitted to yearly data implicitly assumes that, apart from stochastic variations, individuals with the same wage and age (to take just two variables) would choose to work the same number of hours per year. While this is not unreasonable, what if a person could reasonably expect to double their wage next year? Surely this ought to have some effect on the current labour supply decision? Likewise, a woman who intends to have a child next year knows that her opportunity cost of time then will be higher. This ought to have some influence on current period hours of work. If such influences are sufficiently prevalent and if there is sufficient scope for varying labour supply over time a static labour supply model may yield biased estimates of substitution and income effects.

Another reason for explicitly taking account of the intertemporal dimension of labour supply is to account for the stylized facts we observe over the individual's lifetime. As explained in Chapter 4, the time profile of a person's hours of work, wage rates and earnings per year over their lifetime are all concave. In the case of males, however, ignoring the schooling and retirement phases, all the variables noted above tend to rise rapidly early in life, have a long drawn-out peak and show a slight decline as the normal retirement age approaches. In the case of females, the time profiles are more complex: some spend little or no time in the workforce; others alternate between market and non-market work; and a third group show time profiles of hours, wage rates and earnings which correspond closely to the male pattern more or less continuously since leaving school. An important objective of empirical research has been to develop a single coherent model which accounts for all of these stylized facts.

The pioneering work in this field is Mincer's (1962) model of female labour supply. According to Mincer's model women's labour supply decision is based on permanent wage rates and non-labour income. Of course, over the lifetime exogenous factors cause variations in the opportunity cost of working, like the presence of children and business cycle effects on wages and spouse's income. But these transitory changes affect only the timing of labour supply. The volume of labour supply over the lifetime depends only on the permanent wage rates and non-labour income. As Mincer puts it

> the quantity of labour supplied to the market by a wife is the fraction of her married life during which she participates in the labour force. Abstracting from the temporal distribution of labour force activities over a woman's life, this fraction could be translated into a probability of being in the labour force in a given period of time for an individual, hence into labour force rate for a large group of women. (p. 68)

The crucial assumption here is that the participation rate measures the fraction of lifetime labour supplied to the market. That is, observing an increase in aggregate female participation rate from 50 to 60 per cent is taken to mean that the typical woman has increased her lifetime working hours by 10 percentage points, and that this increase can be understood as representing the effects of changes in the permanent wage rate and non-labour income. This assumption enabled Mincer to claim that the parameters in a model of aggregate female participation rates represented estimates of income and substitution effects which take account of the life-cycle aspect of the decision-making process.

As Heckman (1978) has shown, strong assumptions are required to justify the Mincer procedure. Also, since the theory has nothing to say about the timing of labour supply over the life-cycle it cannot account for the stylized facts that we previously referred to. For such reasons subsequent work on life-cycle labour supply has taken another route, being explicitly derived from the theoretical models introduced in Chapter 4.

As explained in Chapter 4 the theory of dynamic labour supply suggests that individuals would find it advantageous to work more when their wage is high and enjoy more leisure during periods when their wage is low. The positive relationship between wage rate and labour supply over time arises because individuals consume more leisure when time is cheap and less leisure when time is expensive. That is, cheap time is substituted for expensive time, over time. Therefore, this relationship is often referred to as the intertemporal substitution effect even though it is not strictly speaking a substitution effect in the sense this term is normally used. Other authors have called it the efficiency effect – it is efficient to work when wages are high. This obvious consideration also fits well with observed lifetime profiles of earnings. It is not, however, the only consideration affecting the time profile of labour supply. As discussed in Chapter 4, two other considerations impinge on the temporal allocation of work: the rate of interest and the individual's subjective rate of time preference. The higher the rate of interest the more advantageous it is to work more early in life and invest the proceeds to be enjoyed in the future. On the other hand, the higher the subjective time preference, the more an individual would prefer to enjoy leisure now and seek to postpone work to the future.

Life-cycle models of labour supply based on this framework can be extremely complicated. The starting point is the proposition that at each point of time, individuals maximize a utility function over their remaining lifetime. The corollary of this is that, in principle, current labour supply depends on all past and future wage rates. This fact presents the researcher with a seemingly impossible problem, since, at best, individuals can normally only be observed over a short space of time. Notwithstanding these difficulties, empirical models can have a very simple form that follows from a number of simplifying assumptions. First, most research in this field has assumed an exogenous wage; that is, the wage at a point in time does not depend on previous labour supply decisions. This assumption permits the separation of the labour supply from human capital decisions. Second, the lifetime utility function is normally assumed to be addictively separable. This assumption is less restrictive than Mincer's perfect substitute assumption but still places strong restrictions on how wages in other time periods are related to current labour supply. These assumptions give rise to what is, at least superficially, a very simple empirical model – a regression of the change in hours on the change in the wage rate:

$$\Delta \ln H_{it} = \text{const} + \gamma\Delta \ln w_{it} + u_{it} \tag{6}$$

where the coefficient on the wage rate, Δ, represents the intertemporal substitution effect.

To estimate models of this type MaCurdy (1981) used a sample of married men for whom annual observations were available over a 10 year period. His point estimates of γ ranged from a low of 0.14 to a high of 0.45 depending on the particular specification and sub-sample used. This range is rather wide for a common data set which reflects the fact that the estimates are fairly sensitive to both the precise specification and the method of estimation. The estimates were not very precise either, but the conclusion that the intertemporal substitution effect is positive but small is on fairly safe grounds.

The findings by MaCurdy have been confirmed by other studies, using both the same and different approaches. Altonji (1986) provides an exhaustive analysis of different approaches using 14 yearly observations from the same panel data set as MaCurdy, and repeating the work, he obtained very similar estimates. Alternative estimation methods produced slightly different results. Altonji put more confidence in estimates which used the hourly rate as an instrument for the wage variable in (6) (annual earnings divided by hours). This method gave a lower estimate of γ, around 0.05. He also produced compelling evidence that instrumental variable estimation is essential to avoid bias. Least-squares estimation of (6) resulted in an estimate of γ of –0.32 with a very small standard error. But this strong negative relationship arises from the common measurement errors in hours and wage rates and is entirely spurious.

There is less evidence on the intertemporal substitution effect for females. Heckman and MaCurdy (1980) report an elasticity of 0.41, which is at the upper end of the corresponding range found for males. As most empirical studies have found that female labour supply is more responsive, it would not be surprising that the greater responsiveness applies to intertemporal substitution as well, at least historically.

To get some feel for what these findings mean, consider the typical time path of a graduate's earnings over the life-cycle. Typically, graduates in their forties and fifties would earn twice as much as they did in their twenties. If we take γ to be 0.15, this would imply that male graduates would work 15 per cent more hours, or 2 hours more per week, later in life owing to this higher wage. Most researchers would be inclined to interpret this to mean that there is little scope for intertemporal substitution and by implication that static models, which ignore this dimension, are quite adequate. However, as Heckman (1993) points out, most empirical studies in this field have ignored the entry and exit decisions. The parameters are estimated from samples of persons who worked positive hours during the whole period. But we know from aggregate data that most of the variation in aggregate person hours comes from variations in employment (i.e. from people exiting and entering jobs), rather than from variations in hours per person. If this former source of variation were to be taken into account, the scope for intertemporal substitution would be much larger and we would expect a larger estimate of the intertemporal substitution effect.

8 Summary

The primary concern of empirical research on labour supply has been to obtain estimates of the magnitudes of wage and income responses. The empirical models used in this research are very closely aligned to the basic theoretical model of individual labour supply described in Chapter 3. However, the theory on which the models are based has become more sophisticated in a number of respects, not least in the treatment of the tax regimes, the consideration of family labour supply decisions and the dynamics of labour supply over the individual's lifetime. The econometric methods for estimation of labour supply models have also undergone many important developments and extensions. Most significant have been the techniques to correct for sample selection bias, as well as the estimation methods that take account of progressive tax systems. In addition the data sets have become more informative, for example, about personal and family characteristics, and about the individual's financial position. Some data sets contain detailed information about the tax position of individuals, and panel data sets in which individuals are followed over a number of years are used to estimate dynamic labour supply models.

Notwithstanding these developments, the early findings of a backward-sloping supply curve for males but weak wage and income effects, alongside a more responsive female labour supply to wages and income, have proved to be quite robust. But these findings are subject to a number of qualifications. It is now recognized that a concern with a single parameter, whether the supply is backward bending or not, is somewhat misplaced. If we wish to evaluate the effects of a change to a very complex tax system on labour supply there is no alternative but to compute the predicted effect on each individual's labour supply. The aggregate effect of such a change bears a very complicated relationship to both wage and income elasticities and to the distribution of individuals across income and tax brackets. It is also recognized that low estimates of wage and income elasticities, which pertain to a typical individual, can give a misleading impression. The labour supply of a typical individual, a full-time–full-year worker, may well be quite insensitive to wage and income changes. Aggregate effects, however, depend as much on the behaviour of the marginal workers whose entry and exit decisions can be very sensitive to both wages and income.

With respect to the more responsive female labour supply, the early studies tended to give an exaggerated view. One reason for this was the failure to correct for the sample selection problem. Later research suggests that the male/female differences may not be all that large and much of it arises from more females being marginal workers who enter and leave the labour force more frequently than males. This factor, the degree of attachment to the labour force, seems more important than the gender distinction itself. According to one of the most prominent researchers in this field, Heckman (1993), the most important lesson from empirical work during the past decades has been that wages and income exert their strongest influence at the extensive margin – at the margin of entry and exit from the labour force.

CASE STUDY 1 Fixed costs and the labour supply of married females

Most people incur some costs in attending work. Some of these costs are fixed, that is do not depend on the number of hours worked. These fixed costs are likely to have a large impact on the labour supply behaviour of married females. They include things like transport to and from the place of work, meals outside the home, suitable clothing, and child care arrangements. In an innovative study, Cogan (1981) sought to estimate the impact these fixed costs have on the labour supply behaviour of married women.

To induce a woman to work the offered wage rate must be above the reservation wage w^r. Second, income from work, the wage rate times hours, must be sufficient to cover the fixed money and time costs. This implies that a woman will not work below some minimum number of hours, termed reservation hours (H^r). The consequence of this is that the labour supply equation will be discontinuous at H^r as depicted in Figure 5.1. The size of this discontinuity depends on the individual's preferences as well as on the level of non-labour income and the magnitude of the fixed money and time costs.

To estimate the size of the discontinuity without any information about the costs incurred by participants (or non-participants), Cogan specified a two-equation model – a labour supply (hours) equation and a cost of work equation.

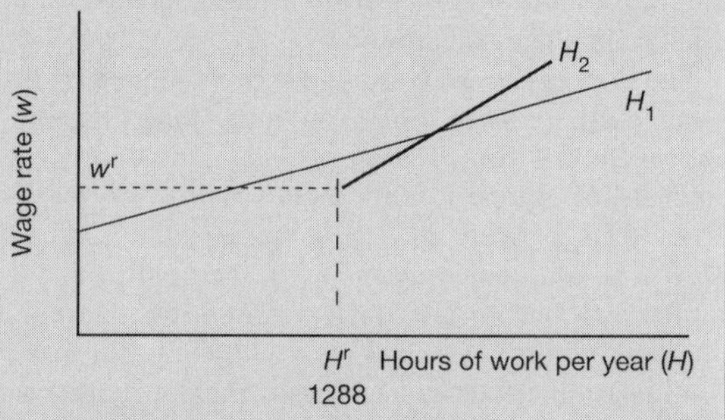

Fig 5.1

Together these two equations imply a reservation wage equation from which H^r can be derived.

Cogan found the estimated mean reservation hours to be very large for both working and non-working women in his sample. On average it was estimated at 1288 hours per year, which is substantially more than half-time work. Note, however, that this refers to the average woman in the sample. The reservation hours for some persons would be considerably lower. The findings can also be expressed in terms of the annual fixed costs of work for the average woman:

continues

CASE STUDY 1 continued

	Annual cost of work	Change in cost of work due to an additional child aged 0–6	Change in cost of work due to an additional year of education
Workers	$907.74	$337.15	$112.29
Non-workers	$1080.97		

Note: All effects are evaluated at the sample means. The average annual earnings in the sample was $4000 (in 1966)

The annual participation cost is clearly fairly high, although not unreasonably so. For working women it comes out at 28.3 per cent of the average annual earnings. The presence of pre-school-age children has a predictably large effect and this factor alone accounts for most of the difference in the fixed costs between those not working and those who work. More surprising is the fairly strong effect of education. Cogan explains this by higher-educated women living further from central business districts where most of the jobs are, and the higher value they place on their non-market time.

Cogan also compared his fixed cost model with a conventional supply of hours model which ignores the fixed costs. He is able to show that the conventional model results in a labour supply function which looks like H_1, that is, the effect of the wage on hours is quite large. In contrast, the fixed cost model resulted in a much smaller estimate of the wage elasticity represented by the steeper function H_2 in Figure 5.1. This suggests that the large wage elasticities commonly found in empirical studies are a result of ignoring the fixed costs of working. However, a note of caution is also sounded. The hours function may be non-linear, being relatively flat at low wages and steep at higher wages, and the fixed cost model wrongly attributes this to fixed costs. This possibility cannot be confidently dismissed without actual observations of the fixed money and time costs of working.

Source: Cogan (1981)

References

Altonji, J. (1986). 'Intertemporal Substitution in Labour Supply: Evidence from Micro Data'. *Journal of Political Economy*, 94, 176–215.

Ashworth, J. and D. Ulph (1981). 'Household Models'. In C. Brown (ed.) *Taxation and Labour Supply*. London: Allen and Unwin.

Blomquist, N.S. and U. Hansson-Brusewitz (1990). 'The Effect of Taxes on Male and Female Labour Supply in Sweden'. *Journal of Human Resources*, 25, 317–357.

Bourguignon, F. and T. Magnac (1990). 'Labour Supply and Taxation in France'. *Journal of Human Resources*, 25, 358–389.

Burtless, G. and J. Hauseman (1978). 'The Effect of Taxation on Labour Supply: Evaluating the Gary Income Maintenance Experiment'. *Journal of Political Economy*, 86, 1103–1130.

Cogan, J. (1981). 'Fixed Costs and Labour Supply'. *Econometrica*, 49, 945–964.

Colombino, U. and D. del Boca (1990). 'The Effect of Taxes on Labour Supply in Italy'. *Journal of Human Resources*, 25, 390–414.

Hauseman, J. (1985). 'Taxes and Labour Supply'. In A. Auerbach and M. Feldstein (eds) *Handbook of Public Economics*, Vol 1. Amsterdam: North-Holland.

Heckman, J. (1978). 'A Partial Survey of Recent Research on the Labour Supply of Women'. *American Economic Review* (Papers and Proceedings), 68, 201–207.

Heckman, J. (1993). 'What Has Been Learnt About Labour Supply in the Past Twenty Years?'. *American Economic Review* (Papers and Proceedings), 83, 116–121.

Heckman, J. and T. MaCurdy (1980). 'A Life Cycle Model of Female Labour Supply'. *Review of Economic Studies*, 47, 47–50.

Killingsworth, M. (1983). '*Labour Supply*'. Cambridge, MA: Cambridge University Press.

Kosters, M. (1966). 'Income and Substitution Effects in a Family Labour Supply Model'. Report No. P-3339. Rand Corporation.

Kosters, M. (1969). 'Effects of an Income Tax on Labour Supply'. in A.C. Harberger and M.J. Bailey (eds) *The Taxation of Income from Capital*. Washington, DC: Brookings Institute, pp. 301–324.

MaCurdy, T. (1981). 'An Empirical Model of Labour Supply in a Life-Cycle Setting'. *Journal of Political Economy*, 89, 1059–1085.

MaCurdy, T., D. Green and H. Paarsch (1990). 'Assessing Empirical Approaches for Analysing Taxes and Labour Supply'. *Journal of Human Resources*, Summer, 25, 415–490.

Mincer, J. (1962). 'Labour Force Participation of Married Women'. In H. G. Lewis (ed.) *Aspects of Labour Economics*. New York: National Bureau of Economic Research.

Mroz, T. (1987). 'The Sensitivity of an Empirical Model of Married Women's Hours of Work to Economic and Statistical Assumptions'. *Econometrica*, 5, 765–800.

Triest, R. (1990). 'The Effect of Income Taxation on Labour Supply in the United States'. *Journal of Human Resources*, 25, 3, 491–516.

van Soest, A., I. Woittiez, and A. Kapteyen (1990). 'Labour Supply, Income Taxes, and the Hours Restriction in the Netherlands'. *Journal of Human Resources*, 25, 517–549.

PART III Labour Demand

CHAPTER 6 Introduction to labour demand

1 Introduction

The demand for labour is a 'derived demand'. In other words it depends critically on the level and nature of the demand for the final product or service. By implication, the technology of production is important, linking factor inputs, including labour, to output via the production function. The production function can be thought of as a technological relationship that determines the possible combinations of labour, capital and other inputs which can be used to produce a given level and quality of product or service. It rarely, by itself, provides a unique answer about the amount and type of labour a firm will demand. Normally, it indicates a range of technically feasible options for labour demand. The choice of inputs is further narrowed by economic factors which are influenced by the firm's goals. Given that market structure has an important impact on how firms behave, it is not surprising therefore to find that it is also an important determinant of the demand for labour.

The production function and labour demand can be viewed in the short run, long run and very long run, depending upon whether capital and technology are assumed to be fixed or variable. However, during the course of this part, we begin to move the discussion away from the idea of a unidirectional relationship which runs from product demand, through the technology and goals of the firm, to labour. In practice, labour or, more accurately, the inventive and entrepreneurial skills embodied in labour, are key factors which lead to changes in the range and nature of the products and processes available. Thus, we return to labour's involvement in various dynamic activities both later in this part and throughout the remainder of the book (see especially Chapter 29).

Section 2 of this chapter outlines the distinction between the short, long and very long run, which underpins the issue of how costly and thereby how quickly different types of inputs can be varied. Section 3 discusses the firm's demand for labour under conditions of perfect competition. It lays down the micro underpinnings of the firm's decision-making process, before examining the main characteristics of the demand for labour curve at the industry level. Section 4 introduces different market structures, moving away from the simplifying assumption of perfect competition. This is important in two respects, first, because differences in market structure influence the demand for labour even if the assumption of profit maximization is maintained; second, the move away from highly competitive markets allows firms to adopt alternative goals, such as sales or growth maximization. Section 5 considers a number of further extensions to the theory of labour demand. In particular, it introduces the idea of different dimensions of the labour input (i.e. hours versus employees) and, in addition, examines the demand for different occupations, education levels, etc. Finally, we briefly outline why it is important to consider the very long run, discussing the potential impact of different rates and directions of technological change for labour demand.

2 Short run and long run

Table 6.1 illustrates some of the lags associated with changing the inputs of labour and capital. It is often argued a priori that capital generally takes longer to adjust than labour, and that both of these inputs can be changed more quickly than the underlying technology of production. As a direct consequence, economists generally define: the short run – as a period long enough to vary the labour but not the capital input; the long run – as a period of time sufficient to vary both labour and capital, but not long enough to alter the technology of production; the very long run – as sufficient to change not only inputs but also the technology. Examples of fixed and variable factors under this taxonomy are set out in Table 6.2.

Table 6.1 Lags in adjusting capital and labour

Labour	Capital
i decision ii advertising (and other means of search) iii interview iv training	i decision ii search iii producer's construction time iv installation and trial

Table 6.2 The short, long and very long run

Period	Examples of variable factor	Examples of fixed factors
Short run	Labour	Capital Technology
Long run	Labour Capital	Technology
Very long run	Labour Capital Technology	

In practice, a single cut-off point between the short and the long run (or between the long and the very long run) may be unrealistic for a number of reasons. First, different factors of production can be varied at different rates (e.g. it may be easier to vary manual than non-manual workers). Second, different dimensions of the service flow from a particular factor can be varied at different rates (e.g. hours of work may be more readily altered than numbers of workers). Third, the speed with which a particular factor can be varied will be different at different points in time (e.g. it may be easier to vary the labour input when the labour market is relatively slack). Nevertheless, while these reservations are important, for simplicity in the theory developed in the initial stages of this part of the book, we assume that: (i) there are only two inputs (e.g. capital and labour); (ii) both inputs are homogeneous (e.g. every worker is identical to every other worker); (iii) labour can be varied in the short run, capital can only be altered in the long run, and the technology of production can only be changed in the very long run. These rather restrictive assumptions are gradually relaxed in succeeding chapters.

3 Firm and market demand for labour under perfect competition

The demand for labour by the firm is dependent upon the price people are willing to pay for the product in the market place, the productivity of labour and the wage rate (*vis à vis* other alternative factor inputs). The basic theory of the demand for labour by the firm (i.e. the way in which the firm chooses its optimal amount of labour) is developed in Chapter 7. The chapter outlines the role played by differences in the technology of production and then the way in which the technology of production and the demand for the product jointly determine the amount of labour demanded, both in the short run and the long run. Again, to simplify the exposition, the initial development of a theory of labour demand is based upon the assumption of perfect competition in both the product and labour markets. As a consequence, the goals of the firm are essentially restricted to profit maximization, although we do explore the special cases of output maximization subject to a cost constraint and cost minimization subject to an output constraint. In Chapter 7 we also demonstrate how the market demand for labour is determined, by aggregating the firms' labour demand curves. When we do this, even in perfect competition, product prices are no longer exogenous. This has to be allowed for in deriving the market demand curve for labour under perfect competition. It becomes clear that the aggregate demand for labour depends crucially on the nature of the associated product market. The linkages between the two are formalized in terms of the four 'Marshallian Rules'.

4 Demand for labour under different market structures

The discussion of the Marshallian Rules leads us to consider other market structures including monopoly. We would naturally expect market structure to be an important influence on labour demand. For one thing, monopolies have an incentive to restrict output below the competitive market level in order to force up prices and earn abnormal profits, with consequent implications for market demand. Historically, at least prices under oligopoly have been argued to be 'sticky', and we would expect some of this inflexibility to be reflected in the labour demand schedule. Of course, as soon as the assumption of perfect competition is relaxed, and we allow some degree of product market power, it becomes possible for the firm to adopt goals other than profit maximization. While we only investigate a small number of the alternatives, they can be shown to have potentially quite radical implications for labour demand, although the competitive outcome often appears as a special case of these theories.

5 Further extensions of the theory of labour demand

Up to this point we have assumed labour to be homogeneous. We demonstrate in Chapter 9 that, when this assumption is dropped, the basic theory has to be extended to allow for a number of different forms of heterogeneity. First, there is a distinction between the number of persons and the number of hours per person. The extra output produced by employing more workers may differ from the extra output resulting from employing more hours per person. Also the cost of (additional) employees will be different from the costs of a higher number of hours. Hiring, for example, involves training and recruitment costs, while asking employees to work additional hours may require overtime premiums to be paid. Another interesting distinction is between production and non-production workers, although this is somewhat clearer for manufacturing than for services. In the case of non-production workers, for example, the technological link between product and labour demand is less clear. This becomes even more important in the case of employees involved in dynamic activities, such as research and development (R&D) personnel. Here the output of the employees is a change in the range or nature of the products and processes available to the firm. Nevertheless, the productivity literature links dynamic firm performance, such as total factor productivity growth, to various R&D inputs, 'as if' there is a technological link between the two – the so-called 'knowledge production function'. This issue is also raised in Chapter 9, and we return to it in more detail in both Chapters 10 and 29. Finally, Chapter 9 goes on to give a brief introduction to the effect of subjective discrimination, for example against women, and its implications for the demand or labour curve. This topic is developed further in Part VII of the book in a chapter on segmentation and discrimination.

6 Technological change and labour demand

Chapter 10 considers the very long run, and the effect of technological change on labour demand. We show how different rates and types of technological change have different implications for labour demand. In general, there is an important distinction between product and process change. In addition, process change can be relatively capital or labour saving, although, historically at least, it has tended to displace labour. Thus, Chapter 10 explores the implications for labour demand of different types of factor-saving bias (including the forms assumed by Harrod, Solow and Hicks). Again, however, an important aim of Chapter 10 is to establish the idea that causality runs in both directions: technological change has important implications for labour demand, but labour itself is crucially involved in the successful production and adoption of new technologies.

7 Conclusions

This chapter sets the scene for the whole of Part III of the book. Most of the material in Chapters 7 to 10 is theoretical, while Chapter 11 reviews the empirical evidence on labour demand. This parallels the structure of the discussion of labour supply, found in Part II above. There is one further important similarity: normally that consideration of labour demand in isolation requires some assumptions about the underlying nature of labour supply (i.e. a perfectly elastic supply of labour curve) – remember in the labour supply part of the book we assumed a perfectly elastic demand for labour. These assumptions simplify the presentation, allowing us to analyse separately labour demand independently of labour supply. They cannot be fully relaxed until Part IV, when we investigate the interaction of supply and demand.

CHAPTER 7 Demand for labour under perfect competition

1 Introduction

This chapter develops the basic theory of the firm's demand for labour. Section 2 demonstrates that the labour demand relationship depends crucially on the firm's technology of production, represented by the firm's production function. There is a close analogy between the role of the production function in underpinning the labour demand curve and the individual utility function in determining labour supply, as we showed in Part II of the book. In the case of labour demand, the distinction between the short and long run turns on whether the capital stock is fixed (short run) or can be varied (long run). Other properties of the labour demand function can be traced to the presence (or absence) of economies of scale in production and to the ease of substitution between capital and labour. Section 3 introduces factor costs, in particular the wage and the price per unit of capital. This enables the analysis to focus not only on the technically feasible factor demands, but on the economically most viable combinations. This involves the introduction of a specific goal of the firm. Given the adoption of perfectly competitive environments in both product and labour markets in this chapter, the only compatible goal is profit maximization. However, for simplicity in exposition, we also use output maximization subject to a cost constraint and cost minimization subject to an output constraint. In later chapters we further examine the equilibrium of the firm under alternative goals of the firm. Section 4 derives the firm's labour demand curve under perfect competition in the short and in the long run. While Sections 2–4 primarily focus on the firm-level decision process, Section 5 turns its attention to the industry. While a number of the firm fundings simply carry across to the industry level, some do not. In particular, it is no longer generally possible to assume that product price is fixed because, for example, as all firms in the industry expand, aggregate output increases and product price is forced down. Finally, Section 6 draws the main conclusions of this chapter.

2 Technology of production

2.1 Production function

The production function describes the link between the firm's output(s) and its consumption of various factor services. The relationship holds for some specified period: it might refer to a particular instant in time or to a day, week or year. It is really, therefore, a 'flow relationship', involving the rate of production and the flows of factor services consumed, although, as we will see, flows are in practice often proxied by corresponding stocks. The production function is a technical relationship by which inputs (such as land, labour, capital and enterprise) are efficiently transformed into physical outputs (e.g. tons of steel, bushels of wheat, etc.). It can be thought of as a 'blue print' or a 'recipe': a set of instructions that inform the producer how most effectively to combine the various flows of inputs in order to produce the required quantities and qualities of output in each period.

As it is supposed to be a technical relationship, output should be measured in homogeneous physical units (e.g. a study of the coal mining industry might adopt tons of coal). There are, however, important conceptual and practical problems of accounting for variations in the quality of output, even within the manufacturing sector. Outside of manufacturing, for example in services, these difficulties assume even greater importance. While some proxy for output can invariably be constructed, the problems of measuring output in areas such as education and health, or in functions such as research and development, have been sufficient to deter some economists from even admitting the existence of a production relationship of the type that we describe below for these activities.

Factor services are generally categorized into four broad types: capital, labour, land (and raw materials) and enterprise. The breakdown is somewhat arbitrary as the labour input often reflects human capital (i.e. knowledge, skills, motivation), and the distinction with enterprise becomes blurred. In addition, it seems unlikely, in practice, that inputs in each of these categories will be homogeneous. There are, however, a number of ways in which these four basic groups can be further sub-divided. First, each of them may be broken down into more detailed types; capital, for example, may be divided into vehicles, plant and machinery, and buildings. Second, inputs can be separated into 'stock' and 'flow' dimensions: labour services can be thought of as comprised of numbers of employees and the 'intensity' with which employees work. The use of the term 'stock' here may be a bit misleading as both employment and capital refer to the stock available for use in production over a given period (i.e. day, week or year). Finally, the intensity of work for labour can be further sub-divided into the number of hours of work (at a given level of work effort) and the amount of effort put into their work (for a given length of working day, week, etc.).

The production function stipulates the maximum outputs that can be obtained from each possible combination of inputs, in a given period of time. While there are important deficiencies with the chosen specification, economists often work with a production function of the form

$$Y = \mathbf{f}(K,L) \qquad (1)$$

where: Y denotes net output or value added; K is the input of capital services per period; L is the input of labour services per period. In practice, the specification chosen for equation (1) is associated with important problems of measurement and aggregation; in particular, there are problems in calculating Y in a way that is meaningful within the confines of the explicit specification chosen in place of **f**( ), and in aggregating both K and L, whenever the two inputs are not perfectly homogeneous.

2.2 Isoquant

Figure 7.1 shows a three-dimensional representation of the two-input/one-output production function. All points beneath the surface are technically inefficient, giving lower output per unit of input than points on the surface. The shape of the production surface depends on the specification of the production function adopted. An isoquant is derived by drawing a contour line (such as the line *ab*) at a given height above the (K,L) plane (e.g. associated with a given level of output, Y_0). This line is then projected vertically downwards onto the (K,L) plane, yielding the isoquant *a'b'*. Each isoquant therefore represents all of the combinations of K and L that yield a given level of output.

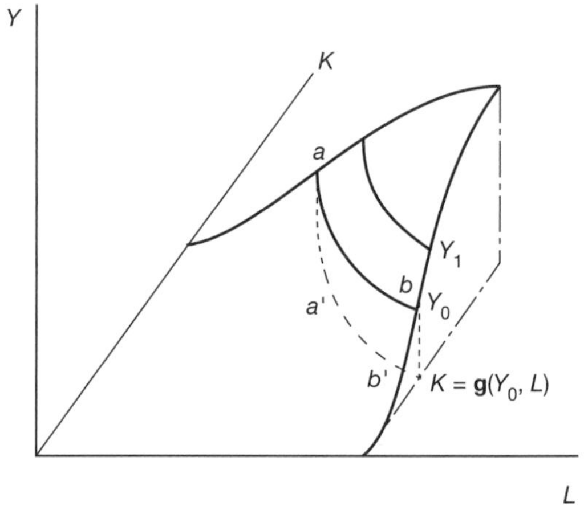

Fig 7.1 Contour map.

If we look at the associated mathematics, it involves restricting the production function represented by equation (1) to a given level of output, $Y = Y_0$. Hence, the isoquant can be written as

$$K = \mathbf{g}(Y_0,L) = \mathbf{h}(L) \qquad (2)$$

If we look at the isoquants associated with a variety of output levels, such as Y_0, Y_1, ... then we obtain the isoquant map, illustrated in Figure 7.2.

Particular production functions have their own characteristic isoquant maps, as we demonstrate below. At this stage, however, the figures are derived from neoclassical production functions, where capital and labour are imperfect substitutes in the production process. The general properties of iso-

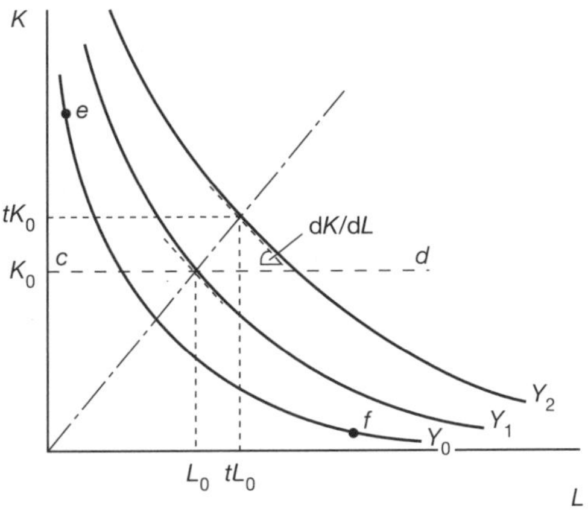

Fig 7.2 Isoquant map.

quants assumed in the literature are: (i) outputs and inputs are homogeneous and measurable; (ii) isoquants further from the origin represent higher levels of output; (iii) isoquants slope downward and to the right in the (K,L) plane, at least for technically efficient combinations of inputs; (iv) isoquants do not intersect along their downward-sloping sections; (v) isoquants are convex to the origin, that is to say that the absolute slope of the isoquant increases as we move to the left and decreases as we move to the right around the isoquant.

2.3 Returns to one factor

The returns to one factor (sometimes called the 'law of variable proportions') is a short-run concept: the firm is assumed to have no choice with regard to the amount of capital it has available. Thus, varying the level of output can only be achieved by altering the amount of labour that it uses in conjunction with the fixed amount of capital. In the short run, the firm expands (or contracts) along a horizontal line such as *cd* in Figure 7.2, changing its labour input and, thereby, attaining new output levels. The relationship between output and labour along such a line is referred to as the returns to labour. This can be derived mathematically from equation (1) by setting $K = K_0$, where K_0 is a constant,

$$Y = \mathbf{f}(K_0,L) = \mathbf{j}(L) \qquad (3)$$

The precise form of the returns to labour function clearly depends on the specification of the production function and, thereby, the nature of the isoquant map. If we imagine moving along a short-run expansion path, such as *cd* in Figure 7.2, noting the associated levels of output and labour input, then these values can be replotted as in Figure 7.3(a). The plotted line corresponds with a returns to labour function, consistent with equation (3).

The returns to labour function is generally referred to as the total physical product of labour curve, TPP_L: the total amount of output, Y, produced at each level of labour input, L, holding capital at some constant level, $K = K_0$. TPP_{L0} in Figure 7.3(a) shows: (i) an early range of increasing returns to labour (e.g. the curve *ab*, where output increases at a faster rate than labour as we move around the TPP_L curve); (ii) a point (though it could be a range) of constant returns to labour (i.e. point *b*, where output increases at the same rate as the labour input); (iii) a range of diminishing returns to labour (i.e. *bc*, where output increases at a slower rate than labour); (iv) a point (though it could be a range) of zero returns to labour (i.e. *c*, where an increase in the labour input produces no addition to output); (v) a range of negative returns to labour (i.e. *cd*, where, if the firm pushed its labour input to higher levels, a decline in production would occur). If the firm started with a greater amount of capital services, such as K_1 in Figure 7.2, then a higher returns to labour curve, TPP_{L1} (not shown in its entirety), would result.

The marginal physical product of labour, MPP_L, is the change in output caused by a small variation in the labour input, holding the stock of capital constant. The MPP_L curve, shown in Figure 7.3(b), is derived from the TPP_L curve in Figure 7.3(a): the height of the MPP_L curve is equal to the corresponding slope of the TPP_L curve at each level of the labour input. Thus, the MPP_L curve rises during the region of increasing returns to the labour input, reaches a maximum at the point of inflexion of the TPP_L curve (i.e. at the point of constant returns to labour), at a labour input of L_0, and cuts the horizontal axis when the TPP_L curve reaches a maximum.

The average physical product of labour curve, APP_L in Figure 7.3(b), is constructed as the total physical product divided by the corresponding value of the labour input (e.g. TPP_L/L). The height of the APP_L curve at any particular level of the labour input is equal to the slope of a ray drawn from the origin to the point on the TPP_L curve vertically above that level of the labour input. If we picture a series of rays being drawn from point *a* to points further and further to the right along the TPP_L curve, then the slopes

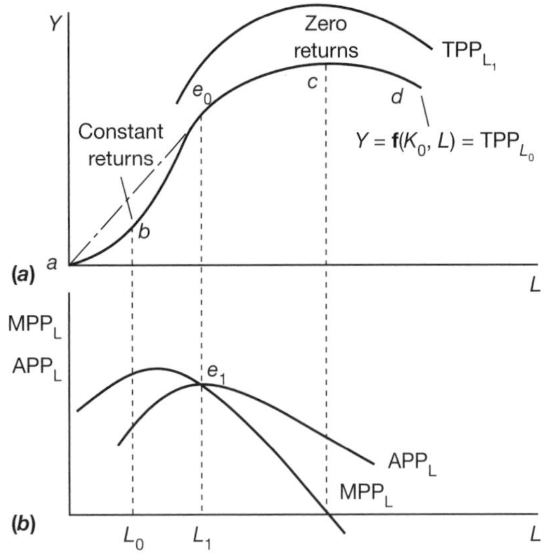

Fig 7.3 (a) Total physical product of labour. (b) Marginal and average physical products of labour.

increase up to ray ae_0 and then begin to decline again. Thus, the highest point on the APP_L curve occurs at a labour input L_1, associated with ray, ae_0, which is tangential to the TPP_L curve in Figure 7.3(a).

Clearly, as the ray ae_0 in Figure 7.3(a) is tangential to the TPP_L curve, the APP_L is equal to the MPP_L at that level of labour input. This is represented by the point of intersection, e_1, in Figure 7.3(b). The MPP_L curve cuts the APP_L curve from above, as shown in Figure 7.3(b), as the slope at point b is higher than that at point e_0, and point b lies at a lower level of the labour input than point e_0. Intuitive proof of the relative positions of the APP_L and the MPP_L curves, however, can be obtained from the following reasoning: if the next worker can be expected to produce more than the average of existing workers, if that person is employed, then the average physical product will rise; if, on the other hand, the next worker will produce less than the average of existing workers, if the individual is employed, the average physical product will fall. In other words, if MPP_L lies above APP_L, then the APP_L curve is rising, but if MPP_L is lower than the APP_L, then the APP_L curve is falling. By implication, the two curves must intersect at the maximum point on the APP_L curve.

Before leaving this subject, it is worth adding that most of the analysis of labour demand is based on the assumption of the law of diminishing returns. In other words, it is assumed that successive additions to the labour input (holding capital constant) will result in smaller and smaller additions to the output of the firm. This is not just a simplifying assumption; there is a strong economic reason for believing that, even in the case of production functions which exhibit some range of increasing returns to one input, the firm will invariably choose to operate in a region of diminishing returns. This is discussed further below.

CASE STUDY 1 Alternative forms of the production function

The shape and position of isoquants depend upon the specification of the production function. It is already clear that a variety of different types of production function have been used to underpin labour demand functions. Table 7.1 describes four of the most common, along with their main properties. They are effectively distinguished by their elasticities of substitution, although all four are constant elasticity of substitution (CES) functions: fixed-coefficient (or Leontief) function, $\sigma = 0$; perfect substitutes, $\sigma = \infty$; the generalized CES function, where σ is constant, but can take any non-negative value ($0 < \sigma < \infty$). Thus, the fixed-coefficient and linear additive functions are specific, polar cases of the generalized CES; the Cobb–Douglas is a specific, intermediate case, where $\sigma = 1$ throughout the isoquant map.

The examples reviewed in Table 7.1 are a sample of a very diverse set of specifications in the factor demand literature. We do not have time to discuss other extremely interesting alternatives, such as the Johansen production schema and vintage production functions in any detail. However, we note that there is a strong intuitive belief that the real world is best characterized by vintage production functions. In a vintage world, new technology is assumed to be (in the simplest case) unchangeably embodied in the capital stock at its date of construction. However, it is probably fair to say that the a priori support for a vintage approach has not

continues

CASE STUDY 1 continued

Table 7.1 Some functional forms and their main properties: a summary

	Fixed coefficient	Cobb–Douglas	CES (general constant elasticity of substitution)	Perfect substitution
Functional form	$Y = \min f(K,L)$ $Y = aK = bL$ (1)	$Y = f(K,L)$ $Y = AK^{\alpha}L^{\beta}$ (2)	$Y = f(K,L)$ $Y = \zeta(aK^{-\rho} + bL^{-\rho})^{-\theta/\rho}$ (3)	$Y = f(K,L)$ $Y = aK + bL$ (4)
Technical parameters	a,b	A,α,β	ζ,a,b,ρ,θ	a,b
Isoquant	$K = \frac{b}{a}L$ Fig 7.4 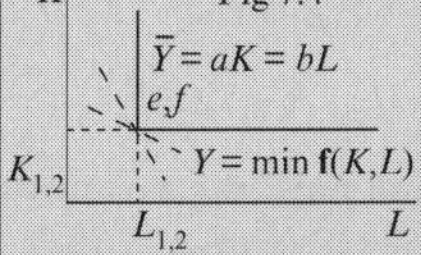	$K = A^{-1/\alpha}\,Y^{1/\alpha}\,L^{-\beta/\alpha}$ Fig 7.5 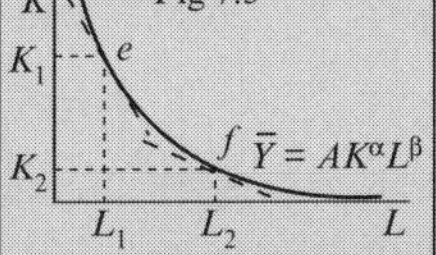	$K=\left[\frac{1}{a}\left(\frac{Y}{\zeta}\right)^{-\rho/\theta}-\frac{b}{a}L^{-\rho}\right]^{-1/\rho}$ Fig 7.6 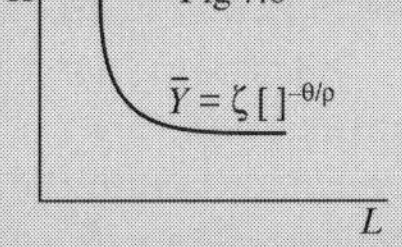	$K = \frac{\bar{Y}}{a} - \frac{b}{a}L$ Fig 7.7 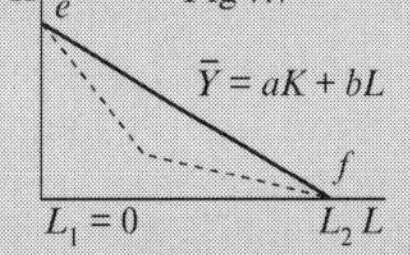
Returns to one factor	$\frac{\partial Y}{\partial L} = 0$ $\frac{\partial Y}{\partial K} = 0$	$\frac{\partial Y}{\partial L} = \beta\frac{Y}{L}$ $\frac{\partial Y}{\partial K} = \alpha\frac{Y}{K}$	$\frac{\partial Y}{\partial L} = \theta\zeta[\,]^{-\theta/\rho-1}\,bL^{-\rho-1}$ $\frac{\partial Y}{\partial K} = \theta\zeta[\,]^{-\theta/\rho-1}\,aK^{-\rho-1}$	$\frac{\partial Y}{\partial L} = b$ $\frac{\partial Y}{\partial K} = a$
Returns to scale	Constant returns to scale everywhere	Decreasing $\alpha + \beta < 1$ Constant $\alpha + \beta = 1$ Increasing $\alpha + \beta > 1$	Decreasing $\theta < 1$ Constant $\theta = 1$ Increasing $\theta > 1$	Constant returns to scale everywhere
Elasticity of substitution	$\sigma = 0$	$\sigma = 1$	$\sigma = \frac{1}{1+\rho}$ $= \text{const } 0 \le \sigma \le \infty$	$\sigma = \infty$

been matched by equally strong empirical evidence of its validity. Johansen has shown that the point input/point output (fixed- coefficient) technology at the micro level (e.g. plant or firm) may still be consistent with production functions exhibiting neoclassical properties at the macro level (e.g. industry or economy wide). One of the most important advances in the production function literature has been the adoption of flexible functional forms. One example is the transcendental logarithmic production function,

$$\ln Y = a_0 + \Sigma_i a_i \ln X_i + \tfrac{1}{2}\Sigma_i\Sigma_j b_{ij} \ln X_i \ln X_j \qquad (1)$$

Where X_i and X_j denote the *i*th and *j*th inputs. In general, flexible functional forms of this type are able to provide local second-order approximations to any production function and do not impose any restrictions on the specification of the production function at that point. In other words, the functional forms outlined above are special cases, nested within the translog, and can be derived by imposing restrictions on the parameter values. For example, if all but the coefficients on the X_i terms are insignificantly different from zero, equation (1) collapses to the Cobb–Douglas production function. We return to estimates of the production parameters in Chapter 11 below (see Berndt, 1991, Chapter 9; Johansen, 1972; Heathfield and Wibe, 1987).

2.4 Returns to scale

Returns to scale is a long-run concept analogous to the short run-returns to one factor described above. By its very nature, it is more concerned with the optimal scale of plant than with the optimal amount of labour employed in a plant of given size. In order to establish the magnitude of returns to scale, we explore what happens to the volume of output when all inputs are expanded (or contracted) at the same time. In order to place some limits on the number of cases to be investigated, it is assumed that all inputs are expanded (contracted) in the same proportion. Thus, if the firm is initially at a point such as (K_0,L_0) in Figure 7.2, all other points of interest lie on a ray from the origin and can be represented by (tK_0,tL_0), where t is any constant, $t > 0$ (note that $t > 1$ for expansion and $t < 1$ for contraction).

The nature of returns to scale turns on the relative amounts by which both inputs and outputs change. In this instance, inputs increase by a factor t, $t > 1$, and output expands by a factor y, which we define as $y = Y_2/Y_1$. There are three primary cases of interest: (i) increasing returns to scale, where $y > t$; (ii) constant returns to scale, where $y = t$; (iii) decreasing returns to scale, where $y < t$. Imagine, for the sake of argument, that $t = 2$ (e.g. all inputs have been doubled); then whether there are increasing, constant or decreasing returns to scale depends on whether $Y_2 > 2Y_1$, $Y_2 = 2Y_1$ or $Y_2 < 2Y_1$ (e.g. $y > 2$, $y = 2$ or $y < 2$) respectively.

The same phenomenon can be illustrated mathematically from the general form of the production function, equation (1). We know that $Y_0 = f(K_0,L_0)$ is one possible point on the production function. If inputs are now increased by a factor t, then a new level of output, say Y_x, results:

$$Y_x = \mathbf{f}(tK_0,tL_0) \qquad (4)$$

where $Y_x = Y_0$ at $t = 1$. Returns to scale can again be categorized in the same manner as before, (i) increasing returns to scale, where

$$Y_x > tY_0 \text{ or } y = (Y_x/Y_0) > t \qquad (5)$$

(ii) constant returns to scale,

$$Y_x = tY_0 \text{ or } y = (Y_x/Y_0) = t \qquad (6)$$

(iii) decreasing returns to scale,

$$Y_x < tY_0 \text{ or } y = (Y_x/Y_0) < t \qquad (7)$$

Two important questions arise. First, would we observe the same measure of returns to scale if the firm sets off from the same isoquant, but from different points on that isoquant (e.g. along different rays)? Second, is the magnitude of returns to scale the same for a given ray, when the firm sets off from different output levels (e.g. are returns to scale the same everywhere along a given ray)? The majority of production functions used to underpin theoretical and empirical work on labour demands adopt fairly straightforward specifications. In such functions, we can invariably discount the first of these problems, but the second question is more open. The precise result involves the concept of homotheticity.

Returning to equation (4), the functions found in the literature are generally homothetic and this implies that we can write

$$Y_x = \mathbf{f}(tK_0,tL_0) = \mathbf{g}(t)\mathbf{f}(K_0,L_0) = \mathbf{g}(t)Y_0 \qquad (8)$$

Such functions have the property that each isoquant is a radial projection of other isoquants and the slope of each isoquant, dK/dL (see Section 2.5), is the same along any radian (see Figure 7.2). The classic case of a firm with a technically optimal scale of production is represented by a value of $\mathbf{g}(t)$ which first increases along the ray, then becomes constant, and then declines. Even this, however, is a rather complicated function and often, for mathematical simplicity, $\mathbf{g}(t)$ is assumed to increase or decrease monotonically with the overall level of activity. Such functions are homogeneous of degree θ, where equation (8) can be written

$$Y_x = \mathbf{f}(tK_0,tL_0) = t^{\theta}\mathbf{f}(K_0,L_0) = t^{\theta}Y_0 \qquad (9)$$

Increasing, constant or decreasing returns to scale now turn on whether $\theta > 1$, $\theta = 1$ or $\theta < 1$, respectively.

There are a wide range of possible causes of economies (and diseconomies) of scale, which fall under three broad headings: (i) technical economies; (ii) managerial (or organizational) economies; (iii) financial economies. In terms of the production function, the technical economies are paramount, but in terms of the demand for labour at the firm or industry level, all three types are potentially important. Transaction cost theory suggests that the optimal size of the firm depends upon the relative costs of internal versus external transactions. Where certain activities are undertaken more efficiently or cost effectively within the company, they are internalized, otherwise they are left to external markets. A full discussion of these concepts can be found in most industrial economics textbooks.

2.5 Shape of the isoquant I: slope and convexity

In this section we develop a measure that gives an indication of the shape of an isoquant. It enables us to look in greater detail at both the negative slope and the convexity of neoclassical isoquants (see rules iii and v of Section 2.2). Once the measure is established, it can be used as an aid to exploring the different functional forms used to represent the technology of production (see Case Study 1).

The slope of the isoquant at any particular point is equal to the ratio of the marginal physical products of the two factors. Beginning from any particular point (K,L) and, initially, holding capital constant, the addition to output, dY, caused by a small variation in the labour input, dL, can approximately be written

$$\mathrm{d}Y = (\partial Y/\partial L)\mathrm{d}L = \mathrm{MPP}_L\,\mathrm{d}L \qquad (10)$$

where: d denotes a small change; $(\partial Y/\partial L)$ is the partial derivative of output with respect to labour, and denotes the change in output brought about by a (small) unit change in the labour input, holding other inputs constant (see Section 2.3). Equation (10) can therefore be given an intuitive interpretation: the total change in output experienced (at some given level of capital stock) is equal to the change in output caused by a (small) unit change in the labour input holding capital constant, MPP_L, multiplied by the number of units that the labour input changes, dL. The equivalent output change caused by varying capital, but holding labour constant, is

$$\mathrm{d}Y = (\partial Y/\partial K)\mathrm{d}K = \mathrm{MPP}_K\,\mathrm{d}K \qquad (11)$$

Around the isoquant, both K and L are changing. In order to remain on the same isoquant, however, the two changes must be in opposite directions and exactly offset one another, leaving output unaltered, dY = 0. Hence,

$$\mathrm{MPP}_K\mathrm{d}K = -\mathrm{MPP}_L\mathrm{d}L \qquad (12)$$

and the slope of the isoquant can be written

$$\frac{\mathrm{d}K}{\mathrm{d}L} = -\frac{(\partial Y/\partial L)}{(\partial Y/\partial K)} = -\frac{\mathrm{MPP}_L}{\mathrm{MPP}_K} \qquad (13)$$

Where the slope, dK/dL, is the change in capital, dK, necessary to remain on the isoquant, given some small change in the labour input, dL (see Figure 7.2).

Property (iii) of the production function, outlined in Section 2.2, indicated that the isoquant would slope downwards left to right in the (K,L) plane. Equation (13) shows that a positive slope would require the MPP of one of the two inputs (but not both) to become negative. In other words, the firm would have to push its consumption of one of the inputs to such a high level that the addition of one more unit would actually reduce the level of output. Clearly, where inputs have positive prices, no rational producer would behave in this manner. Thus, although a positive slope may be technically feasible, it will lie outside of the range of options that the firm considers.

Property (v), outlined in Section 2.2, concerned the assumption that isoquants would be convex to the origin. Compare the slopes at points e and f in Figure 7.2. At point f, there is a relatively high level of labour input and a low level of capital. Under the assumption of diminishing returns to one input (see Section 2.3), the MPP_L will tend to be relatively small and the MPP_K relatively large. Thus, according to equation (13), the (absolute) value of the slope of the isoquant will be close to zero. At point e, on the other hand, there is a relatively large amount of capital and small amount of labour. As a result, the relative sizes of MPP_K and MPP_L are reversed, and the (absolute) value of the slope is high. The change in the (absolute) value of the slope from low at point f to high at point e is sufficient proof of convexity for our purposes.

2.6 Elasticity of substitution

The elasticity of substitution, σ, is a summary measure of the shape of the isoquant and, thereby, of the ease of substitution between the various inputs. It is measured as

$$\sigma = -\frac{\text{percentage change in the ratio of capital to labour}}{\text{percentage change in the slope of the isoquant}}$$
$$= -\frac{\text{percentage change in the ratio of capital to labour}}{\text{percentage change in the ratio of } \mathrm{MPP}_L \text{ to } \mathrm{MPP}_K} \qquad (14)$$

There are three important features of the elasticity of substitution: (i) σ is symmetrical with respect to the two factors; (ii) σ is always non-negative; (iii) σ is inversely related to the degree of curvature of the isoquant. Figures 7.4–7.7, which appear in Table 7.1, illustrate the isoquants associated with alternative values of σ.

1 Figure 7.4 represents the case of perfect complements, $\sigma = 0$. The point of interest on the 'right-angled' isoquant is the corner, as all other input combinations are technically inefficient (e.g. associated with more capital or more labour without producing any greater output). For this reason, economically meaningful substitution between inputs is not possible. It can be seen that, for an extremely small change in the capital/labour ratio around this corner point, the percentage change in slope is nevertheless large. Thus, from expression (14), for a sufficiently small change in K/L, $\sigma = 0$.

2 Figure 7.7 represents the opposite extreme, the case of perfect substitutes. In this instance, we can choose as large a percentage change in the capital/labour ratio as we like, it is clear that the slope of the isoquant does not alter and substitution between capital and labour is extremely easy. Putting this information into expression (14) indicates a ratio of some positive number divided by zero and, hence, $\sigma = \infty$.

3 Figures 7.5 and 7.6 both represent intermediate cases between 1 and 2 above. These isoquants belong to the broad class of imperfect substitutes; both are neoclassical isoquants of the type used in the analysis to date. In this class of functions, $0 < \sigma < \infty$; and substitution between inputs becomes easier as σ changes from 0 towards ∞.

3 Equilibrium of the firm

3.1 Three alternative goals

The principal goal of the firm which underlies much of economic theory is profit maximization, in part, because it is consistent with perfect competition. When exploring the equilibrium of a profit-maximizing firm, however, it is also useful to understand equilibrium under conditions of output maximization subject to a cost constraint and cost minimization subject to an output constraint. The latter two goals can be viewed as special cases which, under certain circumstances, give the same solution as profit maximization. They are particularly useful where profit maximization does not give a determinate solution. One such case is in the long run where there are constant returns to scale, with the result that small production units are just as profitable as large, and it is impossible to determine the optimal scale of an individual firm's activities and, thereby, its factor demands. In addition, the other two goals may be more relevant for certain enterprises that do not operate under competitive market conditions, such as government departments or nationalized industries.

3.2 Output maximization subject to a cost constraint

Figure 7.8 depicts the isoquant map of a particular firm,

$$K = g(Y_i, L) \tag{15}$$

where output is fixed at some particular level, Y_i, for each isoquant ($Y_i = Y_0, Y_1, \ldots$, where successive subscripts denote higher levels of output per period). The firm's costs of production can be written

$$C = rK + wL \tag{16}$$

where: C denotes the total cost of employing the input combination (K,L); r is the rental per unit of capital; w is the wage rate.

Under this goal, the firm has to operate within a total cost constraint $C \leq C_1$. Setting C at its maximum value of C_1, then the budget constraint line can be written as

$$K = \frac{C_1}{r} - \frac{w}{r}L \tag{17}$$

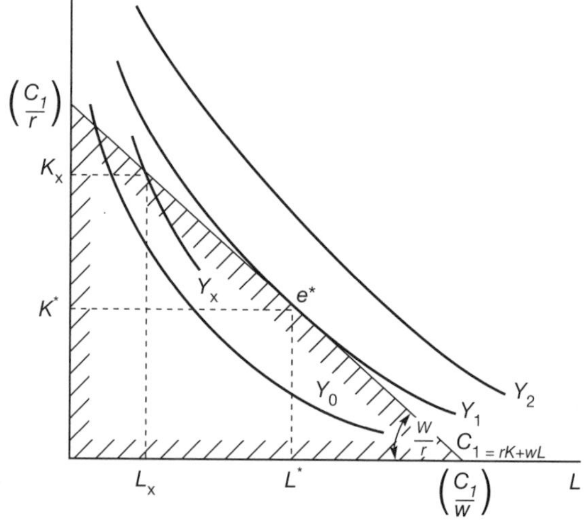

Fig 7.8 Output maximization subject to a cost contraint.

which, for given wage and rental, represents a straight line, downward sloping from left to right in the (K,L) plane, intersecting the K axis at value (C_1/r) and the L axis at (C_1/w). The slope of the line is constant at a value of $(dK/dL) = -(w/r)$, which is the ratio of the factor prices. Equation (17) is termed the isocost line, for any particular value of C.

Given its budget constraint, the firm can afford to buy any combination of the two inputs lying on the boundary formed by equation (17) or nearer to the origin and, thus, feasible points are shown by the shaded triangle. As an output maximizer, the firm searches for the highest isoquant that it can reach and still satisfy the constraint C_1. It is clear that the firm could produce Y_0, but this would not be the highest level of output attainable; even in the short run, with capital K_x, it could produce Y_x. It can produce Y_0 without spending all of the budget C_1, and it can therefore afford to hire more inputs and produce more output. While it would ideally like to move to an output level such as Y_2, or higher, it is not able to do so, because no input combination associated with this output level falls within its budget constraint. The highest output the firm can reach, when it is able to vary both of its inputs, is Y_1, and point e^* therefore is a point of long-run equilibrium for the cost-constrained output maximizer.

The long-run equilibrium position is at the point of tangency between the given isocost line and the highest attainable isoquant. The convexity of the isoquant and linearity of the budget constraint line ensure that (K^*,L^*) are the only values of the inputs that satisfy both the cost function C_1 and the output level Y_1. Because it is a point of tangency, the slope of the isoquant at e^* is the same as the slope of the budget constraint line,

$$\frac{dK}{dL} = -\frac{MPP_L}{MPP_K} = -\frac{w}{r} \qquad (18)$$

This is a necessary condition for long-run equilibrium, which has its counterparts in the constrained cost-minimizing and the profit-maximizing cases outlined below. It is clear from above that, in the short run, the firm may already have a given stock of capital, such as K_x, which may not be consistent with long-run equilibrium. If the firm is committed to paying for this fixed stock of capital from its fixed budget, C_1, its highest output is Y_x, employing a labour input of L_x.

3.3 Cost minimization with an output constraint

The firm is now assumed to have a particular output in mind, Y_1, that it wants to produce at lowest possible cost. In effect, the firm searches through alternative (K,L) combinations, consistent with the specified output level

$$K = \mathbf{g}(Y_1, L) \qquad (19)$$

until it finds the pairing with the lowest cost. Figure 7.9 shows the isoquant, Y_1, which is assumed to be the desired level of output. The alternative cost levels are represented by a series of isocost lines,

$$C_i = rK + wL \qquad (20)$$

where $C_i = C_0, C_1, C_2, \ldots$.

In the long run, the constrained cost-minimizing behaviour of the firm leads to the point of equilibrium, f^*, with optimal input levels, (K^*,L^*), and associated cost level C_1. Any other combination of inputs would have resulted in either: (i) a higher cost than necessary in order to produce output Y_1 (e.g. at the cost level C_2); or (ii) a cost level which does not enable the firm to purchase enough of the two inputs to produce the desired level of output (e.g.

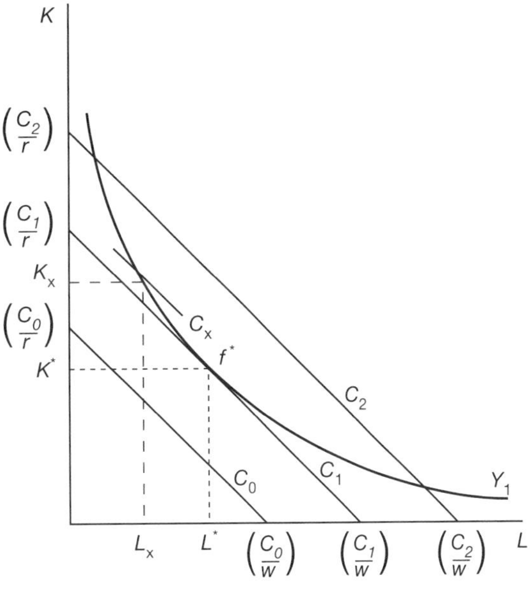

Fig 7.9 Cost minimization subject to an output constraint.

the cost level C_0). Thus, the result is very similar to the constrained output maximization problem reported in Section 3.2: the long-run equilibrium is a point of tangency between an isocost line and an isoquant, as in equation (18) above. If, by chance, the output maximizer chose the same isoquant as the one to which the cost minimizer was constrained, then the resulting equilibria would be identical, other things being equal. In the short run, however, the cost minimizer may be committed to some sub-optimal level of capital, such as K_x in Figure 7.9. Thus, in order to meet its output constraint, Y_1, the firm is forced to a short-run equilibrium, employing K_x of capital and L_x of labour, incurring a higher than long-run cost of C_x.

3.4 Profit maximization

Figure 7.10 illustrates the outcome for the unconstrained profit maximizer. In finding this more general solution, we draw on our experience from the previous two cases. Both of the earlier results indicate that long-run equilibrium involves a point of tangency between the isoquant and isocost lines. Any other points are associated with either: (i) a lower level of output for a given level of cost; or (ii) a higher level of cost for a given level of output. The profit-maximizing solution therefore must be point of tangency. The question is, simply, which one?

The profit maximizer will find the optimal combination of inputs by comparing all of the points of

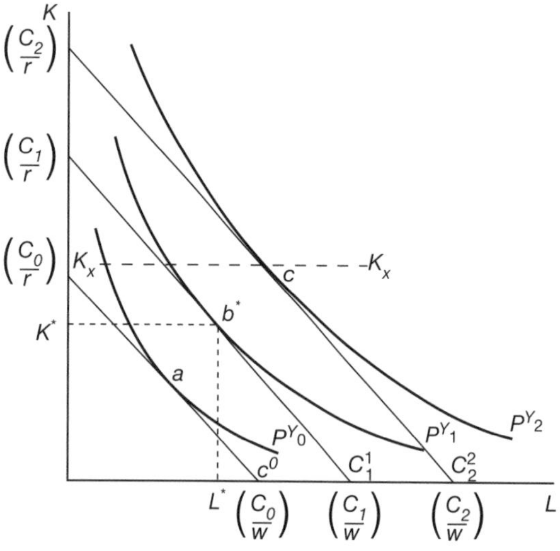

Fig 7.10 Profit maximization.

tangency consistent with equation (18). At each point of tangency, the entrepreneur calculates the profit level,

$$\Pi = pY - C \tag{21}$$

where Π denotes total profit level and p is the price per unit of the firm's output. Thus, the calculation is repeated at points a, b, c, etc., which form the long-run expansion path of the firm, which is searching for the largest difference between revenues and costs. In this instance, this profit-maximizing position is assumed to be at point b^*, associated with the long run optimal input combination (K^*,L^*). In the short run, however, the firm will be committed to some level of capital, such as K_x. In this case, the entrepreneur cannot compare points of tangency, but only points along the short-run expansion path for the firm, represented by the horizontal line at level K_x. Nevertheless, the entrepreneur uses basically the same technique as in the long run (although along a different path) in this case, to isolate the short-run profit-maximizing position, as at point c.

4 The demand for labour by the firm under perfect competition

In this section we take the analysis to the next stage of drawing the firm's demand curve for labour under perfect competition, first in the short run and then in the long run.

4.1 Short run

4.1.1 Deriving a point on the labour demand curve

This section focuses on the demand for labour as output is expanded, but the amount of capital, the fixed factor, is constant. The firm is assumed to be a profit maximizer. This short-run expansion path of the firm can be used to relate the concept of firm equilibrium with the demand for labour and, thereby, to derive the demand curve for the variable input. Figure 7.11 links the isoquant map, cost and revenue curves with the demand curve for labour. Figure 7.11(a) shows the equilibrium of the firm using the traditional isoquant map. The firm sets off from point a, which is assumed to be the profit-maximizing equilibrium position. K^* becomes the effective constraint on the capital input, $K^* = K_0$. Following the analysis reported in Section 2 above, Figure 7.11(b) shows the returns to labour curve (i.e. the total physical product of labour curve), $Y = \mathbf{f}(K_0,L)$, and the total revenue product curve, $p\mathbf{Y}(\ )$, where p is the price of the product, which is a constant under perfect competition.

The marginal revenue product, MRP_L, is the change in total revenue brought about by a small change in the labour input, and can be defined as

$$\mathrm{MRP}_L = \frac{\partial \mathrm{TRP}_L}{\partial L} = \frac{\partial (p\mathrm{TPP}_L)}{\partial L} = \frac{\partial (pY)}{\partial L} = \frac{\partial p}{\partial Y}\frac{\partial Y}{\partial L}\mathbf{f}(\ ) + p\frac{\mathrm{df}(\ )}{\partial L} \quad (22)$$

Assuming a perfectly competitive product market, the price of output is constant, and the change in price caused by a small change in the labour input is

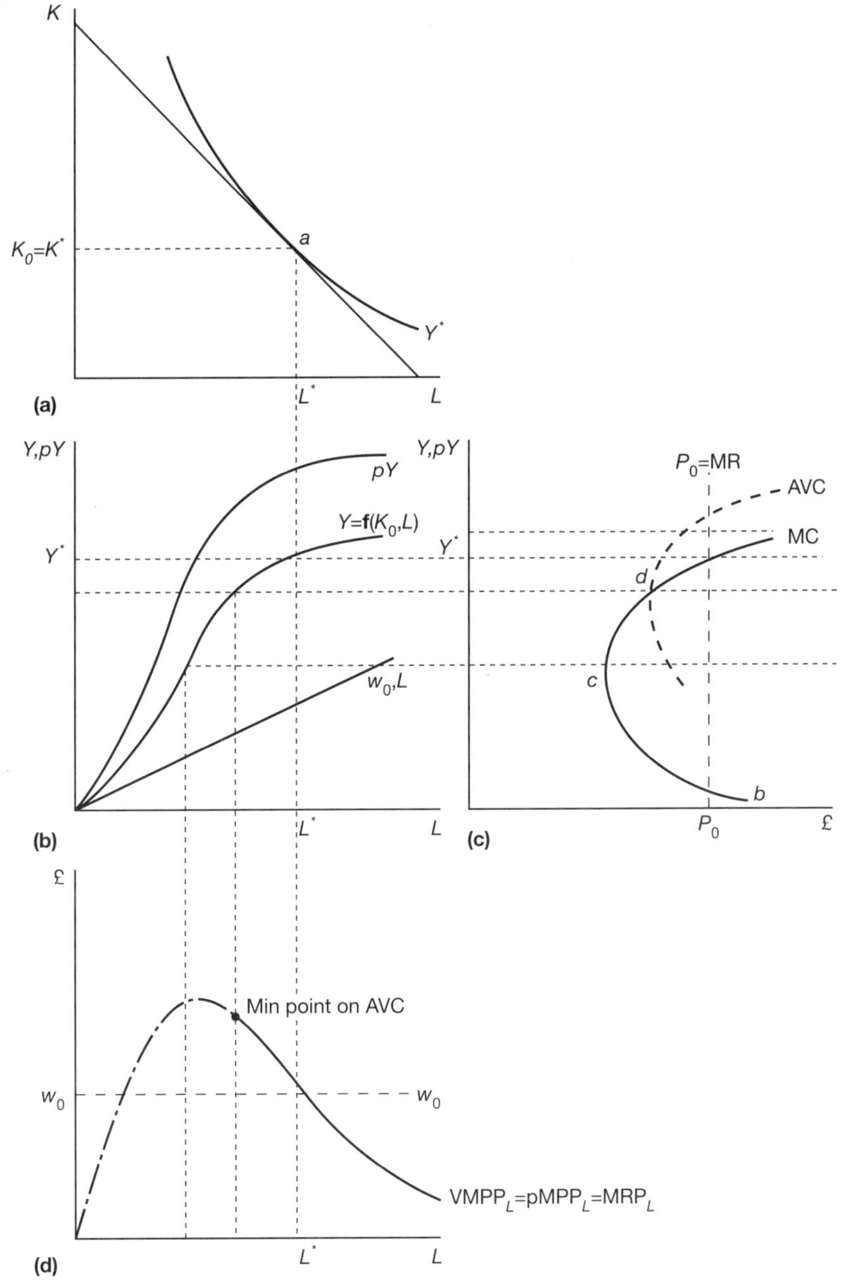

Fig 7.11 Firm equilibrium and the demand for labour.

zero and the price change term in equation (22) disappears. Thus, under competitive conditions,

$$\mathrm{MRP}_L = p\mathrm{MPP}_L = p_0\,\mathrm{MPP}_L \tag{23}$$

The value of the marginal physical product, VMPP_L, is defined as

$$\mathrm{VMPP}_L = p\mathrm{MPP}_L = p_0\mathrm{MPP}_L \tag{24}$$

and, under competitive conditions, the MRP_L and the VMPP_L are identical for a given firm in the short run. Denoting the total revenue product, $p\mathbf{f}(K_0,L)$, it is apparent that the slopes of the TRP_L and TPP_L curves are different; the slope of the TRP_L curve is greater than the slope of the TPP_L curve (i.e. $p\mathrm{MPP}_L > \mathrm{MPP}_L$). This implies that, for all positive output prices, the value of the marginal physical product curve lies above the marginal physical product curve. Figure 7.11(d) shows the VMPP_L curve (= MRP_L under perfect competition). The VMPP_L curve reaches a maximum at the point where the TRP_L curve is steepest, that is at the point of inflection.

Figure 7.11(c) shows the corresponding marginal cost curve of the firm, formed as

$$\mathrm{MC} = \frac{w_0}{\mathrm{MPP}_L} \tag{25}$$

Given that w is constant because of the highly competitive nature of the labour market, then the MC curve reaches its minimum at point c, corresponding with the point of inflection of the TPP_L curve (i.e. at highest MPP_L). This occurs at the same labour input as the maximum point on the VMPP_L curve. As the return to labour falls towards zero, the marginal cost becomes very large and the associated MC curve approaches an asymptotic value of Y. Thus, the MC curve is 'U shaped', as shown by bcd in Figure 7.11(c).

The equilibrium of the firm can now be visualized in any one of four ways. In Figure 7.11(a), using the production function the firm can be seen to be in short- (and long-)run equilibrium at point a. Figure 7.11(c) includes the going price per unit of output, $p = p_0$, which is also the marginal revenue of the firm, MR,

$$\mathrm{MR} = \frac{\mathrm{dTR}}{\mathrm{d}Y} = \frac{\mathrm{d}(pY)}{\mathrm{d}Y} = \frac{\mathrm{d}p}{\mathrm{d}Y}Y + p \tag{26}$$

where, under perfect competition, $p = p_0$; hence, $\mathrm{d}p/\mathrm{d}Y = 0$ and $\mathrm{MR} = p = p_0$. The firm is in equilibrium where MR = MC, that is

$$p_0 = \frac{w_0}{\mathrm{MPP}_L} \tag{27}$$

If it turned out that MR < MC (i.e. $p_0 < w_0/\mathrm{MPP}_L$) then the last unit produced would have made a loss and the firm would contract; if, for the next unit, MR > MC (i.e. $p_0 > w_0/\mathrm{MPP}_L$) then a further unit of output would cost less to produce than it would earn in revenue and the firm would choose to expand. Only at MR = MC would the firm be in equilibrium. In Figure 7.11(d), on the other hand, the firm is in equilibrium where the value of the marginal physical product is equal to the wage, $\mathrm{VMPP}_L = w_0$, that is

$$p_0\mathrm{MPP}_L = w_0 \tag{28}$$

If the revenue generated by the last unit of labour is lower than the cost of the labour, $\mathrm{VMPP}_L < w_0$, then the firm will choose to contract its labour force. If, on the other hand, the firm found that $\mathrm{VMPP}_L > w_0$ on the next unit of labour, then the firm would choose to expand its labour force. Only where equation (28) holds will the firm be in equilibrium. Examination of equations (27) and (28) shows the two equilibrium conditions to be identical.

Finally, Figure 7.11(b) can be used to show the same equilibrium position. In this case, the point of equilibrium can be derived by comparing the TRP_L curve with a labour expenditure (or wage bill) curve, w_0L. Given that w_0 is a constant, w_0L will be a ray through the origin. The profit-maximizing firm chooses the maximum distance between the TRP_L curve and the total labour expenditure, w_0L, curve. It just so happens that this distance is a maximum when the slope of the TRP_L curve is equal to the slope of the w_0L curve. The slope of TRP_L is the VMPP_L, where product prices are constant, and the slope of w_0L is w_0. This again yields the same equilibrium position $w_0 = \mathrm{VMPP}_L = p_0\mathrm{MPP}_L$.

Comparison of Figures 7.11(c) and 7.11(d) indicates that the profit maximizer will never operate on the upward-sloping part of the VMPP_L curve. This section of the VMPP_L curve corresponds to the downward-sloping part of the MC curve. As the average variable cost curve must lie above the MC curve at every level of output on the downward-sloping part of the MC curve (i.e. b to c in Figure 7.11(c)), then under perfect competition where p_0 = MC, the price per unit of the product is always less than the average variable costs on this section of the curve and the firm maximizes its profitability (i.e. minimizes its losses) by closing down. The two figures also make it clear that the profit-maximizing firm will not consider all of the downward-sloping part of the MRP_L curve but only that part of the MRP_L curve associated with the MC above the AVC curve.

4.1.2 Deriving the whole labour demand curve

So far, the analysis has established just one point on the demand curve for labour. Normally, the complete demand curve can be thought of as a continuous relationship between w and L, downward sloping from left to right in the (w,L) space. Figure 7.12 illustrates the short-run-constrained, cost minimization and profit maximization equilibrium positions as w is changed. Consider a fall in w from w_0 to w_1. The firm

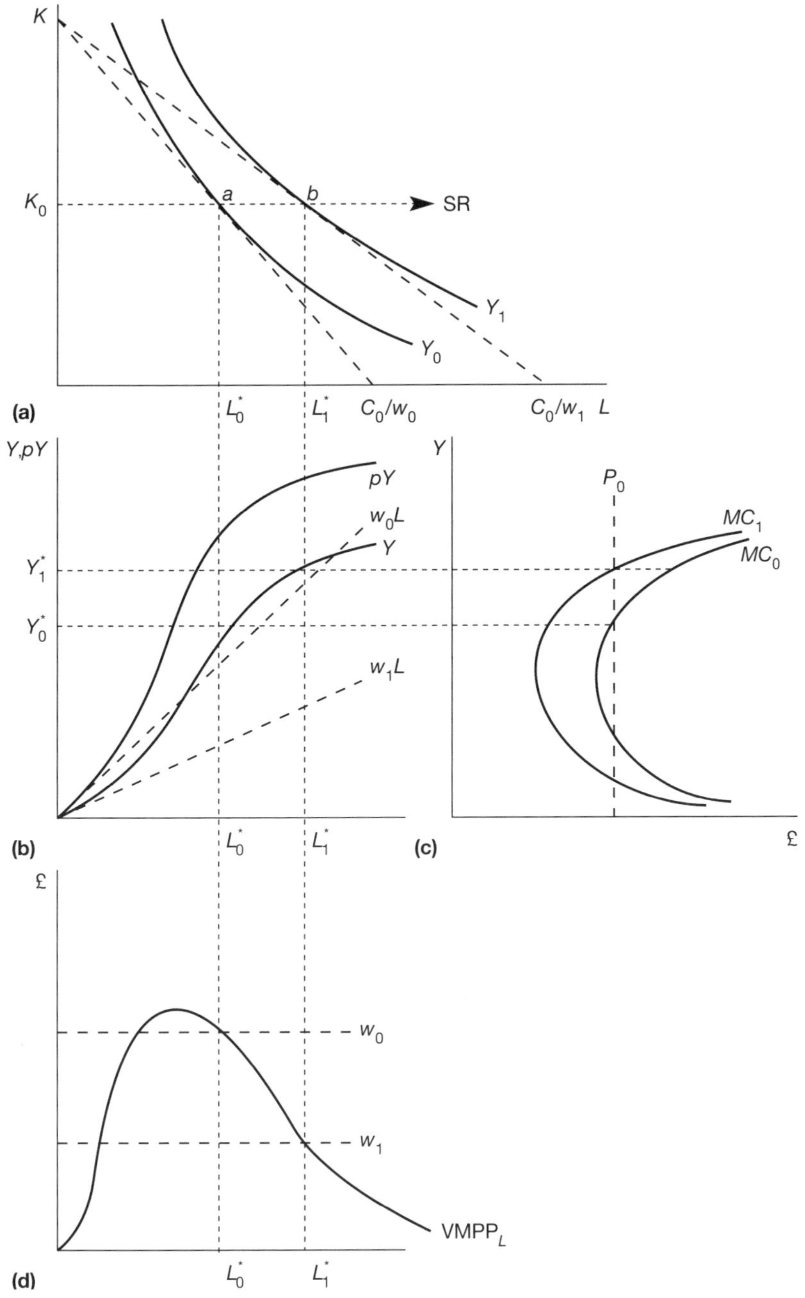

Fig 7.12 Establishing all points on the firm's demand curve for labour.

moves from its original short-run (and long-run) equilibrium position, at point *a* and labour demand L^*_0, to the new short-run position at point *b* and labour demand L^*_1. As the output price p_0 is fixed and the returns to labour curve is unchanged, then the MRP_L curve is also fixed. The original wage, w_0, is replaced by w_1 in Figure 7.12(d) and the new equilibrium is L^*_1. The new output level, from Figures 7.12(a), 7.12(b) and 7.12(c) is Y^*_1. In terms of Figure 7.12(c), the lower wage w_1, shifts the marginal cost curve from MC_0 to MC_1. In this case, Y^*_1 is also associated with $MR = MC_1$ where the $p_0 = MR$ curve has remained unchanged. In Figure 7.12(b) the labour cost radian has pivoted from w_0L to w_1L, causing the labour input at which the distance between TRP_L and w_L is a maximum to change from L_0^* to L_1^*.

The principal conclusion of this section is that the demand curve for labour corresponds to a part of the $VMPP_L$ curve. The upward-sloping part of the $VMPP_L$ curve can be dismissed, as it is associated with the downward-sloping (and, hence, loss-making) part of the MC curve. Even the early part of the downward-sloping section of $VMPP_L$ (i.e. where MC lies below AVC) should also be discounted: the demand curve for labour is therefore formed from part of the right hand tail of the $VMPP_L$. Note also that only the positive part of the right hand tail is relevant as labour has a non-negative price. A formal derivation of the labour demand curve is set out in Case Study 2.

CASE STUDY 2 Formal derivation of labour demand function

It seems useful to undertake a somewhat more formal derivation of the labour demand curve (see Silberberg, 1978). In this instance, we assume that the firm minimizes costs subject to an output constraint in a two-factor input model:

$$c = \sum_{i=1}^{2} w_iX_i \text{ s.t. } Y_0 = \mathbf{f}(X_1,X_2) \quad (1)$$

which can be written as the Lagrangian problem,

$$\text{Min } \mathscr{L} = w_1X_1 + w_2X_2 + \lambda(Y_0 - \mathbf{f}(X_1,X_2) \quad (2)$$

Thus, setting the derivatives of $\mathscr{L}$ with respect to X_1, X_2 and λ equal to zero for a minimum,

$$\frac{\partial \mathscr{L}}{\partial X_1} = \mathscr{L}_1 = w_1 - \lambda f_1 = 0 \quad (3)$$

$$\mathscr{L}_2 = w_2 - \lambda f_2 = 0 \quad (4)$$

$$\mathscr{L}_\lambda = Y_0 - f(X_1,X_2) = 0 \quad (5)$$

We have three equations ((3), (4) and (5)) in three unknowns (X_1, X_2, λ).

The second-order condition for an interior minimum is that the bordered Hessian determinant, Δ, formed by the second partial derivatives of the Lagrangian, $\mathscr{L}$, with respect to X_1, X_2 and λ, should be negative,

$$\Delta = \begin{bmatrix} -\lambda f_{11} & -\lambda f_{12} & -f_1 \\ -\lambda f_{12} & -\lambda f_{22} & -f_2 \\ -f_1 & -f_2 & 0 \end{bmatrix} < 0 \quad (6)$$

These second-order conditions are normally satisfied where factor prices are constant (i.e. independent of X_1 and X_2) and where the underlying technology of production is 'well behaved' (i.e. a neoclassical function, with isoquants convex to the origin).

Equations (3)–(5) form a system of three equations in three unknowns (X_1, X_2 and λ). The implicit function theorem implies that if the Jacobian (see equation (6)) is non-zero, then solutions for X_1, X_2 and λ will exist (although they may prove difficult to derive in practice). Thus, by implication, if the second-order conditions for a minimum hold, then explicit solutions for X_1, X_2 and λ exist.

Solving (3)–(5) yields equations

$$X_1 = X_1\,(w_1, w_2, Y_0) \quad (7)$$

$$X_2 = X_2\,(w_1, w_2, Y_0) \quad (8)$$

$$\lambda = \lambda\,(w_1, w_2, Y_0) \quad (9)$$

Even with this very general model, it is possible to show that $\frac{\partial X_1^*}{\partial w_1} < 0, \frac{\partial X_1^*}{\partial w_2} > 0$ and $\frac{\partial \lambda_1^*}{\partial w_1} \gtrless 0$. While it may seem curious to pay much attention to λ^*, which appears at first sight just a mathematical 'trick' to obtain the minimum, in practice it turns out to be the marginal cost function of the firm.

Source: Silberberg (1978)

CASE STUDY 3 Factor demand function based upon CES function

This case study briefly explores the factor demand function derived from an underlying CES production function under conditions of constant real factor prices and cost minimization subject to an output constraint. The problem is to *minimize*

$$w_1X_1 + w_2X_2 \text{ s.t. } Y_0 = \xi[aX_1^{-\rho} + bX_2^{-\rho}]^{-\theta/\rho} \quad (1)$$

(see Table 7.1 for a discussion of the interpretation of the parameters). The Lagrangian problem can be written

$$\text{Min} = w_1X_1 + w_2X_2 + \lambda\,[Y^0 - \xi(\ )^{-\theta/\rho}] \quad (2)$$

and the first-order conditions can be derived as

$$\mathscr{L}_1 = w_1 - \lambda(-\theta/\rho)\,\xi\,[\ ]^{(-\theta/\rho)-1}\,a(-\rho)\,X_1^{-\rho-1} = 0 \quad (3)$$

$$\mathscr{L}_2 = w_2 - \lambda(-\theta/\rho)\,\xi\,[\ ]^{(-\theta/\rho)-1}\,b(-\rho)\,X_2^{-\rho-1} = 0 \quad (4)$$

$$\mathscr{L}_\lambda = Y - \xi\,[aX_1^{-\rho} + bX_2^{-\rho}]^{-\theta/\rho} = 0 \quad (5)$$

It is a common feature of CES functions that most of the terms in equations (3) and (4) are identical. Hence, dividing equation (3) by equation (4),

$$\frac{w_1}{w_2} = \frac{a}{b}\left(\frac{X_1}{X_2}\right)^{-\rho-1} = \frac{a}{b}\left(\frac{X_2}{X_1}\right)^{1+\rho} \quad (6)$$

Using $\sigma = \frac{1}{(1+\rho)}$ (see Table 7.1),

$$X_2 = \left(\frac{w_1}{w_2}\right)^{\sigma}\left(\frac{b}{a}\right)^{\sigma} X_1 \quad (7)$$

Substituting X_2 into equation (5) and using $\sigma = \frac{1}{(1+\rho)}$,

$$X_1^* = \left(\frac{1}{a}\right)^{1/\rho}\left(\frac{Y_0}{\xi}\right)^{1/\theta}\left[1 + \left(\frac{b}{a}\right)^{\sigma}\left(\frac{w_1}{w_2}\right)^{-\rho\sigma}\right]^{1/\rho} \quad (8)$$

4.2 Long run

4.2.1 Constrained output

If a production function characterized first by increasing and then by decreasing returns to scale is assumed, then, in perfectly competitive long-run equilibrium, the firm is forced to choose the technically most efficient scale of plant. In the long run each firm is 'pinned' to this optimal scale and, at this point on its cost curves, it experiences constant returns to scale. The industry expansion (or contraction) is therefore a special case where, in the long run, existing firms add nothing in terms of extra production; all additional output arises through an increase in the number of firms.

As the analysis in this section deals with the long-run expansion path, it can no longer be assumed that the firm expands and contracts along a given 'returns to labour' curve. In the long run, the firm adjusts its stock of capital and moves from one 'returns to labour' curve to another. Figure 7.13(a) shows that, if the firm is constrained to a technically optimum level of output, Y^*, the long-run equilibrium of the firm is at point a when the wage is w_0, but at point b when the wage is w_1. As the wage falls from w_0 to w_1, the firm increases its demand for labour from L_0 to L_1. There is only a substitution effect present and this implies directly, from the underlying properties of the isoquant, that the demand curve for labour will be downward sloping from left to right.

Figure 7.13(b) demonstrates that the demand curve will be downward sloping. At a wage rate w_0, the firm was on a short-run expansion path Y_0 at a point a_1. After the wage change from w_0 to w_1, the firm moves to a new short-run expansion path. Its lower capital stock implies a 'returns to labour' curve Y_1. After the change in wage, the firm is at point b_1 along Y_1 (i.e. output is constant at Y^*). In terms of its total revenue product, the initial equilibrium is at a_2 and the new equilibrium at b_2. Although the demand curve for labour, DL, shown in Figure 7.13(d) is certain to be downward from left to right, the precise way in which that result arises depends on what has happened to the marginal physical product of labour as the firm moves away from point a on isoquant Y^* and towards point b. In other words it depends crucially on the elasticity of substitution between capital and labour (this was discussed in Section 2.6). The result also depends on what happens to the price at which output sells, because, while the individual firm's output is 'pinned' by its technically efficient scale, the lower wage (other things being equal) will lower costs and price, demand will rise in the market and new firms will enter.

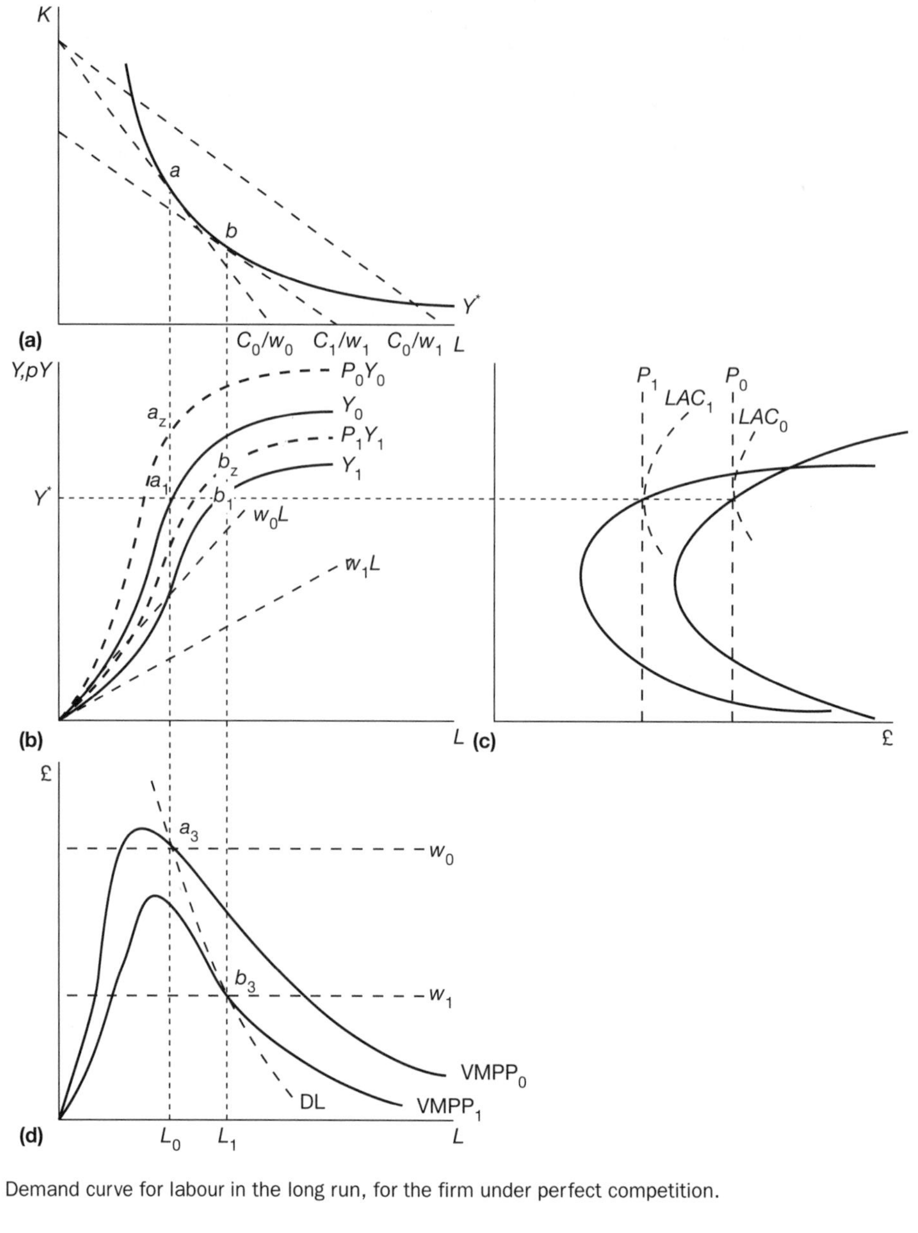

Fig 7.13 Demand curve for labour in the long run, for the firm under perfect competition.

The likely outcome is shown in Figure 7.13(d). For well-behaved production functions, the marginal product of labour is higher at point *a* than at point *b* in Figure 7.13(a). Thus, the slope of Y_0 at a_1 in Figure 7.13(b) is greater than the equivalent slope of Y_1 at b_1. Hence, a move from *a* to *b* is associated with a shift in the position of the value of the marginal physical product curve from $VMPP_0$ towards $VMPP_1$ in Figure 7.13(d). It might be possible to conceive of less well-behaved functions where this is not the case. Nevertheless, the reduction in the wage causes a downward movement of long-run average costs from LAC_0 to LAC_1 in Figure 7.13(c) and the product price on this competitive market falls in the long run. This result reinforces the movement from higher to lower $VMPP_L$ curves. Thus, in terms of Figure 7.13(d), the firm moves along its labour demand curve DL. Under the circumstances described, the long-run demand curve tends to be less elastic than each of the $VMPP_L$ curves. This is because the firm is 'pinned' to its optimal scale in the long run and is unable to expand its output in the same manner that it did as a short-run response in its search for transitory profits.

4.2.2 Constant returns to scale everywhere

The case of constant returns to scale everywhere is a peculiar one in a market where all firms face the same prices (both output and input). While the size of the industry is determined by the intersection of the market supply and demand curves, the size of any one firm is indeterminate. In Figure 7.14(a) the firm sets off from an arbitrarily given equilibrium, *a*. Surprisingly, perhaps, it is possible to say quite a bit about the nature of the demand curve as long as restrictions are placed upon the possible expansion of the firm. Assume initially that firms in the industry react to a fall in the going wage, not by moving from

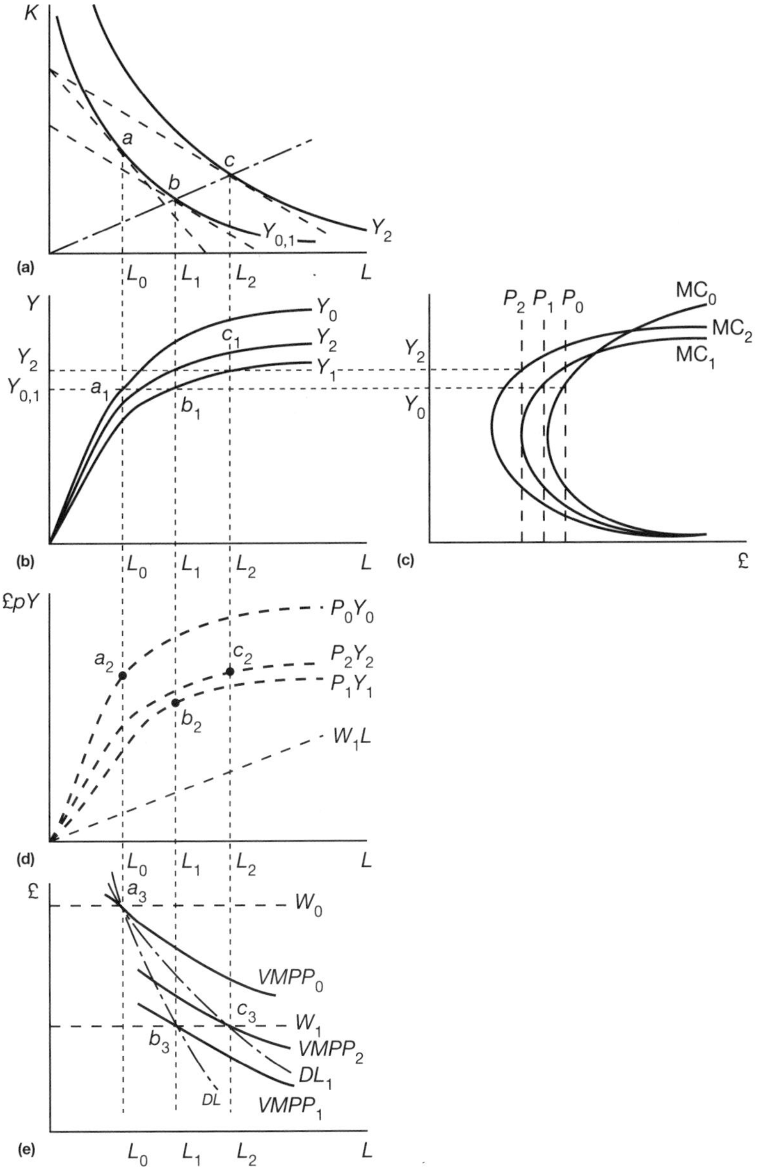

Fig 7.14 The demand curve for the constrained output maximizer.

a to b, but by attempting to maximize output subject to a budget constraint. When the wage-rate falls from w_0 to w_1, the firm moves from a to c.

For well-behaved production functions, the MPP_L is higher at point a than at b. In addition, if the production function is linearly homogeneous, the MPP_L is the same at point b as at point c. This is reflected in the slopes of the returns to labour functions in Figure 7.14(b): the slope at a_1 is greater than the slope at b_1; the slopes at b_1 and c_1 are the same. Ignoring the effect on product prices for a moment, the movement from a to b is a pure substitution effect of size $L_1 - L_0$, which by itself would result in a downward-sloping demand curve such as DL in Figure 7.14(e). In addition, however, there is an output expansion effect of size L_2–L_1 which must also be taken into account. Overall the substitution and output effects result in the demand curve DL_1 in Figure 7.14(e). Ignoring price changes for a moment, DL_1 is more elastic than DL because of the effects of the output expansion.

Clearly, however, at the same time there are price changes brought about by the lower wage, which has reduced average costs of production in the market. In the long run, this will result in a lower price of output through the effects of competition. The initial equilibrium price, $p_0 = LAC_0$ in Figure 7.14(c), is replaced by a new and lower product price, $p_1=LAC_1$ because the lower wage itself reduces costs and competition reduces prices, but, in addition, the output expansion effect further reduces this to P_2. These changes are again reflected in the position of the $VMPP_L$ curves, resulting in the shift from $VMPP_0$ to $VMPP_1$ and then $VMPP_2$. The final result is seen as a movement from a_2 (to b_2) to c_2 in Figure 7.14(d) and as a movement from a_3 (to b_3) to c_3 in Figure 7.14(e).

5 Elasticity of labour demand: Marshallian Rules

5.1 The industry demand curve under perfect competition

In the short run new firms cannot enter, and any increase in output must be supplied by firms already in the market. If all firms in the industry experience a reduction in the wage rate (i.e. because of an outward shift in the supply curve of labour), the result will be an outward shift of the upward-sloping part of each firm's MC curve, as shown in Figure 7.14(c) (which is the same as in Figure 7.12(c), i.e. the perfectly competitive firm's supply curve). This in turn results in an outward shift in the industry supply curve (i.e. sum of individual firm's MC curves). The going price of the product is set by the intersection of the industry demand (i.e. average revenue) curve and supply curve (i.e. $\Sigma_i MC$, where $i = 1, \ldots, n$ denote the firms in the industry). Assuming the industry demand schedule to be downward sloping, left to right in the p,Q space, the result will be a fall in the price of the product. There is very little to add about the difference between the short and long run in this particular instance. The industry's long-run demand curve is now the summation of all the individual firms' long-run demand curves. In the short run, each firm's demand curve for labour could be different from all other firms because of differences in technical efficiency. In the long run, however, if there is a unique scale of output (caused by first increasing followed by decreasing returns to scale) technical efficiency and costs are equalized under conditions of perfect competition. In the case of some unique scale of the firm (i.e. where the production function is characterized by first increasing then, at higher output levels, decreasing returns to scale) the industry demand is formed as the summation of the firms' demands where the amount of labour services demanded is identical for all firms. In the case of constant returns to scale everywhere the size of output and the size of labour demands of each firm are indeterminate. The size of the industry, however, is determined by the intersection of market supply and demand and the individual demands, equal or not, must sum to the total fixed by market forces.

In this section, attention focuses on the own-price elasticity of demand for a particular factor at the industry level. Labour is assumed to be one of two factor inputs (i.e. labour and capital) and labour services are assumed to be perfectly homogeneous. It is already clear from the previous sections that the elasticity of demand for labour is likely to depend on the elasticity of substitution between capital and labour and on the product's own price elasticity of demand. As we demonstrate below, these features underpin two of the Marshallian Rules determining the elasticity of labour demand at the industry level. The Marshallian Rules state that, within an industry, the (absolute) elasticity of demand for labour varies with: (1) the elasticity of substitution between the two inputs; (2) the own-price elasticity of demand for the output produced by the factor; (3) the share of labour in the cost of production; (4) the elasticity of supply of the other factor used in production.

5.2 Elasticity of substitution between inputs

Marshall's first law is that the demand for any particular factor is more elastic, the more readily substitutes for that input can be obtained (other things being equal). This is a clear consequence of the shape of the isoquant: the substitution effect caused by a given change in the wage rate, other things being equal, will be larger the less curved the isoquant. Figures 7.4 and 7.5 illustrate the effect of different elasticities on the demand for labour for an output-constrained cost minimizer. In each figure, the solid line shows the isoquant, while the two dashed lines indicate the alternative factor price ratios (i.e. the more steeply sloped in absolute terms has a higher labour to capital price than the more shallowly sloped). Figure 7.4 shows that, in the case of perfect complements, the relative prices have no impact on the choice of factor intensity. Figure 7.5 indicates that the same change in factor prices results in a shift from e to f (L_1 to L_2), while the change in Figure 7.7 is even more marked (from $L_1 = 0$ to L_2).

5.3 Own-price elasticity of demand for final output

The second law states that the demand for a particular factor is likely to be more elastic, the greater the own-price elasticity of demand for the output it produces. This proposition arose directly from the fact that the demand for labour is a derived demand and, therefore, the amount of labour depends directly in the volume of output demanded in the product market (other things being equal). The second law therefore relates to the output effect rather than the substitution effect. A fall in the wage rate lowers costs and prices and, thereby, causes an increase in the market demand for the product. The more elastic the product demand curve, the greater the increase in the overall level of activity, other things being equal. This was illustrated in Figure 7.13(c), where the precise slope of the labour demand curve was shown to depend on the rate at which the product price was forced down. If the demand for the product is totally inelastic then a fall in the wage only produces an increased demand for labour in the industry as a whole through the substitution effect, as there is a zero-output effect. The more elastic the demand for the product, other things being equal, the greater will be the additional output taken up by the market for any given reduction in product price. Under such circumstances, there is, overall, a larger output effect and hence a more substantial rise in the demand for labour. It is worth adding that the own-price elasticity of demand tends to be greater in the long run than the short run and, hence, so too is the elasticity of demand for labour.

5.4 Share of the factor in the cost of production

Marshall's third law (sometimes called the 'importance of being unimportant') is that the demand for a particular factor is likely to be more elastic the more important that factor figures in total production costs. The law might be widely accepted as it is very similar to the argument applied to the own-price elasticity of product demand (i.e. that the smaller the proportion of consumer income devoted to that product, the more inelastic the product demand). Even so, this is the only one of the four laws that appears to have required slight modification. By an oversight in the translation of his mathematics, Marshall failed to appreciate that the law was not unequivocally true. Hicks, using a more sophisticated formula that included a term for the elasticity of substitution, later proved that the validity of this proposition turns on the relative sizes of the price elasticity of demand for the product, ξ_p, and the elasticity of substitution between inputs, σ. The Marshallian proposition is correct whenever the elasticity of product demand is greater than the elasticity of substitution between inputs, $\xi_p > \sigma$, but the reverse is true whenever $\xi_p < \sigma$. In essence the sign reversal is driven by the relative ease with which individual can adjust the basket of goods which they consume (represented by ξ_p) *vis-à-vis* the case of substitution between inputs used by producers (represented by σ).

5.5 Price elasticity of supply of other inputs

Marshall's fourth law is that the demand for a particular input will be more elastic, the more elastic the supply of cooperating factors of production. If the two inputs are substitutes then a fall in the wage rate will produce a substitution towards labour in the production process and away from capital, other things being equal. Assume for a moment that the output expansion effect is negligible; then the substitution effect reduces the demand for capital. If the supply of capital to the industry is highly elastic, then the rental is approximately constant and the full substitution effect is observed. If, however, the supply of capital is inelastic, the same substitution effect results in a relatively large fall in the rental and the change in the slope of the isocost line is not as severe. The same argument applies where there is an output expansion effect. Any substitution away from capital caused by the fall in the wage rate is to a smaller or larger extent offset by the capital using effects of the output expansion. If the substitution away from capital tends to give rise to a relatively large fall in the rental, this will reinforce the pressure for an output expansion and the net effect will be a more elastic demand for labour.

6 Conclusions

In this chapter we have laid the foundations for the analysis of labour demand. In particular, we have derived the firm's demand curve for labour under perfect competition, in the short run and in the long run, as developed in marginal productivity theory. Subsequent chapters look at the demand for labour under alternative market structures, allow for the heterogeneity of labour, and consider the very long run and thereby the role of technological change.

References

Berndt, E.R. (1991). *The Practice of Econometrics: Classic and Contemporary*. Reading, MA: Addison-Wesley.

Heathfield, D. and S. Wibe (1987). *An Introduction to Cost and Production Functions*. London: Macmillan.

Johansen, L. (1972). *Production Functions: Short-Run and Long-Run, Micro and Macro*. Amsterdam: North-Holland.

Silberberg, E. (1978). *The Structure of Economics: a Mathematical Analysis*. New York: McGraw-Hill.

CHAPTER 8 Labour demand under different market structures

1 Introduction

Chapter 7 developed the basic theory of the demand for labour by the firm under perfect competition. The present chapter extends the analysis in a number of ways. While the assumption of a perfectly competitive product market is relaxed, the assumption of a perfectly competitive labour market is retained throughout. The earlier results based upon perfect competition remain important for a number of reasons, providing a benchmark for the efficient (static) operation of companies and markets, and forming a necessary condition for Pareto optimality. Even a casual look at the real world, however, suggests that perfect competition is relatively rare. While the majority of firms are small to medium sized, most markets tend to be dominated by a relatively small number of large firms, which often possess considerable market power. This has immediate implications for labour demand, even if such companies maintain the goal of profit maximization. Section 2, therefore, looks at the theory of labour demand by profit-maximising firms under non-competitive product market conditions, including non-discriminating and discriminating monopoly and oligopoly. It is fairly obvious that, if a firm has market power that enables it to earn abnormal profits, it is possible for it to adopt goals other than profit maximization. This issue is linked to the divorce between ownership and management, giving rise to principal–agent problems. In other words, the managers of the company may pursue their own ends, which may not be in the best interests of the shareholders. In order to illustrate the importance for labour demands, Section 3 provides some simple examples of labour demands for different types of organization and goals of the enterprise, including managerial goals and worker-managed firms. Finally, Section 4 provides the overall conclusions.

2 Profit maximization in non-competitive product markets

2.1 Introduction

This section investigates the demand for labour by private profit-maximizing companies which operate under less than perfect competition in the product market. From the range of possible product markets, this section investigates labour demands under conditions of pure monopoly and oligopoly. Even then, it is impossible to consider all of the possible variants for each product market structure. The student interested in investigating the nature and implications of alternative product market regimes is recommended to read one of the microeconomics or industrial economics textbooks that deal with this topic (see, for example, Tirole, 1990), although the reader should not be too surprised if such books fail to develop the implications of the goal of the firm for factor demands in any detail.

2.2 Non-discriminating monopoly

This section analyses a market where there is a single seller of the product. By outlining a theory of firm demand therefore, the discussion also analyses a theory of market demand. As a monopolist, the producer faces the product market demand curve and this is assumed to be a negative relationship between price and quantity. The present section deals with the non-discriminating monopolist, which is distinguished by the fact that the producer is forced to sell the whole of its output at the same price. The implication of this is that, as the firm expands its level of activity, it not only forces down the price at which it can sell its additional produce, but it also has to accept this lower price on all of the existing units of output that it sells. The discriminating monopolist, on the other hand, can charge different prices to different segments of the market. We turn to this special case in Section 2.2.3 below.

2.2.1 Short-run demand curve for labour

The first thing to note is that where there is some degree of monopoly power, this produces a distinction between the marginal revenue product of labour, MRP_L, and the value of the marginal physical product, $VMPP_L$. If we look back to equation (22) of Chapter 7, it is possible to see that the price of the monopolist's output depends upon the quantity produced. In other words, $\partial p/\partial Y.\partial Y/\partial L.\mathbf{f}(\ )$ is non-zero. In fact, it is negative, because, as the firm adds more workers and increases output, the firm can only sell this output by reducing the price of its product, $\partial p/\partial Y < 0$. The outcome is that the MRP_L curves are more inelastic than the $VMPP_L$ as the latter assume price to be fixed. Bearing this in mind, Figure 8.1 illustrates the derivation of the short-run demand curve for labour in the case of non-discriminating monopoly. The short-run expansion path is again along a line such as K_0K_0 in Figure 8.1(a) and this picks out a particular 'returns to labour' curve, Y, in Figure 8.1(b). The movement along K_0K_0 is caused by a falling wage and this results in a series of MC curves in Figure 8.1(c); lower wage rates result in lower MC curves. The demand curve faced by the firm is now represented by D in Figure 8.1(c) and shows price to fall as output rises. Firm equilibrium for the profit maximizer occurs where marginal revenue of the firm is equal to marginal cost, MR = MC, at the prevailing wage rate. As the wage rate falls, the MC curve as a whole shifts downwards and the upward-sloping part of the MC curve, in effect, moves outwards. This causes equilibrium output to rise and product price to fall. Hence, Figure 8.1(b) shows that the total revenue product curve approaches the total physical product as price falls (and would cut it at the output level at which the demand curve cuts the output axis, although, for obvious reasons, a monopolist would clearly never push output this high). Clearly, the normal monopoly incentives reduce the level of output substantially below what it would be in a perfectly competitive economy. At a wage w_0, only L_0 of labour services are demanded; at a wage w_1, L_1 of labour services are demanded. The non-discriminating monopolist demand for labour curve is represented by DN in Figure 8.1(d). The closest it is possible to get to a competitive demand curve is DD (by setting MC = AR at each wage in Figure 8.1(c). Clearly DN lies inside DD at every wage rate, and the gap between the two reflects the normal monopoly incentive which acts to reduce output (and, thereby, labour demand) in order to raise product price and profits.

2.2.2 Long-run demand for labour

The essential difference between monopoly and perfect competition in the long run is that monopoly precludes the entry of new firms and no forces exist that would push the price of the product to the minimum level of average total costs. Natural monopolies are generally associated with increasing returns to scale everywhere, or at least across all relevant outputs given the overall size of the market. Increasing returns form a natural barrier which tends to preclude the entry of small new competitors. Positive profits can be earned by the monopolist despite the increasing return because the firm is able to price output above marginal cost (and thereby above average variable costs). While it is generally not possible to assume the existence of decreasing returns to scale everywhere (as this results in a constant incentive for the market to move towards an infinite number of infinitely small firms), constant returns cause no real problems (unlike under perfect competition where the scale of any particular enterprise was indeterminate) as long as the monopolist has some other mechanism of maintaining barriers to entry, such as advertising, patents, etc. Thus, in summary, there is no reason why the monopolist should choose a plant of technically optimal scale; indeed, choosing a larger scale may be one mechanism the monopolist uses to deter new entry. The downward shift in LMC caused by the fall in wage is shown in Figure 8.2(c); this changes the long-run equilibrium from an output Y_0 to Y_1. To simplify the figures a little, the production function is assumed to use the same capital stock at c as at point a and, hence, c lies along the short-run expansion path K_0K_0 in Figure 8.2(a) and along the same total physical product of labour curve, TPP_0, as a in Figure 8.2(b). The fall in wage from w_0 to w_1 is shown in both Figures 8.2(a) and 8.2(b) to produce a change in equilibrium from a to b if output is main-

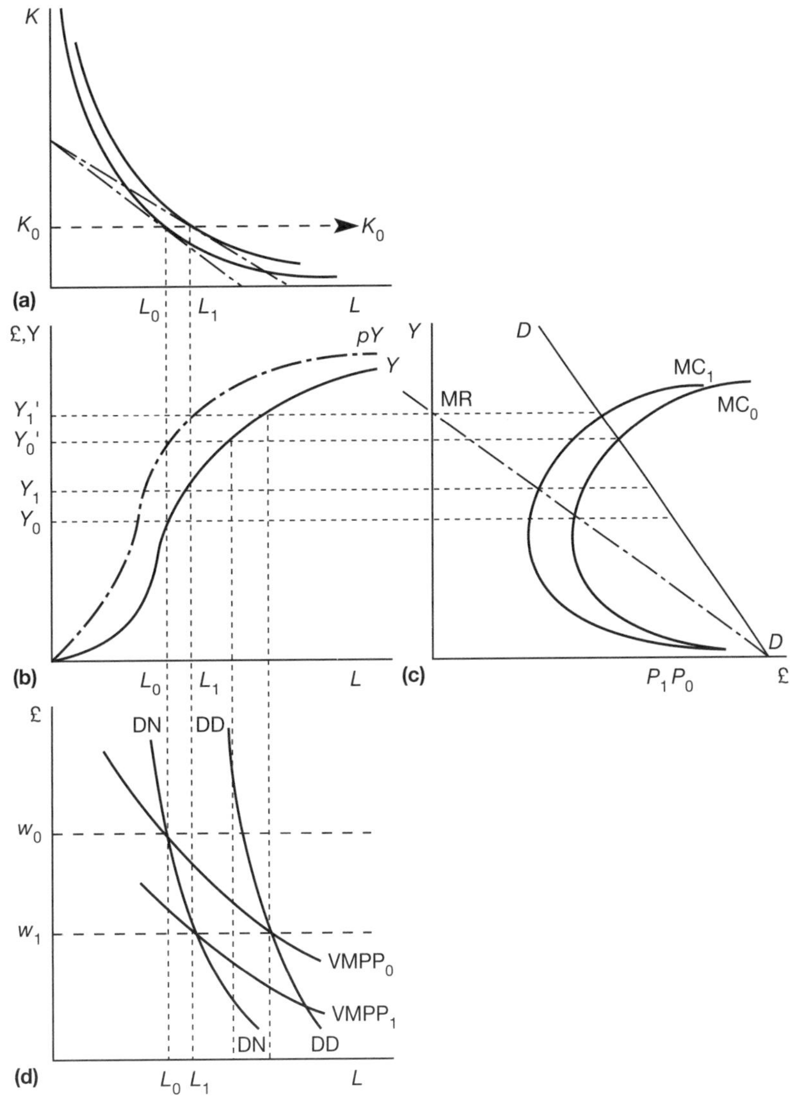

Fig 8.1 Short-run equilibrium of the monopolist.

tained at the level Y_0. The output expansion effect, however, moves the firm up to point *c*, which restores the firm to TPP_0 in Figure 8.2(b). Finally the movements from *a* to *b* and from *b* to *c* are translated into a demand for labour curve, DN in Figure 8.2(d).

2.2.3 Discriminating monopoly

If the monopolist is able to discriminate between buyers for every unit purchased, the firm is able to charge a variety of prices even though the output is homogeneous. In the case of first-degree price discrimination, the price obtained for each unit of output is the maximum amount of money the consumer is willing to pay for it. Under this form of discrimination, although the monopolist supplies to those willing to pay most and every additional unit sells at a lower price, the monopolist is not forced to reduce the price of existing units and therefore suffers no loss of revenue on existing sales. The firm's demand curve for its product is therefore also its marginal revenue curve. Figure 8.1 above shows that

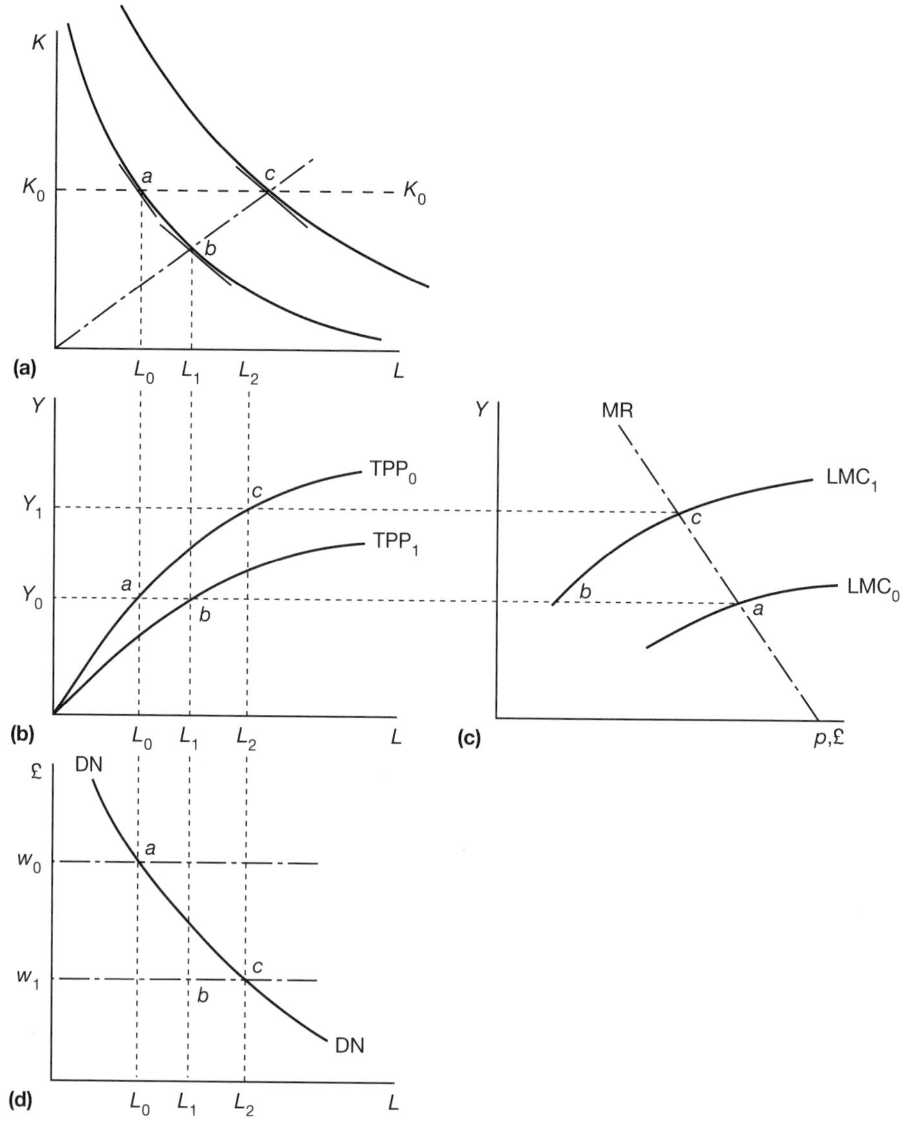

Fig 8.2 Long-run demand for labour under conditions of non-discriminating monopoly.

this implies directly that the discriminating monopolist, setting MC = AR, will expand its output further than the corresponding non-discriminating monopolist (i.e. to a level Y_0' when wages are w_0 and Y_1' when wages are w_1). The resulting labour demand curve, DD in Figure 8.1(d), is equivalent to the labour demand curve of the perfectly competitive industry and lies to the right of the equivalent non-discriminating demand curve DN at every wage. Note, however, that the implications for consumer welfare are quite different, with the monopolist capturing all of the potential consumer surplus.

2.2.4 Regulated industries

In a sense, most monopolies have, in one way or another, operated under some form of regulatory control. During the early post-war period, many of them were run as nationalized industries and, as such, their prices were controlled to levels that just enabled them to achieve a target rate of return. In terms of Figure 8.1, therefore, labour demand would generally have been closer to DD than DN. Indeed if the target rate of return is set lower than the level that competitive firms would demand, the demand curve might lie even further to the right. However, there are few incentives for nationalized industries to remain efficient. This has unpredictable results for labour demand, as increased costs can be in the form of expensive capital projects or greater labour inputs. In general, however, greater inefficiency implies higher per unit costs and prices and, thereby, lower demand and output. By the 1980s, there was both a realization of the inefficiencies coupled with the political will to change. The result was a programme of privatization in a number of countries, such as the UK and New Zealand, coupled with various measures to increase competition and/or some form of regulation. The form of regulation differs somewhat between countries.

Privatization, therefore, has reoriented the companies towards profit maximization. There is some evidence that there have been resulting improvements in labour productivity. After the initial shock of privatization, however, what happens to the demand for labour over time depends crucially on the form of regulation. In the UK, the privatized natural monopolies are jointly controlled, to varying degrees, by an appointed regulatory body (such as OFTEL, OFFER, OFWAT, etc.) and the Monopolies and Mergers Commission. Other sectors are only regulated by the MMC.

In the UK, there is a form of price regulation based upon variants of the RPI – x formula, originally proposed by the Littlechild Report. As its name suggests, the company is allowed to raise its prices along with the rate of inflation represented by the retail price index, RPI, minus an amount that reflects the scope for productivity improvements. Clearly, the choice of x is likely to have important implications for the time path of labour demand in the industry. This occurs for at least three reasons. First, in the period between price reviews, there is an incentive for the company to maximize profits for a period, subject to the impact of this on the regulator's view about future prices. Thus, there is likely to be a period when the natural monopoly incentives apply, shifting the labour demand curve inwards. However, costs will be allowed to rise prior to the review, in an attempt to convince the regulator that there is little scope for price reductions. This may have the effect of shifting the demand for labour curve outwards. Second, the regulator's choice of x is crucial via the effect it may have on labour productivity. Higher values of x are likely to result in a lower demand for labour over time. Third, in the longer term, RPI – x effectively collapses into some form of profit or, more likely, rate of return regulation, as the value is set to restrict the magnitude of abnormal profits. If, for example, the outcome is to set a regulated return above the cost of capital (although below the unregulated rate) there is an incentive for the firm to substitute towards capital and away from labour, as each additional unit of capital earns a super-normal profit. This results in the Averch–Johnson effect in which labour productivity grows, but there is overcapitalization and total factor productivity is lower.

3 Oligopoly

3.1 Theories of oligopolistic behaviour

Oligopoly is a market structure where rivalry and the interdependence of firms are all important (except perhaps in the extreme case of collusive oligopoly which takes the form of joint profit maximization, where the market situation is analogous to the multiplant monopolist). A full theoretical treatment of oligopoly would seem to require a game theoretic approach and, if so, the derivation of a simple labour demand function would seem unlikely. Nevertheless, it is possible to say a number of things about labour demand under oligopoly, in particular under the rather special case of the kinked product demand curve. While such a theory does not isolate a unique equilibrium position for the oligopolist it is a useful way of visualizing sticky price–output and wage–employment situations.

3.2 Kinked demand curve analysis

The early theories of oligopoly adopted the concept of a kinked product demand curve in order to show stickiness in firms' pricing and output decisions. Figure 8.3(c) shows that at the going market output Y_0 (isolated by MC = MR) the demand curve has a distinct kink: if the firm lowers its price, other things being equal, its rivals will be forced to lower their

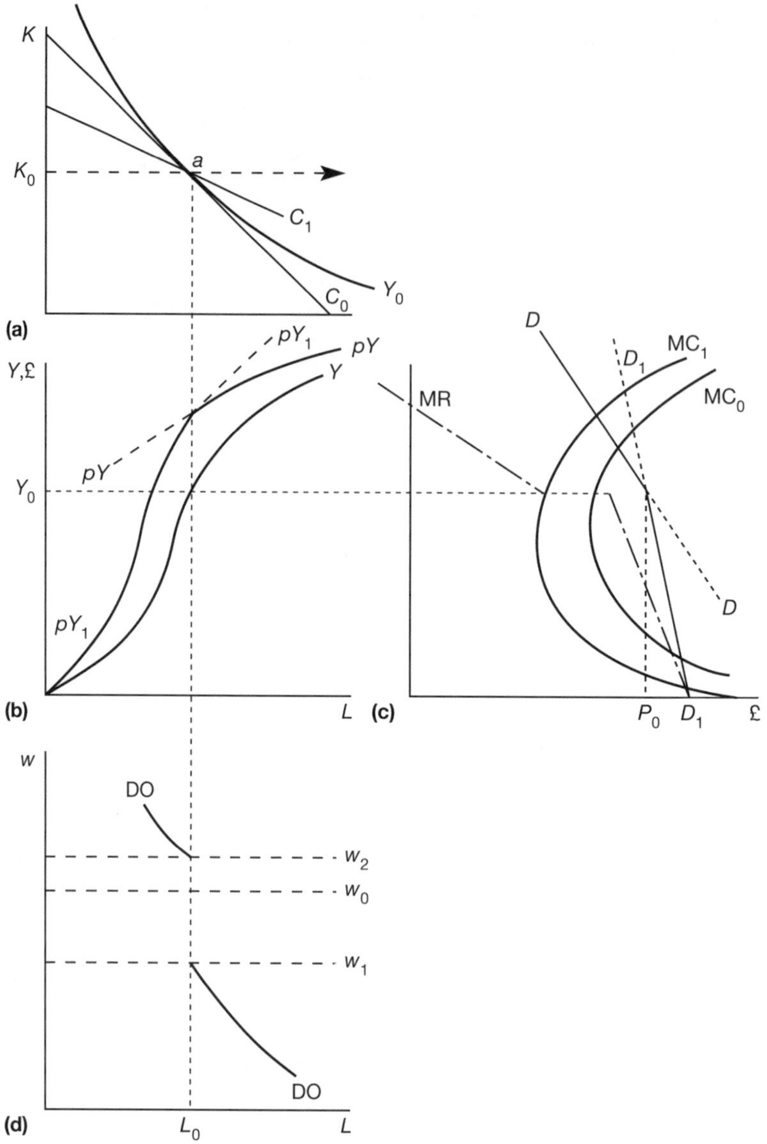

Fig 8.3 Oligopoly, simple interdependence and the demand curve for labour.

prices and the firm's product demand curve will be relatively inelastic; if, on the other hand, the firm raises its price, its competitors are under no compulsion to follow suit and the firm's demand curve will be relatively elastic. Under these circumstances, the firm faces a 'kinked' demand curve for its product at the current equilibrium price, p_0. However, a kinked demand curve for the product not only suggests stickiness in product prices and output, but also in wages and employment. The kink in Figure 8.3(c) occurs at the equilibrium output level Y_0 with an associated labour input L_0 shown in Figures 8.3(a), 8.3(b) and 8.3(d). As in the case of monopoly, the product price is not constant at different output levels; in general, higher output levels result in lower prices and the TRP_L curve in Figure 8.3(b) again cuts the TPP_L curve at the output level at which the product demand curve cuts the axis. As in the case of monopoly, this is of hypothetical interest only, as output would never be pushed that high. A more interesting feature is that the total revenue product of Figure 8.3(b), and the labour demand curve in Figure 8.3(d) are also discontinuous at a level L_0 and equilibrium occurs at the intersection of MRP_L and w_0 (again, more accurately, w_0 passes through the discontinuity in the MRP_L curve). After a fall in the wage rate from w_0 to w_1, the firm finds that its marginal cost of producing each scale of output has fallen from MC_0 to MC_1 in Figure 8.3(c). Nevertheless, the optimal scale of output has not changed and, for this particular change in the wage rate, there is no change in the firm's demand for labour. A slightly larger fall in the wage rate, however, would have forced the firm outwards to a higher output level along K_0 in Figure 8.3(a), down the sloping part of MR in Figure 8.3(c) and, similarly, down DO.

In practice, one of the weaknesses of the kinked demand curve theory is that, once the firm is forced outside the product market discontinuity (i.e. by a change which takes w above w_2 or below w_1), it is not clear, from the confines of the model, what new equilibrium will emerge, because, as it adjusts its output, so will its rivals; the outcome is uncertain. Neither does the model explain how the original equilibrium came about in the first place. It seems that the theory must turn to a game theoretic approach to determine the equilibrium. Nevertheless, the model illustrates that, at least in the short run, the oligopolist demand for labour may be 'sticky' in the face of even quite large changes in the wage rate.

It is fairly easy to show that the kink in the labour demand curve disappears in the long run, even if the oligopolist still feels bound by the same output and price. Figure 8.4 uses the same kinked product demand curve and equilibrium occurs, in this instance, where LMC_0 cuts the discontinuous marginal revenue curve, MR. Figure 8.4(a) shows that the firm is now able to adjust its capital stock from K_0 to K_1, moving from point a to point b around the isoquant Y_0, in response to the change in wage from w_0 to w_1. Because of this, the reduction in the costs of the firm will be more substantial in the long run than in the short run (i.e. in the short run the firm was restricted to a sub-optimal combination of capital and labour in the face of the revised factor price ratio). The analysis continues to assume that the associated downward shift in the long-run marginal cost curve from LMC_0 to LMC_1 in Figure 8.4(c) still produces an intersection in the discontinuous region of MR. Hence, the firm still chooses to produce Y_0 of output. The firm has, however, moved from a to b, onto a lower TPP_L curve in Figure 8.4(b) because it has moved to an expansion path with a smaller stock of capital in Figure 8.4(a). The total revenue product curve shifts in a similar way (not shown) because output and price are unchanged. Figure 8.4(d) shows that, in effect, the discontinuous demand for labour curve has shifted to the right from DO_0 to DO_1. The new wage w_1 now (just) intersects a discontinuous part of the DO_1 curve, associated with a higher level of labour demand of L_1. The effective demand for labour curve is now the continuous function DO^*.

3.3 Models of inter-dependent oligopoly

It is clear from the previous section that a full treatment of labour demand under oligopoly requires some form of game theoretic approach which determines the time path of output, prices and labour demand, as well as the long-run equilibrium output (if one exists). There are several related models of oligopoly that purport to explain the equilibrium of the firm on the basis of a specified market demand curve for the product and a given set of behavioural rules that lay down how one firm reacts to the behaviour of its competitors. The Cournot model, for example, assumes that each firm behaves as if its competitors are going to maintain their output at a constant level; in the corresponding Bertrand model, each firm assumes that its competitors maintain their prices at a constant level. By implication, each firm has a set of output levels (in the Cournot model) or price levels (in the Bertrand model) which maximize its profits given its competitors' chosen output or price levels respectively. This set of optimal points lie along each firm's reaction curve. For certain relative slopes of the reaction curves, their intersection can be shown to be a stable equilibrium. The simple, traditional Cournot duopoly game is illustrated in Figure 8.5 – a detailed exposition can be obtained from most industrial economics textbooks (and more advanced models are available; see, for example, Fudenberg and Tirole, 1986; Thépot and Thiétart, 1991).

The π_1 and π_2 curves are isoprofit lines for firm 1 and 2 respectively. For any level of its competitors output, the firm in question will always attempt to reach the highest profit. This occurs by picking the isoprofit line closest to the horizontal axis for firm 1 and the vertical axis for firm 2. Because of the shape

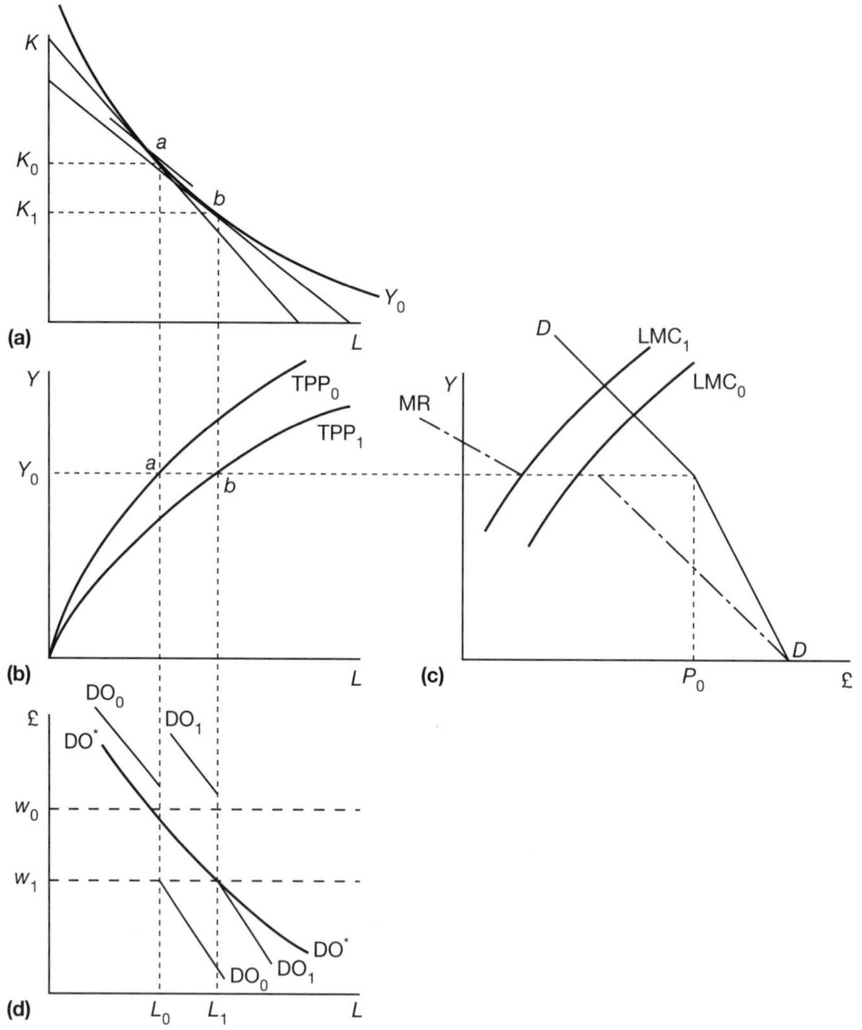

Fig 8.4 Long-run demand for labour under conditions of oligopoly.

of the isoprofit lines, it always involves being on the 'highest' point of the U-shaped curve. Thus, if firm 2 chooses $Y_2 = 0$, firm 1 chooses point a on π_1^0; if firm 2 chooses Y_2^*, firm 1 chooses point b on π_1^*. The lower the competitor's output, the higher the profit for the other firm. Thus, firm 1 can earn π_1^0 if $Y_2 = 0$ (i.e. firm 1 is a monopolist) and, likewise, firm 2 can earn π_2^0 if $Y_1 = 0$. By implication, $\pi_1^* < \pi_1^0$ and $\pi_2^* < \pi_2^0$. Joining the peaks of the π_1 gives firm 1's reaction curve, R_1^0 – the set of outputs the firm will choose depending on the output of firm 2; similarly, joining the peaks of π_2 gives R_2^0 – the set of outputs firm 2 will choose given the output of firm 1. The only output combination that satisfies both firms occurs at point b, where R_1^0 intersects with R_2^0. Thus, under rivalry, the equilibrium output levels are Y_1^* and Y_2^*. This information, along with relative factor prices, will determine the firms' demands for labour in equilibrium. Note, however, the optimal would be better for one or both of the companies if they colluded. They could now move to a point such as c, where π_1^{**} is tangential to π_2^{**} ($\pi_1^{**} > \pi_1^*$ and $\pi_2^{**} > \pi_2^*$). The implication is that labour demand would be higher under rivalry than collusion. The natural monopoly incentives again act to shift the labour demand curve for one or both firms downwards.

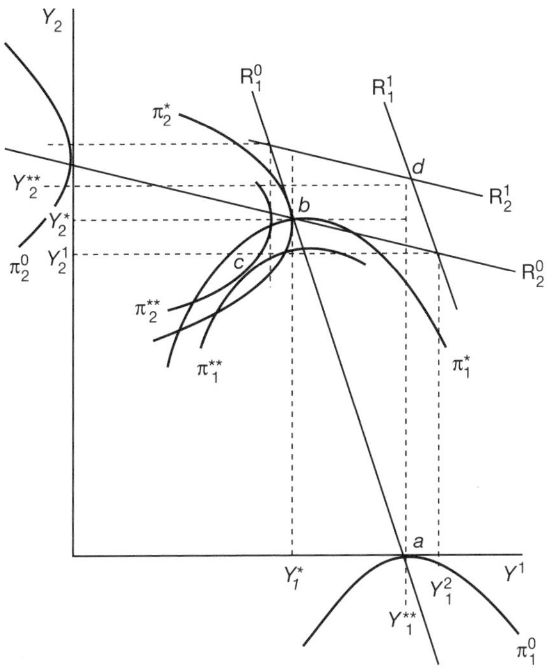

Fig 8.5 Traditional Cournot equilibrium under conditions of falling wage.

We can now illustrate the implications of a reduction in the wage for labour demands. First, a fall in the wage has the normal substitution effects, leading to a higher demand for labour (and lower capital). The magnitude of this effect, as always, turns on the value of the elasticity of substitution. Second, the wage reduction has an impact on output. In effect, if firm 2 produces Y_2^*, a given profit level, such as π_1^* can now be achieved at a higher output level by firm 1; in other words, firm 1's reaction curve shifts from R_1^0 to R_1^1. Likewise, a fall in firm 2's wage results in a shift from R_2^0 to R_2^1. If only firm 1 experiences the reduction, its output grows to Y_1^2, while firm 2's shrinks to Y_2^1. Thus, other things being equal, firm 1 will increase and firm 2 will reduce its demand for labour. The net effect depends upon the relative slopes of the reaction curves, as well as the underlying substitution effect, although intuitively we expect overall labour demand to rise. However, if we maintain the assumption of competitive labour markets, both firms experience the reduction in wage. The new equilibrium occurs at point *d* where R_1^1 intersects R_2^1. Output is now higher for both firms and, given the substitution effect works in the same direction, labour demand will rise.

While the model has not been developed to the full, it is possible to say a number of things about the demand for labour curve. First, a fall in the wage can be expected to result in the normal kinds of substitution effects, towards labour and away from capital. Second, it is possible to demonstrate that (for normal revenue and cost curves) the reaction curves in the Cournot model shift to the north east, and the reaction curves in the Bertrand model shift to the south west, implying a higher level of output and labour demand for each firm experiencing the wage reduction. The substitution and output effects for the independent oligopolist are therefore acting on the demand for labour in the expected direction. Finally, other things being equal, the demand for labour curve where the firms cooperate to ensure a position of profit maximization will generally be lower at every wage rate than in the case of the independent oligopolist.

4 Types of organization, goals of the enterprise and labour demands

4.1 Introduction

If companies are small in size compared with the market, privately owned, owner managed (or closely controlled by their shareholders) and possess no market power, then they will be constrained to follow a common profit-maximizing goal. While it seems uncertain whether this was ever a close description of companies, even in the 'Golden Age of Competition', it is certainly not an adequate representation of the position observed in many sectors of modern industry and commerce. Large, professionally managed companies remain extremely important in the UK, despite the recent growth in self-employment and decline in the size of manufacturing units. Some of the large multinational companies have output in excess of some of the smaller industrialized countries.

Large firms with monopoly power have the potential to earn abnormal profits. Where there is a divorce between ownership and control, not all of these potential profits are likely to find their way back to shareholders as managers appropriate some part of them to finance goals of their own. The principal–agent problem in this context is essentially how to ensure that management (the agent) acts in the best interests of the owner (the principal). In general, owners are interested in the profits earned by the company, which determine the discounted sum of dividends and the share price. Managers, on the other hand, have goals of their own linked to their career development and life style. Thus, where managers exercise discretion over the firm's funds, the outcome (both in terms of the level of employment and the structure of the workforce) may differ from the case of profit maximization. The issue of Corporate Governance therefore, amongst other things, involves the design of managerial contracts and reward structures which bring management objectives more closely in line with shareholders. These types of employment contracts are touched upon in Part VI of the book. However, we should not forget that principal–agent problems arise in a whole range of other situations than commercial companies, such as government departments, the health service, etc. As the theories of the firm relaxed the assumption of profit maximization, two schools of thought emerged: managerial and behavioural theories. The managerial models assume that managers attempt to optimize some stated goal (i.e. maximize sales revenue, growth, etc.) which is more in line with their own aspirations. The behavioural theories, on the other hand, reject the idea of optimization and the firm is viewed as an amalgam of diverse groups with differing goals. According to the behavioural theories, managerial teams are not maximizers, but satisfiers.

Despite these reservations, economic theories of the firm based on the assumption of profit maximization remain of immense importance. There are still many small, owner-managed businesses in particular sectors that correspond closely to the sort of firm described by profit maximization theory. In addition, this particular goal may provide the basis of normative theories of the firm, a benchmark of behaviour by which to compare actual levels of technical and allocative efficiency. In addition, as we shall see below, profit maximization becomes a special case of a wide range of managerial goals and behaviour, forced upon managers when market conditions are too tight to allow other forms of behaviour to emerge. Finally, the increased degree of international competition appears to have reorientated the goals of many large companies back towards profit maximization. While the remainder of this section deals mainly with the employment implications of the professionally managed firms (comparing the outcomes with those of profit maximizers), we also recognize a further strand of the theory. A number of small firms and, indeed, historically at least, one or two larger firms have been run as cooperatives. Such forms of enterprise are more common outside the UK, particularly in Spain, Italy and the previous Communist Bloc countries. The cooperative nature of the enterprise introduces new goals with potentially quite different implications for labour demand.

4.2 Managerial theories of the firm

4.2.1 Alternative managerial goals

The economics literature has thrown up a wide range of alternatives to profit maximization. In this section, two of the earliest managerial theories are reported just to illustrate their implications for labour demand. The first of these is the sales revenue maximization theory (see Baumol, 1967). The second model is a theory of managerial utility maximization reported by Williamson (1964). Further discussion of other managerial theories, including more recent developments, can be found in most industrial economics textbooks. Note again, however, that most of the original theories pay little attention to labour demands.

4.2.2 Sales revenue maximization

There are a number of reasons why the manager, after ensuring that the firm achieves some minimum profit level that satisfies the shareholders, might attempt to maximize sales revenue rather than profits. First, it has been suggested that the salaries of managers may be linked more closely to sales rather than to profits. Second, the maximization of sales may ensure the highest possible market share, which is often used as an index of the firm's performance and market power. Third, while it may be possible to justify a reduction in sales on profit grounds in the short run, it is often interpreted as a sign of growing unpopularity of the product with adverse longer-term consequences. Fourth, larger firms may find fund raising from external sources easier than small firms. Fifth, the long-run profitability of the firm is difficult to quantify and sales may be the best available indicator of performance.

Figure 8.6 shows the derivation of the labour demand curve of an output maximizer using the four quadrant set of diagrams developed above. Figure 8.6(b) shows the total revenue curve of the firm, pY, and the total costs of the firm, comprised of variable costs, w_0L, capital costs, r_0K_0, and a minimum acceptable profit, π_0. Note that prices fall along the demand curve as the firm moves from lower to higher outputs;

$p = \mathbf{p}(Y)$, and the total revenue curve approaches the total physical product curve at higher output levels. The following discussion treats output and revenue maximization as synonymous. In practice, this is only the case for regions of the product demand curve where a 1 per cent increase in output produces less than 1 per cent decrease in the product price. Thus, the output and revenue-maximizing results are only the same for equilibrium solutions which occur to the left of the point at which the total revenue curve, pY, in Figure 8.6(b) reaches a maximum.

Figure 8.6(c) shows the firm's average cost curve, AC_0, inclusive of a minimum profit, π_0. The firm's average revenue curve is its demand curve, D. A profit maximizer would choose the level of output Y_π^*, where MR=MC (see Figure 8.6(c)) and where the vertical distance between revenue and total cost is greatest (see Figure 8.6(b)). The revenue maximizer, on the other hand, increases output until Y_R^* is reached. At this level of output, the firm's revenues are just sufficient to cover its costs inclusive of the minimum profit; this occurs at $AC_0 = D$ in

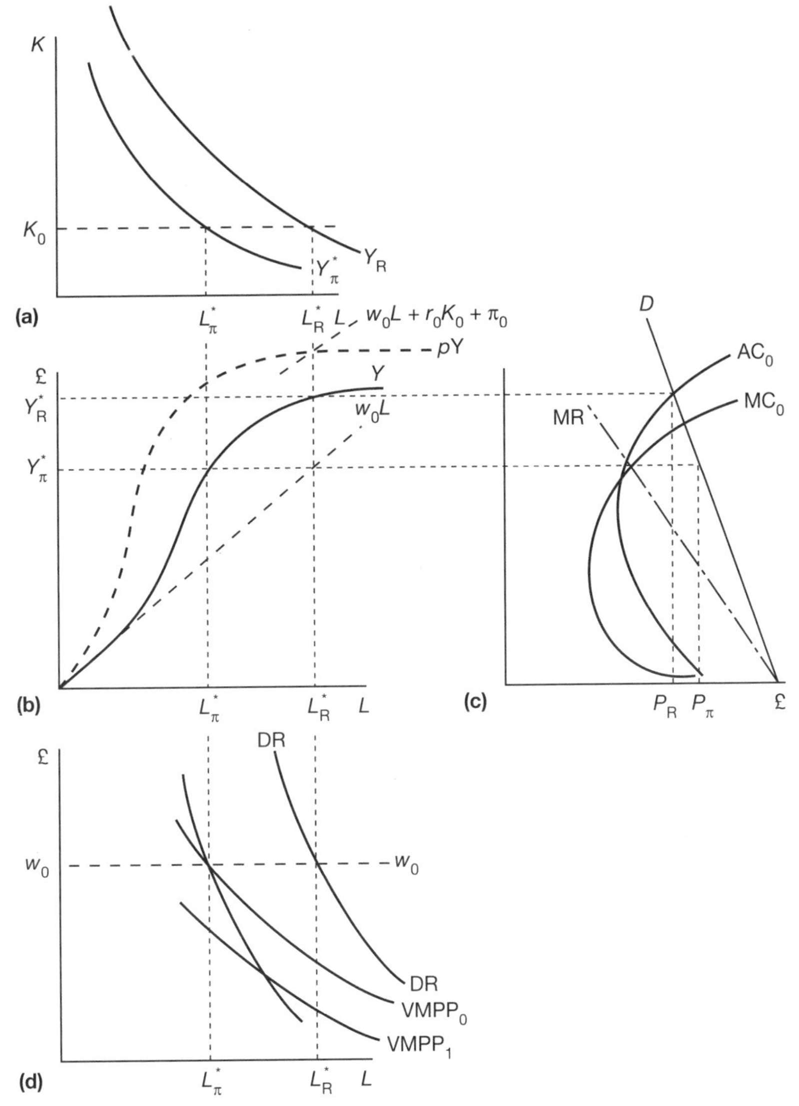

Fig 8.6 Sales revenue maximization and short-run employment.

Figure 8.6(c) and $w_0L + rK_0 + \pi_0 = pY$ in Figure 8.6(b). The need to meet the minimum profit requirement constrains the revenue maximizer to Y_R^* (any further increase in output above Y_R^* breaks the profit constraint, π_0).

As the model applies to the large, professionally managed corporation which possesses some degree of monopoly power, Figure 8.6(c) shows a downward-sloping demand curve, D, for the firm's product. For simplicity, however, the firm is assumed to face a perfectly elastic supply of labour at the competitive wage, w_0, in Figure 8.6(d). The profit maximizer sets MC = MR at output Y_π^*, and the equilibrium level of employment is at a level L_π^*, corresponding to the point of intersection between w_0 and $VMPP_1$ in Figure 8.6(d). The revenue maximizer, on the other hand, continues to expand output up to the point where $p = AC_0$ resulting in a higher level of output, Y_R^*, and lower price, p_R, associated with a lower value of the marginal physical product curve, $VMPP_1$, in Figure 8.6(d). The short-run equilibrium labour demand for the revenue maximization, however, is not a point of intersection between w_0 and $VMPP_L$. In this case, employment is expanded to a level where $VMPP_L < w_0$ (although, more generally, $VMPP_L \leq w_0$). In other words, the revenue maximizer uses 'potential' operating profits to fund additional workers over and above the profit-maximizing level. The exact position of the revenue maximizer's demand for labour curve, DR, is fixed by the intersection of the average cost (inclusive of profit constraint) and product demand curve. Tracing this point of intersection around from Figure 8.6(c) to 8.6(d) indicates that, at wage w_0, the sales revenue maximizer demands L_R^* of labour. At every possible wage, the revenue maximizer's labour demand curve lies to the right of the profit maximizer's except where market conditions or shareholder pressure raise π_0 to the profit-maximizing level.

Advertising activity forms an important feature of the sales-revenue-maximizing model. This is only natural insofar as advertising is an important instrument that the firm uses to manipulate its level of demand at any given price. It is now possible to imagine the firm to be faced by a whole series of revenue curves (R_0, R_1, R_2, ...), each of the type used in Figure 8.6(b) above, each formed as the result of successively higher levels of advertising, denoted by A_0, A_1, A_2, ..., respectively. These constant increments of advertising are added onto the production costs of the firm (the latter are assumed to depend only on the level of output and not on the level of advertising). It is assumed that equal additions to advertising expenditure yield successively smaller and smaller additions to revenue (i.e. shifts in the revenue function) at any given level output. In other words, there are diminishing returns to advertising. It is clear that the profit maximizer will choose an advertising expenditure associated with the maximum vertical distance between any pair of corresponding revenue and cost curves (where the revenue curve reflects the impact of the advertising and the associated cost curve includes the expenditure on advertising). The revenue maximizer, on the other hand, continues to expand advertising beyond the profit-maximizing level as each additional unit of advertising continues to shift the revenue curve upwards. The revenue maximizer therefore carries on expanding its advertising until it reaches the highest possible level of revenue on any of the revenue curves R_0, R_1, R_2, ... (although, in practice, this is not generally a point on the highest revenue curve). Given diminishing returns to advertising everywhere, the equilibrium will always be a constrained revenue-maximizing position. By implication, the revenue maximizer is likely to employ more workers in non-production activities such as market promotion, although it should be borne in mind that many firms sub-contract a significant proportion of their market promotion activities.

The labour demand implications can be traced from the optimal levels of output and advertising in the revenue-maximizing model. In practice, both activities are likely to be higher than under profit maximization and, if the technologies of each activity are identical for the profit and revenue maximizer, then the model predicts that a greater number of both production and non-production workers will be demanded by the revenue maximizer. Thus, the demand curve for non-production workers of the revenue maximizer will lie at least at the same level and generally at a higher level than the corresponding demand curve for the profit maximizer, other things being equal. However, it is also possible to imagine conditions under which π_0 is forced higher, for example by increasingly active shareholders. In the extreme $\pi_0 = \pi_{max}$, and it can be seen that profit maximization occurs as a special case.

4.2.3 Managerial utility maximization

Williamson (1964) argued that managers follow their own best interests and attempt to maximize their own utility, which is only partly related to the reported profits of the firm. In the simplest form of utility-maximizing model, managerial utility may be assumed to be a function of reported profits, π^r, the expenditure on staff directly under the manager's control, S, and the level of perks, M. A variety of reasons can be put forward to justify these variables: S, for example, may reflect the power or prestige of the manager; π^r might be included because it reflects on the competence of the manager; M is an indication of non-pecuniary income. Each of the arguments of the function is assumed to give rise to diminishing marginal utility, leading to diminishing marginal rates of substitution between any pair of benefits and resulting in indifference curves that are convex to the origin.

In order to focus on the employment consequences of the model, it is initially assumed that perks are zero. Staff in the model are assumed to be non-production workers and, as in the sales revenue maximization model, such employees can affect both the level of output and the price at which the product sells. As the manager's utility is assumed to arise out of activities financed from operating profits (ie. revenues minus operating costs), the manager ensures that the firm behaves efficiently in production. This assumption is somewhat suspect in real life, as the manager may associate disutility with ensuring maximum productive efficiency and may therefore be willing to trade off some operating profits for an 'easier life'.

Figure 8.7 shows that, for each level of staff expenditure, there is a corresponding maximum reported profit curve that the firm can achieve represented by the π^{r*} curve. The manager's indifference curves are represented by u_0^u, u_1^u, ..., showing a trade-off between reported profit and staff. The equilibrium position of the utility maximizer (where perks are constrained at zero) is at the point of tangency between the profit curve π^{r*} and the indifference curve u^{u*}. Higher levels of utility, such as u_1^u, are not feasible and lower levels, such as u_0^u, are not optimal. The utility maximizer chooses a level of staff S^{u*}, which is associated with a point where the marginal utility of the last £1 of reported profit given up is identical to the marginal utility of the additional staff on which this £1 is spent. The profit-maximizing owner–manager, on the other hand, only obtains utility from reported profit and not from staff *per se*. Their indifference curves are therefore horizontal, represented by u_0^π, u_1^π, u_2^π ... , in Figure 8.7. The point of maximum utility for the owner–manager is at $S^{\pi*}$, where $u^{\pi*}$ is tangential to π^{r*}. It is clear from the figure that the utility maxi-

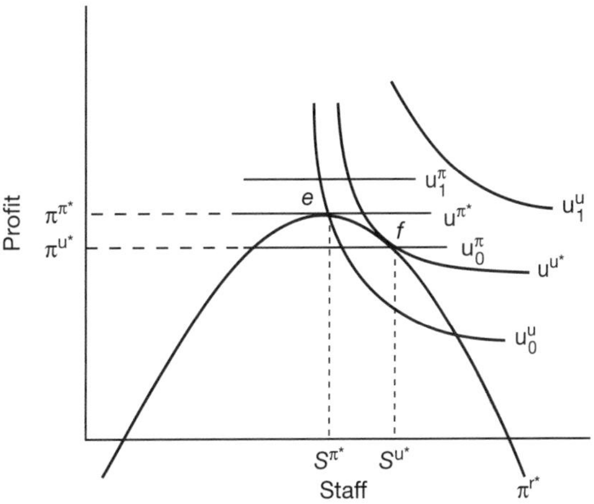

Fig 8.7 Staff model.

mizer will in general employ a greater number of staff than that of the profit maximizer. As the firm is assumed to behave efficiently in production activities in both models, then the ratio of non-production to production staff will also be higher for the utility than the profit maximizer.

Figure 8.7 also makes it clear that the utility-maximizing professional manager will report lower profits than the profit-maximizing owner–manager, other things being equal. By implication, if the professional manager is forced to maximize profits at point e, they would experience a level of utility $u_0^u < u^{u*}$. Likewise, as the owner–manager experiences no utility from employing any staff over and above that necessary to maximize profits, they would be on utility level u_0^π if they were 'forced' to employ $S^{u*} > S^{\pi*}$.

The full model also allows the professional manager to obtain utility from perks. The utility-maximizing manager may be able to raise their overall level of utility by giving up some profits and/or some staff and receive a higher level of perks. Each £1 spent on perks is £1 less that can be declared as reported profits or £1 less available to be spent on staff, but the marginal utility of perks starts off from a high level when perks are small. Hence, utility maximizers generally trade off some staff and reported profit for higher non-pecuniary income. The owner–manager, on the other hand, is assumed to obtain no benefit from perks or additional staff and the utility maximizer still chooses a solution with more staff (and perks) than the corresponding profit maximizer.

4.2.4 Worker-managed firms and labour demands

The behaviour of the worker-managed firm was investigated in the late 1950s and early 1960s, particularly as a consequence of the (then) Yugoslavian experiments with market socialism. Interest revived in the UK in the 1970s, following the establishment of a number of worker cooperatives, whose goals were recognized to be different to the traditional owner-managed capitalist firm and probably more akin to the Yugoslavian firms. Interest was stimulated again with the evolution of a number of examples of localities where small, cooperative firms have emerged and apparently thrived, such as the Emilia Romana region of Italy, and by the increased importance of self-employment and small and medium-sized enterprises (SMEs) in, for example, the UK.

Following the early work in this area (Ward, 1958; Domar, 1966), initially it is assumed that the worker–managers adopt the short-run goal of maximizing income per employee. Product prices are set by the market (they are assumed constant at the firm level) and the interest on capital is set by the state. The workforce is homogeneous and the wage per employee, W, is formed as two parts, the wage payment w set by the state and some share of profits, π/L,

$$W = w + \frac{\pi}{L} \tag{1}$$

Thus, in the case where the firm has one variable input (labour) and one fixed input (capital), the production function can be represented by

$$Y = \mathbf{f}(L) \tag{2}$$

The worker-managers are assumed to attempt to find the level of output and employment that maximizes their own wage income,

$$S = \frac{pY}{L} - \mathrm{w} - \frac{i}{L} \tag{3}$$

where i is the interest charged.

It is possible to represent the solution using Figure 8.8. Equilibrium occurs at the maximum vertical distance between the average revenue per worker curve R, and the average cost per worker curve C. In other words, at the labour input L^{w*} where the slope of R is equal to the slope of C. This can be obtained from equation (3) by differentiating with respect to L and setting the resulting expression equal to zero:

$$\frac{dS}{dL} = \frac{p(L\,dY/dL - Y) + i}{L^2} = 0 \tag{4}$$

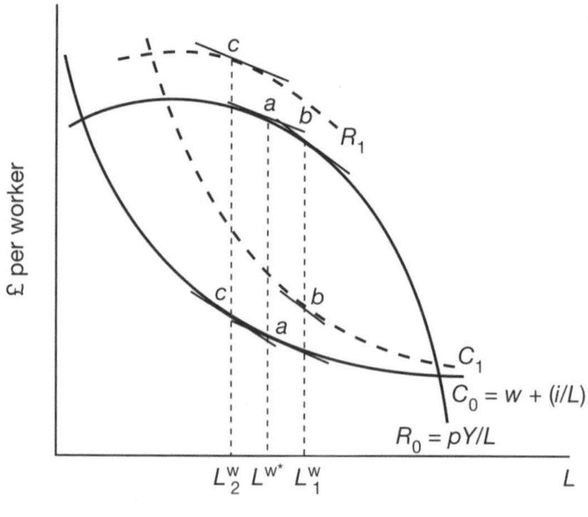

Fig 8.8 Equilibrium of the worker-managed firm.

that is,

$$\frac{Y}{L} - \frac{dY}{dL} = \frac{i}{pL} \tag{5}$$

Using Figure 8.8 and equation (5) it is possible to analyse what happens to the equilibrium solution as the state changes the rate of interest or as the price per unit of the product alters. It is possible to show that output and labour input change in the same direction as i (i.e. as i is increased, so too is Y and L in the firm). This is shown intuitively by the move from equilibrium L^{w*}, with the maximum vertical distance *aa* between the revenue per worker, R_0, and average cost per worker, C_0, curves, to the new equilibrium L_1^w, and maximum vertical distance *bb* between R_0 and C_1. In terms of equation (5), a higher i must be met by an increase in L, pushing down dY/dL faster than Y/L and increasing the gap ($Y/L - dY/dL$). It is also possible to show that output and labour input change in the opposite direction to product price in this one variable factor world (i.e. as p is increased, Y and L both fall). Again, this can be intuitively seen from Figure 8.8, where an increase in price raises the slope of R at every level of L (on the downward-sloping part of the curve). This causes a movement from L^{w*} to L_2^w, to a new maximum gap of *cc* between the revenue, R_1 and cost curve C_0. Using equation (5), it is clear that an increase in p lowers the gap between average and marginal products of labour and this occurs by decreasing the labour input, increasing dY/dL faster than Y/L. Thus, in a one-variable factor input world, the supply curve of the product is backward bending, which can, under certain circumstances, be associated with an unstable market equilibrium. The danger of instability is less in a world where there is more than one variable input, when the likelihood of instability depends on the importance of labour in the total costs.

Equation (5) can be rewritten as

$$\frac{pY-i}{L} = p\frac{dY}{dL} \tag{6}$$

which states that the average (net) revenue product of labour (ARP_L) is equal to the value of the marginal physical product. More generally, under conditions where the firm can affect the price of the product, it can be shown that the ARP_L is equal to the marginal revenue product of labour, MRP_L,

$$\left(p + \frac{\partial p}{\partial}Y\right)\frac{dY}{dL} = \frac{pY-i}{L} \tag{7}$$

Thus, it is possible to show that the outcome from the income-maximizing worker–management model is a special case of Fellner's union–management model (Law, 1976) below. Figure 8.9 shows the ARP_L and MRP_L, curves. Fellner suggests that unions will have some map of wage–employment trade-offs, where each curve represents combinations that are considered equally preferable (represented by a series of indifference curves u_0^u, u_1^u, ..., where each curve shows a given level of satisfaction and, because of its shape, corresponds with a constant total wage bill).

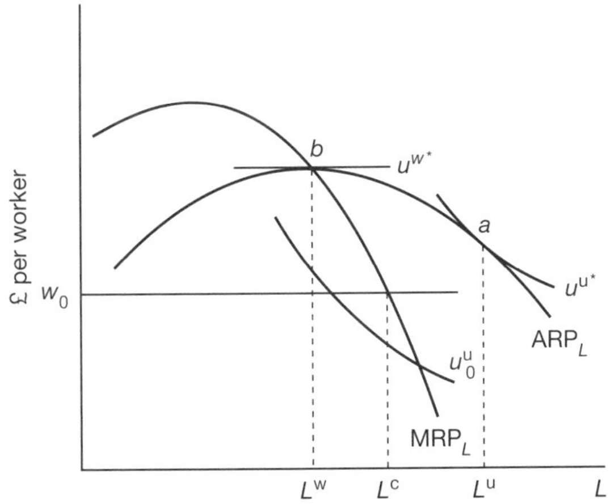

Fig 8.9 Comparison of the worker- and the union-managed firm.

Fellner suggests that there will be some minimum acceptable wage–employment trade-off, u_0^u, and some maximum that the union can obtain without bankrupting the firm, u^{u*}, (tangential to ARP_L). Point *a* can be considered to correspond to an outcome that would be most preferable in a worker-managed/union-managed firm, where wage and employment are the arguments of the 'utility' function. This compares with the outcome *b* in the income-maximizing worker-managed firm, where the indifference curves are horizontal (shown as u_0^w, u_1^w, ... with the optimal shown by u^{w*}) because employment is not an argument in the utility function.

It is somewhat difficult to conceive of a demand curve for labour in a worker-managed firm. Certainly, for most values of *w* (the arbitrarily set wage payment per worker before profit sharing) the demand for labour is unaffected. Only when *w* is set at a level (i.e. because of minimum wage legislation) that there is no profit surplus left to divide between workers (i.e. associated with the maximum ARP) will it have a direct impact on the demand for labour. In such a case, if *w* exceeds the ARP_L the firm will close down. If, on the other hand, *W* is assumed to be the effective wage, then manipulation of *W* in the worker-managed firm will move the firm around the ARP_L curve. This is something of an artificial demand curve, however, as the income-per-head maximizing firm would only choose a single point in the curve. Only if the management develops a social conscience about unemployment and thereby acts by changing *W* to alter the employment level (along the lines of Fellner's model) will a demand curve be observed.

If 'equivalent' capitalist and worker-managed firms are now compared, the demand for labour curves would generally be very different. However, it is very difficult to compare like with like. Perhaps the most satisfactory assumption is that the competitive wage, w_0, in the capitalist industry is the same as the minimum wage in the equivalent worker-managed firms. Thus, referring to Figure 8.9, the employment under the capitalist system would be L^c, compared with L^w under the income-per-head-maximizing regime. This is simply because, in effect, labour is cheaper under the capitalist regime as it has no profit-sharing scheme. On average, under the adopted goals, firms will be of a smaller size with lower employment in the income-maximizing worker-managed system. Clearly, however, if the worker–managers allowed the level of employment also to enter as an argument in their utility function, then employment might be lower than, equal to or higher than in the capitalist system.

4.2.5 Behavioural theories of the firm

Behavioural theories of the firm reject the idea of optimization (much of the literature stems from the seminal work of Cyert and March, 1963). The firm is viewed as an amalgam of diverse groups with differing interests and goals. The various groups within the firm come into conflict and, while their differences are never fully resolved, compromises are worked out that make use of pecuniary or non-pecuniary 'side-payments'. The diversity of goals would probably be sufficient, in itself, to preclude optimization of any kind. In addition, however, the behavioural theory recognizes the existence of imperfect information and uncertainty. According to the behaviouralists, managers are not maximizers, but satisfiers. Problems faced by the firm are ranked in order of importance and only invoke managerial response when they rise above a certain threshold level. Once they merit a response, managers search for solutions, concentrating on the more important problems first, attempting to reduce them below the threshold level. Where such actions are particularly successful (or unsuccessful) the aspiration levels of the management team may be adjusted accordingly (i.e. downward where the 'drive' for improvement is unsuccessful).

Each separately identifiable group within the firm may have their own goals and each goal (or set of goals) may, in turn, have its own implications for labour demands. In the theory put forward by Cyert and March (1963), five main goal areas are distinguished: production; inventory; sales; market share; profit. The multiplicity of goals and the fact that they are imperfectly rationalized preclude precise statements about any outcome. The production goal for example seems to be interpreted as both the number of employees sufficient to produce the target output and some sort of smoothing of variations in the level of output in order to minimize adjustment problems. Perhaps the only clear statement that the behavioural theory has to offer is associated with the existence of organizational slack. The theories of profit maximization assume that the least cost combination of inputs is always chosen. The existence of organizational slack means that, in effect, the cost curves of the firm are higher at each level of output than is strictly necessary on technical and economic grounds. When abnormal profits are earned, the labour force is thought to follow goals inconsistent with maximum profit (i.e. leisure pursuits). Management is forced to consider ways of increasing the efficiency of labour, but there may be little incentive to do so and such 'policing' activities cost money. When profits sink towards or below some accepted level, then there is an efficiency drive. Thus, the theory points to less than perfect efficiency and a greater variability of output than employment, consistent with the real world.

5 Conclusions

In this chapter we compared the basic theory of the demand for labour by the firm under perfect competition, developed in the previous chapter, with the demand for labour under different market structures and different goals of the firm. It was argued that although the assumption of perfect competition may be of relatively limited real-world value, there are some product markets in which high levels of competition can be observed. In addition, perfect competition yields an outcome of normative importance, as it is one in which prevailing market conditions force firms to be efficient, at least in a static sense. Thus, such firms could be visualized as minimizing production costs at each level of output or maximizing output at any given cost level.

Once the assumption of perfect competition in the product market is relaxed, there are a plethora of alternative market structures, each with its own implications for the demand curve for labour. This variety of outcomes occurs even before the assumption of profit maximization is relaxed. General results are hard to find, but certain conclusions can be drawn. First, at the industry level, the labour demand curve under a competitive regime, other things being equal, tends to lie further from the origin than under a non-competitive regime. Second, while it is difficult to say how an oligopolistic industry might reach an equilibrium position, once it is there the short-run stickiness in the price–output position is reflected in stickiness in the wage–employment outcome. Third, a non-collusive oligopoly is likely to have an industry-level labour demand function that lies further from the origin than its collusive counterpart, other things being equal. Fourth, the labour demand curve of a non-discriminating monopoly lies below that of a discriminating monopoly at every wage. We noted, however, that where monopoly power is likely to be excessive, various forms of regulation come into play which have the effect of shifting the labour demand curve (some way) back towards the competitive position.

It is even more difficult to draw general conclusions about the shape and position of labour demand curves in firms that adopt goals other than profit maximization. In the professionally managed (as opposed to owner-managed) firm, the sales-revenue maximizing model suggested both a higher demand for production employees at any given wage and a higher demand for non-production workers. The managerial utility-maximizing model reinforced the conclusion about non-production staff and, although it assumed a profit-maximizing level of production staff, this conclusion could easily be modified if managers experience disutility in strictly policing productive efficiency. The behavioural theories of the firm throw further light on the issues of X-inefficiency and costs and benefits of policing efficiency. Finally, it was shown that labour-managed firms appeared to behave in quite a distinct manner. This group of theories are quite heterogeneous, although they have the common characteristic of intertwining labour supply and demand. If anything the demand for labour in the income-per-head-maximizing firm will be less than or equal to the perfectly competitive, profit-maximizing firm. This conclusion, however, is modified if the level of employment is introduced alongside income per worker in the worker–managers' utility function. The solution now becomes indeterminate *vis-à-vis* its capitalist counterpart.

References

Baumol, W.J. (1967). *Business Behaviour, Value and Growth.* Revised Edition. New York: Harcourt, Brace and World.

Cyert, R.M. and J.E. March (1963). *A Behavioural Theory of the Firm.* Englewood Cliffs, NJ: Prentice Hall.

Domar, E. (1966). 'The Soviet Collective Farm as a Producer Cooperative'. *American Economic Review*, September, 734–757.

Fudenberg, D. and J. Tirole (1986). *Dynamic Models of Oligopoly.* Chur: Harwood.

Law, P.J. (1976). 'The Illyrian Firm and Fellner's Union Management Model'. *Warwick Economic Research Papers*, No. 94. Coventry: University of Warwick.

Thépot, J. and R.A. Thiétart (eds) (1991). *Microeconomic Contributions to Strategic Management.* Amsterdam: North-Holland.

Tirole, J. (1990). *The Theory of Industrial Organisation.* Cambridge, MA.: MIT Press.

Ward, B. (1958). 'The Firm in Illyria: Market Syndicalism'. *American Economic Review*, 48, September, 566–589.

Williamson, O.E. (1964). *The Economics of Discretionary Behaviour: Managerial Objectives in a Theory of the Firm.* Englewood Cliffs, NJ: Prentice Hall.

CHAPTER 9 Further extensions to the theory of labour demand

1 Introduction

This chapter extends the analysis of labour demand in a number of significant ways. Section 2 examines the important distinction between employees and hours of work and the related issue of the time pattern of work. If there is an increase in the demand for labour will it be filled in the form of extra employees or extra hours of existing employees? The associated marginal products and marginal costs may be quite different. This section also introduces the idea of adjustment costs, which affect the paths of employment and hours over time. This is more formally dealt with by dynamic (or multi-period) factor demand models. Section 3 examines what determines the number of operating hours in the day and the associated shift system. Section 4 explores the implications of the fact that labour is heterogeneous in the sense that there are different occupations, skills and education levels. In doing so, we consider the distinction between production and non-production workers. Marginal productivity theory, on the face of it, appears to apply to the employment of workers who add directly to output. What does it have to say about non-production workers? This topic is further developed in Chapter 10 which deals with the issue of technological change and labour demand. Section 5 considers the possibility that employers may use observable differences in labour (i.e. gender, race, religion, etc.) as a basis for discrimination. This topic is developed in Chapter 24 on segmentation and discrimination, and further extended in Chapter 28 which shows that firms may use the duration of unemployment as an indicator of employability. Finally, Section 6 draws the main conclusions of this chapter.

2 Employment and hours

In choosing the amount of labour services, the firm can vary at least three dimensions of the labour input: the number of people employed; the number of hours worked by each employee; and the degree of effort that each employee puts into the job. The analysis of worker effort is largely dealt with by efficiency wage theory, which we deal with in Part VI below. This section focuses on the first two of these dimensions, employment and hours. The firm's choice between the two depends crucially on the structure of labour costs and the relative productivity of persons and hours.

2.1 Labour costs

The wage payment is only one of a large number of dimensions of labour costs. Non-wage costs, in principle, can include items such as National Insurance Contributions (NICs), Selective Employment Taxes (SETs), redundancy payments, private social welfare payments, hiring and firing costs, training costs, and payments in kind. Despite the apparent diversity of types of costs, the literature tends to classify them under three headings: variable costs (i.e. the hourly wage rate), quasi-fixed costs (i.e. employer lump sum payroll taxes) and adjustment costs (i.e. hiring and firing costs, such as training costs and redundancy payments). The discussion below illustrates the importance of 'quasi-fixed' labour costs for the employment and hours decision.

Figure 9.1 illustrates the cost structure faced by the firm in choosing between alternative lengths of the working week. Following the taxonomy developed in the previous paragraph, the costs are comprised of:

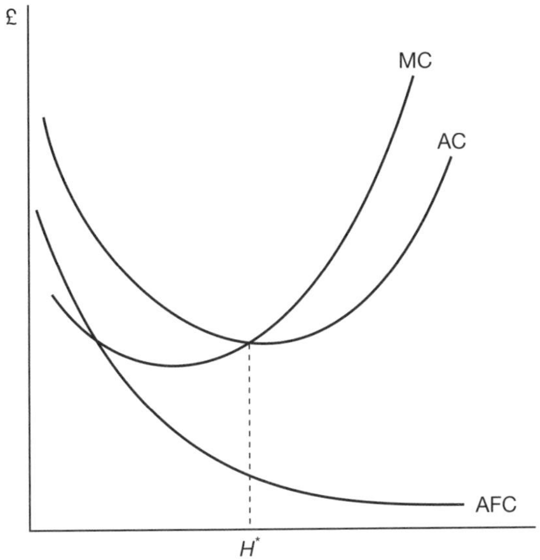

Fig 9.1 Labour costs per hour: calculated over various lengths of working week.

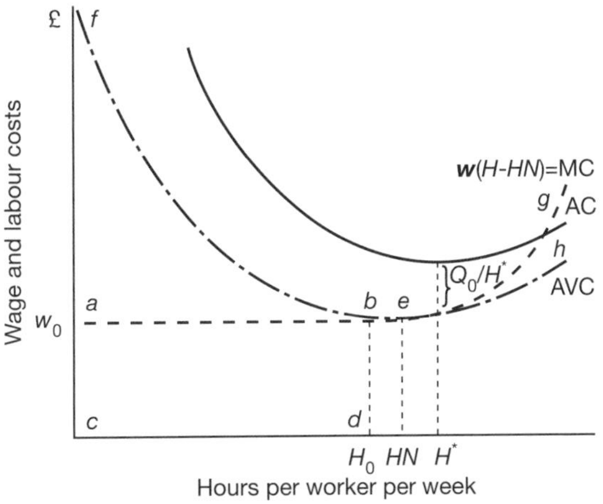

Fig 9.2 Structure of labour costs.

1 a fixed part, FC, which is a lump sum payment per worker, independent of the number of hours worked, which is, therefore, 'spread more and more thinly' as hours of work increase (shown by average fixed costs, AFC);

2 a variable part, VC, whose size changes with the length of the working week (shown by marginal costs, MC).

Calculating costs per hour for each worker, it is possible to obtain average fixed labour costs ($AFC = FC/H$) and average variable labour costs ($AVC = VC/H$), and, by definition, $AC = AFC + AVC$. While it is useful to think of the categorization of costs in this way, the resulting curves should not be confused with the traditional cost curves of the firm, which are calculated on a 'per unit of output' basis.

Figure 9.2 provides greater detail about the structure of labour costs. The variable parts of wage costs are essentially: (i) the basic wage, w_0 per hour, which operates below normal hours; (ii) the basic wage augmented by the overtime premium, w_1, above normal hours. The basic wage is constant up to normal hours, HN. Thus, in the absence of guaranteed payments of any kind, the average variable cost per hour is equal to marginal cost, $AVC = w_0H/H = w_0 = MC$, and shown by the line *ae* in Figure 9.2. Many contracts specify some normal hours, particularly in manual jobs, providing both the employer and employees information about the commitment of hours which can typically be expected. The proportion of jobs specifying normal hours has fallen as the ratio of manual to non-manual jobs has fallen and with the introduction of more flexible work patterns. Historically, in the UK, employment contracts, particularly in the unionized sector, specified some level of guaranteed pay, for short-time working, $G = w_0H_0$ (where $H_0 \leq HN$). In this case, once the firm is committed to hiring a given employee, its marginal cost is zero up to H_0 (shown by the line *cd* in Figure 9.2), and is then equal to the basic wage (between *b* and *e*). In a world of guaranteed wage payments, however, average variable costs fall progressively with the number of hours up to H_0, $AVC = w_0H_0/H$ (which approaches the vertical axis as $H \to 0$ and w_0 as $H \to H_0$).

We now turn our attention to overtime working, which occurs when firms demand hours above HN. Historically, in most industrialized countries, these additional hours have attracted an overtime premium, particularly amongst manual workers in the unionized or covered sectors. Again, more recently, overtime premiums have become somewhat less common with the reduction in unionization, the changing occupational structure and the flexibilization of labour markets. Nevertheless, the type of payment remains an important feature of many employment contracts. Thus, above HN, the hourly wage rate rises progressively with the number of hours, $w = \mathbf{w}(H - HN)$, where $dw/dH > 0$ for $H > HN$. In the real world, these increases generally take place in a whole series of steps (i.e. time and a quarter for the first five hours of overtime, time and a half between, say, six and ten additional hours, etc.) but for simplicity we approximate this by the continuous curve $w(H)$ in Figure 9.2. By implication, as $w(H - HN) > w_0$ for $H > HN$, then this increasingly high marginal cost of hours pulls the average variable cost of hours upwards as hours increase (see the difference between *eh* and *eg* in Figure 9.2).

Finally, we turn our attention to quasi-fixed labour costs (QFLCs), Q_0. An example QFLC would be a lump sum employer National Insurance Contribution (NIC), imposed in the UK prior to 1975 (a tax paid by the employer for each worker, independent of the number of hours worked). Subsequently, employer NICs became a function of the earnings of workers and therefore their hours of work, but there are still upper and lower limits to the payments that introduce a quasi-fixed element of cost. Guaranteed wage payments have certain of the characteristics of a QFLC: they are a fixed cost per worker, independent of the number of hours worked. However, because guaranteed payments are only operative below normal hours, they do not affect the position of the minimum point of the average wage curve. QFLCs are added to the wage costs to yield the user cost of labour. The more important the fixed element of labour costs in Figure 9.1, the higher is AFC and the more steeply sloped is the AC curve to the left of H^* and, for any given AVC curve, the higher is the number of hours at which the AC curve reaches its minimum point, $H^* > HN$ as shown in Figure 9.2. Thus, the minimum cost of employing an individual worker occurs at H^*, associated with the lowest point on the AC curve (i.e. the distance between the two curves in Figure 9.2 is Q_0/H, which clearly falls as H rises).

2.2 Productivity and firm equilibrium

If there is no difference in productivity between employees and hours, then the production function can be written

$$Y = \mathbf{f}(K, EH) \tag{1}$$

where: Y is output; K is capital stock; and EH are employee hours. In this case, the firm will treat the two dimensions of labour services (hours and employment) as homogeneous inputs into the production process. Given a perfectly elastic supply of labour to the firm at each wage rate and assuming that there are no other costs involved (i.e. costs of adjusting the labour force), then, as far as possible, the firm will alter its employment level to ensure that every worker remains at H^* in Figure 9.2 (see Ball and St Cyr, 1966). Where existing employees are on H^*, it is always cheaper to employ one extra worker for H^* hours per week than to ask existing employees to work additional (overtime) hours. While H^* will be linked with normal hours, the existence of QFLCs (at least, under the assumptions we have made above) will ensure that $H^* > HN$ and an average of $H^* - HN$ of overtime per employee will be worked.

If there are differences in the productivity of employees and hours at the margin, then the firm will not treat them as homogeneous in the production process, and this will influence the level of demand for the two factors. In order to distinguish the influence of productivity differences from that of QFLCs, we assume a constant user cost of labour per hour. Separating employment and hours in the production function,

$$Y = \mathbf{f}(K, E, H) \tag{2}$$

enables the marginal productivity of employees, $\partial Y/\partial E$, to be distinguished from the marginal productivity of hours, $\partial Y/\partial H$. Under these conditions, the firm will be willing to expand the number of hours worked above HN if $\partial Y/\partial H > \partial Y/\partial E$ at HN. A necessary condition for profit maximization is that

$$\frac{\text{MRP}_\text{H}}{\text{MRP}_\text{E}} = \frac{w_\text{H}}{w_\text{E}} \tag{3}$$

where: MRP denotes the marginal revenue product; subscripts H and E denote hours and employment respectively. Employment and hours are adjusted such that their contributions to total revenue at the margin are equal to their marginal costs. Thus, the firm that finds that, at H_N, the productivity of hours exceeds the productivity of employment will expand the hours of its workforce and reduce employment levels. This produces a movement towards equilibrium in two ways as it reduces the ratio of the productivity of hours over employment. If wages also increase with hours, it also increases the per unit cost of hours disproportionately as the firm has to pay higher rates of overtime premiums.

2.3 Adjustment costs, employment and hours

At any given point in time, the firm may not be in equilibrium, which has implications for the observed balance of inputs, including employment and hours. The path which the firm chooses back towards long-run equilibrium reflects both the costs of maintaining a given level of employment and the costs of adjusting the employment level. It is generally assumed that the costs of adjusting employment (i.e. costs of search, hiring, firing, training, etc.) will be significantly higher than those of adjusting hours of work. The magnitude of these costs will depend partly on demand features (i.e. how efficiently firms search for new employees) and partly on supply (i.e. the tightness of the particular labour market and the search behaviour of employees). A failure to achieve the long-run, desired level of, say, employment, may lead to sub-optimal levels of other inputs, such as hours and capital utilization in the short run.

Figure 9.3 shows that the immediate position of the firm can now be seen in terms of two sets of costs: first the costs of failing to employ the (long-run) optimal number of workers, E^*_t, at prevailing factor prices; second, the costs of moving from the existing level of employment, E_t, to the desired level, E^*_t. Both cost functions can be expected to be approximately quadratic in shape: the cost per employee of not achieving E^*_t will rise with the magnitude of the discrepancy; the cost per employee of moving away from E_t will rise the greater the magnitude of the change involved in each period. The costs of altering the level of employment at time t are shown by the curve AA, which does not necessarily reach its minimum point at employment level E_t because the firm experiences natural wastage of labour. Thus, the firm has to pay some search, hiring and training costs even to maintain employment at E_t. There is a point below E_t, such as E_t', where the curve touches the horizontal axis. In other words, adjustment costs fall to zero if the firm simply allows natural wastage to take place. It is assumed that the firm is faced by a 'U'-shaped average labour cost curve BB associated with the production process itself, which, in the period in question, reaches a minimum at point a. This point represents the minimum production costs of a firm wishing to produce a given level of output Y^*, with fixed capital stock. Hours act as a buffer whenever employment is not at its desired (long-run) level. If the firm has a smaller than optimal labour force, in order to produce the given level of output, it resorts to working a higher number of hours and, thereby, overtime payments. If the firm has too many workers, it reduces hours, but may be faced by guaranteed wage payments.

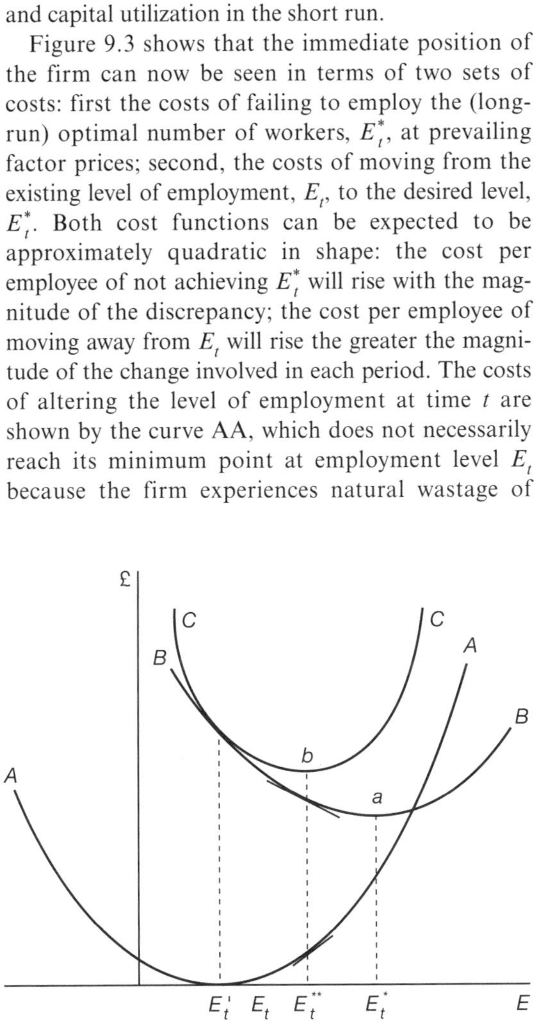

Fig 9.3 Adjustment costs and firm equilibrium.

In order to provide a solution to the problem, we assume that the firm attempts to minimize costs. The current employment level implies a substantial level of overtime working, $H_t > H^*$, if the firm is to produce Y^*. The high penalty imposed by overtime premiums induces the firm to move away from E_t, towards E^*_t, but, as it does so, it experiences higher and higher adjustment costs. In this simple, one-period model, the movement towards E^*_t ceases to reduce overall costs within the period when the reduction in costs of moving along BB towards point d is equal to the additional costs caused by the increased costs of adjustment of moving around AA. This occurs where the slope of AA just equals the absolute slope of BB and coincides with the point b, where the overall cost curve, CC, reaches a minimum. At a point such as b, the firm employs a smaller number of workers than it desires in long-run equilibrium, $E^{**}_t < E^*_t$, for a greater number of hours, $H^{**}_t > H^*_t$.

The introduction of an adjustment cost, however, raises the question of the dynamics of the movement from E_t to E^*_t. In minimizing the overall costs (i.e. of not being at the long-run optimal employment level and of the change in employment) for the single time period, the analysis omits to consider the whole of the adjustment from E_t to E^*_t. In moving from E_t to E^{**}_t, the firm has only completed a part of the total adjustment – there is still a further $E^*_t - E^{**}_t$ left. The firm is therefore faced by the prospect of paying additional adjustment costs (and perhaps incurring further costs associated with not having achieved the long-run optimal level of employment) in later periods. Nevertheless, the result is consistent with the idea of the partial adjustment of labour, period by period, to its desired, long-run equilibrium level. This kind of movement has been accounted for by lagged adjustment models in the empirical literature (see Chapter 11).

In the model outlined above, we assumed that the firm minimized costs subject to some output target. A number of models have developed measures of desired output (rather than current, actual output), often based on a lagged function of past output experience. This represents the first step on the road to making output endogenous and jointly determined with factor demands. Seen in this light, output itself may fall below (or rise above) its long-term desired level. The extent to which this occurs will depend on the costs of adjusting output *vis-à-vis* inputs, and, thereby, on the costs of longer (shorter) waiting lists, lost (new) orders and changes in stock levels. It is a noticeable feature of many industries that one common means of adjustment is either to allow order books to shorten or lengthen or for there to be variations in the inventories of work in progress and finished goods.

2.4 Multi-period labour demands

The previous section introduced the idea of the adjustment of inputs in response to labour market shocks, including changes in factor prices. While the previous analysis allowed adjustment, all of the costs involved related to the period in question and the resulting model was clearly static in the sense that it did not examine the path of output and factor demands over time. Returning to Figure 9.3, it is possible to see that, in principle, the cost-minimizing firm will calculate the discounted sum of costs associated with each alternative time path from E_t to E^*_t, and then choose the least cost alternative. Without extra information, there is no way of knowing whether the firm will chose a series of relatively small adjustments (i.e. perhaps minimizing the combined production and adjustment costs in each period) or make a single, relatively large jump directly from E_t to E^*_t. Some general pointers to the firm's choice are that:

1 the more rapid the growth in adjustment costs (i.e. the greater the rate of increase in the slope of AA) the more likely the firm is to adopt a piecemeal approach towards *e*;

2 the lower the production cost penalty (i.e. the more 'shallow' the 'U'-shaped BB curve) the more likely the firm is to adjust gradually.

In addition, however, it seems likely that the costs of adjustment may affect the long-run outcome. Imagine, for example, that a particular occupation is associated with particularly high adjustment costs. It is possible to imagine that this is likely to result in a long-run solution involving a smaller proportion of such people as their 'inflexibility' will give rise to higher costs in the long term in a situation where demand varies over time. This suggests that we need a more complex model that explicitly allows for the dynamics of adjustment. Following Nickell (1986), a simple 'dynamic' model for the price and wage taker can be written,

$$\text{Max PV} = \int_0^\infty e^{-\rho(t)}\{p(t)\mathbf{R}[E(t),t] - w(t)E(t) - C(X(t))\}dt \quad (4)$$

$$\text{s.t. } \dot{E}(t) = X(t) - \theta E(t) \quad (5)$$

where: initial employment $E(0)$ and the wage rate in each period, $w(t)$, are given exogenously; adjustment costs, C, are strictly convex (as outlined above); and ρ is the discount factor.

Equation (4) is based on the assumption that the firm maximizes the present value of the company where revenues and costs are discounted back to the time the decision is made. The discount factor is based on the rate of interest that the firm could earn from investing its money in some acceptable alternative (such as the bank). The discount factor at time t is the cumulative interest that can be earned from investing in this alternative over the period 0 to t. **R**[ ] is the net revenue function, which is defined as the amount of revenue left over having paid for the 'flexible' inputs. The labour costs accounted for in equation (4) include the wage bill, wE, and the costs of adjusting the labour input, $C()$. Equation (5) refers to the net change in employment, $\dot{E}_t$, which is the gross change, $X(t)$ (i.e. recruitment at time t if the firm is expanding its employment), minus wastage, $\theta E(t)$ (where θ is the wastage rate).

Nickell (1986) argues that the nature of the optimal path of employment over time can be deduced intuitively. Along this path, the addition of one employee results in no increase in the present value of the firm because the additional revenue net of wage generated by the worker is just offset by the costs of hiring the worker. Similarly, along this path, the subtraction of one employee from the workforce does not affect the present value of the firm, as the lower revenue net of wage caused by the loss of the worker are offset by the costs of firing the worker. The associated stationary equilibrium level of employment, E^*, satisfies

$$pR_E(E^*) = w + (r + \theta)C'(\theta E^*) \quad (6)$$

Thus, a unit increase in employment at the stationary equilibrium has the following implications: on the left hand side we have the value of the marginal product; on the right hand side, we have additional wage costs of w per period; a once and for all hiring cost, C'; a steady state increase in hiring of θ arising from the greater wastage associated with the slightly larger workforce, generating an associated cost flow of $\theta C'$ (note that r is the real rate of interest). It is interesting to compare this result with the equilibrium conditions of the static models outlined earlier. If, for example, $r = \theta = 0$, then equation (6) collapses to

$$pR_E(E^*) = w \quad (7)$$

which corresponds with the static equilibrium where there are no costs of adjustment. Note, however, that equation (6) shows that the dynamic adjustment costs, $(r + \theta)C'(\theta E^*)$ will affect the stationary equilibrium level of employment, E^*. Intuitively, equation (6) suggests that the marginal revenue product of labour will need to be higher than in the case of the static equilibrium without adjustment costs in order to 'pay' for the costs of hiring and firing. This implies that the level of employment in dynamic equilibrium will be lower than the corresponding level in the absence of adjustment costs. In essence, the adjustment costs raise the effective per unit price of labour *vis-à-vis* other inputs.

3 Work patterns and the demand for labour services

3.1 Shiftwork

Work patterns are a composite of different dimensions of employment, such as the time of work and length of shift. We exclude from the discussion, for the moment, other dimensions of work patterns such as payment by results and worker effort. In addition we might look at the issues of casual, temporary and outside work, including sub-contracting, which have become an increasingly important feature of the UK labour market. These are largely dealt with in later chapters of the book, although there may be some connections with the present section. For example, the demand for casual and temporary workers may be a response to peaks in product demand. The 'time of work' may refer to the times during the day, week or year when the firm consumes the labour services that it hires. Its choice of the times to open and shut the establishment, to work its capital stock and consume its labour services is crucially dependent on a variety of influences, including: the ability to store its product; rhythmically varying factor prices; and rhythmically varying product demands, particularly where the output cannot be stored.

The firm's choice of the time of shift and the length of shift are often inextricably intertwined. In certain production processes, they jointly determine the period over which the capital of the firm is manned and are, therefore, closely related to capital utilization where capital must be manned when it is operating. Under such circumstances, higher capital utilization can be achieved by: increasing the number of hours worked per employee; maintaining (or even reducing) hours of work in combination with a move from a less to a more intensive shiftwork pattern (i.e. from one to two or from two to three crews working).

Shiftworking can be defined as a situation in which one worker replaces another on the same task within a 24 hour period. There are a great variety of shift systems currently in operation. The more traditional ones include: 'four-crew three-shift' (covering about 168 hours per week), 'three-shift' systems (three crews covering a 24 hour period for five days a week); two-shift systems, such as 'alternating day and night', 'permanent day and permanent night' and 'double day' (two crews covering between about 16 and 20 hours, although sometimes covering the full 24 hours per day); evening shifts for part-time workers. In addition to the different types of system there are other possible variations. A particular system may operate with split shifts, where work periods are timed to coincide with peaks in demand, leaving the employee free between peaks. Certain systems may be made to rotate (or alternate), with one crew first working one shift and then another. The speed of rotation can also be varied.

It seems difficult to ignore shiftworking in most industrialized economies. In the UK, for example, around 25 per cent of manual workers in manufacturing industry were employed on one form of shift system or another by 1990. While, on average, the incidence of shiftworking is known to be higher in manufacturing, it is not restricted to this sector alone, and a number of the occupations with the very highest incidence of shiftworking are in the non-manufacturing sectors (i.e. coal miners, ambulance drivers, train drivers, telephonists, etc.).

As some of the hours worked on a shift system occur outside of the normal working day, they generally command a higher premium (or penalty) rate. The wage rate varies rhythmically over the day, as illustrated in Figure 9.4. The employer now faces higher marginal and average labour costs per hour outside of the normal working day, and this will influence the firm to try and concentrate its operations at relatively inexpensive times of the day. For example, other things being equal, Figure 9.4 indicates that $\tau_0 \rightarrow \tau_1$ will be preferred to $\tau_1 \rightarrow \tau_2$ or $0 \rightarrow \tau_0$. The sinusoidal curve representing the rhythmically varying price of labour does not in itself provide any insights about the optimal choice of work pattern. The optimal work pattern, however, can be explored using the concept of the least cost labour envelope, shown in Figure 9.5, which can be constructed from information about overtime and shift premiums. The envelope represents the least cost way of maintaining (machine) coverage by a single worker at any given time during the operating day or week. This does not mean that it is necessarily the same worker present at all points during the operating period; the model allows one worker to replace another on a shift system. It is particularly applicable to situations in which machines require workers to be present in order to operate.

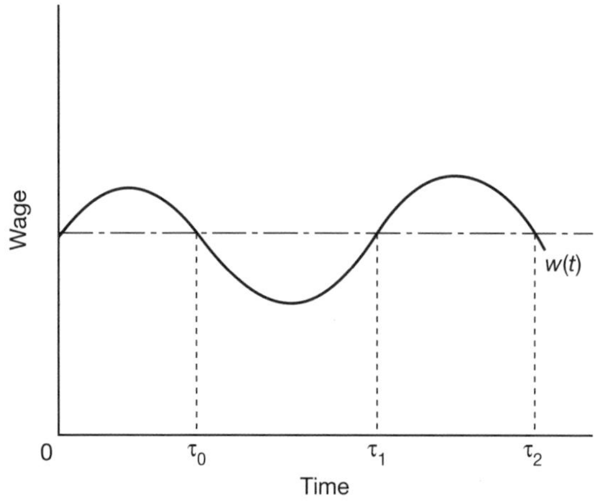

Fig 9.4 Rhythmically varying wage.

The first concept therefore is the average cost per hour of ensuring that one worker is available in the plant during all of the hours that the machinery is running. For any particular system, such as the one-shift, 'normal day plus overtime', the costs faced by the employer can be divided into the two broad cate-

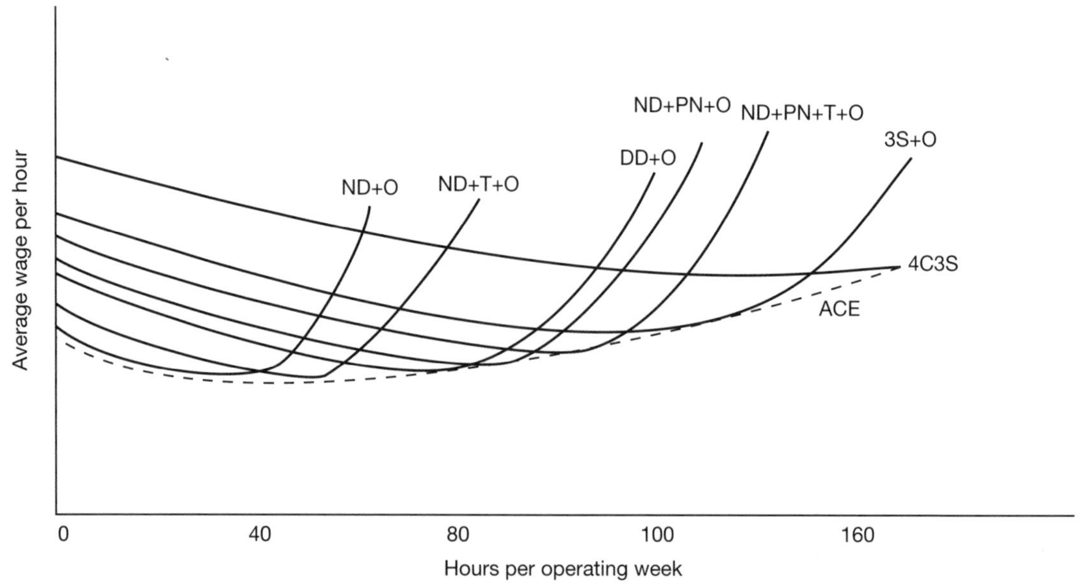

Fig 9.5 Average cost envelope: 168 hour operating week.

gories, quasi-fixed and variable (see Section 2). The burden of quasi-fixed labour costs is spread increasingly thinly over larger and larger number of hours, while variable labour costs rise disproportionately as the length of working day increases (i.e. moving to higher and higher overtime rates). Average labour costs per hour decline with the length of operating day up to the point where the higher hourly rates associated with overtime just offset the declining fixed costs per hour. Thus, a 'U'-shaped curve can be expected for each shift system with a minimum point at, or just after, the length of day covered by normal hours, as shown in Figure 9.5.

The average labour cost curves for progressively more intensive work patterns begin at higher and higher levels on the vertical axis because an *S*-shift system carries *S* times the quasi-fixed labour costs of the single-shift system. The more intensive systems also reach their minimum points at higher average wage levels because they command higher shift premiums. Figure 9.5 shows seven alternative shift systems, including part-time work, found in the real world. Each system is formed from a combination of: ND – normal day working; T – twilights; DD – double day (e.g. 6 a.m.–2 p.m. and 2 p.m.–10 p.m.); PN – permanent nights; 3S – three-shift non-continuous (6 a.m.–2 p.m., 2 p.m.–10 p.m., 10 p.m.–6 a.m., Monday to Friday); 4C3S – four-crew three-shift (as 3S but seven days per week); O – overtime working. Other systems, which are not illustrated, are built up from variants of these (i.e. alternating day and night), where evidence suggests that the curves lie in a fairly well-behaved manner and it is possible to envisage a 'minimum cost' or 'best practice' situation represented by the average cost envelope function, ACE. This frontier represents the average labour cost of providing one-worker cover for all alternative lengths of operating hours. The Ball and St Cyr (1966) wage–hours relationship now appears as a special case (i.e. when normal day plus overtime, ND + O, is the only shift option available). Thus, having decided its optimal operating hours per week (i.e. capital utilization), the firm simply reads off the associated least cost work pattern from Figure 9.5. At 40 hours per week, the firm would choose ND + O, but at 95 hours per week it would opt for the more complicated combination of ND + PN + T + O.

Substitution of the wage–utilization envelope, ACE, for the wage–hours function shown in Figure 9.2 makes no fundamental difference to the analysis of optimal employees and hours. Under these conditions the firm still opts for the minimum point on the wage relationship, which is the same for both functions. On the other hand, incorporation of the revised wage relationship in models that allow different returns at the margin between employment and hours, and substitution between capital and capital utilization, give rise to a different outcome. In the second of these cases, increases in utilization result in increased overtime or shift premiums payments (as well as higher levels of depreciation), but they are also likely to reduce the stock of capital required to produce the desired level of output. Figure 9.6 helps to illustrate the result. The least cost labour envelope is represented by ACE and is associated with a marginal cost of an extra hour of utilization of MC. However, expansion of utilization produces capital savings: in the simplest case (i.e. ignoring depreciation), one machine working for 16 hours produces the same volume of capital services as two machines operating for eight hours each. Marginal capital savings are represented by MKS and equilibrium occurs when MKS = MC; an additional operating hour costs as much in terms of higher labour costs as it saves in terms of the capital input. Having determined KU^*, it is then possible to return to Figure 9.5 in order to read off the corresponding optimal work pattern.

It is fairly easy to generalize the factor demand equation developed in the absence of shiftworking, equation (2) above. If continuous manning of capital

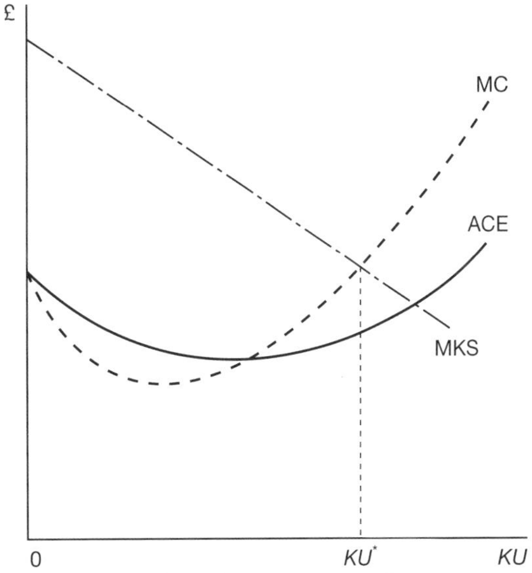

Fig 9.6 Costs and benefits of capital utilization: optimal level of capital utilization.

(i.e. workers must be present when capital is utilized and capital is utilized when workers are present) is assumed, capital utilization is measured as the number of hours that the factory is manned. Thus, $KU = H.S$, where H is average hours per operative and S is the number of shifts operated. The production function can be simplified to

$$Y = \mathbf{f}(K, KU, EM) \tag{8}$$

where: Y, K and KU are defined above; EM denotes the number of workers in the factory at any given point during the operating period, KU. If the firm minimizes its costs of production subject to an output constraint, optimal capital utilization can be written

$$KU^* = \mathbf{h}(w, c, Y^*, w', \delta') \tag{9}$$

where: $w = \mathbf{w}(KU)$ is defined by the wage–utilization envelope function shown in Figure 9.6; c is the user cost of capital and $\delta = \delta(KU)$ is the depreciation of capital caused by changes in utilization; w' and δ' are defined as $\mathrm{d}w/\mathrm{d}KU$ and $\mathrm{d}\delta/\mathrm{d}KU$ respectively; both are positive in the relevant range. Substituting the optimal level of capital utilization, KU^*, from equation (5) into the wage–utilization envelope, $w = \mathbf{w}(KU)$ yields the optimal (cost–minimizing) combinations of shiftwork, S^*, and hours, H^*. Each of the equations can be shown to collapse to the traditional factor demand result where various restrictions are placed on the shape and nature of $\mathbf{w}(KU)$ and $\delta(KU)$ functions.

It is possible to show that increases in shift premiums tend to result in a higher proportion of the envelope being associated with overtime working. Likewise, increases in overtime premiums raise the importance of shiftwork *vis-à-vis* overtime around the envelope.

3.2 Extensions to the shiftwork model

The choice of work pattern should be seen as part of a more general optimization problem. First, there is an important question mark against the implicit assumption that wages are the only rhythmically varying price. Second, the earlier discussion assumed that the product (and work in progress) can be stored at zero cost, or that the consumer is happy to receive it as and when it becomes available. Finally, previous discussion abstracts from any problems concerning the need for certain processes to be operated for some minimum/maximum period because of technological constraints.

In the real world, many intermediate products and services consumed by the firm are also associated with rhythmically varying prices. The cause is not difficult to find: firms tend to concentrate their production at certain times of the day/week/year and, thereby, set up peak demand problems for their suppliers. The suppliers react by varying the prices of their outputs. Examples include electricity and telephone charges. Figure 9.7 illustrates the case of a dual, rhythmically varying price situation, where the pattern for labour costs, $w(t)$, is almost the mirror image of electricity charges, $e(t)$, where the electricity is used to power the firm's capital. By implication, capital (electricity)-intensive firms will have an incentive to concentrate their production at night or at weekends when per unit electricity charges are low (i.e. as in the case of iron and steel making) and labour-intensive firms will have an incentive to undertake production during the daytime, Monday to Friday, when per unit labour costs are lowest. The incentive to move to one time or the other is accentuated by increases in the amplitude of the input price functions. Finally, note that there is an incentive for firms to search for organizational and technological changes that allow it to operate its capital and labour independently at different times of the day or week (thus, machines may be 'loaded' during the day and operated at night).

At one extreme, there are products which can be stored at zero cost and the only problem for the firm is to decide when to produce them; at the other extreme, there are products or services which cannot

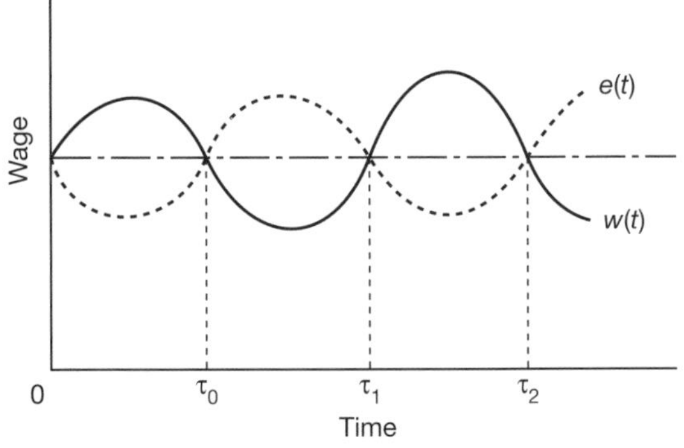

Fig 9.7 Multiple rhythmically varying prices.

be stored and must be produced at the time they are to be consumed. There are many examples involving the provision of services such as hospital treatment or transport services. In all these examples, the level of demand is either cyclical or time specific and the output cannot be stored. Thus, the firm has to decide whether to consume the labour services and produce its output at the time it is demanded or not. The fact that these demands can occur at 'unsocial' times of the day or week implies that firms may have to pay penalty rates for the labour it uses in the production process. On the other hand, in some instances, the price which the firm can ask for the product may also shift up at these times as the instantaneous demand curve moves outwards (i.e. as in the case of peak-time travel on the railways). Where time of day price tariffs are not possible, supplying companies have found a strong incentive to search for technological changes which separate the times at which labour services are supplied and times at which the product or service is delivered (i.e. as in the case of cash dispensers at banks).

Another notable feature of many of the associated demands is that they are often concentrated over a short period (i.e. the 'Friday night peak' of activity at hospital casualty, the demand for transport services during the morning and evening rush hours, etc.). Historically, such peaks have often given rise to split shifts, but increasingly the problem has been solved by using part-time workers. Similar seasonal patterns (i.e. in tourism) have been met by casual and, to some degree, by outside labour (i.e. migrant workforces). Interest in this area provided considerable debate over the issue of Sunday trading in the UK. Here there is an underlying flow of individuals who prefer shops to open on Sundays; in addition, the volume of potential Sunday trading shows seasonal patterns. Under such circumstances, firms that open at unsocial times capture business from those that remained closed, even if total trade is no higher. Sunday trading laws were liberalized in the UK in the early 1990s.

Finally, we note that certain processes may be technologically determined. If a chemical reaction is involved it may not be feasible simply to shut the process down mid-way through. The effects might be unfortunate, to say the least, in the production of iron and steel, adhesives or cement, or in the middle of surgery! The associated work patterns in some instances are therefore geared directly to fulfil the technological constraints of the associated processes.

4 Demands for different types of labour

4.1 Types of labour

The emphasis of the discussion is now changed from the choice between employees and hours towards the choice between different categories of workers. 'Different categories' may mean a variety of things, in particular: occupations or skill groups; individuals with different educational attainments; males versus females; core versus peripheral workers; etc. It is fairly easy to incorporate different types of workers where they are employed directly in current production, but it is somewhat more difficult in the case of indirect or non-production groups and considerably more difficult in the case of workers employed in dynamic functions, such as research and development (R&D). The distinction between current and dynamic activities is likely to be particularly relevant in discussing the demands for workers with different educational attainments. Even in the case of current production employees, the distinctions between different types of workers has become more blurred as firms have moved to leaner, flatter organizational forms with decentralized decision making and multi-skilling.

4.2 Demands for direct production workers

The choice between labour of different types is treated in much the same way as the static treatment of the choice between capital and labour or between employment and hours outlined above. The production function is respecified as

$$Y = \mathbf{f}(K, L_1, L_2) \qquad (10)$$

where L_1 and L_2 denote the inputs of two different types of direct production workers. The short-run demand function, with costs of adjustment, may reveal that one type of labour (i.e. the more highly skilled or, perhaps, core workers) is less easily varied in the short run.

Consider the case in which labour services (measured in person hours) can be varied, but capital is fixed. Figure 9.8 illustrates the demand curve for L_1 type labour under two assumptions: cost minimization subject to an output constraint; output maximization subject to a cost constraint. Both L_1 and L_2 are variable, but w_2 (the wage of the second type of labour) is fixed and w_1 (the wage of the first type of labour) is falling. As the wage falls from w_1^1 to w_2^1 and then to w_3^1, the output-constrained cost minimizer moves from *a* to *b* and then to *c* in Figure 9.8(a) and along the demand curve for labour D_1 in Figure 9.8(b). The cost-constrained output maximizer, faced by the same changes in wage, moves from point *a* to b_1 and then to c_1 in Figure 9.8(a) and along the demand curve for labour D_2 in Figure 9.8(b). The outcome can be interpreted in the following way: in order to produce any particular level of output with fixed capital, the firm requires a particular input of labour services; if different types of labour are imperfect substitutes for one another, the total service input can be made up from various quantities of the two labour inputs, as shown by the isoquant in question; the firm chooses the combination of labour types that produces the total of labour services required at least cost.

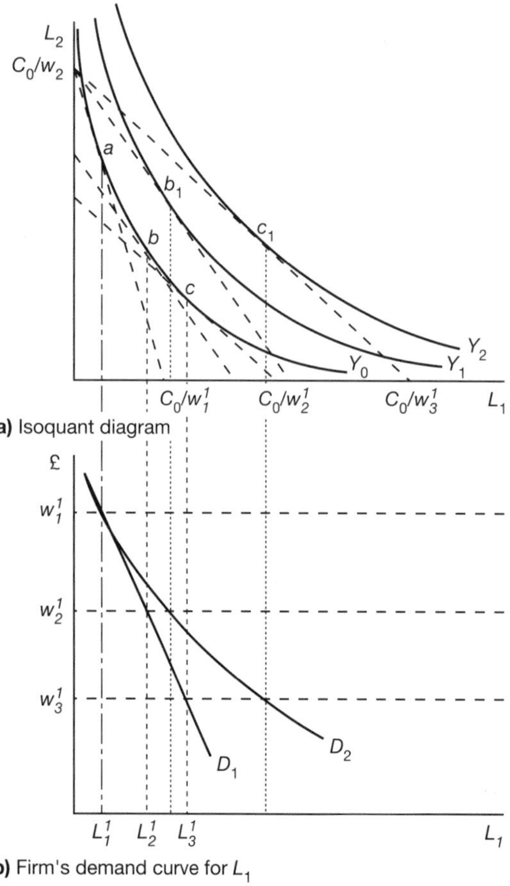

Fig 9.8 Demand for L_1 where w_1 varies.

Labour types L_1 and L_2 might refer to core and peripheral workers. Core workers, for example, are more likely to be represented by trade unions, with relatively long service records and covered by a variety of protective legislation. Peripheral workers are more likely to have shorter service records, less likely to be union members and largely exempt from protective legislation. Thus, differences in the quality of the two types of workers may affect the shape of the isoquant map and differences in their per unit cost affect the slope of the isocost line. There are other important considerations which are likely to impact on the choice between the two. First, there are likely to be important differences in the structure of the labour cost curve between peripheral and core workers. As part-time workers do not generally command a time of day premium, at least in the UK, their employment can enable the firm to increase capital utilization without incurring higher per unit labour costs. In addition, because part-time workers tend to be peripheral rather than core, the costs of adjusting their numbers is comparatively low. Both the premium and the low costs of adjustment make them a source of a flexible response to changing conditions in the product market. The same is broadly true of other groups, such as casual workers, home-workers, freelance workers, etc., and there are strong connections between the employment of these groups and part-time workers. Clearly, while there are important supply side factors operating, which explain the major growth in these categories of workers in recent years, there is also a strong demand side element caused by the need for flexibility in a more competitive, uncertain and rapidly changing economic environment.

4.3 Indirect labour inputs in current production

This section again focuses on those employed in current activities, but an attempt is made to distinguish between direct and indirect workers. Indirect workers are defined as those who work in support of direct workers. They might involve people in personnel functions, those dealing with payroll and tax issues, secretaries, etc. The production function can still be represented by equation (10), but, in this instance, indirect workers, L_2, may be complementary to both L_1 and K. Disaggregated studies of the demands for non-production workers (for example) have revealed some occupations, such as secretaries, where the dominant feature is their dependence on other occupations (and indirectly, therefore, on the causes of employment in these other occupations). There are occupations, such as scientists and technologists, where the dominant factors appear to be a set of industry characteristics (i.e. as is suggested by the structure–conduct–performance models of industrial economics). Finally, occupations such as managers show dependence both on other occupations and on industry characteristics. Even this approach appears to be an oversimplification. First, the stock of plant and machinery itself requires its own support workers. Machinery that requires maintenance may involve both direct and indirect workers. Second, the employment of indirect workers in the firm may affect the productivity of its direct production workers. While this sort of effect may be more important for indirect workers in dynamic functions, it cannot be ruled out for indirect workers in current functions.

4.4 Non-production workers, administrative overhead and dynamic functions

A number of researchers have treated administrative, technical and clerical staff (ATCs) as a 'fixed' and production workers as a 'variable' cost. It has been argued that their fixed nature can be seen insofar as the proportion of non-production workers within total employment falls during boom periods and rises during recession. The reason is that, while certain non-production activities (i.e. quality control, wage clerks, transport workers, etc.) are closely tied to output, others (i.e. sales, marketing, research and development, etc.) are not. The empirical evidence, however, probably suggests that the adjustment of ATCs is more discontinuous or lumpy, with lags in adjustment, followed by significant shakeouts during periods of recession. In recent years, firms have made considerable attempts to reduce the scale of administrative overheads, introducing flatter forms of organization with more devolved decision making.

A number of these workers, however, are in dynamic functions which involve an investment decision by the firm where the higher costs incurred in the current period are reflected in long-run differences in the productivity and profits of firms. Empirical evidence supports the view that in the long run, labour productivity is related to the density of non-production workers; higher levels of labour productivity are consistently found, over a wide range of industry groups, in firms employing relatively large proportions of ATCs. However, this result probably mainly reflects the capital intensity of the production process, which does not impact so dramatically on non-production workers insofar as their employment is tied to the stock of capital or output of the firm.

The work on the demands for workers with different educational attainments has resulted in largely unsatisfactory results, partly caused by the omission of an explicit supply function and partly from the failure to account for the dynamic nature of the tasks undertaken by more educated workers. A more extensive literature has grown up around the 'R&D' or 'knowledge production function'. Here investments in R&D, training, etc., impact on future productivity and company profitability. Thus, the demand for labour in dynamic activities is determined by a comparison of the current cost with the discounted stream of future returns. We deal with this issue in detail in Chapter 10.

Every time a firm takes on a new worker (even unskilled workers who may require no formal training) it may make an investment of a dynamic kind. Initially the firm might find their employment unprofitable at the level of productivity they exhibit on commencing work. However, such workers may experience substantial learning-by-doing effects and, at their later, higher productivity levels, their employment may turn out to be profitable. Where learning effects are important, labour turnover and the need to adjust the level of employment in the firm may have an important bearing on the profitability of employing such labour. The importance of learning by doing may reflect the fact that many of the skills (i.e. specific skills) that the firm requires may not be available on the open market and this will involve the firm in training (which we return to in Part V of the book).

5 Discrimination and labour demand

The discussion to date has suggested that the employer may wish to distinguish the demands for various groups (i.e. by function, education, occupation, etc.), because of differences in the nature of their contribution or their productivities. It is also possible that the employer may wish to distinguish between other groups, such as male and female or black and white, on non-economic grounds (i.e. for reasons outside of their contribution to the production process). In doing so, the employer is discriminating against certain groups and in favour of others. The socio-psychological literature defines discrimination as behaviour not motivated by an objective consideration of fact. This is not a watertight definition, however: a man is not accused of discrimination if he prefers to look at a beautiful rather than an ugly woman (beauty is in the eye of the beholder!); but may be accused of discrimination if he prefers to live next door to a person of the same ethnic origin. In this section it is argued that discrimination is a situation in which an individual acts 'as if he were willing to pay something either directly or indirectly or in the form of a reduced income, to be associated with some persons instead of others' (Becker, 1971, p. 14).

Employers may discriminate if they choose not to employ certain workers even though their marginal revenue products exceed their associated wage rate. In order to show the effects of such action, the concept of a discrimination coefficient, Ω, is introduced. Faced by a user cost of labour w, the discriminating employer behaves as if the 'real price' of the factor is $w(1 + \Omega)$, which is termed the 'net wage'. Thus, Ωw represents the employer's money evaluation of the non-pecuniary price element of employing this factor. Where Ω is positive, the employer associates a positive disutility with this factor, but where Ω is negative the employer associates positive non-monetary returns with this factor. Purely objective behaviour by the employer would be based on a comparison of the marginal revenue product of the employee and the wage. The employer acts in a discriminatory manner against the ith factor if they decide on the labour demands using $w_i(1 + \Omega_i)$, where $\Omega_i \neq 0$. In doing so, however, the employer forfeits profits, a factor that may, to some extent, deter discriminatory behaviour.

In a simple model, the producer faces competitive factor markets and adopts a fairly straightforward goal, such as minimizing the costs of producing a given level of output. Figure 9.9 shows the choice of input combination, a, associated with the minimum isocost line C^*C^*, where $C^* = w_1L_1^* + w_2L_2^*$. At point a the ratio of marginal products of any two factors (i.e. the slope of the isoquant) is equal to the ratio of factor prices (i.e. the slope of the isocost line). Discrimination in this simple model implies that the market prices of factors are altered by a percentage mark-up which we have called the discrimination coefficient. We assume a 'mark-up' of Ω_1 for the first type of labour and Ω_2 for the second type, where $\Omega_2 < \Omega_1$. The entrepreneur may now be thought of as minimizing costs subject to an output constraint, where the costs are based on the 'net factor prices' $w_1(1 + \Omega_1)$ and $w_2(1 + \Omega_2)$. The minimum 'effective' cost line of the discriminating firm is shown as B^*B^* in Figure 9.9 and the firm is in 'equilibrium' at point b. Assuming a given price of product, the equilibrium of the firm at b is given by

$$\frac{\text{VMPP}_1}{\text{VMPP}_2} = \frac{\text{MP}_1}{\text{MP}_2} = \frac{w_1(1 + \Omega_1)}{w_2(1 + \Omega_2)} \tag{11}$$

If the buyer discriminates more heavily against L_1 than L_2, there is a substitution away from the former and towards the latter. It is quite plain that the higher the elasticity of substitution between L_1 and L_2, the greater will be the impact of any particular percentage mark-up of any one factor above the other. A second feature is that the discriminatory firm is forced into a higher cost situation than the non-discriminatory firm. The factor market still charges the factor prices w_1 and w_2 and so the discriminating firm's cost level is represented by C_1C_1 (where $C_1 > C^*$).

Clearly the firm's demand curve for a factor which it discriminates against is depressed below the equivalent profit-maximizing curve. At the going market wage w_1, the demand by the firm undertaking discrimination is L_1', compared with L_1^* for the non-

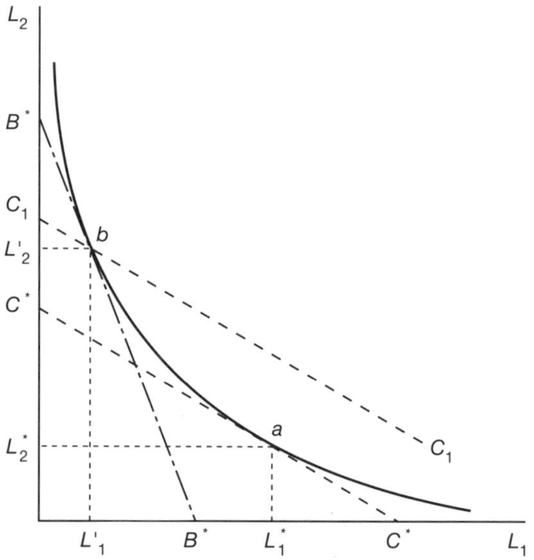

Fig 9.9 Effects of discrimination on the demands for labour services.

discriminatory firm, $L_1^{'} < L_1^{*}$. The greater the degree of discrimination, the more depressed the demand curve for this group of workers becomes and assuming that the higher costs of discrimination are not reflected in a contraction of the level of activity, the more buoyant the demand for the substitute group becomes. However, we can see that there will be some market-level effects. For one thing, systematic discrimination by employers in a given sector will rise and, other things being equal, increase prices and reduce demand. In addition, the wages will tend to fall amongst the group discriminated against, increasing their attractiveness to employers, and rise amongst the group which is favourably treated, reducing the incentive to hire them.

Note that there are certain similarities with some of the managerial theories of the firm, as discrimination could be represented by an indifference curve of managers showing the trade-off between different types of labour. A further similarity is that discriminatory behaviour is unlikely under highly competitive product market conditions. The existence of discrimination under perfect competition would require that all producers behave in the same way, attaching the same Ω_i. It would only take one producer to set $\Omega_i = 0$ for it to have a competitive advantage, removing other producers from the market or altering their behaviour. One prediction of this model is that discrimination is more likely to be concentrated in sectors which have greater degrees of market power.

A further form of discrimination occurs where the introduction or growth of a minority group of employees causes an adverse reaction amongst the existing (majority) workforce, which affects the performance of the firm. In effect, employee discrimination impacts on the marginal physical productivity of the minority group, resulting in an unwillingness amongst managers to employ such workers, other things being equal. Figure 9.10 illustrates the nature of employee discrimination. The isoquant would be represented by YN_0 in a world where no discrimination took place. In this case, it is assumed that the two types of workers, L_1 and L_2, are perfect substitutes such that they can be exchanged one for one in production, maintaining output constant. Thus, YN_0 has a slope of 45°. Clearly, no type 1 workers will be employed as long as the wage of this group is higher than the wage of type 2 workers. In the case of the isocost line C, therefore, where $w_1 > w_2$, equilibrium occurs at point a with $L_1 = 0$. By implication, under

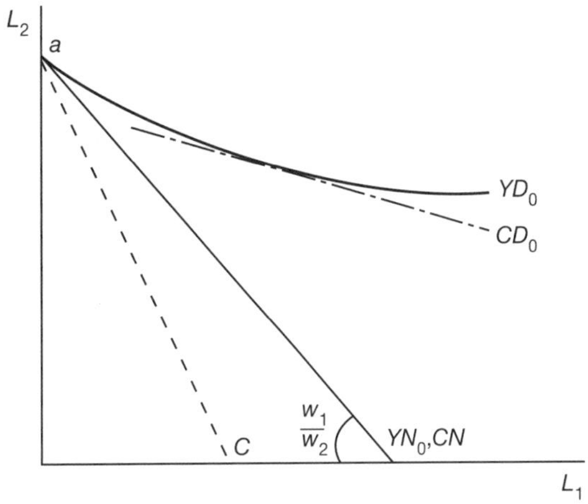

Fig 9.10 Effects of employee discrimination.

these conditions, if w_1 fell below w_2, $w_1 < w_2$, then only type 1 workers would be employed. Market forces would normally ensure that $w_1 = w_2$, and then the manager is indifferent between hiring type 1 and type 2 workers. Discrimination by employees, however, will mean that the effective isoquant (i.e. the isoquant perceived by the manager) is YD_0 rather than YN_0. This may occur because type 2 workers can affect the productivity of type 1 workers or because the introduction of type 1 workers into the firm lowers the overall productivity of employees and, therefore, the net marginal product is lower than might have been expected. Thus, at the going relative wages, w_1/w_2, only type 2 workers are employed. Employment of type 1 workers now requires their wage to be lower, in order to offset these productivity effects. The greater the employee discrimination the more shallowly sloped is the isoquant, YD_0, and the larger the wage reduction required in order that type 1 workers are employed. If the YD_0 curve becomes horizontal (or positively sloped), then there is no positive wage at which type 1 workers will be employed.

6 Conclusions

This chapter has explored a number of extensions to the theory of labour demand. We have shown how the choice of employment and hours are jointly determined and their paths over time are interrelated. We also demonstrated that the choice between factors are not only influenced by their current costs and productivity, but also by their costs of adjustment. During the course of the discussion it became clear that the hours–employment decision could only be properly understood in the context of a more general model of work patterns. The chapter then showed how the employment decision could be generalized to examine the demand for different types of labour. Finally, we built upon this model to illustrate the implications of employer and employee discrimination for labour demands.

References

Ball, R.J. and E.B.A. St Cyr (1966). 'Short Term Employment Functions in British Manufacturing Industry'. *Review of Economic Studies*, 33, July, 179–208.

Becker, G.S. (1971). *The Economics of Discrimination*. Chicago: Chicago University Press.

Nickell, S.J. (1986). 'Dynamic Models of Labour Demand'. In O. Ashenfelter, and R. Layard (eds) *Handbook of Labour Economics*. Amsterdam: North-Holland.

CHAPTER 10 Technological change and labour demand

1 Introduction

It has long been realized that technological change is a major influence on the labour market. In the very long run, not only is the firm able to alter its capital and labour inputs, but it can also change its technology of production and the technical characteristics of its products. In this chapter, therefore, attention focuses on the principal ways in which technological change can influence the demand for labour. The subject became extremely topical during the debate concerning the extent to which the new information technologies have altered the level and structure of labour demands. However, it would be wrong to portray this as a unidirectional process. The introduction of new technologies can certainly have significant implications for the level and structure of labour demands. On the other hand, technological change is partly endogenized, as firms can decide to invest in research and development (R&D) and to innovate. This also alters the number of employees and the balance of labour demands across skills and discipline areas. Thus, we build upon the discussion of the demands for different types of labour, making a key distinction between static and dynamic activities.

Section 2 continues by providing definitions of invention, innovation and diffusion, as well as embodied and disembodied technological change, and factor-saving biases. In Section 3 we introduce the idea that investment in research and development, and the associated human capital, gives rise to changes in firm performance over time. In particular, higher current levels of R&D result in greater firm efficiency and increased future sales. Section 4 returns to the theme that technological change often impacts upon factor demands. In particular, these changes may be labour saving, capital saving or neutral in their impact on the key inputs. Some thought is also given to product and process change, and to the impact of new technology on the skill structure of the firm. Section 5 considers the impact of technological change at the industry level. Section 6 explores the influence of new technology on factor demands at the economy level and, finally, Section 7 provides the main conclusions of this chapter.

2 Some important definitions

Technical change, in principle, can be distinguished from technological change: the term technical change is reserved for changes in technique where newly adopted technologies may already be known and not newly invented; on the other hand, technological change involves new technology and, hence, an associated inventive step. As a rough guide: the changes around a given production function (e.g. around an isoquant) represent technical changes, while alterations to the production function itself (e.g. a shift of the isoquant map) represent technological change and form the subject of this chapter. As the distinction between the two terms implies, technological change can mean additions to the 'book of blue prints', which widen the choice of *ex ante* alternatives, but which may, in practice, never be used.

From an analytical point of view, it is important to distinguish between invention, innovation and diffusion, although, in practice, the boundaries between these three are not always clear cut. The following can be used as working definitions: (i) an invention involves the formulation of a new product or process, where the underlying principle is not a part of the 'state of the art' (i.e. it is not known by those who are recognized to be well versed in that particular product area or production technique); (ii) an innovation denotes the first industrial or commercial application of an invention (or more broadly, the successful application of new ideas); (iii) the diffusion process relates to the pattern of adoption of a given invention, for example amongst firms in a given industry or region (perhaps even worldwide).

A further distinction is between product and process change. In essence, the majority of product changes involve alterations to the set of technical characteristics that comprise the product. On occasion, in the rarer case of radically new products, entirely novel technical characteristics (or combinations of characteristics) may be involved. Process change, on the other hand, is associated with an alteration in the method of producing the good. While it may be possible to think of examples of pure product (i.e. involving no process change) or pure process innovation (i.e. involving no product change), in the real world, technological change often involves a mixture of both. It must also be remembered that, insofar as each product may be used as an input into other production processes, one firm's product innovation may well be another firm's process innovation.

The models developed below for the most part assume that process technological change is disembodied: improvements affect all units of the firm's existing capital and/or labour. However, it is important to recognize the possible existence of embodied technological change. In this case, new technology is generally assumed to affect only the latest vintage of capital; existing capital embodies older vintages of technology. In a vintage world, the introduction of new technology involves the firm in investment activity and its labour demands at any given point in time depend on the 'portfolio' of vintages that it holds and the degree to which it chooses to utilize each vintage. Clearly, the demand functions for labour built on the vintage hypothesis are generally more complicated than those which adopt the assumption of homogeneous capital and disembodied technological change. It has also been argued that labour itself may exhibit vintage effects, with individuals educated or trained more recently (often younger individuals), embodying higher levels of human capital.

Finally, it is worth bearing in mind that technological change may manifest itself in any way within the production function. At its simplest, it may appear as factor-augmenting technological change, an increase in the efficiency of one or more of the inputs: the existing workforce can produce more output or the same output can be produced by fewer workers, other things being equal. At its most complicated, it could, in principle, alter every technology parameter of the production function, including the elasticity of substitution. Empirically, changes in the production parameters caused by moving around the production function can be difficult to disentangle from the effects of technological change.

3 Dynamic activities and the demand for labour

In this section, we consider the firm's demands for labour in dynamic activities. The example we take is research and development, but we equally might apply the same principles to other functions, such as training. An understanding of investments of this type are crucial to a full appreciation of the level and structure of labour demands, because the employment of some workers is not linked in any way to the level or even the nature of the firm's current output. The outputs of R&D workers presently employed by the firm may not occur for many years into the future. In addition, the timing and the nature of the outputs are, in general, more uncertain, sufficiently so as to induce some researchers to deny the existence of a production function relationship between R&D inputs and outputs.

We are going to abstract from these difficulties and assume away problems of measuring inputs and outputs. Indeed, throughout this section, we assume that R&D can be represented by R, the number of research workers. This enables an 'R&D' or a 'knowledge' production function to be written, which, for simplicity, we assume to be log-linear:

$$Y_t = A_t K_t^{\alpha} E_t^{\beta} RD_{t-1}^{\gamma_1} \, RD_{t-2}^{\gamma_2} \ldots RD_{t-n}^{\gamma_n} \qquad (1)$$

where A, α, β and γ, $i = 1,\ldots, n$, are constants. Thus, differentiating with respect to time in the normal way,

$$\frac{1}{Y}\frac{\mathrm{d}Y}{\mathrm{d}t} = \frac{1}{A}\frac{\mathrm{d}A}{\mathrm{d}t} + \alpha\frac{1}{K}\frac{\mathrm{d}K}{\mathrm{d}t} + \beta\frac{1}{E}\frac{\mathrm{d}E}{\mathrm{d}t} + \sum_{i=1}^{n}\gamma_i \frac{1}{RD_{t-i}}\frac{\mathrm{d}RD_{t-i}}{\mathrm{d}t} \qquad (2)$$

Thus, it can be immediately seen that total factor productivity growth depends on past R&D and, perhaps, to some degree via $(1/A)$ $(\mathrm{d}A/\mathrm{d}t)$, on exogenous technological change which does not arise directly as a result of the firm's own R&D activity. The contribution of R&D is more clearly seen by partially differentiating equation (1) with respect to R_{t-i},

$$\frac{\partial Y_t}{\partial R_{t-i}} = \gamma_i \frac{Y_t}{R_{t-i}} \tag{3}$$

and γ_i is the marginal divided by the average product (i.e. the percentage change in output attributable to a given percentage change in R&D).

Note that, if the effects of R&D as represented by the parameters $\gamma_1, \ldots, \gamma_n$ are fixed over time, then we can look at the impact of an extra R&D worker at a given point in time, R_t, in terms of its impact on current and future output,

$$\frac{\partial Y_{t+i}}{\partial R_t} = \gamma_i \frac{Y_{t+i}}{R_t} \tag{4}$$

Then, applying an appropriate discount rate, ρ, the overall impact of the additional research worker at time *t* can be written as, MY_R, where

$$MY_R = \sum_{i=1}^{n} (1-\rho)^i \gamma_i \left(\frac{Y_{t+i}}{R_t}\right) \tag{5}$$

Thus, we can think of MY_R as the gross present value of employing an additional R&D worker and, hence, the firm invests in R&D as long as

$$MY_R \geq W_R \tag{6}$$

where W_R is the wage rate of research workers. Given estimates of MY_R, however, it is possible to use equations (5) and (6) to determine R_t^*, the optimal number of R&D workers, which occurs where R_t is increased until expression (6) becomes an equality. Clearly, while it may be possible to work out the *ex post* returns to R&D, it is much more difficult for the firm to carry out the *ex ante* calculation and invest optimally. While equations (5) and (6) give the marginal condition, the overall contribution of research workers at time *t* is given by the difference in output with and without R_t. In other words,

$$TY_R = \sum_{i=1}^{n} (1-\rho)^i Y_{t+i}\left(1 - \frac{1}{R_t^{\gamma_i}}\right) \tag{7}$$

In general, given that the average always exceeds the marginal product in a Cobb–Douglas world (see equation (3)), the firm makes a profit on its R&D investment.

Clearly, company managers form an expectation about TY_R, but so do City analysts and investors. Thus, current investments in R&D are reflected in the market value of the company, MV. There is a clear linkage between the knowledge production function outlined above and market value. This linkage can be traced to the fact that past R&D drives a wedge between the value of output and the costs of inputs used in current production activity. We define this gap as economic profit, Π_E, which is used to make discretionary investments which can be expensed, such as advertising, AD, and R&D, *R*. What is left is accounting profit, Π_A, which is distributed between such items as dividends, funds retained for investment and corporate tax liabilities. In a steady state growth situation, where a constant proportion of Π_E goes to each activity, dividends will grow proportionally with economic profit. The final link is that, in the long run, the market value of the company reflects the discounted sum of future dividends. Thus, we should find with sufficient information that MV should be positively related to R&D insofar as this activity has a positive impact on productivity and firm profits.

The use of market value can be traced back to Tobin's '*q*' (Tobin, 1969), which is basically the ratio of the market value to the book value of capital. While earlier theories concentrated on the relationship between MV and the tangible assets of the firm, more recent work has focused on intangible assets including R&D. The result is a model in which

$$MV_t = \mathbf{f}(K_t, G_t) \tag{8}$$

where: K_t denote the stock of tangible assets: and G_t denote the stocks of intangibles. Thus, changes in MV will reflect the expected discounted sum of future profits which arise because of changes in both tangible and intangible assets. Imagine, for simplicity, that the stock of intangibles can be written

$$G_t = G_{t-1} + \gamma R_{t-1} - \delta G_{t-1} \tag{9}$$

where: *R*, research and development employment, is used as a measure of investment in intangibles; δ is the rate of depreciation of intangibles which is assumed constant; γ and δ are constants determined by the regression (while it plays a similar role, note that γ is not the same as in equation (2)). Again, as long as the relationship remains unchanged over time, it is possible sequentially to substitute for G_{t-1}, G_{t-2}, ..., and, as a result, we obtain

$$G_t = (1-\delta)^n G_{t-n} + \gamma R_{t-1} + \gamma(1-\delta)R_{t-2} + \gamma(1-\delta)^2 R_{t-3} + \ldots + \gamma(1-\delta)^{n-1} R_{t-n} \tag{10}$$

Given that $0 \leq \delta \leq 1$, then for sufficiently large *n*,

$$G_t = \gamma[R_{t-1} + (1-\delta)R_{t-2} + (1-\delta)^2 R_{t-3} + \ldots + (1-\delta)^{n-1} R_{t-n}] \tag{11}$$

Again, we see that the intangible asset measure is formed as a sum of past R&D, where the weights reflect the rate of depreciation of R&D. By implication, it should be possible to derive future market values from current and future R&D employment (altering intangible assets) and investment in plant and machinery, etc. (altering tangibles). We would anticipate that market value would be maximized if the firm follows the profit-maximizing rule set out in equation (6). However, there is significant potential for asymmetric information which means that (potential) shareholders may have a different view about such investments. In essence, the shareholders may be apparently more risk averse or short termist. Given that the firm has to look to its market value, not least because of takeover raids, it may be more inclined to pick values of R&D which maximize MV rather than TY_R where the two differ.

4 Employment consequences of technological change at the firm level

Having looked at some of the potential driving forces behind technological change, we now turn to its implications for labour demands at the firm level. The impact on labour clearly depends on the rate of technological change, but also on its nature, for example whether it is product or process. In the case of process change, it is also important to consider the concept of neutrality, which concerns the degree to which technological change is factor saving (or using). Most of this debate has surrounded the balance between capital and labour, but it also has implications for the skill mix of the firm.

4.1 Process change and neutrality

This is generally treated as a relative concept and, thus, interest centres not only on changes in the overall consumption of each factor service, but also on the change in demand for one factor relative to another. Two equivalent ways of defining the relative factor-saving nature of technological change are adopted here: the first focuses on the changing slope of the isoquant (e.g. the changing ratio of the marginal physical products) at a given capital/labour ratio; the second looks at the change in the capital/labour ratio for any given slope of the isoquant (e.g. for any given ratio of the marginal physical products). In the analysis which follows, both factor and product prices are assumed to be constant, although these assumptions are relaxed somewhat in later sections.

Figure 10.1(a) shows the case of a neutral technological change: t is used to denote the pre-invention and $t + 1$ the post-invention position. The pre-invention equilibrium is at point a, where the isoquant Y^0_t and isocost lines are tangential. After the invention, the firm is able either to produce the same output, Y^0_{t+1}, with a smaller volume of inputs, or to produce a larger volume of output, Y^1_{t+1}, with the same volume of inputs (or some combination of these two). The technological change is neutral because: the slope of the isoquant (e.g. the ratio of marginal products, MPP_L/MPP_K) is the same at point b as it is at point a, along the radian $(K/L)^0$; the capital/labour ratio remains the same on the new isoquant for the given ratio of marginal physical products experienced at point a.

The precise change in the firm's demand for labour depends on its goal. As factor prices are assumed to remain unchanged, Figure 10.1(a) shows that the cost-minimizing firm producing Y^0 of output would move to a new equilibrium at point b. On the other hand, the output maximizer subject to a cost constraint would choose to produce Y^1 at point c (where $a=c$). Figure 10.1(b) indicates that the labour demand curve shifts inwards from D^0_t to D^0_{t+1} as a result of the technological change, under the goal of cost minimization subject to an output constraint. Figure 10.1(c) shows the case of the output maximizer subject to a cost constraint. As this firm has experienced no change in its factor prices, it can now achieve the higher output level, Y^1_{t+1}, and the effect of this is to maintain the demand for labour curve unchanged, $D^1_{t+1} = D^0_t$, under this particular goal of the firm.

Figure 10.2 illustrates the case of labour-saving technological change. Figure 10.2(a) relates to the labour-saving case because the new isoquant, Y^0_{t+1}, has a smaller slope (e.g. a lower ratio of MPP_L/MPP_K) at the capital/labour ratio $(K/L)^0$. The ratio of marginal physical products originally located at point a is found at a higher capital/labour ratio, $(K/L)^1$, after the technological change. Other things being equal, labour-saving technological change implies a more substantial downward shift in the firm's demand curve for labour than the corresponding neutral case. The cost minimizer, in maintaining an output level Y^0, moves from point a to point b in Figure 10.2(a), which is associated with a substantial downward shift in the demand curve for labour from

D^0_t to D^0_{t+1} in Figure 10.2(b). In essence, the technological change causes an additional substitution effect away from labour and towards capital at the going factor price ratio, as it reduces MPP_L relative to MPP_K. The output maximizer subject to a cost constraint maintains expenditure on the isocost line going through point *a* in Figure 10.2(a), and this goal is associated with a smaller downward shift in the demand curve for labour, in Figure 10.2(c) than in 10.2(b), because of the higher level of production involved.

Figure 10.3(a) illustrates the analogous capital-saving case. Figure 10.3(a) indicates that the change is capital saving because: the change raises the MPP_L relative to the MPP_K at the old capital labour ratio, $(K/L)^0$; and the old ratio of marginal physical products is now to be found at a lower capital/labour ratio, $(K/L)^1$, on the new isoquant. The case of the output-constrained cost minimizer is shown by the change in equilibrium from *a* to *b* in Figure 10.3(a), and this is associated with a relatively small downward shift in the demand curve for labour, from D^0_t to D^0_{t+1}, in Figure 10.3(b). In fact, if the technological change had been slightly more capital saving (labour using), it might actually have caused an outward shift in the labour demand curve, even with this rather restrictive goal of the firm. Figure 10.3(c) indicates that for the output maximizer, the substitution towards labour (caused by the relative increase in MPP_L) and the increased level of production produce an outward shift in the demand curve for labour from D^0_t to D^1_{t+1}.

The discussion has helped to show that there are a variety of possible outcomes and, in particular, the position of the new labour demand curve depends on: the nature of the invention (e.g. whether it is capital saving, labour saving or neutral); the goal of the firm (e.g. whether it is one of cost minimization subject to an output constraint or output maximization subject to a cost constraint).

4.2 Process change and the skill structure of the firm

Innovative activity affects not only the level of employment and the balance between capital and labour, but also the skill structure of the firm. It is quite easy to visualize a three-dimensional isoquant map, where the firm has two different types of labour inputs, in addition to its capital stock. Focusing on the (L^1,L^2) plane, it is then possible to assess the relatively L^1 saving (or relatively L^2 saving) technological change, in much the same way as the relatively capital- or labour-saving change outlined in Figures 10.1 to 10.3. In addition to labour used directly in the production process, however, the innovation process itself may affect the skill structure of the firm: the installation and 'debugging' of machinery, even where it is bought 'off the shelf' requires relatively highly qualified personnel; research and development is an even more skill-intensive process.

There is still a considerable debate about whether technological change produces a pervasive trend in labour demand which is skill raising, deskilling or associated with the polarization of skills within the firm. The debate is largely unresolved, for several reasons. First, technological change is itself heterogeneous; there are many different types of changes going on at any one time, with different implications for the skill structure. Second, the precise implications of any particular new technology depend as much on organizational factors as on the inherent characteristics of the change itself. In other words, it depends on the way in which the firm chooses to use the new technology. In the case of the introduction of numerically controlled machine tools or machine cells, for example, the consequences for labour demands depend on whether management decides to separate the tasks of programming and operating the machines or to combine them so that they are both undertaken by the employees who operate the machines. If the tasks are separated, a further question arises as to whether the programming is undertaken 'in house' or sub-contracted to specialist computer software firms. The former option would not generally be deskilling within the firm (though it may polarize skills), while the latter would be deskilling at the firm (and perhaps the industry) level, but not necessarily within the economy (if the software specialist is a domestic firm located in the services sector). Obviously, decisions of this type are not independent of economic factors; for example, the choice will depend to some extent on the most cost-effective option open to the firm. There is evidence, however, that the successful introduction of technologies of this type requires new skills amongst existing members of the workforce, which often involves training and retraining.

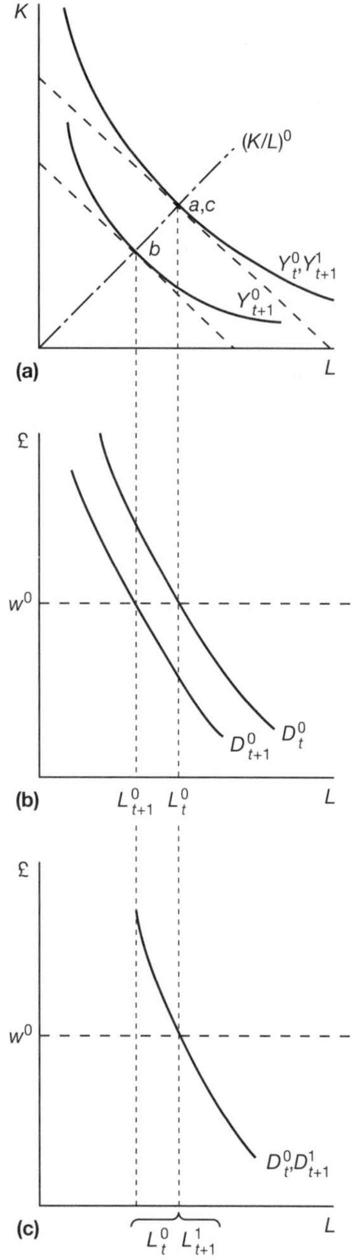

Fig 10.1 Neutral.

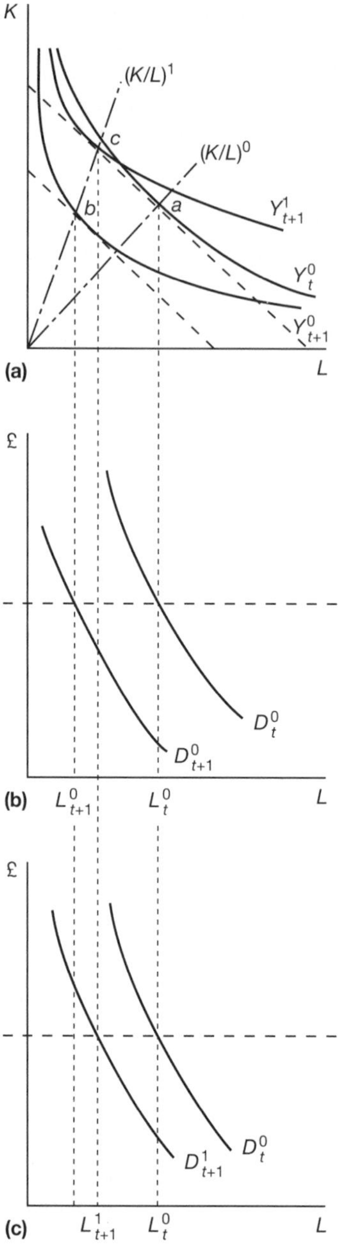

Fig 10.2 Labour saving.

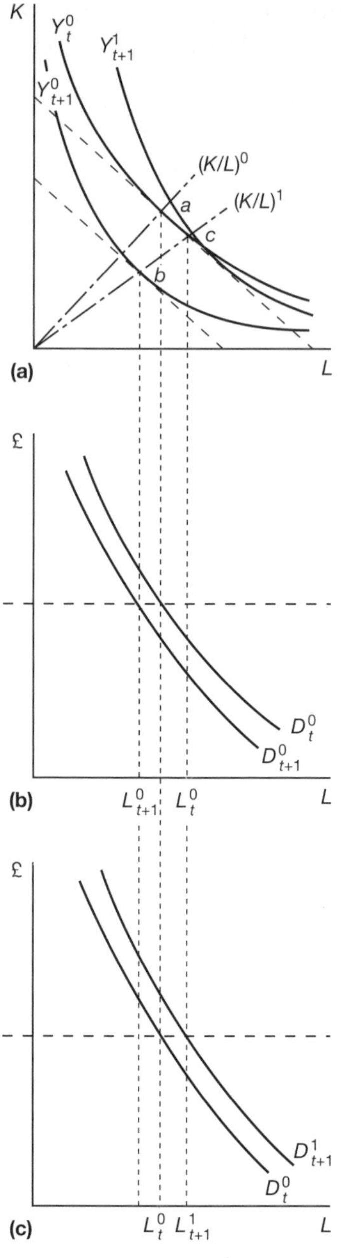

Fig 10.3 Capital saving.

4.3 Product change

Other things being equal, a product change can be expected to be demand increasing. Of course, there may be exceptions to this rule. Given the risks of invention and innovation, the firm may unwittingly replace a successful product by a relatively unsuccessful one, as in the case of the Ford Edsel or the introduction of Corfam by Courtaulds. In other instances, the firm might intentionally switch from a

CASE STUDY 1 Harrod, Hicks and Solow neutral change

The Harrod, Hicks and Solow neutral definitions of technological change have been found useful in the context of developing growth models. Harrod focused on a purely labour-augmenting type of progress,

$$Y_t = f(K_t, g(t)L_t) \qquad (1)$$

where, $g' = (1/g)(dg/dt)$ is the rate of labour-augmenting technological change at time t, and $g' > 0$. Since $g(t)$ increases over time, a given output can be obtained from a given input of capital services and a smaller and smaller input of labour services. It is as if, after the change, one worker can produce $(1 + g')$ the amount produced by a worker prior to the change. Solow neutral progress is analytically identical, except that it is purely capital augmenting,

$$Y_t = f(h(t)K_t, L_t) \qquad (2)$$

where, $h' > 0$ is the rate of capital augmentation (i.e. $h(t)$ increases with the passage of time). Of course, both types of factor-saving change can occur simultaneously,

$$Y_t = f(h(t)K_t, g(t)L_t) \qquad (3)$$

and the relative factor-saving effect depends on the sizes of g' and h'. The special case where $g' = h' = j'$ is the case of Hicks neutral progress and, assuming a homothetic production function,

$$Y_t = f(j(t)K_t, j(t)L_t) = k(t)f(K_t, L_t) \qquad (4)$$

where both $j' > 0$ and $k' > 0$ cause an upward displacement of the whole production function and, in the linear homogeneous case, $j' = k'$. Of the three alternatives explored, intuitively, the Harrod neutral change would appear to have the most important implications for the reduction in demand for labour.

In the special case of a Cobb–Douglas technology, all three types of neutrality described in the previous section produce analytically identical results,

$$Y_t = AK_t^{\alpha}[g(t)L_t]^{\beta} = [g(t)]^{\beta}AK_t^{\alpha}L_t^{\beta} = A\{[g(t)]^{\beta/\alpha}K_t\}^{\alpha}L_t^{\beta} \qquad (5)$$

though the rates of augmentation differ. Thus, in the CD case despite the fact that technological change was assumed to be labour augmenting, thus reducing the labour demanded at every output level, it does not alter the optimal long-run ratio of capital to labour. With a Cobb–Douglas technology, Harrod neutral change at rate g' is exactly equivalent to Solow neutral change at some other rate, h', or Hicks neutral change at rate j'. In practice, despite its extremely restrictive nature, the CD function is widely used not only in production theory, but also as an underpinning for growth accounting measures of the residual factor, which attempt to isolate an upper limit for the rate of technological change. The use of the function, however, raises a number of questions concerning the accuracy of such measures of technological change.

high-volume, low-profit area to a low-volume, high-profit product. In this section, however, the discussion concentrates on the more likely outcome of a demand-increasing product innovation.

The outcome is simplified if the innovation is a pure product change, with no alteration to the technology of production. In this case, the firm faces the same isoquant map (where output is measured in terms of the physical number of units of the product). In the short run capital is fixed, say, at K_0, and the expansion path of the firm is along a single total physical product of labour (TPP_L) curve. Although the TPP_L curve is unchanged, as the demand curve for the product shifts outwards to greet the introduction of the new product, the price of the product increases at every level of output, and this causes the TRP curve to shift upwards. The effect on the demand for labour can again be shown in a number of different ways, as shown using Figure 10.4. If point a_1 on TRP_0 in Figure 10.4(b) is used to represent the initial equilibrium position, then the outward shift in the product demand curve causes the TRP curve to assume a greater slope at every level of labour input, resulting in TRP_1. As the nominal wage bill line remains unchanged, at w_0L, the two now have the same slope at a higher level of the labour input, corresponding with point b_1 on TRP_1. Alternatively, the same result can be shown in Figure 10.4(c), where the higher product price is represented by an outward shift in the VMPP curve to $VMPP_1$, and equilibrium occurs at point b_2, where this curve intersects the nominal wage line w_0. The overall effect of the pure product innovation is an increase in labour demand from L_0 to L_1.

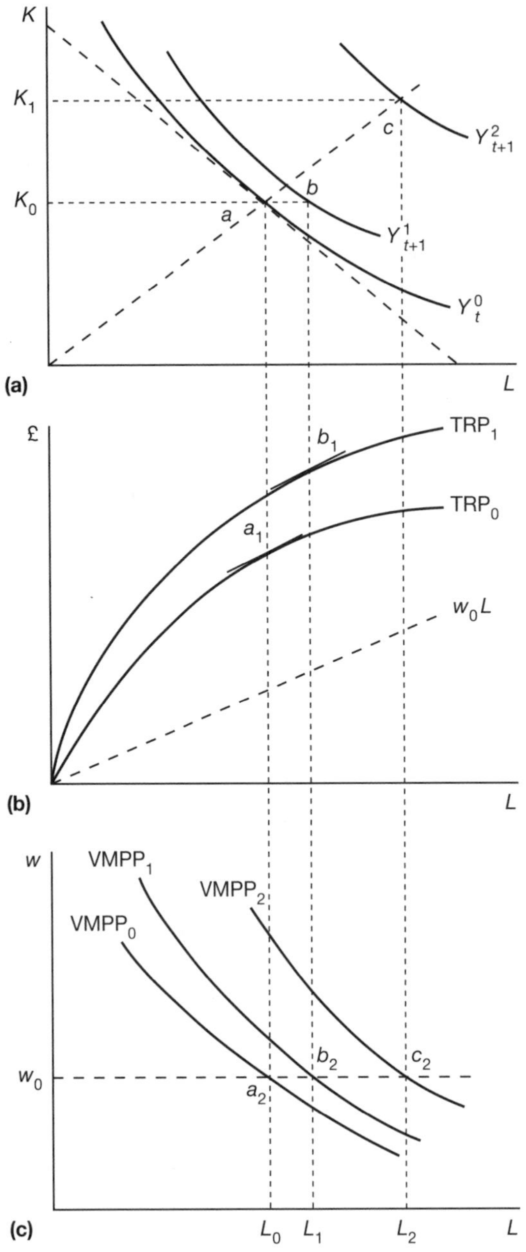

Fig 10.4 Product change and labour demand.

An alternative way of viewing this is to look at the effect of product price changes on the real factor prices of the firm's inputs. From the establishment's point of view, real wage costs can be written *w*/*p* and real rental as *r*/*p*, where *p* is the product price. It is clear that point *b* in Figure 10.4(a) cannot be a point of long-run equilibrium as relative factor prices have not changed. What the long-run equilibrium turns out to be, as always, depends on the goal of the firm, but the lower real price of inputs could allow the output maximizer subject to a cost constraint to move outwards further as movements to higher capital (redressing the capital/labour imbalance) shift the TRP curve outwards and the point of tangency further to the right. Thus, the final equilibrium could be as high as L_2. We later show that the precise outcome also depends upon market structure.

The real world is further complicated by the fact that product innovation generally goes hand in hand with process and organizational change. The new product line may greatly alter the isoquant map. It might, for example, imply a switch from one-off to batch, continuous or mass production methods or vice versa. In addition, it may cause changes in the types of materials and machinery used by the firm. All these things will tend to have important educational and occupational consequences for the workforce the firm wishes to hire. Finally, analogously to process change, the product innovation itself will almost certainly involve other types of labour input, such as qualified scientists and engineers, managerial effort and marketing people.

5 Impact of technological change at the industry level

5.1 Diffusion and labour demand

In considering the impact of technological change on the demand for labour at the firm level, it was possible to adopt a partial equilibrium framework. In essence, the firm operated either under the old technology or under the new. It was assumed that the path by which the firm moved from one state to another was not of prime importance. There are obvious dangers of adopting this assumption even at the firm level (particularly in large, often multi-plant, sometimes multinational, companies): there may be costs associated with moving from the old to the new technology, resulting in prolonged adjustment, with consequent implications for the labour demand curve; there may be considerable uncertainty about the nature of the new technology, which leads to the firm 'experimenting' with it, introducing it a 'bit at a time'.

If these sorts of questions are important for the firm, they are even more crucial at the industry level. The innovation, no matter how radical for the firm, may be relatively minor in the context of the industry, where the rate of imitation (e.g. the diffusion path) may be the more significant phenomenon. The influences on the rate of diffusion therefore will also be influences on the demand for labour. The diffusion process generates labour demands of its own. The spread of microelectronics technologies, for example, gave rise to demands for electronics and software engineers which, in the UK, transcended the downturn in economic activity centred on 1980–1981. The introduction of such technologies, however, had quite profound effects on the demands for certain products (i.e. clockwork watches) and for certain skills such as biotechnologists. A wide variety of factors are known to influence the rate of diffusion, including the proportion of firms that have already adopted the new technology; the profitability of installing the new technology; the size of the investment; the underlying rate of invention (e.g. affecting expectations about the appearance of competitive or complementary technologies), which may slow down the diffusion process until the technology in that area stabilizes.

The resulting diffusion curve (showing, for example, the proportion of potential user firms having adopted the invention over time) is generally sigmoidal (a flattened 's') in shape, with increasing rapid diffusion of the technology at the beginning, but slower and slower rates of adoption towards the end The faster the rate of diffusion, the more radical the implications for labour demand; slow rates may be accommodated by natural wastage (or by lower rates of recruitment), but rapid rates of change may result in the firm incurring abnormally high costs of adjustment.

The operation of the labour market, adjusting through the movement of real wages, will clearly affect the diffusion process. Suppose, for example, that a new labour-saving technology becomes available. Under the pre-innovation factor price regime, it may well be profitable for innovation to take place. Following the innovation, as succeeding firms adopt the invention, greater amounts of labour are freed from the industry, causing a cumulative fall in the real wage. As real wages fall, the incentive to adopt the new technology is itself reduced and the diffusion process slows. Clearly, the opposite is true where particular skills or disciplines are complementary to the new technology. The extent to which the rate of diffusion is affected by labour market factors depends upon the pervasiveness of the technology, the flexibility of wages and the responsiveness of flows through the education and training system.

It should also be noted that the impact of process change on labour demand may be different at the firm and the industry levels. The initial innovators (and perhaps some of the early imitators) may experience increases in demand that more than offset the labour-saving effects of a process change. These increases arise from their ability to lower their prices after the adoption of the new technology, thereby gaining a larger market share. Where gains in market share can be consolidated (e.g. by means of advertising and other barriers), the early adopters may be able to maintain labour demand, even when the diffusion process is well advanced. On the other hand, non-innovators are, come what may, faced by the prospect of reduced demand, because their market share will decline in the face of successful innovation and imitation by competitors if no action is taken. Of course, there are dangers in being amongst the first adopters; after all, innovation and early imitation are often risky, especially before a given standard is accepted for the technology. It is the heterogeneity of firms, including the differing qualifications and degrees of risk aversion amongst managers, which in part explains the extended pattern of the diffusion process. There is a direct analogy with this argument at the national level, discussed below.

5.2 Rate of change in labour demand

Here we report on a model which builds upon the discussion of neutrality and factor-saving biases, outlined in Section 4, from a paper by Stoneman (1987). The model is based on a number of fairly restrictive assumptions: there are a fixed number of identical firms in the industry; all firms introduce the technology at the same time; there are constant returns to scale; the elasticity of demand for the product is a constant; technological change is factor augmenting; there are only two inputs, capital and labour. Under these assumptions, the expression for the rate of change in labour demand, $\mathrm{d}L/L$, is the same for both the industry and for each (identical) firm in the industry,

$$\mathrm{d}L/L = \alpha_K(\sigma - \varepsilon_{\mathrm{p}})(c' + h' - w' - g') + g'(\varepsilon_{\mathrm{p}} - 1) - w'\varepsilon_{\mathrm{p}} \quad (12)$$

where: α_K is the share of capital in output; σ is the elasticity of substitution between capital and labour; ε_{p} is the own-price elasticity of demand for the product; $c' = \mathrm{d}c/c$ is the rate of change in capital prices;

$w' = dw/w$ is the rate of change in wage rate; $g' = dg/g$ is the rate of labour augmentation; $h' = dh/h$ is the rate of capital augmentation. An analogous expression can be found for the rate of change in the demand for capital. The first thing we note is that the rate of change in labour demand depends upon the rate of introduction of the new technology, which is itself a function of the part of the sigmoidal diffusion curve the industry is on. In addition, the result depends on the relative magnitudes of the elasticity of substitution between inputs and the elasticity of product demand – a finding first derived in the absence of technological change (see, for example, the discussion of the Marshallian Rules). Indeed, it is apparent that not only the size but the sign of dL/L changes.

There are several ways in which expression (12) can be explored. It can be simplified in a variety of ways, for example by assuming that $w' = c' = 0$ (e.g. $dw/w = dc/c = 0$). Thus, the expression collapses to

$$dL/L = \alpha_K(\sigma - \varepsilon_p)(h' - g') + g'(\varepsilon_p - 1) \quad (13)$$

and some further progress is made by looking at the neutrality of technical change. In the discussion below, it is assumed that technical change is neutral in an absolute sense (e.g. if $h' > 0$ then $g' = 0$ and vice versa). Hicks neutrality therefore implies that $g' = h' = j'$, and equation (13) further collapses to

$$dL/L = j'(\varepsilon_p - 1) \quad (14)$$

and the sign for the rate of growth in labour demand simply turns on the size of the elasticity of demand for the product. In this case, $dL/L \gtreqless 0$ as $\varepsilon_p \gtreqless 1$. The result indicates that, as might be expected on the basis of earlier findings, higher elasticities of product demand are more favourable to the growth in labour demand. The Solow neutral case has $g' = 0$ and $h' > 0$, with the result that,

$$dL/L = -\alpha_K(\varepsilon_p - \sigma)h' \quad (15)$$

and the sign of the rate of employment growth depends on the relative sizes of the elasticity of substitution and elasticity of product demand, $dL/L \gtreqless 0$ as $\varepsilon_p \lesseqgtr \sigma$. Finally, the Harrod neutral case has $g' > 0$ and $h' = 0$, with the result that,

$$dL/L = g'\,[\alpha_K(\varepsilon_p - \sigma) + (\varepsilon_p - 1)] \quad (16)$$

It is immediately clear that the rate of growth in labour demand will be positive if $\varepsilon_p > 1$ and $\varepsilon_p > \sigma$. The similarity between this and both the Hicks neutral and the Solow neutral case is immediately apparent. As might be expected, the Harrod neutral case is the least favourable to the growth in labour demand. While this may be true, the dual inequality ($\varepsilon_p > 1$ and $\varepsilon_p > \sigma$) is too restrictive, and it is sufficient, from equation (16), to write, $dL/L \gtreqless 0$ if $\varepsilon_p \gtreqless (1 + \alpha_K\sigma)/(1 + \alpha_K)$. It is clear from this expression that the rate of growth in demand for labour can be positive even with Harrod neutral progress. Indeed, this could occur with quite low values of ε_p, if the elasticity of substitution is sufficiently low. As expected from our earlier discussion, if the underlying technology is assumed to be Cobb-Douglas, $\sigma = 1$, then the condition for positive growth in labour demand in both the Solow and Harrod neutral cases can be seen to be the same as in the Hicks case.

5.3 Labour demand and monopoly power

The technological change literature has paid a great deal of attention to the role of market power as an influence on the rate and direction of technological change. Much of this debate is attributed to the seminal work of Schumpeter. While the precise interpretation has differed from author to author, broadly speaking, the issue has been whether larger firms with greater monopoly power are a more significant source of invention and innovation. Neither the theoretical nor the empirical findings have proved conclusive. However, while the earlier empirical findings, on balance, tended to provide support for the Schumpeterian hypothesis, more recent work, particularly based upon panel data sets and including both firm and industry effects, has found little support.

In this section, however, we are more concerned about the impact of market structure on employment opportunities. For simplicity, the comparisons are limited to the cases of perfect competition and pure monopoly. It is fairly easy to demonstrate that the two market structures will generally have different output expansion effects in the face of a cost-reducing technological change. Which is the larger turns on the precise characteristics of the demand curve, although, in general, the output expansion effect under monopoly can be expected to be smaller than under perfect competition.

Figure 10.5 compares the equilibrium under these two market structures both prior to and following a process innovation. In Figure 10.5(a), competitive equilibrium under the old technology takes place at point a_0, where the supply curve of the product, S_0, which is the sum of the marginal cost curves of the individual firms, cuts the market demand curve D. Under monopoly, Figure 10.5(b) indicates that equilibrium occurs at point a_1, where the marginal cost curve MC_0 cuts the marginal revenue curve MR, associated with point c_1 on the demand curve. Given the same demand curves and cost structures ($S_0 \equiv MC_0$) under the two market regimes, the restrictive nature of monopoly is already obvious, insofar as $YC_0 > YM_0$. Thus, as we demonstrated earlier, the traditional monopoly restriction on output implies, other things being equal, a lower level of labour demand.

Following a cost-reducing process innovation, the supply curve under competition shifts outward from S_0 to S_1, with a change in equilibrium from point a_0 to point b_0. The analogous change in costs results in a downward shift in the marginal cost curves of the monopolist from MC_0 to MC_1, changing the point of intersection of marginal cost and revenue to point b_1, associated with point d_1 on the demand curve. It is clear from Figures 10.5 (a) and 10.5 (b) that, for the particular curves chosen, the technological change produces a smaller reduction in price (both absolute and percentage) under monopoly than perfect competition. For the curves illustrated, the absolute increase in output is smaller under monopoly than competition (although the percentage change is more difficult to judge, because of the smaller output produced under monopoly). It can be seen from this exercise that the degree of monopoly power has an important role to play in determining the size of the output expansion effect, with its associated implications for the change in demand for labour, and the price reduction it will pass on to its customers.

6 Impact of technological change at the economy level

6.1 Circular flow and labour demands

At the economy level, technological change has the potential to produce not only overall changes in the demand for labour, but also major structural changes. It should be borne in mind that occupations and regions are linked with particular industries, with the result that shifts in the balance between industrial sectors have direct consequences for the distribution of labour demands by occupation and by region. The movement of goods from firm to firm and firm to household will ensure that the effects of a given technological change are, in the final analysis, transmitted to the rest of the economy. There is no guarantee what the final outcome may be, for a number of reasons.

First consider the case of a product innovation. A product innovation by one firm will, in many instances, appear as a process innovation by another

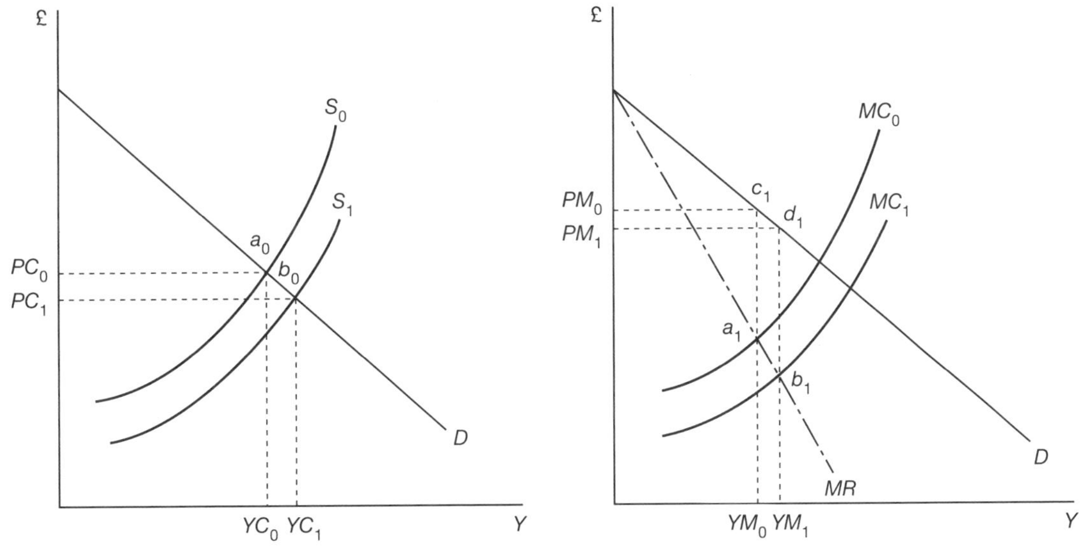

(a) Competition **(b)** Monopoly

Fig 10.5 Market structure, technological change and labour demand.

firm. In this case the output expansion effect of the product innovation in the producing firm or sector may not be replicated by a similar change in the user firm or sector. If it is assumed, for the sake of argument, that the innovation appears as a Solow neutral change in the using sector (with no factor price changes), then the outcome in that sector depends solely on the relative sizes of the price elasticity and the elasticity of substitution, according to inequality (15). Any further transmission from the initial user to other industries will be in the form of price reductions. This is discussed further below.

A process innovation which strongly reduces labour demand in one sector may or may not be labour demand reducing in the economy as a whole. In this instance, the initial process change is being passed on to other sectors in the form of lower prices of its output. Returning to equation (12), it is possible to assume that it will appear as a reduction in the price of the capital goods it purchases, $c' < 0$, and, in the simplest case, it is assumed that the factor augmentation terms and the wage change term are zero. Thus, the original equation collapses to

$$\mathrm{d}L/L = \alpha_K(\sigma - \varepsilon_{\mathrm{p}})c' \tag{17}$$

which is equivalent to the Solow neutral change condition for a growth in labour demand, as $\mathrm{d}L/L \gtreqless 0$ if $\varepsilon_{\mathrm{p}} \gtreqless \sigma$. What has happened is that the user firm now finds its capital input is cheaper and this causes a substitution away from labour, the extent of which is determined by σ. On the other hand, lower input prices reduce its costs, lower its own product price and raise the demand for its product, the extent of which is determined by ε_{p}. The net effect turns on the relative magnitudes of σ and ε_{p}. Of course, the price elasticities and elasticities of substitution differ between sectors, and so the outcomes between the original innovating sector and the user sectors could be in the same or in the opposite direction.

The sizes of the ripples caused by a technological change in one sector that pass through the economy appear likely also to depend on the degree of monopoly power of each of the sectors. The discussion of Section 5.3 indicated that the precise result of monopoly power on the transmission of the benefits of a process innovation to its customers would depend on the mix of monopoly and competition in the economy. In general, however, the suspicion remains that a monopoly will tend to take a part of the cost reduction for itself, in the form of higher profits. In terms of the argument developed in the preceding paragraph, c' will generally be expected to be smaller in absolute terms for the industry buying from a monopoly than from a perfectly competitive sector. However, it should be noted that Schumpeterian theory suggests that the flow of inventions might be greater from the monopoly than from an equivalent competitive industry.

Finally, the discussion touches on one further distinction between the micro and macro outcomes. Labour-saving change within a given industry may produce a substitution towards the output of that industry and away from other industries' products. If, even after the labour-saving innovation, the industry retains a higher than average labour to capital ratio, the effect may nevertheless be to increase the overall labour/capital ratio in the economy. If, on the other hand, the innovating industry is itself relatively capital intensive *vis-à-vis* the remainder of the economy, then the effect of the labour-saving technological change may just be the forerunner of an overall increase in the capital/labour ratio in the economy.

6.2 Verdoorn's Law

The picture painted to date is one of different sectoral reactions to technological change. A situation of rapid productivity growth and stagnant demand (e.g. caused by low own-price and income elasticities or the general economic situation) seems to be a likely breeding ground for large-scale job losses and redundancies. To some extent this has been the situation in the UK manufacturing sector over the 20 or 30 years from the mid-1960s; while output in manufacturing has increased, the sector's employment has declined secularly. In the early 1950s, manufacturing provided over 50 per cent of jobs in the UK, while, by the beginning of the 1990s, this had shrunk to less than 25 per cent. A similar phenomenon now seems set to occur in a number of services, including banking and finance.

Nevertheless, there is some evidence that the industries with faster productivity growth also tend to be those with the higher rates of output growth, a relationship known as Verdoorn's Law. Its existence mitigates some of the worst effects of productivity growth on labour demand. The relationship has generally been estimated in the form

$$\frac{1}{(Y/L)} \cdot \frac{\mathrm{d}(Y/L)}{dt} = f\left(\frac{1}{Y} \cdot \frac{\mathrm{d}Y}{dt}\right) \tag{18}$$

where: Y denotes the level of output; L is the labour input; and t is time. In fact, the principal direction of causality has been hotly disputed and the relationship has been widely criticized as an *ad hoc* representation of the production relationship over time. A number of explanations for the relationship have been put forward: growth in demand may open up ranges of increasing returns in the production function that the firms in the industry would take much longer to reach via merger activity in a static demand situation; fast growth means an expansion of the capital stock and firms are able to change their portfolio of vintages of capital by buying the most up to date plant and machinery; periods of recession may be associated with labour hoarding and an increase in the rate of growth may result in a more intensive use of labour, giving rise to short-term productivity increases; faster growth industries, through higher productivity, may be able to support greater levels of R&D, resulting in subsequent productivity increases; learning effects may be more important in faster- than in slower-growing industries; productivity growth, when passed on to the consumer, may result in a more rapid growth in demand and output.

If empirical investigations had revealed the opposite result (e.g. that high labour productivity growth industries are those with slow output growth), then the disruptive influence of technological change on the labour market would have been much more important. What the empirical evidence does show, however, is that the Verdoorn relationship has been changing over time. This in itself suggests that the Verdoorn relationship is an imperfect representation of a more complex link between production and labour productivity.

6.3 Global distribution of labour demands

Labour demand in the domestic economy depends crucially on relative productivity growth *vis-à-vis* the rest of the world. If foreign companies achieve faster productivity growth or greater improvements in product quality, then domestic producers will find themselves facing increased import penetration and lower export performance. In this case, productivity growth simply does not lead to an equivalent growth in demand, because foreign competitors are doing better. There is a fairly close analogy between the consequences of firm innovation for labour demand and that of national innovative performance: each country can be viewed as a single producing unit within a whole set of other producers (e.g. the other countries in the world economy). It is possible for the fastest innovating country, as well as perhaps the early imitators, to experience quite different employment consequences to the world as a whole. Even if the innovations occurring within a country are labour saving, the expansion in demand that comes from being at the forefront of change may well offset these adverse effects. The principle of demand expansion offsetting the inherent labour-saving bias of technological change is just as appropriate at the national level as it is at the firm level. It has been suggested that a three-fold taxonomy of countries can be adopted: (i) the principal inventing and innovating nations, creating and using the latest technology; (ii) the rapid imitators, which, while not at the forefront of invention, keep abreast of the latest technologies; (iii) a group of countries which not only fail to invent and innovate, but are slow to imitate. Certainly, the last group is likely to feel the major burden of labour-saving changes as they are concurrently faced by stagnant demand caused by declining shares of world markets, either through lower job opportunities or declining wages.

7 Conclusions

In this chapter we have examined an additional range of extensions of the basic theory of labour demand to allow for the further effects of technological change. We have made a key distinction between the role of labour in the production of new technologies and the impact that technological change has on labour demand. In addition, we have demonstrated that even inherently relatively labour-saving innovations may not reduce employment opportunities. At the micro level, the result turns crucially on the elasticity of substitution between factors and, particularly, the own-price elasticity of demand. At the macro level, the picture is complicated by the interindustry flows. However, international trade patterns suggest that labour-saving innovation can lead to higher exports and lower imports which can lead to higher employment in the domestic economy, especially if the home country is an early rather than late innovator.

References

Stoneman, P.A. (1987). 'An Analytical Framework for an Economic Perspective on the Impact of New Information Technologies'. In P. Stoneman (ed.) *Information Technology and Economic Perspectives*. Paris: OECD, pp. 70–93.

Tobin, J. (1969). 'A General Equilibrium Approach to Monetary Theory'. *Journal of Money, Credit and Banking*. 1, February, 15–29.

CHAPTER 11 Demand for labour services Empirical evidence

1 Introduction

This chapter provides an examination of the empirical evidence relating to the demand for labour. It explores a variety of factor demand relationships which do not explicitly specify or estimate a supply function. The chapter highlights some of the more practical problems of data and specification. In doing so, it provides an overview of the way in which the empirical literature has evolved, both in terms of less restrictive functional forms representing the underlying model of production and the increasingly sophisticated treatment of the dynamics, given that there are significant costs of adjustment for most, if not all, inputs. The reader is referred to two excellent reviews of empirical labour demand: Berndt (1991, Chapter 9), which also provides information about many of the statistical methods and tests; and Hammermesh (1993, especially Chapter 3) which gives a rigorous coverage of the resulting parameter estimates.

Section 2 touches upon issues of measurement, aggregation and the key parameters to be estimated. Section 3 investigates the use of non-stochastic techniques for isolating the labour demand curve, linking the approach with the marginal productivity debate. This section also looks at the use of special labour market conditions, such as binding minimum wages legislation, when observed employment lies along the demand for labour curve. Section 4 outlines a variety of single-equation models, 5 discusses the incorporation of adjustment costs and lagged adjustment processes into the empirical specifications and 6 examines inter-related factor demand models. Section 7 reports on the development of more flexible functional firms and Section 8 outlines a number of key findings. Finally, Section 9 draws the main conclusions of this chapter.

2 Measurement, data and specification

2.1 Alternative approaches

There are essentially two main approaches to the estimation of the parameters of the production and factor demand functions. The first is via the production function and the second begins with the dual cost function. For a number of functions, such as the Cobb–Douglas and CES, it is possible to move fairly easily between the production and cost formulations; in other cases, it is more difficult if not impossible. There is an important distinction between the assumptions that underlie the two approaches: in the production function approach, output is endogenous and input quantities are exogenous; in the cost function, input prices and output are exogenous, while production costs and input quantities are endogenous. Thus, one approach can be more appropriate than the other depending on the nature of the firm or industry in question.

There is a vast literature on the direct estimation of production functions, which offers valuable insights about number of the key parameters of the factor demand equations (see Heathfield and Wibe, 1987, Chapter 9; Hammermesh, 1993). The labour economics literature, however, has focused upon the first-order conditions resulting from the firm optimization problem. In the case of the production function approach the solution of the first-order conditions normally results in a set of (reduced form) input demand equations in terms of factor prices and (where it is not endogenized) output. In the case of the cost function approach, the derivation of the factor demand function is made relatively straightforward by the application of 'Shephard's

Lemma'. In essence, this states that the optimal (i.e. cost-minimizing) input demand is obtained simply by differentiating the total cost function with respect to the price of the factor in question. Note, however, that both the production and cost approaches result in a set of factor demand equations. In general, it may not be possible to estimate one of the equations (i.e. labour demand) independently of the others.

Finally, we add to this list of alternative approaches the direct estimation of the labour demand function by means of natural experiments. By this we mean that there may be particular circumstances when, for some reason, observed wage–employment combinations are believed to lie along the demand curve. This type of approach is less common, partly because of the dearth of natural experiments when we can be sure that the outcome is pinned to the demand curve and partly as consequence of a preference amongst economists for the application of sophisticated econometric techniques.

2.2 Key parameters

In essence, the aim is to produce an empirical specification which accurately describes the firm's demand for labour at different wage rates, holding other factors constant. From such models it is possible to derive a number of key production parameters which throw light on the ease of substitution between labour and other factors (especially capital), the sensitivity of labour demand to changes in the wage, the ease of substitution between different types of labour (occupations, skill levels, etc.). A priori the demand curves are expected to be downward sloping and the sensitivity of labour demand to a change in the wage rate is an empirical question. Thus, for homogeneous labour, economists are particularly interested in isolating the constant output demand elasticity, η_{EE}. Following Hammermesh (1993, p. 61), this can be written

$$\eta_{EE} = -(1 - S)\,\sigma < 0 \tag{1}$$

where there are constant returns to scale. S is the share of labour in either total cost or total revenue (depending on the approach adopted) and, in the two-input case, σ is the elasticity of substitution between capital and labour. Thus, the constant-output elasticity of labour demand is closely related to the elasticity of substitution for labour in the production function, but they are not identical concepts. Nevertheless, production function studies which yield estimates of σ throw some light on η_{EE}. In general, the constant-output elasticity of labour demand is greater (i.e. more negative) the higher the elasticity of substitution between labour and other factors of production. By implication the cross-elasticity of demand for labour associated with a change in the price of capital can be written as

$$\eta_{EK} = (1 - S)\;\sigma > 0 \tag{2}$$

Thus, the cross elasticity is larger the smaller is the share of labour in output.

A number of empirical studies, however, estimate the total demand elasticity, η'_{EE}, which does not hold output constant,

$$\eta'_{EE} = -(1 - S)\;\sigma - S\eta_{\text{p}} \tag{3}$$

where η_{p} is the own-price elasticity of product demand. In general, a given increase in wage has a larger negative effect on labour demand if we do not hold output constant, because, in addition to the substitution away from labour, the higher wage raises firm costs and prices, and reduces the demand for its product, Marshall's 'second law'. Equation (3) therefore divides the overall elasticity of labour demand into its two key components: the substitution, $(1–S)\sigma$, and scale, $S\eta_{\text{p}}$, effects. A similar revision is now needed for the overall cross-elasticity of

$$\eta'_{EK} = (1 - S)(\sigma - \eta_{\text{p}}) \tag{4}$$

demand; again see the Marshallian Rules discussed above.

2.3 Measurement issues

Early studies tended to be based on more restrictive functional forms, estimated using aggregate time series information, but, over time, the literature has moved to more flexible production functions to underpin the factor demand equations. Less restrictive functions tend to be extremely 'data demanding', but their development and adoption has been aided by the growing availability of large micro cross-sectional and panel data sets. Today the tendency is to estimate the most general functions possible in the light of data constraints and then to test various restrictions which imply simpler production technologies.

A priori there is no reason to think that time series or cross-sectional data should yield superior estimates of labour demand functions. In general, time series data are more suited to the exploration of short-run phenomena, estimating the dynamics of employment (i.e. adjustment processes); cross-sectional data are thought to reflect longer-term relationships. Panel data sets (pooled cross-section time series data) potentially offer the best of both worlds, and they have been increasingly used in empirical work.

What is clear, however, is that the estimates of key parameters vary with the type of data used (Berndt, 1991, pp. 454–457). In particular, the cross-sectional data based upon labour demand equations suggest $\sigma \simeq 1$. In the case of time series data, however, estimates of the elasticity tend to be smaller. If, as we have suggested, time series reflect short-run and cross-sectional reflect long-run estimates, part of the answer appears to lie in adopting appropriate lagged adjustment mechanisms in time series data. While early evidence rejected this as the source of the difference, in retrospect, adjustment costs appear to be an important part of the empirical story. Further support for this can be found in the cross-sectional findings where the value of the elasticity tends to be smaller in the capital than the labour equations (capital stock taking longer to adjust than the labour input).

We might anticipate that micro data must be superior to aggregate information, but, in practice, the realized benefit depends upon how the data are used. The level of aggregation is an important issue because factor demand functions are based on an assumption of a common underlying cost or production function; if not, then the parameters being estimated will vary across the units or over time. The aggregation problem is potentially just as great whether units are 'added together' to form one observation in a time series or they are used to estimate a single empirical specification in which the parameters are assumed the same across units. A given establishment may use a variety of technologies and it is an interesting question whether these can be aggregated together. The problem is further compounded in the case of multi-establishment firms. Given the way in which establishment, firm or government statistics are constructed, the aggregates constructed are often inconsistent with the production function that underlies the empirical specification. Examples include the use of measures of total employment (where individuals are heterogeneous and differently productive) or net output constructed additively (i.e. subtracting the values of raw materials and intermediate goods from gross output) when the underlying production function is not additive and separable. Related issues concern the allocation of firms to industries or skills to occupational categories in official statistics. While such allocations should, in principle, be made on the basis of cross-price elasticities, in practice, these are largely unknown, and other considerations influence the final allocations. Indeed, this is a 'Catch 22' type of problem, because, if such elasticities are known, there is little need to estimate production or factor demand functions.

There are other, perhaps even more basic, problems of measuring variables which are treated with varying degrees of rigour. In general, the literature uses an average wage, which is not, in general, the same as the user cost of labour given that not all remuneration is in the form of wages (a company car, private health insurance, etc.) and, in addition, the employer generally pays other 'on-costs', including payroll taxes (in the UK these would include National Insurance Contributions). The observed wage may be affected by the amount of time spent on training during the work period (see Chapter 16 below). Average wages may, anyway, not be the most appropriate measure; the marginal wage may be more relevant. In the case of hours of work, for example, the marginal wage may reflect the need to pay an overtime premium or a shift component. Again, for some groups the construction of an hourly wage from monthly or hourly data may lead to a correlation between the 'price' variable and the error term in much the same way that we discussed in the case of labour supply. Even more acute problems arise in measurements of the volume and the corresponding 'price' of capital services. There is some evidence, for example, that the error in measuring the price of capital tends to bias estimates of the constant-output demand elasticity towards zero.

3 Non-stochastic estimates of demand

This section considers a number of attempts to produce direct estimates of the demand for labour curve. The first involves the use of questionnaires which ask employers about the various influences on their demand for labour. The second also uses a questionnaire approach, but, this time, focuses on the employers' planned levels of demand under various economic scenarios. Finally, there are studies which rely on the existence of special labour market conditions when it can be argued that observed employment lies along the demand rather than the supply curve (e.g. 'natural experiments', such as the existence of binding minimum wages legislation).

3.1 Marginalist debate

Under fairly reasonable assumptions, the marginal productivity doctrine yields a downward-sloping demand curve (e.g. a negative relationship between the wage and the quantity of labour services demanded). Early attempts to test the validity of the marginal productivity doctrine and the existence of a negatively sloped demand curve for labour using a questionnaire approach led to an extremely heated debate (Lester, 1946; Machlup, 1946). Lester set the ball rolling by trying to glean information about the main influences on the demand for labour using a questionnaire sent to employers drawn from a sample of manufacturing firms in the USA. He argued that the replies were largely inconsistent with the marginalist view of the world. It appeared that, in reaching their employment decisions, employers appeared to be much more concerned about the state of product demand than about the level or changes in real wage rates.

Prior to the time of the questionnaire, the southern USA experienced relatively low wage rates *vis-à-vis* the north, although the differential had been narrowing. According to Lester, firms operating plants in both regions indicated that relatively low wages in the south had not induced more labour-intensive production in that region. In addition, the firms' reactions to the relative rise in the wage in the south appeared to emphasize the need to increase sales efforts (rather than to lower their output levels, alter price or to change product quality) and increase all-round technical efficiency (rather than just to introduce labour-saving machinery). Lester argued these responses did not support the marginalist school. He proposed that, in many concerns, it is either infeasible or too expensive to adjust employment in response to changes in wages in the way suggested by the marginalist approach.

Employers decide the demand for labour and, hence, their reactions to any particular economic change are important. Nevertheless, the Lester evidence can be criticized on at least two grounds. First, Machlup was highly critical of the way in which the questions used by Lester had been formulated and argued that a questionnaire approach was unlikely to be a reliable means of testing the marginalist view. Machlup also attacked Lester's interpretation of the answers. He suggested that the importance placed on product demand (particularly as product demand tends to fluctuate more sharply than the wage level), on the willingness to introduce labour-saving machinery in the face of rising wages and to vary both price and quality (hence, indirectly, leading to lower employment), were all consistent with the marginalist theory. Second, while employers may wish to react in a certain way, economic circumstances may force them to respond differently: where they do not minimize costs or maximize profits, competition may ensure that only the most efficient survive.

Lester, however, gave some empirical evidence that, at one stage, was thought to be difficult to explain within the confines of the marginal productivity doctrine. He showed that there had been a significant rise in the southern wage *vis-à-vis* the north in the footwear and clothing industries between 1937 and 1941, but employment in the south had increased faster than in the north. In addition, employment had increased most quickly in those firms where wages rose most. At the time it was thought that Machlup's criticism did not answer this question. In retrospect, however, the observed trends could still be a direct reflection of market forces. Whether employers believed that the south's relatively low wage influenced them to use more labour-intensive techniques or not, the observed trends were consistent with an outward shift in the demand curve for labour in the south relative to the north as plants were relocated or plants in the south expanded, causing wage rates in the south to catch up with the north. Other explanations might link wages with productivity in a variety of ways (see Part VI of the book).

3.2 Planned labour demands

Attempts have been made to establish points on individual demand relationships by asking employers about their (future) demands for labour under various, alternative scenarios. The rationale for this work is that, if the demand relationship can be isolated, it can then be used in comparison with the analogous supply position in order to establish whether shortages or surpluses are likely to occur. Questions of this type have been asked by a number of UK Government Committees, including those concerned with the three-year medium-term forecasts of scientific personnel. Employers were asked how many people with scientific and engineering qualifications they 'would aim to employ in three years time, assuming ... that the required number of recruits will be available?' The question is phrased in a way to suggest that the firms will be faced by a perfectly elastic supply curve of labour, illustrated by the line S_0S_0 in Figure 11.1. In response, firms indicate that (in total) they might expect to be at point *a*, on the market demand curve, *D*. The outcome is compared with exogenously produced evidence about the supply of labour (based on knowledge of existing stocks of qualified personnel, adjusted for flows through the education system, deaths, retirements, etc.), represented by the perfectly inelastic supply curve S_1S_1 in Figure 11.1. The result is an expected shortage of *ab*.

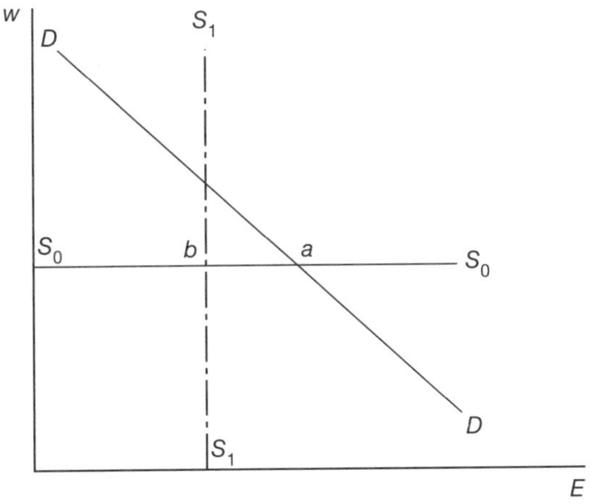

Fig 11.1 Planned labour demands.

A similar sort of approach has been applied with respect to the employment consequences of technological change, including a series of surveys by the Policy Studies Institute in the 1980s (e.g. Northcott and Rogers, 1984; Northcott and Walling, 1988). Questions about employment plans appeared alongside those about the introduction of new product and process technologies. Such surveys, in part, attempt to highlight potential shortages of key skills (e.g. electrical and electronic engineers, computer specialists, etc.), as well as examining the general implications of expected technological change for the overall level of firm employment and skill structure.

The early studies using this approach were open to considerable criticism, given that nothing was known about the reasons underlying the firms' decisions and how they might be modified as conditions changed. The original studies provided no guidelines to firms about the future paths of relative salaries or economic activity. As a consequence, firms made inconsistent assumptions about the growth of their industry and future market shares. Such techniques have improved with experience and use. In particular, forecasts are likely to become more accurate where firms are provided with alternative scenarios about growth in demand, technological change, etc. Further improvements can be achieved using Delphi-style techniques, feeding information back to employers to allow them to modify their decisions in the light of other employers' responses.

3.3 Special labour market conditions and the demand curve

The existence of special labour market circumstances may enable the demand for labour function to be isolated. Imagine a market in which legislation brings about a binding minimum wage, producing a perfectly elastic supply of labour curve, at least in the relevant employment range. In Figure 11.2, *D* represents the market demand curve and S_0S_0 is the market supply curve prior to government intervention. Interaction of supply and demand produces a

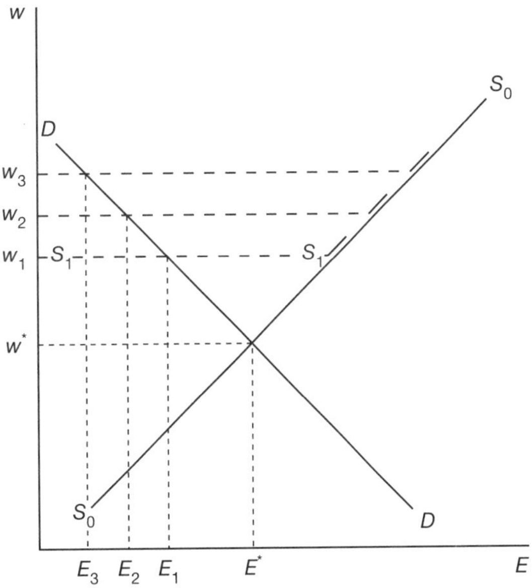

Fig 11.2 Employment and labour demand under minimum wages legislation.

free market equilibrium at wage rate w^* and employment E^*. However, the government intervenes and introduces a minimum wage, w_1, making the effective supply curve, S_1S_1, perfectly elastic in the relevant range, at a new wage rate, w_1. If the government now changes this minimum wage at regular intervals (e.g. from w_1 to w_2 to w_3), while the demand curve remains stable, the observed combinations of wage rate and employment lie along the demand curve for labour. This simple supply and demand model illustrates the original result of Stigler (1946) that the imposition of a wage above the market equilibrium level ($w_1>w^*$) reduces employment ($E_1<E^*$). The validity of the argument and the effects of minimum wages on the number and nature of jobs available in the economy are important in the light of the EU's positive attitudes towards this policy, and the UK Labour Party's intention to reintroduce such a policy in the UK.

The Reynolds and Gregory (1965) study of Puerto Rico included 37 industries between 1949 and 1954, and 50 industries between 1954 and 1958. They argued that conditions in Puerto Rico at this time came very close to those outlined in Figure 11.2: the government had introduced minimum wage legislation; minimum wage rates were changed frequently; separate minimum wages were set for each industry and appeared to be operative in the majority of industries (i.e. the minimum exceeded the 'free market' wage). Thus, the 'covered' sector (i.e. the proportion of economic activity for which there was a binding minimum) in Puerto Rico was extensive; unemployment was high, consistent with a perfectly elastic supply of labour curve. Thus the wage–employment combinations observed in Puerto Rico at that time appeared to represent points on the various demand for labour curves.

Unfortunately, this very neat result is complicated by the fact that demand conditions did not remain unchanged. Figure 11.3 shows that, if the shifts in demand are not taken into account, the observed wage–employment combinations are not an accurate representation of the demand curve. The D curve is formed from the intersection of D_t and S_t, at point a, and the intersection of D_{t+1} and S_{t+1} at point b. The observed wage–employment curve appears more inelastic than the 'true' demand curve. Indeed, it is possible, for sufficiently large shifts in the demand curve, that the observed D curve could have a perverse, positive slope. In order to isolate a 'pure' demand relationship, the authors corrected the observed employment levels for changes in demand conditions in each industry group. The method is illustrated in Figure 11.4, where, in this instance, D_1 is used to denote the demand curve at time 1 and D_2 the analogous curve at time 2. As the minimum wage is altered from w_1 to w_2, the observed equilibrium changes from c to d, associated with a change in employment from E_1^b to E_2^a (note that the output expansion effect actually makes employment rise in this example).

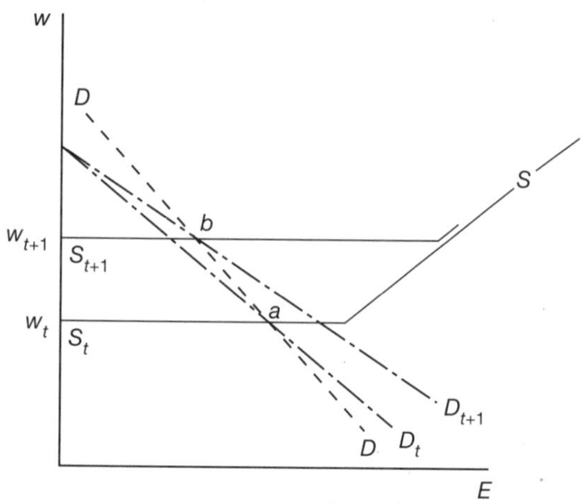

Fig 11.3 Impact of changes in demand conditions.

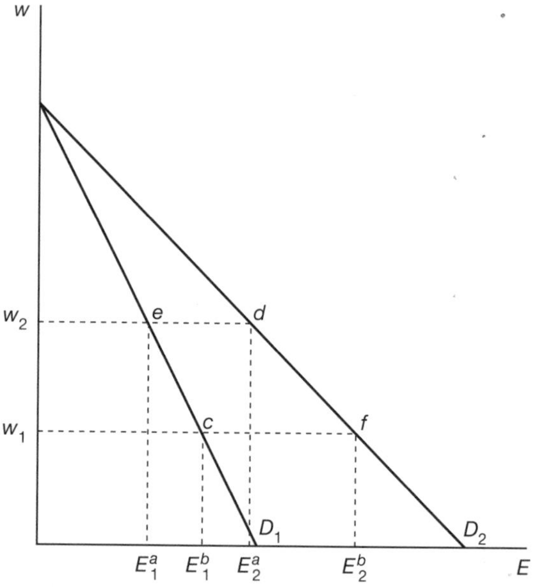

Fig 11.4 Adjusting for changes in demand conditions.

By adjusting E_2^a downwards in accord with the changed demand conditions, point *d* is recalculated as point *e*, along D_1. Alternatively, by adjusting E_1^b upwards, in accordance with the changed demand conditions, point *c* is recalculated as point *f*, along D_2. In order to derive a simple solution, the authors assumed that each industry was characterized by a linear homogeneous production function (exhibiting constant returns to scale everywhere) and changes in demand conditions were independent of the minimum wage set for each industry. The adjustment to the labour input was carried out by multiplying E_1^b by the ratio of output in year 2 to year 1 (e.g. to obtain E_2^b) or by dividing E_2^a by the same ratio of outputs (e.g. to obtain E_1^a). The results of this exercise indicated that a 1 per cent rise in the wage rate in Puerto Rico, on average, produced a slightly greater than 1 per cent fall in the demand for labour, consistent with a downward-sloping demand curve for labour.

While we have used the special conditions invoked by minimum wages to explore a non-parametric method of isolating the demand curve, it seems appropriate at this point to mention the more general (mainly econometric results) relating to the impact of minimum wages on employment. The early econometric models of this relationship, which are rather *ad hoc* in nature, focus on a relatively small number of disadvantaged economic groups, such as teenagers (see Hammermesh, 1993, pp. 186–187). The US results tend to point to fairly low employment elasticities with respect to the minimum wage, of the order –0.1 and –0.3, and estimates for the UK, Canada and Puerto Rico are generally of the same order of magnitude (Hammermesh, 1993, Table 5.3). One set of higher estimates for Puerto Rico appear to reflect the relatively high minima and the magnitude of 'covered' *vis-à-vis* 'uncovered' employment. Some studies have even suggested that minimum wages can increase the employment of adult workers, a line of argument that can be traced back at least to the work of Hammermesh (1982). In part this may be a reflection of differences between, for example, teenage and adult markets. A study of the effects of French minimum wages suggests a similar or somewhat higher absolute value of the elasticity for young people to that reported above, but a negligible value of the elasticity for adults (Bazen and Martin, 1991). In addition there may be positive multiplier effects of higher minimum wages, especially if the absolute value of the elasticity of demand for labour is relatively small.

4 Single-equation models

4.1 Employment and person hours

This class of models has been used to explain one or more of the following: the number of workers, *E*, hours of work per person, *H*, and the number of person hours, *EH*. The early work in this area chose to explain either *E* or *EH*; only later were the two dimensions of labour services treated on a more equal footing. Whether an input is considered to be exogenous or endogenous often depends on the length of time it takes to vary. These models are often characterized by tiers of decision making: explanations of the factors most rapidly adjusted may assume other inputs which are slower to adjust as exogenously given, for example hours and inventories are jointly determined, but other factors (including capital and employment) are exogenously given. There is a certain asymmetry here which is absent from the inter-related factor demand systems, which tend to treat all of the factors of production as jointly determined.

4.2 Models of labour hoarding

One approach focuses on the existence of excess labour at various points in the business cycle. It assumes labour hoarding to be caused by the costs of adjusting the labour input to its desired level. Such costs prevent the firm from attaining its technically efficient output (e.g. it is not on its production function) except at peaks during the business cycle, when labour is assumed to be fully utilized. Adoption of a fixed-coefficient production function bypasses the problem of substitution of capital for labour services in the short run. In the longer term, substitution is made implicit in the time path of the technical output–labour relationship. The assumption that the peak of any cycle is on the production function allows

$$b^* = Y^*/(E^*H^*) \tag{5}$$

to be calculated for each peak, denoted *. Thus, the value of *b* can be isolated for succeeding peaks in output per person hour and a time series of linearly interpolated peak-to-peak estimates of b_t can be calculated. The technically minimum employment in each period, E_t^* can now be isolated,

$$E_t^* = (1/b_t)(Y_t/H_t^*) \quad (6)$$

H_t^* is approximated by normal hours (where wage costs per hour are assumed to be minimized), or trend hours to allow for the existence of permanent overtime working. E_t^* can be defined as the number of employees that would be required to produce that level of output if they are working to their full capacity at normal (or trend) hours of work.

The computed value of E_t^* can then be substituted into an employment function, which includes a variable representing expected output. Fair (1969) estimates a model of this type for each of 17 US manufacturing industries. Overall, the model appears to provide a reasonably good explanation of employment behaviour, although its performance is better for manual than non-manual workers. While the author claimed that the model is statistically superior to its single-equation counterparts, the alternative specifications used in the comparison did not include the expectational hypothesis incorporated in the 'preferred' model. A similar approach adopts a production relationship consistent with the cubic cost curves of microeconomic theory (see, for example, Hazledine, 1978). Using these values as the desired input levels: $E_t < E_t^*$ represents undermanning; $E_t = E_t^*$ represents optimal manning; $E_t > E_t^*$ represents overmanning. Costs of deviating from the optimal levels of employment and output can then be expressed as a quadratic penalty function,

$$(Y_t/H_tE_t) = a - b(E_t - E_t^*)^2 \quad (7)$$

In a series of papers, Hazledine estimates a number of alternative specifications based upon equation (7) for UK, Canadian and New Zealand industries. The results broadly support the hypothesis of a 'U'-shaped productivity function, consistent with the cubic cost function of microeconomic theory which generally performed better than an equivalent Ball and St Cyr (1966) model.

4.3 Models based upon first-order conditions

In much of the early work, the first stage of deriving the specification of the employment relationship required the inversion of the underlying production function. In empirical work, the technology of production was often drawn from the CES class of functions but more recently from translog functions. Inversion of the production function yields

$$E_t = \mathbf{j}(Y_t, K_t, Z_t) \quad (8)$$

where Z is a vector representing the input of other factor services. By adopting a cost-minimizing or profit-maximizing goal, the technically efficient input combinations are restricted to those which are economically optimal,

$$E_t^* = \mathbf{k}(Y_t^*, K_t^*, Z_t^*, R_t) \quad (9)$$

where * denotes planned or desired values of the associated variables. The variables with a shorter decision time than employment are replaced by relative factor price terms, R; those with longer decision times may appear as exogenously given variables (e.g. K and Z). The particular variables which enter equation (9) vary from study to study, depending on the assumptions adopted. Desired values of the independent variables, where they appear in the estimated function, are often represented by their actual values. In the case of the exogenously given output term, some experimentation has occurred with alternative measures, including: (i) both current and lagged output; (ii) actual values of future output; (iii) sales, rather than output; (iv) orders and deliveries. A necessary condition for profit maximization where no market imperfections exist is that,

$$\frac{\partial Y}{\partial E} = \frac{w}{p} \quad (10)$$

where w and p denote the competitive wage rate and product price respectively and Y is the optimal scale of output. Equation (10) indicates that differentiating partially with respect to E and setting the result equal to the real wage, the desired level of employment, E^*, can be written as

$$E_t^* = \mathbf{m}((w/p)_t, Y_t^*, t) \quad (11)$$

or the equivalent specification,

$$E_t^* = \mathbf{n}((w/r)_t, K_t^*, t) \quad (12)$$

where: r denotes the per unit rental cost of capital; and t is a time trend picking up the effects of technological change.

In the seminal paper by Ball and St Cyr (1966), only the costs of deviating from the optimal combination of inputs are made explicit, and this is achieved by means of a total cost function,

$$C_t = wEH_t + F_t \quad (13)$$

where: F denotes the fixed costs of production; and C is the total cost. The wage rate is not constant, but varies with the number of hours worked, according to a quadratic relationship,

$$w = \mathbf{w}(H) = a - bH + cH^2 \quad (14)$$

As we noted in an earlier chapter, this brings the choice between employees and hours more clearly into focus: whenever employment is not at its optimal level, hours act as a buffer, but this has an associated cost, as the average wage rate exceeds its minimum value, w_0. Thus, there is an incentive for firms to move to the desired employment level. However, there are costs of adjusting employment and, although these are not treated explicitly in the model, they imply $E \rightarrow E^*$ gradually over time and are therefore accounted for by means of the lagged adjustment of employment (see Section 5 below). The production function is defined as

$$Y_t = Ae^{gt}K_t^{\alpha}(EH)_t^{\beta} \quad (15)$$

although, in the original work, the authors used a time trend to summarize both changes in capital, K, and technological change, t. Substituting w from equation (14) into (13) and, in the resulting function, further substituting H_t from (15), results in a revised version of the total cost function. Differentiating total costs with respect to E and setting the result equal to zero, for a minimum, yields the cost-minimizing level of employment,

$$E_t^* = Be^{-gt/\beta} K_t^{*-\alpha/\beta} Y_t^{*1/\beta} \quad (16)$$

where $B = (2c/b)A^{-1/\beta}$.

4.4 Hours of work and the structure of labour costs

The work of Whybrew (1968) was amongst the first to highlight the long hours of overtime being worked in the UK and attempted to attribute this mainly to institutional factors. It was argued that overtime is allocated to a relatively small number of individuals because of links built up between this group and the management. Once this has occurred, a ratchet effect comes into play as individuals become reliant on overtime earnings which they treat as permanent rather than transitory income. While the econometric explanations of hours of work tend to place less emphasis on institutional factors, they are often not too far below the surface in these models. The roles played by guaranteed pay, normal hours and overtime premium rates are implicit in the quadratic wage–hours sub-model of Ball and St Cyr (1966). Desired hours are therefore crucially linked to normal hours, although quasi-fixed labour costs drive a wedge between them. The higher the overtime premiums, the steeper is the wage–hours function and the greater the costs of not being at the desired-level hours and therefore the more rapid the adjustment of employment.

In the Ball and St Cyr (1966) model, however, the quadratic is assumed to be invariant, implying no changes in guaranteed pay, normal hours or overtime premiums over time. We noted that the cost-minimizing number of hours can be derived from equation (14) as $H_0 = b/2c$, a constant. However, the authors expressed concern over this, arguing that H_0 might be related to output, and other authors noted that H_0 is likely to be related to institutionally determined normal hours, which have exhibited a secular downward trend in the post-war period. As we have noted the existence of quasi-fixed labour costs implies $H_0 > H_N$ leading to a higher optimal level of hours and a smaller optimal level of employment. Several studies at the micro level in the USA and the UK conclude that quasi-fixed labour costs have not been sufficiently large to affect the minimum point on the wage–hours function or the optimal hours of work of the typical worker and seem unlikely to have affected the optimal level of employment, although more aggregate empirical work using regression techniques has tended to find a more significant role for quasi-fixed labour costs.

Attention has also focused on improving the specification of the labour input. This was one of the ways in which it was hoped to account for the unexpectedly high estimate of the marginal product of labour. In particular, at a fairly early stage, authors were concerned to allow the elasticity of output with respect to the number of employees, β_E, to differ from the elasticity with respect to the average number of hours per person, β_H. It was argued that the revised results might indicate that $\beta_E < 1$ and $\beta_H > 1$, and that a priori we might expect $\beta_H > \beta_E$ because: higher H will go hand in hand with higher capital utilization (other things, including shiftwork patterns, being equal); non-productive hours (e.g. set-up time, work breaks, etc.) do not rise proportionately with the number of hours officially worked. On the basis of cross-sectional data for 24 UK industries in three different years, Feldstein (1967) found that $\beta_H > 1$, but $0 < \beta_E < 1$. Using a quite different sample of quarterly time series data for the US economy, Craine (1972), found decreasing returns to both employment and capital, but increasing returns to hours. In such models the expansion of overtime hours is limited by the resulting disproportionate increase in overtime costs.

Other authors argued that the magnitude of β commonly found in empirical work is caused by a misspecification of the input of capital services. While the stock of capital is exogenous in the short run, capital utilization can be varied, in much the same way as labour hours. Adopting a CES function, no binding constraints on either capital or labour over time, and that assuming the ratio of the cost of utilizing capital to labour remains approximately constant, the mix of total hours worked to capital utilization lies on a linear expansion path function identical to the one used by Ball and St Cyr (1966). However, β, previously interpreted as the returns to labour, now represents returns to scale, which explains why it takes a value greater than unity (Smyth and Ireland, 1967). If this interpretation of β is correct, however, the estimates found in the literature are often still too high to be plausible.

5 Adjustment costs and lags

The idea that inputs may only adjust gradually towards their desired levels was suggested at an early stage (see, for example, Neild, 1963; Brechling, 1965). However, there were problems of isolating data on the costs of adjustment, as well as the difficulties of explicitly building such costs within the models. As a consequence they were incorporated implicitly via lagged adjustment mechanisms. Suppose that the cost of: (i) not hiring the desired (e.g. long-run optimal) number of employees increases quadratically with the difference between actual and desired levels, $E^*_t - E_t$; (ii) adjusting the input increases quadratically with the magnitude of the change in employment in any given period, $E_t - E_{t-1}$ (see Chapter 9). Then the total costs can be represented by their two elements,

$$C_t = b_1(E^*_t - E_t)^2 + b_2(E_t - E_{t-1})^2 \tag{17}$$

where b_1 and b_2 are constants. Setting $\mathrm{d}C_t/\mathrm{d}E_t = 0$ and rearranging,

$$(E_t - E_{t-1}) = \Gamma(E^*_t - E_{t-1}) \tag{18}$$

where $\Gamma = b_1/(b_1 + b_2)$ is a constant. This is an additive form of the Koyck adjustment mechanism, which has the characteristic that the firm adjusts a constant amount of the discrepancy between desired and actual employment in each period. The analogous log-linear version of the Koyck mechanism can be written as

$$\frac{E_t}{E_{t-1}} = \left(\frac{E^*_t}{E_{t-1}}\right)^{\Gamma} \tag{19}$$

where E adjusts to its desired level, E^*, at a constant rate, Γ, $0 \leq \Gamma \leq 1$. When $\Gamma = 0$, there is no adjustment within the period and, when $\Gamma = 1$, adjustment is complete. The adjustment mechanism represented by equation (19), however, is derived from a less plausible underlying cost function than equation (18).

Substituting for E^*_t from equation (19) into equation (16), the Ball and St Cyr model can be rewritten as

$$E_t = B\Gamma e^{-\Gamma gt/\beta} K_t^{*-\Gamma\alpha/\beta} Y_t^{*\Gamma/\beta} E_{t-1}^{1-\Gamma} \tag{20}$$

Similar equations have been estimated by a large number of other authors. The results have a number of consistent features: they indicate $0 < \Gamma < 1$, in line with a priori expectations about adjustment costs and the associated partial adjustment of employment towards its desired level; $\beta > 1$, in contradiction to the traditionally assumed law of diminishing returns to labour; where t and K are included separately, the time trend has indicated a secular increase in output per unit of input. It should be borne in mind that the inclusion of a one-period lagged dependent variable gives rise to potentially important econometric problems. When the model is estimated in absolute form (e.g. explaining the level of employment), it is fairly clear that the current value of the dependent variable will generally be closely related to its value one period previously. There is the possibility that significant values on E_{t-1} will be interpreted as support for the adjustment cost hypothesis, when this variable is proxying for omitted variables.

Subsequently, complicated lag structures have been estimated, where current employment is influenced by the levels of employment in more than one past period,

$$E_t = \mathrm{l}(E^*_t, E_{t-1}, E_{t-2}, \ldots) \tag{21}$$

where desired employment is replaced by some observable function of desired output and relative factor prices. While this may help to ensure a better dynamic specification of the model it may result in a number of empirical problems (e.g. multi-collinearity between the lagged dependent variables, making it difficult to isolate the precise lag structure, as well as problems in forecasting and policy analysis). In the early studies, which were often based upon rather limited time series data, the more general lag structures significantly reduced degrees of freedom. However, some of the problems of more complex lags may be avoided where the lag coefficients are related, allowing the lag structure to be summarized by a simple polynomial, saving degrees of freedom. Whether or not this is a useful approach depends on the extent to which the adjustment parameters follow some simple distributional pattern.

Partial adjustment mechanisms try to account for a diverse mixture of both product and labour market influences and, in all probability, fail to fulfil this task entirely. The rate of adjustment appears to vary as the underlying economic conditions change. There is tentative evidence that, historically at least, adjustment is faster upwards than downwards (consistent with the high fixed costs incurred by employers at that time in terminating existing employment contracts). There is perhaps stronger evidence that adjustment costs are not constant over the business cycle and, in particular, that they vary with the 'tightness' of the labour market, for example as reflected by the rate of unemployment, vacancies or hours of work. These attempts to improve the adjustment process have links with the work on equilibrating models which separate the sample into sub-periods of excess supply and excess demand (see Part IV below).

In more recent years, the issue of adjustment costs (and lagged adjustment) has become tied up with the testing of general dynamic specifications (Hendry, 1995). The first stage is to consider the issue of stationarity. If the associated series are not stationary then the normal statistic requirements needed for the application of standard regression techniques (constant mean, variance and covariance) are not fulfilled. This requires a test of the order of integration of the data set – the so-called unit-root tests (such as the Dickey–Fuller and augmented Dickey–Fuller tests). Normally, economic series are integrated of order 1 ($I(1)$) and, hence, are only stationary after first differencing. The next stage is to search for a cointegrating regression $Y_t = \beta X_t$ that is $I(0)$, in other words, X_t and Y_t do not move too far away from one another over time. If the error term, μ_t, is also $I(1)$, clearly a long-run relationship has not been established. Finally, there remains the problem of defining a general dynamic specification. This is normally based on an overparameterized model, which for $I(1)$ data contains all of the variables in first difference form, lagged first-differences and lagged exogenous variables in absolute values. This can clearly be very data demanding; however, some saving of degrees of freedom can be made by replacing the absolute values of the lagged exogenous variables by an error correction term (formed from the residuals from the long-run relationship). The overparameterization allows the search for a more parsimonious form (i.e. general to specific modelling). An example of this approach can be found in Case Study 1.

CASE STUDY 1 Dynamic specifications of the employment function

This case study gives a recent example of the estimation of employment functions for nine UK engineering industries using annual data covering the period 1954–1987, using cointegration techniques (Briscoe and Wilson, 1991). A review of the literature suggested an empirical specification in which employment was determined by

$$E_t = f(Y_t, w_t, m_t, c_t) \quad (1)$$

where: E is employment; Y is output; w denotes (real) wage rate, m is raw material prices and c the user cost of capital. The inclusion of a range of lagged dependent and independent variables could also be justified (i.e. expectations about the level of demand for the product might be represented by current and lagged output). The authors had a wider range of variables from which they could draw their chosen empirical specification.

Examination of the time series data revealed that they were only stationary after first differencing (i.e. they were integrated of order 1, I(1)). The search for a long-run relationship led to the exploration of a number of alternative specifications of the cointegrating regression. Their preferred specification was

$$E_t = \alpha_0 + \alpha_1 Y_t + \alpha_2 w_t + \alpha_3 H_t + \alpha_4 f_t + \alpha_5 r_t \quad (2)$$

where: H denotes hours of work; f is real oil prices and r is bank rate. The choice is surprising in that our earlier discussion suggested that average hours of work appear likely to be endogenous to the system and determined by broadly the same independent variables as E. The authors make no comment on this issue. They specify the general dynamic form of the equation as

$$\Delta E_t = \alpha_0 + \alpha_1 \Delta Y_t + \alpha_2 \Delta Y_{t-1} + \alpha_3 \Delta W_t + \alpha_4 \Delta W_{t-1} + \alpha_5 \Delta H_t + \alpha_6 \Delta H_{t-1} + \alpha_7 \Delta f_t + \alpha_8 \Delta f_{t-1} + \alpha_9 \Delta r_{t-1} +$$

continues

CASE STUDY 1 continued

$$\alpha_{10}\Delta r_{t-1} + \alpha_{11}\Delta E_t + \alpha_{12}\Delta E_{t-1} + \alpha_{13}\Delta E_{t-2} + \alpha_{14}Y_{t-1} + \alpha_{15}W_{t-1} + \alpha_{16}H_{t-1} + \alpha_{17}f_{t-1} + \alpha_{18}r_{t-1} + \alpha_{19}E_{t-1} \quad (3)$$

This general dynamic specification ran into a degrees of freedom problem and the authors chose to estimate the equivalent error correction form,

$$\Delta E_t = \alpha_0 + \alpha_1\Delta Y_t + \alpha_2\Delta Y_{t-1} + \alpha_3\Delta w_t + \alpha_4\Delta w_{t-1} + \alpha_5\Delta H_t + \alpha_6\Delta H_{t-1} + \alpha_7\Delta f_t + \alpha_8\Delta f_{t-1} + \alpha_9\Delta r_t + \alpha_{10}\Delta r_{t-1} + \alpha_{11}\Delta E_t + \alpha_{12}\Delta E_{t-1} + \alpha_{13}\Delta E_{t-2} + \alpha_{14}EC_{t-1} \quad (4)$$

where EC is the error correction term (i.e. the residuals from the long-run relationship) and can be seen to replace the last tranche of variables in absolute form from equation (3). Based upon the results from each of the nine industries, the authors conclude that over the sub-period 1954–1965, output played a particularly important role in determining changes in employment; in the period 1965–1976, the importance of output was considerably lower, with real wages playing a dominant role; finally, in the most recent sub-period, both output and real wages played important roles in most industries.

Source: Briscoe and Wilson (1991)

6 Inter-related factor demand models

The basic approach has been to develop a cost-minimizing specification in which the demand functions for employees, hours, capital stock and capital utilization are jointly determined and their adjustments towards long-run equilibrium values are interdependent (Nadiri and Rosen, 1969). By assuming that desired output is exogenously given, rather than determined endogenously within the model, the optimal solutions for the factor inputs appear as a set of recursive equations. Inter-related partial adjustment does not upset this feature of the model because only past values of the other dependent variables appear in the factor input equations. The resulting factor demand models treat the various dimensions of factor services on a more equal footing, as jointly determined, and the adjustment path of one is dependent on the adjustment of the others. We can trace the implications of the inter-relatedness of the factor adjustments diagrammatically using the case of hours and employment outlined above. A more rigorous treatment of the four-factor case is presented in Case Study 2.

The Nadiri and Rosen (1969) problem is based on cost-minimizing behaviour subject to an output constraint. Thus, at time t, Figure 11.5 shows the firm to be in long-run equilibrium at point e_t, with H_t,E_t. A favourable demand shock now hits the firm and its desired output shifts to Y^*_{t+1} and, given that factor prices have not changed, long-run equilibrium occurs at e^*_{t+1}. However, the high costs of changing the labour in the short run mean that E_t is almost fixed. Thus, the majority of the burden of adjustment falls upon hours (in our two-input example). Indeed, in order to meet the output constraint, hours have to be increased to H_{t+1}. However, gradually, over time, the firm is able to move employment towards E*. By period t + 2, for example, the outcome is at H_{t+2},

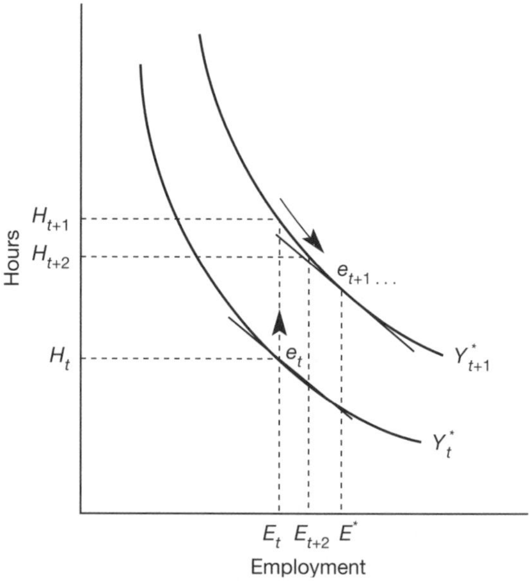

Fig 11.5 Short- and long-run equilibrium with inter-related adjustments.

E_{t+2}, as the firm moves around the isoquant Y^*_{t+1}, meeting the output constraint in each period. Figures 11.6(a) and 11.6(b) clearly show the inter-relatedness of the two paths. The inflexibility of employment causes hours to overshoot their long-run equilibrium value, H^*_{t+1}, in the short run as shown in Figure 11.6(a). However, as employment begins to change, as shown in Figure 11.6(b), then hours fall back from their peak, H_{t+1}, towards the long-run equilibrium value, H^*.

The models outlined to date effectively assume that the observed or actual output is the same as the planned output. In certain instances, such an assumption may be fairly accurate, for example where the product or service cannot be stored and demands must be satisfied. The inherent problem with this approach is that the production function parameters implied by each of the different factor demand equations may be inconsistent. This can be avoided by the joint estimation of factor input and production functions. Thus, a production function (with current output appearing as the dependent variable) is added to the factor input equations and estimated simultaneously. However, there is a potentially more fundamental reason for endogenizing output. In general, demand and production can, to some extent, vary independently where the firm holds stocks with important implications for factor demands. Stocks are not the only source of flexibility, driving a wedge between production and demand. In particular, consumers may be willing to wait for the delivery of certain types of goods, and,

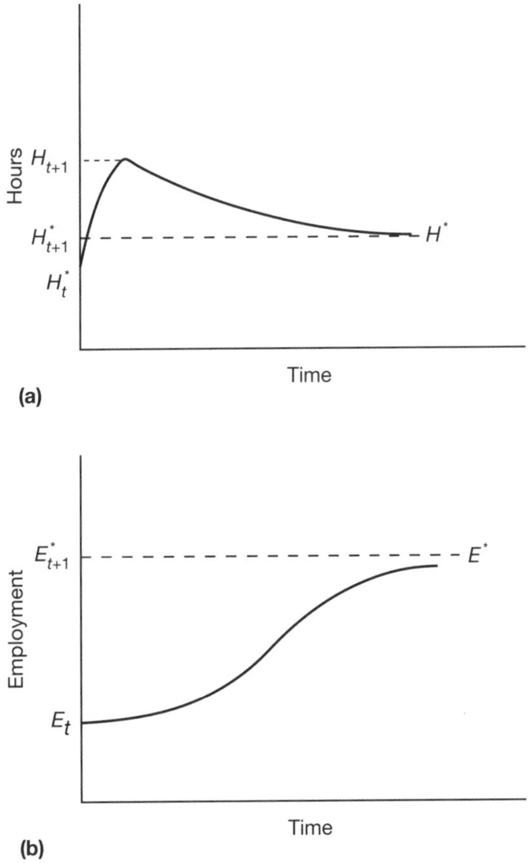

Fig 11.6 Paths of hours and employment with inter-related factor demands.

CASE STUDY 2 Inter-related factor demand models

This case study considers the implications of inter-related factor adjustments in the case where the firm is faced by four inputs: capital (*K*), capital utilization (*KU*), employment (*E*) and hours per worker (*H*). Following Nadiri and Rosen (1969), the goal is to minimize costs subject to an output constraint. The Lagrangian expression can be written as

$$\mathcal{L} = w(E_tH_t) + sE_t + cK_t + \lambda\,[Y^*_t - \mathbf{q}(K_t, KU_t, E_t, H_t)] \quad (1)$$

where: Y^*, the desired level of output, is assumed equal to actual output and is given exogenously; $\mathbf{q}(\,)$ is the production function,

$$Y = AK^{\alpha}KU^{\phi}E^{\beta}H^{\theta} \quad (2)$$

and *K*, *KU*, *E* and *H* denote capital stock, capital utilization, employment and hours respectively; *w*, the wage per person hour, varies with the number of hours worked, $w = \mathbf{w}(H)$; *s* denotes quasi-fixed labour costs; *c* is the user cost of capital, $c = p_K(i + \delta)$, where p_K is the price of capital, *i* is the interest rate, and δ is the rate of depreciation of the stock of capital, $\delta = \delta\,(KU,t)$.

Differentiating expression (1) with respect to the five unknowns, setting the resulting expression equal to zero to find a minimum and solving for the optimal input levels, E^*, H^*, K^* and KU^*, yields

continues

CASE STUDY 2 continued

$$E_t^* = (Y_t^*)^{1/\rho} (w/c)^{\phi/\rho} (c/s)^{(\alpha+\theta)/\rho} \left(\frac{i+\delta}{\delta'}\right)^{-\phi/\rho} = E^* (Y^*, R) \quad (3)$$

$$H_t^* = (s/w) \left(\frac{\beta}{\theta}(1+\varepsilon) - 1\right)^{-1} = H^* (R) \quad (4)$$

$$K_t^* = (Y_t^*)^{1/\rho} \left(\frac{w}{c}\right)^{\beta/\rho} \left(\frac{s}{w}\right)^{(\beta-\theta)\rho} \left(\frac{i+\delta}{\delta'}\right)^{-\phi/\rho} K^*(Y^*, R) \quad (5)$$

$$KU_t^* = \left(\frac{(i+\delta)}{\delta'}\right) \frac{\phi}{\alpha} = KU^* (R) \quad (6)$$

where, to simplify the notation, we have $\rho = \alpha + \beta$, $\delta' = (\partial\delta/\partial KU)$ and $\varepsilon = (dw/w)/(dH/H) \geq 0$. A number of other changes were also made: time trends were added to each equation; the various relative factor price terms were proxied by a single wage/price ratio; an output term was included in the flow (as well as the stock) equations; and a general Koyck adjustment mechanism was adopted to allow the path of each dependent variable to be related to the paths of the other variables,

$$\begin{vmatrix} X_{1,t} - X_{1,t-1} \\ \cdot \\ \cdot \\ \cdot \\ X_{4,t} - X_{4,t-1} \end{vmatrix} = \begin{vmatrix} \Gamma_{11} & \Gamma_{12} \ldots \Gamma_{14} \\ \Gamma_{21} & \\ \cdot & \\ \cdot & \\ \Gamma_{41} & \Gamma_{42} \ldots \Gamma_{44} \end{vmatrix} \begin{vmatrix} X_{1,t}^* - X_{1,t-1} \\ \cdot \\ \cdot \\ \cdot \\ X_{4,t}^* - X_{4,t-1} \end{vmatrix} \quad (7)$$

where X_i denotes the log of the ith input and $i,j = 1, \ldots, 4 = E, H, K, KU$. Under these conditions, the change of X_i between period $t-1$ and t depends not only on its own partial adjustment, Γ_{ii}, but also on the partial adjustment of all other inputs, Γ_{ij} (for $i \neq j$).

Taking logs of equations (3)–(6) and denoting the resulting expressions as

$$X_j^* = X_j(Y^*, R, t) \quad (8)$$

where R denotes the appropriate factor price ratio, then, substituting into equation (7), and adding a stochastic error term, $\mu_{i,t}$,

$$X_{i,t} - X_{i,t-1} = \sum_{j=1}^{4} \Gamma_{ij} [X_j(Y_t^*, R_t, t) - X_{j,t-1}] + \mu_{i,t} \quad (9)$$

Bearing in mind the approximations made in moving from the theoretical to the empirical specification, the Nadiri and Rosen (1969) model produces a number of plausible results. The estimated periods for adjusting input levels to their desired values are shortest for capital utilization, longer for hours, longer still for employment and longest of all for capital stock. Clearly, however, the model does not cope adequately with the complexities of capital utilization, when there may be technical fixities between the times at which capital can be operated and workers must be present in the plant. A more important problem concerns the opposite signs on the lagged hours and lagged capital coefficients to be found in the hours and employment equations. Finally, a positive and significant coefficient appears on one of the factor price variables, which is not consistent with the traditional neoclassical hypothesis. However, in their later work the authors manage to isolate a coefficient that is significantly negative for the durable goods industries, although not for non-durables.

Source: Nadiri and Rosen (1969)

when production exceeds (is less than) demand, waiting lists decline (grow). All of these extensions suggest that actual output will tend to desired output gradually over time: the speed of adjustment will depend on the costs of not meeting current demand within the period, and the costs of adjusting output from its existing level.

7 Flexible functional forms

Much of the early work on factor demands was based on the Cobb–Douglas function. While these results are of some interest, the CD imposes a unitary elasticity of substitution on the technology and alternative forms of biases in technological change appear analytically identical. However, the CD function yields estimates of marginal products and factor shares but even here there is some doubt whether the restricted functional form simply approximates the underlying accounting identity ($pY = rK + wL$). The only way in which it is possible to test whether the CD is an accurate description of the real world is in the overall fit of the equation and the significance and meaningfulness of the estimated parameters. Tests of this type can be misleading and, given the subsequent advances in the specification of the production function, more rigorous tests are now available by placing restrictions on more general functional forms.

Results based on the CES function offer the immediate benefit of saying something about the ease of substitution between capital and labour. While the function is still, in certain respects, highly restrictive, even the simplest form allows elasticities other than unity and more complex CES functions allow different elasticities between alternative pairs of inputs in a three- (or more) input function. This modification requires the replacement of the simple, two-input measure of the elasticity of substitution with an analogous partial elasticity of substitution. This measure, attributed to Allen and Uzawa, considers the impact of a change in the price of one factor on the quantity demanded of another, holding everything else constant (e.g. output and other factor prices). A number of examples can be given of applications of this model. First, given the importance for educational planning, particularly in the context of a developing country, a number of CES studies have been concerned with the question of substitutability between individuals with differing educational attainments. They tend to indicate quite high levels of elasticities of substitution (though less than perfect) but with a large variation in the estimated values. Incorporation of a supply function results in more consistent, though still high, elasticities. Second a separate, though related, debate has focused on possible shortages of key occupations or skills (e.g. engineers and technicians). Again, fairly high values for the elasticities of substitution were obtained. Third, studies which focus on the elasticities of substitution between labour of different skill levels and capital suggest that labour in higher skill categories is complementary with capital, and lower-skilled workers are substitutes for capital. Finally, other authors have focused on union and non-union labour, different races, etc.

CASE STUDY 3 Flexible functional forms

We now turn to more flexible functional forms, related to the translog function introduced in Chapter 7. The example we take is that of a non-homothetic translog cost function, described in detail by Berndt (1991, Chapter 9),

$$\ln C = \ln\alpha_0 + \sum_{i=1}^{n}\alpha_i \ln p_i + \tfrac{1}{2}\sum_{i=1}^{n}\sum_{j=1}^{n}\gamma_{ij}\ln p_i \ln p_j +$$

$$\alpha_y \ln Y + \tfrac{1}{2}\gamma_{yy}(\ln Y)^2 + \sum_{i=1}^{n}\gamma_{iy}\ln p_i \ln Y \qquad (1)$$

where: p_i and p_j denote the prices of the ith and jth inputs; C is total cost; Y is output; and the various α and γ are constants to be determined by the regression. A number of restrictions have to be imposed for the cost function to be well behaved; in particular, it has to be homogeneous of degree 1 in prices for any given Y, which requires

$$\sum_{i=1}^{n}\alpha_i = 1;\ \gamma_{ij} = \gamma_{ji};\ \sum_{i=1}^{n}\gamma_{ij} = \sum_{j=1}^{n}\gamma_{ji} = \sum_{i=1}^{n}\gamma_{iy} = 0 \qquad (2)$$

Other restrictions can be tested empirically to see whether the data can be described by a simpler (less flexible) technology.

As noted above, such functions are generally not estimated directly. Differentiating with regard to input prices and using Shephard's Lemma, it is possible to derive the cost share equations for each input. For simplicity, assume that the inputs are capital, K, employment, L, energy, E, and raw materials, M. We have retained this notation in the case study simply because this form has become known as the 'KLEM model' in the literature. The four input equations can be written,

$$\begin{aligned} S_K &= \alpha_K + \gamma_{KK}\ln p_K + \gamma_{KL}\ln p_L + \gamma_{KE}\ln p_E + \\ &\quad \gamma_{KM}\ln p_M + \gamma_{KY}\ln Y \\ S_L &= \alpha_L + \gamma_{LK}\ln p_K + \gamma_{LL}\ln p_L + \gamma_{LE}\ln p_E + \\ &\quad \gamma_{LM}\ln p_M + \gamma_{LY}\ln Y \qquad (3) \\ S_E &= \alpha_E + \gamma_{EK}\ln p_K + \gamma_{EL}\ln p_L + \gamma_{EE}\ln p_E + \\ &\quad \gamma_{EM}\ln p_M + \gamma_{EY}\ln Y \\ S_M &= \alpha_M + \gamma_{MK}\ln p_K + \gamma_{ML}\ln p_L + \gamma_{ME}\ln \\ &\quad p_E + \gamma_{MM}\ln p_M + \gamma_{MY}\ln Y \end{aligned}$$

Where $S_i = p_iX_i/C$. The symmetry restriction requires that $\gamma_{ij} = \gamma_{ji}$. The restrictions necessary for the cost function to be well behaved imply the four α must sum to unity (down the first column of coefficients on the right hand side) and the γ across each row must sum to unity. The various restrictions reduce the number of para-

continues

CASE STUDY 3 continued

meters to be estimated from 24 down to 12. Error terms are added to equations (3). However, given that $\Sigma^4_{i=1}S_i = 1$, then only three of the four equations need to be estimated and symmetry and summation restrictions on the coefficients need not be imposed.

Berndt (1991, p. 475) reports estimates based upon equation (3), using UK manufacturing data for the period 1947 to 1971. The resulting Allen partial elasticities of substitution are set out in Table 11.1, and the corresponding own- and cross-price elasticities are reported in Table 11.2. The findings imply that capital and energy are complementary inputs, capital and labour are substitutes and energy and labour are substitutes.

Table 11.1 Allen partial elasticities of substitution for 1971, σ_{ij}

	K	*L*	*E*	*M*
K	−6.99	0.97	−3.60	0.35
L		−1.51	0.68	0.61
E			−11.74	0.83
M				−0.39

Table 11.2 Price elasticity estimates for 1971, ε_{ij}

	K	*L*	*E*	*M*
K	−0.34	0.29	−0.16	0.21
L	0.05	−0.45	0.03	0.37
E	−0.17	0.20	−0.53	0.51
M	0.02	0.18	0.04	−0.24

Source: Berndt (1991, Chapter 9)

A number of functional forms, such as the translog, have been developed which subsume the CES as a special case (see Case Study 3). Again, a number of patterns emerge. On the positive side the functions appear to provide reasonable explanations of factor demands. In addition, elasticities of substitution often vary and differ from unity and, hence, the assumption of a CES (let alone a CD function) is generally rejected when explicitly tested. On the negative side, there are still inconsistencies such as the differences in results between time series and cross-sectional databases and between the supposedly equivalent production and dual cost functions. In addition the approach is demanding in terms of data and gains in terms of the theoretical richness of the specification are lost where models are estimated on inadequate data sets. While the translog gave the ability to test for the existence of factor saving/using technological change, without the need for restrictive assumptions about the underlying technology, it proved extremely difficult to disentangle the effects of technological change from other features of the production function. In practice, researchers have often been forced to impose untested restrictions on the underlying technology of production and nature of technological change (e.g. appearing as a simple time trend). Jorgenson (1983) finds that technical change is capital using in 25 and labour using in 31 US industries. The work of Denny *et al.* (1980) is interesting because of its micro nature, developing explicit indicators of technological change and analysing production changes at Bell Canada. The authors found some evidence of labour-saving bias, but argue that the main productivity gains could be attributed to exploiting increasing returns to scale, rather than technological change *per se*.

8 Key parameter estimates: a summary

8.1 Aims and scope

Hammermesh (1993) provides a review of key parameter estimates found in the literature. These are derived from all the kinds of models described above, as well as equilibrium and disequilibrium models – which we deal with in Part IV of the book. His taxonomy throws some light on why different studies report different parameter values including: the type of model (i.e. direct estimates of the production function, first-order conditions, etc.); the underlying technology of production; the level of aggregation of the data, etc.

Here we provide only the briefest of summaries of these key parameters, but refer the interested reader to Hammermesh's excellent discussion.

8.2 Studies using highly aggregate data

A review of 15 major studies of the elasticity of substitution between capital and labour produces a wide range of results, although the majority suggest an absolute value of the elasticity somewhere in the range 0.3 to 0.78, which is consistent with fairly low elasticities of substitution. However, four of the studies suggest higher elasticities, certainly over unity. Hammermesh concludes that direct estimation of σ is not a very promising route.

The second group comprises 32 studies of the constant-output (short-run and long-run) total elasticities of demand for labour, again all estimated using highly aggregate data. The results are again diverse. Ignoring the niceties, such as differences induced by the various approaches and sources of data, the vast majority of the estimates indicate a fairly low value of the constant-output elasticity of demand. Bearing in mind that some of the studies produce multiple values (i.e. for different groups), just under 60 per cent of the 29 estimates reported in this category take values less than or equal to 0.4; a further 30 per cent lie between 0.4 and 1.0; the remainder lie outside of this range. In the case of short-run elasticities, there are a number less than or equal to an absolute value of 0.3, but the majority lie above unity. The number of total elasticities is quite small, but the lowest are around 0.4 and the high values again above unity.

Hammermesh (1993, Table 3.3) also reports constant-output elasticities of demand for a number of studies which he describes as 'based on equations systems using data on aggregates or large industries'. Again, there are multiple estimates for some of the studies based upon the results for different groups and, here, we use all of the estimates available. In this instance, all of the results lie in the absolute range 0 to 1, but the vast majority are clustered around 0.5 to 0.7. Certainly, 60 per cent of the estimated parameters lie between absolute values of 0.4 and 0.8. Based upon nearly 70 studies included in this category, Hammermesh concludes that:

> A simple mean of the estimates of σ is 0.75, while the mean estimate of $-\eta_{EE}$ is 0.39. Ignoring for the moment issues of aggregation, nearly all the studies produce estimates below 1, and in most the estimates are below 0.75. At the other extreme, few studies produce estimates below 0.15 ... These considerations and an estimate that $S_L \approx 0.70$ in developed economies suggest that a reasonable confidence interval for $-\eta_{EE}$ is (0.15, 0.75). We can be fairly sure that the true value *at the aggregate level* is in this range. If one were to choose a point estimate for this parameter, 0.30 would not be far wrong (though picking a single estimate is not a good idea) .... Interestingly ... the 'best guess' value of $-\eta_{EE} = 0.30$ is consistent with the Cobb-Douglas production function (since the implied σ is 1.0). The immense literature that estimates the constant-output demand elasticity for labour in the aggregate has truly led us 'to arrive where we started and know the place for the first time'. (Hammermesh, 1993, p. 92).

8.3 Disaggregated studies of homogeneous labour

Hammermesh (1993, pp. 92–104) reviewed two sets of estimates in this broad group: 19 based upon data on small industries and 23 based upon firm- or plant-level data. Again, for a variety of reasons, some of the papers covered produce more than one parameter estimate. The results can be divided into those that produce estimates of the elasticity of substitution, σ, the constant-output elasticity of demand, η_{EE}, and the total elasticity estimate, η_{EE}'. Again we focus on the areas where there are sufficient studies to attempt to form an overview of the magnitudes of the various parameters.

In the case of the small industry groups, the seven estimates of σ lie between 0 and 0.75, and six of the seven lie in the range 0.26 and 0.75. Only two of the reported firm- or plant-level studies estimate σ directly, and both values are approximately 0.5. The results again tend to suggest an elasticity of substitution for labour well below unity. The estimates of the constant-output elasticity of demand at the small industry level suggest absolute values between 0.1 and 1.0. Again, however, 12 of the 16 parameter estimates are in the range 0.23 to 0.61. A broadly similar conclusion about the range of estimates of $-\eta_{EE}$ is found in the case of the firm- or plant-level estimates. Here, there are 28 estimates of $-\eta_{EE}$, of which 85 per cent lie in the range 0 to 1, but the vast majority cluster between 0.2 and 0.6 (about 57 per cent of the total).

The results of the various micro studies are broadly in line with the aggregate outcomes reported in Section 8.2. On balance, the mean value of σ is slightly lower than the earlier estimates, at about 0.5, but the estimated value of $-\eta_{LL}$ is slightly higher, at about 0.45. Hammermesh (1993, p.103) suggests that, 'Concluding that $-\eta_{LL}$ is probably between 0.15 and 0.75 for the typical firm remains warranted.' In other words, whilst recognizing that each firm or industry will have parameter estimates which reflect its own particular situation, if we randomly selected a firm or industry, it would probably show values lying in this range. Of course, this also indicates that the more disaggregated studies add to our stock of knowledge by reflecting the special production or labour demand circumstances in which certain firms or industries operate.

One final, though important, finding comes from a range of studies that explore the demand for a whole range of factors of production. Such studies suggest that, in general, labour is a price substitute for every other major group of factors, including capital, energy and raw materials. We touched upon the KLEM group of models in Case Study 3.

8.4 Heterogeneous labour

In many respects, the more disaggregated the level, the more difficult it is to provide an overview of the existing results, at least giving likely values of the estimated parameters. In addition, throughout his review of the empirical results, Hammermesh (1993) points to the somewhat different functional forms adopted by such studies and the inherent difficulties of comparison with the earlier results reported above. Nevertheless, these more detailed studies are linked to significant policy questions and, despite the difficulties associated with empirical investigation, there is enormous interest in the results. In the main, while there is a substantial amount of disagreement between particular studies, on balance they appear to suggest that: (i) the elasticity of demand is higher for less skilled workers and lower at higher skill levels; (ii) unskilled workers are substitutes for capital and skilled workers are complements. It is perhaps even more dangerous to propose generalizations based upon the diverse educational demand literature, and the reader is advised to explore the discussion in Hammermesh. However, on balance, the studies seem to point in broadly the same way as the occupational results (after all, there is a considerable degree of linkage between occupations, skills and education). In addition, there appears to be a degree of complementarity between more skilled labour and the use of newer technologies. Finally, as an example of other work in this area, we consider the results of the studies of different age groups, particularly in the context of the demand for young people. Again the results are quite diverse. However, there is some support for the earlier finding that the demand elasticity tends to fall as skill level increases. Given that skills are acquired over time, it is not surprising perhaps to find that a number of the studies in this area tend to find high elasticities for young people, and that own-wage elasticities tend to fall with age (at least in moving from youth to adult).

9 Conclusions

In this chapter we have reviewed a wide range of empirical evidence relating to the input of labour services. We began by discussing a number of empirical issues, such as problems of measurement of key variables (such as the price of hours and the user cost of capital). However, the discussion was more positive about the developments in both larger and richer databases, and the improvements to econometric techniques in estimating the demand side relationships. The chapter also outlines the evolution from fairly restrictive functional forms to general specifications of the underlying production technology that enable specific restrictions to be explicitly tested. The movement from Cobb–Douglas to CES and translog functions can be seen in this light. Similar improvements have occurred in the shift from single-equation models (such as those that focus on employment) to systems of equations which attempt to explain simultaneously both the demand for all types of factor services, as well as the inter-related adjustments of factor demands towards their optimal or desired levels. Finally, we undertook a brief review of the range of estimates of the key parameters of the labour demand functions, including the constant-output elasticity of labour demand.

The main conclusions would appear to be that (Wilson, 1984a and 1984b): the majority of studies find that input demands respond to relative factor price changes in the anticipated way; the resulting parameter estimates are generally consistent with the axioms of production theory; while a wide range of estimates of partial elasticities of substitution between inputs have been obtained, particularly for the estimated elasticities of substitution between capital and labour, they tend to average out at about unity, but explicit tests based on less restrictive functional forms tend to reject the Cobb–Douglas technology; functions that allow for, and can therefore test for, more than one elasticity of substitution tend to reject the hypothesis of a single elasticity throughout; the greater the degree of commonality between the characteristics of the different groups distinguished in the production function, the higher tends to be the degree of substitutability; the studies which distinguish explicitly between capital, manual (blue collar) and non-manual (white collar) labour tend to find that manual workers and capital appear to be substitutes, while non-manual workers and capital are complements; nearly all studies that have attempted to isolate biased technical change have established its existence, but it has not always been in accordance with a priori expectations and the direction of bias has often been contradictory between studies.

References

Ball, R.J. and E.B.A St Cyr (1966). 'Short Term Employment Functions in British Manufacturing Industry'. *Review of Economic Studies*, 33, 179–207.

Bazen, S. and J. Martin (1991). 'The Impact of the Minimum Wage on Earnings and Employment in France'. *OECD Economic Studies.* 199–221.

Berndt, E.R. (1991). *The Practice of Econometrics: Classic and Contemporary*. Reading, MA: Addison-Wesley

Brechling, F. (1965). 'The Relationship Between Output and Employment in British Manufacturing Industries'. *Review of Economic Studies*, 34, 187–216.

Briscoe, G. and R. Wilson (1991). 'Explanations of the Demand for Labour in the United Kingdom Engineering Sector'. *Applied Economics*, 23, 913–926.

Craine, R., (1972). 'On the Service Flow from Labour', *Review of Economic Studies*, 40, pp. 39-45.

Denny, M. *et al.* (1980). 'Productivity, Employment and Technical Change in Canadian Manufacturing: The Case of Bell Canada'. Chapter VI in *Groups of Experts on Economic Analysis of Information Activities and the Role of Electronics and Telecommunications Technologies* Vol.II, Background. Paris: OECD, pp. 241–365.

Fair, R.C., (1969). *The Short Run Demand for Workers and Hours*. Amsterdam: North-Holland.

Feldstein, M.S. (1967). 'Specification of the Labour Input in the Aggregate Production Function'. *Review of Economic Studies*, 34, 375–386.

Hammermesh, D.S. (1982). 'Minimum Wages and the Demand for Labour'. *Economic Inquiry*, 20, 365–379.

Hammermesh, D.S. (1993). *Labour Demand*. Princeton, NJ: Princeton University Press.

Hazledine, T. (1978). 'New Specifications for Employment and Hours Functions'. *Economica*, 45, 179–193.

Heathfield, D. and S. Wibe (1987). *An Introduction to Cost and Production Functions*. London: Macmillan.

Hendry, D.F. (1995). *Dynamic Econometrics*. Oxford: Oxford University Press.

Jorgenson, D.W. (1983). 'Modelling Production for General Equilibrium Analysis'. *Scandinavian Journal of Economics*. 85, 2, 101–112.

Lester, R.A. (1964). 'Shortcomings of Marginal Analysis for Wage Employment Problems'. *American Economic Review*, 36, 63–82.

Machlup, F. (1946). 'Marginal Analysis and Empirical Research'. *American Economic Review*, 36, 547–554.

Nadiri, M.I. and S. Rosen, (1969). 'Inter-related Factor Demand Functions'. *American Economic Review*, 59, 452–471.

Neild, R.R. (1963). *Pricing and Employment in the Trade Cycle: A Study of British Manufacturing Industry, 1950-61*. Cambridge: Cambridge University Press.

Northcott, J. and P. Rogers, (1984). *Microelectronics in British Industry: The Pattern of Change*. London: Policy Studies Institute, Report No. 625.

Northcott, J. and A. Walling (1988). *The Impact of Microelectronics: Diffusion, Benefits and Problems in British Industry*. London: Policy Studies Institute.

Reynolds, L.G. and P. Gregory, (1965). *Wages Productivity and Industrialisation in Puerto Rico*, Homewood, IL: Irwin., pp. 41–103.

Smyth, D.J. and N.J. Ireland, (1967). 'Short Term Employment Functions in Australian Manufacturing'. *Review of Economics and Statistics*, 49, 537–544.

Stigler, J. (1946). 'The Economics of Minimum Wage Legislation'. *American Economic Review*, 36, 358–365.

Whybrew, E.G. (1968). 'Overtime Working in Britain, Royal Commission on Trade Union and Employee Associations.' Research Paper No. 9, London: HMSO.

Wilson, R.A. (1984). 'Evidence from Econometric Studies of Production Functions'. Section 3 in P. Stoneman (ed.) *Information Technology and Economic Perspectives*, Paris: OECD.

Wilson, R. (1984). 'The Impact of Information Technology on the Engineering Industry'. Research Report, Institute for Employment Research, University of Warwick.

PART IV Operation of Labour Markets

CHAPTER 12 Introduction to equilibrium, disequilibrium and adjustment

1 Introduction

The previous two parts of the book examined the supply of and the demand for labour, and now we bring these two components together. A labour market exists where buyers and sellers of labour meet or communicate to agree on a price (a wage) at which they are willing to exchange a given volume of labour services. We will see in Part VI of the book that the employment relationship, or nature of the 'labour contract', is often complex and rarely characterized by the kind of 'spot market' transactions that occur in the case of the market for other kinds of goods. Thus our definition of a labour market, offered above, is perhaps simplistic, but nonetheless represents a good starting point, which leaves the complexities of long-term relationships, information problems, uncertainty, etc., to later chapters. The analysis of labour markets offered in this part draws mainly upon mainstream neoclassical market economics. The supply and demand curves are brought together to theorize about wages and employment under different market conditions. Initially we assume equilibrium outcomes, but we go on to consider the possibility of disequilibrium and the process of adjustment.

The use of these supply and demand curves in standard neoclassical economics is sometimes referred to as the wage competition model. Suppliers of labour are competing for the highest wage they can obtain and buyers of labour are seeking the highest productivity labour at the lowest wage. It also implies that the buying and selling of labour services takes place in an open or 'external' labour market. Alternative frameworks have been put forward such as that of the job competition model (see Chapter 24) and internal labour markets (see Chapter 19). However, a great deal of mainstream labour economics proceeds on the basis of wage competition in external labour markets and, while this might be a little simplistic and ignore certain important features of labour markets, it provides a useful framework for analysing a range of labour market issues.

This introductory chapter considers the definition of a labour market, the classification of labour markets and their boundaries. In doing so, it provides a useful background to the subsequent chapters which tend to take the definition of labour markets as given, but often focus on different markets, such as 'the youth labour market' or the 'aggregate labour market'. Section 3 briefly outlines the problems that arise in aggregating across individuals to form a labour supply function and across producers to form the labour demand function. Section 4 looks at the problem of identifying the supply and demand functions from observations which are the outcome of their interaction. Up to this point, the discussion assumes that the wage is the mechanism by which the market moves to equilibrium and clears. Section 5 however, makes the point that individuals receive wages net of tax and firms have to pay various on-costs over and above the wage.

2 Existence and classification of a labour market

In many ways the labour market is no different to the market for other products, although, as we pointed out in Chapter 1, it has a number of peculiarities. A labour market can be said to exist when buyers and sellers meet or communicate in an attempt to agree on a price (in this instance a wage) at which they are willing to exchange a given volume of goods or services (in this case, labour services). In a competitive labour market, buyers and sellers are in close enough contact that an agreement between any pair of them can affect the terms on which the others trade. To talk about a labour market, it must be possible to distinguish the particular buyers and sellers involved. We can at least be clear about hypothetical situations where it would be realistic to argue that a labour market exists: imagine, for example, a geographical region isolated from the outside world where there are a large number of individuals with identical skills and a large number of firms wishing to hire workers of this type.

The purity of a particular labour market depends essentially on mobility in its broadest sense: it is of little use talking of a local labour market if there is a substantial flow of people into and out of the area in question; it is not entirely clear what we mean by an occupational labour market if there are other skills available that are extremely close substitutes in the production process. The existence of a labour market generally turns on the degree of mobility: it makes much more sense to talk of an occupational labour market (e.g. for technicians) than an industrial labour market (e.g. for all people in the engineering industry), but it is only a matter of degree. The purist might argue that it is not possible to think of a single labour market in isolation as all markets are linked together and an agreement made by a buyer and seller in any market affects the terms on which all the others trade. Again, the real world lies somewhere between the two extremes: there are certain cases where it is safe to talk of a labour market (e.g. certain localities and certain occupational groups) and other instances where this is not true (e.g. where migration is possible or where close substitutes exist).

Chapter 1 promised that a somewhat more rigorous definition of a labour market would be provided later in the book. Now seems an appropriate time. In practice, relatively little work has been carried out on the optimal classification of markets and most empirical work to date has settled for using official classifications (i.e. examining the supply of and demand for a particular occupation as defined in official statistics). However, it seems worth while to provide some intuitive explanation of the issues underlying an 'optimal' classificatory scheme, even if this requires further refinement. Such a scheme relies upon measures of 'distance' between individuals (and groups of individuals). These measures of distance are used to aggregate individuals into groups which maximize the internal homogeneity of the group (i.e. minimize the distance between individuals within the group) and maximize the heterogeneity of the groups (i.e. maximize the distance between individuals in different groups). Classifications in official statistics tend to be based on largely subjective, experiential measures of distance which cannot be easily quantified. Occupational boundaries, such as the Standard Occupational Classification, are based on subjective assessments of similarities between job types, bearing in mind responsibility levels, educational requirements, etc. (rather than, for example, definitions based on cross-price elasticities between individuals or groups of individuals).

CASE STUDY 1 An economic geographer's approach to defining labour markets

In general, economic geographers have somewhat different goals in mind when defining local labour market areas (LLMAs). Nevertheless, the two approaches are closely connected. For example, in the UK LLMAs are widely accepted as the most appropriate areal units for the analysis of unemployment. Of these, the most commonly used are the travel-to-work areas (TTWAs), which are the smallest units for which official unemployment statistics are produced. From a more general economic perspective, these can be justified on the grounds that: for many individuals it is important to find employment within a certain travelling distance, otherwise jobs become too inconvenient or too costly to reach given the going wage; likewise, employers are likely to prefer individuals who live closer rather than further away, other things being equal,

> TTWAs are relatively self-contained LLMAs within which the majority of residents work (supply-side self containment) and the majority of jobs are filled by local residents (demand-side self containment). (Flowerdew and Green, 1993, p. 289)

The Department of Education and Employment use a variety of criteria in defining the TTWAs: (i) 75 per cent of journey-to-work trips should start and end in the area (with some flexibility – larger

continues

CASE STUDY 1 continued

resident workforces, over 20,000, having lower containment, 70 per cent); (ii) minimum resident size of 3500; (iii) should be mutually exclusive; (iv) should cover the whole of country.

The construction of the TTWAs is undertaken using a complex algorithm. The key stages in the derivation of TTWAs is illustrated in Figure 12.1 although the guidelines and the associated algo-

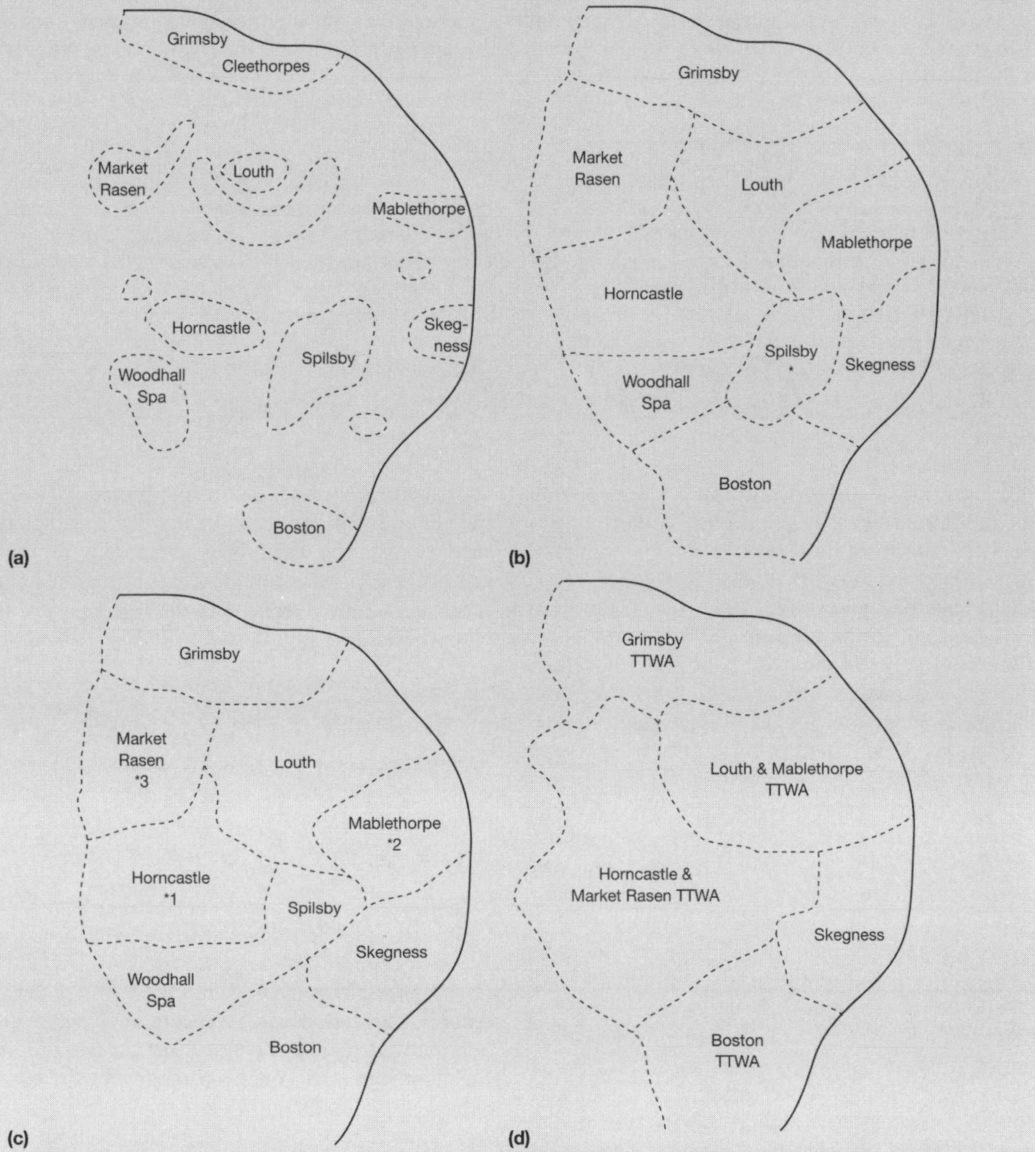

The asterisks indicate which areas do not meet statistical criteria necessary to qualify as TTWAs.
Figure (a) shows *proto* TTWAs. The expansion of *proto* into *provisional* TTWAs is illustrated in Figure (b). Spilsby *provisional* TTWA, marked by an asterisk, is the weakest of the areas not satisfying the statistical criteria, so it is dismembered and the component wards reallocated, mainly to Woodhall Spa *provisional* TTWA, as displayed in Figure (c). Horncastle, Mablethorpe and Market Rasen *provisional* TTWAs, marked by asterisks, do not satisfy the satistical criteria to qualify as TTWAs, so are, in turn, dismembered and the component wards reallocated. Eventually, all meet the statistical criteria to qualify as TTWAs, as illustrated in Figure (d).

Fig 12.1 Key stages in the derivation of travel-to-work areas: the example of the Lincolnshire wolds and marshes.

CASE STUDY 1 continued

rithm have been changed in the light of the availability of the 1991 Census of Population.

The official TTWAs are defined based on all journeys to work. In practice, however, different groups of the population have different joumey-to-work patterns, and empirical evidence suggests that there would be fewer TTWAs for males than for females, and for more highly educated and skilled than for less. In addition, it appears that metropolitan areas tend to be more complex, with inconsistent and overlapping TTWAs for different sub-groups. Finally, there is an issue of basing TTWAs on journeys to work, as this will be influenced by the unemployment rate, given that unemployment tends to be concentrated amongst less skilled and educated individuals. Thus, the shape of the 'map' might differ significantly at different points in the cycle. For a discussion of some of these issues, see Coombes *et al.* (1987).

Given that it is often difficult to work with the complete listing of TTWAs (there were 322 developed for use with the 1981 Census of Population), economic geographers have attempted to produce typologies, grouping together similar local areas. Typologies are often developed using some form of cluster analysis, such as the eight-fold one reported in Green and Owen (1988), which suggests 10 groupings, including: (i) manufacturing towns; (ii) declining centres; (iii) high-tech growth centres; (iv) male employment centres; (v) unemployment black-spots; (vi) resorts; (vii) in-migration nodes; (viii) relatively prosperous areas; (ix) service growth areas; (x) established service centres. Such clusters can be enormously useful in quantitative empirical work, but have the disadvantage of being subject to change as socioeconomic conditions vary.

Sources: Coombes *et al.* (1987); Flowerdew and Green (1993); Green and Owen (1988).

Perhaps the most rigorous empirical work to date has been undertaken by geographers attempting to specify the extent of local labour markets, for example using 'travel-to-work areas' (Coombes *et al.*, 1987; Flowerdew and Green, 1993 – see Case Study 1). These, as their title suggests, are based on the idea of travel-to-work distances, times or patterns, reflecting actual (spatial) labour mobility. The same principle is adopted in studies of the classification of occupations, which attempt rigorously to aggregate from the most detailed occupational classification in the *Labour Force Survey* (Sanderson, 1987). Groups which exhibit the greatest actual inter-occupational mobility are added together; those showing least inter-occupational mobility are kept apart. This approach to 'optimal aggregation', however, appears to have a number of inherent problems, in particular the measures: compound supply and demand side factors; fail to distinguish between the underlying causes of mobility, such as relative factor rewards or changes in socioeconomic ranking of different occupations, etc.; relate to actual rather than to potential mobility – potential mobility is only reflected in actual mobility if an appropriate market signal (such as a change in relative factor prices) is given, otherwise there may be no movement between groups even if they are close substitutes.

In order to illustrate the idea of potential mobility, we adopt the concept of 'wage distance', which is consistent with a wage–competition model. However, the general principles can be applied to other measures of distance, which may be more appropriate to non-wage adjustment models. At the aggregate level therefore, we are interested in the percentage of individuals changing from state 1 to 2,

$$E_{1,2} = \frac{\text{\% changing from state 1 to 2}}{\text{\% change in relative factor prices}} \qquad (1)$$

At the unit record level, we are interested in the percentage wage change required before there is a change in state,

$$S = S_1 \text{ if } (\partial w_2/w_2) < (\partial w_2/w_2)^* \qquad (2)$$

$$S = S_2 \text{ if } (\partial w_2/w_2) > (\partial w_2/w_2)^* \qquad (3)$$

Where w_2 denotes the wage in state 2 and we assume, for simplicity, that the wage in state 1 (where the individual is currently located) remains constant.

Note that the wage change necessary to produce the change in state is defined relative to the starting values of relative factor prices.

It is fairly easy to show that there are both supply and demand dimensions to the issue of distance:

1 demand side – if the firm currently employs individual i at wage w_i, in preference to individual j at a wage w_j, what would be the change in w_i/w_j necessary for the firm just to prefer employing individual j?

2 supply side – if individual j does not currently work for firm x at wage w_x, but prefers to work for firm y at wage w_y, what would be the change in w_x/w_y necessary for the individual just to prefer working for firm x?

Figure 12.2 illustrates the demand side. The line Y_0 represents an isoquant, showing the various combinations of hours of type i and type j individuals which would be required to produce that level of output. In practice, we assume that the firm cannot employ a mix of the two people (i.e. some hours of i and some of j), they hire either individual i or individual j. The firm currently employs individual i (amongst others), who works H_i hours per period and is paid a wage w_0. If the firm sacked individual i, its output loss would be Y_0 (i.e. the marginal product of that individual) and its cost saving would be C_0. If the firm replaced individual i with j, maintaining its output at Y_0, individual j would have to work H_j hours (again, note, we assume that the firm cannot employ some proportion of both i and j, which, with this isoquant, would be more efficient under certain wage regimes). Clearly, at current wage relativities, a switch from i to j would not be cost effective (the cost curve would shift outwards parallel with C_0 until it passed through point a). However, if the wage of w_j fell, causing the wage line to swing outwards by the percentage $(dw_j/w_j)^*$ to intersect the horizontal axis just to the right of a, the firm would prefer individual j to i. Thus, Figure 12.2 makes clear that the wage distance depends on the starting values, w^0_i and w^0_j and the productivity of the two individuals at the margin.

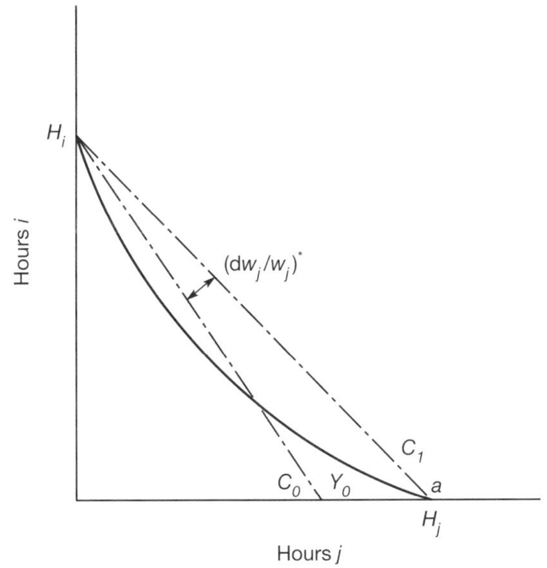

Fig 12.2 Threshold wage change necessary to induce a switch between workers.

Imagine that the firm can compare all other individuals against i and plots the distribution of $(dw/w)^*$ across all workers. The result might well be something like Figure 12.3, where the observed distribution is shown by the dashed line, x. However, this distribution is formed from individuals with certain characteristics who can be grouped together. The most appropriate groupings could be isolated by cluster analysis, revealing the common characteristics that place individuals in one group rather than another. Figure 12.3 suggests three distinct groups (A, B and C), which might minimize internal heterogeneity and maximize the differences between groups. Note that there may well be an endogenously determined optimal number of groupings. If the number of groups is too small, internal heterogeneity will be too high; if the number of groups is too large, differences between some of the groups will be too small. The groups A, B and C would be the wage–competition labour market equivalents to the travel-to-work areas used by geographers. The characteristics of these groups, however, might be defined on a range of factors such as education level, skills, experience, etc.

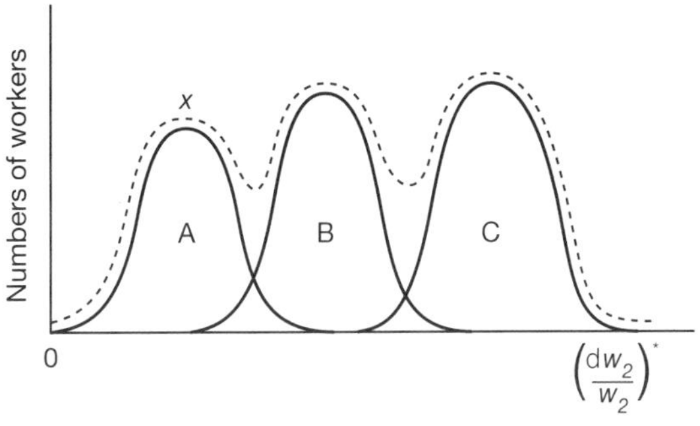

Fig 12.3 Numbers of workers who become 'more suitable' than worker i as relative wages change.

This analysis emphasizes the distinction between potential and actual distance. Starting from given wage rates for the two individuals, a switch is never observed unless the absolute value of (dw_2/w_2) is greater than the absolute size of $(dw_2/w)^*$, no matter how small $(dw_2/w_2)^*$. This will clearly be the case where the wage relativities for i and j are maintained unchanged: potential substitution is then not translated into actual mobility.

Even considered from the demand side alone, the question of optimal classification is difficult enough. However, there is also a supply side issue. Under what conditions would individual j be willing to work for firm x? At current wage relativities, how much would w_x have to rise relative to w_y in order to induce individual j to switch allegiance? Group A from Figure 12.3 might be relatively skilled and therefore potential substitutes in production for existing workers. However, this group might require a large rise in relative wages before they would be willing to switch. Thus, there is an analogous distribution $(dw/w)^*$ on the supply side, which determines the potential mobility of individuals into firm x.

By implication, the optimal classification of markets depends on the joint distribution of $(dw/w)^*$ across individuals (for a given firm) and across firms (for a given individual). Figure 12.4 attempts to illustrate this intuitively: the horizontal axis indicates the wage rise necessary to make various (groups of) individuals willing to supply themselves to the firm; the vertical axis indicates the wage falls necessary to make various (groups of) individuals attractive to the firm. Measuring wage distance as the length of any ray from 0, group B now appear as being 'closer' than either A (individuals unwilling to supply, except under major shifts in relative wages) or C (firms unwilling to demand, except under major shifts in relative.wages).

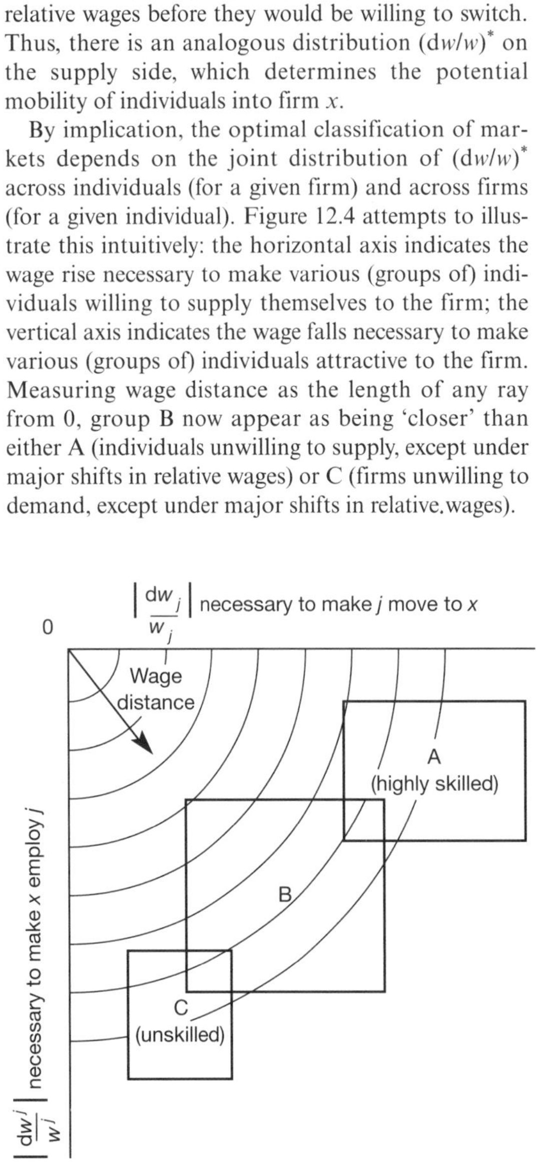

Fig 12.4 Concept of wage distance on both supply and demand sides.

3 Issues of aggregation

Having defined the dimensions of the labour market, the task is one of adding together the individual supply curves to yield market supply – and adding together the individual (i.e. firm) demand curves to yield market demand. What is clear, however, is that there is no a priori reason why the market-level curves should be of the same simple form (i.e. linear) or even have the same properties (i.e. an upward-sloping supply and downward-sloping demand relationship between the wage rate and quantity of labour services) as the underlying micro functions. The conditions that must be met before it is possible to draw a market-level function of exactly the same form as the underlying micro relationships are extremely stringent. It is worth adding that aggregate statistics are rarely, if ever, compiled in a way which complies with the conditions laid down for rigorous aggregation.

In the case of the demand for a particular occupational group, for example, it seems likely that the derivation of the market demand curve may involve aggregating across firms in different industries, using different technologies and therefore having different labour demand functions. In addition, each industry is likely to have a different market structure, goals of the firm and may behave quite differently. Consequent differences in the effect on output and labour demand will be reinforced where the industries have different price elasticities of demand. Drawing 'well-behaved' shapes for the market functions is an act of faith, undertaken for analytical simplicity. While there are clearly going to be circumstances when this is possible, they may turn out to be the exception rather than the rule. These words of warning over, the discussion continues on the following assumptions: first, market supply and demand functions can be drawn; second, they are continuous curves in the wage–labour services space; third, except where the assumption is specifically countermanded, the market demand curve is a decreasing function of the wage and the market supply curve is an increasing function of the wage rate.

4 Identification of labour supply and demand schedules

In order to simplify the analysis, the discussion begins by assuming that the labour market clears instantaneously (although this assumption is later dropped). Isolation of a demand relationship at the market level, without jointly estimating a labour supply function, effectively requires that the demand curve remains stationary in the face of a shifting supply curve. Such a situation is illustrated in Figure 12.5, where the labour demand curve varies only slightly around D, bounded by D_0 and D_1. The supply curve, on the other hand, has shifted over the whole length of the demand curve, between S_0 and S_1. In this case, market equilibria, which are represented by points of intersection between the two curves, all lie on or close to the labour demand curve, D. In the extreme case, where there are no shifts in the demand curve, all of the observed combinations of wage and employment lie on the demand curve, D. Clearly, the opposite applies if the points are to lie along a labour supply function (i.e. the demand should be volatile and the supply curve stable).

Even in the less extreme version, in the case of demand, if a curve was fitted through points such as a, b and c, it should approximate fairly closely to the demand curve. Contrast this result with the one shown in Figure 12.6. In this case, the demand curve has also shifted to a significant extent and the various points of intersection, representing market equilibria, are scattered widely throughout the (w,E) space. If a single curve was fitted through these points without any further restrictions or information, there is no guarantee that it would approximate the demand function at all closely. It would be a hybrid of supply and demand. In response a number of models attempt to provide a full model of the labour market with both supply and demand curves represented (see Hammermesh, 1993, pp. 79–80, and Chapter 14 this book for examples).

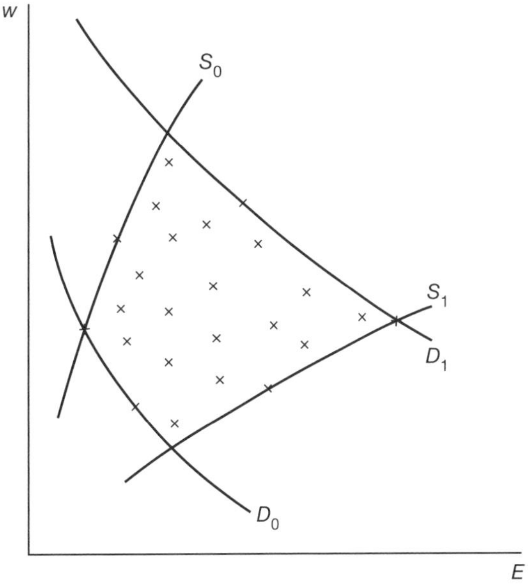

Fig 12.6 Failure to identify demand curve.

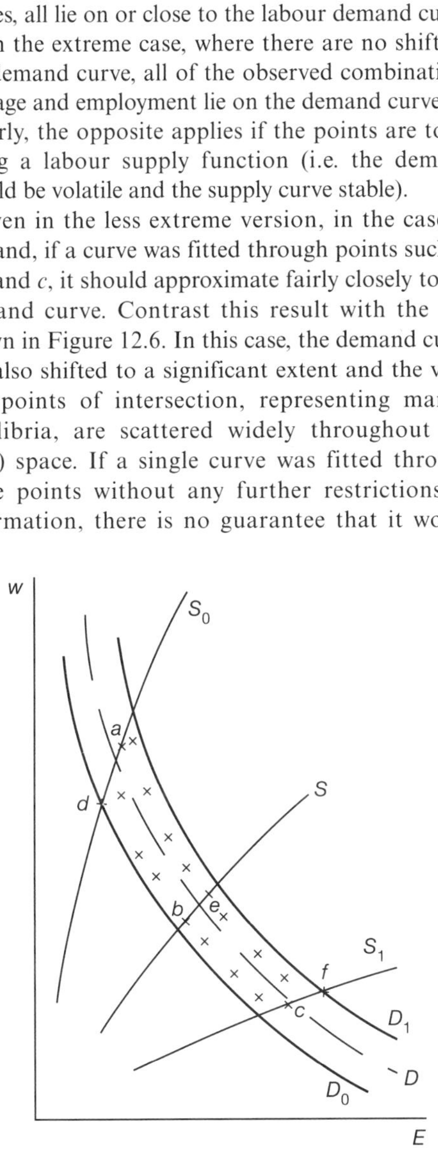

Fig 12.5 Identification of demand curve.

There are several other problems that are worthy of note. One question concerns non-random error around the demand curve, D. For example, if the positions of the supply and demand curves in Figure 12.5 are not independent, then some degree of bias will be introduced into the estimate of the demand curve. Suppose, just for the sake of argument, that during periods of low economic activity both supply and demand were shifted closer to the origin than during periods of high activity. In this case the points of intersection might be at d, e and f (associated with the intersection of S_0,D_0, S,D and S_1,D_1, respectively). In this instance, the estimated curve will be biased, appearing more elastic than the real demand curve. Clearly, the potential bias from such a source increases with the degree to which the demand curve itself shifts. Again, a similar argument applies when isolating the supply curve.

Perhaps the most important problem concerns the assumption introduced at the beginning of this section, that the market clears instantaneously. Figure 12.7 illustrates the outcome when wages only adjust slowly in the face of shifting supply, even though there is a stationary demand curve, D. The problem arises when the market becomes supply constrained, as in the case where the supply curve shifts from S_0 to S_1. Instantaneous adjustment implies a shift from an equilibrium at e^* to one at g^*, but a partial adjustment of wages means that the market will initially move out to a point such as f on S_1 and then gradually (as wages adjust upwards in the face of excess demand) move from f to g^*. In effect, when the market is (temporarily) held at point f, it is supply constrained. In other words, there is an excess demand for labour of fe^* at wage w^*, and inherent pressure for the wage to rise. We might also imagine an outward shift in supply from S_0 to S_2, which, if wages adjusted slowly, might produce an additional supply of e^*i of workers. However, the market is, in this instance, demand constrained. At a wage w^*, employers will only hire E^* of workers (or labour services) and there is an excess supply of labour on the market. As the wage rate gradually declines towards w_2, employment moves along the demand curve from e^* towards h^*. Thus, where wages adjust only slowly in both directions (upward and downward), the observed outcome is asymmetric. The potential asymmetry may make the phenomenon difficult to model using simple partial adjustment mechanisms, suggesting the need for a more explicit treatment of supply. Similarly, there may be a further asymmetry in the flexibility (i.e. the rate of change) of wages in the two directions

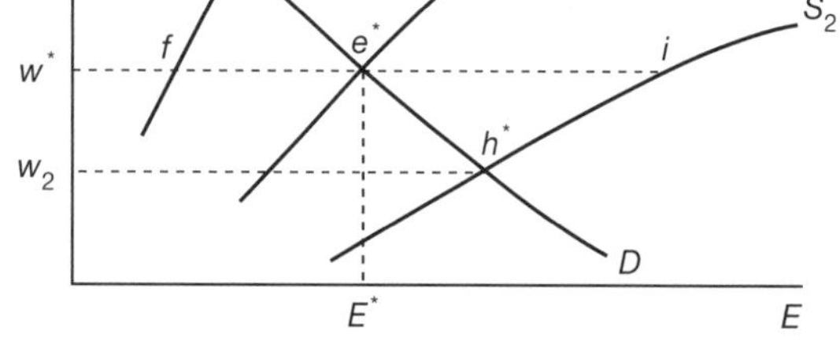

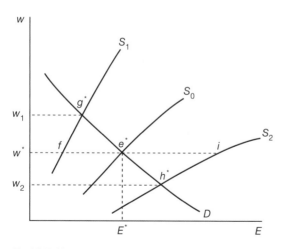

Fig 12.7 Market clearing and identification.

(employees may be more reluctant to see wages fall than rise; employers may exhibit the opposite preference). We return to both of these issues in later chapters. A move to a point such as f not only is a long way off the demand curve, but also appears to involve a major decline in observed employment, followed by a gradual rise (depending on the rate of adjustment of wages and the elasticity of the supply curve).

5 User cost, earnings and the market outcome

One thing that needs to be borne in mind when bringing together supply and demand is that the observed wage may not be an adequate measure of either the producer's perceived per unit cost of labour or the worker's perceived reward for supplying labour services. The demand decision is more likely to be based on the per unit user cost of factors and the supply decision on net real earnings (i.e. the pecuniary and non-pecuniary take-home pay). Two important factors causing a divergence between the observed wage and the actual remuneration are: (i) fringe benefits; (ii) income and payroll taxes.

The remuneration perceived by the individual is the money wage, augmented by any non-pecuniary payments (i.e. perks, such as a firm's car). Clearly, non-pecuniary payments are viewed as an additional benefit by employees and cost by employers, thereby affecting both the effective take-home pay and user cost of labour. A natural reaction would seem to be to construct remuneration and cost variables by valuing the fringe benefits and adding them to the wage in each period. This may only be a first approximation, however, as an additional £1 of fringe benefits may have a different impact on the supply of labour services (or on the demand for labour services) than an extra £1 of wage. In the case of supply, for example, fringe benefits may be subject to a lower rate of tax than the equivalent money payment, but they may not leave the same freedom of consumer choice as extra wages. A rigorous model of the market might, therefore, specify the supply and demand curves as functions of both money wages and fringe benefits. For simplicity, however, we assume that fringe benefits can be translated directly into equivalent money wages. Under this assumption, the adoption of remuneration and user cost measures will mean that fringe benefits will not require separate treatment in the models.

Even allowing for fringe benefits, there are other influences which are relevant. The government's involvement in the labour market through taxes and subsidies affects the perceived costs and rewards of employment. Income taxes (and subsidies) affect the level of take-home pay and, thereby, the individual's labour supply decision. Payroll taxes (and subsidies) affect the per unit cost of labour to the firm thereby influencing the firm's demand decision. At the micro level, where taxes exceed subsidies, they tend to shift both supply and demand curves inwards and, thereby, reduce employment below the free market level. At the macro level, however, this need not be true as the taxes raised may be spent in a manner that creates employment.

The implications of these payments for a particular labour market can be analysed using Figure 12.8. The lines S_0 and D_0 denote the supply and demand relationships where the wage is an adequate measure of employee remuneration and of user cost. The free market equilibrium occurs at point *e*, at a wage w_e^* and employment level E_e^*. Now introduce a government which taxes both employers and employees. Employers now pay payroll taxes. While they are not willing to pay a higher amount at each level of employment, part of what they would have paid now goes to the government rather than the individual. It is as if the demand curve has shifted in from D_0 to D_1; the employer receives less labour for each amount it is willing to pay. Employees pay income taxes and this makes their perceived remuneration lower than the wage at every employment level. Employees still require a take-home pay represented by points along S_0 for each level of employment. Given that the government now taxes them, the amount of labour supplied is lower at any given gross wage and the effect is to shift the supply curve inwards from S_0 to S_1. Market equilibrium now takes place at a wage w_f^* and employment level E_f^*. At this point: the perceived costs per employee to the employers are w_g and they are willing to pay w_f^* in wages (the effective tax rate on employers is a/w_g). The gross pay of the employee is w_f^*, which is seen as a perceived remuneration of w_h after tax (and the effective tax rate on the employee is b/w_h^*). Thus the levels of employment supplied and demanded at the gross wage w_f^* are equal.

Finally we note the employment effects of these tax burdens. At a wage w_f^*, for example, without payroll taxes employers would have hired an additional *c* workers. Similarly, at this wage rage, in the absence of income tax, a further *d* employees would have supplied their services. Given that free market supply and demand are equal at point *e*, the overall impact of taxation is to lower employment from E_e^* to E_f^*. Thus, there is a natural tendency for governments to restrict the tax burden in order to raise employment. However, this tendency is simplistic because the taxes may be moving the market closer to a point where social welfare is optimized (i.e. if employment imposes net welfare costs which are borne by society, such as the health costs of work-related illnesses) and the tax revenues are spent and, thereby, create employment.

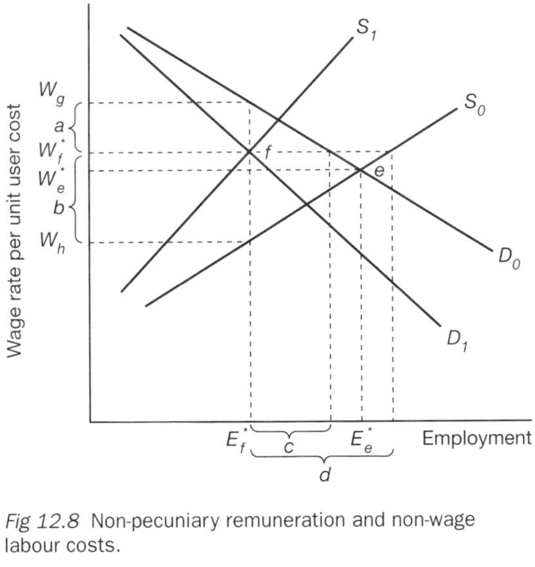

Fig 12.8 Non-pecuniary remuneration and non-wage labour costs.

6 Conclusions

This chapter considered the difficulties which surround the more rigorous definition of a labour market. In addition, it outlined a number of issues surrounding the identification of the supply and demand curves, including issues of aggregation. Finally, the discussion illustrated the simple 'wage–competition' model, indicating the impact that government taxation may have on observed wages, user cost and employment levels. The discussion continues, at least initially, on the assumption that it is possible to isolate a particular, pure labour market. Partial equilibrium analysis is adopted where the inter-relationship with other labour markets can be ignored. As mentioned in this introduction, this 'wage–competition' model of such 'external labour markets' does not take into account some of the idiosyncrasies of the employment relationship, and the possibility, for example, that the supply of and demand for labour occurs within a particular firm. We consider various aspects of the employment relationship, including internal labour markets, in Part VI of the book.

References

Coombes, M.F., A.E. Green and D.W. Owen (1987). 'Substantive Issues in the Definition of "Localities": Evidence from Sub-Group Local Labour Market Areas in the West Midlands'. *Regional Studies*. 22,4, 303–318.

Flowerdew, R. and A. Green (1993). 'Migration, Transportation and Workplace Statistics from the 1991 Census'. In A. Dalt and C. Marsh (eds) *The 1991 Census Users' Guide*. London: HMSO, pp. 269–294.

Green, A. and D. Owen (1988). *The Development of a Classification of Travel-to-Work Areas*. Project Report. Institute for Employment Research. Coventry: University of Warwick, July.

Hammermesh, D.S. (1993). *Labour Demand*. Princeton, NJ: Princeton University Press.

Sanderson, J. (1987). 'Defining Functional Occupational Groups'. *Environment and Planning A*, 19, 1199–1220.

CHAPTER 13 Static equilibrium under different market structures

1 Introduction: aims and scope

In this chapter we assume that it is possible to identify separate labour markets of the 'ideal' type outlined in Chapter 12, in other words where we can consider one market in isolation from all others. Thus the chapter adopts a partial equilibrium approach and uses comparative static analysis to examine the wage and employment outcomes predicted when we bring supply and demand functions together under different market structures. We simplify the analysis by assuming hours are fixed and examining the market for persons. By different market structures we mean that we observe different degrees of market power on each side of the labour market. A number of stylized situations suggest themselves. For example, we might observe: perfect competition in both supply and demand; a single buyer (a monopsonist) facing a perfectly competitive supply; a single supplier (trade union) facing a large number of small employers; or a situation in which both suppliers and buyers have some degree of market power (i.e. oligopoly and oligopsony). The ideas are introductory and developed further in later sections of the book. In particular, the case of a trade union having a monopoly on the supply of labour is taken up in Part VII of the book. Section 2 continues with a discussion of the basic outcome under perfect competition in the labour market. Section 3 considers the case of monopsony, in other words, a situation in which there is power on the buyer but not the supplier side. Monopoly, dealt with in Section 4, is the mirror image of this, with power on the supplier but not the buyer side of the market. Bilateral monopoly occurs where a single buyer faces a single supplier, and is the subject of Section 5. The final situation we deal with is oligopsony, which is similar to bilateral monopoly, but with a small number of agents on each side of the market. Section 7 draws the main conclusions of this chapter.

2 Perfect competition

The simplest case is the market in which there are many buyers and sellers, so that no one buyer or seller can, individually, exert any influence on the wage rate. The other rules of perfect competition must apply to allow the outcome. For example, each unit of labour is homogeneous, buyers and sellers possess perfect knowledge of the market and are perfectly mobile. Under these circumstances the wage rate and level of employment are determined by the intersection of the market supply and demand curves as shown in Figure 13.1. The outcome under such circumstances is straightforward. At wages below w_1,

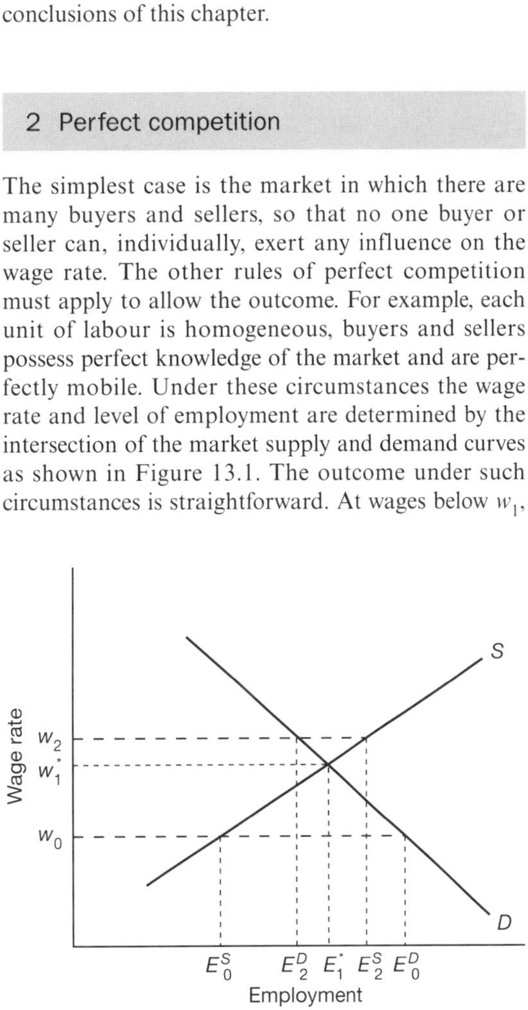

Fig 13.1 Market equilibrium under conditions of perfect competition.

such as w_0, labour demand, E^D_0, exceeds labour supply, E^S_0, there is a shortage of labour in the market and a natural incentive exists for firms to bid up wages. This incentive continues until wages reach a level w_1, at which supply equals demand. If, by chance, wages are set at a level w_2, an almost mirror image situation arises, with labour supply, E^S_2, in excess of labour demand. Now there are not enough jobs to go around and individuals, in their search for employment, have an incentive to offer their labour services at a wage lower than w_2. Thus, wages fall below w_2. This incentive to bid down wages continues until wages fall to w_1. However, at w_1, all incentives for further change disappear; both sellers and buyers are happy with the outcome.

We described the model as if some form of adjustment takes place when disequilibrium occurs. Clearly, if such adjustment takes a considerable while, the market can be thought of as being in disequilibrium. Generally in competitive markets, however, adjustment is assumed to be rapid, indeed perhaps so rapid that the adjustment process itself can be ignored. In the extreme we might imagine that the wage–competition outcome is analogous to the 'price auction' or 'spot market' models of product markets. In this case buyers and sellers bid as part of a *tâttonnement* process, the auctioneer settles on w_1 as the market clearing wage and exchange duly takes place at the equilibrium values (w^*_1, E^*_1); effectively disequilibrium is never observed in the market.

CASE STUDY 1 Labour market structure

Labour market structure depends on the power of both buyers and suppliers of labour services. Thus, the market outcome seems likely to depend on both the degree of monopsony (buyer) and monopoly (supplier) power.

There is likely to be some relationship between the degree of market power of firms in the product and labour markets (i.e. between product market monopoly and labour market monopsony), if only because some skills are firm or industry specific. Generally, however, firms in different industries to some degree compete for the same labour. Thus, a monopolist in the product market may nevertheless have to compete intensively for certain types of workers. In the case of monopsony, we need to know the number and size of firms competing in each labour market. In practice, this type of information is not available. However, some insights can be obtained by looking at the degree of 'firm dependence' for each skill,

$$\zeta_i = \sum_j (E_{ij}/\sum_j E_{ij})^2 \tag{1}$$

where: E denotes employment, i is the ith skill and, in principle, j denotes the jth firm. Given the similarity with Herfindahl indices, the measure lies in the range $0 \leq \zeta_i \leq 1$, taking a value of 0 under perfect competition and 1 under perfect 'firm dependence' (i.e. where the skill is hired by a single firm).

In practice, firm-level data are rarely if ever available, but it is possible to gain some insights by constructing a measure of 'industry dependence', which indicates the extent to which the employment of each of the 569 occupations (the four-digit occupational grouping available in the *Labour Force Survey* in the 1980s) is concentrated at the four-digit industry level. See Table 13.1. Given that even four-digit industries contain a number of firms, ideally the results should be combined with product concentration data at this level. Given the way it is constructed, the absolute value of the index is influenced by the classification which is being used to code the industrial and occupational data. Relative values across occupations and over time will be unaffected except where there are significant classification changes.

Most of the groups show significant falls in the index between 1983 and 1987. The decline is large for both the professional (0.48 to 0.42) and the associate professional and technical occupations (0.36 to 0.29). Sales occupations and clerical and secretarial showed somewhat different patterns. Finally, managers and administrators, and plant and machine operatives, showed some reversal of the general downward trend between 1986 and 1987 (though this may partly reflect changes in coding procedures). In summary, the index says more about the outlying groups than about the bulk of the occupations (which tend to take on a fairly standard set of values, around 0.3–0.4). In particular, the services of professionals are purchased by a relatively small group of buyers compared with

continues

CASE STUDY 1 continued

Table 13.1 Index of industrial dependency

Occupation	1983	1984	1985	1986	1987
1 Managers and administrators	0.44	0.42	0.37	0.37	0.39
2 Professional occupations	0.48	0.45	0.45	0.43	0.42
3 Associate professional and technical occupations	0.36	0.32	0.32	0.32	0.29
4 Clerical and secretarial occupations	0.04	0.04	0.05	0.05	0.04
5 Craft and skilled manual occupations	0.35	0.35	0.33	0.33	0.29
6 Personal and protective service occupations	0.39	0.36	0.35	0.36	0.36
7 Sales occupations	0.29	0.32	0.32	0.33	0.32
8 Plant and machine operatives	0.19	0.17	0.17	0.17	0.21
9 Other occupations	0.36	0.34	0.34	0.33	0.32

the average for all occupations. This may be linked with the lack of adjustment in markets such as those for professional engineers, during periods of perceived shortages. Plant and machine operatives have a low index, but the lowest value of all is associated with the clerical and secretarial group. Other things being equal, we expect these markets to be highly competitive on the buyer side. While these results seem broadly in line with expectations, further work is required to pull together all of the information relating to monopsony power, including firm size and concentration.

An analogous measure of monopoly power can be constructed based on the extent to which a given industry is dependent on the supply of a particular skill – an index of 'occupational dependency'. The measure takes a value of unity when the industry is wholly dependent on one skill and zero when its factor demands are spread across a wide number of skills. While occupational dependency is of interest and potential importance, it influences monopoly power through its interaction with other factors. In particular, in principle, certain occupations may be more indispensable insofar as they are complementary with key pieces of capital equipment, while having no close substitutes amongst other occupations employed by the firm. Any such index must also be supplemented by information concerning the existence and power of trade unions and/or professional institutes. It is often argued that the degree of monopoly power can be proxied by trade union membership, coverage by collective agreements, etc. The decline in union power over the period since 1979 has certainly been a crucial influence on the extent of monopoly power. However, even where union membership is high, the result may differ depending on the number of trade unions representing the workers in question, whether the unions have similar (or dissimilar) goals and the degree to which they are willing to cooperate. The progress and outcome of a dispute over the regrading of nurses in the 1980s was almost certainly influenced by the existence of three unions with differing goals and strategies. In addition, the movement to single-plant bargaining has shifted the balance of power away from trade unions in multi-plant (often multinational) producing situations. Finally, the declining power of the TUC in recent years may further undermine the ability to coordinate strike action effectively, further reducing union power.

Source: Bosworth and Warren (1989)

3 Monopsony

Monopsony occurs in a market where there is one buyer of labour and many sellers – see Case Study 1. In a market of this type, a monopsonist can offer any wage rate it chooses. The supply curve indicates how much labour will be forthcoming at that wage. Assuming that the employer must pay the same wage to all employees the supply curve is equivalent to the average cost of labour to the monopsonist. Assuming a positively sloped supply curve, with average cost rising, the marginal cost of employing the labour will be higher than the average cost and both are increasing functions of the quantity of labour. In other words, when the wage paid is increased in order to attract more labour, the wage bill rises because this higher wage is paid not only to newly employed labour, but also to existing workers. Figure 13.2 shows the supply of labour curve S_0, and the marginal cost of labour to the monopolist is represented by the MLC_0 curve.

The profit-maximizing monopsonist will equate the marginal cost of labour with its marginal revenue product, which, for any given wage, is represented by the demand curve. Thus, the monopsonist will choose to employ E_2^* of labour at a wage w_2, the wage indicated by the supply curve. One implication of this is that it is not possible to identify a demand curve for labour under monopsony, because there are many wage rates consistent with a given level of employment dependent on the elasticity of the labour supply curve. This can be demonstrated quite easily by looking at the labour supply curve S_1 and its associated marginal labour cost curve MLC_1. Here the equilibrium employment would be E_2^*, as before, but the wage paid to employees would be w_3.

Despite the absence of a demand curve under monopsony, we are able to undertake a comparison with the outcome under perfect competition, as long as the MRP curve of the monopsonist is the same as the demand curve for the perfectly competitive market (i.e. assuming that the existence of monopsony power does not affect the position of the curves). Under these circumstances, it is clear that the monopsony outcome is associated with a lower wage rate and a lower level of employment than under perfect competition, $E_2^* < E_1^*$.

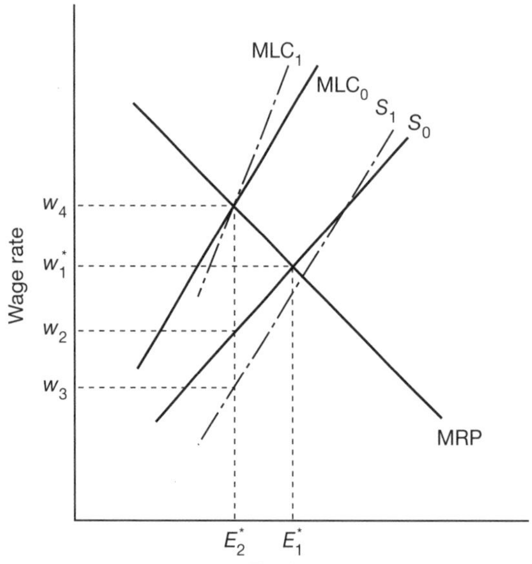

Fig 13.2 Market equilibrium under monopsony.

The difference between w_1 and w_2 has been called the measure of Pigouvian exploitation. Given that workers are, in some sense, being 'exploited', this suggests that there may be some beneficial effects from the introduction of a minimum wage. This can again be demonstrated using Figure 13.2. Based on the labour supply curve S_0 and marginal revenue product curve MRP, it can be seen that the firm chooses a wage rate w_2. If, however, the government sets a minimum wage, w_m, above w_2, this will increase employment at least up to the point where $w_m = w_1$. Above this level, however, employment is determined by the intersection of w_m and MRP, and employment falls back below the competitive maximum, E_1^*, although it will continue to generate employment levels above E_2^* until $w_m \geq w_4$. A minimum wage $w_m < w_2$, has no effect. There are, of course implications for the costs of production of introducing an effective minimum wage.

Up to this point we have assumed a non-discriminating monopsonist. However, first-degree discrimination would mean that the employer would be able to pay each employee the minimum wage necessary to induce them to supply their labour. Under this form of perfect discrimination, S_0 represents the marginal cost of labour curve, as the monopsonist does not have to increase the wage of existing employees when it offers a higher wage to attract an additional worker. Given that the employer continues to set MLC = MRP (where MLC is now represented by S_0), then the outcome is the wage–employment combination (w_1^*, E_1^*). At first sight this looks identical to the outcome under perfect competition. However, there is a crucial difference, and that is that the firm appropriates all of the potential welfare surplus that would have accrued to those employees who, under the non-discriminatory regime, were paid w_2, but would have worked for less. Now all of the area under the MRP curve and above the *S* curve contributes to firm profit, rather than being divided partly between profits and wages.

It seems unlikely that a situation of perfect discrimination would be observed in the real world. For one thing, many workers do identical jobs and inequalities in pay lead to conflict or differences in effort. However, the idea that a monopsonist might be able to differentiate in its treatment of several groups who are similarly productive within the company appears more realistic. This might happen, for example, where firms can discriminate between, say, males and females, whites and ethnic minorities, core and peripheral workers, etc.

The outcome in a two-market case is illustrated in Figure 13.3. If the monopsonist is not able to discriminate between the two markets, the supply of labour is simply amalgamated, S^A+S^B, and the associated marginal labour cost curve is represented by MLC^A+MLC^B. The result is that the wage offer is the same to both markets, $w_0^A = w_0^B = w_0$, and employment outcomes are E_0^A, E_0^B, with a total of $E_0^A + E_0^B$. If the monopsonist is able to discriminate, however, this enables the firm to set MRP equal to MLC separately in each market. Thus, the firm sets $m_0^A = m^B{}_0 = m_0$, with differential wage outcomes, $w_1^A > w_0 > w_1^B$, and employment, $E_1^A > E_0^A$ and $E_1^B < E_0^B$ (but both $E_1^A < E_c^A$ and $E_1^B < E_c^B$, where subscript c denotes the competitive outcome). These outcomes reflect the position and relative elasticities of the two labour supply curves. In essence, it pays the firm to expand its employment further in market 1, with the more elastic curve. Even though some individuals in market 2 would be willing to work for lower wages, the increase in wage at the margin soon makes expansion through route 2 very expensive. Finally, we can again see that the competitive outcome has higher wages and employment in both markets than either of the monopsony outcomes. This idea of segmented markets and employer discrimination are discussed again in Chapter 24.

4 Monopoly

It is interesting to compare the monopsony outcome with that of monopoly. Under monopoly there is just one seller (we can think of this as a group of individuals belonging to a trade union) and many buyers. The outcome of the very simplest of models is illustrated in Figure 13.4. The demand curve for labour represents the monopolist's average revenue curve. In other words, if the union chooses to supply a given amount of labour, say, E_1, the set of firms in the market will pay a wage of w_1. To find the market equilibrium, however, we add the marginal revenue curve. The marginal revenue curve is important because it reflects the fact that, each time the union chooses to supply another unit of labour, it not only forces down the wage for the additional worker employed, but for all existing employees. The monopolist supplies E_2^* of labour, where the marginal revenue curve cuts the supply curve of labour, and the wage paid, w_2^*, can be derived from the demand curve at that level of employment. Thus, in keeping with the traditional theory of monopoly, the effect is a restriction of supply below the perfectly competitive level, E_3, at a higher price (w_2 compared with w_3).

It is unrealistic to assume that the objective of a trade union is to maximize profits by setting the marginal cost of supplying labour equal to the marginal revenue. For one thing, the supply curve is not a marginal cost curve in the traditional sense. What is

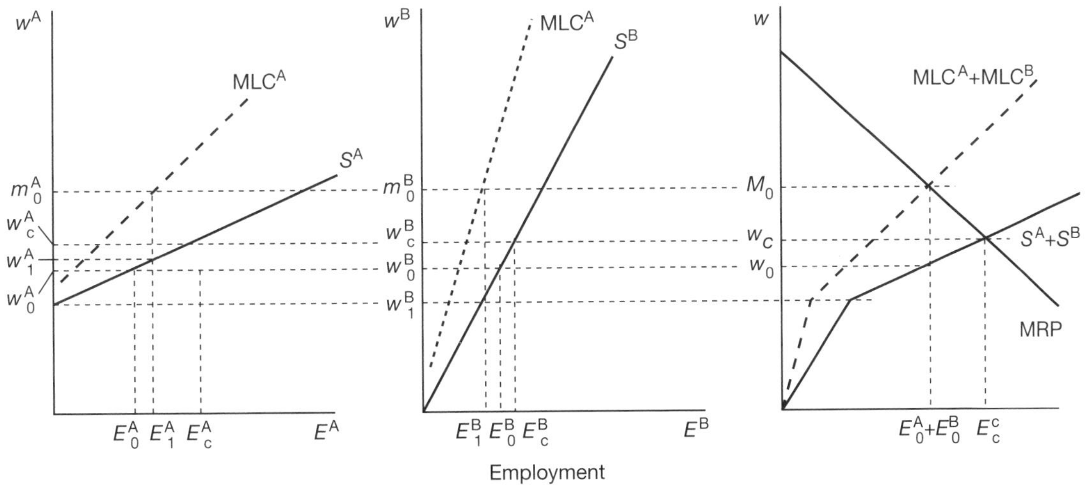

Fig 13.3 Discriminating monopsonist: two-market case.

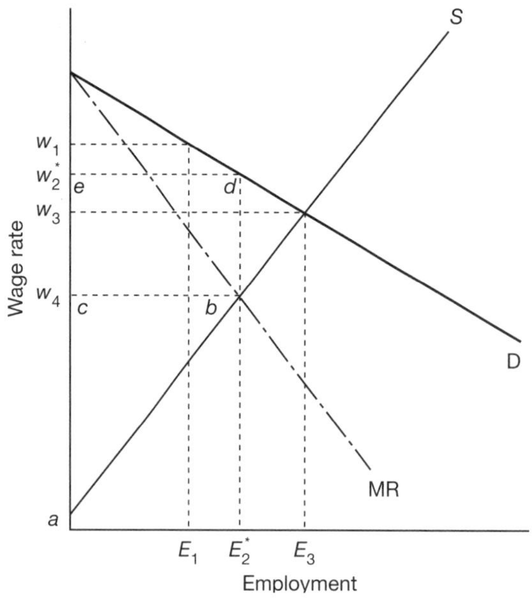

Fig 13.4 Market equilibrium of the profit-maximizing monopolist.

happening here is that the supply of labour curve is based upon the utility maximization of the union (monopoly supplier) members. Thus, each member can do no better in terms of their leisure-income trade-off than be on the supply curve. What the union does, however, is to attempt to maximize the economic surplus paid to its members. Clearly, at a wage w_4, members receive a surplus of *abc*. However, with united action, they can increase this by *abde*. There are numerous question marks about the assumptions we have made, such that a union will behave in this way. More realistic objectives of trade unions are discussed at greater length in Chapter 25 of the book.

One reason for maximizing these 'monopoly rents' is that in doing so, it creates the largest value of surplus that can be used to pay union membership fees. However, unions represent their members and may adopt a variety of different goals, bearing in mind that they are characterized by principal–agent problems analogous to the shareholder–management case noted above. One example might be that once in the union, 'insiders' restrict the membership in order to maximize their wage rate. Just to illustrate the possible effects of different union goals on market wages and employment, however, we explore the outcomes of three alternative goals: wage bill maximization; wage rate maximization subject to a minimum employment constraint; and employment maximization subject to a minimum wage constraint. The resulting equilibria from each of these objectives are shown in Figure 13.5. A union which attempts to maximise the wage bill (total 'revenue' of union members) will, by definition, seek that level of employment E_1 at which marginal revenue (the addition to the wage bill caused by employing an additional unit of labour) equals zero. The resulting wage rate is w_1. If the union maximizes the wage rate subject to a minimum employment constraint of, say, E_2, then the wage will be w_2. If, however, the union is concerned to maximize employment subject to a minimum wage constraint, w_3, then it will expand supply to E_3.

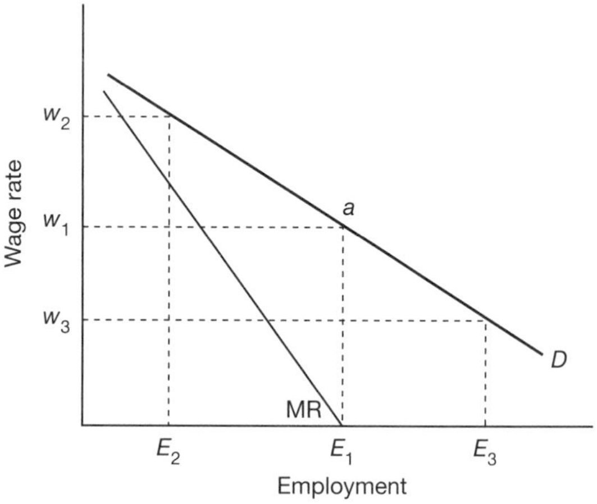

Fig 13.5 Wages and union goals.

5 Bilateral monopoly

Bilateral monopoly exists where there is a monopsonist on the demand side (a single buyer of labour) and a monopolist (a single supplier or union) on the supply side of the labour market. If both are profit maximizers then the situation is as illustrated in Figure 13.6. The monopsonist wishes to employ E_1 labour at wage rate w_1; the monopolist wants to supply E_1 at a wage rate w_2. The figure has been drawn so that the desired level of employment is the same for both the monopolist and the monopsonist, although, in general, this would only happen by accident. The main feature is that both buyers and suppliers want to restrict the volume of employment below the competitive level but for different reasons:

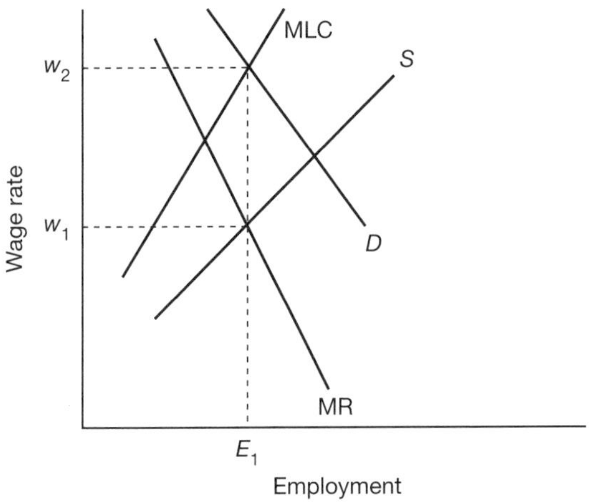

Fig 13.6 Bargaining range under conditions of bilateral monopoly.

the monopsonist wants to do so in order to lower the wage below the competitive market level and the monopolist to raise the wage above this level. Without imposing any additional structure on the problem the most that can be said is that the outcome is likely to lie somewhere between by the two wage rates w_1 and w_2. The eventual settlement will depend upon the bargaining strength of the two parties. The bargaining process and the economics of strike action are again dealt with in Part VII below.

Using the same comparative static framework for the analysis, however, it is possible to consider the outcome of bilateral monopoly under the alternative assumptions considered above, for example where the monopsonist attempts to maximize profits and the monopolist attempts one of the following: wage bill maximization, wage rate maximization subject to an employment constraint and employment maximization subject to a wage constraint. The three different outcomes, one for each of the three alternative goals of the monopolist, are illustrated in Figures 13.7(a)–(c). In all three cases, we have assumed that the monopsonist would prefer to set a wage rate of w_1, with employment E_1, as described in Section 3 above. In setting these different goals, however, the unions may produce situations of greater or less conflict between the workers and management. As might be expected, wage rate maximization subject to a minimum employment constraint of E_3 produces the greatest potential conflict with the employer about the wage rate if the wage demand is pushed high enough (i.e. depending on what the union perceives to be the minimum level of employment) (see Figure 13.7(b)). Indeed, in this instance, the monopolist is seeking a lower level of employment, E_3, than the monopsonist, E_1. Conversely the union which seeks to maximize employment subject to the minimum wage rate constraint seeks a higher level of employment, E_4, than the monopsonist, E_1 (see Figure 13.7(c)). In this case,

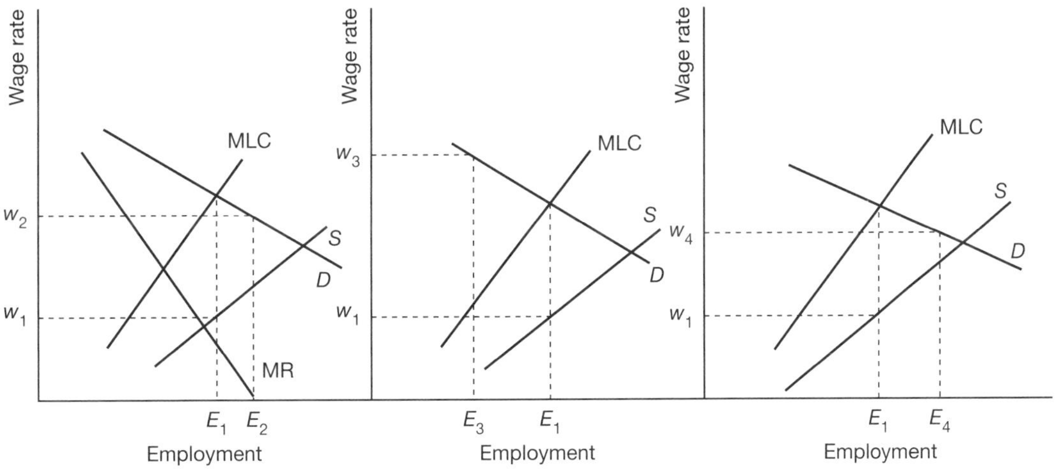

(a) Wage bill maximization

(b) Wage rate-maximization subject to a minimum employment constraint of E_3

(c) Employment maximization subject to a minimum wage constraint of w_4

Fig 13.7 Bilateral monopoly under different assumptions about the monopolist.

while the monopolist still attempts to set a higher wage rate than the competitive level, it is not as high as in the wage rate maximizer subject to an employment constraint. The outcome for the wage bill maximizer (shown in Figure 13.7(a)) lies between the other two examples.

6 Oligopolistic market

Up to this point, this chapter has considered market structures characterized by extreme conditions of market power. In the real world, however, it is unlikely that most labour markets will conform to these extreme types, but will be characterized by intermediate degrees of market power or dominance. On the demand side of the labour market, oligopsony is probably a more widespread market structure with workers being hired by a relatively small number of employers. Oligopsony should be dealt with using some form of game theoretic approach. However, the literature in this area is relatively underdeveloped. Limited insights can be gained using kinked demand curve theory (Coyne, 1975). The precise outcome of this model depends on whether the oligopsonist is an oligopolist in the product market and whether the suppliers of labour also possess market power (e.g. the supply of labour might be oligopolistic).

The rationale for this specification is very similar to that of the standard kinked demand curve model of oligopoly. The oligopsonist does not expect other firms to follow a wage decrease. Therefore, a wage reduction would lead to a relatively large fall in the supply of labour to the firm. However, it expects other firms to follow a wage increase and hence the supply function is much steeper for wages above w_0. Figure 13.8 therefore shows the supply curve to be kinked at w_0,E_0, and relatively elastic in the range *ab*, but inelastic in the range *bc*. This produces a discontinuity in the marginal labour cost curve, MLC.

In the first instance the oligopsonist is assumed to be a perfect competitor in the product market and is not faced by any labour union possessing market power on the supply side. The outcome is illustrated in Figure 13.8. The employer sets marginal labour cost, MLC, equal to the marginal revenue product, MRP_1, which occurs at level of employment E_0 (or, more accurately, MRP_1 passes through the discontinuity in MLC at that level of employment). The

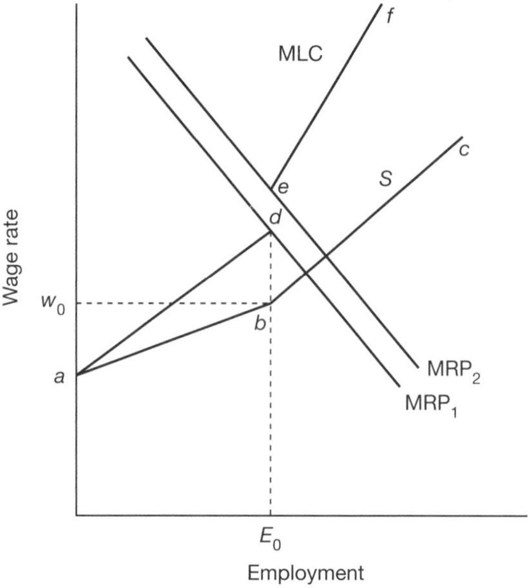

Fig 13.8 Market equilibrium under conditions of oligopsony.

outcome is interesting because (as in the case of the kinked demand curve under oligopolistic product markets), the resulting wage–employment outcome is 'sticky'. Any movement of the MRP curve between MRP_1 and MRP_2 has no effect on wages or employment. As a consequence, when demand increases the employer enjoys an increased surplus. If this is followed by a fall in demand still within the discontinuity *de*, there is no reduction in employment. That is to say that no labour is laid off. This provides one possible explanation of both 'labour hoarding' in the downswing of the trade cycle and wage rigidity. However, other explanations have taken precedence, as we will demonstrate in Part VI of the book

If the assumption of oligopsony in the labour market is augmented by an oligopoly in the product market, the prediction of wage rigidity is reinforced. An oligopolist in the product market facing a kinked demand curve for its product possesses a kinked average revenue product curve for labour, and a discontinuous marginal revenue product of labour, such as the MRP curve in Figure 13.9. The demand curve can now shift upwards in such a way that point *d* coincides with point *b* or downwards so that point *a* coincides with point *c*, without affecting wages. The size of such a shift is $2ad + bc$. The conclusion about wage rigidity is now even stronger with two discontinuities combining.

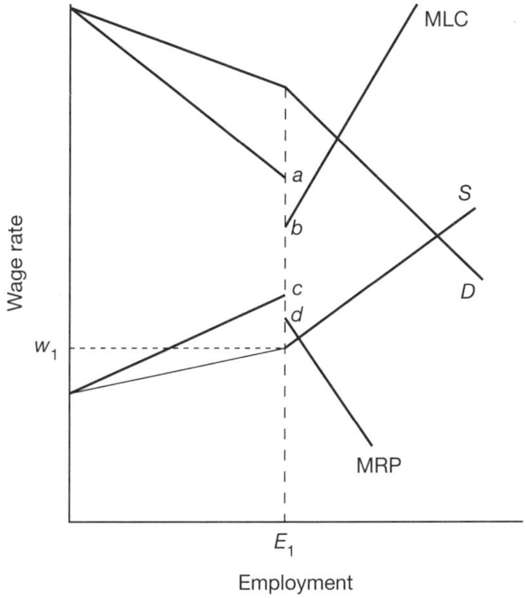

Fig 13.9 Market equilibrium: oligopoly and oligopsony.

7 Conclusions

This chapter has examined a number of possible labour market outcomes associated with different degrees of market power amongst both enterprises hiring employees and the workforce. While a number of the models are highly stylized and simplistic, the range of different outcomes should at least convince the reader that market structures, both in terms of the product and labour markets, will be crucial to modelling wages and employment.

References

Bosworth, D.L. and P. Warren (1989). *Labour Markets: Operation and Failure*. Project Report. Institute for Employment Research. Coventry: University of Warwick.

Coyne, J. (1975). 'Kinked Supply Curves and the Market'. *Journal of Economic Studies*, 2, 2, 139–151.

CHAPTER 14 The dynamics of equilibrium, disequilibrium and adjustment

1 Introduction

This chapter examines the way in which labour markets adjust towards equilibrium. It focuses more on the issues of skill shortages than underemployment or unemployment, although they are, broadly speaking, mirror images of one another. We further develop the discussion of skill shortages in Chapter 15 and unemployment is given special treatment in Chapters 28 and 29 below. The present chapter divides into two broad elements. The first considers traditional wage adjustment and the second deals with other forms of adjustment, such as delivery lags, inventories, etc.

The discussion of the traditional wage–employment adjustments models begins by describing shortages and surpluses in the internal labour market (ILM), outlining how these spill over into the external labour market (ELM). Section 3 explores the interaction between internal and external labour markets. Section 4 focuses explicitly on shortages in the ELM and deals with both short- and long-run, static and dynamic shortages. Section 5 considers some of the issues which arise in estimating constrained equilibrating models of the ELM, which have both disequilibrium and market-clearing outcomes nested as special cases.

The second half of the chapter, found in Section 6, refocuses the discussion away from the wage to consider what other forms of intentional or unintentional adjustment take place if the market is not in wage–employment equilibrium. The section deals with employment, hours, effort, inventories and delivery lags, as well as a number of other forms of adjustment. It develops these ideas further by considering the so-called 'flexibilization' of the labour market, where the emphasis has been on a reduction in various rigidities (including hiring and firing costs) to bring the market more rapidly towards its equilibrium position.

2 Internal sources of adjustment in the labour market

Firms have a potential pool of labour services that they can call on from among their existing employees. Broadly speaking, at any one time, this pool can be thought of as being fixed, although some firms may have fairly flexible arrangements with a group of workers that they call upon from time to time, or can mirror such arrangements with occasional subcontracting. Thus, if product demand is not fixed, the firm is likely to experience skills imbalances or skills gaps as the level of its activity in different areas varies. There is an important distinction between a skill shortage and a skills gap, although there are obviously connections between the two. The former refers to the inability of the firm to find a suitable person to fill a particular position, even when attempting to recruit in the external market. The latter refers to a more general lack of adequate skills across a section (or all) of the firm's workforce. In the main, this chapter focuses on the first of these two issues; we return to the second issue elsewhere, including Chapter 29 below. The precise nature of the problem of skills imbalances differs between the firm's current production activities and its undertaking of investments associated with its future growth and development. This section deals with current production activities, rather than the dynamic investment activities of the firm which we return to below.

As we have seen in Chapter 11, the literature on inter-related factor demand models suggests that,

$$Y = \mathbf{f}(K, KU, E, H) \quad (1)$$

where: Y denotes current output; K is capital stock; KU is utilization; E denotes employment; and H is hours of work per employee. Increases in product demand, reductions in normal hours of work and unplanned wastage of employees produces a gap between current and desired factor demands. Equation (1) gives a clue as to how firms may react. In the short run the firm can raise hours of work by reducing short-time working, increasing overtime and/or switching employees from part-time to full-time contracts. This may be associated with increases in capital utilization, KU. The firm may introduce more intensive shift systems which can result in higher operating hours of equipment even in the face of lower average hours per employee. Finally, it is possible to alter incentive systems to increase the amount of worker effort, driving a wedge between the number of employee hours, EH, and effective worker effort, $E'H'$.

One of the principal adjustment mechanisms available to firms is hours of work, which can generally be varied at short notice. In addition, at least in some countries, there are few social, legal or economic constraints on the use of overtime working as a response to an increase in demand for a firm's products, although there are upper limits, for example in certain areas of activity where health and safety issues arise (i.e. number of hours a bus driver can work) and in countries signed up to the Social Chapter (with its 48 hour ceiling per week). Where individuals are covered by collective agreements, firms often pay a premium rate, for example time and a quarter, time and a half or double time. Finally, there may simply be physically upper limits to the number of hours that can be worked, especially in the longer term where workers become disenchanted with long hours. While there are clearly limits, variations in hours are often preferable to employers because of the more important problems they face in varying wages and employment. Blandy and Richardson (1982) found considerable evidence of the use of hours as an adjustment mechanism in Australia. It was not uniformly important, however; for example, overtime showed up strongly as an adjustment mechanism for skilled tradespeople, but much more weakly for the police. The legal professional also showed considerable use of hours as an adjustment mechanism, although in this case, overtime was not paid and the adjustment can also be thought of as a variation in effort.

While worker effort has became an increasing focus of the conceptual and theoretical literature, it is probably fair to say that, empirically at least, it remains one of the big 'unknowns' in labour economics. The potential importance of effort dispels the notion of a fixed technological relationship between inputs and outputs. Worker effort is, in much the same way as hours of work, a feature of the internal labour market (although, again, it may spill over into the external market insofar as, for example, potential workers see how hard employees have to work for a given wage). The 'efficiency wage' hypothesis is based on the premise that worker effort can be varied by altering wages. If this is so, then there will be some optimal level of wage payment (i.e. where the additional wage cost is just equal to the value of the additional output at the margin caused by the extra effort). Again, we return to these issues in detail in Part VI of the book.

Work patterns, including part-time work and shift-working, are closely inter-related with hours of work and capital utilization. It is possible to show how the firm can respond to changes in demand for its product by increasing labour hours and capital utilization in the short run, and moving to a more intensive shift system with lower average hours per worker in the long run. However, for an existing firm an increase in shiftworking appears to require that the firm hires more workers to form additional crews (and this response is dealt with under the heading of 'external labour' markets below). If the (instantaneous) capital/labour ratio is flexible in the short run, however, it may be possible to spread the existing workforce across a larger number of shifts. If so, it would raise the capital/labour ratio at any given moment in time and should have the effect of increasing labour productivity. The additional disutility of the increases in capital utilization for the workers is compensated by overtime premiums in the short run (until the shift system is modified) and by replacing overtime by shift premiums in the long run. A movement towards more intensive shiftwork may be rational even if the final solution is to move to introduce a more capital-intensive form of production with a smaller number of workers, as it is normally most cost efficient to use newer, more expensive equipment for longer periods of time. While there have been important changes in shift patterns over time, the associated changes often require planning and negotiation. Thus, it appears that, with some exceptions, increases in shiftwork have been used more as a longer-term method of maintaining capital utilization in the face of falling hours per employee, than as a method of providing short-run flexibility (Anxo *et al.*, 1995).

In general, it is more useful to treat output as endogenous; indeed firms can adjust either the quantity or the quality of output. A study of engineers found that five of the 12 firms surveyed would curtail production rather than use a 'constrained' adjustment mechanism (wage structure, job structure or allocative procedures) to respond to a shortage (Mace and Taylor, 1975). A priori we might anticipate that quantity reflects a short- and quality a long-run response. This is oversimplistic, however, as many firms vary the quality of their output (intentionally or unintentionally) with throughput (i.e. as the rate of production increases, quality controls may not be able to cope with the rate of production). One response to a shortage of teachers (or to a reduction in teachers as school budgets are squeezed) is to allow class sizes to rise. This is a potentially destabilizing response to shortage as it promotes other reactions, such as a fall in job satisfaction, which exacerbate the initial shortage. Other authors have detected increases in output quality in markets exhibiting increasing levels of excess supply. Changes in the quality of output will also be a natural outcome of modifying hiring standards during periods of imbalance.

Demand and production can vary independently, however, where the firm is willing to allow the length of its order book to vary. Increasing the length of waiting lists is not a costless response to the increase in demand for the firm's product, however, as unsatisfied customers cancel their orders, and long lists act as an incentive for new firms to enter the market. While waiting lists add a degree of flexibility, this is limited, particularly in the downward direction, as such lists cannot take negative values. Inventories provide a further mechanism for evening out variations in labour demand in some areas of production. When output exceeds demand, stock levels grow, and when output is less than demand, stock levels fall. However, inventories also incur costs. The inputs that were used in the production of the semi-finished and finished products which are stored were paid for in an earlier period, with no associated revenue return and consequent impacts on the cash flow and profitability of the company. In addition inventories take physical space and may require special conditions (of temperature, dust protection, etc.) to keep them in good condition. They may be subject to depreciation or obsolescence. In some product areas, the costs of storage may be sufficiently high (effectively infinite) to preclude this method of adjustment (i.e. electricity generation).

Firms may respond to changed market conditions by altering the technology used in production. In particular, they may respond to increasing levels of demand for their products or shortages of particular skills by introducing new production processes which reap economies of large-scale production or which economize on scarce skills. This is likely to be a longer-term response to major and prolonged changes in market conditions. A broadly neoclassical literature has grown around the idea of induced technological change. In the simplest models, shortages of particular factor inputs are reflected in relative factor prices and such changes act as a signal to inventors about the direction of technological change. A somewhat more institutional version of this can be found in the form of evolutionary theories of technological change (Nelson and Winter, 1982). There is a body of evidence that some firms have adopted such strategies in response to exogenous shocks. On the other hand, the econometric evidence concerning induced change is very mixed, which may be the result of the fact that skill shortages are themselves a barrier to innovation and diffusion (see Chapter 15 below). Indeed, labour markets for the highly qualified often have a number of complicating features, especially where such individuals work in dynamic functions – see Case Study 1.

CASE STUDY 1 Labour markets for the highly qualified

A number of features associated with the more highly educated make the task of modelling their labour markets quite distinct and thereby make questions of shortages or surpluses particularly difficult to resolve. In particular, they compile a number of the various aspects of shortage discussed in more detail in Section 4, including: (i) substitution between inputs; (ii) dynamic functions of qualified personnel; (iii) education and training lags and the nature of the supply function; and (iv) cobweb cycles. A number of the issues raised below about career ladders and training are also relevant.

continues

CASE STUDY 1 continued

The elasticity of substitution is such a central question from a growth and development perspective (given the potentially crucial role played by highly qualified labour), and from an educational planning and training viewpoint, that a considerable amount of empirical evidence has been accumulated in this area. The evidence divides into two parts: one concerned with substitution between occupational groups and the other between levels of educational attainment. Both sets of evidence tend to point in the same direction, consistent with there being relatively high elasticities of substitution although the estimated elasticities drop markedly where both the supply and demand functions are explicitly estimated. In addition, such exercises are often undertaken at a fairly aggregate level and we would expect to find a higher degree of substitution between broad groups than between more specific categories of labour. Finally, a number of the cross-sectional studies probably reflect long-run results. These are likely to produce higher elasticities than in the short run where jobs cannot be redefined and redesigned and where there is insufficient time for other forms of adjustment to take place. Insofar as the empirical evidence suggests fairly high elasticities, this does not concur with the generally held view that substitution would be relatively low, for the relatively highly skilled and qualified groups. Nor is it consistent with the often voiced disenchantment of employers faced with what they argue to be shortages of certain types of personnel. There is, however, greater evidence of the lower substitutability between the more skilled workers and capital, as well as the link between education, training and innovation. It is well known, for example, that the ratio of non-production to total employment in the firm is linked to the productivity performance of the firm.

The main problem, however, is that the static underpinnings of the traditional factor demand functions become increasingly suspect as we transfer our attention to more highly skilled and educated groups. These labour groups tend to be more involved in activities that enhance the performance of the firm over time, such as: research and development; installation of new capital; advertising and product promotion; and general management functions. In these cases, demand functions that are formed from a simple inversion of the production function are likely to be misleading (Bosworth and Wilson, 1978). This is a quite different phenomenon to the factor-saving (or using) changes caused by process innovation (or more generally by the diffusion of process change) which take effect through modifications to the production function. We are talking about the demands for labour that are themselves a function of the firms' attempts to alter the (perceived or actual) technical specification of their products or processes, the scale of the firms' activities and, thereby, the relationships between inputs and outputs. The essential feature of these demands is that they are proactive rather than reactive.

We can perhaps illustrate this point by looking at one attempt to incorporate R&D activity within the production function (Schott, 1978). It can be interpreted as a 'proactive' theory in the limited sense that firms have undertaken these past investments in R&D with a view to modifying the current relationship between inputs and outputs. R&D enters via its impact on the level of knowledge, N, of the firm,

$$N_t = \mathbf{f}(RD_t, RD_{t-1}, \ldots, RD_{t-z}) \quad (1)$$

where: N_t denotes the stock of knowledge at the end of period t; RD denotes R&D activity; t is time; and z is the age at which technical knowledge becomes obsolete. Output Y can be written as

$$Y_t = \mathbf{g}(K_t, KU_t, E_t, H_t, N_t) \quad (2)$$

where, in addition, KU denotes capital services; E is employment; H denotes average hours of work per employee; and N is the level of know-how. Based upon cost minimization subject to an output constraint, the solution of the first-order conditions yields a recursive system of five equations determining the optimal levels of the five factor inputs in terms of the exogenous variables. Ingenious as this approach is, it has a number of peculiarities: (i) knowledge is treated as an input like any other; (ii) while this allows it to influence total factor productivity, changes in knowledge do not affect the coefficients on the traditional inputs of capital and labour; (iii) the model is reticent about product and process change – the simplest interpretation is that the relevant measure of R&D relates only to process change expenditures; and (iv) it is not immediately clear how to measure employment, E – it seems possible that these should only be production workers but at least the variable should exclude R&D workers who appear implicitly under RD. For a recent review, see Griliches (1995).

Sources: Bosworth *et al.* (1992); Bosworth and Wilson (1978); Schott (1978); Griliches (1995)

3 Interaction of internal and external labour markets

The empirical results from the inter-related factor demand literature support the argument that hours and capital utilization can be adjusted most rapidly, followed by employment and, finally, the stock of capital. Once the firm attempts to alter the number of employees, it has shifted its response from the internal to the external labour market, releasing workers on the downturn or recruiting on the upturn. Lags in recruitment mean that in the short run the firm may have no choice but to meet its requirements from the ILM. In effect, the costs of response through the ELM increase disproportionately with reductions in the period of recruitment. These costs arise from advertising, interview time, etc. (hiring costs). Clearly the firm will tend to look to external recruitment when the ELM can supply the required labour services more cost effectively than the ILM. Both routes involve increasing costs at the margin. The firm may feel that there are skill shortages if the costs of meeting some target recruitment in some set period of time are considered to be excessive. This view is more likely to arise during periods when ELMs are tight.

Bosworth and Warren (1990) discuss a potential disequilibrium situation in which the supply of overtime hours is positively related to the premium offered, allowing the firm to meet (partly) increased product demand from extra labour services generated in the ILM. This is costly for the firm, however, the more so the longer product demand is sustained. It would seem obvious that in the longer term the firm should recruit additional employees and reduce overtime working. Firms may, however, face a backward-bending supply of labour amongst existing workers. This happens if, when they attempt to raise basic wages in order to attract more applicants from the ELM and to reduce overtime hours, they may face a lower internal supply of hours at current overtime premium rates. Such firms experience an important dilemma – whether to: allow output to fall below the potential level of demand; raise both basic rates and overtime rates; attract workers by sustaining above normal hours so that workers expect permanent overtime working.

The discussion in the previous section treated labour services in the ILM and ELM as being identical. In practice, ILMs are often associated with heterogeneous labour and career ladders. Firms recruit externally at relatively low skill levels, where possible, filling vacancies at higher levels internally. Career and wage progression often results from a mix of seniority and ability, where the latter is influenced by learning by doing and training. Shortages can now arise where the continuum of flows up the ladder is not maintained. Disproportionate wastage at a higher level can mean that there is not a sufficient number of individuals at a lower level to fill the vacancies created. More importantly, there may be a 'quality gap': there may be sufficient numbers of individuals but they are 'not sufficiently senior', 'not experienced enough', or 'have not received adequate training'. Resort to the ELM is complicated by the need for individuals at that level to have significant levels of firm-specific training. It may also be problematic insofar as such recruitment mechanisms at higher rungs of the career ladder may not be well developed or regularly used. In addition, the introduction of outsiders can disrupt a general ethos of internal opportunity and promotion.

4 Types of shortages in external labour markets

4.1 Static shortages

The discussion contained in this section adopts a traditional, partial equilibrium framework. In other words, it assumes that it makes sense to analyse what happens in a single market in isolation from all other markets. Figure 14.1 shows the supply and demand curves for labour services in a particular market (e.g. for a given skill in a given region). The supply curve, *S*, shows the volume of labour services individuals are 'happy' to supply at a given (real) wage rate, w. To simplify the exposition, we discuss the case of employment (i.e. for the moment we will use the term employment rather than labour services). The demand curve, *D*, indicates the amount of labour services entrepreneurs are 'happy' to hire at the given wage rate, w. Note that we abstract from questions of taxation and its effects on labour supply and demand which we discussed earlier in this part of the book. The market-clearing wage is w^*, at which both groups are satisfied with exchanging E^* of labour services.

If for some reason the going wage is either w_0 or w_1, the market is not in equilibrium and either the suppliers or buyers are not satisfied with the outcome. A wage, w_1, is associated with a position of

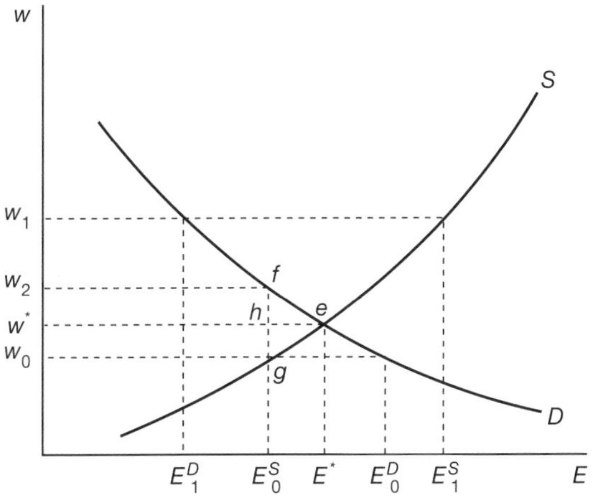

Fig 14.1 Static shortages.

surplus, $E_1^S > E_1^D$, while w_0 is associated with a position of shortage, $E_0^D > E_0^S$. Concentrating on the second of these cases (we deal with issues of unemployment later in the book), we turn to the question of how the magnitude of the shortage might be expressed. Traditionally, the shortage has been thought of in terms of some absolute difference, $E_0^D - E_0^S$, although a percentage measure might also be revealing insofar as it allows for the absolute size of the market. For example, $(E_0^D - E_0^S)/E_0^S$. However, in this wage model, it is equally valid to measure disequilibrium in terms of wage rates, either in absolute form (e.g. $w_2 - w_0$) or as a percentage $((w_2 - w_0)/w_0)$. While w_2 is not known to the researcher, the employer might hypothesize what wage rate it would be willing to pay if the supply of labour was fixed at E_0^S. This is clearly related to the value of labour services to the firm at the margin, and may be a strong influence on the entrepreneur's perception of the magnitude of the shortage.

The labour services measure is generally chosen because more detailed data are available about this dimension (e.g. employment, unemployment and vacancies) than about wages, and because of the difficulties faced by the researcher in isolating the unobserved rates, such as w_2. Nevertheless, it is possible to show that it may be extremely misleading to attempt to measure the magnitude of any shortage from the labour services dimension alone. Figure 14.2 illustrates two markets of roughly equal size, $E^* = E^{A*} = E^{B*}$, both experiencing shortages at the going wage rate, $w_0 = w_0^A = w_0^B$. Judging by the criterion of the absolute (or percentage) difference between labour services supplied and demanded, the shortage is more severe in market A than in B. Other things being equal, we would expect employers in A

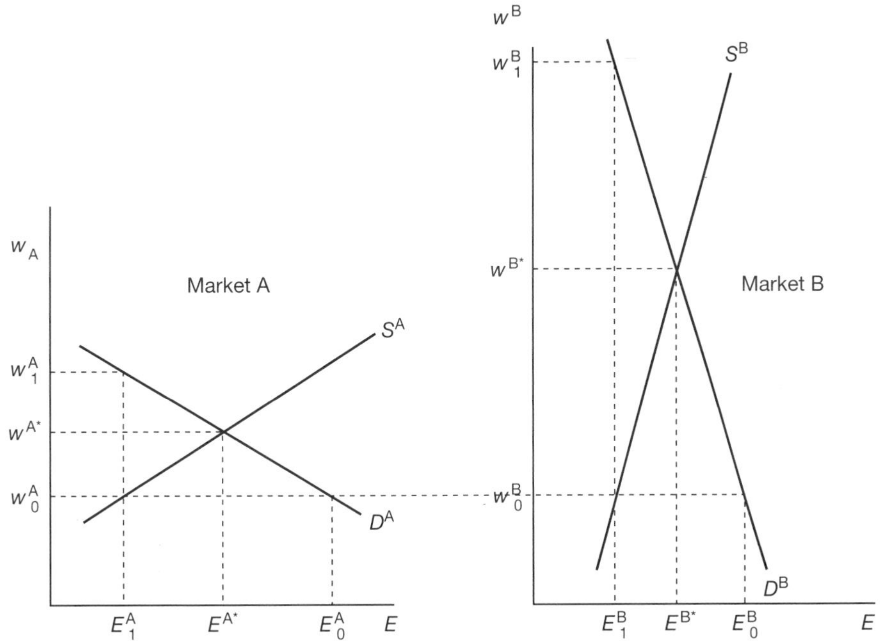

Fig 14.2 Dimensions of shortages.

to be more vociferous about the shortage. However, the absolute wage measures indicate a larger maladjustment in market B $(w_1^B - w_0^B) > (w_1^A - w_0^A)$ and $(w_1^B - w_0^B)/w_0^B > (w_1^A - w_0^A)/w_0^A$. Thus, while a fairly small adjustment to wages will bring market A back into equilibrium, a major adjustment is required in market B.

4.2 Short-run disequilibrium/long-run equilibrium

The type of disequilibrium position envisaged above should be relieved by an adjustment of wages towards equilibrium over time, $w_0 \rightarrow w^*$. In other words, firms bid up the going wage rate to attract additional labour services. In this static analysis the area *efg* in Figure 14.1, is a deadweight welfare loss. This is comprised of an area of (lost) labour surplus, *hef*, and a corresponding area of producer surplus, *heg*. The dynamic analogue of this welfare measure of shortage is the discounted sum of (similar) triangles, *efg*, over the period that the shortage prevails. Clearly, the size of the triangle can be expected to shrink over time as wages and employment adjust. Thus, firms will be complaining about transitory shortages (or surpluses) during the period of adjustment. The magnitude and longevity of the problem depends upon the speed of adjustment of wages. In general, firms do not instantaneously raise their wage offers sufficiently to remove the shortage, perhaps because of outside interference (e.g. incomes policies) or internal constraints (e.g. difficulties in altering salary structures). The result is an 'administered price shortage'.

The concept of dynamic shortages was introduced in the work of Arrow and Capron (1959), and is an extension of the shortage concept outlined above. In this instance, the wage adjusts slowly towards its long-run equilibrium position and the equilibrium changes over time forming a 'moving target' (e.g. as the demand curve shifts, say, persistently outwards). This situation is illustrated by the steady outward shift of the demand curve over time, $D_t \rightarrow D_{t+1} \rightarrow D_{t+2}$, in Figure 14.3. Depending on the assumptions about the rate at which the demand curve shifts and the rate of adjustment of wages (and whether the rate of adjustment is in some way related to the magnitude of the shortage) it is possible to generate situations of growing shortages. Figure 14.3 shows that, although $w_t \rightarrow w_{t+1} \rightarrow w_{t+2}$, shortage increases from $0 \rightarrow (E_{t+1}^D - E_{t+1}^S) \rightarrow (E_{t+2}^D - E_{t+2}^S)$. This type of situation was associated with the market for engi-

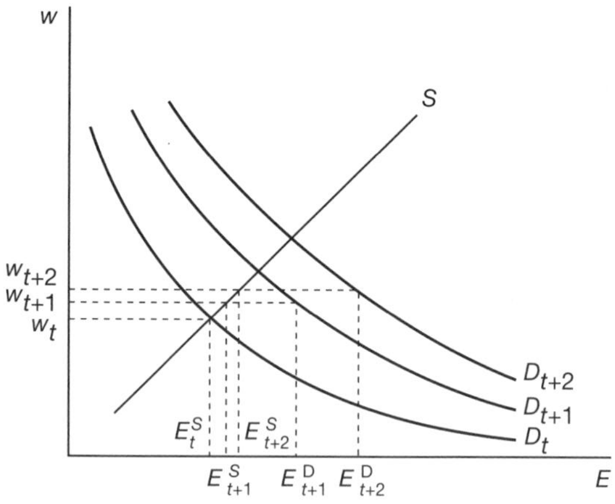

Fig 14.3 Dynamic shortages.

neers in the early post-war period and, subsequently, for electronic and software engineers. For example, the pervasive trends in the introduction of microelectronic technologies into both products and processes in the UK gave rise to trends in the derived demand for electronics and software engineers that even transcended the deep recession of 1981.

The link between product and labour demand is an important one, as the former is a desired output level. Thus, if actual output persistently falls below the target level (or rate of increase) the firm's output aspirations may be revised downwards. Alternatively, if product quality or production efficiency do not improve at the planned rate, then the desired level of demand may not materialize anyway. This gives rise to the 'ephemeral' shortages described by Senker (1992). The link with the dynamic performance of firms is brought home even more clearly by the fact that successful innovatory activity is skill intensive. Both UK data and international comparative information suggest that innovatory firms are more likely to experience skill shortages and, by implication, a lack of skills can be a severe brake on the rate of technological change and improvements in firm performance (see Chapter 15). These failures carry over from the micro- to the whole-economy level.

4.3 Education and training lags: short- and long-run supply

The third major feature associated with skilled or highly qualified persons concerns the length of time required to educate or train (retrain) labour. The implication of this is that we can distinguish between the short- and long-run supply curves of qualified labour, as shown in Figure 14.4. Given a limited stock of individuals possessing the relevant skill or qualification, the short-run supply curve will become increasingly (perhaps totally) inelastic at higher levels of labour services, as shown by the curve S^{SR}. However, this short-run constraint on supply is avoided in the long run as new entrants enter the stock through the education and training system, shown by S^{LR}. In the extreme, the short-run supply curve may be maintained throughout the education/training period, shifting in a discrete once-and-for-all way at the end of the period as new entrants flow onto the market. If the period of education or training is particularly lengthy, this appears to give rise to potentially long periods of shortage or surplus when wages fail to adjust or do so only slowly. Even where wages adjust quickly to short-run conditions there may remain a long-run imbalance such as the gap between demand and long-run supply at the going wage rate. This is illustrated by the difference $E_1 - E_0$ at the wage w_0, in Figure 14.4.

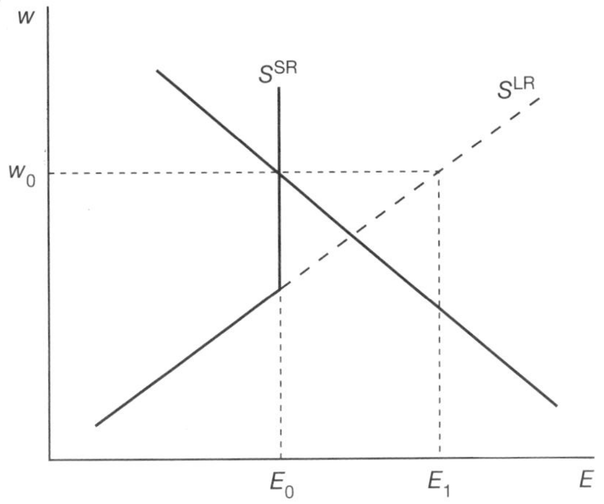

Fig 14.4 Short-run and long-run supply.

The cobweb phenomenon is well known and we will give no more than the briefest of outlines of the associated theory. Figure 14.5 assumes that the demand for labour curve has recently shifted from its previous position (which formerly intersected the supply curve at the kink in S^{SR}) to D. Thus, at time t, the supply of labour is represented by S^{SR} which is wholly inelastic in the relevant range. The short-run equilibrium wage is w_t and E_t of labour services are traded on the market. However, at a wage w_t, many

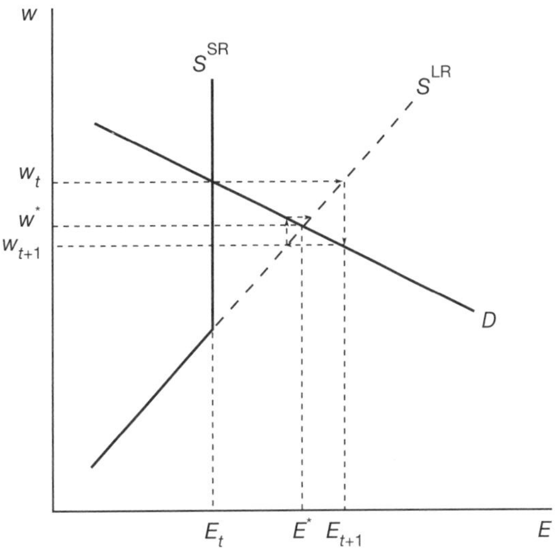

Fig 14.5 Cobwebs.

individuals who currently do not have the requisite skills feel that it is worth undergoing training or education. This number is represented by the difference between the short- and long-run supply curves at the going wage rate, w_t. Eventually, therefore, a further $E_{t+1} - E_t$ of qualified labour flow onto the market (e.g. at time $t + 1$). In fact the market is not willing to take up such large numbers as this at the going wage. If this number supply themselves, the market finds a new (short-run) equilibrium wage at w_{t+1}. However, at this wage some qualified people will withdraw from the market in the long run, and the market eventually moves to a new position on S^{LR} at the wage w_{t+1}. Thus, the (in this instance, convergent) cobweb cycle begins to emerge, as shown by the dashed, arrowed line in Figure 14.5. If such cobwebs exist, at least in the form indicated by this simplistic theory, they should be fairly easy to isolate empirically. Not only does the overall market swing from periods of excess demand to excess supply and back again, but the position of new entrants should be even more clear cut, experiencing complete reversals of fortune in successive periods.

Cobweb models have been estimated with some success in the USA (Freeman, 1971, 1975 and 1976). In their simplest form they focus on new entrants and, in particular, on the starting salaries of graduates. The success of the work done in the USA in this area and the lack of comparable UK results stems from a variety of factors, not least of which is the availability of information about employment and wages for detailed occupational and qualified groups in the US economy. In addition, historically at least, the greater flexibility of the US market allows greater short-run changes in wage rates, acting as a signal for individuals to train (see, for example, Freeman, 1981). If wages crept much more slowly upwards or downwards, the inherent forces leading to the generation of the cobweb would be undermined. There are, nevertheless, some unanswered questions about the cobweb phenomenon even in the USA. In particular, where do the previously trained workers who are not taken up by the market in the current period go? Are they taken up by other markets that do not use their special skills, and does this mean that they do not return to their primary market when excess demand appears in the subsequent period?

It is important to note that, in the real world, there may be other influences on the position of the supply curve which may make this dichotomous short-run/long-run assumption somewhat implausible. One possible cause of shifts is the existence of immigration and emigration. Such international flows may prove to be an especially important safety valve where the markets operate freely, given that labour markets for highly qualified individuals are often much less localized than for other groups. The conditions of the Treaty of Rome and the subsequent introduction of a single market since 1994 have increased the flows of highly qualified persons across Europe, although they are still limited by differences in the level and nature of qualifications in different countries.

The cobweb cycle model suggests that wages adjust to short-run supply and demand conditions, providing a market signal, which induces education or training to take place. While the adjustment process is inefficient, even the simplest models suggest that it will normally be convergent, an outcome which is virtually assured where the actors in the market are not assumed to be myopic and allowed to learn from past 'mistakes'. In certain markets, however, short-run disequilibrium signals (such as increased relative wages) may go unheeded and the necessary education or training may not take place. This may be the result of 'poaching', where firms rely on the recruitment of trained personnel in the external labour market rather than on their own training programmes. We return to this in detail in Part V of the book, below.

This suggests that employers' returns to training and, hence, the associated volume of activity depend on the extent of turnover of employees. In this type of model, optimal wages and training are endogenized as higher wage offers reduce turnover and, up to a point, raise the rate of return to training. An alternative way of looking at this issue, however, is that government policy, in the UK at least, has, if anything, moved in the direction of increased flexibility (and mobility) in the external labour market and less support for in-house training (i.e. the abandonment of statutory training organizations). This has the effect of pushing up the wage that firms would have to pay to keep the employees that it trains, to a level that makes training non-viable.

There appear to be examples of markets broadly of this type. The market for craftspeople, for example, has been in long-term decline over the period since the late 1960s. As craftspeople have been made redundant or voluntarily left their jobs they have also often left the industry entirely. However, there is some evidence that supply has been reducing more rapidly than demand and that training has not been able to keep pace with such losses. The downward shift in supply can be traced to job uncertainty, which is often a cause of psychological stress. In effect, some individuals (including a proportion that would in practice have retained their jobs) 'jump before they are pushed', and, often, it is the higher-quality people who choose to go first, as they find it easier to obtain alternative employment. Clearly, the downward trend in the demand for labour is not conducive to encouraging individuals to undertake training; intense product market pressures, and the higher wastage rates from otherwise relatively secure jobs, discourage individual firm-funded training; and the rate of perceived net outflows from the sector may discourage industry-funded training (through statutory training organizations – such as the old Industry Training Boards). Thus, the number of new trainees in each period is not sufficient to counter the net losses. This may in turn influence the ability of firms to meet potential product demand, thereby losing potential customers, and may in a dynamic sense influence the position of the demand for craftsmen and women in future periods. To call this problem one of training failure is, however, something of a misnomer – it is really a 'turnover and training problem'. Nevertheless, it is interesting that the UK appeared to experience quite persistent shortages in craft skills in a market where the demand for craftspeople and the number employed was declining quite rapidly.

5 General models of the labour market

Goldfeld and Quandt (1986) refer to a 'now standard version of (the econometric disequilibrium) model' as having the form

$$D_t = \alpha_1 w_t + \beta_1 X_{1t} + \mu_{1t} \quad (2)$$

$$S_t = \alpha_2 w_t + \beta_2 X_{2t} + \mu_{2t} \quad (3)$$

$$w_t = w_{t-1} + \phi(D_t - S_t) + \beta_3 X_{3t} + \mu_{3t} \quad (4)$$

$$Q_t = \min (D_t, S_t) \quad (5)$$

The omission of (4) would be equivalent to assuming the price, w_t, of the 'commodity' to be exogenous. Given such an assumption, a model consisting of (2), (3) and (5) alone might be thought of as particularly useful for examining markets with externally regulated prices (i.e. markets in the formerly centrally planned economies, or markets with price ceilings).

The inclusion of a price adjustment equation such as (4), however, makes it possible to represent D_t, S_t and w_t in a number of ways: in terms of their own past values, the past values of the stochastic terms, μ_{1t}, μ_{2t} and μ_{3t}, and the vectors of exogenous variables, X_{1t}, X_{2t} and X_{3t}. Given time profiles for X_{1t}, X_{2t} and X_{3t}, it is possible to derive expected time profiles for D_t, S_t and w_t. The evolution of such profiles over time would involve periods of excess supply and excess demand, during which only the quantities on the short side of the market would be observed being transacted (ensured by equation (5)). While disequilibrium will be the general case, it is possible to see from equation (4) that at least two special cases exist. First, the traditional market-clearing outcome, where the change in price, $w_t - w_{t-1}$, makes up for the whole of the potential disequilibrium, $D_t - S_t$, within the period. Second, where $w_t = w_{t-1}$ and there is no adjustment to wages to move the market towards a new equilibrium. More generally, however, interest focuses on the speed with which wages adjust, particularly *vis-à-vis* the magnitude and frequency of any shocks which impact on the market. This issue is at the heart of the debate about the neoclassical (wage–competition) and more institutionalist approaches.

Two approaches have been used depending on whether the sample period is separated into periods of excess supply and demand exogenously or endogenously. In the case of exogenous separation, for example, the sample is divided into situations of excess demand or supply depending on whether the real wage rate is rising or falling (or by some proxy such as unemployment and vacancy data). The two sets of observations are then used separately to estimate the supply equation (during periods of excess demand) and the demand equation (during periods of excess supply). In addition, some authors compare the single-equation employment function estimates from the two sub-samples with the estimates for the combined data set, testing for significant differences in the results. Endogenous separation is undertaken using two-stage least squares or a full information maximum likelihood technique enables all four equations, (2), (3), (4) and (5), to be estimated simultaneously on the complete sample. In both cases, however, the key to the successful estimation of disequilibrium models lies in correct separation of the sample into regimes of excess supply and excess demand. Quandt (1982) stresses the importance of any observable variable that has 'a one-to-one correspondence to periods of excess demand or excess supply' as a means of data separation. It has been variously postulated that the presence of rising wages, above-average levels of overtime working or below average unemployment/vacancies ratios are indicative of excess demand and can be employed as criteria for data separation.

While there were a number of problems with the estimates, one of the strongest features of the results is the existence of disequilibrium in UK labour markets. In other words, wages adjust relatively slowly to disequilibrium, especially when viewed in the context of the size of the shocks affecting labour markets. A second key finding is that there appears to be a more rapid adjustment of wages in an upward direction, but relatively slow in the downward direction. This clearly suggests, at least in the case of the UK, that, historically at least, wages are fairly rigid in the downward direction. In many respects the more recent estimates are more acceptable than the early findings for the USA (Rosen and Quandt, 1978), in which a number of key coefficients are either insignificant or have unexpected signs and, more fundamentally, indicate excess demand for labour for the period 1930 to 1946 and excess supply continuously from 1956 to 1973, which seems counter-intuitive. The 'preferred version' of the model reported in Hall *et al.* (1985) appears to work reasonably well and gives some interesting results with regard to the periods designated excess demand and excess supply. In this model, the long-run elasticity of demand with respect to output is very close to unity and the analogous coefficient with respect to the real wage is –0.33. These results are not only extremely interesting from a policy viewpoint, but are also close to those reported using other labour market models (Layard and Nickell, 1985). The model suggests that supply and demand were reasonably close to one another throughout much of the period 1964–1980, which is consistent with the market being in equilibrium. However, the period 1980–1982 exhibits a large and increasing excess supply caused by a major decline in the demand for labour.

Quandt and Rosen (1985) present a disequilibrium model of the labour market and test the unconditional probability that there is excess supply in each period. The model is slightly more sophisticated than the one reported above, with six equations (i.e. demand for labour, supply of labour, observed quantity of labour represented by the minimum of supply and demand condition, wage adjustment, price adjustment and vacancy/unemployment rate adjustment). The main point of this paper is the discussion of the new test statistics. The data reject the hypothesis of 'chronic excess supply' in US labour markets in the recent past, and the authors argue that not all of the observations lie on the demand curve (Quandt and Rosen, 1985, p. 197).

One of the major problems with a number of these studies has been associated with the high level of aggregation at which they are undertaken. However, the approach has also been applied to specific labour markets, as described in Case Study 2.

CASE STUDY 2 Youth labour market

The youth labour market, perhaps more than any other, is associated with disequilibrium. There is a tendency for employers to switch recruitment of personnel on and off like a tap, depending on the state of the business cycle. The downturn severely constrains recruitment activity, which might be expected to have severe consequences for potential new entrants, such as young people finishing their education. There is certainly some evidence of this amongst young people leaving the higher education system.

The youth labour market has also been affected by longer-term trends in employment opportunities. Merrilees and Wilson (1979) argue that in the case of youth labour markets, the evidence is not so much that of short-lived switching between excess supply and demand, but a period of continuous excess demand in the 1950s and 1960s, followed by excess supply since around 1970 (1969 for males and 1971 for females). They argue that the econometric models endogenizing the allocation of observations to supply- or demand-constrained regimes are not particularly suited to handling this 'once-and-for-all' switch in the youth labour market. They use a priori information to divide their sample into two halves and they test the sensitivity of their results to the choice of switch point. Thus, they estimate: (i) an equilibrium model based on the supply and demand equations; (ii) supply and demand functions separately for the two subperiods, up to and after 1970. Comparison of the results strongly suggests that the equilibrium model does not perform at all well. During the period up to 1970, there is excess demand and the supply function is identified; during the period after 1970, there is excess supply and the demand function is identified. Some evidence is given that relative wages adjust in the appropriate direction to restore equilibrium, but the equation does not perform particularly well. Merrilees and Wilson (1979) conclude that, in the past decade, high relative wages and the recessions have contributed to the large rise in youth unemployment, while government employment and training programmes have only counteracted this trend slightly.

Essentially the same technique has been applied more recently by Wells (1983), with basically the same results. However, the emphasis of the conclusions was somewhat different. Wells argues that the relative wages of young people do not appear to adjust rapidly in response to changes in their market position. On the other hand, labour costs have changed significantly over time and demand has been sensitive to these changes. Thus, the author argues that the reduction of the age range over which youth, rather than adult, wages are paid and the growth of youth relative to adult pay were both detrimental to youth employment prospects. Junankar and Neale (1984) used the same database and re-

continues

CASE STUDY 2 continued

estimated the equations using maximum likelihood methods. The parameter estimates were very similar to those reported by Wells, but there were some interesting differences in the implied periods of excess supply and demand, indicating a more complicated 'switching' between regimes. Nevertheless, all of the authors appear to favour a disequilibrium view of the youth labour market and this gives some support for the need for government intervention.

In practice, since these studies were undertaken, youth labour markets, particularly in the UK, have changed quite significantly. Not only have labour markets become more flexible, but institutionalized youth wages are now much less important a feature and most forms of unemployment benefit have been removed, so young people aged 16 or 17 who might have been unemployed are now more likely to appear in other economic states. Thus, we are highly unlikely to see a simple switching between employment and unemployment. Figure 14.6, taken from various *Youth Cohort Studies*, gives the main trends.

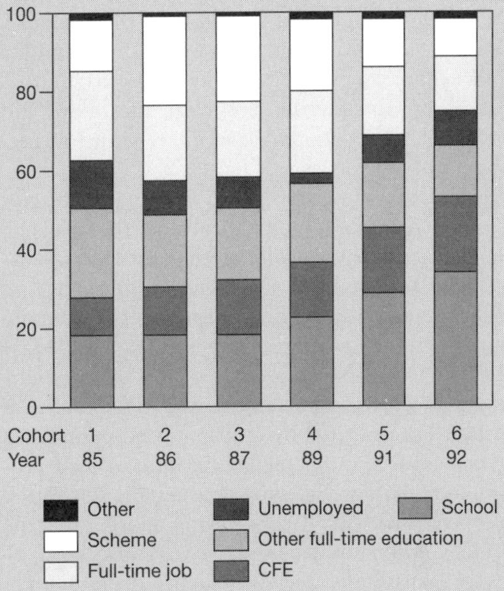

Fig 14.6 Activities of young people 16–17 years old.

Source: *Employment Gazette*, June 1993

6 Employment and other forms of adjustment

The discussion to date has focused primarily on wages as the principal adjustment. However, academics who take a more institutional perspective would point to other sources of adjustment, and might even argue that wages are a relatively unimportant mechanism. Indeed, they are given some support for this stance by the evidence of disequilibrium (or, at best, slow adjustment towards equilibrium) that arises from the empirical models outlined above. They would argue that the highly constrained nature of wages as an adjustment mechanism inevitably means that adjustment may be concentrated on other variables. One approach is to alter the number of persons employed through changes in the firm's hiring or firing policies. Changes in such activities, while often considered from an institutionalist angle, have important economic implications, for example, there are clearly increasing marginal costs of expanding (or contracting) the hiring activity beyond what is normal for the firm.

Such changes can take a number of forms. In periods of shortage, the firm might expand its personnel division, advertise more extensively or use the help of a specialist recruitment agency. In addition, the firm can consider its hiring standards. Again, during periods of shortage, the firm may lower the 'specification' relating to the type of person that it is seeking; during periods of surplus, it may raise its hiring standards. This might involve the firm taking on individuals without key skills that it would normally require and, then, provide training (or retraining). In periods of surplus, firms can lay workers off from their jobs temporarily when there is a reduction in demand for their products. This form of activity underlies a number of the implicit contract models, as individuals and firms maintain a continuing commitment to one another despite the fact the individual is not currently in the firm's employment. However, temporary lay-offs seem to be more common in the USA than in the UK or Europe. Within the UK context, permanent redundancies and dismissals are more common than temporary lay-offs. Evidence from the 1970s suggests 48 per cent of unemployed persons were either made redundant or sacked from their last job, a figure which would have been even greater but for the fact that many women left their jobs for 'domestic reasons'. In practice, it is clear that many job separations are involuntary and are regarded as permanent by both parties.

Redundancy can occur in two main ways: the closure of a plant or organization and the selective redundancy of members of a given plant or organization. The former is more obvious although it is probably the latter which represents the more common method of employment adjustment. Mass redundancy can also be used as a form of wage bargaining by firms, especially in the USA, but is a constant latent threat by multinational companies that can shift the geographical location of their production activities. Selective redundancy is often voluntary, involving firms paying more than the statutory minimum. Redundancy can also be compulsory unilaterally decided by employers or by a procedure laid down in the awards relating to the firm. Historically, the most common procedure was 'last in, first out' which uses reverse seniority to decide who is made redundant. More recently, however, with the reductions in the penalties for redundancy, age appears to have become a disadvantage, and seniority is no guarantee of security.

Plant- and firm-level redundancy can be viewed as a form of market-induced substitution. The adjustment of labour markets to exogenous shocks is theoretically feasible even if none of the agents within the market choose to adjust. In particular, there is switching between agents in the market from non-responsive firms which go into receivership to other firms which are more efficiently structured for the new conditions. Hence, if the firm does not adjust, then the market eventually forces some form change of its own (Johansen, 1972). The UK has experienced significant changes in the ratios of factor inputs and productivity via the scrapping of the least efficient production units. In certain industries, such as textiles and metal manufacturing, the number of separate production units in existence fell dramatically from 1966 through to the early 1980s (Bosworth, 1987). Production activity was increasingly concentrated in a smaller number of more efficient units, which tended to be utilized for longer hours. It was argued that, in these industries, a considerable proportion of the productivity growth that occurred could be traced to the scrapping of inefficient machinery rather than to the introduction of new machines. However, there has been a continued downsizing of companies through the 1980s and early 1990s, as firms concentrated on their core business.

'Flexibilization' is a word used to describe the process by which policies have been introduced to remove and reduce various rigidities in the labour market. In the UK, for example, various governments since the early 1970s, but especially during the early post-1979 Conservative administration, have reduced the power of trade unions and lowered the quasi-fixed labour costs which influence firms' propensities to hire and fire. One consequence has been the subsequent casualization of the workforce. Casualization is in many respects diametrically opposite to the introduction of new technology as an adjustment mechanism. In essence it is a means of reducing costs by undertaking work on a casual and temporary basis, avoiding the higher 'on-costs' or 'non-wage' costs generally associated with permanent jobs. Note that, in Australia, however, casual workers are paid a premium in order to compensate for their lack of security and absence of redundancy and other longer-term benefits. A related strategy is to employ more part-time staff, given that part-timers typically receive lower non-wage benefits in the UK (although, again, not in Australia). We return to the issue of 'flexibilization' in the final part of the book.

7 Conclusions

This chapter has touched upon a crucial area of debate in the study of labour markets and within labour economics itself. This concerns the issue of the role played by the wage rate in 'clearing the market'. Institutionalists argue that the wage is relatively unimportant, which, they believe, undermines much of the traditional neoclassical analysis. In the main, neoclassical economists accept that the labour market is, to some degree, special and does not operate as a 'spot market', but that its special features, including the partial adjustment of wages towards their equilibrium level, can be allowed for explicitly in the analysis. The empirical evidence reviewed in this chapter throws some light on the debate, but does not entirely resolve it. At the present time the results appear more consistent with market failure than, say, spot markets. The truth probably lies somewhere in between, but precisely where has yet to be resolved. This will require further improvements to the disequilibrium (equilibrating) models. In addition, much of the empirical work to date has been at a relatively high level of aggregation, and it is not clear that the results relate to an identifiable labour market. The discussion is, therefore, part of a broader debate on how labour markets operate, in particular the role of more institutional factors in the operation of the labour market. Even within a more neoclassical framework, it has become recognized that wages may play more than one role, for example in the supply of person hours and in the supply of effort (see Part VI of the book). As such the whole discussion is a part of a broader debate about labour market flexibility (see Part VIII of the book).

References

Anxo, D., G. Bosch, D. Bosworth, G. Cette, T. Sterner, and D. Taddei (eds) (1995). *Work Patterns and Capital Utilisation: An International Comparative Study*. Boston: Kluwer Press.

Arrow, K.J. and W.M. Capron (1959), 'Dynamic Shortages and Price Rises: the Engineer-Scientist Case', *Quarterly Journal of Economics*, vol. 73, no. 2, pp. 292–308.

Blandy, R. and S. Richardson (1982). *How Labour Markets Work: Case Studies in Adjustment*. Sydney: Longman Cheshire.

Bosworth, D.L. and P. Warren (1990). 'Disequilibrium, Basic Wage Rigidity and Adjustment'. *Journal of Employment and Productivity*, 2, 1, 46–58.

Bosworth, D.L. and R.A. Wilson (1978). 'Some Evidence on the Productivity of Qualified Manpower in Britain: a Note'. *Bulletin of Economic Research*, 30, 45–49.

Bosworth, D.L. (1987). 'Capital Stock, Capital Usage and Supply-Side Constraints'. In R.M. Lindley and R.A. Wilson (eds) *Review of the Economy and Employment*. Institute for Employment Research. Coventry: University of Warwick, Chapter 3.

Bosworth, D., R. Wilson and P. Taylor (1992). *Technological Change: the Role of Scientists and Engineers*. Aldershot: Avebury.

Freeman, R. (1971). *The Market for College Trained Manpower*. Cambridge: Cambridge University Press.

Freeman, R. (1975). 'Supply and Salary Adjustments to the Changing Science Manpower Market'. *American Economic Review*, 65, 1, 27–39.

Freeman, R. (1976). 'A Cobweb Model of the Supply and Starting Salary of New Engineers'. *Industrial Labour Relations Review*, January.

Freeman, R. (1981). 'Response to Change in the U.S.'. in R.M. Lindley (ed.) *Higher Education and the Labour Market*. Guildford: Society for Research into Higher Education.

Goldfeld, S.M. and R.E. Quandt (1986), 'The Econometrics of Rationing Models'. Econometric Research Program. Research Memorandum No. 322. Princeton University, Princeton, NJ.

Griliches, Z. (1995). 'R&D and Productivity: Econometric Results and Measurement Issues'. In P. Stoneman (ed.) *Handbook of the Economics of Technological Change*. Oxford: Blackwell, pp. 52–89.

Hall, S.G., S.G.B. Henry., A. Markandya and M. Pemberton (1985). 'The UK Labour Market: Expectations and Disequilibrium'. Discussion Paper. London: National Institute for Economic and Social Research.

Johansen, L. (1972). *Production Functions: An Integration of Micro and Macro Short-run and Long-run Aspects*. Amsterdam: North-Holland.

Junankar, P.N. and A.J. Neale (1984). 'Relative Wages and the Youth Labour Market'. Conference on the Young Persons' Labour Market. Institute for Employment Research. Coventry: University of Warwick.

Layard, R. and S. Nickell (1985). 'The Causes of British Unemployment' *National Industrial Economic Review*, Febuary, 62–85.

Mace, J.D. and S.M. Taylor (1975). 'The Demand for Engineers in British Industry: Some Implications for Manpower Forecasting'. *British Journal of Industrial Relations*, 13, 2, 175–192.

Merrilees, W.J. and R.A. Wilson (1979). 'Disequilibrium in the Labour Market for Young People in Great Britain'. No. 10. September. Discussion Paper. Warwick University, Coventry.

Nelson, R.R. and S. Winter (1982). *An Evolutionary Theory of Economic Change*. Cambridge (MA): Harvard University Press.

Quandt, R.E. (1982). 'Econometric Disequilibrium Models'. *Econometric Abstracts*, 7–64.

Quandt, R.E. and H.S. Rosen (1985). 'Is There a Chronic Excess Supply of Labour? Designing a Statistical Test'. *Economic Letters*, 19, 193–197.

Rosen, H.S. and R.E. Quandt (1978). 'Estimation of a Disequilibrium Aggregate Labour Market'. *Review of Economics and Statistics*, 40, 371–379.

Schott, K. (1978). 'The Relations Between Industrial Research and Development and Factor Demands'. *Economic Journal*, 88, 85–106.

Senker, P. (1992). 'Skill Shortages and Britain's International Competitiveness'. In D.L. Bosworth, P.A. Dutton and J.A. Lewis (eds) *Skill Shortages*, Chapter 2. Aldershot: Avebury.

Wells, W. (1983). *The Relative Pay and Employment of Young People*. Research Paper. No. 42. London: Department of Employment.

PART V Human Capital

CHAPTER 15 Introduction to human capital

1 Introduction

This part of the book is concerned with the role of skills and expertise in economic performance. There has been a growing realization of the central role that a highly skilled and qualified workforce plays in the successful introduction of technological and organizational changes. Equally, there has been mounting evidence of the inadequacies, if not the failure, of the UK training system in the post-war period. This introductory chapter sets the scene by discussing the concept of the skills base of the economy. It outlines the problem of skill shortages that occurs each time the economy recovers from recession, but also points to more persistent and perhaps fundamental types of shortage. In particular, certain types of skills may be in short supply even during periods of recession. More importantly still, the economy may experience 'skill gaps' that reflect the inability of current employees to meet the businesses' objectives. We therefore investigate the link between the skills base, training and various other dynamic investments of the firm. This chapter argues that the 'market for training' is a complex one which is characterized by imperfections and prone to failure. This suggests a potentially important role for government intervention.

The two subsequent chapters in this part of the book develop a more rigorous conceptual framework for examining the decision to invest in education and training. Chapter 16 considers the decision process from both the individual and firm viewpoints. In doing so, it follows the traditional distinction between general and specific skills. However, it argues that the distinction between the two is not so clear cut in the real world, where individuals often stay with the same employer for quite long periods. The chapter also provides evidence about the rate of return to investments in education and training, and explores the use of econometric methods to establish the impact of training schemes.

Chapter 17 moves from the individual employee or firm level to consider the concept of a 'market for training' in greater detail. It makes a clear distinction between the market for training and the market for trained individuals. It then examines the extent and nature of market failure, and conditions under which the government might wish to intervene. The chapter outlines the key distinction between private and social rates of return. It argues that, out of line with the standard wisdom, there may be some grounds for the government to intervene in support of specific (as well as general) training. Finally, the chapter outlines some evidence drawn from various evaluations of government education and training schemes.

2 Skills base

Evidence from surveys of skill shortages in the UK demonstrate at least two things. First, the nature and extent of skill shortages over the business cycle. Too rapid growth appears to run into capacity constraints to meet potential demand from domestic sources, with consequences for export performance and import penetration, as well as for inflationary pressures. Second, skill shortages not only have a short-term impact which puts an effective break on economic growth, but they also have long-term consequences for the introduction of new technologies. Thus, skill shortages limit the capacity for innovation and future growth. The policy message is really one which relates to the debate over short termism in the UK – the long-term prosperity of the economy depends crucially upon a long-term strategy which provides a stable environment for the production and exploitation of skills, and, thereby, for the successful introduction of technological and organisational changes.

It is perhaps surprising how little we know about the UK skills base. Unlike research and development, which is covered by the accounting standard SSAP13, company accounts do not generally itemize expenditure on human resource development. That is not to say that there is no information at all; for example, there are self-reported data about qualifications available from the *General Household Survey* and *Labour Force Survey* along with some information about training activities (see Figure 15.1). There was an attempt to undertake a national skills survey in the mid-1980s (Training Agency, 1989), which was quite widely criticized as overestimating training activity in the UK, although it should be acknowledged that certain types of investment (such as on-the-job training) are notoriously difficult to define and measure. A number of localities have tried to map their existing skills and human resource development requirements in an attempt to improve employment prospects in the area (Elias and Healey, 1991). In addition, there is an accumulation of comparative, international, case study information that we discuss in more detail below. Some attempts have been made to bring the available training data together (see for example Employment Department, 1990, which provides a useful listing of the major sources), but the data remain diverse, heterogeneous and incomplete. As a consequence, it is perhaps not surprising that, even in the mid-1990s, the government announced the need for an audit of the UK's skills base – despite its potential political consequences, given that the government of the time had been in power since 1979.

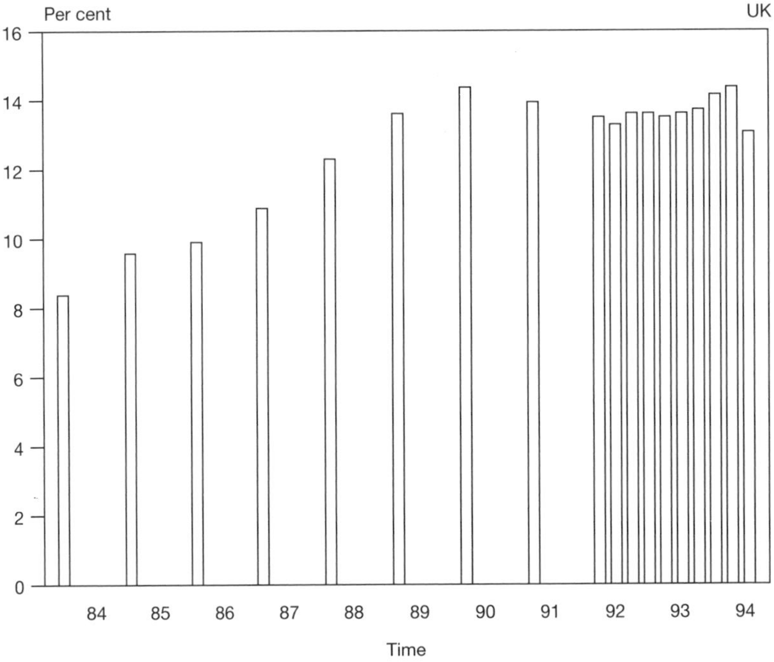

Notes:
1. Employees of working age receiving job-related training (on or off the job) in the last four weeks (seasonally adjusted).
2. Working age is defined as men aged 16–64 and women aged 16–59.
3. 1984–1991 Spring data only. 1992 onwards Spring, Summer, Autumn, and Winter of each year.

Fig 15.1 Trends in job-related training.
Source: 'Labour Market Information'. *Skills and Enterprise Executive Summary*, Issue 1/95, January 1995, p. 7.

More complete information is available about skills imbalances. There are a variety of sources of data about unemployment and vacancies, which to some extent reflect skill surpluses and shortages. In addition, there is a long-running time series of data from the CBI *Quarterly Industrial Trends Survey*. In recent years, much more detailed results about skill shortages have become available from the *Skill Needs in Britain* surveys.

3 Cyclical and secular shortages and skill gaps

Skill shortages are a recurring theme in the UK economy. Short-run problems are partly the result of the relative volatility of the UK economy *vis-à-vis* its main industrial competitors, at least in the period from the mid-1960s to the late 1980s – see Case Study 1. More surprisingly, however, they are also the consequence of longer-term influences that stem from the fact that periods of unsustained rapid growth have been punctuated by slow and often negative growth during recession. The resulting job losses make specific skills (i.e. those linked to the employing company) redundant. The structural changes, with the major shift in employment from manufacturing to services, can devalue more general skills. The pervasive long-term occupational changes illustrated in the forecasts in Table 15.1 provide an indication of the likely magnitude of commitment needed to education and training. Even within occupations, however, skill levels change. The joint effect is illustrated in Figure 15.2.

Table 15.1 Detailed projected change in employment by standard occupational classification (SOC): 1993–2001 (UK)

Occupation	SOC		Per cent
Managers and Administrators	1.1	Corporate managers and administrators	24
	1.2	Managers/proprietors in agriculture and services	11
Professional occupations	2.1	Science and engineering professionals	23
	2.2	Health professionals	13
	2.3	Teaching professionals	14
	2.4	Other professional occupations	43
Associate professional and technical	3.1	Science and engineering associate professions	15
	3.2	Health associate professionals	0
	3.3	Other associate professionals	30
Clerical and secretarial	4.1	Clerical	–4
	4.2	Secretarial	–2
Craft and skilled manual	5.1	Skilled construction trades	15
	5.2	Skilled engineering trades	–13
	5.3	Other skilled trades	–5
Personal and protective	6.1	Protective service occupations	15
	6.2	Personal service occupations	28
Sales	7.1	Buyers, brokers and sales representatives	0
	7.2	Other sales occupations	4
Plant and machine operatives	8.1	Drivers and mobile machine operatives	–4
	8.2	Industrial plant and machine operatives	–5
Other	9.1	Other occupations in agriculture, etc.	–11
	9.2	Other elementary occupations	–13
All occupations			**7**

Source: *Labour Market Quarterly Report*, Employment Department, February 1995

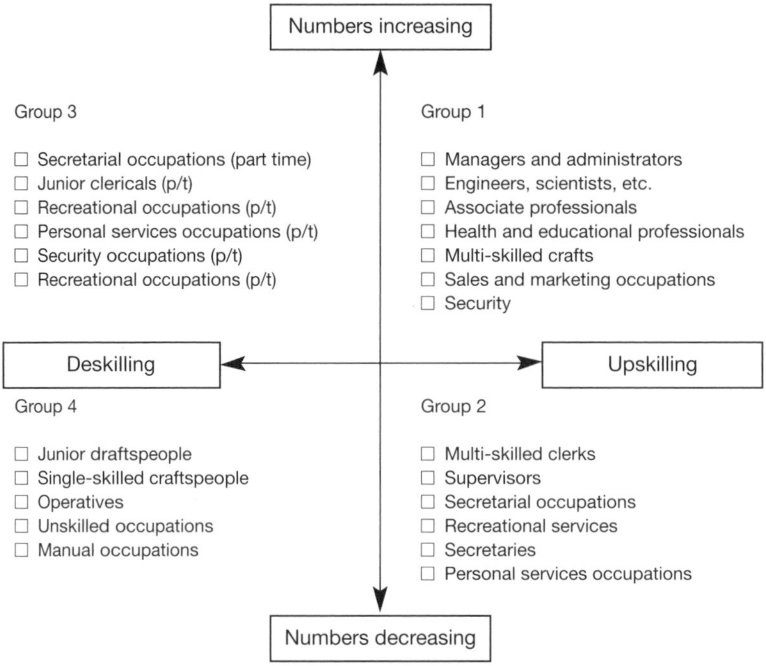

Fig 15.2 Jobs affected by changes in numbers and skill levels.
Source: Data compiled from the *Skill Needs Survey* database

CASE STUDY 1 Skill shortages and the business cycle

Evidence of the cyclical nature of skill shortages can be found in Figure 15.3 which shows information about expected skill shortages, taken from the CBI *Quarterly Industrial Trends Survey*. The data here relate to manufacturing companies and are based on a question about whether firms expect a lack of skilled labour to limit their output over the subsequent four months. The data reveal the low levels of shortage in the years immediately following the recessions of 1981 and 1990, with a major peak in late 1988/early 1989. The proportion of firms reporting shortages fell to 5 per cent or less in both of the troughs, rising to nearly 30 per cent at the peak. Similar peaks have occurred before, such as the one in 1979, and the peak of 1974 was even higher. The upturn in shortages following the last recession is clearly visible.

Table 15.2 reinforces this result, setting out the changing pattern over the 1990s, based upon a question concerning hard-to-fill vacancies, taken from the *Skill Needs in Britain* surveys. By Spring 1994, around 11 per cent of employers

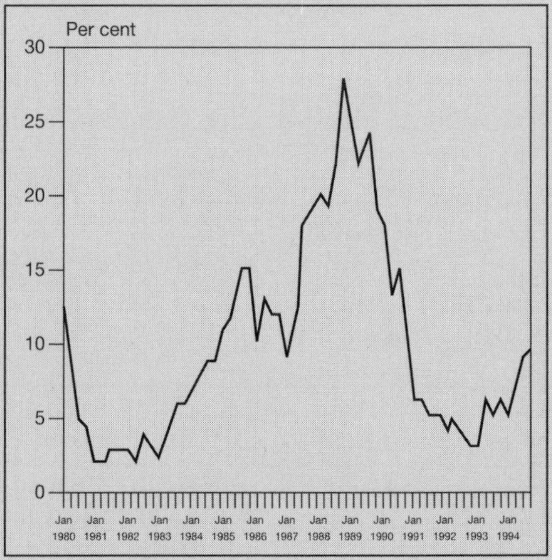

Fig 15.3 Expected skill shortages.
Source: CBI Quarterly Industrial Trends Survey

continues

CASE STUDY 1 continued

Table 15.2 Hard-to-fill vacancies at the time of the interview

Industry sector	Proportion of firms reporting hard-to-fill vacancies				
	1990	1991	1992	1993	1994
Manufacturing	23	6	5	7	11
Mining, utilities and construction	22	8	2	4	5
Distributing and consumer services	20	8	7	11	14
Finance and business services	20	7	3	5	8
Transport, public administration and other services	22	7	6	5	10

Source: *Skill Needs in Britain* – from *Labour Market Quarterly Report*, Employment Department, February 1995

were experiencing hard-to-fill vacancies, well below the level of 21 per cent in 1990, but above the recession levels of between 5 and 7 per cent. In 1994, there were just under three hard-to-fill vacancies per affected employer. The survey also provides a breakdown by area, which indicates that, by 1994, the South East had re-emerged as one of the areas of greatest shortages only surpassed by the East Midlands. On the other hand, Wales, Scotland and the South West still exhibited well below the national average of hard-to-fill vacancies.

Engineering was particularly hard hit by skill shortages in the late 1980s. The ranking of industries in terms of their reported problems at that time was (highest to lowest): engineering; production and construction; distribution and other consumer services; finance and business services. The ranking during recession was somewhat different, although shortages were still most acute in engineering and least important in financial and business services. The continued low level of shortages in construction reflected the slowness of that sector to recover out of recession. The percentage of employers reporting hard-to-fill vacancies also varies across occupational groups. Here the effects of the cycle are marked by greater changes in the rankings. At the peak of the cycle, clerical and craft-related shortages were the most important, with professional and associate professional close behind. By 1991, with the onset of the recession, professional and associate professional formed the most important areas of skill shortage. In 1990, the South was one of the areas of greatest skill shortage, but, with the onset of recession in 1991, the picture looked significantly different. By 1994, however, the South East had re-emerged alongside the East Midlands as the area of highest shortage.

A key indicator of the intensity of a given area of shortage is the length of time that it takes to fill the vacancy. It should be recognized that different occupational groups use different methods of advertising and recruitment, with different degrees of background checks on the individual's references and personal history. More importantly the tightness of the labour market may also mean that some occupations take longer to recruit than others. When this dimension of intensity is taken into account, a somewhat different picture emerges. While professional and associate professional groups still stand out, as do craft and related, considerably more emphasis is placed upon shortages of managers and administrators.

Skill shortages are a complex problem, the causes of which range from poor pay and conditions, through the unreasonably high expectations of potential employers, to pervasive technological changes which reorientate the demands for skills and know-how. Perhaps one of the most interesting things is that, even when employment is falling sharply, some hard-to-fill vacancies are reported. Such shortages are often an indication of a longer-term problem. Skill gaps may be an even more fundamental problem, given that they relate to particular groups or all existing employees in a company rather than to a relatively small number of individuals that the company may be trying to recruit. Indeed, skills gaps may be under-reported insofar as the top executives and managers of a company themselves have skill inadequacies, and do not recognize the existence of a skill gap – see Case Study 2.

CASE STUDY 2 Management qualifications, skills base and training

The quality and skills of top executives appear to be crucial in the process of human resource development. For one thing, poor-quality managers may not even recognize the need to recruit certain types of individuals or the existence of a skills gap within a company. Thus, it may be that, the poorer the management team, the greater will be the under-reporting of skill imbalances in the statistics. In addition, however, it seems likely that more highly qualified decision makers will be more willing to invest in training. For one thing, more highly qualified individuals tend to adopt longer-term planning horizons, as shown in Figure 15.4.

Table 15.3 is taken from a survey of over 700 UK companies and shows the qualification of the MD and the training intensity of each group of staff in the company. It shows that over 30 per cent of companies whose MDs are qualified scientists, engineers or social scientists undertake relatively high levels of investment in employee training. On tbe other hand, those companies wbose MDs are 'self-made', rather than having formal qualifications, tend to invest less in all categories of training, thus underscoring the point that they perhaps do not put as much emphasis on investment in human capital and take shorter-term views. The ratios of high levels/no training are even more revealing. Companies whose MDs are qualified scientists or engineers (QSEs) have a higher ratio than the others, indicating that they invest in more training for all categories of staff

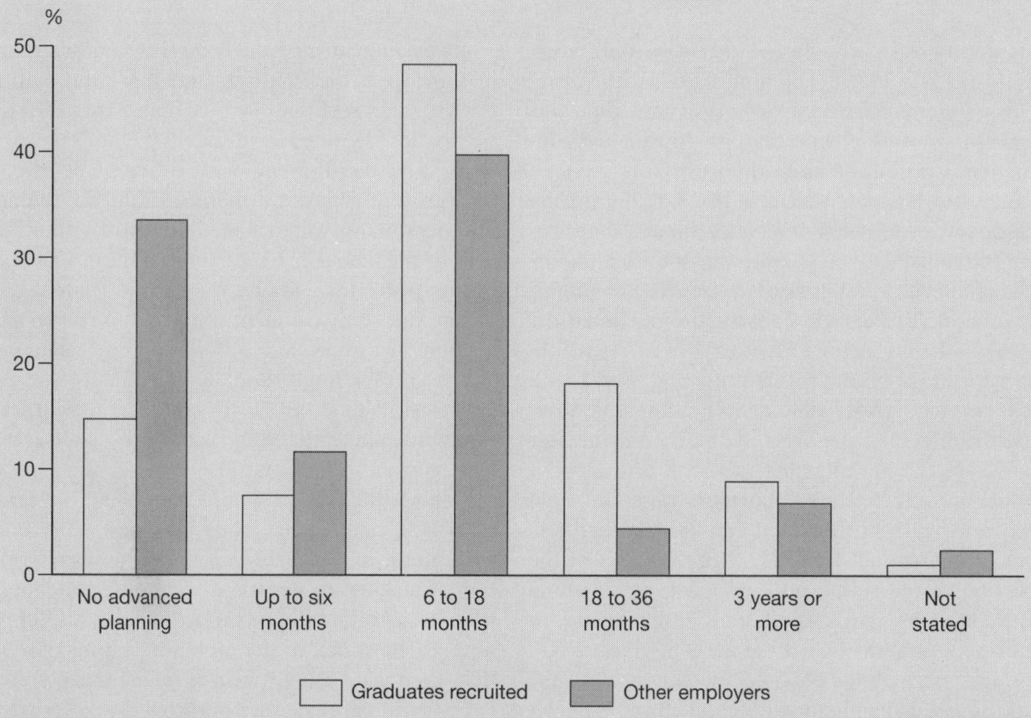

Fig 15.4 Planning horizons of private sector employers who recruited new graduates in 1988.
Source: Rigg *et al.* (1990).

continues

CASE STUDY 2 continued

compared with companies with MDs with other or no qualifications.

Table 15.4 shows the corresponding link between the composition of the Board of Directors and staff training. The results show that intensive training for all categories of staff (except others) is highest for companies with QSEs on the Board. Those without QSEs are also more likely not to have any training for their QSEs, graduates and other staff. The ratios of high level/no training confirm these results. Broadly similar results apply to comparisons between those Boards with and without graduates.

Sources: Tan and Bosworth (1995); Bosworth *et al.* (1992); Bosworth and Jacobs (1989)

Table 15.3 MD qualification and training intensity

MD qualification	Science /Eng.	Social science	Self-made	Unknown	Overall Average
Employee training					
None	1.7	3.0	11.0	9.8	6.3
Intense	31.5	31.3	18.5	24.5	26.6
Intense/none	18.5	10.4	1.7	2.5	
QSE training					
None	5.6	6.0	4.8	5.6	5.8
Intense	25.3	16.9	6.2	18.9	16.8
Intense/none	4.5	2.8	1.3	3.4	
Graduate training					
None	3.9	4.8	4.87	6.3	4.8
Intense	23.6	20.5	8.2	20.3	
Intense/none	6.1	4.3	1.7	3.2	
Others training					
None	0	3.0	6.8	2.1	2.9
Intense	12.9	9.6	5.5	11.9	10.5
Intense/none	–	3.2	0.8	5.7	

Source: Tan and Bosworth (1995)

Table 15.4 Structure of the board and training intensity

Board composition	QSEs		Graduates		Technical	
	None	Some	None	Some	None	Some
Employee training						
None	6.4	2.9	9.5	2.5	7.3	4.1
Intense	19.2	43.3	14.3	37.8	18.2	34.9
Intense/none	3.0	14.9	1.5	15.1	2.5	8.5
QSE training						
None	10.3	4.7	2.4	7.1	9.1	6.2
Intense	9.0	33.9	2.4	28.6	7.3	24.5
Intense/none	0.9	7.2	1.0	4.0	0.8	4.0
Graduate training						
None	6.4	1.8	0	4.2	1.8	4.6
Intense	14.1	35.1	4.8	32.4	16.4	26.6
Intense/none	2.2	19.5	–	7.7	9.1	5.8
Others training						
None	2.6	2.3	0	2.9	0	3.7
Intense	11.5	16.4	0	17.2	14.5	12.9
Intense/none	4.4	7.1	–	5.9	–	3.5

Source: Tan and Bosworth (1995)

4 Training and other dynamic investments

The initial discussion in this chapter acknowledged the lack of hard information about the UK's skills base. In this section we report further evidence from the *Skill Needs in Britain* surveys relating to the extent of investment in various dynamic activities, including training. The dynamic activities relate to the following areas: (1) investment in automating production processes; (2) increased use of computers; (3) moving up market, producing higher-value-added products or services; (4) providing more off-the-job training; (5) diversifying into new market or product areas; (6) placing greater emphasis on customer care or quality management programmes. The extent of activity in each of these areas is based upon a five-point scale, which can be interpreted as ranging from insignificant through to extremely high levels of a particular activity.

The main feature of the results is the relatively high proportion of establishments that report low levels of the six dynamic activities distinguished. Figure 15.5, for example, shows the proportions of establishments reporting on the extent to which they are moving 'up market' into higher-value-added products. The vast majority of establishments (over 65 per cent) report little or no activity in this area. In other investment areas, the lack of activity is even more marked. Over 83 per cent of establishments report that they are not making greatly increased use of computers. At first sight, this may not appear particularly surprising given the extent of diffusion of computers by the early 1990s. Nevertheless, advances in computers and software continue to open up a whole range of new applications. Further proof of this is given in Section 5 below.

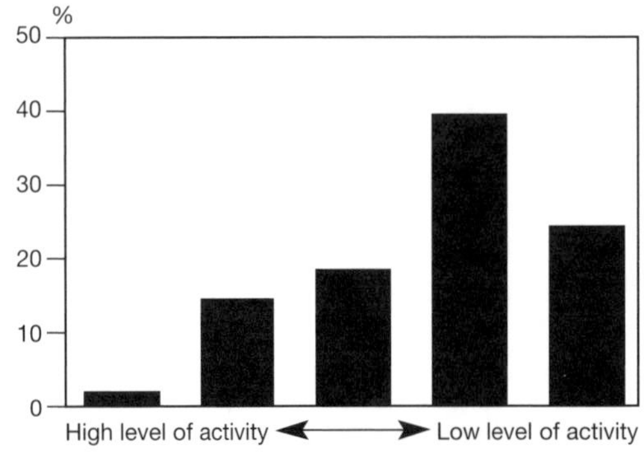

Fig 15.5 Moving up market by providing added value products or services.
Source: *Skill Needs in Britain, 1991.*

A similar pattern emerges with regard to quality management programmes, where 87 per cent of establishments fall into the bottom two levels of activity categories. In practice, the bottom two levels of activity categories are the most frequently reported for all six of the dynamic activities, including off-the-job training. In the case of training, however, there were a significant minority of establishments that believed themselves to be doing more than in earlier years.

The question arises as to whether dynamic activities are concentrated in a small proportion of all establishments (i.e. if the establishment replies that it is investing heavily in one of the areas, it is also likely to be investing in the others). Figure 15.6 is constructed by weighting the level of activity (0 = most active and 5 = least active) for each of the six areas and adding the total up for each establishment. If above-average responses in some areas balanced out lower levels of activity in others, establishments would all be concentrated at about the overall average. If, on the other hand, some are better in all and some are worse in all areas, the dispersion of establishments would be significantly higher. Figure 15.6 shows that the distribution ranges from 0 (i.e. major dynamic investments in all six areas) to 30 (i.e. no dynamic investments in any area). However, the distribution is clearly skewed towards lower levels of activity, and the modal value is 22. Thus, the average modal response is nearly 4 across the six areas, consistent with relatively low levels of dynamic activity.

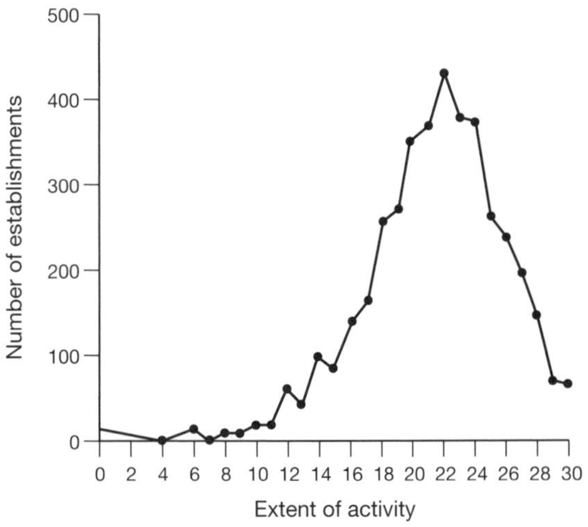

Fig 15.6 Extent of dynamic activities amongst UK establishments
Source: *Skill Needs in Britain, 1991.*

Given that training is of particular interest in the context of skill shortages, Table 15.5 illustrates the types of results obtained when comparing the emphasis placed upon training with each of the other areas of dynamic activity. Take the case of investment in computers and investment in training. In this instance, 38 per cent of establishments reported the same level of activity for both areas; about $53\frac{1}{2}$ per cent of establishments reported a higher level of activity in the training area than in terms of computers; finally, only $8\frac{1}{2}$ per cent of companies felt that they had recently had a higher level of activity in the case of computers than training. Indeed, there is tentative evidence that greater emphasis was being placed upon higher levels of training than on increased use of computers, higher-value-added products and diversification of the product range. However, all of these results should be seen in the context of the apparently overall low levels of activity in all of the areas.

5 Skill shortages and dynamic investments

This section investigates the relationship between the extent of each of the six dynamic activities and the existence of skill shortages. The basic pattern of the findings is the same across all six areas and other measures of skill shortage, such as acknowledging that a 'skill gap' exists, also give consistent results. We therefore simply illustrate the outcome with just one area of dynamic activity, that of moving 'up market' by providing higher-value-added services or products, although we return to the case of training itself in Section 6 below.

Figure 15.7 indicates that the proportion of establishments reporting the need for increased skills rises from 45 per cent amongst establishments most actively seeking to move up market to $72\frac{1}{2}$ per cent amongst the group of establishments least active in moving up market. A similar result applies in the case of the 'skills gap' measure. The proportion of establishments indicating a 'skills gap' rises from 13 per cent in the highest investment activity group to 23 per cent in the lowest. The most obvious explanation is that significant levels of dynamic activity require the presence of an adequate skills base. However, the evidence presented in Sections 4 and 6 also suggests that establishments in the UK are perhaps not doing enough to overcome prevailing inadequacies in the skills base.

While we have not reported it in detail, the results show that establishments that have lower skill deficiencies are also more actively introducing computer technologies. This is consistent with other evidence on information technologies (IT):

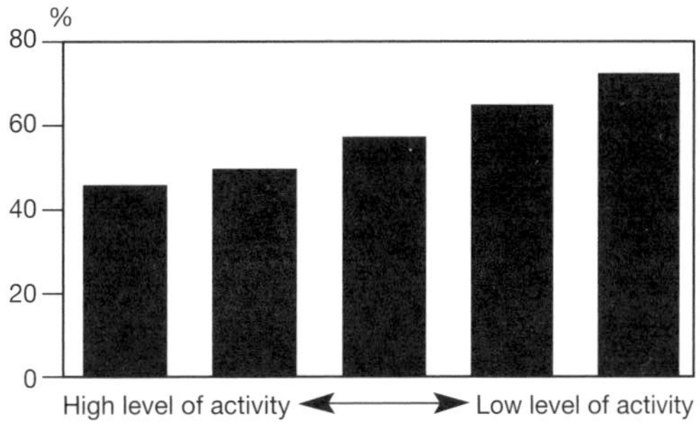

Fig 15.7 Extent of moving up market by providing added value products or services (horizontal) increasing skills needed (vertical).
Source: *Skill Needs in Britain, 1991*

Table 15.5 Relative emphasis on training and other specific dynamic activities

Increased	More emphasis on increased training (than:)	Same emphases on increased training (as:)	Less emphases on increased training (than:)
Automation	$30\frac{1}{2}$	35	$34\frac{1}{2}$
Computers	$53\frac{1}{2}$	38	$8\frac{1}{2}$
Higher-value-added products	41	39	$19\frac{1}{2}$
Diversification of the product range	31	41	28
Customer care/quality management	$5\frac{1}{2}$	35	59

Note: Numbers do not always sum to 100 because of rounding error

> An adequate supply of skills in IT is essential for any business committed to growth and competitiveness. But even some of the best-equipped organisations are struggling to exploit IT because employees at all levels are lacking in these critical skills. The number of computer users has grown rapidly in recent years as has the pace of technological development. Employers must be sure of what IT skills are required and by whom, then decide the best methods of developing them. A major study of over 700 private sector employers by the West London Training and Enterprise Council concludes that unskilful introduction and use of IT will inhibit sales, slow expansion and reduce profitability – the opposite of its intended effect. Shortfalls in IT skills are a significant barrier to growth. ('Lack of IT Skills a Barrier to Growth', 1993.)

6 Role of education and training

The evidence presented to date (and that found in subsequent chapters) suggests that high levels of qualifications and skills are central to successful innovatory activity, firm performance and growth. In addition, the UK appears to have experienced both cyclical and secular shortages and gaps which have limited both the length of the upturn and reduced the potential for long-term growth. All of this suggests the need for major investments in education and training, a theme we take up in earnest in the next two chapters.

While education, training and work experience are crucial in determining the occupations and functions open to individuals, there are no hard and fast rules: intelligence and natural ability may carry one individual into an activity or job where another person would require training; many individuals have qualifications that they do not fully utilize in their jobs. Thus, it is unrealistic to attribute skill differences entirely to this source. Variations in ability, whether innate or developed in childhood before training, allow some people to earn more than others. This is most noticeable where 'scarce talents' exist, for example in the case of sportsmen and women or entertainers. Even if tastes were identical and the long run were considered, exceptional sportsmen and women and entertainers would earn a return reflecting their high level of skill, referred to as 'rent to a scarce talent'. Nevertheless, in general, the more education or training that the individual receives, the further up the occupational/functional hierarchy they can reach. It is interesting to note that even the most skilled sportsmen and women undertake intensive training. In its simplest form, human capital theory suggests that, if individuals are indifferent between jobs (i.e. on the assumption of identical preferences regarding the non-pecuniary advantages and disadvantages of occupations), the long-run wage differentials are just sufficient to compensate for the costs of the training required to achieve the relevant skills. Of course, other factors also influence wage differentials in the real world (see Chapter 26).

By implication, as we noted in the discussion of labour supply models, individuals can to some extent determine their income profiles over their lifetime by investing in education and training. Most of the investment occurs during the earlier stages of career development. There is evidence, for example, that the early experience and attainment of children are particularly influential and carry over into their subsequent school careers (Mortimore *et al.*, 1988). However, the relative importance of investment in human capital at different stages of the life-cycle is changing as jobs become less secure and as the concept of 'lifetime learning' becomes more important. Thus, in general, education and training should be viewed as a sequence or continuum of inter-related investments. The essential feature of human capital models is unchanged, however, as individuals give up income during the period of education or training in return for increased future earning power.

An almost identical situation faces employers, given that higher levels of education and skill amongst their workforce lead to improved firm performance from which, in principle, they can pay higher salaries. Higher economic profits also lead to a greater potential to retain funds for investment in training, research and development, etc. Such investments raise the future monopoly power of the company, increasing future profits and creating a virtuous circle.

7 Market for training: imperfections and failure

The succeeding chapters in this part of the book therefore address the issue of human resource development, both from the individual and firm perspectives. It is possible to think of there being both a demand for and supply of additional skills, and, thereby, in some sense a 'market for training'. The market is complex, not only because there are important institutional factors at play, but also because the demand for higher skills may come from either the individual employee or the employing institution. In addition, the price at which 'skill development' is traded is also complicated, including both the direct costs of training (such as course fees) and various opportunity costs (such as a lower salary, incurred by the employee, or lower output, incurred by the firm, during the training period).

Complex, institutionalized markets seem likely to have imperfections which might lead to lower than socially optimal levels of activity. In Section 5 above, we noted the relationship between the level of investment in dynamic activities and the availability of skills within the establishment. Perhaps the best illustration of this result can be found in the case of training itself: by far the highest proportion of establishments reporting the greatest need for increased skills or the existence of a skills gap also reported the lowest levels of training activity. Figure 15.8 shows that, in the case of training, 40 per cent of those who report the highest additional off-the-job training also reported the need to increase skill levels in the establishment to operate effectively, but 77 per cent of establishments where the least additional training was taking place reported the need to increase skills to operate effectively. Likewise, the proportion of establishments reporting skill shortages over the previous 12 months rises from 18 per cent in the case of establishments with the largest additional training to $29\frac{1}{2}$ per cent amongst establishments with the least additional training. In other words, the establishments which recognize that they have the greatest need to improve the skills of their workforce are doing least about it.

As we will see in subsequent chapters, there are a variety of possible causes of market imperfections and failure. In particular, there are externalities and spillovers. The greater the number of establishments involved in quality training, the higher is the return to training. We will argue that the UK training system became trapped in a vicious cycle of decline, with increasing numbers of firms relying on recruiting skills in the market place, rather than developing the human resources already employed by the company. At its worst, this involves the poaching of workers from other employers. A survey of engineering labour shortages in the North West in the 1980s, for example, found that 80 per cent of the firms interviewed looked to poaching as a key way of meeting their skills needs. Of course, increased levels of poaching activity reduce the rate of return to training by companies and undermine the extent and quality of this type of investment activity. This phenomenon is clearly illustrated in Figure 15.9, which compares how employers in the UK and Germany tackle their skills problems.

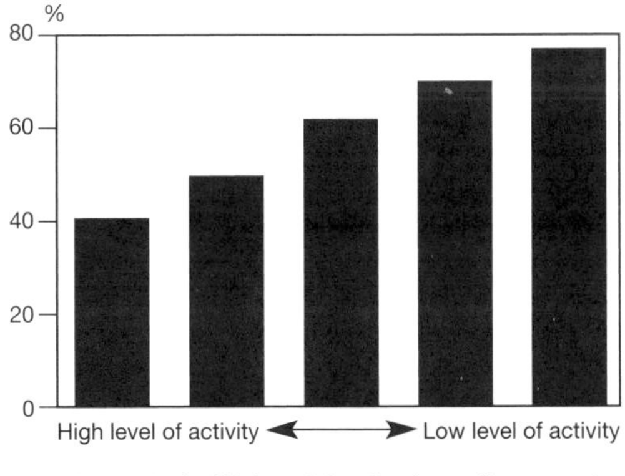

Fig 15.8 Level of off-job training (horizontal) amongst firms reporting skill shortages (vertical).
Source: *Skill Needs in Britain, 1991*

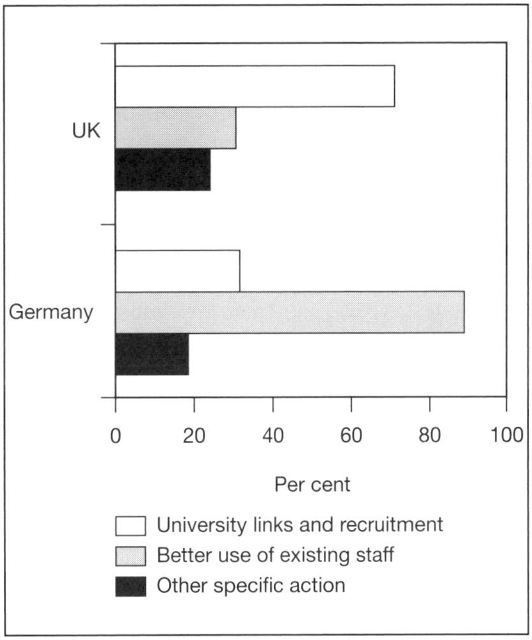

Fig 15.9 The skills problem and how employers tackle it in Germany and the UK.
Source: 'German Attitudes to Research and Training Help their Businesses to Innovate'. *Skills and Enterprise Briefing*, Issue 12/93, March 1993, Figure (3).

8 Government intervention

If markets are inefficient or fail, then there may be a need for government intervention. In practice, the government funds much of the formal education of young people, as well as a wide range of training programmes, paid for from general taxation and, in turn, society reaps the benefit in terms of lower unemployment, greater competitiveness, and faster rates of growth of GDP. This raises the important distinction between private and social rates of return: the private rate of return to education and training is calculated from the costs and benefits borne by the individual, the social rate of return is calculated from those borne by society as a whole. Of course, it is natural that the government would choose to become involved where the social diverges from the private rate of return. However, there are often less quantifiable reasons why the government might choose to intervene, for example to maintain cultural heritage or, alternatively, as part of a social engineering exercise to alter the balance of power relationships within a country. The involvement of governments in the funding has led to considerable interest in the effectiveness of education and training programmes. The present part of this book therefore addresses a number of the problems which arise in evaluating the impact of education and training schemes.

Human capital theory is based on the premise that it is the content of education or training that increases the individual's productivity and, thereby, the willingness of employers to pay out higher wages. However, not all economists take this view: some believe in the 'screening hypothesis', which suggests that what the employer is looking for is a variety of personal attributes, including innate ability, motivation, ability to work under pressure, etc. These are almost impossible to observe directly (i.e. during the course of an interview) and employers use success in the education system as a proxy. Educational attainment is therefore merely a selection device and the educational content makes no direct contribution to productivity or income. The screening hypothesis represents a major challenge to the human capital approach, and particularly to the social rate of return. From the individual's point of view, they earn higher wages after the education, whether it was the content of the course or the fact they obtained a qualification that caused it. The same is not true from society's point of view, as the additional education does not increase the individual's real output or productivity. This raises a number of important issues which will be discussed in the course of this part of the book.

9 Conclusions

In this introductory chapter, we have attempted to show why the skills base of a country is so important. In particular, the role of skills in successful innovation has been emphasized. Evidence has also been provided that, historically, at least, the UK skills base has been inadequate. Indeed, tentative evidence was provided to suggest that those firms with the greatest problems tended to be those doing least about it. The remainder of this part of the book is taken up with the development of a more formal conceptual framework to estimate the rates of return to investment in education training and the evaluation of training schemes. We return to the broader issues of the contribution of skills to examine performance and growth in Chapter 29.

References

Bosworth, D.L. and C. Jacobs (1989). 'Management Attitudes, Behaviour and Abilities as Barriers to Growth'. In J. Barber, J.S. Metcalf and M. Porteous (eds) *Barriers to Growth in Small Firms*. London: Routledge, pp. 20–38.

Bosworth, D.L., R.A. Wilson and P. Taylor (1992). *Technological Change: the Role of Scientists and Engineers*. Aldershot: Avebury.

Elias, P. and M. Healey (1991). *People and Work in Coventry*. Coventry: City of Coventry.

Employment Department (1990). *Training Statistics*. London: HMSO.

Industrial Facts and Forecasting (1991). *Skill Needs in Britain, 1991*. London: IFF.

'Lack of IT Skills a Barrier to Growth'. *Skills and Enterprise Briefing*. Issue 27/93. September. Employment Department Group.

Mortimore, P., P. Sammons, L. Stoll, D. Lewis and R. Ecob (1988). *School Matters: The Junior Years*. Somerset: Open Books.

Rigg, M., P. Elias, M. White and S. Johnson (1990). *An Overview of the Demand for Graduates*. London: HMSO.

Smith, E. (1990). *Skill Needs in Britain, 1990*. London: IFF.

Tan, H.C. and D. L. Bosworth (1995). 'Scientists and Engineers, Dynamic Activities and Business Performance'. Economics Group Working Paper. Manchester School of Management, UMIST.

Training Agency (1989). *Training in Britain*. HMSO: Sheffield (*(i) Individuals' Perspectives; (ii) Employers' Perspectives on Human Resources; (iii) Employers' Activities; (iv) Market Perspectives*).

CHAPTER 16 Human capital and the private returns to education and training

1 Introduction

This chapter sets out a conceptual framework for understanding the education and training investment decisions of both individuals and firms. Given that economists tend to focus mainly on the quantifiable costs and benefits, it is generally possible to calculate a rate of return to such investments. The individual's perception prior to the investment is summarized by the *ex ante* rate of return, while the *ex post* rate of return can be calculated from the actual (observed) costs and benefits resulting from the investment. The two differ for a variety of reasons: the investment is often long term (affecting lifetime earnings) and taken on the basis of highly imperfect information. In addition, the outcome depends on the market for educated and trained individuals and, thereby, on the investments of other individuals. The longevity of the investment can have important implications for the market clearing process, giving rise to the possibility of cobweb cycles. The difficulties of calculating the *ex ante* rate of return have led some economists to question the whole concept of human capital theory.

Section 2 develops the idea of education and training as private investment decisions based upon net tax income and expenditure flows. It outlines the associated concept of the rate of return to education and training which we first touched upon in the labour supply chapters. It explores the differences between *ex ante* and *ex post* rates of return, emphasizing the importance of imperfect information in long-term decisions of this type. Section 3 shows that the underlying rate of return can also be estimated using an earnings function approach, an idea taken up in detail in Chapter 26 below. It is particularly useful to introduce the approach at this stage, however, as it is widely used in the evaluation of training programmes. Section 4 introduces a firm perspective on training. In doing so, it considers the distinction between specific and general training. This raises some important questions about who will finance the investment, the firm or the individual. This section also says something about the links between training and internal labour markets, and company evaluation of the returns to training. Finally, Section 5 draws the main conclusions of this chapter.

2 Investment decisions

2.1 Costs and benefits

To simplify the exposition, we begin by discussing education and training investments from an individual perspective. It is clearly an investment activity because it gives rise to both costs and benefits that are distributed over a number of time periods. The pecuniary costs can be divided into two broad groups: first, direct expenditures (such as outlays on tuition fees, books, materials, etc.); second, the opportunity cost associated with lower productivity and earnings. Of course, there may be other, non-pecuniary costs, such as social upheaval, stress, etc. The returns are those factors that raise the individual's present and future welfare: the learning process may be enjoyable (i.e. a consumption benefit); there may be a lower chance of experiencing unemployment during the individual's lifetime; future net of tax earnings may be higher; there is a greater chance of obtaining a more prestigious and enjoyable job with a lower intrinsic disutility of work. While non-economic factors may be important our attention focuses primarily on the quantifiable economic effects of education and training on factors such as productivity and earnings.

If, after allowing for differences in the timing of the costs and benefits, the decision maker calculates that the benefits exceed the costs, then the additional education or training will generally be undertaken. The investment decision is incremental in nature. This turns out to be extremely important as there is a crucial distinction between the average and marginal rate of return. The difference in income stream of someone with a PhD and someone without a first degree might far outweigh the costs of obtaining a PhD, and the associated average rate of return might be high. On the other hand, we might find that the major part of this can be attributed to the first degree, less to the Master's level and the rate of return to the PhD itself might be lower than alternative investments the individual can make. It is therefore important to think of the marginal contribution of each subsequent investment. Past expenditures are sunk costs that do not enter the rate of return calculation directly. However, they are important in the sense that investments are often sequential (i.e. in the UK individuals generally require A levels before they are admitted onto a degree course). Bearing in mind the need to calculate marginal rather than average rates of return, at certain key intervals, individuals choose a new portfolio of education–training options stretching into the future, which may be subsequently revised.

2.2 Rate of return calculation

Ideally both the income streams (i.e. with and without education or training) should relate to the future experience of the same individual, but in practice, this is clearly impossible, because at any given point in time, an individual may either invest or not invest, but not both. Even information about the income stream associated with the chosen route is rarely (if ever) known for the particular individual undertaking the decision. In general, this longitudinal dimension is proxied by cross-sectional data about incomes of comparable people, relating to individuals of different ages and observed at the time of the investment decision. Using cross-sectional data avoids problems posed by inflation insofar as all the income and cost streams are in terms of the prices of the year in which the decision is taken. This approach largely ignores the question of whether actual cross-sectional values at that point in time reflect either the perceived (*ex ante*) or actual (*ex post*) time series values. However, the emergence of major panel data sets is beginning to throw some light on this issue:

> analysis of earnings profiles over the working lives of individuals revealed that the well-known parabolic profile of earnings by age which is exhibited in cross-sectional analyses (i.e. the fact that earnings rises with age until the mid forties then declines until retirement) is also reflected in the working life experience of individuals. (Elias and Gregory, 1994, p. i).

Figure 16.1 indicates two groups of individuals who differ only with regard to their level of education or training. $W(M)$ denotes the earnings stream 'expected' without the additional training and $W(T)$ is the equivalent earnings stream with investment in education or training. In order to simplify the analysis, however, Figure 16.2 is used as a first approximation: *dg* denotes the 'expected' earnings stream without the additional investment; *abef* is the equivalent stream with investment in education or training. Broadly the same analysis can be applied to the individual or to the firm: in the case of the individual, W may denote various levels of wage; in the case of the firm, W might refer to various levels of the value of the marginal physical product captured by the firm. We return to the firm's investment decision later in this chapter.

Assuming that the non-monetary costs and benefits are insignificant then the investment will be undertaken if,

$$\sum_{t=\tau_1}^{\tau_2} \frac{[W(T)-W(M)]_t}{(1+i)^t} > \sum_{t=\tau_0}^{\tau_1} \frac{[W(M)-W(0)]_t}{(1+i)^t} + \sum_{t=\tau_0}^{\tau_1} \frac{\kappa_t}{(1+i)^t} \quad (1)$$

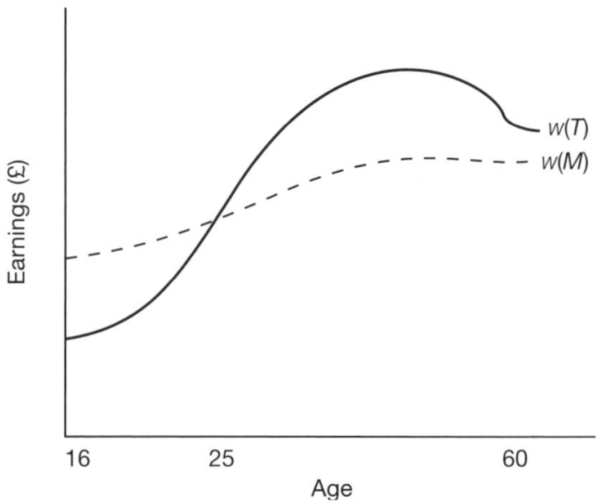

Fig 16.1 Cross-sectional cohort's income streams.

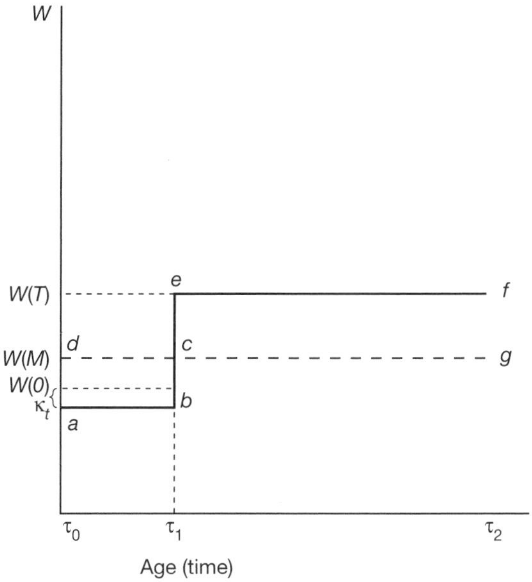

Fig 16.2 Investment and income streams and the rate of return.

where: $W(0)$ is the wage per period during training; $W(M)$ is the 'without-training' wage level; $W(T)$ is the post-training wage level; κ denotes the direct costs per period borne by the individual; i is the rate of discount; t denotes the particular point in time that a given cost or benefit can be expected to occur. The period of training is $\tau_1 - \tau_0$ and the period over which returns accrue is $\tau_2 - \tau_1$. Inequality (1) is interpreted as showing that, for the investment to be undertaken, the discounted future stream of benefits (i.e. *gcef* appropriately discounted) must outweigh the similarly discounted stream of costs (i.e. *abcd*, appropriately discounted, where *abcd* represents the sum of the income forgone and the direct expenditure on education borne by the individual). In other words the net present value of the investment must be greater than zero. If, by chance, at discount rate i, the inequality was replaced by an equality, then the decision taker would be indifferent about the investment.

An alternative approach is to calculate the rate of return, r, which ensures,

$$\sum_{t=\tau_1}^{\tau_2} \frac{[W(T) - W(M)]_t}{(1+r)^t} = \sum_{t=\tau_0}^{\tau_1} \frac{[W(M) - W(0)]_t}{(1+r)^t} + \sum_{t=\tau_0}^{\tau_1} \frac{\kappa_t}{(1+r)^t} \quad (2)$$

and then compare r with the rate of interest, i. The rate of interest, i, represents the return the individual would have received if they had invested the same amount of resources into the best alternative available. Investment will be profitable if $r > i$, but the individual would not invest when $r < i$ and would be indifferent when $r = i$. This simple analysis clearly ignores issues of risk and uncertainty. A simple but imperfect method of allowing for risk would be to adjust the required interest rate by a risk premium (i.e. $i + \delta$, where δ is the adjustment for risk), or to choose a value of i that reflects an equally risky investment.

Figure 16.3 illustrates the dynamic nature of the interaction between education and/or training investments and wages. Period 0 represents the end of compulsory education, at which time the anticipated earnings stream without further investment in education or training is represented by the horizontal line W_0. At this point in time the individual may perceive an investment of size *abb'a'*, which is more profitable than any available alternative. This investment lowers actual earnings to Y_0, but raises future (potential) earnings to W_1 starting at time 1. The second investment, of size *cdd'c'*, however, lowers the observed earnings in period 1 from W_1 to Y_1, but raises potential earnings to a level W_2 starting at the beginning of period 2. The curve *abcd....* illustrates the actual income stream. It is clear from this argument that observed income streams in the real world reflect the combined effects of investment in both education and training. At any point in time, the observed income level is raised by past investments, but reduced by the size of the current investment activity. In general, the majority of the investment activity takes place early

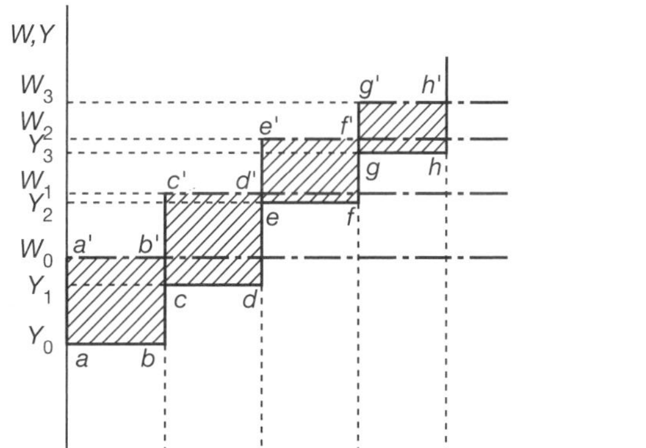

Fig 16.3 Investment portfolio: potential and actual earnings.

in the individual's career, reaping the benefits in later years, although, as we noted above, this is becoming somewhat less clear cut, at least in the UK; as tenure falls, the number of job changes increases and a shift occurs towards 'lifetime learning'.

2.3 Empirical evidence

2.3.1 *Ex post* rates of return

A considerable body of evidence has accumulated about the average private rate of return to undertaking a degree or equivalent qualification in various countries, (for UK evidence, see, for example, Wilson, 1980, 1984 and 1987). The internal rate of return is isolated by solving for r in equation (2), where τ_0 denotes age 16 (or 18) and τ_2 relates to retirement, at age 65. It is worth noting that earnings forgone are, in practice, subject to considerable problems of measurement given that the two groups involved (i.e. those who do and do not undertake the educational investment) are comprised of different individuals. Willis and Rosen, for example, argue that

> it is well understood that college and high school graduates may have different abilities so that income forgone during college by the former is not necessarily equal to earnings of the latter. (Willis and Rosen, 1979, p. S8)

We return to this issue in detail in Section 3.3 below. In most of the empirical studies, a number of adjustments are made to the flows, for example, concerning student grants, summer earnings, etc. Table 16.1 reports a summary of the associated results derived by Wilson.

The results are interesting both in terms of the diversity of the values observed and their distinct movements over time. The first feature of the table concerns variations in the rates of return across professions. This may reflect differences in the non-pecuniary aspects of the associated jobs. In addition, each market may be characterized by some degree of disequilibrium (with excess supply in cer-

Table 16.1 Private rates of return for different professions

<table>
<tr><th>Profession</th><th>1955</th><th>1970</th><th>1980</th><th>1985</th></tr>
<tr><td>All graduates</td><td>17.5</td><td>12.5</td><td>9.0</td><td>8.5</td></tr>
<tr><td>Chemists</td><td>20.0</td><td>12.5</td><td>9.5</td><td>9.0</td></tr>
<tr><td>Physicists</td><td>20.0</td><td>13.5</td><td>11.0</td><td>10.0</td></tr>
<tr><td>Engineers</td><td>14.5</td><td>13.0</td><td>10.0</td><td>10.5</td></tr>
<tr><td>Architects</td><td>13.5</td><td>13.5</td><td>7.0</td><td>6.0</td></tr>
<tr><td>Quantity surveyors</td><td>16.0</td><td>15.0</td><td>5.5</td><td>10.5</td></tr>
<tr><td>General medical practitioners</td><td>21.0</td><td>15.5</td><td>12.5</td><td>n/a</td></tr>
<tr><td>Consultants</td><td>22.0</td><td>16.0</td><td>12.4</td><td>n/a</td></tr>
<tr><td>Other hospital doctors</td><td>13.0</td><td>10.5</td><td>7.5</td><td>n/a</td></tr>
<tr><td>General dental practitioners</td><td>35.0</td><td>24.5</td><td>17.5</td><td>n/a</td></tr>
<tr><td>Solicitors</td><td>14.0</td><td colspan="2">11.5</td><td>n/a</td></tr>
<tr><td>Barristers</td><td>10.5</td><td colspan="2">10.5</td><td>n/a</td></tr>
<tr><td>Lawyers in industry</td><td colspan="2">17.0</td><td>18.0</td><td>17.0</td></tr>
<tr><td>Primary school teachers</td><td>6.0</td><td>4.0</td><td>–ve</td><td>n/a</td></tr>
<tr><td>Secondary school teachers</td><td>10.5</td><td>8.0</td><td>1.5</td><td>n/a</td></tr>
<tr><td>Further education teachers</td><td>15.0</td><td>11.0</td><td>4.0</td><td>n/a</td></tr>
<tr><td>University lecturers, etc.</td><td>20.5</td><td>13.0</td><td>10.5</td><td>n/a</td></tr>
<tr><td>Accountants</td><td>16.0</td><td>16.0</td><td>13.5</td><td>n/a</td></tr>
<tr><td>Economists</td><td>18.5</td><td>22.5</td><td>16.0</td><td>n/a</td></tr>
<tr><td>Statisticians</td><td>21.0</td><td>22.0</td><td>12.0</td><td>n/a</td></tr>
<tr><td>Patent agents</td><td>n/a</td><td>18.5</td><td>13.5</td><td>15.5</td></tr>
</table>

Note: The data are subject to a number of detailed adjustments and the dates should be treated as approximate

Source: Bosworth and Wilson (1988) based on results from Wilson (see text)

tain areas and excess demand in others). This feature may be accentuated by differences in the extent to which there are restrictions on entry to the various professions and, thereby, in the monopoly power of the associated group. Such factors may be important in explaining the different rates of return to teachers and lawyers in industry. The second main feature of the table is that the estimated values have clearly changed over the period. After the mid-1960s, rates of return fell quite dramatically and, for some groups, dropped below zero. The general downward movement was the product of the major outward shift in the supply function during a period in which demand stagnated. The subsequent revival of rates of return reflected the economic recovery at that time.

2.3.2 *Ex ante* versus *ex post* rates of return

A number of studies have addressed the question of students' perceived costs and benefits at the time of making the investment decision. It is perceived rather than actual flows that are at the heart of the decision whether to invest or not. However, the collection of data about perceived income streams is associated with a number of important problems. The choice boils down to asking either how the (potential) student or trainee expects their (net) income (or the income of some essentially identical person) would progress over time with or without the educational investment or, alternatively, how the analogous incomes would differ at different ages at the time of the investment decision. The first way of phrasing the question has the advantage of being technically correct, but has problems in ensuring the flows are in constant prices; the second form of the question has less of a problem coping with inflation and the results are more directly comparable with the majority of *ex post* studies. One advantage of this type of survey is that, in principle, the two income streams are for the same person, unlike the majority of *ex post* studies where the income stream for the non-educational investment group is generally more *ad hoc*.

There are several interesting features of the results relating to investment in a first degree (Bosworth and Ford, 1985). First, the perceived income streams by both routes (i.e. with and without investment) tend to show fairly rapid growth in the early years of the career, levelling off in later life. However, the graduate stream overtakes the non-graduate stream within the first few years of the adopted career. Second, the associated rates of return in some studies tend to be high *vis-à-vis ex post* rates of return. For fairly obvious reasons to do with the self-selection process, the estimate of Williams and Gordon (1981), based on a broad cross-section of school children, gave a lower estimate (13 per cent for males and 10 per cent for females) than Bosworth and Ford's study of new entrants to university (23 per cent and 21 per cent respectively). Third, the estimated *ex ante* rates differ across groups of the population. In particular, as in the case of *ex post* rates of return there are differences in perceived incomes and rates of return between males and females, although the differences in rates of return appear less clear cut by the time individuals reach university. In addition, there are major differences in *ex ante* rates of return to different subject areas. In the university new entrant sample, business and finance topped the scale at 25 per cent, compared with arts at 15 per cent (and a mixed group of subjects at only 12 per cent). Finally, the perceived income streams and, by implication, the rates of return exhibited a skewed distribution of the type traditionally associated with actual incomes (see Chapter 26).

3 Earnings functions and returns to education and training

3.1 Introduction

In this section, we focus on the use of earnings functions to estimate rates of return to education (see Chapter 26). Mincer derived an equation to establish the influence of schooling and work experience in human capital (Mincer, 1974), which has been widely used on UK data. This involves regressing the log of annual earnings on schooling and work experience (and its square) – in other words an 'earnings function'.

3.2 Choice of functional form

The semi-log form is derived from the fact that the specification of the earnings function should reflect the skewed nature of the income distribution observed in the real world, with a relatively high proportion of individuals on low incomes and a relatively small proportion on high incomes (i.e. the mean income exceeds the mode). A simple justification for the most common specification can be found in the work of Roy (1951):

> if each of the relevant abilities is normally distributed but earnings vary with the product of two or more uncorrelated kinds of ability, then the logarithm of earnings, rather than earnings themselves, will be normally distributed. (Berndt, 1991, p. 161).

Of course, this result is crucially dependent on the assumption that the underlying 'abilities' are normally distributed.

If the (compound) rate of return to education can be written as r, then the earnings function can be written as

$$\ln W_s = \ln W_0 + rs + \mu \tag{3}$$

where: s is a measure of the investment in schooling (i.e. the number of years of schooling, which acts as a proxy for forgone earnings); μ is a random error term (Berndt, 1991, p. 162). In this equation, W_0 represents the estimated level of earnings without education. The percentage return to the first year of schooling can be written as

$$r_1 = \frac{W_1 - W_0}{W_0} \tag{4}$$

or, alternatively, this expression can be rearranged as

$$W_1 = (1 + r_1)W_0 \tag{5}$$

It is easy to see that subsequent years of investment result in a compound growth in earnings of the form,

$$W_s = (1 + r_1)(1 + r_2) \ldots (1 + r_s)\, W_0 \tag{6}$$

Finally, based upon the assumption of a constant rate of return in each year ($r_1 = r_2 = \ldots = r_s = r$),

$$W_s = (1 + r)^s W_0 \approx e^{rs} W_0 \tag{7}$$

which is equivalent to equation (3) above.

Results for the USA and the UK show that if work experience, X, is not included in the analysis the explanatory power of schooling on earnings is very low. However, inclusion of X and X^2 increases the explanation to 30 per cent and when weeks worked per year are included as well, explanatory power further doubles. This result conforms with expectations since there is a negative correlation between schooling and experience which gives rise to an underestimate of the effect of schooling unless experience is allowed for. Even so, such earnings functions still require careful interpretation since the coefficient on schooling may reflect other factors (i.e. the amount of schooling may depend on innate ability or family background). In particular, things like drive, enthusiasm, etc., can be important determinants of earning power, and may be correlated with years of schooling thus leading to an overestimate of the returns to education (again, see the earlier discussion of the screening hypothesis). Clearly, other variants are possible,

$$\ln W = \ln W_0 + \beta_1 s + \beta_2 X + \beta_3 X^2 + \beta_4 sX + \mu \tag{8}$$

where labour market experience not only enters in a non-linear (quadratic) form, but also interacts with the level of schooling (Berndt, 1991, p. 163). Berndt notes that a sufficient condition for the experience–earnings profiles of the more educated to be steeper is that $\beta_4 > 0$.

Statistical earnings functions can be specified in a manner which can test for earnings differentials between different sub-groups of the population,

$$\ln W_i = \mathbf{f}(s_i, X_i, Z_i) + \mu_i \tag{9}$$

where, in addition to the variables defined above: Z is a vector of other possible influences; μ is a random error term (reflecting unobserved random influences not accounted for directly); $i (= 1, \ldots, n)$ denotes the ith individual in the sample. Despite some tentative links with Roy's (1951) theory, it is difficult to derive a simple form of this type based upon a dynamic optimization model of individual behaviour. Nevertheless, functions based on equation (9) have been used to estimate the effects of a wide range of influences (such as race, gender, training schemes, region, etc.). We will return to these estimates at various times throughout the remainder of the book. The associated differentials are often picked up by the coefficient estimated on a dummy variable (representing the particular influence in question, i.e. it generally enters as a simple shift variable, with all the limitations that implies):

> Let us remember the unfortunate econometrician who, in one of the major functions of his system, had to use a proxy for risk and a dummy for sex. (Machlup, 1974; quoted in Berndt, 1991, p. 150).

For those interested in the appropriate specification of such equations, and a discussion of their strengths and limitations, see Maddala (1992, Chapter 8).

Equation (9), for example, might test for the effects of training by the inclusion of a training dummy, T,

$$\ln W_i = \ln W_0 + \beta s_i + \alpha T_i + \gamma Z_i + \mu_i \tag{10}$$

where $T_i = 1$ if the ith individual has received training and $T_i = 0$ otherwise. Clearly, earnings differences, amongst other things (such as the probability of obtaining work), are taken as measures of the success (or failure) of particular government programmes and are, therefore, central elements in the evaluation of such programmes and policies. There are many examples of evaluation exercises that throw light on individuals' earnings, employment, occupation, etc., which we cover in depth in the following sections. In the main, we can distinguish: first generation, where no account was taken of the effects of non-random selection of individuals onto different programmes; second generation, where attempts were made to allow for selection in a variety of ways.

3.3 Omitted variables and selection biases

Ideally, the calculation would be undertaken for each individual, knowing what their income stream would be both with and without the investment. Clearly, this is not possible: once the individual has received the education or training, we will never know what their income stream would have been without it; if they don't receive it, their alternative income stream with education or training is not observed.

> [Esme Weatherwax] 'Of course not! It didn't happen. But the point is, it might have happened. You can't say "if this didn't happen then that would have happened" because you don't know everything that might have happened. You might think something'd be good, but for all you know it could have turned out horrible... The point is you'll never know. You've gone past. So there's no use thinking about it. So I don't.'
>
> [Ridcully] 'Trousers of Time. One of you goes down one leg, one of you goes down the other.'
> (Terry Pratchett, *Lords and Ladies*. Discworld Novel. London: Victor Gollancz, p. 162)

The issue of selection biases, which has assumed a central importance in the empirical literature, concerns, in particular, the self-selection of individuals into particular groups. This issue, which has been a recurring theme throughout the book, is especially important in terms of earnings functions. While individuals do not normally choose their gender, they (their parents, employer or the government) choose whether they continue in education or enter a training scheme. The key issue is whether the selection of individuals is non-random, in other words, dependent on some set of observed or unobserved characteristics which influence their ability to absorb successfully and exploit the education or training programme.

One obvious omitted variable is the innate ability of the individual in question, but there may be others, such as motivation and drive. Such omissions make it difficult to determine whether the educational investment causes the higher income level. If, for example, individuals who undertake the investment have higher innate ability then some, if not all, of the higher income would have been experienced anyway. In this case, the return to post-compulsory education would be lower than suggested above. In a study of examination performance, for example, it is shown that young people who are selected (self-selected) into the group which take examinations have characteristics which make them more likely to attain a higher examination score than those selected into the non-exam group (Bosworth, 1994).

Selection issues have particularly come to the fore in the case of the evaluation of training schemes. Here, a variety of selection procedures may come into play (Barnow, 1987, p. 180):

> *Application* by eligible individuals (potentially influenced by those who run the programme);
> *Acceptance* onto the programme by those in a position to accept or reject applicants;
> *Activity assignment* by negotiation between the applicant and administrator (i.e. course, course content, etc.);
> *Participation* the decision by the individual to enroll, and to turn up.

The question is what can be done to correct for such omissions and sample selection biases. The choice is not innocuous. Barnow (1987) documents and explores the sources of the wide range of results regarding the impact of the US *Comprehensive Employment and Training Act* programmes on earnings. Two main causes of differences are isolated: (i) hypotheses tested; (ii) methodology adopted to account for selection biases (Barnow, 1987, p. 175). Of these, variations in methodology accounted for the majority of the differences, of which the treatment of selection issues by experimental and non-experimental methods was most important.

In the experimental approach a large number of candidates are randomly assigned to the 'recipient' and the 'control' groups (unlike medicine, it is difficult to think of a 'placebo' group who think they receive training but don't). We would then observe the two cohorts over time. In practice, there are many problems in applying these experimental methods. There is the cost involved (this is particularly the case where treatments are multi-stage, such as where individuals become eligible for a higher-level training after successfully completing the first stage of the programme). In addition, there are practical issues about individuals who leave or do not respond to questions about the programme (i.e. non-random attrition). More importantly, there are ethical issues about offering potentially beneficial treatments to part of the population, while keeping this help from the control group. Experimental methods, at least in the social sciences, have been much more extensively used in the USA than in, say, the UK. The advocates of experimental methods are often sceptical about the accuracy of non-experimental methods:

> policy makers should be aware that the available non-experimental evaluations of employment and training programmes may contain large and unknown biases resulting from specification errors. (LaLonde, 1986, p. 617; see also Fraker and Maynard, 1987).

Nevertheless, non-experimental (or stochastic) methods have been more widely used, and improvements in methodology have evolved. To illustrate the general approach, we follow Heckman and Robb (1986), where the 'treatment' is a course of training. The individual can, in principle, receive training at a specific point during their careers (i.e. at time k). This training takes one period, during which they earn no income from paid employment. Thus, at the beginning of time period k, based upon information available to the individual at time $k - 1$, the expected present value of the individual's income stream without training can be written as

$$\mathrm{PV}(M) = E_{k-1}\left[\sum_{\tau=0}^{\infty}\left(\frac{1}{1+r}\right)^{\tau} Y^{*}_{i,k+\tau}\right] \tag{11}$$

where, in this case, r is used to denote the rate of interest, which is assumed to be common across all individuals, i. The present value of the income stream with training can be written as

$$\mathrm{PV}(T) = E_{k-1}\left[\sum_{\tau=1}^{\infty}\left(\frac{1}{1+r}\right)^{\tau} Y^{*}_{i,k+\tau} + \sum_{\tau=1}^{\infty}\frac{\alpha}{(1+r)^{\tau}}\right] \tag{12}$$

where α is the impact of training on earnings in each subsequent period. The individual is given a subsidy of S_i if they undertake training (clearly, the 'subsidy' could be negative if the individual pays the direct costs of training). What is important for the present purposes, however, is that the subsidy is comprised of two parts: the first is determined by a set of observables, Z_i, and the second by unobservables, ν_i. Thus, we can write,

$$S_i = Z_i\phi + \nu_i \tag{13}$$

Clearly, the net return to training can be written as the difference between the two present values,

$$R_i = \mathrm{PV}_i(T) - \mathrm{PV}_i(M) = E_{k-1}(S_i - Y_{ik} + \alpha/r) \tag{14}$$

To simplify the exposition, it is assumed that the individual's expectations are fulfilled and, thus, the expected values of S, Y and α/r can be replaced by their actual values.

Thus, the individual's training decision can be represented by

$$T_i = 1 \text{ iff } S_i - Y_{ik} + \alpha/r = Z_i\phi + \alpha/r - X_{ik}\beta + \nu_i - \mu_{ik} > 0 \tag{15}$$

$$T_i = 0 \text{ otherwise} \tag{16}$$

As Heckman and Robb (1986, p. 252) point out, if (Z_i, X_{ik}) is distributed independently of $(\nu_i - \mu_{ik})$, then equations (15) and (16) correspond to a standard discrete choice model. Heckman and Robb (1986) go on to discuss a number of alternative methods of estimating the impact of treatment on outcomes where enrolment into the treatment and non-treatment categories is non-random. Nevertheless, they caution

> In the absence of genuine experimental data, some assumptions must be invoked to solve the problem of selection bias. The choice of an appropriate assumption requires appeal to content, a priori beliefs, and prior knowledge. There is no content-free solution to the problem of selection bias despite claims to the contrary in the recent literature in statistics which solves selection problems by imposing *ad hoc* mathematical structures onto the data. (Heckman and Robb, 1986, p. 283)

Finally, we note another potential form of self-selection bias. Many of the more recent evaluations use cohort data, such as the *Youth Cohort Study* matched samples in the UK, which are often subject to significant problems of attrition. In many instances, the effects of sample attrition have not been tested directly. In some papers where they were tested, they did not appear to be significant, but other investigations have suggested that sample attrition is far from random.

3.4 Empirical results

An interesting paper by Willis and Rosen (1979) attempts to isolate the marginal effects of college education on earnings, allowing for self-selection factors. Their aims are therefore two-fold: first, to estimate lifetime earnings conditioned on actual school choices that are purged of selection bias; second, to examine the relative importance of family background and financial constraints in determining future earnings prospects. The authors argue that up to two-thirds of the variance in earnings in earlier studies can be attributed to unobserved components or person-specific effects, which can often persist over much of the life-cycle. The authors suggest a four-equation framework,

$$W_{ij} = \alpha_j(X_i, v_i) \tag{17}$$

where W_{ij} represents the potential lifetime earnings of the ith individual, having chosen school level j; X_i is a vector of observed measures of ability; v_i is an unobserved talent component; α_j indicates that the lifetime earnings outcome will differ between routes (i.e. high school versus college). Second, the wealth generated by this process is written as

$$V_{ij} = \mathbf{g}(\alpha_j, Z_i, \Omega_i) \tag{18}$$

which translates the earnings from choice j into a present value measure, V_{ij}, conditioned on observed, Z_i, and unobserved, Ω_i, components of family background (reflecting tastes and financial barriers to schooling). The selection rule is given by

$$i \in j \text{ if } V_{ij} = \max(V_{i1}, V_{i2}, \ldots, V_{in}) \tag{19}$$

which indicates that the ith person chooses the educational route that maximizes their wealth. Finally, equation (20) specifies the distribution of the unobservables,

$$(\alpha, \Omega) = \mathbf{F}(\alpha, \Omega) \tag{20}$$

The authors argue that

> Since observed assignments of individuals to schooling classes are selected on (X,Z,v,Ω) earnings observed in each class may be non-random samples of the population's potential earnings, because those with larger net benefits in the class have a higher probability of being observed in it. (Willis and Rosen, 1979 p. S10)

This idea has obvious links with the theory of comparative advantage. One implication of this selectivity problem is that considerable care should be taken in using the traditional rate of return measures outlined in Section 2 above as investment guidelines. The authors argue that

> population mean 'rates of return' among alternative school levels have no significance as guides to the social or private profitability of investments in schooling. For example, a random member of the population might achieve a negative return from an engineering degree, yet those with appropriate talents who choose engineering will obtain a return on the time and money costs of their training which is at least equal to the rate of interest. (p. S11)

The Willis and Rosen (1979) sample was a group of about 5000 individuals who applied for the Army Air Corps in the USA. The authors calculate lifetime earnings based on the assumption of a constant geometric process for each individual, based on information soon after entry into the labour force and a further observation 20 years later. A dichotomous split is then made between measured personal characteristics, X, which are assumed to affect only lifetime earnings potential, and a vector of family background and tastes, Z, representing financial barriers to school choice, and which impact only on the discount rate. The authors argue that this broadly corresponds with Becker's distinction between factors that shift the marginal rate of return to investment schedule and those that shift the marginal supply of investment funds schedule. A Heckman two-stage procedure is adopted to allow for sample selection biases. The first stage of this procedure involves estimation of a (reduced form) probit equation, explaining the probability that the individual will stay on at college. This equation is used to construct the selectivity bias correction factors. The second stage is to estimate the wage equations, which include the correction factors as least-squares regressors.

The results of the reduced form probit equation revealed that the individual's mathematics score had a strong positive effect on college attendance, whereas their mechanical score had a strong negative impact. The individual was more likely to attend college if their mother worked when they were aged 6–14 years, probably relaxing the financial constraints on the individual's education process. The authors conclude that the probit results support the hypothesis that the expected gains in lifetime earnings influence the decision to attend college. Earnings equations are estimated at the point of entry and at the 20 year point in their career, separately for both high school and college groups. Equations were also estimated for the rate of growth in earnings. The results vary somewhat according to the dependent variable adopted. The authors conclude, however, that the results show positive sorting/selection bias in observed earnings of both groups:

> those persons who stopped schooling after high school had better prospects as high school graduates than the average member of the sub-population and that those who continued to college also had better prospects than the average member of the sub-population. That is, the average earnings at most points in the life cycle of persons with given measured characteristics who actually choose B exceeded what earnings would have been for those persons (with the same characteristics) who chose A instead. Conversely, average earnings for those who chose A were greater than what earnings would have been

> for measurably similar people who actually chose B had they continued their schooling instead. ... The most attractive and simplest interpretation is the theory of comparative advantage. (pp. S28–S29)

It is not surprising in the light of the finding of positive selection that the rate of return to a typical type A person (college) differs from that of a typical type B person (high school only). The authors report that

> Assuming that persons with the average characteristics of those who choose B would have exhibited the same values of experience and initial year of earnings as those who actually chose A and vice versa, the average rate of return for persons of type A is 9.9 per cent, while the average is 9.3 per cent for persons of type B. Thus, those who actually chose A had measured abilities that were more valuable in A than those who actually chose B. (pp. S30–S31).

CASE STUDY 1 Matched samples and natural experiments

One further approach to the issue of controlling for selection biases in calculating the returns to education and training is to use some form of matched sample. One example of this has been an attempt to take indivduals, separately from trained and untrained groups and to match them according to a wide range of discernible characteristics (Payne, 1990, Appendices 2 and 3). The outcome is therefore a comparison of the effects of training controlling at least for the observable characteristics. This approach, however, does not avoid the criticism of its failure to control for non-observables, which, according to a number of authors, may explain a considerable degree of the variation in outcomes (see Section 3.4).

An alternative approach which has appeared in the literature is the use of identical twins (Behrman *et al.* 1980; Blanchflower and Elias, 1993; Ashenfelter, 1994). Using identical twins appears a neat way of controlling for unobserved heterogeneity. According to Blanchflower and Elias (1993, p. 3)

> twins present the so-called 'natural experiment' to studying differences in schooling and earnings controlling for genetically based characteristics and for childhood socialisation effects.

While they appear to be a 'natural experiment' twins do pose a number of statistical problems. In the case of identical twins, for example, differences between pairs tend to be small and particularly susceptible to errors of measurement (Griliches, 1979). In addition while there is evidence that identical twins show higher correlations for IQs, etc. the association suggested by a review of the literature is far from perfect (Blanchflower and Elias, 1993, p. 3). Indeed, the authors provide a number of interesting insights about the special nature of 'twin' data sets. For one thing, they show that the inclusion of an ability test score reduces the estimate of the economic gain from a year of schooling by as much as 30 per cent. More importantly, however, they show that twins appear to have discernible differences in education and labour market behaviour to non-twins. Finally, there are important differences between identical twins which are both measurable and correlated over time.

Behrman *et al.* (1980) suggest that differences in education levels between identical twins were virtually unconnected with differences in their income levels. In their results, each additional year of schooling yields about a 2 per cent higher income for the better-educated twin. This is contested by Ashenfelter in a study of 500 twins from the National Twins Festival in Twinsburg, Ohio. Controlling for the effects of the special measurement errors in twin data, Ashenfelter (1994, p. 8) concludes that

> on average, an additional year of education has a very sizable effect on the earnings of twins and may be as large as 14% for each additional year

There are some interesting question marks, however, about whether the NTF sample is itself special and non-random. The results from 'twin' data have yet to be reconciled.

4 Firm investment in education and training

4.1 Type of training and the role of the firm

The treatment of human capital would be incomplete without a discussion of the role of the firm in the education and training process.

> For many years, the economics of training was narrowly focused, being mainly concerned with the benefits to individuals of training, and with evaluations of government training schemes. Since most training is provided by firms, and has a considerable informal element to it, this emphasis was recognised by many economists as either incomplete or inappropriate. (McNabb and Whitfield, 1993, p. 4)

In this section we attempt an explicit treatment of the firm's training decision. As we will see, given that the individual worker is the unit in which the additional human capital is embodied, the decision is not entirely in the hands of the firm's managers. In addition, in this section, we deal with various dimensions of training. In particular, formal versus informal and specific versus general.

Training is a heterogeneous activity, which differs in extent (quantity) and quality. It also differs in terms of its content (curriculum), method of 'teaching' and location. While all these dimensions are important, economists attempt to summarize their most important features by distinguishing between informal and formal training. Informal often takes place on the job and is often of short duration and low quality. Formal more generally occurs off the job, following an established curriculum with well-laid-out teaching methods, often leading to a recognized qualification, and is often thought to be of higher quality. Some care should be taken in this, however, as some informal training can be of high quality and exactly targeted and suited to the training needs of specific types of personnel. It is a question of 'horses for courses'.

Specific training raises the productivity of the employee within the firm providing the training, but not in other firms that the employee might work for. All firms are to some degree different, and skills based on the specific characteristics of the firm (i.e. based on knowledge of its internal structure and *modus operandi*) may not be useful elsewhere. In the case of specific training the wage that the employee can obtain outside the firm is determined independently of the amount of training received. General training, on the other hand, results in skills that are useful in any firm, quite independent of which firm provides the training. Workers with certain skills (e.g. computing) are unlikely to be tied to any one industry let alone to a firm that provided training.

In a competitive labour market, with perfect labour mobility, no firm is likely to choose to fund general training. Any firm that provides such training will be put at an economic disadvantage. In order to recoup its outlays on training, the firm would have to hold down the worker's wage below the level associated with their post-training level of productivity. This is not possible in a traditional, competitive labour market: the non-training firms will be willing to pay a higher wage and the trained worker will be induced to switch allegiance between companies. The firm that provided the training can only retain the worker if it pays the competitive wage. Thus, in anticipation that the going market wage will not allow firms to recoup any expenditures they make, they refrain from investing in general training. A company would only consider providing general training where exogenous forces create immobility of labour between firms. In effect, however, immobility makes all training to some degree specific in nature. If the firm will not finance general training, then the burden is placed on the individual (or their family) or on the government.

4.2 Optimal investment by the firm

Under conditions of perfect competition in both the product and labour markets, with a homogeneous workforce, employees will be paid a real wage, W, in accord with their marginal physical product of labour, MP, at time t,

$$MP_t = W_t \tag{21}$$

If training opportunities for the workforce exist, the current production from workers under training may fall to zero in the case of full-time formal training or may be reduced below the normal level for part-time formal or informal training. At the same time, training can be expected to raise the current expenditure of the firm above its level in the absence of training. Clearly, training has an adverse effect on the immediate profitability of the firm. Nevertheless, taking a longer-term view, training will still be undertaken if it raises future receipts (or reduces future expenditures) sufficiently, compared with their levels without training.

In order to develop a simple model of the training decision, both the product and factor markets are assumed to be perfectly competitive. The output of a trained employee is represented by their marginal product, $MP(T)_t$, where t denotes the time period; the output of untrained labour is $MP(M)_t$. The real wages are $W(T)_t$ per person per period for trained labour and $W(M)_t$ for untrained. The expenditure on training is κ_t per period for $\tau_1 - \tau_0$ periods. The costs and returns to training take place within a total of $\tau_2 - \tau_0$ periods. Note, however, that τ_2 in particular may not take the same value for the individual and the firm; τ_2 may refer to the working life of the individual, whereas in the case of the firm it refers to the remaining period of tenure of the individual. The going rate of interest or discount is represented by i per cent per period. Training is profitable for the firm if,

$$\sum_{t=\tau_0}^{\tau_1} \frac{MP(0)_t - MP(M)_t}{(1+i)^t} + \sum_{t=\tau_1}^{\tau_2} \frac{MP(T)_t - MP(M)_t}{(1+i)^t} > \sum_{t=\tau_0}^{\tau_1} \frac{\kappa_t}{(1+i)^t} + \sum_{t=\tau_0}^{\tau_1} \frac{W(0)_t - W(M)_t}{(1+i)^t} + \sum_{t=\tau_1}^{\tau_2} \frac{W(T)_t - W(M)_t}{(1+i)^t} \quad (22)$$

This indicates that the addition to the output of the firm (appropriately discounted) must exceed the expenditure on training plus the additional wages paid to trained workers (both flows again appropriately discounted). The difference is that the flows associated with trained employees are divided separately into the training period (i.e. MP(0) and W(0)) and the post-training period (i.e. $MP(T)$ and $W(T)$). The firm continues to train additional workers until inequality (22) is replaced by an equality for the very last trainee. The first term on the left hand side of the inequality is the present value of the loss in output incurred during the training period. This loss may take into account not only the trainee's reduced productivity, but also the reduced output of other employees involved in the training process (not already included in κ). The second term on the left hand side represents the present value of the employee's increased productivity during the post-training period. The first term on the right hand side is the present value of direct expenditures on training (excluding productivity losses already accounted for). The second term on the right hand side is the present value of the extra wage costs paid to the trainee during the training period. If $W(0) < W(M)$ this term represents a saving in costs. The final term on the right hand side is the present value of the additional wages paid to trained employees in the post-training period.

4.3 General training

Where training is perfectly general, under competitive conditions, both trained and untrained labour are paid their marginal products (see Section 4.1). First, this implies that $W(T)_t = MP(T)_t$. Hence, rearranging inequality (22) yields

$$\sum_{t=\tau_0}^{\tau_1} \frac{W(M)_t - W(0)_t}{(1+i)^t} > \sum_{t=\tau_0}^{\tau_1} \frac{\kappa_t}{(1+i)^t} + \sum_{t=\tau_0}^{\tau_1} \frac{MP(M)_t - MP(0)_t}{(1+i)^t} \quad (23)$$

The present value of the saving in labour costs through paying trainees less during the training period must be greater or equal to the present value of the costs of the training (both direct expenditures and lower productivity). Second, however, this is not the end of the story, because with competive markets $W(M)_t = MP(M)_t$ and

$$\sum_{t=\tau_0}^{\tau_1} \frac{MP(0)_t - W(0)_t}{(1+i)^t} > \sum_{t=\tau_0}^{\tau_1} \frac{\kappa_t}{(1+i)^t} \quad (24)$$

In effect, in the absence of some third party (such as the government), the employee must accept a wage sufficiently lower than the marginal product during the training period to finance the direct and indirect costs of training. In other words, under the assumed market conditions, the employee must pay for general training. In the case of the individual, inequality (1) applies, and this will determine whether the individual undertakes general training.

4.4 Specific training

In a situation where the training is completely specific then the firm will tend to finance the training itself (bearing in mind the caveats concerning labour mobility outlined in Section 4.1). In this instance, the employer realizes that, although the employee's productivity within the firm is raised by training, productivity within other firms remains at the pre-training level. In effect, the employer can pay labour at the outside wage $W(M)_t$ in every period, even though the employee's contribution to the output of the firm after training would suggest a higher remuneration. Hence, $W(0)_t = W(T)_t = W(M)_t$ and inequality (22) can be rearranged to form,

$$\sum_{t=\tau_1}^{\tau_2} \frac{\text{MP}(T)_t - \text{MP}(M)_t}{(1+i)^t} > \sum_{t=\tau_0}^{\tau_1} \frac{\kappa_t}{(1+i)^t} + \sum_{t=\tau_0}^{\tau_1} \frac{\text{MP}(M)_t - \text{MP}(0)_t}{(1+i)^t} \tag{25}$$

which indicates that the firm will choose to invest in training (when it bears the whole cost of training and reaps all the benefits) as long as the present value of the additional future productivity is greater than or equal to the present value of the training outlays (both direct expenditures and lower productivities during the training period). Assuming that $W(0)_t = W(M)_t = W(T)_t$, then the individual would never choose to fund training. This can be demonstrated by substituting these values of W into inequality (1) above. However, as argued above, this is not the only possible outcome with imperfect mobility, as the employee might fund some of the training but reap some of the benefits. This, however, requires that the individual reaches some agreement with the employer that wages will differ from marginal productivity. The precise balance of funding might depend on the relative importance of voluntary and involuntary turnover of employees, and on the outcome of implicit or explicit bargaining between the parties (Bosworth *et al.*, 1993).

If the firm is unlikely to finance general training, can it be assumed that it will finance specific training? After all, specific training raises the productivity of employees within the firm, but not elsewhere. In a situation of high voluntary turnover, a firm investing in training may not experience a sufficiently long payback period to recoup its expenditure. In this case, the greater burden of the investment, if it is to be undertaken at all, might still fall on the employee. In a situation of high involuntary turnover, workers may find themselves laid off before recouping their investment in training. Under such circumstances, the burden of investment, if it is to be undertaken at all, would fall on the firm rather than on the employee. The 'best' outcome is that the funding may be shared, the worker expecting expenditure to be repaid in the form of higher future incomes (reflecting, in part, their increased productivity) and the employer recouping its expenditure by paying a future income lower than the individual's productivity would suggest. Asymmetric and imperfect information about the probability that the individual will leave or the probability that the firm will make the individual redundant, however, seem likely to result in underinvestment in training.

This discussion points to the crucial role played by labour turnover. A priori, we would expect that the private rate of return to individuals and firms will be lower in economies where turnover is relatively high (i.e. economies characterized by a highly volatile business cycle or major restructuring). We return to this issue below. First, however, we note that turnover is not entirely exogenous: it depends on the wage offered by the employer *vis-à-vis* the wage offered in the highest paid alternative employment. The firm might restrict voluntary turnover by increasing the wage above the external competitive norm insofar as it can be financed by a reduction in adjustment costs (i.e. search and hire costs). This might create a situation of excess supply of workers which the firm can react to by rationing jobs, raising hiring standards, or by shifting some of the burden of training costs onto employees. The last course has the advantage of further locking employees within the firm, until they have recouped their own investment.

4.5 Links with the internal labour market

Part VI of the book further investigates the concept of an internal labour market (ILM), which is characterized by a predominance of jobs being filled internally, by promotion. Our analysis of the training process with a certain specificity of training, emphasizing the costs of turnover and the breakdown of the simple, static marginal productivity doctrine, is consistent with behaviour within an ILM. Specificity of training is clearly linked with the procedure of filling jobs internally, by promotion. It can also help to explain why most ports of entry tend to be low down in the job hierarchy. It would seem that skill specificity is a factor that helps create and maintain an ILM. Equally, however, the existence of an ILM (where employees are 'locked in' for other reasons) may give rise to higher levels of firm-specific investments in human capital as it makes such investments more profitable.

Throughout our discussion of labour demands, we were careful to emphasize that the firm must be seen as involved in a wide variety of functions, in effect, producing a number of different outputs. Quite outside of their traditional role in the product market, firms also appear as suppliers of training and experience. In other words they produce their output and training as joint products. The degree to which the firm funds training and shares the benefits with its trainees is part of the 'income' (in its broadest sense) perceived by workers in their supply of labour decision. The individual's supply of labour to the firm therefore contains an implicit demand for training. The degree to which workers are willing to pay for their own training and share the benefits with employers who train them influences the firm's demand function for labour (through the perceived user cost of labour). Hence, the firm's demand for labour contains an implicit supply of training (i.e. it makes a wage and a training offer to individuals). It is possible therefore to conceive of a hidden market for inservice training. Individuals are willing to offer different amounts of labour services, depending on the wage and training offer by the firm; firms are willing to offer to hire different amounts of labour services from the individual, depending on the wage they have to pay, existing human capital and 'trainability'. This view of the world has a number of similarities with Thurow's model of the operation of labour markets (Thurow, 1975). The situation has, historically, been made more complicated by government intervention in training. To some extent, if the government subsidizes the training function, some firms may become providers of general training to individuals who they may not plan to employ.

4.6 Evaluation of company level training

We suspect that many companies are far from systematic in their monitoring and evaluation of training activities. There is evidence to suggest that the UK training of apprentices appeared to be more a short-term response to skill shortages than planned human resource development (Lindley, 1975). A series of case studies of the Youth Training Scheme revealed a haphazard approach amongst UK companies (Dutton, 1986). A similar picture appears to emerge in other countries, however, as revealed by the Advisory Council for Adult Education's in-depth interviews of 50 Dutch companies (Koning, 1993, p. 92). In the UK, the first systematic cost–benefit calculations appear to have been carried out by the Engineering Industry Training Board (1972) – now called the Engineering Training Authority (EnTrA).

A considerable amount is known about differences in company-level training, skills and firm performance in the UK thanks to a series of international comparative case studies carried out by the National Institute for Economic and Social Research. A series of Anglo-German comparisons provide comparative evidence for engineering, furniture making and clothing (Daly *et al.*, 1985). All three studies link the higher average levels of labour productivity in German plants to the greater skills and knowledge of their workforce. Interestingly, we began with a view that UK and Dutch firms might both be disorganized in their evaluation of training. A recent set of case studies of 12 UK and nine Dutch plants in three metal-working sectors, however, revealed that output per hour worked was around 25 to 30 per cent lower in the UK than in the Netherlands (Mason and van Ark, 1994, p. 66). The authors trace the reason to the UK's

> slower investment in new capital and lower average levels of workforce skills and knowledge (p. 66).

However, much of this may be the result of the Dutch system of education and training rather than company-level activity. Nevertheless, it is important to see how these two dimensions of the training infrastructure interact:

> The higher skill levels found throughout the Dutch engineering industry primarily reflect that country's widespread provision of full-time courses of education and training. As elsewhere, trainees completing full-time courses of vocational schooling still need to undergo programmes of structured on-the-job training when they first enter employment. However, the relatively high attainment of students at junior and intermediate technical schools in the Netherlands give Dutch employers a considerable head start over their British counterparts in terms of the trainability of their workforce, both as new entrants to the labour market and subsequently as adult workers who may need retraining and updating ... . In this context Dutch employers are able to carry out training to given standards more quickly and cost effectively than is possible in Britain, and in many cases they are able to set their training standards much higher than is feasible for their British counterparts.

Other studies have pointed to the education and training failure at the highest levels in UK companies. While there are examples of highly qualified Boards of Directors, managing directors and CEOs at this level, UK companies appear to be underqualified at the same level and this acts as a key barrier to growth, What seems more important is that this impacts on the introduction of new technology and the dynamic performance of the company.

5 Conclusions

The concept of human capital theory, and the individual's decision about how much investment to make in education and training, was introduced in

Part II of the book concerned with labour supply. In this chapter we have developed this idea further with a special emphasis on the measurement of the rate of return to human capital investment. Empirical evidence on *ex ante* and *ex post* private rates of return to education in the UK was discussed. In general *ex ante* rates of return (expected rates of return, for example by those considering possible investment in higher education) vary in ways that are similar to the variations in *ex post* returns, calculated from information about individuals who have already made the investments, although there are some differences in the estimates; for example, in some studies, the estimated *ex ante* returns are quite high relative to the *ex post* returns. Rates of return also vary, of course, according to the population group analysed, partly for reasons associated with self-selection. Having considered the individual's decision, we went on to discuss the decision to train within firms. Here the distinction between general and specific training has been important in the literature. Again empirical evidence from a number of countries was discussed. It appears that in some countries and in some companies the training decisions have been more systematic than in others. The empirical evidence suggests, however, that high levels and quality of education and training have been an important source of productivity performance and competitive advantage in countries such as Germany.

References

Ashenfelter, O. (1994). 'How Convincing is the Evidence Linking Education and Income?'. *Journal of Employment and Productivity*, 6, 1, March, 1–12.

Barnow, B.S. (1987). 'The Impact of CETA Programs on Earnings: A Review of the Literature'. *Journal of Human Resources*. 22, 2, 157–193.

Behrman, J., P. Taubman, Z. Hrubec and T. Wales (1980). *Socioeconomic Success: a Study of the Effects of Genetic Endowments, Family Environment and Schooling*. Amsterdam: North-Holland.

Berndt, E.R. (1991). *The Practice of Econometrics: Classic and Contemporary*. Reading, MA: Addison-Wesley.

Blanchflower, D.G. and P. Elias (1993). 'Ability, Schooling and Earnings: Are Twins Different?'. Discussion Paper. Institute for Employment Research. Coventry: University of Warwick.

Bosworth, D.L. (1994). 'Truancy and Pupil Performance'. *Education Economics*, 2, 3, 243–264.

Bosworth, D.L. and J. Ford (1985). 'Income Expectations and the Decision to Enter Higher Education'. *Studies in Higher Education*. 10, 1, 21–31.

Bosworth, D.L. and R.A. Wilson (1988). *Infrastructure for the Protection of Intellectual Property: Patent Agents and Patent Monopolies*. Research Report. Institute for Employment Research. Coventry: University of Warwick.

Bosworth, D.L., R.A. Wilson and A. Assifa (1993). 'The Market for Training: a Human Capital Approach'. *International Journal of Manpower*. 14, 2/3, 33–46.

Daly, A., D. Hitchen and K. Wagner (1985). 'Productivity, Machinery and Skills in a Sample of British and German Manufacturing Plants'. *National Institute Economic Review*, February.

Dutton, P.A. (1986). *The Impact of YTS on Engineering Apprenticeship: a Local Labour Market Study*. Research Report. Institute for Employment Research. Coventry: University of Warwick.

Elias, P. and M. Gregory (1994). *The Changing Structure of Occupations and Earnings in Great Britain, 1975-1990*. Employment Department. Research Series 27. London: HMSO.

Engineering Industry Training Board (1972). *The Costs of Training: a Preliminary Report*. Occasional Paper No. 2. Watford: EITB.

Fraker, T. and R. Maynard (1987). 'The Adequacy of Comparison Groups for Evaluation of Employment Related Programmes'. *Journal of Human Resources*, 22, 2, 194–227.

Griliches, Z. (1979). 'Sibling Models and Data in Economics: Beginnings of a Survey'. *Journal of Political Economy*, 87, 5, October, S37–S64.

Heckman, J.J. and R. Robb (1986). 'Alternative Identifying Assumptions in Econometric Models of Selection Bias'. *Advances in Econometrics*, 5, 243–287.

Koning, J. de (1993). 'Evaluating Training at the Company Level'. In R. McNabb and K. Whitfield (eds) *The Economics of Training Part 1. International Journal of Manpower*, Special Edition, 14, Nos. 2/3, pp. 85–93.

LaLonde, R.J. (1986). 'Evaluating the Econometric Evaluations of Training Programmes with Experimental Data'. *American Economic Review*, 76, 4, 604–620.

Lindley, R.M. (1975). 'The Demand for Apprentice Recruits by the Engineering Industry: 1951–71'. *Scottish Journal of Political Economy*, 22, 1, 1–24.

Machlup, F. (1974). 'Proxies and Dummies'. *Journal of Political Economy*, 82, 4, July/August, 892.

Maddala, G.S. (1992). *Introduction to Econometrics*. (Second Edition). New York: Macmillan.

Mason, G. and Bart van Ark (1994). 'Vocational Training and Productivity Performance: An Anglo–Dutch Comparison'. *The Economics of Training, Part II. International Journal of Manpower*, 15, 5, 55–69. (Reprinted in R. McNabb and K. Whitfield (eds) *The Market for Training*. Aldershot: Avebury, 335–355.)

McNabb R. and K. Whitfield (1993). 'Key Issues in the Economics of Training'. *The Economics of Training. Part II. International Journal of Manpower*, 14, 2/3, 4–16.

Mincer, J. (1974). *Schooling, Experience and Earnings*. New York: Columbia University Press.

Payne, J. (1990). *Adult Off-the-Job Skills Training*. Research and Development Paper 57. Sheffield: Training Agency.

Roy, A.D. (1951). 'Some Thoughts on the Distribution of Earnings'. *Oxford Economic Papers*, 3, June, 135–146.

Thurow, L. (1975). *Generating Inequality: Mechanisms of Inequality in the US Economy*. London: Macmillan.

Williams, G. and A. Gordon (1981). 'Perceived Earnings Functions and *Ex Ante* Rates of Return to Post Compulsory Education in England'. *Higher Education*, 10, 2, 199–227.

Willis, R.J. and S. Rosen (1979). 'Education and Self Selection'. *Journal of Political Economy*, 87, 5, S7–S38.

Wilson, R.A. (1980). 'The Rate of Return to Becoming a Qualified Scientist or Engineer in Great Britain, 1966–1976'. *Scottish Journal of Political Economy*, 21, 41–62.

Wilson, R.A. (1984). *The Declining Return to Professional Status in the British Economy (with Special Reference to Scientists and Engineers)*. PhD Thesis. Coventry: University of Warwick.

Wilson, R.A. (1987). 'Rates of Return to Entering the Legal Profession: Some Further Evidence'. *Scottish Journal of Political Economy*, 34, 174–191.

CHAPTER 17 Human capital, social rates of return and government intervention

1 Introduction

Chapter 16 concentrated on human capital investment from the point of view of the individual and the firm. We now turn to market-level issues. A key distinction is made between the market for training and the market for trained individuals, although the two are clearly related. This leads naturally to a consideration of the possibility of market imperfections, and even market failure (both in the market for training and the market for trained individuals). This lays the foundations for the discussion of social rates of return and government intervention which look at human capital issues from society's point of view, as well as the theory and evidence of government intervention.

In Section 2 we consider a number of market-level concepts including the 'market' for training and the market for educated and trained individuals. In addition it outlines the concept of market failure as applied to education and training, and the case for government intervention. In Section 3 we discuss the distinction between private and social rates of return. In Section 4 we look at some empirical evidence about social as opposed to private rates of return. We also present a case study of the policies to revise vocational education and training. Finally, Section 5 presents the main findings of this chapter.

2 Market-level issues

2.1 Market for training

The way in which the discussion above has evolved makes it clear that there is implicitly, if not explicitly, a market for training. The market for training is quite distinct, though clearly related to the market for trained individuals. Some workers are looking to improve their education or skills and seek an employer who is able to satisfy their needs. In doing so, they are generally forced to accept a lower wage as, the higher the training component, the lower their current productivity in the employing firm. Full-time, formal general education can be seen as one extreme case of this, where employees have to finance the whole of the 'training' as their productivity within the firm falls to zero. Wholly specific training forms the opposite extreme, where individuals are unwilling to pay for the training, insofar as the whole of the benefit is reflected in increased productivity of the firm but not in the individual's income. Clearly these can be seen as extreme cases bearing in mind that, in previous sections, we have shown that, as the uncompleted duration of spell in employment can be quite long, both individuals and firms may be willing to pay some part of both types of training. How much individuals are willing to pay for their training depends upon the nature of the market for trained individuals.

In the same way, some employers may be willing to offer jobs with a training component. The difference between the wage without and the wage with training reflects the supply price of training. In the main, higher amounts and/or qualities of training will exact a higher price. Of course, the price the firm charges to the individual will reflect the balance of specific versus general training and/or the likely tenure of the individual within the training firm. Again, purely formal educational establishments can be seen as firms which wholly specialize in the supply of education and/or training. Insofar as formal educational establishments have no other outputs, the education or training is wholly 'general' in nature and students (or the government) pay the whole of the costs of such education.

Figure 17.1 therefore, gives a neoclassical interpretation to the market for education and training. The vertical axis denotes the price of training and is represented by the proportion of the wage for the job given up at various intensities of training (represented here by the proportion of time spent on training). In principle, this has an upper limit of $W(M)$, the going rate for the job without training, unless the individual (or the government) subsidizes the training period. The figure distinguishes between three mixes of general and specific training. On the supply side: S^S denotes wholly specific; S^I is a mix of roughly equal proportions of specific and general; S^G denotes a higher mix of general training. The supply curves with higher proportions of general training $S^S \rightarrow S^I \rightarrow S^G$ require the employee to give up a higher proportion of their potential pay at any given intensity of training.

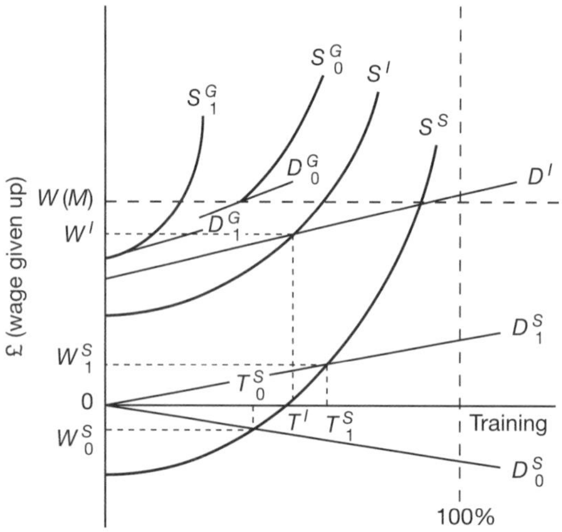

Fig 17.1 Market for training

Figure 17.1 also shows the position of the demand curves for various types of training. What individuals are willing to pay depends crucially on the net benefits they perceive from the investment (as described above). D_0^S represents a demand curve where the majority of potential trainees see little personal benefit from the highly specific nature of the training (e.g. they see non-pecuniary disadvantages of undertaking the training, such as the stress of the course, the changing nature of the tasks they will be asked to do). In this case the market outcome, where D^S_0 intersects S^S, suggests that the firm will have to pay the individual a subsidy in order to train. In fact, they have an addition to their wage which makes their total wage $W(M) - W_0^S$. If individuals view the specific training more favourably, however (as we suggested, signalling their commitment to the firm in return for some perceived future benefit, such as increased job security), the demand curve might be of the type D_1^S, and the market outcome suggests that employees are willing to pay some (small) proportion of their wages in order to do so ($W_1/W(M)$). Traditional theories of specific training tend to ignore such effects; the individual is assumed to be indifferent between training and work, and the outcome is where the S^S curve cuts the horizontal axis (the individual gives up no wage, receives no benefit and the outcome is determined by the returns to training to the firm of different intensities of training).

The intermediate mix of specific and general training has supply and demand curves S^I and D^I respectively. The demand curve has shifted upwards as the employee perceives higher future income as a consequence of the training. However, the supply curve also shifts up, as the higher proportion of general training means that the firm perceives the individual to be the greater beneficiary and expects it to be funded by a greater reduction in the wage. The outcome would be W^I, T^I. An example of this type of outcome might be newly qualified graduates studying, for example, for professional accountancy qualifications. Indentured staff receive a mix of specific and general training and accept lower wages as a consequence.

What happens at higher ratios of general to specific training clearly depends on the relative shifts of supply (inwards) and demand. Two outcomes suggest themselves. First, where the intersection of the two curves occurs along the vertical axis, as in the case of D^G_1 S^G_1. Here there is no point of agreement between employees and employers that leads to a positive training outcome. Second, at the intersection along $W(M)$, the employee works for free for some part of the week, in return for training for the remainder of the period. Any intersection above $W(M)$ requires the individual (or the government) to subsidize the firm.

How does formal education fit into this picture? It is clear from this discussion that the price to the individual of receiving more general training becomes higher in the sense that they are asked to give up a greater proportion of the wage. This can be treated as a cost which can be compared with the opportunity cost of the wage forgone in entering full-time education. However, there is a second component of cost to be taken into account. As the supply curve shifts to the left, the firm expects the individual to spend a higher proportion of their time working, which makes the attainment of a given standard of achievement less efficient in a firm setting. Finally, comparative advantage suggests that firms will be relatively more efficient in providing training with higher proportions of specific training and formal educational institutions more efficient in providing more general skills. Thus, at some sufficiently high ratio of general to specific training, the advantage of being paid a wage becomes so low (i.e. the income received and/or the proportion of time spent training) that it pays to switch out of employment and into full-time education.

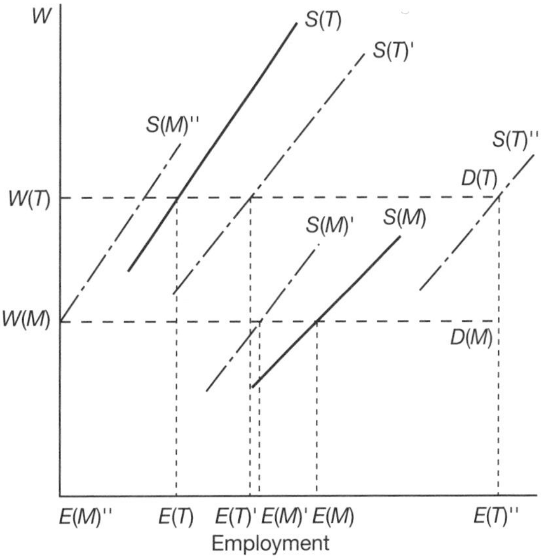

Fig 17.2 Perfectly elastic demand curves and returns to education and training.

2.2 Market for trained individuals

The analysis in Chapter 16 assumed that the individual (or firm) decision to undertake the education or training does not affect the anticipated level of future earnings. Where there is a single investor, this may be a reasonable approximation, but the assumption appears less acceptable where relatively large numbers of individuals react at the same time and in broadly the same way to the observed market signals. Thus, the analysis outlined in previous sections would only be theoretically rigorous if the demand curves for labour associated with both levels of education or training are perfectly elastic. Figure 17.2 illustrates this special case. Prior to any new recruits entering training, the supply and demand curves for the lower-educated/trained workers are represented by $S(M)$ and $D(M)$ respectively; the supply and demand curves for the more educated/trained workers are represented by $S(T)$ and $D(T)$ respectively. The prevailing wage regime prior to the entry of new trainees is shown by $W(M)$ for the lower and $W(T)$ for the higher group. Figure 17.2 shows that, at this stage, there are $E(M)$ less trained individuals in employment and $E(T)$ of the more highly trained. Assuming that the '*M*' cohort is the only source of potential trainees, then, as some individuals enter into training, $S(M)$ shifts inwards to $S(M)'$ and, as training is completed, $S(T)$ shifts outwards to $S(T)'$. At this stage, employment in the two groups is $E(M)'$ and $E(T)'$ respectively. Under these special circumstances, the wage regime remains unaltered at $W(T)$ and $W(M)$ and the rate of return based on the observed pre-training levels remains valid in the post-training situation.

Assuming that there are no differences between individuals (i.e. in their abilities, perception of wages over time, rates of discount, etc.), then, if it is profitable for one person to change from '*M*' to '*T*' status, it is profitable for the whole *M* cohort. As far as this cohort is concerned, $S(M)$ will eventually shift to $S(M)'' = 0$ and $S(T)$ to $S(T)''$. Thus, for these cohorts, employment eventually reaches $E(M)'' = 0$ and $E(T)''$. This does not necessarily imply that the '*M*' group eventually disappears, as it may form an essential rung on the career ladder leading to '*T*' status or above. Hence, other employees, with lower than '*M*' status, may be undertaking similar investment decisions that will create a new cohort of '*M*' workers, tending to shift the $S(M)$ curve outwards.

In the presence of a downward-sloping demand curve, however, the investor must take into account the number of individuals who are likely to undergo training. If large numbers transfer from '*M*' to '*T*' status, this will almost certainly depress the post-training productivity and wage of '*T*' workers and raise the post-training wage of '*M*' workers, other things being equal. Figure 17.3 illustrates this more general case. The *ex ante* market positions are again represented by $S(M)$ and $D(M)$ for the lower level of education or training and $S(T)$ and $D(T)$ for the higher level. The perceived pre- and post-investment wage regimes are represented by $W(M)$ and $W(T)$ respectively. In this more general case, however, as members of the 'M' cohort invest in education or training (assuming that it is profitable for at least one of them to do so), then, *ex post*, the inward shift of $S(M)$ to $S(M)'$ raises the wage of those remaining in the 'M' cohort to $W(M)'$, while the outward shift of $S(T)$ to $S(T)'$ lowers the wage of the 'T' cohort to $W(T)'$.

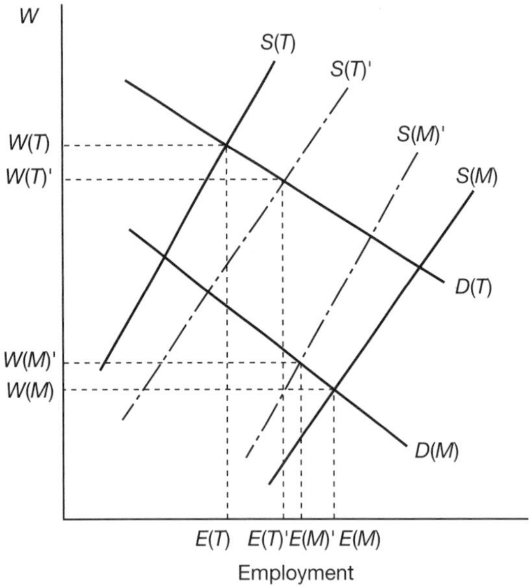

Fig 17.3 Downward-sloping demand curves, wage rates and the rate of return.

The movements of the supply functions, when coupled with downward-sloping demand for labour curves, squeeze the wage levels together and make education and training less and less profitable for the remaining potential investors. At the same time, the rising $W(M)$ will make investment by workers of lower than 'M' status more profitable, other things being equal, and will make further investment by 'T' status workers appear more profitable in order to reach higher rungs of the ladder. Thus, other flows from the T category (upwards) and into the M category (from below) may restore the differentials. However, the analysis does illustrate the potential for a divergence between *ex ante* and *ex post* rates of return, and emphasizes the importance of the rates of flow between jobs with different education and training levels.

It is also possible that the size of the flow into training at each level will affect the cost of training per person and, thereby, the 'price' charged for training. In terms of the discounting procedure, these early flows are weighted heavily and have an important bearing on the overall profitability of the investment. Economies of scale in the education or training process would tend to lower the cost per person as larger numbers train; diseconomies of scale would have the opposite effect. A further implication is that, with imperfect information about the number and timing of new entrants, *ex ante* and *ex post* rates of return will diverge and marginal investors may find that they have made a mistake. Finally, we note that the labour market for highly qualified labour has a number of characteristics, such as imperfect information and lags in supply (because of the period of training), that may give rise to a cobweb adjustment process whenever the market is not in equilibrium (Freeman, 1971 and 1976). We have dealt with this concept in some detail in Chapter 14 and we do not repeat it here. The creation of cobweb cycles, however, is only one dimension of imperfections, and other factors, such as constraints on the capacity of the education and training sectors, may also affect the operation of the labour market.

2.3 Failure and government intervention

The classic argument for a free market depends on the assumption of long-run perfectly competitive equilibrium which results in a position that is Pareto optimal: even if such conditions do not prevail in the real world, strictly speaking, a necessary condition for government intervention appears to be that it should make some people better off without making anyone worse off. Even then, a complete justification requires proof that direct government intervention is the most efficient way of achieving this welfare aim.

It is interesting to explore which of the Pareto conditions, if any, are met in the case of education (see Blaug, 1972, Chapter 4). (i) There is little evidence to support general increasing returns to scale in education which would make education a natural monopoly on a national scale (although there is also the possibility of regional or local monopolies). (ii) Parental ignorance of the benefits of education may be argued to be sufficient justification for state intervention, at least in the provision of more complete and accurate information. (iii) Education would appear to be a quasi-public good (a pure public good would involve joint and equal consumption, quite independent of whether the consumer pays for it or not). It is associated with externalities and hence a free market would provide too little investment. Amongst the plethora of spillover benefits (Blaug, 1972, p. 108), educated parents to some extent teach their own children and educated workers raise the productivity of the less educated members of their team. This idea forms the basis of the 'New Growth Theories' which we return to in Chapter 29 below. (iv) The returns to education may look very different from the perspective of the individual receiving the education and the head of the household (who funds and makes the education decision). As a consequence, the head of the household may underinvest in the young person's education and the state would be required to intervene. (v) If education is provided by the market, it must be funded from income (or wealth) or from borrowing. Given imperfections in the capital market, low-income families can expect their children to experience lower future incomes than the children of high-income families. This results in a low-income–education 'poverty trap'.

Two further arguments point at least to state intervention and, possibly, to state provision of education. First, intervention requires coordination of the various policies, the provision of a legislative framework and, more particularly, a means of overseeing the operation of the education system (to ensure that societal quantity–quality criteria are met) and obtaining feedback from it. Second, the education system can result in 'social cohesion' insofar as it may instil common values in tune with the needs and aspirations of society. An example of this would be the EC-funded Human Capital and Mobility Programme. The social gains from cohesion, however, need to be traded off against any benefits of diversity and reduction in the freedom of choice.

Similar issues surround government intervention in training. Again support for intervention requires proof that the market fails to provide the socially optimal quantities or qualities of trained workers and that the resulting system achieves a 'better' outcome than when left to the free market. It is interesting therefore to explore some of the arguments for government intervention. (i) Historically, training was linked with the guilds and, later, the trade union movement. In the past, there were rules regarding the numbers of trainees or the ratio of trainees to qualified workers and, in earlier years, unions, or professional institutes, were able to manipulate the volume of training in order to achieve objectives favourable to their members. (ii) Empirical evidence suggests that UK employers were neither enlightened nor farsighted in their training decisions. Firms tended to overestimate the costs of training, even when they had spare capacity which could be used for this purpose. They also failed to undertake a rigorous investment appraisal of training. UK apprentice intake, for example, was better explained by current shortages of trained workers than by future labour needs. (iii) The price mechanism fails to send the right signals. At certain times during the post-war period, downward inflexibility of wages has been augmented by upward rigidity caused by incomes policies. (iv) There may have been economic reasons as there are several ways in which firms can obtain skilled personnel, in particular they can train them or 'poach' them from other firms. The choice depends on the relative costs of each strategy – poaching is clearly not cost free as it involves search and recruitment costs. Poaching also imposes a cost on the firms that do finance part of the training. The more poaching that exists, the lower the rate of return for training firms and the smaller their training effort. The adoption of the poaching rather than the training route appears to have undermined training in the UK. (v) During the business cycle, there may be a large pool of unemployed whose retraining cannot be justified on purely economic grounds; the government may choose to finance remedial programmes on equity grounds (even when it might have achieved a higher rate of growth by upgrading the skills of those in employment). (vi) On a cynical note, the government may view the removal of individuals from the unemployment register during the training period (independent of what happens to them in the job market afterwards) as a political benefit of training.

3 Private and social rates of return to education and training

3.1 Individual and society

There is no reason why private and social rates of return should be the same. Even if they were, the (risk-adjusted) rate of interest with which they are compared might still differ. In practice, the two rates of return are unlikely to be equal. The individual cal-

Table 17.1 Individual and societal returns

	Society	Individual
Benefits	Direct (i.e. pre-tax) gains in production + psychic benefits + externalities and spillovers	Take-home (i.e. post-tax) earnings + psychic benefits
Costs	Production forgone during the education period + total costs of tuition	Lost of earnings (i.e. post-tax – grants to students + costs of tuition borne by individual

culates the private rate of return to education or training using information about take-home pay (i.e. earnings net of tax including fringe benefits) and the direct costs of education borne by the individual; the government calculates the social rate of return using gross (i.e. pre-tax) pay and the total costs of education including those borne by the government. Table 17.1 summarizes a number of differences between the individual and social returns to education.

In the discussion which follows, we continue to use W as the net wage and introduce W' as the gross wage. Hence, $W = (1-\rho)W'$ where ρ is the (average) rate of taxation for the individual we are observing. Hence, the individual, undertaking their private calculus, will undertake investment as long as

$$\sum_{t=\tau_1}^{\tau_2} \frac{[1-\rho(T)]W'(T)_t - [1-\rho(M)]W'(M)_t}{(1+i)^t} > \sum_{t=\tau_0}^{\tau_1} \frac{\kappa_t}{(1+i)^t} \quad (1)$$

where: $\rho(T)$ and $\rho(M)$ denote the tax rates for the higher and lower education levels respectively (where, in general, $\rho(T) > \rho(M)$); κ denotes the direct costs of education borne by the individual. Note that in comparison with inequality (1) in Chapter 16 that the decision rule has been simplified for expositional purposes. In particular we assume that the individual receives the 'M' wage during training, but pays some part of this wage to the trainer, which is now subsumed within κ. This expositional change is maintained throughout the remainder of this section. The government, on the other hand, acting in the best interests of society as a whole, calculates the social rate of return. This is based on providing the amount of education that creates the largest net addition to the wealth of society. From society's point of view, education is profitable if

$$\sum_{t=\tau_1}^{\tau_2} \frac{W'(T)_t - W'(M)_t}{(1+i)^t} > \sum_{t=\tau_0}^{\tau_1} \frac{\kappa'_t}{(1+i)^t} \quad (2)$$

where κ' are the total direct costs of the education (i.e. those borne by society as a whole). For the moment, inequality (2) uses the same rate of interest, i, as (1), an issue discussed further below. Investment takes place up to the point where expression (2) becomes an equality, which is the socially optimal level.

It is possible to show that the expression for the social rate of return is the sum of the individual and government elements. From inequality (2) we can write

$$\sum_{t=\tau_1}^{\tau_2} \frac{[1-\rho(T)]W'(T)+\rho(T)W'(T)-[1-\rho(M)]W'(M)-\rho(M)W'(M)}{(1+i)^t} > \sum_{t=\tau_0}^{\tau_1} \frac{\kappa_t+\gamma_t}{(1+i)^t} \quad (3)$$

where γ denotes the direct expenditure on education per student by the government. Hence

$$\sum_{t=\tau_1}^{\tau_2} \frac{[1-\rho(T)]W'(T) - [1-\rho(M)]W'(M)}{(1+i)^t} + \sum_{t=\tau_1}^{\tau_2} \frac{\rho(T)W'(T) - \rho(M)W'(M)}{(1+i)^t} > \sum_{t=\tau_0}^{\tau_1} \frac{\kappa_t}{(1+i)^t} + \sum_{t=\tau_0}^{\tau_1} \frac{\gamma_t}{(1+i)^t} \quad (4)$$

Thus, ignoring non-pecuniary considerations, if individuals invest up to the point where the NPV = 0 for the last trainee, the government's implicit investment decision can be written as

$$\sum_{t=\tau_1}^{\tau_2} \frac{\rho(T)W'(T) - \rho(M)W'(M)}{(1+i)^t} > \sum_{t=\tau_0}^{\tau_1} \frac{\gamma_t}{(1+i)^t} \quad (5)$$

It can be seen that one of the principal factors which drives a wedge between the private and social rate of return is that the individual calculates the rate of return net of tax and the government calculates it gross of tax. This result shows that the government will 'top up' spending on education or training up to the point when inequality (5) is transformed into an equality.

If we imagine a situation in which, in the first instance, all education is paid for privately, then the quantity of education will be determined when expression (1) is replaced by the equivalent equality. However, $W'(T) > W'(M)$ and the government's discount rate is, on average, less than (or equal to) the individual's; then expression (2) will hold as an inequality and welfare will be increased by additional investment. This can be achieved in a number of ways, not least of which is for the government to take over some of the direct expenditure on education, $\gamma > 0$, reducing κ. Given this modification, the private rate of return is increased, attracting a greater number of individuals to invest, which in turn forces the return back down. At the same time, the higher direct expenditure, γ, implies a lower rate of return to the government at the margin. This reallocation of resources can continue until both the individual and social rate of return expressions reach equality.

In general, the government can be expected to use a lower discount rate than individuals. For one thing it operates at a macro level and this avoids the issues of individual risk and imperfect knowledge about the probability of success and, thereby, about the level of future incomes, all of which make personal borrowing to fund investment difficult. Given that, in general, the private discount rate, $i(P)$, from expression (1), is greater than the social discount rate, $i(P) > i(S)$, then, by implication, the government views individuals as underinvesting in education or training and will increase its own spending above the level we originally suggested in inequality (5).

3.2 Firm and society

Taken at face value, inequalities (1) and (5) suggest that neither the individual nor the government would become involved in specific training as $W'(T) = W'(M)$; in other words the firm reaps the benefit and not the individual and, hence, there are no tax gains for the government (see Chapter 16 for a discussion). In practice, this view may be misleading because it looks only at the individual and not the firm calculus. In practice, specific training raises the individual's productivity within the company and thereby raises profits. Thus, insofar as the government also taxes various aspects of company profits (and capital gains), then it will have exactly the same motivation to support specific training. It is not clear that the government recognizes this argument. Indeed, it may seriously underinvest in specific training as economic (or discretionary) profit not only supports dividend payments and company-funded physical investment, but also research and development and firm funded training,

$$\Pi^E = \Pi^R + RD + ADV + TRAIN = DIV + I + TAX + RD + ADV + TRAIN \quad (6)$$

where: Π^E and Π^R denote economic and accounting (or reported) profit respectively; RD is R&D; ADV is advertising; and TRAIN is training expenditure (all of which are written off as current costs); DIV denotes dividend payment, I is investment in physical capital and TAX denotes corporate taxes paid out of profits.

3.3 Government training and unemployment

The present value of training as perceived by the individual (or company) might be entirely different to that perceived by the government. Consider an individual faced by very long-term unemployment if there is no change in their level of skill. The individual will consider retraining to be worth while if

$$\sum_{t=\tau_0}^{\tau_1} \frac{(1-\rho)W'(0)_t - W(U)_t}{(1+i)^t} + \sum_{t=\tau_1}^{\tau_2} \frac{(1-\rho)W'(T)_t - W(U)_t}{(1+i)^t} > \sum_{t=\tau_0}^{\tau_1} \frac{\kappa_t}{(1+i)^t} \quad (7)$$

where: $W'(0)$, $W'(U)$ and $W'(T)$ denote the gross wage levels during training, unemployment and post-training respectively; the remaining variables have been defined above. It is initially assumed that the individual is assured of obtaining employment at wage $W'(T)$ after training. Inequality (7) basically says that the discounted sum of take-home pay after training over and above unemployment benefit must exceed the discounted sum of training costs borne by the individual, having taken into account the difference between the training wage and unemployment benefits.

The expression may simplify in a variety of ways. In general, with government training schemes, it might be assumed that $\kappa = 0$ because the government bears the direct costs of training. The expression is simplified further where the training wage $W'(0)$ falls below the tax threshold. Finally, the training wage is unlikely to differ significantly from unemployment benefit on government schemes; hence, $(1-p)W'(0)_t \approx W(U)_t$. Note that, from the individual's viewpoint, it makes no difference whether it is the government or a firm which pays the training wage.

Investment in training is profitable for society if

$$\sum_{t=\tau_1}^{\tau_2} \frac{W'(T)}{(1+i)^t} > \sum_{t=\tau_0}^{\tau_1} \frac{\kappa'}{(1+i)^t} \quad (8)$$

where $\kappa' = \kappa + \gamma$. The gain to society is the gross wage from the ('guaranteed') post-training employment, and the cost is the direct training expenditure per person. Unemployment benefit does not appear in the expression because it is a transfer payment. The training wage might appear if the individual is making a positive net contribution to economic output during the training period. We make the point about it being net in case the individual's activity displaces someone else. In general, however, it is probably close to zero and inequality (8) appears a good first approximation. We continue with this assumption below. A number of studies have attempted to calculate the internal (social) rate of return that makes expression (8) into an equality – see Case Study 1.

Hence, it is again possible to divide the social rate of return to training into its two components: the individual (private) and government rates of return. Rather than show the combined expression, we report the inequality relating to net present value of the government's own payments and receipts:

$$\sum_{t=\tau_0}^{\tau_1} \frac{W(U) - (1-\rho)W'(0)}{(1+i)^t} + \sum_{t=\tau_1}^{\tau_2} \frac{W(U)_t + \rho W'(T)_t}{(1+i)^t} > \sum_{t=\tau_0}^{\tau_2} \frac{\gamma_t}{(1+i)^t} \tag{9}$$

In this case, the first term on the left hand side shows the government's net change in expenditure during the training period: it makes a saving if this first term is positive (as the training wage is less than unemployment benefit) and incurs a higher cost if it is negative (as the individual receives a net training wage in excess of unemployment benefit). The second term has two components: the first is the saving of unemployment benefit when the individual obtains paid work at the end of the training period, and the second is the additional tax receipts obtained from the individual's

CASE STUDY 1 Social and private rates of return

The empirical evidence which calculates $r(S)$ from expression (8) indicates that social rates of return to higher education are lower than private rates of return. In part this simply reflects the fact that the government applies a lower interest rate as the cut-off in its social rate of return calculation, that is $i(P) > i(G)$ and, thus, $r(P) > r(G)$. Table 17.2 presents some typical results (Wilson, 1983). They again indicate differences between subject areas (and between their associated professions), as well as reinforcing the earlier conclusion concerning a downward trend in rates of return. One other interesting feature of comparisons between a wider range of subject areas is the lack of support for the hypothesis of a shortage of engineers, at least on the basis of these computations.

The simple rate of return methodology does not encompass the dynamic consequences of a social shortage, for example, of the type conceived by Finniston (1980). In effect, Finniston argues that a greater supply will create its own demand, by increasing the rate of growth of the economy (a type of 'Says' Law'). It is argued that this will occur partly because this will raise the status of engineers in society and partly because they will improve the technological dynamism of the economy and, in doing so, this will give rise to externalities by raising the employment and earnings prospects of other groups. Earlier in this chapter we argued that the normal operation of markets suggests that the post-training wage is inversely related to the number of people who undertake training. According to the Finniston argument, however, the after-training wage, W′(T) will be higher the greater the number of engineers trained (and the better the quality of their training).

Table 17.2 Private and social rates of return: scientists and engineers

Year	1967–1968	1970–1971	1972–1973	1973–1974	1974–1975	1976–1977	1978–1979	1979–1980
Private rate of return:								
Scientists	14.0	12.5	–	9.5	–	9.5	–	9.0
Engineers	14.5	13.0	10.0	–	10.5	9.5	9.0	–
Social rate of return:								
Scientists	8.5	8.0	–	6.0	–	6.0	–	6.0
Engineers	7.5	7.0	6.0	–	6.0	5.5	5.5	–

Source: Wilson (1983)

post-training wage. The term on the right hand side is the government's direct expenditure on training. In summing expressions (7) and (9), the first term on the left hand side cancels; the $\rho W'(T)$ in the composite second term and the $W(U)$ cancel, leaving $W'(T)$; finally, on the right hand side, $\gamma + \kappa = \kappa'$. The result is the social rate of return, shown by expression (8).

Expression (7) indicates that the government can raise the individual's willingness to undertake training by lowering tax rates, ρ, unemployment benefit, $W'(U)$, and the individual's contribution towards the direct costs of training, κ, or increasing the training wage, $W'(0)$. As it does so, the number of people participating in the training programme increases, pushing the private rate of return back down towards the cut-off interest rate. The discounting procedure gives more weight to earlier rather than later flows and, thus, the private and social rates of return will tend to be more sensitive to changes in $W'(0)$, $W'(U)$ and κ, than to ρ. Exploration of inequality (9) shows that as the government raises the incentive to the individual by lowering taxes or increasing the proportion it contributes to the direct costs of training, it worsens its own 'return' at the margin. Other things being equal, the government will continue to do this until both the private and social expressions (7) and (8) become equalities. However, if the government can increase the incentive to the individual and reduce the disadvantage to itself by lowering unemployment benefits, this must also be traded off against the social costs of doing so (unemployment and low income have been linked with crime, poorer health and even higher suicide rates).

While these results are intuitively plausible, the analytical framework, as we have developed it up to this point, has a number of potential weaknesses. Not least of these is the assumption that an individual, having completed the training, will obtain paid market employment. Thus, the expressions should be amended by replacing $W'(T)$ by $(Pr)W'(T) + (1-Pr)W'(U)$, where Pr is the probability of obtaining employment. Many evaluations of government training programmes take the probability of finding employment as a key indicator of the scheme's success. Second, there is the question of whether a person who finds employment and, thus, obtains a wage $W'(T)$, displaces someone else who then enters unemployment – one aspect of the displacement effect. There may be a danger that, on some types of scheme, the trainee may be used as 'cheap labour'', by the firm, displacing other existing workers who are paid the full rate (in either the same firm or in other firms, through competitive forces, because of the lowering of average costs in the 'subsidized' company). There is also the possibility that, once trained, the individual might decant an existing worker into unemployment.

Equally, however, it should be noted that the partial nature of the rate of return calculation does not allow any multiplier effects. The individuals finding employment experience a higher net wage, $(1-\rho)W'(T)$, and this creates additional consumption of $c[(1-\rho)W'(\mathrm{T}) - W(U)]$, where c is the marginal propensity to consume, as well as freeing resources for additional government spending $\rho W'(\mathrm{T})+W(U)$. There is also an important question mark about the period over which the rate of return should be calculated, τ_2, given that the new employment is unlikely to be lifelong, particularly amongst young people, while, amongst older people, the remaining length of their working life places a limit on τ_2. Finally, there is the contentious issue of the value of leisure time to the unemployed (i.e. in particular, the 'forced' leisure time). If the hours of unemployment have positive marginal and average utility, then some adjustment of expression (7) (if not also (8)) should be made to take account of this loss when training and subsequent employment begin. However, it is not clear that the higher leisure of the unemployed has a greater value, as they have less income to combine it with to form pleasurable activities. There does not appear to be any strong empirical support for this link between unemployment and leisure. For example, all of the psychological measures suggest higher mental distress amongst the unemployed, which hardly seems consistent with a 'leisured class' (Oswald, 1994).

CASE STUDY 2 International comparisons in education and training

In the late 1980s and early 1990s, the UK was at the bottom of the league in the OECD for 'staying-on' rates as shown in Table 17.3. The UK's staying-on rate in full-time education and training has been below that of all the other countries (the only exception was France at age 16, with a very major difference between the UK and Germany for young people aged 16–18. Table 17.4 further demonstrates that the qualifications held at the time of leaving formal education also differ widely.

continues

CASE STUDY 2 continued

Table 17.3 Participation in full-time education and training (including YT) of 16–18 year olds (percentage of total population by age cohort)

Country	16 years	Average 16–18 years
United States	95	81
Japan	96	79
France	88	77
Germany	100	92
United Kingdom	93	70

Table 17.4 Highest-level qualifications of school leavers: the UK, France and West Germany.

	UK	France	West Germany
No qualification	10	10	10
Low-level school leaver (below one C grade at GCSE)	35	–	–
Intermediate level (one A level and below)	40	55	60
Higher level (university entrance) two or more A levels	15	35	30

In a recent report by the NIESR comparisons are made between France, the UK, Germany and Japan. It was found that 27 per cent of English 16 year olds in 1990–1991 reached GCSE grades A to C in mathematics, the national language and one science subject, compared with 50 per cent in Japan, 62 per cent in Germany and 66 per cent in France. Although it is difficult to compare quality of education, training, managerial skills, innovation and human capacity across countries, the UK has had a major problem which can be traced, in part, to the elitist nature of the education system. An overhaul of the system of National Vocational Qualifications has been carried out in the UK in an attempt to overcome this. An ambitious set of targets has been agreed by the government and the CBI to be achieved by the year 2000. The agreed targets are: by 1997 at least 80 per cent of 16–19 year olds should gain NVQ level 2 which is equal to four GCSEs grade A–C in their foundation year of education or training (normally by age 17 years). They will also have a right to structured training, work experience or education leading to NVQ level 3. In 1990, 45 per cent of 16–19 year olds achieved NVQ level 2 and this increased to 55.1 per cent in 1992 (30 per cent of 16 to 18 year olds achieve NVQ level 3).

For the employer the targets were that by 1996 all employers should take part in training or development activities as the norm, with at least 50 per cent of the employed workforce aiming for a qualification or modules leading to NVQ. By the year 2000 *at least* 50 per cent of the employed workforce should be at NVQ level 3 (in 1990, 33 per cent of the employed workforce had NVQ level 3 or its equivalent). By 1996 at least 50 per cent of medium and large companies (over 200 employees) should qualify as 'Investors in People' (IiP) accredited by TECs/LECs. These targets have been called National Education and Training Targets (NETTS). They are very much like the three main targets of the 1981 New Training Initiative. If so little was gained from the old system between 1981 and 1992 it must be asked if the new ones will be successful.

Source: Bennett *et al.* (1994, p. 144)

In Chapter 15 we touched upon the interaction between the education and training systems:

> A broad conclusion must be that ... the competitive advantage derived by Dutch employers from a system of vocational education and training largely based on full-time schooling compares favourably with the German skills advantage deriving from the long-established 'Dual System' of apprenticeship training. By contrast, in Britain neither type of system is well developed. (Mason and van Ark, 1994, p. 67).

There are at least three lessons to be learnt from this. First, that a high-quality education system with wide access increases the returns to training, in much the same way that basic research aids applied research and development. It seems likely that a reverse causation also exists with higher levels of specific training improving the productivity of subsequent general training. Second, that the social rate of return should not be calculated simply from the individuals' wages. If it is calculated in this way, the government will only consider funding general training. We also should recognize that firms pay a variety of taxes and the corresponding calculation demonstrates that there is a case for government support for firm-based training (see Section 3.2). This perhaps to some extent explains why

> The bulk of British training to craft and technical standards is financed by employers through a traditional apprenticeship system which, however, lacks the institutional and legal foundations of the more successful German system. (Mason and van Ark, 1993, p. 67)

Third, there are significant spill-over effects in training. If all firms train, mobility (and even poaching) becomes less problematic; the loss of a skilled individual is to some extent offset by the ability to recruit another (equally) skilled individual. Of course, there must be some loss of firm-specific human capital, but, as we have noted, the costs of training up new recruits will be much less where such individuals come with high levels of general skills and an orientation to learning. All of these things appear to point to a failure in the market for training in the UK.

4 Evaluation of government education and training schemes

State involvement in training has been a major area of growth in the post-war period and, by the mid-1980s, both the UK and USA operated a plethora of training schemes (Barnes, 1976; Ziderman, 1978; Bennett *et al.*, 1984; Layard *et al.*, 1994). Early evaluations were either crude or non-existent. Certainly, much of the information essential to an accurate calculation, such as displacement rates, was highly speculative, if available at all. The main basis for comparison at that time appeared to be a simple 'cost per person taken off the unemployment register'. Some early work on the UK Government Training Centre Courses suggested quite high rates of return (Ziderman, 1969 and 1978; Thirwall, 1969).

In more recent years there has been a large and growing volume of UK and US empirical work aimed, in part, at evaluating the returns, especially the impact of government training schemes. Such studies generally examine the effects of training on employment probabilities and/or post-training earnings (Main and Shelley, 1988; Whitfield and Bourlakis, 1989; Baker, 1990). As noted above, most recent evaluations attempt to correct for selection biases. In order to do so, they explore the types of individuals who choose to enter or are selected onto training programmes. This information can be used to correct for sample selection biases. It is not immediately apparent in which direction these biases run; for example, individuals may be selected who are most disadvantaged or, alternatively, might be most likely to benefit from the training. Often, however, it seems to be the former – those in most need – rather than the latter who appear on government-run training schemes. Few of these studies, however, look at various aspects of deadweight welfare loss (i.e. as in the case where the training would have been financed anyway) or displacement effects (i.e. where the ex-trainee takes the job of another worker, who then becomes unemployed).

Despite the obvious need for caution, as Barnow's (1987) study highlights, some important conclusions appear to have emerged about the US *Comprehensive Employment and Training Act* programmes:

> Most of the studies found that the programs raised earnings by \$200 to \$600 annually in current dollars. The programs were found to be more effective for women than men, and public service employment and on-the-job training were generally found to be more effective activities than classroom training and work experience. (Barnow, 1987, p. 157).

A study of the *Scottish Young People's Survey (SYPS)* attempted to evaluate the effects of the Youth Training Scheme (YTS) in Scotland (Main and Shelley, 1988). The original *SYPS* data provided information about a cohort of school leavers who entered the labour market in the Summer of 1983–1984. Information about their labour market status was sought in April 1985 and April 1986, and (in subsequent studies) extended to October 1987. Main and Shelley (1988) found that participation on YTS raised the employment probability in April 1986 by about 17 percentage points for an advantaged school leaver and 11 percentage points for a disadvantaged school leaver. The advantaged and disadvantaged groups were defined in terms of differences in educational attainment and local labour market conditions. Despite isolating a significant impact, the authors concluded that the magnitude of the YTS effect was small compared with the influence of certain personal characteristics and circumstances. The effects of YTS on post-training wages were even less clear cut. OLS estimates suggested that YTS lowered wages by about 7 per cent, but the associated coefficient was not statistically significant. Application of a Heckman correction procedure for sample selection biases resulted in an insignificant positive coefficient on the YTS variable.

A parallel study used Cohort 1, Sweeps I–III of the *Youth Cohort Study* for England and Wales (Whitfield and Bourlakis, 1989). The authors adopted a labour queue model, in which employers rank individuals in terms of their trainability. The principal focus therefore concerns whether participation on the YTS improved the individual's position in the 'job queue', although the authors emphasized that the linkages between YTS and the labour queue were likely to be 'extremely complicated'. With regard to sample selection biases, the authors note that 'each decision made by young people introduces a sample selection bias into the analysis' (p. 5). A Heckman two-stage procedure is used in the estimation of the wage equation. Estimation is based on two samples, both comprised of those individuals who have been on YTS combined with one of two alternative control groups, which are designed to distinguish between the 'intended' and the 'actual' populations.

The results were very similar to those of Main and Shelley (1990) and it did not make a great deal of difference which of the two samples (control groups) were used in the estimation. YTS participants had a significantly higher probability of being in employment than non-participants. However, the effects of YTS were only just sufficient to offset the major negative effects of own personal characteristics and circumstances (such as their ethnic background and local labour market conditions). For example, YTS improved the employment chances of individuals by about 21 percentage points; on the other hand, being in an ethnic minority reduced it by 27 points and living in an area of high unemployment reduced it by 30 percentage points. There were no major differences between males and females (this is not so surprising given that young males and females are more similar in their labour market behaviour than slightly older individuals). YTS tended to increase the chances of employment with a scheme employer, rather than in the external labour market.

The wage equations suggested that YTS participants earned less in employment than non-participants: up to 14 pence per hour less amongst those who stopped with scheme employers, but 5 pence less for those who found a non-scheme employer. The Heckman procedure unearthed no evidence of significant sample selection biases. Whitfield and Bourlakis offered a number of explanations for the wage result, including the hypothesis that individuals who went on a YTS scheme were more likely to be in a job with higher amounts of training and, consistent with our earlier discussion, earning a lower wage than individuals in jobs without training.

The *National Child Development Survey* includes data on a cohort of individuals born in 1951 who, by 1981, had a number of years of labour market experience. The wealth of personal and labour market variables available make NCDS an extremely valuable source of information about training (Baker, 1990). The sample has major attrition problems (from 18,000 in 1951 to 12,000 in 1981), although most of these occur in the first part of the period. This type of selection bias is not covered in the empirical work, but self-selection is addressed directly. In a number of earlier studies of wages, investment in human capital is approximated by tenure, which is a highly imperfect proxy that, at best, subsumes the effects of training and learning by doing. NCDS enables the explicit inclusion of a vector of training dummies (reflecting participation in off-the-job, on-the-job and apprentice training) and a vector of duration variables, distinguishing completed and uncompleted time on training. This enables Baker to examine the relative contributions of training and tenure (Baker, 1990). Even then, however, tenure is associated with a variety of competing explanations.

Probit equations were estimated separately to explain the probability that an individual receives off-the-job, on-the-job or apprentice training. Clearly, independent equations are not entirely satisfactory as individuals may be deciding between these three training options (as well as between the training and non-training option). These are major differences in the determinants of the three types of training. For example, off-the-job training is influenced by the length of formal education, local area unemployment rates and size of company, while on-the-job training is affected by marital status, length of experience, etc. The wage equations initially suggested that selection biases were important. However, this result proved to be sensitive to the inclusion of firm size; individuals in small firms receive significantly less training of all types. While the firm size variable can be interpreted in an individual choice framework, its importance again raises the issue of the role of firms in the training decision and the way in which firms influence the selection of individuals who will be offered training (Baker, 1990, pp. 41 and 44). Strictly speaking, training should be modelled sequentially, as the probability that an individual will accept an offer of training, conditional on the firm making the offer

(Baker, 1990; Booth, 1989a and 1989b). Few studies, however, have adopted this approach to date.

5 Conclusions

In this chapter we have discussed the theory and evidence of government intervention in education and training. This has included an outline of the concept of the social rate of return to education and some estimates of this rate are lower than the corresponding private rates. We went on to see, however, that these social rates of return may themselves underestimate the benefits of education and training to society. Government has increasingly monitored and evaluated the effectiveness of its various education and training programmes. Clearly, the effects will reflect the different education systems and cultures. As background to this discussion, therefore, we also looked at some international evidence about participation rates in education and training and presented a case study of the effects of the reorganization of vocational education and training. For further discussion of this important area, see McNabb and Whitfield (1994) and Layard *et al.* (1994).

References

Baker, M. (1990). *The Effect of Training on the Earnings of Young Males: An Analysis of the National Child Development Survey*. Master's Dissertation. Coventry: University of Warwick.

Barnes, D. (Sir) (1976). 'The Reorganisation of Manpower Services in Great Britain'. *International Labour Review*, 113, 1, 97–114.

Barnow, B. S. (1987). 'The Impact of CETA Programs on Earnings: A Review of the Literature'. *Journal of Human Resources*, 22, 2, 157–193.

Bennett, R.J., P. Wicks, and A. McCosham (1994). *Local Empowerment and Business Services*. London: UCL Press.

Blaug, M. (1972). *An Introduction to the Economics of Education*. Harmondsworth: Penguin.

Booth, A.L. (1989a). 'Earning and Specific Learning: What Price Specific Training'. Discussion Paper 8911. Uxbridge: Brunel University.

Booth, A.L. (1989b). 'Employer Provided Training: Who Receives it and What is it Worth?' Mimeo. Uxbridge: Brunel University.

Finniston, Sir M. (1980). *Engineering Our Future*. London: HMSO.

Fraker, T. and R. Maynard (1987). 'Adequacy of Comparison Group for Evaluations of Employment-Related Programmes'. *Journal of Human Resources*, 22, 2, 194–227.

Freeman, R.B. (1971). *The Labour Market for College Trained Manpower*. Cambridge, MA: Cambridge University Press

Freeman, R.B. (1976). 'A Cob-Web Model of the Supply and Starting Salary of New Engineers'. *Industrial and Labour Relations Review*, 29, 2, 236–248.

Layard, R., K. Mayhew and G. Owen (eds) (1994). *Britain's Training Deficit*. Aldershot: Avebury.

Main, B.G. and M.A. Shelley (1988). 'The Effectiveness of YTS as a Manpower Policy'. Discussion Paper No. 8801. Department of Economics. St Andrews: University of St Andrews.

Main, B.G. and M.A. Shelley (1990). 'The Effectiveness of the YTS as a Manpower Policy'. *Economica*, 57, 495–514.

Mason, G. and B. van Ark (1994). 'Vocational Training and Productivity Performance: An Anglo-Dutch Comparison'. In R. McNabb, and K. Whitfield (eds) *International Journal of Manpower*, Special Edition, Part II, Vol. 5, No. 5, 55–69.

McNabb, R. and K. Whitfield (1994). *The Market for Training*. Aldershot: Avebury.

Oswald, A.J. (1994). 'Four Pieces of the Unemployment Puzzle'. Keynote Speech: Sixth EALE Conference, Warsaw, 22–25 September.

Thirwall, A.P. (1969). 'On the Costs and Benefits of Manpower Policies'. *Employment and Productivity Gazette*, November.

Wilson, R.A. (1983). 'Rates of Return: Some Further Results'. *Scottish Journal of Political Economy*, 30, 2, 114–127.

Wilson, R.A. (1984). *The Declining Return to Professional Status in the British Economy (with Special Reference to Scientists and Engineers)*: PhD Thesis. Coventry: University of Warwick.

Whitfield, K. and C. Bourlakis (1989). *YTS, Employment and Earnings: An Analysis Using the England and Wales Youth Cohort Study*. Project Report. Institute for Employment Research. Coventry: University of Warwick.

Ziderman, A. (1969). 'Costs and Benefits of Adult Retraining in Great Britain'. *Economica*, November.

Ziderman, A. (1978). *Manpower Training: Theory and Policy*. London: Macmillan.

PART VI Employment Relationships

CHAPTER 18 Models of the employment contract

1 Introduction

Trade in labour services is one of the most complex forms of market transaction. Workers, even with a modest level of skill, sell a quite complex bundle of labour services. They do not just perform a single task like the employees in Adam Smith's pin factory. Jobs require workers to perform a multitude of tasks drawing on many different skills and abilities – manual dexterity, the ability and willingness to learn from experience, to communicate with co-workers and superiors, to adapt to changing production methods and so on. Two further complications were alluded to in Chapter 1. Labour services are embodied in human beings, and their supply cannot be divorced from the person in which they are present. In addition, the price of labour is the main determinant of an individual's income which in turn has an important influence on their whole life. For reasons such as these, there is a strong theme running through the labour economics literature which holds that the market for labour is different from most other markets.

In this part of the book we focus on some of the things which make the labour market different under the rubric of the employment relationship. The principal focus is on the employment contract: how the trade in labour services is structured given the inherent complexity of the transaction. As we shall see this rules out so-called complete contracts in which every conceivable detail is specified in advance of a person taking on a job. This gives rise to an incentive problem because workers (and employers) can take advantage of the incomplete nature of the contract. But the other two special features of the labour market are also present. The embodiment of labour services in an individual means that the employment relationship is not just a trade between two economic agents, but embedded in a set of social relations within a firm and between different groups in society. The form that this relationship takes cannot be understood without reference to social mores and values. Finally, the fact that most individuals derive their main income from work means that the variability or security of that income is a major issue. The employment contract is not just an agreement about the price at which trade is to take place, but also an instrument for structuring incentives and sharing the risks.

2 Institutional approaches and internal labour markets

For reasons explained in Chapter 1, this book provides a mainly neoclassical perspective on labour economics. In the process, relatively little attention has been paid to the institutional arrangements of labour markets. But the labour market, more than most other markets, is governed by numerous institutional processes. These include the nature of the firm and its employment practices, the strong influence exerted by trade unions and employer organizations, the very extensive regulation of employment matters by the state, and the highly political nature of the underlying conflict between labour and capital. Noting this pervasive influence of institutions, broadly speaking, many would argue that the neoclassical perspective is seriously at odds with the reality and offers a very limited perspective on how labour markets actually operate.

The neoclassical paradigm is at its weakest, and seems most at odds with reality, when we look at the process of adjustments in labour markets – see Case Study 1. According to the competitive theory, it is the price that adjusts to bring supply and demand into balance. Yet, in the labour market it is very difficult to see this presumed adjustment process at work. The internal labour market view is that the internal organization of firms is crucial to the way in which labour markets function. This is most evident in the internal labour market analysis of how labour markets adjust, and in particular the role of wages in the adjustment process. A central idea is that a firm can adjust to labour market imbalances in a number of ways, by varying job allocations, recruitment standards, the training of workers, overtime and subcontracting, etc. These adjustment instruments largely substitute for wage changes leaving little role for wages in the adjustment process.

The concept of an internal labour market can be traced back to the work of Kerr (1954) and Dunlop (1957), and was fully articulated by Doeringer and Piore (1971). It can be defined as an administrative unit (e.g. a workplace or a firm) in which the pricing and allocation of labour is determined by administrative rules and procedures. The internal labour market has a number of characteristics which makes it distinctive. There is a high degree of employment stability, workers tend to remain employed in the same firm for a long time, entry is restricted to lower-level positions while higher-level jobs are filled by internal promotion, specific skills and on-the-job training are important, and the allocative procedures and wage determination are governed by rules and procedures heavily influenced by custom.

Doeringer and Piore emphasized three factors crucial to the emergence of internal labour markets: skill specificity, on-the-job training and customary law. By skill specificity they mean that firm-specific skills are relatively important in comparison with general or transferable skills. The distinction between these two types of skills was introduced in Part V of the book. The second factor is the importance of on-the-job training. Doeringer and Piore argue that by far the largest proportion of blue collar job skills are acquired on the job. This argument could be extended to white collar jobs, with the proviso that a formal education is likely to be a more important pre-requisite. The third factor is the importance of habit and custom in the operation of internal labour markets. Custom is the set of unwritten rules that can govern any aspect of work: the control of absenteeism, disciplinary matters, job allocations, hours of work and most aspects of pay. From an institutional perspective, customs are an integral part of any social organization. In any setting where individuals and groups interact with each other over extended periods of time, conventions governing these interactions evolve. The workplace is no exception. Although primarily an economic organization, created and maintained to pursue a purely economic objective, it is at the same time a social organism.

There have been a number of contributions to the literature which have extended and developed the internal labour market concept (Richardson and Blandy, 1982; Creedy and Whitfield, 1988; Osterman, 1984; Marsden, 1986) but of particular significance is the development in transaction cost economics. The importance of transaction costs was first articulated by Coase (1937), but its further development is primarily due to Williamson (see for example Williamson *et al.*, 1975; Williamson, 1985). The contribution of transaction cost economics is to suggest a holistic rationale for internal labour markets. Economic institutions, including the firm, are seen as mechanisms for economizing on transaction costs. In the case of the employment relationship, the specific skills of the incumbent workforce create a difficulty. This is not unique to the employment relationship, but has parallels in other markets. To cope with the specific nature of this relationship, a particular contractual arrangement is required, and the suggestion is that an internal labour market is such an arrangement. Workers accept the direction of management within certain limits largely determined by rules and procedures that have evolved through custom and habit. Using a key concept of Williamson, the rules and procedures of internal labour markets can be seen as an efficient governance structure – efficient because they balance the need for adaptability with the workers' desire for stability.

3 Implicit contracts

The origins of implicit contract theory can be traced back to a number of stylized facts about the labour market which appear inconsistent with competitive theory and developments in general equilibrium theory. The two critical facts are that wages tend to be rigid over the business cycle while the level of employment varies, and the existence of involuntary unemployment. These two facts are of course central issues of macroeconomics to which numerous answers have been given. However, none of the answers have been entirely satisfactory, and at the time implicit contract theory developed the *assumed* rigidity of wages seemed a particularly weak point. The motivation behind implicit contract theory was to devise a more satisfactory answer.

The conceptual origins of implicit contract theory can be traced back to the theory of general equilibrium under uncertainty developed by Arrow and Debreu. The state contingent claims theory that they developed was concerned with the existence and nature of general equilibrium under uncertainty. The major innovation of implicit contract theory was to view the employment contract as an instrument for the long-term exchange of labour services. Based on the assumption that workers are more risk averse than firms, the theory shows that in an efficient contract the firm will absorb most of the risk and pay workers a wage which insures them from fluctuations in their marginal product (Baily, 1974; Azariades, 1975). Less formally, implicit contract theory views the firm as consisting of three departments. There is a production department which purchases labour services and credits each worker with the value of their marginal product; an insurance department which sells insurance policies and, depending on the state of nature, either debits or credits the worker with an insurance indemnity; and an accounting department which pays each worker a wage net of the indemnity. In good times, the workers receive less than the value of their marginal product, and, in bad times, more.

There is another strand to the literature which has much in common with implicit contract theory. This strand is closely related to the internal labour market concept, in that the focus is on the long term, and to the social nature of the employment relationship. Thurow (1975, 1983) has been a strong critic of the applicability of the price auction model of the labour market. Another prominent contribution is due to Okun (1980, 1981) who coined the term the 'invisible handshake', the implied promise by a firm to continue to employ a worker for the foreseeable future. This 'invisible handshake' is offered by the firms to recover the cost of the 'toll' associated with new hires and to build up reputation as a reliable employer. Another term for this implied promise is relational contracting – referring to the fact that the identity of the parties to an employment contract matters.

4 Incentive problem

4.1 Worker effort

The conventional theory of supply and demand for labour as outlined in Parts II and III is formulated in units of hours or some other measure of units of time – individuals supply hours, firms have a demand for person hours and the price at which exchange takes place is the price for an hour of labour. However, even a moment's reflection would suggest that firms do not want labour hours *per se*; what they require are some services from the workers that they employ. Thus a more natural measure would be to measure labour services in efficiency units. The justification for ignoring the efficiency by which labour time is supplied and used has been that little is gained by recasting the theory in terms of efficiency units. This may well be true as far as the theory of demand goes. But it is possible to see that it is less satisfactory with regard to the supply of labour, as soon as we recognize that workers would normally retain some control over the services that they provide.

Although Robbins (1930), in the first exposition of the backward-bending supply curve, had effort, and not hours, on his horizontal axis, the issue has been largely ignored by neoclassical theory for a long time. It has, however, been a more central part of radical economic analysis. What the capitalist buys in the labour market is the right to a certain amount, measured in units of time, of what Marx called 'labour power', the workers' capacity to perform work. But what the capitalist wants is 'labour', the actual human effort used in the process of production. This distinction was crucial to Marxian analysis of the capitalist economy. It is an essential ingredient of Marxian value theory which is based around the concept of 'surplus value', which is created by the extraction of labour from labour power.

In the analysis of how capitalists extracted labour from labour power, the Marxian analysis tends to emphasize class-based factors. For example, Marx himself put great stress on the 'divide and rule' character of capitalist society. Workers are divided by the division of labour:

> Division of labour within the workshop implies the undisputed authority of capitalists over men, that are but parts of a mechanism that belongs to him.

Allied to and reinforcing this is the autonomy of men in a market economy where labour is not organized, or what Marx referred to as 'anarchy in the social division of labour'.

4.2 Principal–agent models

The modern neoclassical analysis of the incentive issue has developed along a very different route (Hart and Holmstrom, 1986). Most of the economic analysis of the incentive issue has taken place within the principal–agent paradigm. This framework was first used to analyse the incentive for managers to act in the shareholders' interest (Jensen and Meckling, 1976). The framework is quite general, however, and is just as appropriate for analysing incentives faced by the workforce as a whole. In this part of the book the principal is the employer who engages an agent or worker to provide a certain task. The root of the problem is the partially conflicting objectives of the two parties. The employer–principal's objective is to maximize the return net of payment to the worker–agent, while the agent's objective is to maximize their own utility. This utility is assumed increasing in the wage paid and decreasing in the amount of effort that the agent supplies.

Although labour provides a very complex bundle of services in the theoretical models this is subsumed in a unidimensional variable called effort. If effort

CASE STUDY 1 The new economics of personnel

Economists have long regarded the internal operation of the firm as a somewhat mysterious 'black box'. The whole range of institutional practices concerning recruitment, selection, human resource development, job ladders and pay grades, performance appraisals, promotion and design of compensation packages has been taken as given. Being just the institutional mechanism through which the market forces are transmitted, economists have been happy to leave the study of such matters to other disciplines. This attitude is clearly reflected in the language used. While practical people and management academics talk of the organization whose valued employees receive a compensation package, to the economists the organization is a firm which pays its workers a wage determined by impersonal market forces.

But matters are changing. Personnel management has become human resource management, a label which has an economic ring to it. At the same time, many labour economists have turned their attention to matters which were once regarded as being mundane institutional detail: the tendency to hire only at well-defined ports of entry, reluctance to hire older workers, a very low rate of dismissals, rigid adherence to pay scales which do not reflect the local labour market conditions, the prevalent use of promotion-based incentive systems and job ladders, mandatory retirement and generous pensions. In the process it has become clear that these matters are not just an haphazard product of institutional history, but can be understood as a pursuit of economic efficiency. The collective effort of labour economists in this field has come to be known as the 'New Economics of Personnel'.

To take one example, promotion in hierarchical organizations is, as Matthews (1986) points out, so familiar that it is easy to overlook how complicated it really is. Typically it has the following features. There is a system of ranks; responsibility, pay and pension are all linked to rank, promotion is by one step at a time – upwards only, never down; poor performance is penalized by no further promotion, not dismissal; but at the age of retirement, all rights and responsibilities attached to the rank are lost at a stroke.

A number of explanations suggest themselves and have been developed by economists working in this field. The rationale could lie in the learning process of the system. Alternatively it could be seen as a system of screening, or deferred pay to provide incentives or to enable employers to recoup training costs. Other possibilities include a response to incomplete information – those in higher ranks cannot judge the performance of those more than one step below them, or opportunistic behaviour by people in the middle who cannot be expected to recommend the promotion of their subordinates above their own heads.

The 'New Economics of Personnel' has made many important advances in understanding these issues and some of these are taken up in this and the following chapters.

Sources: Main (1990); Matthews (1986)

were observable, the incentive problem has a very straightforward resolution – the firm would simply offer an effort contingent contract. This condition is rarely met, however, as asymmetric information and uncertainty complicate the contracting process. The employer cannot observe the workers' efforts. This calls for a contract contingent on output. However, under conditions of uncertainty there are sources of variations in output which are not directly tied to variations in the input of labour services. Thus, a given level of input can correspond to different levels of output depending on the particular contingency that is realized. In this setting the contract must not only provide incentives for the worker but also allocate the risk between the two parties. Thus, the challenge is to devise contracts which provide incentives for workers to provide labour services at the least cost in terms of inefficient risk sharing.

4.3 Performance-related pay and profit sharing

Most employment contracts do not contain any explicit incentive component. Workers are paid by the hour, week or month depending on the nature of the job (Fama, 1991). However, explicit incentives, usually called incentive- or performance-related pay, are not exactly unusual. The piece rate is the oldest and most common form of individually based performance pay. Usually, the pay is contingent on the number of units produced, subject to a minimum quality standard being attained. This simple principle can become quite complicated when workers perform a variety of tasks and each task must be assigned its own rate or price. A more common form is group-, rather than individually, based performance pay. The major sources of improved efficiency in production are changes in the organization of work, cooperative efforts to uncover and eliminate impediments to productivity and to facilitate the introduction of new processes and techniques. Ultimately the attainment of higher productivity through these routes depends on the behaviour and attitude of workers, and the incentives to provide these services can only come from linking individual pay to an indicator of the performance of a group as a whole.

Profit sharing usually means that a part of a firm's profit is distributed among the workers as an addition to their basic pay. Although it is really a type of group incentive system, the link between the performance of the workers as a group and their pay is very weak. Profit sharing is more about trying to affect the labour–management relations, to play down the 'us and them' attitudes and foster a sense of participation and shared commitment. As such, it should be seen as part of a broader trend of human resource management, the principal aim of which is to establish congruence between the attitudes and behaviour of workers and the firm's objectives.

Profit sharing also has some rather interesting macroeconomic properties. Weitzman (1983 and 1986) argues that a profit-sharing economy is more recession resistant than the conventional wage economy. This is because firms have less incentive to lay off workers in the face of an adverse demand shock. In a conventional wage economy, disequilibrium is reflected in quantities in the sense that workers are laid off and unemployment ensues. In a share economy, workers are kept on and the disequilibrium is reflected in values, lower pay, rather than quantities.

5 Efficiency wages

According to the competitive paradigm all firms pay workers the same wage, at which the supply and demand for labour are equal. These features constitute the two classical laws of the competitive equilibrium: the law of one price and the law that this one price clears the market. Efficiency wage theory questions this second law, and argues that in a competitive equilibrium the wage is above the market clearing wage. The core of efficiency wage theory is the proposition that there is a positive relationship between wages and productivity. Thus, firms may pay workers more than they need to in order to obtain a more productive workforce. In doing so, the wage level is elevated above the market clearing rate and involuntary unemployment is the result.

The stimulus to efficiency wage theory came from a paper by Solow (1979). The objective of this paper was to provide another reason for wage stickiness – the tendency for wages to be stable over the business cycle while the employment varied. His starting point was the assumption that 'you get what you pay for', in other words, that the productivity of workers (the effort provided) depends on the level of wages. Given this assumption he showed that the optimal wage set by firms must be such that the elasticity of effort with respect to the wage is unity. In addition he showed that this wage is invariant with respect to output, meaning that firms would have no reason to drop the wage in a recession.

Solow made no attempt to explain why labour productivity should depend on the wage, beyond mentioning a few possibilities. However, during the 1980s the ideas were picked up by a number of economists. In the process the microeconomic rationale for an effort–wage relationship was developed. It is now common to classify the models that were proposed into four groups depending on the precise reason for the link between wages and effort. In the shirking model of Shapiro and Stiglitz (1984), the reason is that firms pay higher wages to persuade workers not to shirk. In the turnover version, higher wages lead to lower turnover of the workforce and in the adverse selection model firms which pay higher wages attract a higher quality of labour. Finally, there are a number of sociological-type explanations for the wage–effort relationship, the most well known being Akerlof's (1982) gift–exchange model. In this model, higher wages are reciprocated by workers by more effort.

The empirical evidence for efficiency wage theory is mainly indirect. Studies in the USA, notably Krueger and Summer (1988), have documented large and persistent interindustry wage differences. These studies reject the hypothesis that competitive or bargaining theories can account for these differentials. Instead they argue that these differentials reflect industry differences in efficiency wage premiums and take this evidence as supportive of efficiency wage theory. However, critics feel that the link between interindustry wage differences and efficiency wages is, at best, tenuous (Murphy and Topel, 1990). Notwithstanding the lack of solid empirical support, efficiency wage theory has become accepted as a credible additional explanation for unemployment.

6 Conclusions

This chapter has moved the discussion some way from the traditional neoclassical paradigm. It has introduced a number of concepts which are explored at greater length through the remainder of this part of the book. In particular, Chapter 19 considers more institutional approaches linked with internal labour markets and transaction cost approaches. Chapter 20 examines implicit contract theory and various aspects and consequences of the 'invisible handshake'. Finally, Chapter 21 discusses the role of incentives in labour contracts and looks in greater detail at principal–agent models, pay systems and profit sharing.

References

Akerlof, G. (1982). 'Labour Contracts as Partial Gift Exchange'. *Quarterly Journal of Economics*, 97, 543–569.

Azariades, C. (1975). 'Implicit Contracts and Underemployment Equilibria'. *Journal of Political Economy*, 83, 1183–1202.

Baily, M.N. (1974). 'Wages and Unemployment Under Uncertain Demand'. *Review of Economic Studies*, 41, 37–50.

Coase, R. (1937). 'The Nature of the Firm'. *Economica*, 4, 386–405.

Creedy, J. and K. Whitfield (1988). 'The Economic Analysis of Internal Labour Markets'. *Bulletin of Economic Research*, 40, 247–269.

Doeringer, P. and M. Piore (1971). *Internal Labour Markets and Manpower Analysis*. Lexington, MA: D.C. Heath.

Dunlop, J. (1957). 'The Task of Contemporary Wage Theory'. In *The Theory of Wage Determination*, London: Macmillan.

Fama, E. (1991). 'Time, Salary and Incentive Payoffs in Labour Contracts'. *Journal of Labour Economics*, 9, 25–44.

Hart, O.D. and B. Holmstrom (1986). 'The Theory of Contracts'. In T. Bewley (ed.) *Advances in Economic Theory*. Cambridge: Cambridge University Press.

Jensen, M.C. and W.H. Meckling (1976). 'Theory of the Firm: Management Behaviour, Agency Costs and Ownership Structure'. *Journal of Financial Economics*, 3, 305–360.

Kerr, C. (1954). 'The Balkanization of Labour Markets'. In E. Bakke (ed.) *Labour Mobility and Economic Opportunity*. Cambridge, MA: MIT Press, pp. 92–110.

Krueger, A. and L. Summer (1988). 'Efficiency Wages and the Inter-Industry Wage Structure'. *Econometrica*, 56, 259–293.

Main, B.G.M. (1990). 'The New Economics of Personnel'. *Journal of General Management*, 16, 2, Winter, 91–103.

Marsden, D. (1986). *'The End of Economic Man? Custom and Competition in Labour Markets'*. London: Wheatsheaf Books.

Matthews, R.C.O. (1986). 'The Economics of Institutions and the Sources of Growth'. *Economic Journal*, 96, 384, 903–918.

Murphy, K. and R. Topel (1990). 'Efficiency Wages Reconsidered: Theory and Evidence'. Chapter 8 in Y. Weiss and G. Fishelson (eds) *Advances in the Theory and Measurement of Unemployment*. New York: St Martin's Press.

Okun, A.M. (1980). 'The Invisible Handshake and the Inflationary Process'. *Challenge*, 22, 5–12.

Okun, A. (1981). *Prices and Quantities: A Macroeconomic Analysis*. Basil Blackwell: Oxford.

Osterman, P. (1984). *Internal Labour Markets*. Cambridge, MA: MIT Press.

Richardson, S. and R.J. Blandy (eds) (1982). *How Labour Markets Work: Case Studies in Adjustments*. Melbourne: Longman Cheshire.

Robbins, L. (1930). 'A Note on the Elasticity of Demand for Income with Respect to Effort'. *Economica*, 10, 29, 123–129.

Shapiro, C. and J.E. Stiglitz (1984). 'Equilibrium Unemployment as a Worker Discipline Device'. *American Economic Review*, 73, 433–445.

Solow, R. (1979). 'Another Possible Source of Wage Stickiness'. *Journal of Macroeconomics*, 1, Winter, 79–82.

Thurow, L.C. (1975). *Generating Inequality*. New York: Basic Books.

Thurow, L.C. (1983). *Dangerous Currents: the State of Economics*. Oxford: Oxford University Press.

Weitzman, M. (1983). 'Some Macroeconomic Implications of Alternative Compensation Systems'. *Economic Journal*, 93. 763–783.

Weitzman, M. (1986). *The Share Economy: Conquering Stagflation*. Cambridge, MA.: Cambridge University Press.

Williamson, O.E. (1985). *The Economic Institutions of Capitalism*. New York: Free Press.

Williamson, O., M. Wachter and T. Harris, (1975). 'Understanding the Employment Relation: The Analysis of Idiosyncratic Exchange'. *Bell Journal of Economics*, 6, 250–278.

CHAPTER 19

Institutional analysis of the employment relationship

Internal labour markets and the transaction costs approach

1 Introduction

For reasons explained in Chapter 1, this text provides a mainly neoclassical perspective on labour economics. In the process, little attention has been paid to the institutional arrangements, even though the labour market, more than most other markets, is governed by numerous institutional processes. These include the nature of the firm and its employment practices, the strong influence exerted by trade unions and employer organizations, the very extensive regulation of employment matters by the state, and the highly political nature of the underlying conflict between labour and capital. Noting this pervasive influence of institutions, broadly speaking, many would argue that the neoclassical perspective is seriously at odds with reality and offers a limited perspective on how labour markets actually operate. In Chapter 1 we countered some of the implied criticism of neoclassical theory by the argument that while institutional factors channel and to some degree control economic forces, in the long run the economic forces rule supreme. But even if we were to accept this argument, there is still much to be learnt from those who have adopted a different perspective.

The competitive paradigm is at its weakest, and is most at odds with reality, when dealing with the process of adjustment in labour markets. According to the competitive theory, prices adjust to bring supply and demand into balance and yet, in the labour market, it is very difficult to see this presumed adjustment process at work. The presence of large-scale unemployment, with little evidence that wages are moving in an equilibrating direction, is a prime example. But so are several other anomalies such as wage differences between very similar jobs in the same locality, large and small firms, and across industries. In addition, the neoclassical framework lacks a theory of price adjustments. What exists is some *ad hoc* hypothesis appended to the Walrasian system. Typically it is just assumed that if demand and supply are not in balance the price will change, and that the difference between supply and demand determines the speed of adjustment.

These features are less problematic to institutional economists. Their major claims have been that wages are determined by institutional processes in which economic forces play only a minor role and, the corollary, that the allocation of labour is not determined by relative wages. From this perspective, unemployment and other anomalies are not really anomalies at all, but fairly predictable outcomes of institutional processes and impediments.

Rather than providing a comprehensive overview of institutional labour market analysis this chapter focuses on one important model – the internal labour market. This permits a reasonably complete treatment of a very important and influential model. In addition, the internal labour market model introduces a number of issues that subsequently have been addressed by neoclassical economic theory and form the subject matter of Chapters 20, 21 and 22. The present chapter is organized as follows. In the first instance we take up an example of how institutional economists have analysed the wage determination process. This is followed by an extensive analysis of the internal labour market model as developed by Doeringer and Piore. We then turn our attention to transaction cost theory which provides a complementary perspective on why internal labour markets exist and how they operate. The last section of the chapter takes up the 'three pillars' of the Japanese employment system and relates these practices to internal labour markets.

2 Institutional analysis of wage determination: an example

There is a very rich and extensive literature exploring the institutional perspective on wage determination. This literature includes the American institutional school of labour economics with key figures Reynolds, Dunlop and Kerr, while, in Europe, the institutional perspective was developed by trade union economists. The industrial relations perspective on wage determination also has a very strong institutionalist flavour.

As it is not possible to do justice to the many contributions to this debate we use a single example to illustrate the approach. Dunlop's (1957) analysis was based around two key concepts: job clusters and job contours. The first concept, job clusters, was used to describe the internal wage structure of a firm. A job cluster refers to the group of jobs within a firm which are linked by technology, administrative organization or by custom. To analyse the effect of the factors external to the firm he used the concept of a wage contour, a group of firms whose wages are strongly related. The links between the firms could arise because they operate in the same product market, compete for similar types of labour or employ workers who are members of the same unions.

Dunlop's short-run analysis relied on a particular example; the union rates for motor-truck drivers in Boston for July 1951 given in Table 19.1. This table has become a classic in the labour economics literature and has been reproduced numerous times. The problem that the table poses is also a classic, as it shows one type of labour performing almost identical work being paid markedly different wage rates. Dunlop's answer to the question of why the rates differed was that each rate reflects a wage contour. Drivers in the publishing industries do not belong to the same wage contour as those carting scrap iron and laundry, and the reason, he argued, was that the product market characteristics are dominant in determining to which contour drivers belong. Thus drivers in high-paying industries were paid high rates because they were lucky enough to be working in high-paying industries and a couple of reasons were alluded to. One was the force of historical precedent. If, in the evolution of an industry, it had to pay higher wages to attract labour, these higher rates would tend to persist because they were regarded as 'proper'. Another reason put forward was the influence of the wage rate of workers with whom drivers came into contact.

In the longer run, Dunlop saw the structure of wages as determined by the pattern of industrialization. As new industries emerged they had to attract labour from existing employment by offering higher wages. As successive industries have required more extensive skills the overall level of wages has drifted upwards as industrialization has proceeded. The structure and overall level of wages is simply the result of this process. It cannot be understood as the intersection of some aggregate demand and supply curve for labour. Clearly, this long-run perspective, as well as the short-run analysis, accord little weight to supply factors. Dunlop argued that once a wage structure is established, the labour supply tends to adapt itself to the structure, but does not exert much direct influence over it.

Table 19.1 Union scale for motor-truck drivers (Boston, 1 July 1951)

	$ per hour
Magazine	2.25
Newspaper, day	2.16
Oil	1.99
Building construction	1.85
Paper handlers, newspaper	1.83
Beer, bottle and keg	1.78
Grocery, chain store	1.68
.	.
.	.
.	.
Movers, piano and household	1.30
Scrap, iron and metal	1.20
Laundry, wholesale	1.20

Abridged version of Table (1) in Dunlop (1957, p. 21)

3 Internal labour markets

3.1 Background and definition

A centrepiece of institutional analysis revolves around the construct of an internal labour market. This concept has its origin in the writings of Kerr (1950 and 1954) who made a sharp distinction between structured labour markets and those lacking any structural features. The latter were distinguished by there being no attachment between worker and employer and the behaviour of the market closely resembled the competitive model. Structured markets, on the other hand, were those craft and enterprise markets subject to rules and procedures governing wage determination and the allocation of work. The influence of Kerr's writing can be found in many places in the literature, but it was not until Doeringer and Piore (1971) that the internal labour market paradigm received widespread acceptance. This work was very important because it drew together a number of different strands of thought from the institutional school into a coherent framework. It has also become generally accepted and is one of the most widely cited works in the labour economics literature.

From a wider perspective the internal labour market construct as developed by Doeringer and Piore is important for two reasons. First, they provided an analytical description of the internal organization of a firm. This has been an area of comparative neglect by neoclassicists, but one which is receiving increasing attention, some of which is inspired by the internal labour market analysis. Second, their analysis suggests that internal organization is an important influence on the way in which labour markets function. This is most evident in their analysis of how labour markets adjust, and in particular the role of wages in the adjustment process. This aspect of their work extended the earlier institutional analysis of wage determination.

Doeringer and Piore defined an (enterprise) internal labour market to be

> an administrative unit, such as a manufacturing plant, within which the pricing and allocation of labour is governed by a set of administrative rules and procedures ... to be distinguished from the external labour market of conventional economic theory where pricing, allocating and training decisions are controlled directly by economic variables. (Doeringer and Piore, 1971, pp. 1–2).

One of the most important features they highlight concerns the rights and privileges extended to the incumbent workforce, such as exclusive rights to non-entry-level jobs and continuity of employment. Since this shelters incumbents from direct competition the internal labour market is closely related to what others have referred to as industrial feudalism and the balkanization of labour markets. Their definition is most applicable to an internal labour market within an establishment or a firm. They had in mind unskilled and semi-skilled blue collar workers in manufacturing industry, where jobs were arranged along lines of progression for which the establishment was typically the boundary. But the internal labour market construct could also apply to white collar workers in clerical, administrative or managerial functions. In the case of managers, there is often a fairly well-defined career path stretching from trainees to supervisory positions and, from there, on to a series of positions in a corporate hierarchy.

In addition to these internal enterprise labour markets, the craft, occupational or professional labour markets of skilled blue and white collar workers can also be regarded as internal labour markets. As in the case of the enterprise internal labour market, the operation of these markets is also governed by rules and procedures. Often these only govern the entry to the trade, craft or occupation, but, in other cases, they apply to pricing as well, although not to the allocation of labour (i.e. the choice of job by a member of such a market is not usually governed by any rules). Whether or not such markets, or any market for that matter, should be regarded as an internal labour market depends primarily on how useful this construct is for analytical purposes. Doeringer and Piore, for example, argue that the internal labour market is a useful construct when the rules and procedures are rigid, but, if they are not, the obsession with institutional detail can only obscure the operation of the underlying economic forces. Relying on this dictum, we will in the first instance concentrate exclusively on enterprise internal labour markets. We should note, however, that when, as was historically the case in the UK, trade unions are organized along craft lines and have a large influence on the how the markets for craft or trade occupations function, this focus is questionable.

3.2 Factors leading to the development of internal labour markets

Three factors are crucial to the emergence of internal labour markets: skill specificity, on-the-job training and customary law. The effect of these factors according to Doeringer and Piore is very much in accord with what we would expect from conventional neoclassical theory. By skill specificity we mean that firm-specific skills are relatively important *vis-à-vis* general or transferable skills. The distinction between these two types of skills was introduced in Part V of the book. Other economists have supported this presumption of a high degree of skill specificity. Thus Williamson suggests that skill specificity arises out of the interaction between workers and technology. While jobs may well be designed to require only general skills, in the actual operation of a manufacturing process there is a constant modification of the processes with the result that a high degree of task idiosyncrasy develops. Only the worker who has been part of the process for some time can do their job efficiently and only that person can transmit this knowledge to other individuals.

The second factor is the importance of on-the-job training. Doeringer and Piore argue that by far the largest proportion of blue collar job skills are acquired on the job. This argument can, to some degree, be extended to white collar jobs, with the proviso that some type of formal education qualification is likely to be a more important pre-requisite. On-the-job training is closely related to skill specificity. Because of the very specific skill requirements there are very few persons learning a given skill at a particular point in time. Thus, the economies of scale that could in principle be attained through formal training schemes are not available, and informal on-the-job training is usually far more cost effective. Additionally, to the extent that task idiosyncrasy is strong, the relevant knowledge cannot be transmitted through formal instruction.

The third factor is the importance of habit and custom in the operation of internal labour markets. Custom is the set of unwritten rules that can govern any aspect of work including the control of absenteeism, disciplinary matters, job allocations, hours of work and most aspects of pay. From an institutional perspective, customs are usually viewed as a natural part of any social organization. In any setting where individuals and groups interact with each other over extended time periods conventions governing these interactions evolve. The workplace is no exception. Although primarily an economic organization, which is created and maintained to pursue a purely economic objective, it is, at the same time, a social organism. How customs emerge is seldom easy to pin down. To some extent it is just the maintenance of past practices. However, custom does not preserve everything that has taken place in the past; nor are customs entirely rigid – their development is an evolutionary process. Precedent is nevertheless a very important force, presumably due to equity considerations. If a worker has been treated in a certain way before, equity demands that the employee in question or any other worker is afforded the same treatment today.

While Doeringer and Piore regarded skill specificity, on-the-job training and custom as three critical factors in generating an internal labour market, they argued that they operate in conjunction with several other factors. In doing so they essentially provided an efficiency explanation for the operation of the internal labour market. In this they differed from some of their predecessors. Kerr, for example, put more stress on how internal labour markets restricted competition. Their efficiency argument was that an internal labour market confers benefit to both the workers and the firm. The value to the workers derives from the job security, the chance of advancement and the benefits arising from equity and due process that internal labour markets provide. The value to the firm arises from the reduction in labour turnover and efficiencies in recruitment and training.

That there is a cost to labour turnover has long been recognized by neoclassical economists. The issue was first raised by Oi (1962) who argued that labour was a quasi-fixed factor of production on the grounds that a proportion of labour costs were fixed rather than variable. The quasi-fixed nature of labour is reflected in what is normally referred to as labour hoarding, meaning that employment is stabilized over the business cycle by maintaining an excess labour force in recessions to avoid the costs of recruitment and training in an upturn. Institutional economists have not really added much to this analysis except by drawing attention to the fact that skill specificity makes the training cost larger. In addition, Doeringer and Piore also emphasize what they call the technical efficiencies in recruitment, screening and training in an internal labour market. These efficiency gains depend on the management having more information about the incumbent workforce. Their ability, skills and personal attributes are known from their work history. Thus in selecting workers for training, the management knows if an incumbent worker has the required ability and whether they are likely to remain with the firm for some period of time.

3.3 Allocative procedures within an internal labour market

The influence of administrative procedures and rules is best appreciated by looking at the allocative procedures within an internal labour market, for instance how the assignment of workers to jobs takes place. Apart from being a description of how internal labour markets function, this discussion also highlights the tension between arrangements which are valuable to the workforce and those which are conducive to efficiency. We begin with a discussion of two factors which are relevant to what follows: the degree of openness and the pattern of mobility.

The degree of openness of an internal labour market refers to the proportion of jobs that are filled from within the firm as opposed to hiring from the external market. In a closed internal labour market, external hiring is only done for a set of explicitly designated entry positions – the ports of entry. All other jobs are filled internally through transfer, upgrading or promotion. The entry positions would normally be at low levels. Progression to higher levels and more skilled jobs would then be dependent on the acquisition of the skill and experience required for these jobs. Thus, on-the-job training would be a very important feature in a closed internal labour market.

At the opposite end of the spectrum would be an open internal labour market in which all positions are filled or at least open to external applicants. Under this arrangement, all jobs are also a port of entry, the skill requirements are more general and on-the-job training is a much less important feature. While a closed internal labour market shields the incumbent workforce from the competitive pressures of the external labour market, the forces of competition obviously play a much larger role in the open version. Some would argue that an open internal labour market is a contradiction in terms. To be competitive in the external labour market, the wages in all jobs must be at the competitive level, leaving no room for rules and procedures in either the pricing or allocation of labour. Doeringer and Piore, however, consistent with what they regard as a critical feature of an internal labour market, reject this argument. They point to the fact that many matters are still within the control of a firm such as the process of wage determination and allocation of job assignments. There is also a clear distinction between the incumbent and external workforce which is particularly important when work is scarce. These matters are governed by rules and procedures and to the extent that they impose rigidities, the internal labour market construct is useful even if it is of the open type.

This issue is, in any case, not of great practical importance. Most internal labour markets are neither closed nor open, but fall somewhere in between. The degree of openness also varies within an enterprise between both occupational groups and administrative units within a firm. Because these differences are often large, the notion of a single-enterprise internal labour market seldom makes sense. Rather, a firm usually contains a number of distinct internal markets, each subject to its own rules and procedures. The unskilled and semi-skilled blue collar workers may constitute one market, tradespeople another, administrative staff a third and so on.

The second factor concerns the patterns of mobility within an internal labour market: the rules and procedures that govern the assignments to non-entry-level jobs. The term mobility clusters is useful here – the set of jobs between which there is a high degree of mobility, while mobility between clusters is more limited. Jobs within a mobility cluster are usually related, for example in terms of the skill and experience that is required. A typical example is the single line of progression from a machine operator entry position to a leading hand and supervisor within a section or department. But mobility clusters can be more diverse than this; there can be a horizontal as well as a vertical dimension when range and breadth of experience is more important than level of skill. The mobility pattern is also governed by rules about the criterion for internal mobility, for example whether merit or seniority should be given the largest weight in job allocations. Although efficiency considerations would favour merit, seniority may be given a larger weight if custom dictates this. Some evidence of mobility patterns within internal labour markets is provided in Case Study 1.

CASE STUDY 1 Mobility patterns within internal labour markets

To complement the largely abstract discussion of internal labour markets, it is of some interest to look at some concrete examples. Osterman (1984) interviewed 12 employers of mainly white collar workers. They represented the type of firms normally found in a medium-sized city centre. The study focused on four occupational groups: salespersons, low-level managers, computer programmers and clerical workers. These four occupational groups were chosen because they are typical of white collar work, but they also represent different types of employment systems within a firm. The abstract notion of an internal labour market would take the firm as the boundary. However, in reality a single firm often contains a number of internal labour markets, and some employees may not be part of an internal market at all. At the outset of the study

continues

CASE STUDY 1 continued

it was thought that the managerial group would typify the fairly rigid enterprise internal labour market (i.e. a limited number of entry ports and clearly defined career paths based upon on-the-job training and brief internal courses). The clerical group were expected to be at the other end of the spectrum; not really a part of an internal labour market, but in jobs with low skill requirements and no clear links to better jobs. Computer programmers and salespersons were expected to be in an intermediate position (as professional groups they might have a much stronger linkage with their profession than the firm they happen to be working for). Using the terminology of Kerr, they may be best thought of as belonging to a craft internal labour market as opposed to an enterprise internal labour market. However, a firm might choose to internalize such groups for reasons tied up with the advantages of enterprise internal markets.

To provide some evidence on these issues Osterman looked at how open the different job ladders were (i.e. whether jobs at the higher levels were filled from within the firm or from the external market). Table 19.2 shows that the middle and top jobs in the managerial ladder were filled almost exclusively from within. The other ladders were more open, but internal recruitment through promotion was still dominant. Another dimension of mobility is whether the jobs in one occupation are filled from this occupation or from other occupations in the companies. That is, whether there is any movement across different job ladders. The data in the lower part of the table show that there is considerable mobility across different ladders at the entry level. At higher levels, however, both sales and computer occupations are totally closed to internal movement from other ladders, but both the managerial and clerical occupations are fairly open to cross-ladder internal movements.

Two observations can be made about these mobility patterns. First, the data reveal a considerable variety in the openness of white collar occupations and the internal mobility patterns. Occupations within the same firm differ quite sharply in the extent to which outsiders and insiders have access to higher-ranked positions. Thus it makes little sense to speak of uniform internal labour markets; the internal labour market is more like a complex web of sub-systems.

Second, the large proportion of entry-level computer programming jobs filled from elsewhere within the company reflects an effort by firms to internalize the computer programming function. Traditionally, programming was a professional skill that was organized along craft lines, with a progression from programmer to system analyst dependent on professional competence independent of the firms in which computer persons were employed. But as much computer programming has become more routine, many firms have found it to their advantage to lessen their dependence on a craft-orientated workforce with little commitment to the firm for which they work. Thus they have internalized some of the training and thereby opened up a more varied career structure for a group that would otherwise have faced more limited opportunities. This is an example of a situation in which organizational factors, rather than skill specificity, have been the driving force behind the development of an internal market. Consistent with this interpretation, Osterman also found that the degree of firm skill specificity was rather low and did not differ greatly between the four occupational groups.

Source: Osterman (1984)

Table 19.2 The openness of job ladders in a white collar internal labour market (per cent of all cases)

	Sales	Managerial	Computer	Clerical
Entry from outside is common or very common				
Top jobs in ladder	28	10	40	25
Middle jobs in ladder	16	0	50	70
Entry from elsewhere in the company is common or very common				
Top job	0	30	0	27
Middle job	0	22	0	44
Entry job	42	77	60	50

Source: Osterman (1984, p. 172)

The internal allocative structure, as manifested by the degree of openness and the mobility pattern, can take many different forms. Precisely what they are depends on the time and place in question. But what matters most is that rules and procedures determine the allocations. A central tenet of the internal labour market construct is that these are best understood as resolutions to the partially conflicting objectives of employment conditions which are valued by the workforce and technical efficiency. Furthermore, in looking at these issues one should adopt a holistic perspective; one specific feature does not make much sense on its own, but should be understood with reference to the wider context.

Take, for example, the limited ports of entry, a feature which in itself makes little sense from an efficiency perspective. Not being able to hire outsiders, except for designated jobs, clearly limits management's ability to achieve the optimal level of employment and its most efficient allocation. Additionally, insulating workers from the external competition is likely to have adverse incentive effects. The internal labour market answer is that this should be seen in the context of its contribution to the employment security that workers value. This is not, however, a very satisfactory answer to a neoclassical economist. They would argue that to restrict hiring to certain ports of entry is not a first-best solution; having to compromise on static allocative efficiency to such an extent to achieve greater employment stability seems a large price to pay. The retort, by the institutional school, is that static allocative efficiency is a very narrow consideration – a more important consideration is a set of arrangements which are conducive to skill development; a willingness to pass on knowledge to trainees without the threat that the trainee will replace you, incentives for learning, and an internal mobility structure which permits on-the-job training to operate to its fullest extent. Also, in some cases, there is no conflict between objectives. For example, the skill development need should have an important influence on the mobility patterns to ensure that workers who are considered for higher-level jobs have acquired the necessary skills and experience at a lower level. The mobility pattern that results from this may well be compatible with the workers' aspirations for self-development and advancement. They may, however, prefer seniority-based, as opposed to merit-based, promotions because of the greater certainty that results from a process which is not subject to management whims.

The analysis so far indicates that an internal labour market has a number of characteristics that makes it distinctive. There is a high degree of employment stability, workers tend to remain employed in the same firm for a long time, entry is restricted to lower-level positions while higher-level jobs are filled by internal promotion, specific skills and on-the-job training are important, and the allocative procedures and wage determination are governed by rules and procedures heavily influenced by custom. Because many of these characteristics are not directly observable there is a tendency to focus on some specific observable characteristics in identifying and ascertaining the importance of internal labour markets. For example, in studies of job mobility it is typically found that a large proportion of the workforce have been in their present job for a long time and can be expected to remain in this job for a long time to come – see Case Study 2. Many have taken such facts to imply that as much as two-thirds of the workforce are in internal labour markets. This may well be the case. The focus on some observable factors can, however, be somewhat misleading by creating the impression that long job duration *per se* has some direct consequences for how labour markets operate. This would be misplaced. According to Doeringer and Piore the critical features are that (i) the rules and procedures give rise to rigidities which do have implications for market behaviour and (ii) custom is a very important force shaping these rules and procedures.

CASE STUDY 2 Job duration in selected countries

Although we have cautioned against attaching too much weight to a single feature that is associated with internal labour markets, it is still of interest to consider some of the stylized facts about job duration.

Data on aggregate separation rates indicate a fairly high degree of job mobility. A few selected figures relating to the 1980s reveal that mobility

continues

CASE STUDY 2 continued

is comparatively high in the USA with 18.2 per cent of workers leaving a job within a 12 month period. Roughly comparable figures for France and Germany were 13.9 and 15.8 per cent respectively. However, aggregate separation rates are not very informative. For example, the figures could mean that some 15–20 per cent of the workforce change jobs every year while the remaining 80–85 per cent of workers remain in their jobs for ever. The story is not quite as simple as this as is evident when we look at the current job tenure (incomplete duration of jobs) of workers in a few selected countries. Table 19.3 shows that both the USA and Japan differ substantially from the other countries included by the higher (lower) proportion of workers with short job tenure. The differences between the USA and the other countries are not as large in the upper (long-duration) tail of the distribution which suggests that much of the higher mobility of USA workers is due to the high turnover rates of short-tenure workers. The impact of the Japanese lifetime employment system is clearly evident by the comparative data (22 per cent of the Japanese workforce have been in their present job for 20 years or more). Note, however, that the Japanese distribution is not distinctly different from the German one.

The job tenure data in Table 19.3 depict the distribution of the elapsed, or incomplete, duration of jobs – how long the jobs currently occupied have lasted, so far. Some of the current jobs may come to an end shortly, others will last for a very long time. How long depends on the separation rate which is very dependent on job tenure. Given the distribution of job tenure and the tenure-specific separation rates, we can predict the completed or eventual duration of currently held jobs. A few selected estimates, pertaining to the USA and Germany, are given in Table 19.4. These estimates confirm what has been said before – the USA is distinct in that workers with short tenure are much more mobile than comparable German workers. Only 6 per

Table 19.3 Distribution of job tenure (incomplete duration) of male employees in selected countries.

Tenure in present job	Germany	France	UK	USA	Japan	Australia
Up to 5 years	37.0	42.5	48.2	60.4	33.2	52.9
5–10 years	20.9	21.5	22.0	12.4	18.8	17.6
10–20 years	26.8	25.3	19.4	17.3	26.1	18.2
More than 20 years	15.3	10.7	10.4	9.9	21.9	11.2
TOTAL	100.0	100.0	100.0	100.0	100.0	100.0

Sources: Buechtemann (1991 p.19); Australian Bureau of Statistics, *Labour Mobility in Australia During the Year Ending February 1987*. Catalogue No. 6209.

Table 19.4 Estimated probabilities of achieving a job tenure (completed duration) of 20 years or more: males – USA and Germany.

		Current tenure (years)					
Age group	Country	0–1	1–3	3–5	5–10	10–15	15–20
Young persons	USA	5.6	13.3	29.4	19.4		
(20–24 years)	Germany	17.0	29.5	37.9	50.1		
Mid-career persons	USA	12.3	23.7	28.1	47.5	63.5	78.8
(35–39 years)	Germany	40.4	59.7	45.7	83.5	64.5	100.0

Sources: Buechtemann (1991, p. 19)

continues

CASE STUDY 2 continued

cent of young US males who have joined a firm within the last year will remain in that job for 20 years or more, while the corresponding figure for a German is 17 per cent. The picture is very different, however, when we look at males in mid-career – almost half of US workers with 5–10 years' tenure have jobs which will last for 20 years or more.

Thus even the comparatively high mobility of the US workforce is compatible with a large proportion of the workforce remaining in the same job for a long time. Hall (1982) provides more aggregate estimates for the completed duration of jobs in the USA. The estimates show that 58 per cent of the workforce are in jobs that will last for five years or more and 28 per cent of jobs will last for 20 years or more. These figures are of course higher for European countries and higher still for Japan.

Sources: Buechtemann (1991); Hall (1982)

3.4 The wage structure in internal labour markets

The institutional flavour of Doeringer and Piore's analysis is most evident in their discussion of the wage structure in internal labour markets. The analysis revolves around three major factors which influence the internal wage structure: competitive forces which emanate from the external market, factors which are internal to the firm, and social and institutional constraints. With respect to the competitive forces they do not, unlike Dunlop, suggest that these work through some particular channel. In Doeringer and Piore's analysis, competitive influences are pervasive, although this does not mean that these forces determine the internal wage structure. It is rather a question of these forces acting as constraints on the internal wage structure. The analysis that leads to this conclusion is very neoclassical in spirit. Competitive theory would predict that a worker has to be paid at least what they could obtain elsewhere. But having acquired firm-specific skills this constraint is rarely binding. The firm-specific skills, being non-transferable, limit a workers' alternatives to entry positions elsewhere which, by their very nature, tend to be at lower rates. In other words, skill specificity drives a wedge between a worker's wage in an internal labour market and alternative wages. This means that wage rates in jobs filled through internal promotion are insulated from the direct influence of external labour market competition. Instead, the competitive forces act upon entry-level jobs and the whole sequence of jobs that an individual might hold during the course of their employment within a firm. This leaves the rate for any one job indeterminate, but subject to the constraint that the expected income of a worker during their employment with a firm must be competitive.

How the internal factors influence the wage structure is intimately tied up with how an internal labour market operates. In internal labour markets the allocation of labour is determined by a set of administrative rules and procedures. This could mean by management decree, directing which worker should do which job. But such a direct command system of allocation is bound to be inimical to the wider objective of operating an internal labour market. The alternative is a system of voluntary internal allocation, for instance letting the internal market allocate labour subject to the wage structure that the administrative rules and procedures have determined. This is akin to a Soviet-type planned economy. The central planner sets production and prices, and then lets the consumers buy what they wish, or can, at those prices. This only works if the planner sets the 'right' prices, the prices that equate supply and demand. Likewise, the voluntary allocation through the internal market requires the 'correct' wage structure, a structure which ensures that all the jobs are just filled. This clearly constrains the internal wage structure. The wage for every job must be high enough relative to the job from which it is supposed to draw its labour, and low enough relative to the jobs to which it is supposed to supply labour.

The third major influence is associated with the social and institutional constraints on the wage structure. Doeringer and Piore, like most institutional analysts, put a great emphasis on these. Any wage or wage structure which has prevailed over a period of time tends to acquire the force of custom and there is a tendency to view any change as unjust or inequitable. This does not make change impossible, but imparts a rigidity to the wage structure. In a static world this influence would be inconsequential. The competitive wage for any job would come to be regarded as just and fair. However, in a modern industrial economy subject to constant change, rigidity often comes into conflict with economic realities. But customs and habits are not always inimical to economic efficiency. Workers on a career path have expectations about the wages to be gained through promotion. If technology or demand were to dilute the content of these higher-ranked jobs, it may not be efficient to reduce their rank in the wage structure. Doing so would frustrate workers' reasonable expectations, and have adverse implications for morale and work effort which must be taken into account. In the spirit of institutional analysis, one should focus on the benefits of stability, as opposed to rigidity, that custom and habit help to create.

3.5 Adjustments in the internal labour market

The net effect of these considerations is that the internal wage structure is the outcome of a highly institutionalized process that takes all three types of constraints into account. What this institutional process is depends on the time and place in question, but whatever it is, it is not just the institutional form through which competitive market forces set wages. First of all, if we accept the indeterminacy argument, it does what the market cannot do. Second, the process accords greater weight to the internal structure *per se*. The wages of some groups may well be out of line with the market rates, but the firm that operates an internal labour market can cope with temporary shortages by drawing on its internal supply through changes to the job structure (the set of tasks that make up a job), job allocations (who does which job) and on-the-job training. An internal structure that is out of line is, however, more difficult to correct through other forms of adjustments. The converse of this is that in an economy dominated by firms operating internal labour markets, excess supply, for example, would not be eliminated by nominal wage adjustments. Instead, firms finding it easy to recruit labour would respond by less recruitment effort, more intensive screening, more stringent hiring standards, less overtime and less on-the-job training. Thus, at least in the short run, the existing wage structure is locked in place by the internal and social constraints. To describe the long-run adjustments, institutional economists would normally rely on a historical analysis in which social forces play a very prominent role. This gives the appearance that a factor like custom is able to exert an independent influence on wages.

Critics of the institutional analysis of labour market adjustments have made several points. First, the institutional theory of wage adjustment is derived by aggregating up from the behaviour of the firm to the market as a whole. This raises the question of whether the market can really be understood by simply summing the behaviour of individual firms. Second, it is not clear that institutional analysis contains anything new. That long-run adjustments in the labour market do take a very long time to work themselves out is readily accepted by most economists. This still leaves the possibility that social forces determine what the resulting long-run outcome is, but the counter-argument, as put by Hicks (1974), is that differentials which have acquired the force of custom are those which have previously been caused by market pressures. In this, Hicks acknowledges that customs are important, but then questions whether customs have important dynamics of their own.

4 Transaction costs and internal labour markets

4.1 Concept of transaction costs

In his seminal contribution, Coase (1937) pointed out that the essence of the market economy is that the price system allocates the factors of production. Apart from the Walrasian Auctioneer, no coordinating agency is required – the market system works itself. But this description does not apply to a firm. Within a firm, it is not the price system that allocates the resources, but the entrepreneur. Adam Smith's 'Invisible Hand' has been replaced by Chandler's 'Visible Hand'. This consideration led Coase to suggest that the distinguishing mark of the firm is the substitution of the price system by entrepreneurial direction as a system of resource allocation. The question then becomes, 'Why co-ordination is the work of the price mechanism in one case and of the entrepreneur in the other' (Coase, 1937, p.74). Coase's answer to this question was that there must be a cost to using the price mechanism, and that the existence of a firm should be seen as a way of economizing on these (transaction) costs. Coase mentioned three types of transaction cost which he thought were important. The first was the cost of finding out what the relevant prices are. This type of cost has no direct bearing on the argument here, although the reader will recall that this type of cost is central to the theory of job search. But the other two, the cost of drawing up a set of mutually dependent exchanges and the difficulties with long-term contracts under conditions of uncertainty, are highly relevant.

We readily accept that it is technologically efficient to organize the production of most goods so that a high degree of specialization obtains. This is the central theme of the neoclassical theory of costs and production. However, to achieve this, an institution such as the firm is, in principle, not required. It could be accomplished by the cooperation of a number of independent factors of production concluding separate contracts with each of the other factors for every exchange that takes place. Although rather fanciful, we could imagine each worker buying their inputs from other workers, and selling their output to other workers. That capital is normally required in the production process as well does not change this – each worker might own a machine or each machine might be owned by an independent capitalist. In the absence of a firm, each factor of production would have to contract individually with its cooperating factors – those from whom it buys or sells. In the extreme case of n factors, each cooperating with all other factors, $n(n - 1)/2$ bilateral contracts are required. Coase's point was that the transaction costs of this arrangement would be high. A central contracting agent, a firm, may be a more efficient arrangement. The firm enters into separate contracts with each of the n factors of production and directs the factors to their most efficient uses.

The next question is precisely what type of contract would the firm enter into with its workers? The second cost mentioned by Coase, the cost of drawing up contracts, is relevant to this issue as well. This consideration is a sufficient reason for imposing some kind of structure on the relationship between the worker and the firm. Labour exchanges, where firms hire workers for a day, do exist, but they are not the most common arrangement. The reason is easy to imagine – it would be rather costly to have to hire a new group of workers every day. Instead, firms prefer to hire workers on the understanding that they will remain employed for some time to avoid the cost of daily bargaining and negotiation. The reason for doing so is even more compelling if we add skill specificity to the argument. As soon as the job involves even a trivial degree of skill specificity, it would clearly be very inefficient to hire different workers each day.

Having escaped from the need to negotiate new deals continuously, the firm that hires workers on the understanding that employment will continue for the foreseeable future runs into another problem, in particular, the difficulty of drawing up long-term contracts when the future is not certain. In principle, such a contract would be a full contingency contract, which would specify the actions to be taken by both parties in all conceivable circumstances. In practice this is not possible. Employment contracts typically specify the terms of employment in a very general way, such as the type of tasks to be carried out, hours of work, etc., but not which machine a worker will use or even whether they will be making nuts or bolts. This has the advantage of flexibility. Workers accept a certain degree of managerial discretion, so that, if more nuts are required, the management of the firm can switch workers from making bolts to making nuts.

This was as far as Coase took the argument. Having satisfied himself that employment contracts were of this type he had the desired result – within the firm, resources are directed by the entrepreneur. However, the transaction cost story does not end here. Several issues remain unanswered. Why do workers accept the direction of an employer? To answer that they are fired unless they do so is a bit simplistic. In addition, to find out whether directions are followed, the employer must monitor the actions of its workers, but this is costly, and the costs might well exceed the savings on transaction costs which were the reason for forming a firm in the first place. It is also questionable whether direction is at all feasible, particularly when the factors that tend to give rise to internal labour markets are present. If skill specificity is high, and skill development therefore takes place through on-the-job training, its success is too dependent on a willingness to pass on knowledge and to learn to be managed by direction. The alternative is to rely on the initiative and cooperation of the workers. But such compliance cannot be monitored and, thus, the threat of being fired, while not entirely empty, is at least hollow. What is required is a more complex incentive structure.

4.2 Subsequent development in transaction cost economics

While Coase was the originator of transaction cost economics, its further development is closely associated with Oliver Williamson. At the outset a sketch of the basic argument is useful. The essence of Williamson's ideas seems to be that the internal labour market is an efficient governance structure. That is to say, the rules and procedures that Doeringer and Piore refer to form the institutional mechanism by which the relationship between the firm and its workers is managed. The importance of Williamson's contribution to the internal labour market analysis is that he provides a fundamental explanation for the internal labour market construct. Some have called this approach neoinstitutional. While institutional economists argued that institutions are important to the understanding of economic behaviour, they took the institutions as given. The neoinstitutional analysis is more ambitious; it seeks to explain the type of institutions that will emerge to govern the relationships between economic agents.

In his writings, Williamson is very explicit about the behavioural assumptions on which his analysis is based, and puts great stress on these at every available opportunity. To do justice to his work, we therefore have to be equally explicit. The first assumption concerns bounded rationality, that human agents are 'intendendly rational, but only limitedly so' (Simon, 1961). The importance of this assumption is that it rules out so-called complete contingency contracts – those which specify the action to be taken in all states of nature. This is, of course, a significant departure from the neoclassical mode of analysis. The second assumption is that human agents are prone to opportunistic behaviour, by which Williamson means 'self-interest seeking, with guile'. This assumption appears to correspond to neoclassical theory's individualism (economic agents are presumed to maximize their own utility), but stated in a less flattering way (by the qualifying addendum, with guile). However, whether there is a difference or not is a moot point. In addition to these behavioural assumptions, Williamson assumes that the transactions of interest take place under uncertainty and that information is asymmetric. These assumptions merely define the kind of situations in which transaction cost considerations are of interest. In a certain world, an important dimension of the transaction cost problem vanishes. As was alluded to above, the problem with a long-term contract is that *ex post* the circumstances change in a way that is not anticipated at the time the contract is drawn up. This is the reason why a firm cannot bind itself to hire a worker for the next 10 years at a predetermined rate of pay, nor would a worker want to enter into such a contract. But if the future was known with certainty, there would be little difference between a 10 year contract and a contract that expired at the end of each day. Finally, Williamson argues that asymmetric information is the norm rather than the exception. In the case of the employment relationship this is probably correct, and the neoclassical analysis of this issue, under the banner of the principal–agent model, adopts the same assumption.

While Coase was content to list some of the costs of using the price mechanism, Williamson proceeded by identifying the critical dimensions of transactions: (i) frequency of transactions, (ii) degree and type of uncertainty to which they are subject, and (iii) degree of asset specificity. Although all are important, the refutable implications hinge on asset specificity. This is also the dimension which has been most widely accepted and discussed in the literature. For our purposes, it is the fact that specific human capital is an example of an asset that provides the strongest link between transaction cost analysis and internal labour markets. In general terms, specificity refers to the degree to which an asset can be redeployed to alternative uses, and by alternative users, without losing productive value. Its importance is that when a transaction is supported by specific assets a condition of bilateral dependence is created which greatly complicates the contractual relationship.

4.3 A digression: vertical integration

The role of asset specificity as a motive for vertical integration is one of the most widely discussed implications of transaction cost theory. Before returning to the employment relationship there is some value in a brief acquaintance with this issue. The exchange of labour services is held by many to be intrinsically different from the exchange of other services or the exchange of goods. It is true that there are some differences, but there is a gain in drawing parallels when this can be done, rather than to emphasize the uniqueness of a particular issue. The study of the organization of labour turns out to have numerous parallels with, rather than being sharply different from, the study of intermediate goods markets.

The prediction of transaction cost theory is that vertical integration comes about under conditions of asset specificity, because of the conditions for opportunistic behaviour that this gives rise to. To sustain this argument, envisage a firm that has to undertake investments in order to supply another firm with an input, and that this investment is of little value in some other use. Typical examples cited include expenditure on designs, special equipment or just tailoring the product to the buyer's special requirements. It could also be a situation of site specificity – the buyer is located nearby but there are no other buyers within sight and transport costs are prohibitive. Once this investment has taken place, the argument goes, the buyer has an incentive to drive the price down to a level which yields no return to the supplier. In more formal language, the buyer can capture the whole quasi-rent associated with the investment. Realizing that this would happen, the supplier would not undertake the investment in the first place and the buyer would have no alternative but to make this input itself. In the alternative version of this story, the supplier is cast in the role of the villain, but with the same result – the buyer would make the input itself. In the language of transaction cost theory, the market is not an efficient governance structure and vertical integration is called for.

Klein *et al.* (1978) labelled this the 'hold-up' problem. In a bilateral exchange situation, each party is liable to be held up by the other party. The situation described above need not require vertical integration. Coase has argued that the problem of bilateral dependence can be resolved by long-term contracts notwithstanding the complexity introduced by the fact that such contracts must be state contingent. Likewise, Aoki (1990) has shown that long-term contracts seem to work well in the Japanese automobile industry. Aoki used the term quasi-vertical integration to describe the relationships between a major manufacturer and its several layers of sub-contractors. But they all agree that bilateral dependency created by asset specificity is a problem.

The relevance of this to the internal labour market construct is that skill specificity, like asset specificity, creates a bilateral monopoly situation or, more generally, a small numbers exchange problem. The firm is liable to be held up by its incumbent workers – they are the ones who possess the specific skills and they are not easily replaced by outsiders. Likewise, the firm can take advantage of the fact that it is the only buyer of these specific skills. While in the case of physical asset specificity the problem is solved (or at least mitigated) through vertical integration or long-term contracts, the situation is different in the case of human capital specificity. Since human capital is embodied in individuals, it cannot be owned by a firm in the same way as physical capital. Thus, there is no correspondence to vertical integration. While long-term contracts may well be viable in principle, there are at least two features which are particularly problematic to the exchange of labour services. First, if the contract duration is too long, it would approach servitude. Second, the ultimate sanction provided by the legal system, to sue for breach of contract, can never be an effective threat to an errant worker – it is just too costly to use the legal process to settle the score with individuals.

4.4 Transaction costs and the internal labour market

The transaction cost rationale for internal labour markets is most cogently spelt out in Williamson *et al.* (1975). Their arguments fall under three headings. First, consistent with the transaction cost perspective, considerable weight is attached to the possibility for opportunistic behaviour, but they suggest that the small-numbers exchange problem is attenuated by the fact that wages are linked to jobs rather than workers. This, they argue, discourages individual wage bargaining and, thereby, the scope for individual opportunistic behaviour is reduced. Second, they regard the internal allocation procedures (and promotion in particular) as a system of incentives. Thus, workers do not just willy-nilly accept direction, but they do so because of an internal incentive structure which rewards compliance. Third, the limited ports of entry/internal promotion is 'informationally efficient'. That is to say, the firm, by observing its workers over a long period of time, can attain a more efficient allocation of labour than it would have achieved if all jobs were open to external competition. The authors suggest that a firm with an internal labour market can protect itself against 'low-productivity types' who claim to be 'high-productivity applicants'. In this they are implying that there are problems with interfirm communication of ratings, or, to state it more bluntly, that references tend to be too good.

Of these three arguments, neoclassical theory has implicitly accepted the latter two in the sense that more recent theoretical developments are concerned with the incentive and information structure of employment contracts. The first argument is, however, somewhat unsatisfactory. On the one hand, the strong individualistic emphasis is not in keeping with the institutional mode of analysis. Most workers, even though they have specific skills, would not see themselves as being engaged in a bilateral bargain with their employer. Rather, as the whole history of trade unions shows, bargaining strength ultimately derives from the prospect of collective action. The reason is that, even in the presence of skill specificity, it is doubtful whether these specific skills really reside in individual workers. It is probably more accurate to suggest that the large part of specific human capital is embodied in the collective of workers. Any one worker quitting does not take (all) their human capital away – it remains (largely) intact with the collective. On the other hand, even if we accept the individualistic perspective, no real reason has been given for why attaching wages to jobs would effect a fundamental change to the bilateral bargaining situation. Another, and more convincing explanation, for this praxis has also been put forward by neoclassical economists (Malcomson, 1984). The existence of a hierarchy of jobs with wages attached to them constitutes a reasonably credible commitment that workers will be promoted when jobs become vacant. That is, it is a device by which the prospects of promotion are made more credible to the workforce. There is also a more fundamental reason for questioning the emphasis that transaction cost theory has put on the hold-up problem. The fundamental problem is precisely that which bargaining theory deals with and, in a different context, a hold-up would be called a strike. As will be argued in Chapter 25, however, we do not expect a bargain between rational agents to result in a strike, and by the same token there is no reason to expect that one party will hold up the other in any bilateral exchange situation. Bounded rationality and asymmetric information, two of the maintained assumptions of transaction cost theory, do modify this prediction. But, so far, transaction cost theory has not dealt with the challenge posed by bargaining theory.

The contribution of transaction cost economics is to suggest a holistic rationale for internal labour markets. Economic institutions, including the firm, are seen as mechanisms for economizing on transaction costs. In the case of the employment relationship, the specific skills of the incumbent workforce create a difficulty. This is not unique to the employment relationship, but has parallels in other markets. To cope with the specific nature of this relationship, a particular contractual arrangement is required, and the suggestion is that an internal labour market is such an arrangement. It is an incomplete contract, but complete contracts are ruled out because of their transaction cost implications. Workers accept the direction of management within certain limits, largely determined by rules and procedures that have evolved through custom and habit. These rules and procedures complete the contract. This imparts some rigidity to an internal labour market, but custom and habit are not as inflexible as binding contracts. Custom and habit evolve over time in response to changes in the circumstances. Using a key concept of Williamson, the rules and procedures of internal labour markets can be seen as an efficient governance structure – efficient because it balances the need for adaptability with the workers' desire for stability.

5 Internal labour markets: a synthesis

The features of the internal labour market do not exist as independent elements. Rather, the presence of one feature is strongly related to one or more other features. To emphasize this point we summarize our discussion of internal labour markets in Figure 19.1.

Taking as a starting point that a firm has decided to use a technology which requires firm-specific skills to operate, most of the other features follow. First, on-the-job training becomes a natural way to endow workers with the necessary skills that are not readily available in the market place. This is the internalization of a major activity within the firm. Hence, hiring is necessarily restricted to entry-level positions. In view of the importance of on-the-job training, the firm must then provide incentives which are favourable for it to take place. This is important to both the trainees and the trainers. As far as trainees are concerned, effort must be expended in learning, and being firm specific, only the current firm can offer a return for this effort. Thus employment security is important. In part, this employment security comes from the fact that hiring is for entry-level jobs only. Employment security provides incentives for the trainers as well, but, in addition, their interest must be safeguarded by also limiting external wage competition to entry-level jobs. If not, the wages of trainers could be adversely affected by the workers they have helped to train.

Following the arrow that goes to the right side of the figure, we note that skill specificity leads to small-numbers competition. In the extreme case, a bilateral monopoly situation emerges. This might be attenuated by attaching wages to jobs rather than workers. The two sides of the diagram then merge, and the interest now shifts to productive efficiency. The structure which is conducive to on-the-job training shields workers from competitive forces. Similarly, if the

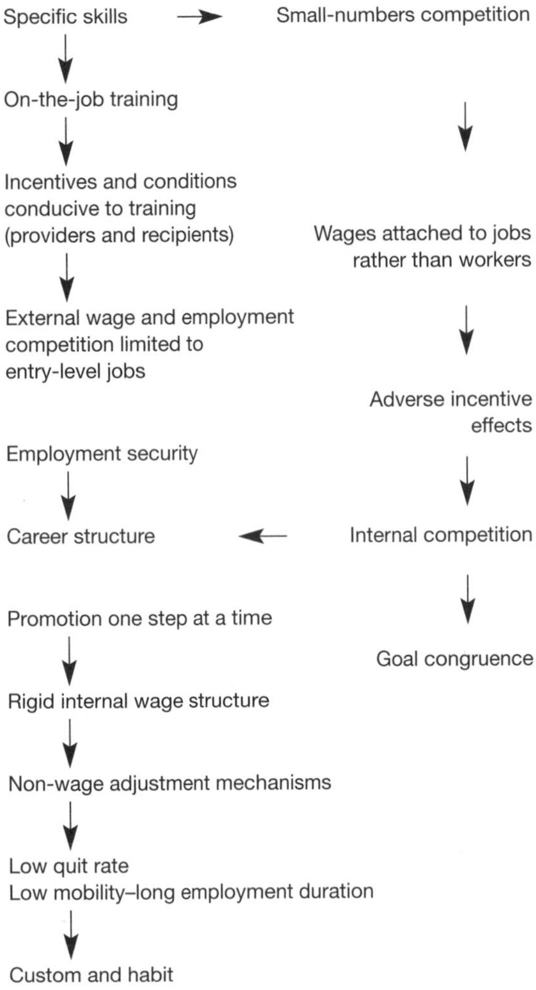

Fig 19.1 Interdependence of the features of the internal labour market.

wage depends on the position that a worker occupies rather than what they do, incentives are weakened. One solution to this is to replace external with internal competition. The competition is for promotion to better-paying jobs. However, since on-the-job training features at all levels, the trainer incentives must be considered. Thus promotion tends to be one step at a time, preventing trainees overtaking their trainers.

Promotion opportunities are normally provided by a hierarchical structure of jobs and wage levels. To preserve the principle that wages are attached to jobs rather than workers, the two cannot be separated. The incentive properties of this system depend on the difference in pay between levels. This makes the wage levels interdependent – it is not possible to change the rate at one level without making corresponding changes at all other levels. This makes for a rigid internal wage structure, which is not responsive to external factors. Because of the employment security that is offered and the low quit rate consequent upon wages reflecting a large component of firm-specific skills, workers take a long-term perspective about promotion prospects. We also observe the factual consequence of this, in particular, low mobility and long tenure in the same firm. This long-term perspective means that the internal wage structure must be fairly stable over time. Having strived for years to reach the top, workers would feel cheated if they were to find that life at the top is not what it once was. However, things cannot remain unchanged for ever. There must be some flexibility to respond to external factors, but to prevent management misusing its discretion in that respect, custom and habit are accorded a high weight.

Having discarded wage flexibility, wages cannot be used as an adjustment mechanism. Instead the firm has to rely on non-wage adjustments. However, since some of these are 'wage like', having indirect effects on workers' earnings, they are also more constrained, in that their use must comply with custom and habits.

The other avenue by which adverse incentive effects are attenuated is through the congruence of the individual worker's and firm's objective. This is a two-way process. Through social conditioning the firm may persuade its workers to identify with the firm, but the firm would also be sensitive to the wishes and aspirations of its workers. This is largely a separate issue, but we just note that it does involve letting custom and habit play a role as opposed to purely economic and technological exigencies.

6 The Japanese lifetime employment system

It is somewhat ironic that the internal labour market construct has been developed mainly by US economists. Mobility in the US labour market is comparatively high and, although this does not mean that internal labour markets are unimportant, their quantitative importance is probably less than in many other developed economies. More to the point, the description of internal labour markets is much more fitting to the employment system used by large Japanese firms than to the arrangements in almost any other country. The system of employment in large Japanese firms is commonly described as resting on three 'pillars': lifetime employment, seniority wages and enterprise unionism. Lifetime employment means that large firms are committed to continue to employ workers until they reach normal retirement age. In a dynamic economy, this is a considerable commitment that has many implications. It ensures recruitment and selection practices that are very rigorous, the internal skill development processes become very important and both the firm and its workers must be very adaptable. The seniority wage principle refers to the practice of ranking and paying workers primarily on the basis of years of service within the particular firm. By implication, individual merit plays a weaker role than in most Western firms. This practice reflects the scant attention given to individual monetary incentives in the Japanese firm. Instead, monetary incentives tend to be collective – for example, semi-annual bonuses based on the firm's performance – and there is a whole battery of features that provide intrinsic incentives by tying individual aspirations to the fortunes of the firm. Enterprise unionism helps to contribute to this, as does the participative decision-making processes, the great value attached to teamwork, quality circles and the paternalistic welfarism of Japanese firms. The whole package is geared to achieve commitment and loyalty from the workforce.

7 Conclusions and summary: status and influence of internal labour market analysis

Japanese employment practices are the *par excellence* of internal labour markets and they have, rightly, attracted considerable attention. The main reason for this is a pragmatic one – the employment practices used must have played at least some part in the Japanese economic success. Thus, there has been much discussion about whether these practices can be transplanted to the more individualistic Western culture. In the late 1980s there was a wide-ranging debate in the academic literature about whether management and industrial relations techniques in the UK were being 'Japanized'. This debate has also taken place in most other Western countries. The Japanese example has probably had less of an influence in labour economics – mainly because the internal organization of a firm has not been the central focus of labour economics. But it is likely that the Japanese example has contributed to the efficiency focus of the internal labour market paradigm. A more important reason for the efficiency focus, however, is that the internal organization of a firm has become a major research agenda for neoclassical theorists. These developments are taken up in Chapter 21. The other issue raised by internal labour market analysis, adjustment processes in labour markets, has become somewhat divorced from the internal labour market construct itself. During the 1980s there emerged a mainly European debate about the flexibility of labour markets. The concept of flexibility includes a consideration of the role that wages play in adjustment processes, but its scope is much broader than wages alone. Some of the issues are the relative efficiency of wage and non-wage adjustments and the role of internal (to the firm) versus external (market) adjustments. This debate has continued and further developed the institutional perspective.

References

Aoki, M. (1990). *Information, Incentives and Bargaining in the Japanese Economy*. Cambridge: Cambridge University Press.

Buechtemann, C. (1991). *Employment Security and Labour Market Behaviour*. New York: ILR Press.

Coase, R. (1937). 'The Nature of the Firm'. *Economica*, 4, 4, 386–405.

Doeringer, P. and M. Piore, (1971). *Internal Labour Markets and Manpower Analysis*. Lexington, MA: D.C. Heath.

Dunlop, J. (1957). 'The Task of Contemporary Wage Theory'. In *The Theory of Wage Determination*. London: Macmillan.

Hall, R.E. (1982). 'The Importance of Life-time Jobs in the US Economy'. *American Economic Review*, 72, 716–724.

Hicks, T.R. (1974). *The Crisis in Keynesian Economics*. Basil Blackwell, Oxford.

Kerr, C. (1950). 'Labour Markets: Their Character and Consequences'. *American Economic Review*, 20, 278–291.

Kerr, C. (1954). 'The Balkanization of Labour Markets'. In E. Bakke (ed.) *Labour Mobility and Economic Opportunity*. Cambridge, MA: MIT Press, pp. 92–110.

Klein, B., R. Crawford and A. Alchian (1978). 'Vertical Integration, Appropriate Rents and The Competitive Contracting Process'. *Journal of Law and Economics*, 21, 297–326.

Malcomson, J.M. (1984). 'Work Incentives, Hierarchy, and Internal Labour Markets', *Journal of Political Economy*, 92, 3, 486–507.

Oi, W.Y. (1962). 'Labour as a Quasi-Fixed Factor of Production'. *Journal of Political Economy*, 70, 538–555.

Osterman, P. (1984). *Internal Labour Markets*. Cambridge, MA: MIT Press.

Simon, H.A. (1961). 'A Formal Theory of the Employment Relationship'. *Economica*, 19, 293–305.

Williamson, O., M. Wachter and T. Harris (1975). 'Understanding the Employment Relation: the Analysis of Idiosyncratic Exchange'. *Bell Journal of Economics*, 6, 250–278.

CHAPTER 20 Implicit contract theory

1 Introduction

The origins of implicit contract theory can be traced back to a number of stylized facts about the labour market which appear inconsistent with competitive theory and theoretical developments in general equilibrium theory. The two critical facts are: (i) the observation that wages tend to be rigid over the business cycle while the level of employment varies, and (ii) the existence of involuntary unemployment in the sense that unemployed workers would like jobs at the current, or even slightly below, level of wages. These two facts are of course the central issues of macroeconomics to which numerous answers have been given. However, none of the answers have been completely satisfactory, and at the time implicit contract theory developed the *assumed* rigidity of wages seemed a particularly weak point. The motivation behind implicit contract theory was to devise a more satisfactory answer.

The theoretical heritage of implicit contract theory can be found in the theory of general equilibrium under uncertainty as developed by Arrow and Debreu. The state contingent claims theory that they developed was concerned with the existence and nature of general equilibrium under uncertainty. Their theoretical developments indicated that for general equilibrium to be attained, there must be *ex ante* agreements which clear the *ex post* markets for all commodities. These agreements they called claims, and they showed that a general equilibrium exists if there is a claim market for each commodity and every state of nature. Of most direct relevance to implicit contract theory is the nature of that equilibrium when individuals differ in their aversion to risk. It can then be shown that the marginal rate of substitution between consumption in different states of nature should be equal for all consumers. This implies that the more risk-averse consumers should carry less of the risk. This result is therefore referred to as the efficient risk-sharing condition.

Implicit contract theory is largely concerned with developing the labour market implications of this result. Conventional theory would predict that under competitive conditions the wages of workers in an industry would vary with the state of the demand. If times are good, the product price would be high as would the value of the marginal product of labour and the wage. In bad times, the converse would hold. Now, if the workers are more risk averse than the firm this is not in accordance with the efficient risk-sharing condition. It would be more efficient for a firm to carry more of the risk by allowing profit to vary more and wages to vary less with the economic conditions. In other words, the employment contract should include an insurance element, insuring workers against bad times by collecting a premium from them in good times.

Two questions arise out of this. First, are workers more risk averse than firms? It is difficult to give an affirmative 'yes' to such a question but there are good reasons for believing that this is the case. Workers' wealth consists mainly of human capital which is not diversifiable – diversification would mean that workers would hold several jobs. The firm, on the other hand, is owned by perhaps a large number of shareholders, each of whom has only a small proportion of their wealth in a particular firm. Thus shareholders can effectively insure themselves against the risk associated with the operation of a single firm. The argument is, in other words, that the risk faced by a particular firm is diversified through the financial markets. Therefore the firm itself can reasonably be assumed to be less risk averse than individuals. The second question is why the employing firm, rather than a separate insurance company, should provide workers with the income insurance that they desire.

As with most insurance matters, asymmetric information and its attendant moral hazard and verification problems intervene. A worker's incentive to do their job diligently would be diminished by the insurance (if the worker is sacked they just collect the insurance) and a specialist insurance company would find it difficult to verify that the bad state of nature, low demand say, has actually occurred. Thus the argument is that the employing firm, having more information than a separate insurer, is much better placed to undertake the insurance function.

From the above outline it is clear that the crucial feature of implicit contract models is how risk is shared between workers and firms. In view of this, to denote these types of contracts as 'implicit' can be confusing. By 'implicit' we normally mean that something is understood to be the case. In case of a contract, an implicit contract has connotations of an informal arrangement which is not written down. The converse of an implicit contract would then be an explicit contract in which everything that matters is clearly specified and written down. It is true that the type of contracts considered by the implicit contracts literature are implicit in the usual sense outlined above. But this is not the crucial feature of implicit contract theory. Instead, the principal concern is how risk should be shared between the two parties, the workers and the firms. For that reason, risk-sharing employment contracts would be a better term, but the use of the term implicit contract to denote risk-sharing contracts is now so entrenched that we adhere to the convention. This has the unfortunate consequence that other types of contracts, in which the implicit dimension is the central feature, cannot be called implicit contracts without inviting confusion. Other authors have used the term 'implicit contracts' to distinguish such contracts from explicit contracts where the distinction turns on whether the contract cannot/can be enforced by a third party. Using a term of Okun (1981), this latter type of contract could perhaps be labelled 'invisible handshakes', which clearly suggests that the contract is an understanding that cannot be enforced in law.

2 The implicit contract model

2.1 Background and assumptions

The theory of implicit contracts was originally developed independently by Azariadis (1975), Baily (1974) and Gordon (1974). Since that time there have been numerous contributions which have taken implicit contract theory far beyond the originators' basic models, and it is now best seen as an important special case of more general contractual models. Several surveys of these developments are also available. Of these, Rosen (1985) and Hart and Holmstrom (1986) focus specifically on implicit contracts. In this chapter we confine our attention to the most basic implicit contract model. Other expositions at about the same level can be found in Azariadis (1981) and Manning (1990).

The setting for the basic implicit contract model is as follows. We envisage a competitive industry consisting of a single firm in which the product price p is a random variable attaining the values $p_1 = 1 - a$ and $p_2 = 1 + a$ $(0 < a < 1)$ in the two states of nature 1 and 2. Without loss of generality we assume that each state is equally likely. There is an inelastic supply of N identical risk-averse workers to the industry with a utility function of the form $u(w + bR)$, where w is the wage rate, b is the value of leisure (per unit of time) and R is the fraction of time devoted to leisure $(0 < R < 1)$. This particular form of the utility function is very restrictive. It implies that consumption and leisure are perfect substitutes with a constant marginal rate of substitution given by b. The conventional labour supply problem has a very simple solution in this setting. If $w > b$ a worker would work all the time $(R = 0)$, while if $w < b$ all the time would be devoted to leisure $(R = 1)$. It follows that b is the unique reservation price of time supplied to market work, that is the reservation wage. The advantage of this formulation is its simplicity – the utility derived from work and leisure can be represented by the same function. If a worker works, the utility is given by $u(w)$; if the worker does not, the utility is $u(b)$. The utility function used here is of the form that was originally used by Azariadis (1975). It has since been found that most of the implicit contract results hold for a more general, but still particular, form of the utility function. In this alternative formulation, R is either unity or zero as before, but the utility when working and not working is represented by two different functions, $u(w) = u(w,0)$ and $v(b) = v(b,1)$. These two functions may differ to the extent that income is valued differently when a worker is unemployed and when employed. The advantages of this more general formulation are that the marginal rate of substitution of income for leisure is not a constant, and it permits b to be interpreted as the value of leisure and/or the amount of unemployment benefit. We continue, however, with the simpler of the two models.

The firm is represented by the single-factor production function $f(E)$ which exhibits decreasing returns to scale. When the firm employs E $(E \leq N)$ workers at a wage of w and sells its output at price p its profit is given by

$$\pi = pf(E) - wE \qquad (1)$$

In the simplest case, the firm is modelled as being risk neutral. Thus, it would only be concerned with maximizing expected profit.

2.2 Spot market contracting

We use the term spot market contracting to denote the situation that would emerge if exchange took place after the state of nature had become known to the two parties. Given the assumptions that we have made, the outcomes are depicted in Figure 20.1. In State 2, when the product price is high, the marginal revenue product curve intersects the inelastic supply curve, N, at the wage w_2^0. In State 1, the lower marginal revenue product curve applies which is drawn under the assumption that

$$(1-a)f'(N) < b < (1+a)f'(N) \qquad (2)$$

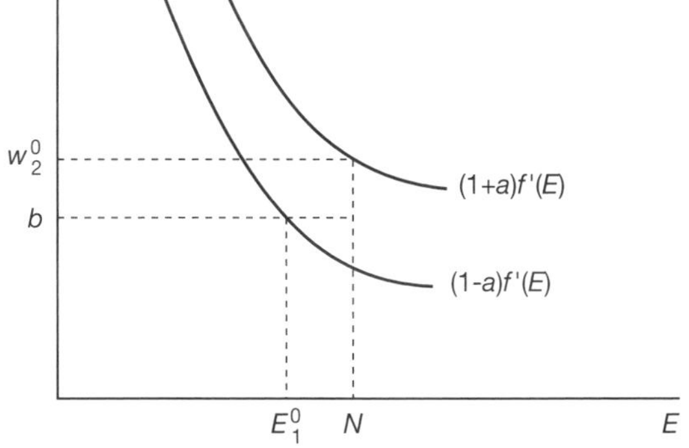

Fig 20.1 Wages and employment under spot market contracting.

That is to say, the marginal revenue product in State 1, if all N workers are employed, is less than the reservation wage. This prevents the spot market wage in State 1, w_1, falling below b. Thus, $w_1 = b$, and the firm maximizes profit by hiring E_1^0 workers. The remaining $N - E_1^0$ workers would be unemployed.

2.3 Pareto efficient contracts

Imagine now that the firm and its workers agree to a contract that mirrors what would happen if spot market contracting were used. That is to say, before the state of nature is known they agree that if State 2 were to occur the firm would pay a wage of w_2^0 and hire N workers, while if State 1 occurred, the wage would be b and employment is E_1^0. A typical worker would then have a certain probability of being unemployed in State 1. Note that the utility of being employed and unemployed is the same because workers in employment in State 1 are only paid their reservation wage, which is only just enough to compensate them for their lost leisure time. Thus, the resulting unemployment could be called voluntary. We denote this contract $\Delta_0 = (w_2^0, b)$.

In Figure 20.2 we depict this contract in a state–space diagram. Assume that this contract yields an expected profit of π_0 to the firm. Given that the firm's costs can be written as the probability-weighted sum of w_1 and w_2, the isocost lines can be drawn as a 45° line where, as we have assumed, the two states have an equal probability of occurring. Thus, the associated isoprofit line can be represented

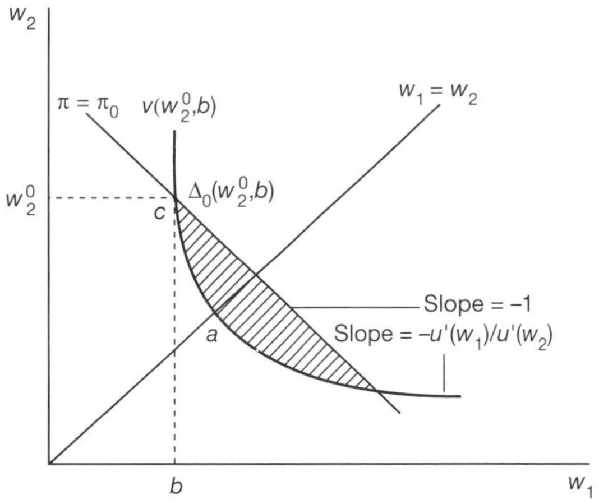

Fig 20.2 Contracts Pareto superior to the spot market.

by the straight line with a slope of –1 drawn through the point Δ_0. The workers' utility of this contract is represented by the curve $v(\Delta_0)$ drawn through Δ_0. The shape of the indifference curve is quite intuitive. If we look at point a, which has the same wage in both states, the risk-averse individual will only be willing to accept a lower wage in, say, State 2, if there is a disproportionate increase in the wage in State 1 (and vice versa). Because of the assumed risk aversion of workers, the slope is less than –1 at point c. More generally, the slope in our simple example is $-u'(w_1)/u'(w_2)$, the ratio of the marginal rates of substitution of wages between the two states of nature.

The implications of this contract can now be ascertained. A worker's utility is increasing in the north-east direction and the firm's profit is increasing in the south-west direction. Thus all contracts within the shaded area bounded by π_0 and $v(\Delta_0)$, are Pareto superior to Δ_0. Furthermore, Pareto efficient contracts must lie on the worker's certainty line where $w_1 = w_2$. It is only on the certainty line that a firm's isoprofit line is tangent to a worker's isoutility curve. So the optimal contract from the firm's perspective, given our starting point at c, occurs at point a. More generally, however, all Pareto efficient contracts lie along $w_1 = w_2$, such that the worker's wage is independent of the firm's output price. In other words, wages are 'rigid'.

2.4 Implicit contracts with unemployment

It is fairly easy to appreciate that risk-averse workers would prefer wage stability to wage variability. However, the certain wage is still subject to uncertainty – there is a chance that a worker will be unemployed in State 1. Many critics of implicit contract theory have focused on this issue. Why, they ask, should workers prefer stable wages which have the effect of increasing the probability of being laid off when times are bad? To deal with this, we have to spell out the rationale for a fixed wage contract more formally.

To incorporate the unemployment concern, we now consider contracts of the form $\Delta = (w_1, w_2, \rho)$, where ρ is the probability of being employed in State 1 – note again that all N workers are employed in State 2. A worker's expected utility from this contract is

$$v(\Delta) = 1/2[\rho u(w_1) + (1 - \rho)u(b) + u(w_2)] \quad (3)$$

and the firm's expected profit is

$$\pi(\Delta) = 1/2[(1 - a)f(\rho N) - w_1\rho N + (1 + a)f(N) - w_2 N] \quad (4)$$

As depicted in Figure 20.3, incorporating the possibility of unemployment explicitly has the effect of making the isoutility and isoprofit curves less steep. The intuitive explanation for this is that although the probabilities of the two states occurring are still the same, the geometry of the change is equivalent to a decrease in the probability of State 1 occurring (and to increase the probability of State 2 occurring). This is because the introduction of unemployment effectively decreases the probability of w_1 being paid. In the case of an isoprofit curve, since the firm does not employ all the workers in State 1, for a given decrease in w_2 it can 'afford' to pay a higher wage to the workers it would employ in State 1. Thus the slope of the isoprofit curve is now $-\rho$. In the case of a worker's utility function the explanation is similar. A given decrease in w_2 must now be compensated with a larger increase in w_1 to keep utility constant, since a worker's probability of receiving w_1 is now diminished by the possibility of being unemployed in State 1.

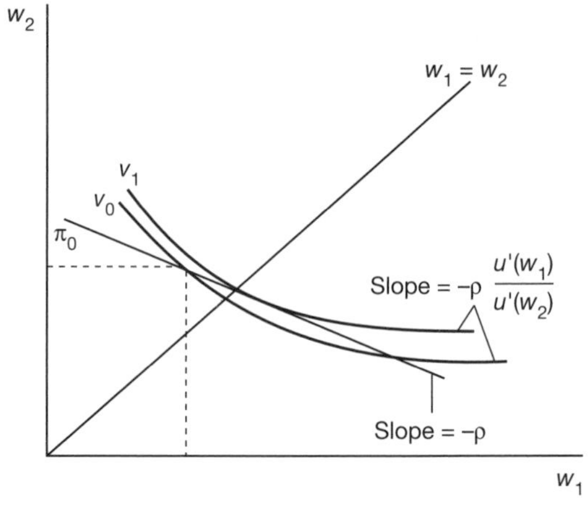

Fig 20.3 Implicit contracts with unemployment.

The tangency condition for an efficient contract is

$$-\rho u'(w_1)/u'(w_2) = -\rho \quad (5)$$

Since the proportionate effect is the same for the two curves the tangency point remains on the worker's certainty line where $w_1 = w_2$. Thus, the possibility of unemployment does not change the wage rigidity result. For any $\rho > 0$ any contract off the certainty line is inferior to one on the line. The next question then becomes: what is the value of ρ in an optimal contract? To answer this question we make use of the

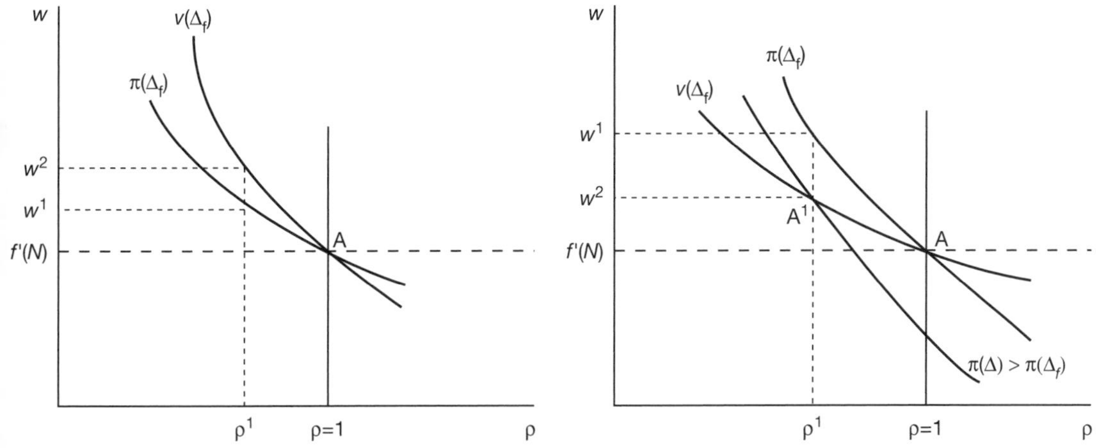

(a) Full employment contract **(b)** Contract with unemployment

Fig 20.4 Full employment and unemployment contracts.

wage rigidity result and consider only contracts of the form $\Delta = (w,\rho)$. This is a contract which commits the firm to pay a wage w to employed persons in either state and nothing to unemployed workers. The workers who agree to such a contract are certain to be employed in State 2, but in State 1 the firm would lay off a fraction $1 - \rho$ of the workforce. Since all workers are identical, $1 - \rho$ is also the probability that a particular worker will be unemployed.

A worker's utility and the firm's profit from this contract are given by substituting $w = w_1 = w_2$ into (3) and (4):

$$v(\Delta) = 1/2[\rho u(w) + (1-\rho)u(b) + u(w)] \quad (6)$$

$$\pi(\Delta) = 1/2[(1-a)f(\rho N) + (1+a)f(N) - wN(1+\rho)] \quad (7)$$

To see whether this contract entails any unemployment, we first consider a full employment contract ($\rho = 1$), and then investigate whether a contract with less than full employment would be more efficient. Having temporarily fixed ρ which, for the moment, we have assumed is 1 (full employment), the optimal full employment contract can be shown to be $\Delta_f = (f'(N),1)$, where the first term in brackets is the value of the marginal product and the second term is the proportion in employment, ρ. This can be rationalized by noting that at $w = f'(N)$ the labour force size which maximizes $\pi(\Delta)$ is equal to the inelastic supply N – the demand for and supply of workers to the firm would be equal. We denote the value of this full employment contract to a worker and the firm by $v(\Delta_f)$ and $\pi(\Delta_f)$ respectively.

Now unemployment would only occur if there is some other contract Δ which is superior to the full employment contract Δ_f. Thus in Figure 20.4 we have drawn the indifference loci for a worker and the firm which are as good as the full employment contract. The slopes of the indifference loci in the w,ρ space are

$$dw/d\rho|v = v_f = -\{1/(1+\rho)\}[(u(w) - u(b)]/u'(w) \quad (8)$$

$$dw/d\rho|\pi = \pi_f = \{1/(1+\rho)\}[(1-a)f'(\rho N) - w] \quad (9)$$

As the formulae imply, these results can be obtained by totally differentiating equations (6) and (7) respectively; setting $dv(\,) = 0$ maintains the individual on the indifference curve and setting $d\pi(\,) = 0$ maintains the firm at the same level of profit; rearranging the expressions then yields equations (8) and (9). Both of these loci are downward sloping and convex in ρ. The full employment contract corresponds to point A in either of the two panels of Figure 20.4.

Looking first at panel (a) we see from the $v(\Delta_f)$ curve by how much a worker must be compensated for a decrease in the employment probability by an increased wage. Likewise, the $\pi(\Delta_f)$ curve shows by how much the firm can increase the wage by having to employ fewer workers in State 1. The panel (a) curves are drawn so that the isoutility curve is steeper than the isoprofit curve. To see the implications of this, consider a contract with an employment probability ρ^1, $\rho^1 < 1$. Given this employment probability, a worker would require $w > w^2$ and the firm $w < w^1$ for this contract to be superior to the full employment contract. This is not possible. Thus, given the slopes of the isoutility and isoprofit curves the efficient contract must be a full employment contract. This is not the case in panel (b), however, where the relative steepness of the two curves is reversed. The wage w^2 that would be sufficient to compensate the worker for a less than full employment contract is now less than w^1, the wage that would yield equal profit to the firm. Thus, A^1 is clearly superior to A – the utility to the worker is the same but the profit is higher.

Whether or not there is unemployment in an optimal contract thus depends on the slope of $\pi(\Delta_f)$ being steeper than $v(\Delta_f)$ at A. From (8) and (9) the condition can be written

$$w_f - (1 - a)f'(N) < \phi(w_f, b), \qquad (10)$$

where w_f is the full employment contract wage and

$$\phi(w_f, b) = [u(w_f) - u(b)]/u'(w_f) \qquad (11)$$

is the marginal risk premium required to compensate a worker for an infinitesimally small risk of unemployment. The left hand side of inequality (10) can be interpreted as the savings to the firm by being able to lay off the marginal worker in State 1 – the wage minus the value of the marginal product. If this 'saving' is larger than the worker's marginal risk premium, a contract with a positive unemployment probability would be more efficient.

It can be seen that such a contract is more likely to result: (i) the lower is the product price in State 1 (i.e. the larger is a), and (ii) the higher is the reservation wage. This makes good sense. A low product price means that the value of the marginal worker employed in State 1 is low. Given that leisure has a value, it is better that the firm asks some workers to go home to enjoy leisure, or to collect unemployment benefit, rather than keeping them employed when their marginal product is low. The case for doing this is stronger the higher is the value placed on leisure.

The nature of the unemployment generated in this model has been a subject of intense debate. Workers have freely entered into a contract which provides a certain wage (if employed) and a certain probability of being laid off should their marginal product become too low. Further, the certain wage contains a risk premium to compensate them for the employment risk they have to carry. In that sense, unemployment, should it occur, is *ex ante* voluntary. However, a worker would rather work at the contracted wage than collect the lower sum b which represents the value of leisure and unemployment benefit. Thus, any unemployment that does occur is *ex post* involuntary.

2.5 Overemployment

Having discovered that an optimal contract may entail positive unemployment, overemployment sounds like a contradiction. In the implicit contract literature overemployment is used to denote that employment is larger than it would have been under competitive spot market contracting. This is still compatible with there being unemployment as well – it simply means that this unemployment is less than under spot market contracting (see Section 2.2).

The overemployment result is a direct consequence of the concavity of workers' utility functions. With reference to equation (11), concavity implies that

$$\phi(w_f, b) < w_f - b \qquad (12)$$

Since the inequality (10) is satisfied in a contract with employment risk ($\rho < 1$), combining (10) and (12) yields

$$(1 - a)f'(N) < b \qquad (13)$$

That is, in State 1 the value of the marginal product is less than the reservation wage. Under spot market exchange (13) holds as an equality. This implies that an implicit contract would result in higher employment than under spot market exchange. With reference to Figure 20.1, employment would be larger than E_1^0. It is tempting to regard this as a virtuous feature – more employment certainly sounds better than less. This is not the case. What is happening is that the insurance aspect of the implicit contract interferes with the employment decision. This is most clear cut if we interpret b strictly as the value of leisure. In this case, b is also the marginal social cost of leisure. In spot market exchange, the private cost of leisure is also b, but in the exchange mediated by an implicit contract this private cost is less, $w - \phi(w_f, b) < b$ to be precise. In the implicit contract the private cost of leisure is lower than the social cost and it is this feature which leads to overemployment. Another way to look at the overemployment result is to note that since workers have to carry an employment risk, an optimal contract should entail compensation for this risk. Part of this compensation comes in the form of a higher State 2 wage. The other part of this compensation comes in the form of a higher than socially efficient level of employment in State 1.

2.6 Unemployment compensation

To summarize the development so far we have derived the three most important propositions of implicit contract theory: (i) efficient risk sharing requires the wages to be the same in all states of nature; (ii) an efficient contract may entail employment risk and that the resulting unemployment may be regarded as involuntary; and (iii) employment is higher than it would be under competitive spot market exchange. Unfortunately, all three of these results are very sensitive to the particular specification of the implicit contract model.

The first result depends crucially on the assumed risk neutrality of firms. This assumption does not have a strong justification, but it is plausible that firms are 'less risk averse' than workers. If we replace the 'strong risk neutrality' assumption with the weaker 'less risk-averse' condition, the strict wage rigidity result does not hold. It is still the case, however, that some of the risk would be shifted to firms and that the implicit contract wage would vary less with the state of nature than under competitive spot market exchange.

With respect to the second result, the issue is not so much its dependence on the assumptions, but its incomplete status. With risk-neutral firms, efficient risk sharing really requires that all the risk, including the employment risk, be shifted onto firms. Thus firms should insure workers against unemployment as well by providing unemployment compensation to workers who are laid off. It is a relatively straightforward task to extend the model to confirm that this is indeed the implication of the theory. Efficient contracts should be of the form $\Delta = (w, \rho, z)$, where z is the amount of unemployment compensation. The precise characterization of the optimal contract is now very sensitive to the choice of workers' utility function. If we use the additive form that we have used so far we obtain the result that z should be such that the workers' utility is independent of their employment status. That is, the value of leisure plus the unemployment compensation is equal to the value of the wage. Note that this does not mean that the income is the same in all states – income is clearly lower when unemployed because of the leisure that would be enjoyed at the same time. The nature of the unemployment is, however, the same as before. It is *ex ante* voluntary and, in principle at least, involuntary *ex post*, but the case for labelling this unemployment involuntary is nevertheless much weaker. For the sake of completeness we should point out that this particular result does not hold for more general utility functions. Unlikely, if not absurd, results, such as employed workers being worse off than unemployed workers, are also possible.

The overemployment result (iii) hinges, as we saw above, on a disparity between the private and social cost of leisure due to the risk premium built into the wage in a contract with employment risk. When the firm provides unemployment compensation, of the form just discussed, this risk premium is no longer there and with it the overemployment result also disappears.

What this discussion reveals is that attempts to summarize the implications of implicit contract theory very quickly run into problems. Having obtained three basic results we find that two of these depend rather crucially on whether firms provide unemployment compensation or not. Since this is obviously an important issue we really should delve a bit further into this matter, but in doing so the plot becomes a good deal more complicated. To bring the matter to a conclusion we have to exclude unemployment compensation from consideration. There are a number of reasons why we might do so even though in theory it would be optimal for firms to provide this. As a matter of fact most workers do not rely on firm-provided compensation when unemployed. This is true even in countries (such as the USA) where unemployment compensation is provided by funds financed by employer contributions. It is even more true in a country like Australia where unemployment benefits are financed by general tax revenue. However, this fact is not a reason, but begs the question, why not? The most convincing reason is probably that the enforcement problem of the implicit contract would be particularly troublesome if it were to include unemployment compensation. This is most transparent if we recognize that workers are most probably heterogeneous with respect to their valuation of leisure. The unemployment compensation that would make the average worker indifferent between working and being unemployed could be extremely attractive to those who value leisure highly.

When we do exclude unemployment compensation the three results summarized above still stand. However, rather than regarding these as being the results of implicit contract theory they are better seen as being typical of the results that have emerged from what is now a vast literature. That is to say, as we vary the assumptions of the model to include unemployment compensation, variable hours of work, different utility functions for workers and firms, to name but a few, the specific results will differ but the broad thrust remains.

3 Enforcement of implicit contracts

Since we do not observe implicit contracts, if they do exist these risk-sharing implicit contracts must also be implicit (understood), as opposed to explicit (written), contracts. This means that they cannot be enforced by a third party, such as a court. In the development of the implicit contract model we simply assumed that contracts could be enforced, although, on several occasions, we have hinted that this is a weak point in the theory. To see what the problem is, suppose that a worker can always quit their job and get another job at the spot market wage. Likewise, a firm can always sack its workers and replace them with new workers at the spot market wage. If there is nothing to preclude this happening, we would expect workers to quit an implicit contract job whenever the spot market wage was higher. Similarly, firms would replace their contract workers with cheaper workers from the spot market whenever the spot market wage was lower then the contract wage. This line of reasoning suggests that the only enforceable contract is one in which the contract wage is equal to the spot market wage! However, there are two principal ways in which to avoid this implication.

The first is to argue that mobility is costly both to workers and the firm. Thus a worker, in deciding whether to quit their job in response to a higher spot market wage, would compare the discounted value of the wage differential with the cost of mobility. If this cost is high, workers would only quit if the spot market wage were much higher than the contract wage. The same consideration also explains why a firm would not replace its contract workers with cheaper workers from the spot market. However, a limitation of the mobility cost argument is that it does not explain why a firm would not lay off workers if the value of their marginal product dropped below their wage.

Another line of reasoning is to take a longer-term perspective on the issue. Instead of conceiving of a single period for which an implicit contract is entered into, we now imagine that both parties enter into a succession of contracts with each other or with others. In this setting, it is reasonable to suggest that somebody who has breached a contract in the past will find it more difficult to find a partner, workers or firms, with which to trade in the future. That is to say that reputation is likely to matter. Opportunistic behaviour, reneging on an implicit contract, may well be optimal in a one-period setting, but if this behaviour affects future opportunities, this is not necessarily the case in a multi-period setting. If the future looms large (i.e. if future opportunities are not heavily discounted), it is possible that concerns about reputation can enforce implicit contracts. The reader is also referred back to the arguments about skill specificity, outlined in Chapter 19.

4 Asymmetric information

Although the basic implicit contract model provides an explanation for involuntary unemployment, there have been several concerns. One is the paradoxical overemployment result – that unemployment of the implicit contract type is accompanied by a larger volume of employment than would be the case under spot market exchange. This is viewed as being somewhat at odds with reality – most would have thought that the level of unemployment during recessions is higher than would occur in a Walrasian equilibrium. A natural response to this and other concerns has been to modify the informational structure of the basic implicit contract model. It is well known that predictions from models of this type are very sensitive to the precise form of the informational structure, and it is highly plausible that the two sides to an employment contract are in possession of private information, which is not known to the other side. The firm, for example, can be expected to know much more about the product market conditions than the workers do.

The literature on implicit contracts with asymmetric information has taken several routes. One has been to investigate the feasibility of contracts contingent on the state of nature even though only one party, the firm, observes it. A central issue then becomes whether the firm can be relied on to tell the truth. It is natural to suspect that this is unlikely. Surely a firm would tell its workers that times are bad, even if they are not, in the hope of getting away with paying them less. However, matters are not quite as simple as this would suggest. In more complex settings than our basic model it is not necessarily the case that a firm would lie – it would tell the truth if, in doing so, its profits are at least as high as they would have been had it reported any other state of nature. This means that the truth-telling requirement does not rule out contracts contingent on the state of nature – the requirement is only an additional constraint on the range of feasible contracts.

Another approach has been to make the contract contingent on a quantity that is observable to both parties. This modelling approach has several parallels in other types of contract models as we shall see in Chapter 21. In the context of implicit contract theory, the most obvious quantity is the level of employment. Thus we consider contracts of the form $\Delta = \Delta(w(E))$, where $w = w(E)$, the wage to be paid in each state of nature, is a function of the level of employment in that state. The idea is of course that the level of employment is correlated with the state of nature – when times are good employment is high and when times are bad employment is low. The level of employment is, in other words, a proxy indicator of the state of nature that is observable to both parties. In contrast to the previous type of contract, now the firm is assumed to be free to choose its profit-maximizing level of employment in each state of nature (i.e. the firm has no commitment to employing some proportion of its workforce in each state).

The basic model we have used so far, with two states of nature and risk-neutral firms, is too simple for analysing the implications of asymmetric information. With only two states of nature, there is a one-to-one correspondence between employment and the state of nature – the workers can infer the exact state of nature from the firm's choice of employment. Thus, the asymmetry is effectively removed. The full implications of asymmetric information can only be seen in a more general model, in which the state of nature is a continuous random variable and firms are less risk averse (but not necessarily risk neutral). Such models are, however, technically very complex and we can only provide an intuitive explanation of the principal results.

In Oswald's (1986) model the intuitive explanation rests on the result that the wage in an optimal contract is an increasing function of employment. When the firm is risk averse, but less risk averse than the workers, some of the risk will be carried by the workers in the form of a variable wage. In good times, when the product price is high, employment and wages would also be high. In bad times the converse applies. The key feature of such a contract is that the contract would specify a higher wage when employment is higher. This feature is also present in the standard monopsony model. The monopsonistic firm that hires more labour has to pay a higher wage. This translates into a marginal cost of labour higher than the wage and when equated to the value of the marginal product of labour, to a lower level of employment than in the competitive case. The employment contingent implicit contract has the same implication. Because the contract wage is higher the higher is the level of employment, it becomes optimal for the firm to employ less labour than it would have done under spot market exchange. Thus, the overemployment result of the basic model with a state contingent contract is reversed and we get underemployment instead.

To summarize the above it is useful to contrast the intuitive explanations for the overemployment and underemployment results, respectively. The overemployment result is really a consequence of a missing insurance market (firms providing unemployment compensation). The workers, not being able to avoid the utility loss if they are laid off, seek compensation for this in two ways. First, by requiring a higher wage when they are employed, and second, by ensuring that the firm hires more workers than it would on grounds on technical efficiency alone. This reduces the risk of unemployment against which complete insurance is not possible. With asymmetric information the state contingent contract is not possible, but a second-best solution is to tie pay to the number of jobs. This is observable by both parties and contains some information about the firm's success in the product market (the state of nature). However, in doing so, the firm will face a wage function which is increasing in employment. It responds to this by hiring fewer workers than it otherwise would have done. Although the outcomes differ – in the first case there is overemployment and in the second underemployment – the cause is similar. Both outcomes are a consequence of a restriction on the range of feasible contracts.

5 Critique and empirical evidence

The relevance of economic theories is ultimately assessed by reference to empirical evidence. In the case of implicit contract theory, discussions about its validity have in the main been concerned with how convincing the explanation of wage rigidity and unemployment really is. This is because the empirical facts are not themselves at issue, but there are a large number of competing explanations. There are, however, some more direct tests of the theory's predictions and we will take up one example.

With respect to the wage rigidity result, the main criticism has been that it is nominal rather than real wage rigidity that has to be accounted for. The implicit contract theory predicts a state invariant real wage. But it is nominal wage rigidity, not real wage rigidity, which is thought to be the central issue in macroeconomics. An aggregate disturbance may make the existing level of real wages untenable, but if nominal wages are rigid the real wage adjustment has to await a rising price level. What has to be explained is why employment contracts fail to set wages as functions of publicly available information, such as an adverse supply shock, but the implicit contract theory does not address this issue.

It has also been argued that the implicit contract explanation for unemployment is unconvincing for a number of reasons (Azariadis and Stiglitz, 1988; Arnott *et al.*, 1988). Why, for example, should reductions in demand lead to lay-offs rather than reduced hours? In the standard model this issue is eschewed by the assumption that workers supply a unit of labour. The standard model is also very restrictive by modelling the contract between a group of N workers and a single firm/industry, but the interaction of these two parties with the rest of the labour market is not explicitly considered. As a consequence, laid-off workers are assumed to become unemployed (i.e. to be completely immobile). This is evidently at variance with observed facts. Although mobility may be costly, interfirm mobility is a very prominent feature of almost every labour market.

While opinions about the relevance of implicit contract theory abound there are very few direct tests of the theory. A notable exception, which touches on the mobility issue, is reported by Beadry and DiNardo (1991). If spot market contracting was the norm we would expect that the current labour market conditions would exert the greatest influence on individual wages – that is, the current unemployment rate should influence a person's wage. Past unemployment rates, however, should not have any impact. In contrast, the implicit contract model would predict that the conditions at the time a contract was entered into would influence the wage while the current conditions should have no influence. But this strict version of implicit contract model only applies to a situation of costly mobility. If the cost of job mobility is low the implicit contract wage would have to be adjusted upwards in tight labour market conditions to prevent workers from quitting – this is, the enforcement problem we have previously alluded to. Thus when workers are mobile, the prediction is that the wage would be correlated with the best labour market conditions since a worker was hired. Using individual panel data, Beadry and DiNardo found that an implicit contract model with costless mobility described the wage determination better than either a spot market approach or an implicit contract model with costly mobility. That is, current wages were found to be negatively correlated with the lowest unemployment rate since workers began a job, and once this effect was controlled for the contemporaneous unemployment rate had no significant effect on wages. The effect of the lowest unemployment rate was quite large – a percentage point increase in the lowest unemployment rate was associated with a drop in entry-level contract wages of between 3 and 7 per cent.

6 Summary

The major innovation of implicit contract theory was to view the employment contract as an instrument for the long-term exchange of labour services. Based on the assumption that workers are more risk averse than firms, the theory shows that, in an efficient contract, the firm will absorb most of the risk and pay workers a wage which insures them from fluctuations in their marginal product.

Implicit contract theory views the firm as consisting of three departments. There is a production department which purchases labour services and credits each workers with the value of their marginal product; an insurance department which sells insurance policies and, depending on the state of nature, either debits or credits the worker with an insurance indemnity; and an accounting department which pays each worker a wage net of the indemnity. In good times, workers receives less than the value of their marginal product, and in bad times more. However, in bad times the workers may be laid off. Whether they then receive anything or not depends on whether unemployment compensation is incorporated in the implicit contract. In principle it should be but, at the same time, there are several reasons why it would not be.

The basic implicit contract model, which excludes unemployment compensation, yields three principal results. First, the (real) wage is rigid or, more precisely, invariant with respect to the state of nature. Second, an optimal contract may result in involuntary unemployment. Third, the level of employment is higher than under spot market contracting. Unfortunately, however, as we have shown, these predictions are very sensitive to the particular specification of the implicit contract model. This sensitivity to the precise assumptions has resulted in a large literature which explores the consequences of different specifications.

The primary motive for the development of implicit contract theory was the twin stylized facts of rigid wages and involuntary unemployment. Although the theory provides an explanation for both of these facts, many have argued that the explanations are lacking. The important wage rigidity result refers to real wages, but it is nominal wage rigidity which seems to be at the heart of the macroeconomic problem of unemployment. Additionally, involuntary unemployment is only obtained through the restrictive assumptions of no variations in hours worked and costly mobility.

Notwithstanding these flaws, implicit contract theory constitutes an important theoretical development. It was the first attempt to incorporate the long-term nature of exchange of labour services into a formal model. Applied labour economists have long been conscious of the fact that the labour market is different from other markets. In Chapter 19 we found that the long-term nature of the employment relationship provided a strong reason why custom and habit would have a large influence on the pricing and allocation of labour. The same feature is also central to several other analyses of labour markets. Another important idea of implicit contract theory is that the employment contract is also a risk-sharing instrument. This strand of thought is taken up in the following chapter where we look at how labour contracts mediate between incentives and risk.

References

Arnott, R., A. Hosios and T. Stiglitz (1983). 'Implicit Contracts, Labour Mobility and Unemployment'. *American Economic Review*, 78, 973–991.

Azariadis, C. (1975). 'Implicit Contracts and Underemployment Equilibria'. *Journal of Political Economy*, 83, 1183–1202.

Azariadis, C. (1981). 'Implicit Contracts and Related Topics: A Survey'. In Z. Hornstein, T. Grice and A. Webb (eds) *The Economics of the Labour Market*, London: HMSO.

Azariadis, C. and J.E. Stiglitz (1988). 'Implicit Contracts and Fixed Price Equilibria'. *Quarterly Journal of Economics*. Supplement.

Baily, M.N. (1974). 'Wages and Unemployment Under Uncertain Demand'. *Review of Economic Studies*, 41, 37–50.

Beadry, P. and J. DiNardo (1991). 'The Effects of Implicit Contracts on the Movement of Wages Over the Business Cycle: Evidence from Micro Data'. *Journal of Political Economy*, 99, 665–688.

Gordon, D. (1974). 'A Neoclassical Theory of Keynesian Unemployment'. *Economic Inquiry*, 12, 431–459.

Gordon, D. (1990). 'Who Bosses Whom? The Intensity of Supervision and the Discipline of Labour'. *American Economic Review*, 80, 28–32.

Hart, O.D. and B. Holmstrom (1986). 'The Theory of Contracts'. In T. Bewley (ed.) *Advances in Economic Theory*. Cambridge: Cambridge University Press.

Manning, A. (1990). 'Implicit Contract Theory'. In D. Sapsford and Z. Tzannatos (eds) *Current Issues in Labour Economics*. London: Macmillan.

Okun, A. (1981). *Prices and Quantities: A Macroeconomic Analysis*. Oxford: Basil Blackwell.

Oswald, A. (1986). 'Unemployment Insurance and Labour Contracts under Asymmetric Information: Theory and Facts'. *American Economic Review*, 76, 365–377.

Rosen, S. (1985). 'Implicit Contracts: A Survey'. *Journal of Economic Literature*, 23, 1144–1175.

CHAPTER 21

Incentives in labour contracts

Principal–agent models, pay systems and profit sharing

1 Introduction – the incentive problem

In the theory of labour demand and supply, firms demand person hours and workers supply hours of work. Labour is measured in units of time. Marx called this labour power. However, what employers really want is labour, the actual physical or mental effort that workers can provide. In modern jargon we would call this labour services. Despite the fact that it is labour services that employers want, the normal *modus operandi* is that workers are generally hired and paid for the time they give up to attend work. It is usually understood, but seldom explicitly expressed, that the workers are to provide a certain amount of labour services to their employer. The reason for the vagueness about the precise amount is that it is intrinsically difficult to be specific about the exact amount and nature of these services. Thus, the normal employment contract is incomplete on a crucial issue and the workers retain some discretion about what and how much they will supply.

From a theoretical perspective this incompleteness seems unsatisfactory. What ensures that workers perform the labour services they are paid for instead of just whittling the hours away? As outlined, the normal employment contract appears to have poor incentive properties. Should not employment contracts incorporate explicit financial incentives to ensure that workers do what they are expected to?

The fact that the majority of workers are engaged and paid according to the time they attend work does not necessarily mean that the normal employment contract is inefficient. There are a number of reasons for this. First, time may be a very good proxy for the amount and nature of the labour services delivered. Second, the threat of dismissal should ensure that the performance of a worker does not fall too far below an acceptable level. Third, and more importantly, a competitive market provides numerous implicit incentives for workers to perform their jobs well even in the absence of explicit monetary inducements. Most of these incentives can be seen as deferred forms of pay, which take the form of assignments to better jobs, promotion, training and career development or better jobs outside the present firm. These deferred rewards can be very substantial. The message boy can rise through the ranks to become the chief executive officer of a major international organization. Some would argue that the implicit rewards are also sufficient. Theoretical work, however, does not support this view, but whether or not implicit rewards are sufficient is ultimately an empirical matter.

Most of the economic analysis of the incentive issue has taken place within the principal–agent paradigm. This framework was first used to analyse the incentive for managers to act in the shareholders' interest. The framework is quite general, however, and is just as appropriate for analysing incentives faced by the workforce as a whole. In this chapter the principal is the employer who engages an agent or worker to provide a certain task. The root of the problem is the partially conflicting objectives of the two parties. The employer/principal's objective is to maximize the return net of payment to the worker/agent, while the agent's objective is to maximize their own utility. This utility is assumed increasing in the wage paid and decreasing in the amount of effort that the agent supplies.

In the case of perfect information the effective resolution of the principal–agent problem is straightforward. Figure 21.1 depicts the agent's indifference curves in the wage-effort space. They have a positive slope reflecting that effort is a 'bad' – everything else being equal, the agent would prefer less rather than more effort. They are also convex to the origin on the reasonable assumption that the marginal rate of substitution of effort for the wage is increasing in effort. If effort was contractible (i.e. observable by both parties) the firm would offer the worker a contract which is at least as good as the best alternative. If the best of the alternatives yields a utility of u_0, any wage–effort pair on the u_0 curve would be acceptable. From amongst all the possibilities the firm would, of course, select the contract that gives the highest profit, and given a profit function π_0 we find that the optimal contract would provide the worker with a wage of w^* on the condition that the worker supplies e^* of effort.

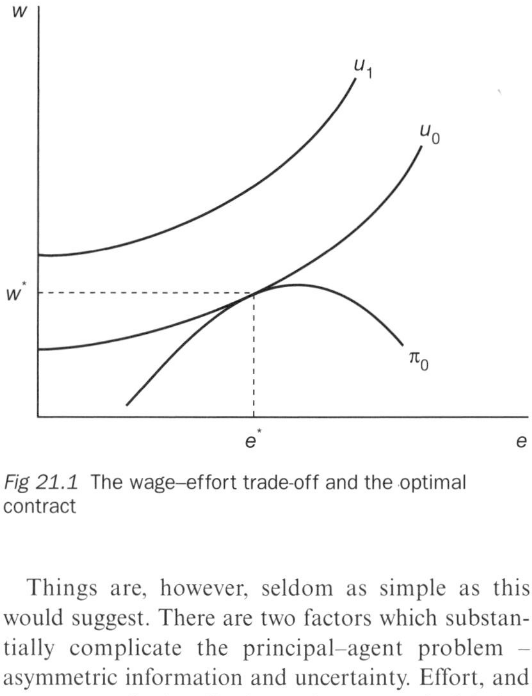

Fig 21.1 The wage–effort trade-off and the optimal contract

Things are, however, seldom as simple as this would suggest. There are two factors which substantially complicate the principal–agent problem – asymmetric information and uncertainty. Effort, and more generally the effective performance of a job, is a nebulous concept. A worker is likely to possess private information about how much effort they exert which is not readily observed by the employer. Are those long telephone conversations really with clients or just a social chat? If it is difficult to tell, effort is non-contractible – the employer can never be sure whether the amount contracted has been delivered. An alternative would be to make pay contingent on the output produced by a worker. In a deterministic world this would entail few problems, but, in general, there are factors outside the control of an individual worker which are likely to affect the output produced and thus the pay. Formally this would be modelled by making output a stochastic variable (i.e. being subject to uncertainty). When the pay is related to a stochastic variable the worker would have to carry some of the risk. As we found in Chapter 20, it might be better for the presumed risk-neutral employer to carry this risk, but then it is difficult to see how employment contracts could contain explicit financial incentives. It is this conflict which is at the heart of the principal-agent problem – how employment contracts should be structured so that there are incentives to perform well, but without burdening the workers with too much of the risk.

In what follows we take up three slightly different principal–agent models. We begin by showing that asymmetric information in itself entails few problems for efficient contracting. This is followed by the standard principal–agent model which, in addition to asymmetric information, incorporates uncertainty. The third model shows how monitoring can improve a principal–agent contract.

2 Model 1 – asymmetric information and certainty

Asymmetric information is not much of a problem in a deterministic world providing that the worker's output is readily observed. Instead of linking pay to effort the obvious alternative is to make pay contingent on output. But this is not as simple as it may seem at first sight. As an introduction to how incentive contracts are modelled, it is useful to spell out why this is not so. In the absence of any incentive issues a firm would offer a worker the lowest acceptable wage. When pay is related to output, however, the firm has to pick a function $w(Q)$ rather than a single number. This makes the problem rather intractable both in theory and in practice. There is no limit to the number of ways in which the wage can be related to output; for any wage function (form of the incentive scheme) that we choose we can never be certain that there is not an alternative function that would be more profitable. In the literature it is common therefore to restrict the firm's alternatives to linear and/or threshold contracts.

A linear contract means that the wage is a linear function of output, that is

$$w(Q) = \alpha + \beta Q \tag{1}$$

while a threshold contract is of the form

$$w(Q) = \begin{cases} \alpha \text{ if } Q < \bar{Q} \\ \beta \text{ if } Q \geq \bar{Q} \end{cases} \quad (2)$$

where $\alpha < \beta$. That is, the higher wage, β, is conditional on output exceeding a certain level $\bar{Q}$. In other words, α is the 'fixed' component of pay and $\beta - \alpha$ (corresponding to βQ in equation (1)) is the 'incentive' element.

In the first instance we restrict our attention to a linear contract, and, without loss of generality, assume that $\alpha = 0$. The firm's problem is to maximize profits (π), which, given that $w = \beta Q$ and $Q = Q(e)$, can be written as

$$\pi = (1 - \beta)Q(e) \quad (3)$$

subject to the constraint that the worker's utility is at least equal to the reservation level u_0, that is

$$u(e,w) \geq u_0 \quad (4)$$

where $w = \beta Q(e)$. To solve this we make use of the fact that the firm moves first; in other words, it decides on β and, then, the worker decides how much effort to supply. This sequential structure makes it possible to approach the problem in reverse. The firm simply works out the worker's optimal effort as a function of the piece rate β. The condition for the worker's optimum effort is $-u'_e/u'_w = \beta Q'_e$, where u_e denotes the partial differential of utility with respect to effort and, similarly, u_w is the corresponding partial differential with respect to the wage. The left hand side of this expression denotes the rate at which effort can be traded for wage while maintaining utility constant (as is obtained by totally differentiating equation (4) and setting $du_0 = 0$). The right hand side of the expression shows the change in the wage that the firm pays for a given change in effort. Knowing this result, the firm selects the lowest value of β which is acceptable to the worker.

Figure 21.2, which is a slight modification of Figure 21.1, depicts the situation. As before, the worker's indifference curves in the wage–effort space are denoted u_0 and u_1. The production function $Q(e)$ depicts the relationship between effort and output; a linear contract implies that the worker receives a fraction β of Q. For each value of β, the worker would choose the level of effort that balances the marginal disutility of effort with the marginal utility of a higher wage. The locus of these optima gives the worker's effort supply function $e_s = e_s(\beta)$. The firm

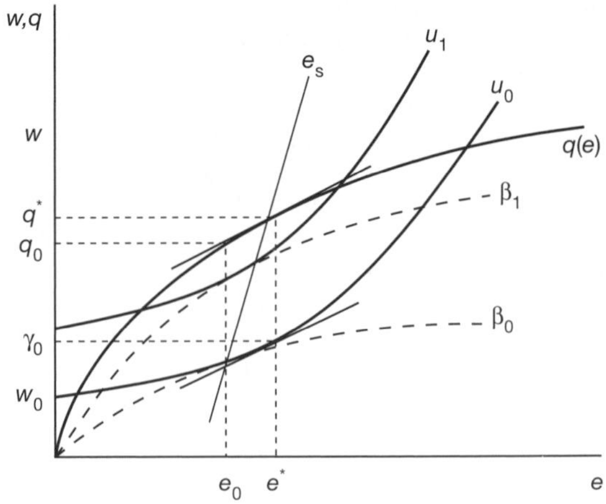

Fig 21.2 Optimal linear and threshold contracts.

then simply picks the value of β, β_0 say, at which e_s intersects u_0. The choice of β_0 would result in the worker providing e_0 of effort and result in Q_0 units of output.

Although β_0 is the optimal piece rate given a linear contract it is not a Pareto efficient contract. From the figure we can see that the horizontal difference between $Q(e)$ and u_0, the firm's profit, is not at its maximum. To the firm the value of additional effort is given by $Q'(e_0)$, but at the margin the cost of effort to the worker is smaller, $\beta Q'(e_0)$ to be precise. The linear contract leads the worker to 'undersupply' effort since they only receive a share of the additional output. A threshold contract can overcome this problem. Given that the worker must receive at least u_0, the level of effort that maximizes the firm's profit is the solution to $-u'_e/u'_w = Q'_e$, e^* say, the level of effort at which the slope of the production function and the worker's wage-effort function are equalized. The threshold contract would thus offer $w = \gamma_0$ if $Q \geq Q^* = Q(e^*)$ and $w < w_0$ if $Q < Q^*$.

To all intents and purposes the solution with a threshold contract is identical to that derived in Figure 21.1. Since there is a monotonic relationship between Q and e, e can be inferred from a knowledge of Q. Both the linear and threshold contract are so-called forcing 'contracts'. The firm by its choice of wage function can make the agent pick any particular effort. This ensures that, notwithstanding the non-observability of effort, an efficient contract can always be found.

3 Model 2 – asymmetric information and uncertainty: standard principal–agent model

3.1 Uncertainty and risk sharing

Under conditions of uncertainty asymmetric information has more profound implications. To see why, we consider the standard principal–agent model in which it is assumed that there is no unique relationship between Q and e. A given level of labour input can correspond to different levels of output depending on the particular contingency realized. Thus, $Q = Q(e,\theta)$, where θ is a random variable, the state of the world, which is assumed unobservable to the principal (it does not matter whether the agent observes θ). θ can represent a wide range of factors such as adverse weather, material supply problems, breakdowns, accidents, etc. The crucial point about this formulation is that the asymmetry is not resolved by both parties being able to observe Q. The principal, not knowing which state of the world has occurred (i.e. how output has been influenced by random factors), cannot infer the level of effort from a knowledge of Q alone.

The efficient risk-sharing condition now implies that the less risk-averse party, here the principal, should assume most of the risk. In the extreme case, a risk-neutral principal should assume all of the risk. The wage would be the same in all states of nature and cannot be made a function of the level of output. As already hinted, this would reduce the worker's incentive to supply effort. When the firm takes on the role of insurer, it cannot be sure of obtaining the labour it has contracted for. What we have here is a problem generic to most forms of insurance – the moral hazard problem. The provision of insurance affects the incentive of the insured to take (or not to take) actions which reduce the chance of the insured against an event (in this case low output) occurring. Having insured your car your incentive to avoid damage is reduced – not by very much perhaps, for example you would still have to carry the risk of serious bodily impairment yourself, but the incentive is still reduced. There is no first-best solution to the moral hazard problem. If the firm provides the insurance (a wage which is invariant with respect to output) there is an adverse effect on the incentive to supply effort. But if the wage is contingent on output the worker has to carry risk associated with variations in output over which the worker has only partial control. This is inefficient. The risk should be carried by the risk-neutral firm, not the risk-averse worker.

There is, then, an inevitable trade-off between the provision of incentives and the sharing of the risk. The challenge is to design a contract that strikes a balance between these two considerations. Such a contract should provide incentives for a worker to supply effort at the least cost in terms of inefficient risk sharing.

3.2 Efficient principal–agent contracts: a formal diagrammatic analysis

The formalization of the principal–agent model is apparently straightforward. The principal's problem is to offer a contract which maximizes expected profit,

$$\max_{w} E\{\Pi\,[Q(e,\theta) - w(Q(e,\theta))]\} \qquad (5)$$

subject to the constraint that the agent's optimal level of effort is given by

$$e = \arg\max E\{u[e, w(Q(e,\theta))]\} \qquad (6)$$

normally referred to as the 'incentive compatibility constraint'. Note that although the solution to the principal's problem depends on the agent's optimal choice of effort which in turn depends on the wage function chosen by the principal, the circularity breaks down because the agent moves second. This makes it possible to embed the agent's optimization problem as a constraint in the principal's objective function.

In addition, the principal's optimization is also subject to a 'participation constraint'; the utility of the offered contract must be at least as large as some alternative contract,

$$E\{u[e, w(Q(e,\theta))]\} \geq \bar{u} \qquad (7)$$

While setting up the problem is straightforward, the solution, at this level of generality, is remarkably complex. To make more rapid progress, we proceed by simplifying the structure so that the problem can be presented in diagrammatic form.

We assume that the output contingent wage can only assume two values w_1 or w_2 (where $w_1 > w_2$) according to whether output is Q_1 or Q_2 (where $Q_1 > Q_2$). If the worker exerts no effort ($e = 0$), the probability of both Q_1 and Q_2 occurring is one-half. However, if effort is exerted, the probability of Q_1, the higher output level, is greater than one-half (ρ>0.5) and the probability of Q_2 is correspondingly smaller. Given this structure we first look at how the worker's choice of the level of effort is determined with the aid of Figure 21.3.

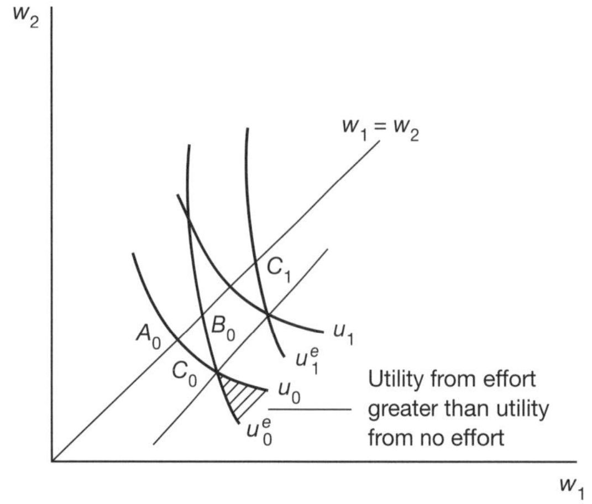

Fig 21.3 No effort and effort indifference curves.

The first, and preliminary, step is to see how the introduction of a choice of effort affects a worker's indifference map. If the worker exerts no effort their indifference curves are represented by u_0 and u_1, they are in other words the 'no effort' indifference curves. These indifference curves are symmetric around the certainty line, where the wages in the two states of nature are the same. At the intersection with the certainty line the slope is –1, reflecting that the two states are equally likely. Now if a worker were to exert effort the indifference map changes in two respects, owing to the disutility of effort and the change in the probability of State 1 (high output) occurring. The first effect means that the worker must generally receive a higher wage when they exert effort to be just as well off as when they choose not to exert any effort. If we restrict attention to situations where $w_1 = w_2$, we note that A_0 represents a w_1, w_2 pair which yields u_0 when the worker exerts no effort. To be just as well off exerting effort, the w_1,w_2 pair must lie further out than A_0, say at B_0. Thus, B_0 can be taken to be one point on the worker's 'with effort' indifference curve $u^e{}_0$ which gives the same level of utility as u_0. The second effect is the higher probability of State 1 occurring when the worker exerts effort. This makes the 'with effort' indifference curves steeper. Again the argument is most transparent if we restrict attention to where $w_1 = w_2$. At A_0 we argued that the slope of u_0 is –1 because the worker is indifferent between an infinitely small decrease in w_2 compensated for by an infinitely small increase in w_1. This is not the case if the probability of receiving w_1 is greater than the probability of receiving w_2. Thus if at B_0, reducing w_2 by Δw_2 is compensated for by a smaller increment in w_1, by $(1 - \rho)/\rho$, which is less than 1 for ρ greater than 0.5. Intuitively, the required compensation is smaller because of the larger probability of receiving w_1.

The net effect of these two factors is that the indifference curve which represents the same level of utility as u_0 when the worker exerts effort intersects u_0 from above at a point such as C_0 which is to the right of A_0.

To aid in the interpretation of the 'no effort' and 'with effort' indifference curves, consider a wage contract which falls in the shaded region where u_0 lies above u_0^e. Given such a contract the worker can obtain a higher utility by exerting effort. Thus, faced with such a contract we would predict that the worker would indeed choose to do so. The simplistic explanation is that w_1, the wage paid when output is high, is sufficiently large relative to w_2 to compensate the worker for the extra effort of trying to increase the chance of high output occurring. If, however, the contract falls in the region where u_0^e lies above u_0, the worker would choose not to exert any effort. In the diagram, C_0 is one point where the worker is indifferent between effort and no effort, and, by extension of the argument, C_1 is another such point. The locus of all such points of indifference is represented by the line drawn through C_0 and C_1, and this locus divides the w_1, w_2 space into two regions. For all contracts to the right and below the locus of indifference, the worker obtains a higher utility by exerting effort; for all contracts to the left and above, utility is higher when no effort is exerted.

Having determined how the worker will choose between no effort and effort as a function of the contract, the solution to this problem can now be embedded in the firm's optimization problem as the incentive compatibility constraint. Figure 21.4 extends the previous diagram by incorporating the firm's isoprofit curves – π_0 when the workers exerts no effort and π_0^e with effort – both representing the same level of profits. The with effort iso-profit curves are further out (when the worker exerts effort the firm can obtain the same level of profit by paying a

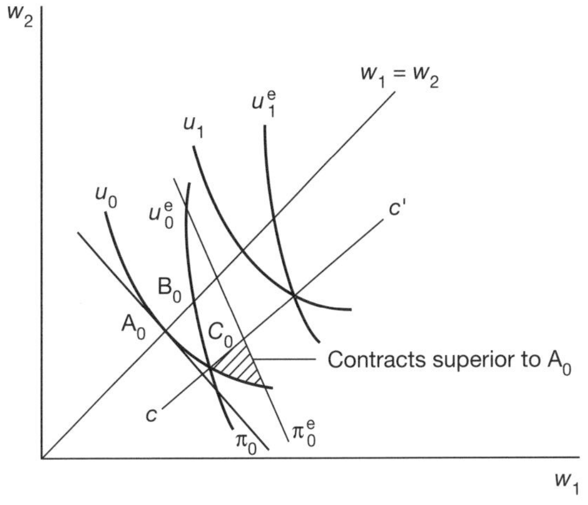

Fig 21.4 Efficient contracts in the principal–agent model.

higher wage) and steeper (to keep expected profits constant a given increase in w_1 must be compensated for by a larger decrease in w_2 because of the higher probability of having to pay w_1). Since the two iso-profit curves represent the same level of profits, any contract in the region where π_0^e is above π_0 yields a higher level of profit to the firm providing that the worker exerts effort. By the argument of the previous diagram, a contract to the right of the locus of indifference *c* – *c*' ensures that the worker will exert effort. If we adopt the convention that workers will exert effort if they are indifferent between doing so and exerting zero effort, the firm would maximize profit by offering a contract which lies as far down on the *c*–*c*' locus as the participation constraint permits. If, for example, u_0 or u_0^e represents the participation constraint, the firm would maximize profit by offering the contract represented by point C_0 in the diagram. If the participation constraint involves a higher level of utility to the worker the optimal contract would lie further out along *cc*'. The common set bounded by u_0, *c*–*c*' and π_0^e, the shaded are a in Figure 21.4, therefore contains the set of contracts which are Pareto superior to A_0. Of these contracts only those along the *cc*' boundary are efficient.

The locus of indifference is thus the core in the principal–agent model. It also represents the incentive compatibility constraint. Efficient contracts will be in the core; precisely where depends on the absolute level of wages that the firm needs to offer, or in the mathematical jargon, the participation constraint. Fixing the participation constraint, at u_0 say, gives a unique optimal contract at the intersection of u_0 and *cc*'.

4 Model 3 – the principal–agent model with monitoring

Since the combination of uncertainty and asymmetric information precludes fully efficient contracts we expect the parties to seek to ameliorate the effect of either or both of these problems. It is natural to approach this by modifying the very strict asymmetry of information in the basic principal–agent model. Even if we accept the idea that the worker is better informed than the employer about the effort that they put in, surely the employer is not totally ignorant about what a worker does. The employer can, and employers normally do, monitor what a worker does in order to provide at least some information about their level of effort.

To get an intuitive grasp of how monitoring can be used to improve the efficiency of a contract it is helpful first to recall what the basic problem is. When effort is not observable the incentive-compatible contract is made contingent on an observable indicator, output, which is subject to stochastic variations. Consequently, the worker is forced to carry some of the risk due to the stochastic variations in this variable.

To incorporate monitoring in the principal–agent model the usual approach is to assume that, while the worker's effort is still unobservable, the employer can observe an indicator, or signal, which is informative about the worker's effort. Informative means that the signal, *s*, and effort are correlated. This makes it possible to base the wage on both *Q* and *s*, in other words, the employer's decision function is now of the form $w(Q,s)$ – the wage to be paid as a function of the joint distribution of *Q* and *s*. Even if s is informative, there is no case for dropping the dependence on *Q*, since *Q*, like *s*, is also informative about effort.

Referring back to Figure 21.4 we found that the incentive compatibility constraint lies to the right of the certainty line. If the worker exerts effort the probability of State 1 occurring is increased and thus the chance of being paid w_1 rather than w_2. But a worker would only do so if w_1 was sufficiently large relative to w_2. How large depends, *ceteris paribus*, on how the worker's effort affects the probability of receiving w_1 rather than w_2. In the absence of monitoring this link between effort and pay can be quite weak if the state of nature is highly variable and/or has a large effect on output relative to effort. If that is the case, the incentive compatibility constraint will lie further out. When the link between effort and pay is weak the chance of actually receiving w_1 by exerting effort is small. This being the case, w_1 must be relatively large to w_2 to induce effort. In the presence of monitoring, and with the wage contingent on the signal s as well as Q, there will be a tighter relationship between effort and pay. Although the uncertainty remains, the state of nature will have a smaller influence on the worker's pay. Therefore, the wage differential $w_1 - w_2$ sufficient to induce effort is smaller. The intuition is that the incentive compatibility constraint will lie closer to the worker's certainty line, and the optimal contract will involve less of a departure from the efficient risk-sharing condition.

A slightly different version of this argument is to note that with monitoring the slope of u_0^e at B_0 is larger than in the no monitoring case. This follows from the probability of receiving w_1 when exerting effort is larger. Since u_0^e is steeper it must intersect u_0 to the left of C_0 and hence the incentive compatibility constraint is closer to the certainty line than in the no monitoring case.

5 Incentive pay in practice

The variety of different models can be confusing, but the need for diversity in modelling is readily apparent as soon as we seek to apply the insight derived from theoretical models to the real world. The real world is far more diverse in terms of the factors that matter to the choice of wage contracts. Sometimes individual output is observable, but in some cases only the output of a group can be observed. The influence of factors outside the control of one or a group of workers is also highly variable. In some cases the output produced is entirely within the control of an individual worker while in other cases the relationship between effort and output is mediated by a large number of other influences. Likewise, the observability of effort, the cost of monitoring and the informational value of monitoring differ from case to case. It is not surprising therefore that we observe a large variety of wage contracts in existence.

As discussed in the introduction, most employment contracts do not contain any explicit incentive component. Workers are paid by the hour, week or month depending on the nature of the job. However, explicit incentives, usually called incentive or performance pay, are not exactly unusual. To give an example, in 1991, 46 per cent of Australian workplaces had some form of performance-related pay. This figure does, however, overstate the importance of performance pay. Not all employees at a workplace are part of a scheme so the proportion of workers with performance pay was much smaller at 15–20 per cent. For these workers the performance component accounted for some 5–10 per cent of their total pay. Thus when the performance component is expressed as a percentage of the total wage bill the figure is only of the order of 1 per cent. These figures are typical of the situation in a number of other countries as well.

5.1 Individual incentive schemes

The piece rate is the oldest and most common form of individually based performance pay. Usually, the pay is contingent on the number of units produced, subject to a minimum quality standard being attained. This simple principle can become quite complicated when workers perform a variety of tasks and each task must be assigned its own rate or price. Piece rates are most common in manufacturing industry where the conditions for its applicability are more often satisfied – output is easily measured, it can be attributed to specific individuals and factors outside the control of a worker do not have a large impact. This latter consideration, the trade-off between the provision of incentives and efficient risk sharing, is nevertheless important in practice as well as in theory. The resolution to this trade-off usually precludes very simple piece rate schemes such as a linear contract. If, in such a contract, the fixed component α is large, in order to avoid shifting too much of the risk onto the worker, β has to be small to keep the total pay within a reasonable limit. However, the contract may then provide insufficient incentives. If the converse is the case, the worker may be carrying too much of the risk. This limitation of a linear contract, while still maintaining simplicity, is often dealt with by allowing the piece rate to come into effect when a certain base level of output is exceeded.

A piece rate system may be very effective in inducing a fast pace of work, but it fails to encourage the care and precision on which product quality depends. Additionally, the single-minded pursuit of higher earnings may lead to excessive usage of non-labour inputs such as material wastage and lack of maintenance and care of capital equipment. These drawbacks with individual piece rates really highlight that what a firm wants from its workers is not unidimensional effort, but a multitude of labour services. Even in the simplest setting it is not just speed that is required but also precision. More generally a firm wants its workers not just to produce certain things, but also to be active participants in the whole production process – to seek out and process information and to make decisions. In principle, it is possible to design a piece rate which tracks precisely the bundle of labour services that the firm seeks to obtain – so much for each unit, so much for each point on the quality index and so on. However, a metering system that seeks to keep track of every dimension of labour services would be hopelessly complicated.

Another common form of individually based performance pay is a commission on the value of sales. Commissions are almost universal for individuals who work independently as sales representatives, but much less common for sales assistants in retail outlets. The reason for this is not difficult to understand. In the former case, sales are highly dependent on individual performance and monitoring is virtually impossible. In the latter case individual sales assistants are part of a team of salespersons and monitoring is relatively easy.

5.2 Group incentive schemes

An incentive scheme based on the output of a group of workers does not directly address the problems associated with individual piece rates, but it does so indirectly. The major sources to improved efficiency in production are changes in the organization of work and cooperative efforts to uncover and eliminate impediments to productivity, including those which facilitate the introduction of new processes and techniques. Ultimately the attainment of higher productivity through these routes depends upon the behaviour of the workers and, thereby, the kind of labour services they supply. These labour services, which include information sharing, innovation, monitoring, coordination and decision making, tend to have more impact on group performance than on individual indicators. In other words, these labour services have external effects (i.e. external to the worker supplying them). As such, they would not show up however encompassing the individual performance indicators were. Thus, incentives to provide these services can only come from linking individual pay to an indicator of the performance of a group as a whole.

For these reasons there has been a marked shift from individual piece rates to group-based performance pay in a number of industrialized countries. In the UK group-based incentive schemes are often known as bonus systems, the bonus being based on the productivity of a small work group or the plant as a whole. One well-known company in which bonus payments were very important during the 1980s was Jaguar Cars. By the end of the 1980s the bonus payments, based on plant productivity and company profits, accounted for 20–25 per cent of a worker's pay. When the incentive component becomes such a large proportion of pay, the worker's ability to cope with a fall in the incentive component if productivity were to slump becomes limited. Under such circumstances the workers may be carrying too much of the risk. In practice this problem is often dealt with, as was the case in Jaguar, by consolidating some of the bonus payments in the basic wage. This limits the workers' 'downside risk', but, of course, if all the bonus payments have been consolidated then the scheme is effectively defunct. By the end of the 1980s, Jaguar Cars almost reached this situation and in the early 1990s management was looking at the possibility of replacing the existing bonus system with some other form of performance pay.

In the USA, group-based payment schemes are normally called gainsharing, reflecting both the management's attempt to sell such schemes to the workforce and their actual operation – the schemes usually take current productivity as the base and any productivity gain above this level is shared between the workers and the firm. Three of the most well-known gainsharing schemes are the Scanlon Plan, Rucker Plan and Improshare. Two are named after their originators, and their respective merits are hotly contested in a bid to get companies to adopt a particular plan. The Scanlon Plan bases bonus payments on changes in the ratio of total payroll costs to the sales value of production. The Rucker Plan is slightly different in that valued added is used in place of value of sales. Improshare is based on a more narrow labour productivity measure – the ratio of actual to 'standard hours', where the latter refers to the number of hours a task should have taken.

Notwithstanding the rising popularity of group-based schemes, their incentive property is diminished by the free rider problem. Free riding means that individual workers who shirk ride on the back of their more industrious team members. The individual free rider obtains all the utility gain from shirking. The cost, however, in terms of forgone output and pay for the team as a whole, is borne equally by all members of the team. From the perspective of individual optimization, the deal seems very favourable to the shirker. In a team of size n, the shirker would only carry a $1/n$ share of the cost. Looked at from this perspective it is apparent that the free rider problem increases with the size of the team. In practical terms this means that group-based schemes are likely to work best in smaller groups, and more so if group cohesion, team spirit, can be relied upon to keep free riding in check.

In theory there is a solution to the free rider problem through the use of a forcing contract (Holmstrom, 1982). In a team context the forcing contract would be contingent on the total (team) output and specify that a certain wage would be paid to team members providing the team output exceeds a certain level. If, however, team output falls short of this given level, the team members would receive nothing (or a very small wage). If the given output level is such that it can only be attained if nobody shirks, the free rider problem vanishes. Shirking by one member would result in that worker (and all other teams members) receiving nothing. The individual worker would, in other words, carry the whole cost of their action. This theoretical solution is of course very difficult to implement in practice. It would, for example, require very precise information about the effort–output relationship. Further problems arise if we introduce uncertainty in the situation just described. The workers would then carry most of the risk, which would violate the efficient risk-sharing condition.

The free rider problem has been the subject of much discussion in the economics literature. As far as one can judge, however, it is less of a problem for the design and the operation of compensation schemes in practice. It may be that team spirit, reciprocal monitoring by team members, social sanctions (i.e. peer-group pressure) and the emergence of norms are quite powerful checks on individual behaviour. In addition, the positive externalities of group performance schemes, the creation of a favourable organizational climate and the stimulus to cooperative behaviour may be sufficiently important to compensate for any free rider effects.

5.3 Profit sharing

Profit sharing usually means that a part of a firm's profit is distributed among the workers as an addition to their basic pay. As such it is really a type of group incentive system, but, because of the special character of profit sharing, it is normally regarded as being distinct from other group-based schemes. The distinguishing characteristic is that profits, in addition to being dependent on the performance of the workforce of the whole enterprise, also depend on the prices of other inputs, the efficiency with which other inputs are used and output prices. Since all these other factors are outside the direct control of most of the workforce, the link between the performance of the workers as a group and their pay becomes very tenuous. For that reason it is doubtful if profit sharing should be regarded as akin to individual or group-based incentive schemes. Profit sharing is more about trying to affect labour–management relations, to play down 'us and them' attitudes and foster a sense of participation and shared commitment. As such it should be seen as part of a broader trend of human resource management, the principal aim of which is to establish congruence between the attitudes and behaviour of workers and the firm's objectives. This is not just a one-way process, the management trying to make the workers think like capitalists, but also one in which the management transfers some of its decision-making prerogative to the workers. One key term that is used is 'empowerment', a mechanism for giving lower-level employees the information and authority to make decisions which traditionally were made at a higher level within the hierarchy. There is an obvious rationale for this. For profit sharing to have any incentive effects, workers must be able to exert some influence on the level of profit. Clearly, an individual worker's ability to do so depends on them being given the authority to use judgement and initiative. For these reasons, profit sharing has a closer link to employee share ownership than it has to other forms of incentive pay.

Profit sharing has also a wide appeal in Conservative political circles for similar reasons. It is seen as a way of lessening the traditional conflict of interest between capital and labour. Thus, in several countries, notably the USA and UK, profit-sharing arrangements have been treated very favourably for tax purposes. This has provided a strong impetus for adopting profit-sharing arrangements. In the early 1980s it was estimated that 450,000 US firms had some kind of profit sharing, equivalent to 25 per cent of enterprises in the private enterprise sector. Among the workers covered by such arrangements, the profit-sharing component amounted to around 9 or 10 per cent of total pay. In the UK profit sharing has been less common but received a considerable boost through tax concessions during the 1980s. In the late 1980s it was estimated that 20 per cent of the UK private sector workforce participated in a profit-sharing scheme (Braddon *et al.*, 1989).

6 The macroeconomics of profit sharing

Another dimension which received considerable interest during the 1980s was the macroeconomic properties of an economy in which profit sharing, or some other type of share system, was extensively used. The originator of this debate was Martin Weitzman who put forward a very persuasive argument in favour of profit sharing in his 1986 book *The Share Economy*. He drew attention to the pervasive unemployment in market economies where, with a conventional wage compensation system, wages are tied to a numeraire (e.g. money) whose value is unrelated to the conditions the firm experiences. This feature of the conventional compensation system means that firms which experience a fall in demand reduce output and employment. This conventional system Weitzman called a 'wage economy'. In contrast, in a 'share economy', workers' pay is tied to the firm's performance, automatically adjusting to changing circumstances. In such an economy, Weitzman argued, adverse shocks automatically lead to reduced pay, and firms respond by reducing prices while maintaining output and employment. The share economy would, in other words, be more recession resistant than a wage economy.

In the UK, Weitzman's ideas fell on very fertile ground. He was invited to address the House of Commons, a very unusual honour, and in 1986 his ideas were taken up in a Green Paper, in which profit sharing was put forward as a solution to the very severe unemployment at the time. To convey the essential property of a share firm we use a hypothetical example.

Suppose that initially the productivity of the GM workforce and the associated price of the cars produced mean that the average revenue per worker is \$36. GM pays its workers the competitive wage of \$24 per hour and, given this wage, it hires workers up to the point where the marginal revenue product of labour is \$24. Now suppose that GM and its workers agree on another type of contract. Instead of a fixed wage of \$24 per hour, the contract now specifies that every worker is paid a two-thirds share of GM's average revenue per worker. In other words, the revenue is split into two parts, two-thirds to the workers and one-third to the firm. Since the average revenue per worker is assumed to be \$36 the workers still receive \$24 per hour and, at first sight, it appears as if nothing has changed.

However, things have changed. With the old contract in place, GM would not want to hire another worker who would be willing to work for \$24 an hour. Assuming, as usual, diminishing marginal revenue product, an extra worker would earn GM less than they cost. Under the new contract, however, GM would be very happy to do so. The additional revenue from this extra worker is of course the same, something a bit less than \$24, but under the share contract GM's total labour costs would only increase by two-thirds of the additional revenue, that is by a bit less than \$16. Thus GM stands to clear a profit of \$8 by hiring an additional worker!

The microeconomics of this example is unsurprising. The example says that you can always find 'employment' as a door-to-door salesperson on commission only. The cost to the firm that employs you is always less than the money that you bring in. If you sell nothing you get nothing, and when you sell something the commission is set to ensure that there is a net gain to your employer.

To emphasize how obvious this is, under a share system a competitive firm's profit can be written as

$$\begin{aligned}\Pi &= pQ(E) - s(pQ(E)/E)E \\ &= (1 - s)pQ(E),\end{aligned} \tag{8}$$

where: p is the product price; E the number of workers; $Q(E)$ the production function; and s the share of the firm's revenue which accrues to the workers.

Maximizing with respect to E yields the first-order condition

$$(1 - s)pQ'(E) = 0 \tag{9}$$

or in more conventional terms,

$$(1 - s)\text{VMP} = 0 \tag{10}$$

which says that employment should be expanded up to the point where the value of the marginal product of labour is zero! This is intuitively fairly obvious, as total revenue carries on rising with the number of employees (as the price of the product is constant), at least up to the point where the marginal physical product of labour becomes zero. Given that the firm's absolute profit is effectively $(1 - s)$ times the total revenue, this carries on rising until total output peaks.

The simplicity of the microeconomics of profit sharing can be deceptive. The willingness of a profit-sharing firm to absorb more workers does have a drawback as far as the workers are concerned – as employment is expanded beyond the point where average revenue per worker is maximized, more workers means that the pay of existing workers falls. Thus the willingness of a profit-sharing firm to take on more labour does not mean that it will be able to do so. The condition given above should not be taken to mean that this is how a profit-sharing firm actually determines its profit-maximizing employment level. It simply means that if a firm could find an additional worker willing to work at the existing share parameter it should take this worker on. But to attract and keep workers the firm must in the long run offer a competitive compensation. Thus the firm cannot think itself free to determine E independently of s. In fact, in the long run, s is the decision variable which the firm sets to attain its profit-maximizing level of employment.

6.1 Long-run equilibrium

To see how a long-run equilibrium is attained in a share economy it is helpful to imagine that there are two processes at work.

Under conditions of perfect competition the law of one wage must hold. In a share economy, in which there is no wage as such, this law applies to the actual pay that a worker receives. We denote the pay by W, which, by the previous argument, depends both on the share parameter and the level of employment and, thus, $W = \mathbf{W}(s,E)$. In a share economy this condition can be met by any set of share parameters by the free movement of labour in pursuit of the highest pay. Workers will leave firms in which the pay is low in favour of firms in which it is high. This process will equalize the pay by the very fact that, when workers leave a firm with low pay, those that remain will find that their remuneration increases; and, when workers join firms with high pay, the remuneration in these firms will fall.

This process, while equalizing the pay for any set of share parameters, does not in itself generate a long-run equilibrium. The resulting allocation might not be efficient. Some firms may have more workers than is consistent with long-run profit maximization, and other firms too few, depending on whether their share parameters are too high or too low. Thus, there is another mechanism at work – a process through which the equilibrium values of the share parameters are attained. Firms try different values of s. If the value they set is too high they will find that they have too many workers (i.e. $\text{VMP} < \mathbf{W}(s,E)$). If that is the case they can increase profits by decreasing s, leading to a loss of workers and an increase in VMP. On the other hand, if $\text{VMP} > \mathbf{W}(s,E)$, they would decrease their share parameter. Thus, through a process of experimenting with different values of s and observing the effects we would expect firms to discover a value of s, s^* say, which results in a workforce E^* that maximizes profits. At those values of s and E, the condition $\text{VMP}_i = \mathbf{W}_i(s_i,E_i)$ holds where the subscript i denotes the ith firm. Since the mobility process guarantees that $W_i = W^*$ for all i, the value of the marginal product is the same in all firms and the allocation of labour is efficient.

The long-run equilibrium in a share economy is the same as for the same underlying wage economy. Firms hire labour up to the point where the value of marginal product is equated to the pay. It is only the process by which this long-run equilibrium is attained that is different from that of a conventional wage economy.

6.2 A diagrammatic comparison of the adjustment processes

Consider a two-sector model with a fixed inelastic labour supply as depicted in Figure 21.5. Sector 1 suffers an adverse demand shock which shifts the value of marginal product curve of the typical firm in the sector from $\text{VMP}_{1,0}$ to $\text{VMP}_{1,1}$, while Sector 2 is unaffected by the disturbance. In a wage economy this would lead to a fall in employment and output, but not so in a share economy. The firms in Sector 1 have no incentive to lay off any workers according to the previous argument. With all workers continuing in employment output is also maintained at its pre-shock level, but due to the lower output price the firm now receives, compensation per worker drops from w_0 to $w_{1,1}$.

This is the short-run effect. With the pre-shock share parameters being maintained there is now a gap between the level of compensation in the two sectors. Thus we expect workers to leave Sector 1 and seek employment in Sector 2, and the firm to adjust its share parameters so that the amount of labour it gets is at the profit-maximizing level. These two processes result in a new long-run equilibrium in which the level of compensation, w_1, is the same in the two sectors.

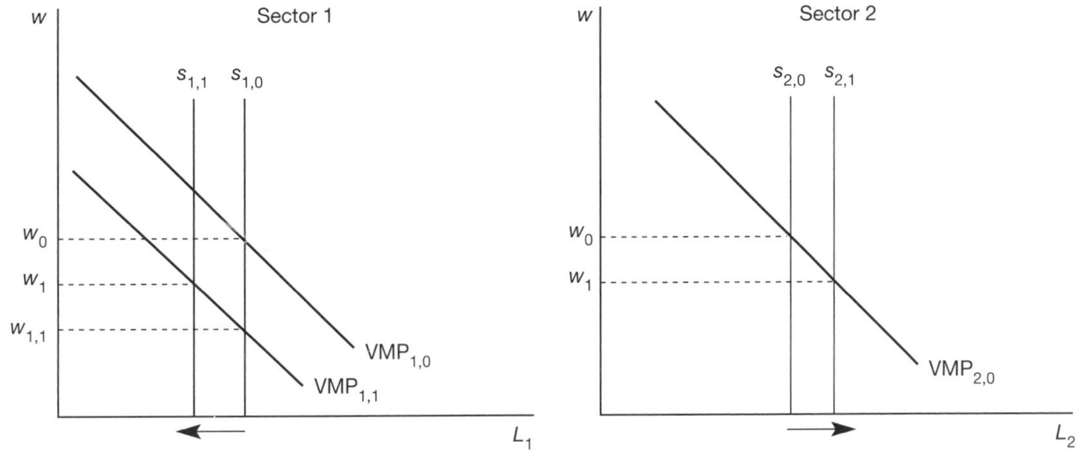

Fig 21.5 The adjustment of pay and employment in a two-sector share economy.

In contrast, in a wage economy there is no automatic tendency to absorb unemployed workers because, in the short run, the compensation is fixed in money wage terms. The workers who are laid off from Sector 1 have to queue for a job in Sector 2, but there is no tendency for the wage in the second sector to fall as a result of a queue of workers outside the gates. It is only through what Weitzman described as a 'complicated, roundabout and extremely problematical long term adjustment' which lowers real wages relative to product prices that leads a wage economy to absorb the unemployed labour. The fall in employment and output in Sector 1 leads to unemployment, which puts downward pressure on money wages, which eventually results in a lower real wage and the absorption of those who became unemployed as a result of the shock. The long-run equilibrium is the same in both types of economies, but the short-run adjustment processes are very different. In the share economy it is the values that adjust, while the quantities (employment and output) remain constant. In a wage economy the prices are kept at their equilibrium values, in the sense that workers are always paid the values of their marginal product, while the disequilibrium is reflected in quantities.

Weitzman offers a much more vivid description of the process: 'In a share economy firms cruise around on vacuum cleaners on wheels, searching in nooks and crannies for extra workers to suck in at existing compensation parameter values' (Weitzman, 1983, p. 777). It is, he argues, much more recession resistant than the wage economy.

6.3 Revenue versus profit sharing

So far we have assumed that it is the firm's gross revenue that is shared between the workers and the firm's owners. However, the properties of the share system remain essentially unchanged whether profits are shared or if the compensation consists of two parts, such as a fixed wage and a share of revenue or profit. To see this, suppose the total pay per worker is given by

$$W = W_g + s[(pQ - W_gE)/E] \qquad (11)$$

where W_g is the fixed, or guaranteed, component of pay and s is the workers' share of average profits per worker – here profit is simply revenue minus the cost of the fixed wage component.

Creating the profit function in the normal way, where $\Pi = pQ - WE$, and rearranging yields

$$\Pi = (1 - s)[pQ - W_gE] \qquad (12)$$

and the first-order condition, the more familiar expression

$$\text{VMP} = W_g \qquad (13)$$

That is to say, the firm would want to expand employment up to the level where the value of the marginal product is equal to the fixed wage component. This still leaves the firm 'labour hungry' in the short run. Since in long-run equilibrium VMP = $\mathbf{W}(W_g,s,E)$, it follows that VMP > W_g, provided that $W_g < \mathbf{W}(.)$, that is the guaranteed component is less than the total pay. Thus the firm would be willing to take on any worker who was prepared to accept employment at the prevailing **W**(.) contract, exactly as in the case for the revenue-sharing firm. The other properties also carry over. The profit-sharing firm would not lay off workers when hit by an adverse demand shock and would display the same employment stability over the business cycle as the revenue-sharing firm.

6.4 Can profit sharing really reduce unemployment?

The claimed advantages of profit sharing have been the subject of considerable scrutiny. In this section we take up three issues contested in the literature: whether a share contract is an efficient risk-sharing arrangement, the status of the excess demand for labour claim, and some empirical evidence about the claimed advantages of a share economy.

A clear weakness of the profit-sharing economy is that workers have to carry their share of the risk of a variable income. This increased exposure to risk is probably one of the reasons why profit-related pay is such a small component of the total in most countries. However, to gain the potential benefit of profit sharing, a pure share system is not required. As in the section above, a guaranteed wage plus a profit-sharing component is sufficient. Even such a system may entail inefficient risk sharing from an individual perspective, but then the argument is that the positive macroeconomic effects are external to individual agents. It has been argued, therefore, that a profit-sharing system should be subsidized by preferential tax treatment on the grounds that the positive macroeconomic externalities compensates for the inefficiency at the level of individual agents.

Another aspect of the share economy that has been the subject of critical scrutiny is the excess demand property. As explained above, in a long-run equilibrium a share firm can be said to display excess demand for labour in that it would be willing to take on additional workers at the existing share parameter. Nordhaus (1988) argues that this property cannot be reconciled with competitive theory, except under highly artificial circumstances. The result is obtained by ignoring the competitive constraint that a firm faces. If a firm's current pay is at the long-run competitive level, taking on an additional worker would result in pay falling below this level. If workers were perfectly mobile in the short run, no firm would want to hire an additional worker since this would result in all other workers leaving the firm. Of course, perfect mobility in the short run is unrealistic, but the excess demand property is difficult to rationalize even with other and more realistic assumptions about labour supply behaviour.

In response to this criticism, Weitzman (1988) retorts that the excess demand property is merely a heuristic device which is useful for thinking about how a share economy might work. Nothing substantive depends on this excess demand property. The key point is not the nature of the long-run equilibrium itself, but that small disturbances in the neighbourhood of a long-run equilibrium are less likely to lead to unemployment in a share economy than a wage economy.

At the empirical level, most of the debate about a share economy has revolved around the Japanese bonus system and the much lower unemployment experienced by Japan in comparison with other developed economies. It is common for workers in large Japanese firms to receive substantial bonus payments once or twice per year. These bonuses have the appearance of being related to the firm's profit and thus the Japanese economy could be said to be an actual example of a profit-sharing economy. From this observation it is tempting to argue that the low unemployment in Japan during the post-war period is evidence that a share system does indeed result in lower unemployment.

The first issue is whether the bonus system is really a form of profit sharing. The empirical evidence is less than compelling and most studies indicate a very weak effect of profits on bonuses (Peck, 1986; Nordhaus, 1986 and 1988; Wadhwani, 1986). The bonus payments are primarily deferred wages, with only a small part being profit related. Whether, in turn, the small profit-sharing component is responsible for the lower Japanese unemployment is more difficult to answer. International comparisons are fraught with problems, but most economists are sceptical of the view that there is a link between lower unemployment and the bonus system (Peck, 1986; Nordhaus, 1986; Wadhwani, 1986).

7 Summary

This chapter began with the observation that the typical employment contract is incomplete. This is important in that the precise amount and nature of labour services to be provided are seldom explicitly specified. Workers are hired and paid per hour, but they usually retain some discretion over precisely what they do. This raises the question of whether employment contracts can or should incorporate more explicit financial incentives.

Labour provides a very complex bundle of services but in the theoretical models this is subsumed in a unidimensional variable called effort. If effort were observable, that is with perfect information, the incentive problem has a very straightforward resolution. The firm would simply offer an effort contingent contract and, providing the firm knows the worker's wage effort trade-off and the effort–output relationship, such a contract would be efficient.

These conditions are, however, rarely met and the three principal–agent models taken up in this chapter show how the combined effect of asymmetric information and uncertainty complicate the contracting process. In the absence of uncertainty, a fully efficient contract contingent on output is possible in principle. However, under conditions of uncertainty there is an additional consideration. There are sources of variations in output which are not directly tied to variations in the input of labour services. Thus a given level of input can correspond to different levels of output depending on the particular contingency that is realized. In this setting the contract must not only provide incentives for the worker but also allocate the risk between the two parties. Thus, the challenge is to devise contracts which provide incentives for workers to provide labour services at the least cost in terms of inefficient risk sharing.

This is the issue dealt with in the standard principal–agent model. To maximize profit the principal selects a wage contract subject to two constraints – the incentive compatibility constraint and the participation constraint. The compatibility constraint arises out of the agent's objective to maximize their (rather than the principal's) utility. The participation constraint reflects the fact that the contract must offer the agent at least as much as can be obtained elsewhere. It is then shown that to satisfy the incentive compatibility constraint the agent must be made to carry at least some of the risk. Thus if, as is normally assumed to be the case, the agent is risk averse and the principal risk neutral, the best contract is less efficient than the optimal contract with perfect information. This inefficiency is, however, reduced when monitoring is possible.

The overview of the explicit incentive schemes used in practice shows that it is difficult to devise pay systems which provide strong incentives but at a low cost in terms of inefficient risk sharing. Individually based schemes such as piece rates can be a very effective incentive mechanism for certain types of labour services. However a number of conditions must be satisfied. The workers must have control of their own pace of work, it must be possible to attribute the output produced to individual workers and the influence of factors outside the control of the workers concerned must be small. As production systems have become more complex and interdependent these conditions are seldom satisfied. Thus there has been a shift to group-based incentive schemes in which the performance component of pay is dependent on the output of a group of workers or even the profit of the firm as a whole. The incentive properties of such schemes are likely to be weaker due to the free rider problem – an individual worker carries only a small part of the cost of their own shirking. On the other hand, this disadvantage may be offset by the positive externalities of group-based schemes.

Although profit sharing is one type of group-based incentive pay the primary motivation is usually not the explicit incentive properties, but a means of fostering participation and shared commitment. Profit sharing also has some rather interesting macroeconomic properties. Weitzman's model of the 'share economy' suggests that a situation in which some part of workers' income is directly dependent on the firm's profit is likely to be more recession resistant than the conventional wage economy. This is because share firms have no incentive to lay off workers in the face of an adverse demand shock. In a conventional wage economy, disequilibrium is reflected in quantities, in the sense that workers are laid off and unemployment ensues. In a share economy workers are kept on and the disequilibrium reflected in values, lower pay, rather than quantities. Whether a share economy would indeed work as predicted by Weitzman is still an open issue. There have been many critics, but there are also many economists who see merit in the idea.

CASE STUDY 1 Performance pay at Volvo

Volvo, the Swedish car manufacturer, has a number of plants in Sweden and elsewhere in Europe. The operations at one Swedish plant, in Kalmar, have attracted more interest than most others. Work at Kalmar began in 1974 and, at the time, represented a very radical development in

continues

CASE STUDY 1 continued

the way cars were assembled. Instead of the traditional assembly line, cars pass from one production group to the next, with each group responsible for the assembly of one major function. Each group is self-managed and enjoys considerable autonomy. This innovative method of production has become widely known, with numerous study visits to the plant by industrial engineers, managers, trade union delegations, study groups, academics, media and others from all over the world. Their impressions have been documented in an extensive literature.

Commensurate with this work organization, the pay system was changed in 1981 to include, as it turned out, a substantial performance component. Initially, only blue collar workers were included in the scheme, but since 1984 all employees have had a performance-related component in their pay. Considerable attention is paid to the measurement of performance. There are no less than seven factors that are taken into account. They are: (1) manual hours per car; (2) office hours per car; (3) waste of materials; (4) materials and tools usage; (5) additional materials required at quality inspection: (6) stock levels; and (7) quality. A standard has been derived for each factor. Improvements above standard are measured and translated into a monetary value that represents a saving in costs, of which 25 per cent is paid to employees.

The pay system has been credited with large productivity gains, of the order of 10 per cent per year following the introduction of the scheme. Likewise, it has led to large increases in pay, so much so that the pay at the plant was out of line with the local labour market conditions and elsewhere within the Volvo group.

The scheme is unusual in that so many factors are measured. The standard objection against this complexity is that it obscures the relationship between performance and pay. However, the view at the plant is that the complicated structure did not lead to any problems.

Other plants within the Volvo group which operate a more conventional assembly line system have simpler performance pay schemes. In the late 1980s a common structure for blue collar workers was a three-part bonus scheme: a production bonus payable on the achievement of yearly production targets, a quality bonus payable on the achievement of agreed quality standards, and a result bonus which is really a profit-sharing scheme. The first two are plant specific, while the other depends on the performance of the Volvo group as a whole. Taken together the three types of bonus payments amount to between 5 and 10 per cent of total pay.

For white collar workers a performance pay component, based on a range of productivity indicators and worth up to 3 per cent of basic pay, was introduced in 1984. White collar workers also participate in the profit-sharing scheme on the same conditions as blue collar workers. Interestingly, white collar workers have been less enthusiastic about performance-based pay and resisted management attempts to increase the share of the performance component in total pay.

References

Braddon, L. *et al.* (1989). *Peoples Capitalism: A Critical Analysis of Profit Sharing and Employee Share Ownership Schemes*. London: Routledge.

Holmstrom, B. (1982). 'Moral Hazard in Teams'. *Bell Journal of Economics*, 13, 324–340.

Nordhaus, W.D. (1986). 'Introduction of the Share Economy'. In W.D. Nordhaus and A. John (eds) *The Share Economy: A Symposium. Journal of Comparative Economics*, 10, 416–420.

Nordhaus, W.D. (1988). 'Can the Share Economy Conquer Stagflation?'. *Quarterly Journal of Economics*. 103, 201–217.

Peck, M.J. (1986). 'Is Japan Really a Share Economy?'. In W.D. Nordhaus and A. John (eds) *The Share Economy: A Symposium. Journal of Comparative Economics*, 10, 427–432.

Wadhwani, S. (1986). 'Profit-Sharing as a Cure for Unemployment: Some Doubts'. London School of Economics, Centre for Labour Economics, Discussion Paper. No. 253. *International Journal of Industrial Organisation*, 6, 59–68.

Weitzman, M. (1983). 'Some Macroeconomic Implications of Alternative Compensation Systems'. *Economic Journal*, 93, 763–783.

Weitzman, M. (1986). *The Share Economy: Conquering Stagflation*. Cambridge, MA: Cambridge University Press.

Weitzman, M. (1988). 'Comment on: Can the Share Economy Conquer Stagflation?'. *Quarterly Journal of Economics*. 103, 218–223.

CHAPTER 22 Efficiency wages

1 Introduction

The fundamental idea underlying the theory of efficiency wages is that firms may gain some benefit from paying their workers more than they need to (i.e. more than is required to secure a certain quantity of labour). Simply paying more can be seen as an alternative solution to the incentive problem which avoids contingent contracts. As is evident from the previous chapters, contingent contracts can be quite complicated and, if simpler contracts can do the trick, we would expect such contracts to be used. Furthermore, the informational requirement for contingent contracts may not be met, for example, where piece rates are not feasible or the cost of monitoring is very high. However, the merit of efficiency wage theory is not so much the simplicity of the contract or more realistic assumptions, but a coherent and convincing explanation for involuntary unemployment. It is this aspect of efficiency wage theory which has attracted most attention.

2 The basic story

According to the competitive paradigm, neoclassical firms pay workers a wage which clears the market for labour. These are two classical laws of the competitive equilibrium – the law of one price and the law of the market clearing price. No one passes up better terms on which to buy or sell. There cannot be any buyers who wish to buy more, even paying a higher price if necessary, yet are frustrated in their attempts to do so. Nor are there any sellers willing to sell more, even at a lower price, yet are constrained from doing so. As we know, this model runs into problems when faced with the fact that there are unemployed workers apparently willing to work at the existing or even a lower wage. It has no entirely satisfactory answer to the obvious questions: why don't the unemployed offer to work for less, and why don't firms lower the wages in the face of an excess supply of labour?

Before dealing directly with these questions, it is instructive to speculate about how the competitive model might actually work in the labour market. Firms and workers would contract at the market clearing wage with an explicit or implicit understanding that the employees provide a certain level of labour services in exchange for the wage. Both parties would then have to keep an eye on the other to ensure that the terms of the contract are adhered to. This is easy for the workers – as long as they are paid the contracted wage the firm has kept its side of the bargain – but not so easy for the firm. Firms would have to monitor the performance of the workers to ensure that they provide the contracted amount of labour services. If a worker is found not to do so, in the absence of penalties for breach of contract, the only punishment that the firm can impose is to dismiss the shirking worker, and we presume firms would do so as a warning to others.

This might work, but in a competitive equilibrium firms would have to exercise extreme vigilance. Recall that in the competitive equilibrium the market clears. This means that, in this stylized world, the worker who is fired can instantly get another job at the same wage. This being the case, the penalty from being found shirking is negligible so the firms would have to watch the workers' every move. Obviously, this extreme vigilance is costly and it may have other adverse effects. Workers naturally resent intensive monitoring and a vicious circle of low morale and ever more intensive monitoring might develop.

The clever firm might then reason that if it were to increase its wage it could cut down on these high costs of monitoring. By paying a higher wage than all other firms, the workers would now have something to lose if they were dismissed. There might be other benefits as well. Turnover costs may fall, not just because there would be fewer dismissals but also because voluntary turnover would fall, and, when the firm hires new workers, it may be able to be more selective about who it recruits. If all goes well the morale of the workers may also improve. With higher wages and less intrusive monitoring, employees should feel better about their situation and this may have positive effects on productivity. All in all, the higher wage might actually increase profit.

Now if one firm can calculate that it can increase its profit by paying a higher wage, then, in principle, so can all other firms. Thus, if one firm were to raise its wage so would all other firms. Each firm calculates that it can increase its profit by doing so, but does this still hold when they all do it? At first sight it would appear not to. The benefits of a higher wage derive from this wage being higher than the wage paid by other firms, so it would seem that each firm's attempt to gain an advantage is frustrated by other firms doing likewise. Worse still, paying a higher wage with no attendant benefits should mean that all firms find that their attempt to increase profits actually lowers profits! But this conclusion is premature. It ignores the employment effect of all firms paying a higher wage, as firms will hire fewer workers. At the same time the higher wage would bring forth a greater supply of labour, or at least not decrease the supply of labour. Therefore, as all firms raise their wages above the market clearing level that previously prevailed the overall supply of labour is going to exceed demand. The resulting unemployment does the same job that each firm expected its higher relative wage to do – to keep shirking under control. In the presence of unemployment, intensive monitoring is not necessary. Workers know that being caught shirking would mean joining the Marxian reserve army of the unemployed for a spell of uncertain duration. Sporadic monitoring would be sufficient to ensure that the risk of being dismissed outweighs the gain from taking advantage of a less intensive monitoring regime, and the firms might be able to pay the higher wages from the savings on monitoring costs.

The consequence of all this is that a competitive equilibrium may entail a wage above the market clearing level. This higher wage, the efficiency wage, arises because firms find it in their interest to pay more than they need to. Thus, efficiency wage theory questions the validity of the classical law of market clearing.

3 The Solow condition

The first modern statement of what we now call efficiency wage theory was made by Solow (1979). His objective was to show that there might be another cause of wage stickiness, in addition to the conventional reasons put forward by macroeconomists. In formalizing this efficiency reason, he showed that at the cost-minimizing wage the elasticity of effort with respect to the wage is unity, a condition which has since become known as the 'Solow condition'.

To derive the Solow condition we write the firm's profit function as

$$\Pi = pQ(eE) - wE \tag{1}$$

where effort $e = \mathbf{e}(w)$, is a function of the wage, w, and, to simplify matters, product price, p, is assumed competitively determined in the product market and, therefore, constant. Note that the production function is assumed to be multiplicative in effort and number of workers. This implies, for example, that if effort were to double the same output could be obtained from half as many workers. Matters are seldom this simple. It may be difficult, for example, for one worker by doubling their effort to operate two machines. The multiplicative form may, nevertheless, be an adequate approximation in most circumstances. In his derivation of the unit elasticity condition, Solow did not assume this multiplicative form, but showed that the production function must have this form for the optimal wage to be independent of output.

Differentiating with respect to E and w we obtain the two first-order conditions

$$pQ'_E(eE) = w/e \tag{2}$$

$$pQ'_w(eE) = 1/e'(w) \tag{3}$$

The first condition determines the optimal level of labour input. It has the usual 'value of marginal product equal to the wage' form, but is now stated in terms of efficiency units. Thus e times E is labour input measured in efficiency units and w/e is the cost of an efficiency unit of labour. The second condition gives the firm's optimal wage and is best understood with reference to Figure 22.1. This depicts what might be a typical effort–wage relationship. We have put the wage on the vertical axis so that the slope of

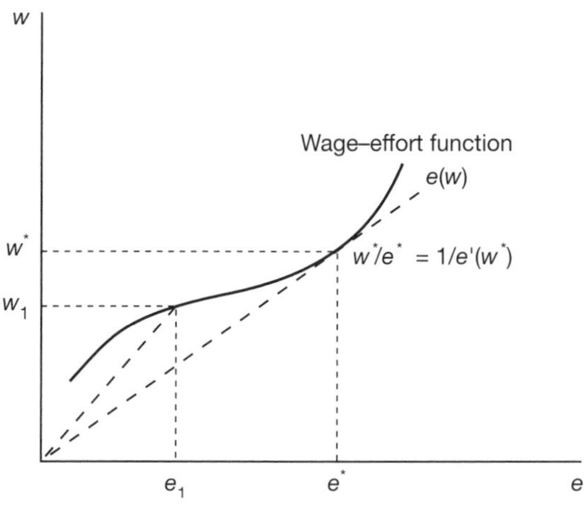

Fig 22.1 The Solow condition.

the curve is $1/e'(w)$ to facilitate the reference to the first-order conditions. The firm's problem is to choose a point on this curve, a particular wage which results in a certain level of effort. First consider the choice of w_1. This would result in a cost per efficiency unit of w_1/e_1 which is represented by the slope of a ray from the origin to the point on the curve. At that point, the effort–wage curve has a slope of $1/e'(w_1) < w_1/e_1$. Thus increasing the wage to w^* yields a relatively large increase in effort. At w^*, the ray from the origin to the curve attains its least slope and coincides with the slope of the wage–effort curve. The first fact means that w/e, the cost of an efficiency unit of labour, attains its minimum value at w^*, and, the second, that at that point $w/e = 1/e'(w)$. The geometry of finding the minimum cost per efficiency unit is identical to the problem of finding the minimum average cost on the total curve. This is precisely the result we obtain by combining the two first-order conditions. Bearing in mind what we have said about the nature of e and E, $Q'_E(\,) = Q'_w(\,)$, and combining (2) and (3), after rearranging, yields

$$(w/e)e'(w) = 1 \qquad (4)$$

In other words, the elasticity of effort with respect to the wage should be unity.

The implication of the unit elasticity result is that, at the optimal wage, a certain percentage change in the wage should lead to the same percentage change in effort. This makes sense. If the latter was greater, a higher wage could be more than recouped from the additional effort that it generates.

It is not, however, the unit elasticity which is the important result, but that the optimal wage depends only on the wage–effort relationship. Consider, for example, how a firm would respond to an increase in its product price, p. Since the optimal wage does not depend on p it would remain unchanged if p changed. Thus we get exactly the same result as in the standard model. The value of the marginal product curve (the left hand side of (2)) would shift out and intersect the (same) w/e at a higher value of E. The firm would simply employ more workers. It would not seek to obtain the additional labour input by inducing more effort from existing workers through a higher wage. If we let variations in p represent business cycle effects the implication is that firms would leave their wages the same whatever the level of output. A contraction in demand would be met by reducing output and laying off workers. Conversely, in a boom, firms would expand output and hire more workers, but they would not vary their wage offers as long as they encounter no constraints on the supply of labour. Thus the model provides an explanation for real wage rigidity over the business cycle. It also suggests that there may well be an unemployment equilibrium. If the efficiency wage is greater than the wage rate at which the labour market clears, firms are not going to lower their wages to take advantage of the excess supply.

The Solow model made no attempt to provide a detailed account why labour productivity should depend on the wage, although it indicated a few possibilities. However, during the 1980s the ideas were picked up and developed by a number of economists. In the process, the microeconomic rationale for the effort–wage relationship was developed more thoroughly. It is now common to classify the models that were proposed into four groups depending on the underlying rationale for the effort–wage relationship. The four types are the shirking model, the turnover model, the adverse selection model and other, including sociological, explanations. These four approaches are taken up in the following sections.

4 The shirking model

The shirking model of Shapiro and Stiglitz (1984) is the most well known and frequently cited efficiency wage model. The model assumes that there is a fixed supply of $\bar{E}$ identical workers whose utility functions can be represented by $u = w - e$. This form of the utility function implies risk neutrality and separability of wages and effort. As in a number of the previous models, we assume that the workers' choice is restricted to two levels of effort, $e = 0$, and some positive level, $e > 0$.

Workers who are employed are paid a wage of w. Those who choose $e > 0$ will always be employed at this wage. Those who shirk, choose $e = 0$, however, face a risk of being caught shirking in which case they will be fired. The probability, per unit of time, of this happening is q. When fired they join the ranks of the unemployed and receive unemployment benefit of b. But the shirkers do not remain unemployed for ever. Having become unemployed they are free to look for another job. The probability of finding another job depends on the state of the labour market – precisely how will be described later.

Because of the many simplifying assumptions the characterization of the workers' choice of effort is very straightforward. Workers who decide not to shirk are employed all the time at a utility $w - e$ per period. A worker who chooses a shirking strategy alternates between employment and unemployment. Suppose that the worker is employed for a fraction θ of the time and unemployed for the remainder, $1 - \theta$. The utility from shirking can then be expressed as a weighted average of the utility when employed and when unemployed.

According to the above arguments the utility of a non-shirker is

$$u^N = (w - e) \qquad (5)$$

while the shirker's utility is

$$u^S = \theta w + (1 - \theta)b \qquad (6)$$

The worker's optimization problem is to choose the strategy that yields the highest expected utility. This means that a worker will not shirk if and only if $u^N > u^S$, known as the 'no shirking condition'. Using (5) and (6) the no shirking condition can be written as

$$w > b + [1/(1 - \theta)]e \qquad (7)$$

The first term on the right hand side is the income that would be obtained from unemployment. Clearly the wage must be larger than that amount. It also has to compensate the non-shirker for the utility loss of exerting effort, which explains the second term on the right hand side. When the shirker is employed they are better off than the non-shirker, by e to be precise. For it to be profitable not to shirk then the difference between w and b must be large enough to make up for this fact. We see from the form of the second term that this difference is larger the smaller is $1 - \theta$, the proportion of time a shirker is unemployed.

To express the no shirking condition in terms of the more fundamental parameters of the model we note that if q is the detection probability per unit of time then $1/q$ is the expected duration of a job. By the same token, if ρ is the probability (per unit of time) that an unemployed worker finds a job, then $1/\rho$ is the expected duration of a spell of unemployment. This makes it possible to express the shirker's alternating employment history in terms of duration. A job of expected duration $1/q$ is followed by a spell of unemployment of duration $1/\rho$. This is then followed by another sequence of employment and unemployment spells of constant expected durations, and so on. Since all jobs and unemployment spells have constant expected durations we can express the expected proportion of time that a shirker is employed in terms of ρ and q as

$$\theta = (1/q)/[(1/q) + (1/\rho)] \qquad (8)$$

Noting that $1/(1 - \theta) = 1 + \rho/q$, the no-shirking condition can be written as

$$w > b + (1 + \rho/q)e \equiv w_0 \qquad (9)$$

Expression (9) has several obvious implications. If employers wish to avoid shirking they must pay a wage which satisfies the no shirking condition (because of the assumption that shirkers exert zero effort employers have no reason for taking a chance on shirkers – there is no point in employing anybody at a wage lower than w_0). Further, the critical wage is higher: (i) the greater is unemployment benefit (b); (ii) the higher is the probability of finding another job (ρ); and (iii) the lower is the probability of being caught shirking (q). All of these results make good sense. When the probability of detection is low firms have to pay a high wage to discourage workers from taking a chance on shirking, and high values of b and ρ mean that the punishment associated with being caught is low: in the first case, because a high unemployment benefit implies a small cost of being unemployed; and, in the case of a high ρ, because a worker does not expect to be unemployed for very long.

For the purpose of this model little is lost by taking the detection rate as exogenous, but the probability of finding another job is crucial to the nature of the equilibrium. Obviously, this probability depends on the state of the labour market. To formalize this, we consider a situation in which there are $\bar{E} - E$ unemployed workers searching for a job. If we assume that there is some exogenous turnover rate (λ) among those employed (for reasons which have nothing to do with shirking), the $\bar{E} - E$ searchers are competing for λE jobs. These assumptions allow us to write the probability that an unemployed worker gets a job (ρ) as

$$\rho = \lambda\, E/(\bar{E} - E) \qquad (10)$$

Alternatively, ρ can be expressed as a function of the unemployment rate $U = (\bar{E} - E)/\bar{E}$. Thus, rearranging equation (10) yields

$$\rho = \lambda(1 - U)/U \qquad (11)$$

Substitution of (10) into (9) gives the aggregate non-shirking constraint

$$w > b + e + e\,[\lambda/q][E/(\bar{E} - E)] \qquad (12)$$

The constraint is depicted in Figure 22.2(a). As can be seen, when full employment is approached, the critical value of w increases very sharply. In the limit, when E approaches $\bar{E}$, there is no wage which is sufficiently high to discourage shirking. Thus, a no shirking outcome is inconsistent with full employment.

Because of the special assumptions made, all firms will offer the lowest possible wage sufficient to induce workers not to shirk (this follows from the assumption that shirking workers supply zero effort). With each firm having a production function $Q = Q(E)$, profit maximization requires $Q'(E) = w_0$, and the total labour demand $E(w_0)$ is found by summing the demands of the N identical firms. This results in the aggregate demand curve depicted in Figure 22.2(b). The equilibrium wage and employment is found at the intersection of the aggregate no shirking constraint and the aggregate demand for labour schedule. At that wage, $w = w^*$, all firms can hire the labour they want. Additionally, w^* is an equilibrium wage. Firms have no incentive to raise the wage above w^*, and nor do they have an incentive to lower the wage. Paying a lower wage would simply induce shirking.

From the workers' point of view the resulting unemployment is involuntary. Those not employed at w^* would be happy to work at this, or even a lower, wage. But no firm will take them on. At w^*, all firms are already employing the profit-maximizing number of workers. Taking on workers at a lower wage is also ruled out by the no shirking constraint. A worker promising not to shirk would not change that. Whatever promises job seekers make, the optimal strategy is to shirk at a wage lower than w^*. Thus, promises not to shirk at a lower wage are not credible and firms just would not listen.

5 The turnover model

The turnover model has much in common with the shirking model and the formal structure exhibits many similarities (Salop, 1979; Stiglitz, 1974 and 1985). As shirking is costly to a firm, so is the turnover of its labour force. Workers who quit have to be replaced, which means that firms have to incur recruitment and training costs. It stands to reason then that a firm should employ a variety of devices to keep turnover at a reasonable level. One such device is to set the wage at a level which inhibits turnover. On the reasonable assumption that workers are more reluctant to quit the higher are their current wages

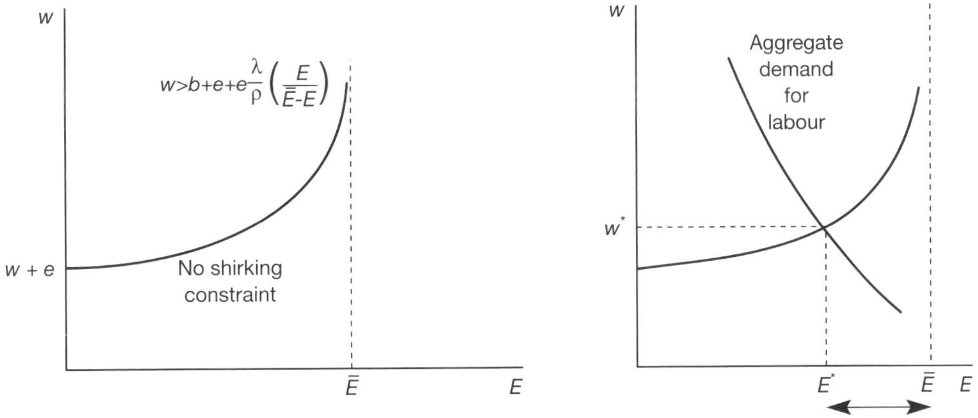

(a) The no shirking constraint **(b)** Unemployment equilibrium

Fig 22.2 The no shirking constraint and unemployment equilibrium in the shirking model.

relative to alternative opportunities, the firm that pays a higher wage should, everything else being equal, experience a lower turnover rate.

The microeconomics of this argument is a straightforward application of the basic efficiency–wage argument. Consider a single firm with production function $Q = Q(E)$ whose turnover cost per worker is given by T which includes recruitment, training and all other one-off costs associated with replacing a worker who quits. A fraction q of the workers quit each period and this fraction is assumed to depend on the firm's wage relative to the average wage paid by other firms. Specifically the quit function is given by $q = \mathbf{q}(w_i/w)$.

Profit per worker is then

$$\Pi/E = \mathbf{p}Q(E)/E - w_i - \mathbf{q}(w_i/w)T \qquad (13)$$

Because of the turnover cost the labour cost has two components: the wage w_i and the turnover cost, amortized over a single period.

Differentiating the profit function with respect to w_i, the optimal wage is given by the first-order condition

$$-1 - q'(w_i/w)T = 0 \qquad (14)$$

which says that the optimal wage is found where at the margin the saving in turnover cost due to a higher wage ($q'(w_i/w)T$) is equal to unity (the cost of the higher wage).

The condition is depicted in Figure 22.3. The firm takes its quit function as given and then decides upon the wage that yields the lowest labour cost. The labour cost is indicated by the two isocost curves C_1 and C_0, $C_1 > C_0$, which have a slope of $-1/T$ (i.e. if w is increased by one unit then q has to fall by $1/T$ to keep the labour cost per worker constant). At a wage of w_1, the quit rate would be q_1 and the labour cost C_1. The lowest-cost wage is found where an isocost line is tangent to the quit function, in other words where the slope of the quit function ($q'(w_i/w)$) is equal to the slope of the isocost curves ($-1/T$). In the figure, the wage corresponding to this point is w^*, the quit rate is q^* and labour cost C_0.

As an aside we can also note that the model implies that firms with higher turnover costs pay higher wages. With reference to Figure 22.3, the larger is T, the flatter are the isocost curves and the larger is the optimal wage. This is as we would expect. Firms with high turnover cost would seek to keep turnover low. In this model they can only do so by paying higher wages.

The microeconomics of this is straightforward, but the equilibrium in an economy consisting of a large number of firms, each setting a wage with an eye on the turnover rate, is more complicated. We will only consider the case where all firms are identical. When firms differ with respect to, for example, turnover cost, an equilibrium would entail multiple wages (see Stiglitz, 1985; Weiss, 1990). This complicates the analysis, but many implications of the single wage equilibrium remain valid. Intuitive reasoning suggests that the equilibrium should be characterized by a number of properties. First, the equilibrium must entail all firms paying the same wage. This wage satisfies certain conditions. In particular no single firm would want to decrease its wage, as this would mean a disproportionate increase in turnover costs which are not compensated for by the lower wage. Second, there should be no quits in equilibrium. Since all employers pay the same wage there is no reason for a worker to quit one firm in favour of another. This allows us to claim that no firm would want to increase its wage above the wage paid by all other firms – since the quit rate is already zero any further reduction through a higher wage is clearly not possible.

There is, however, nothing to ensure that the equilibrium wage clears the market. The argument of why a single firm would not lower its wage stands even in the presence of workers who are offering to work for less. In general we can conceive of a continuum of equilibria bounded, at the lower end, by the workers' reservation wage and, at the upper end, by a wage high enough to make it profitable for a single firm to break ranks and cut the wage. This idea is depicted in Figure 22.4. The turnover cost of a firm that cuts its wage to the lowest possible level (the reservation

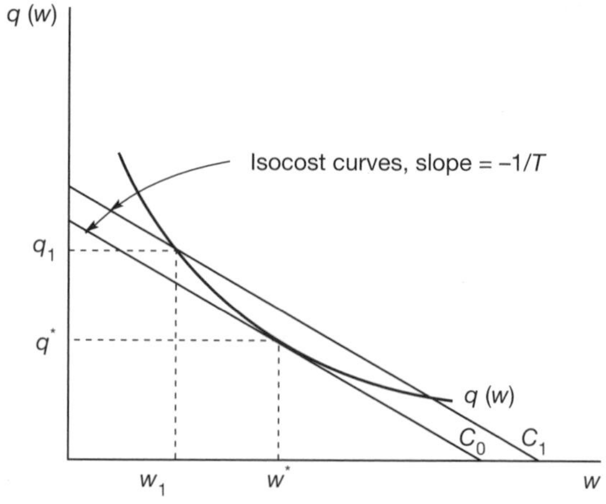

Fig 22.3 The optimal wage in the turnover model.

wage (w^r)) is depicted by the downward-sloping curve $q(w^r/w)T$. It is downward sloping because the higher the wage the lower is employment and, thus, the higher is unemployment. Unemployment exerts a beneficial externality from the perspective of an individual firm – the quit rate that a firm would experience if it were to cut its wage below the market rate is a declining function of unemployment. This translates into a turnover cost function (for a firm paying a given wage) which is declining in the market wage rate. The upward-sloping curve in Figure 22.4 represents the saving in wages by paying w^r rather than w (i.e.$w-w^r$). The argument is then that the equilibrium wage could lie anywhere between w^r and the intersection of ($w-w^r$) and $q(w^r/w)T$ denoted w^{max}. To the right of w^{max}, a single firm's saving from cutting the wage to w^r exceeds the turnover costs that this move would entail.

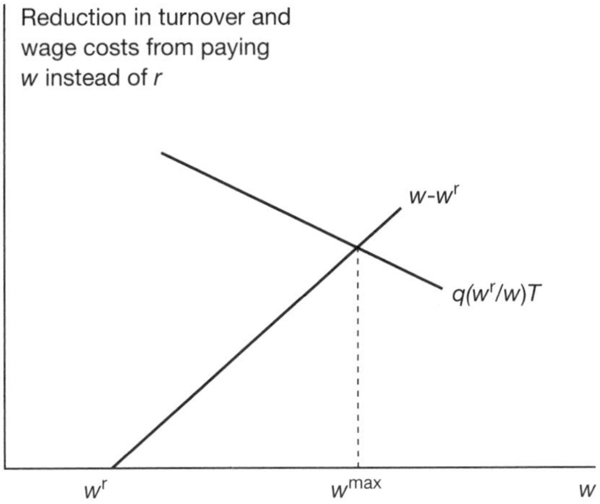

Fig 22.4 The equilibrium wage in the turnover model.

If the resulting equilibrium wage, w^*, is greater than the full employment wage, the model generates involuntary unemployment. There would be unemployed workers willing to work at w^*, but it is not profitable for firms to take them on. An unemployment equilibrium is not, however, a necessary outcome. If w^* is less than the full employment wage, the turnover consideration would be superseded by the need to obtain the required number of workers and the usual competitive (market clearing) solution obtains.

The equilibrium in the turnover model also has the feature that if firms could agree to, or simultaneously changed their wage to, the full employment wage then full employment could be attained. Thus, unemployment is merely a consequence of firms not being able to coordinate their wage setting, leading to an inefficient Nash equilibrium. In the shirking model the unemployment is also inefficient in a first-best sense, but at least it has a function as a discipline device. This redeeming feature is lacking in the turnover model, except that unemployment puts an upper limit on the efficiency wage.

5.1 Turnover cost and wages – an example

Although the logic of the turnover model is impeccable, it is doubtful whether turnover costs are large enough to lead firms to pay above market clearing wages to contain costs. A numerical example illustrates this point. If, in accordance with (13), we write the labour cost per worker per period as

$$c = w + \mathbf{q}(w)T \qquad (15)$$

differentiating with respect to w yields

$$c'_w = 1 + q'(w)T \qquad (16)$$

and the issue is under which conditions c'_w is less than zero (i.e. the cost per worker is decreasing in the wage). Assuming a constant quit–wage elasticity $(w/q)q'(w) = \alpha$, we find after some manipulations that $c'_w < 0$ if $-(1/\alpha) < q(T/w)$.

The inequality is depicted in Figure 22.5 for $q = 0.25$. This figure can be taken to be a fairly typical figure for a firm's yearly turnover rate. As regards

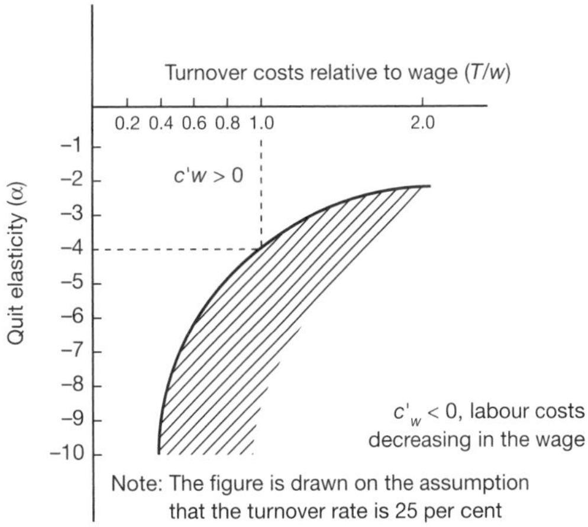

Fig 22.5 Values of the quit elasticity and turnover costs for which the total labour costs are decreasing in the wage paid.

plausible values of T/w we might be guided by the fact that the average firm's expenditure on training is around 2 per cent of the wage bill. If all this expenditure was incurred in training new workers, at a quit rate of 25 per cent the training expenditure per worker would be 8 per cent of the yearly wage. To this expenditure on training should be added the cost of on-the-job training and recruitment costs. If these costs together are of the same order of magnitude, a typical figure for T/w might be 16 per cent, but with considerable variation between firms. The precision of this estimate is in any case not crucial. As Figure 22.5 shows the quit–wage elasticity must be very high for c'_w to be negative for any reasonable values of T/w. Even at $T/w = 1$, when the turnover cost is equal to a whole year's wage, the quit elasticity must be less than –4, At lower, and more reasonable, values of T/w, a reduction in labour cost requires a very high quit elasticity. From the information in Case Study 1 about the effect of Ford's $5 day, we can calculate a quit elasticity of –2.26 (calculated as an arc elasticity). Other, and much more thorough, estimates obtained from econometric studies have found quit elasticities around –1.

The example highlights a potential problem with the turnover model – the turnover cost or the responsiveness of quits to relative wages may not be large enough to yield an equilibrium wage above the reservation wage (with reference to Figure 22.4, the turnover cost function may not intersect w^r in the positive quadrant). The shirking model is subject to a similar objection – the effort–wage elasticity may be below unity for any wage above the reservation wage. Mathematically, the problem is that there might not be an interior solution to the firm's optimization problem. Akerlof and Yellen (1986) provide a counter-argument in the case of the shirking model, but the existence of an interior solution has not been the subject of much discussion in the literature.

6 The adverse selection model

The adverse selection explanation for efficiency wages is based on the idea that the wage, apart from compensating workers, also serves a sorting function. A firm that pays high wages would typically find that it would be more attractive to productive workers. Thus, it would end up having a more productive workforce and the increased productivity might compensate for the higher wage costs that it incurs. The adverse selection model has several parallels in other areas of economics. The most well known is Akerlof's (1970) 'lemons' model, in which the buyers of used cars cannot evaluate their quality (i.e. they don't know if the car is a 'lemon'). But the archetypical model occurs in the insurance field, but then with the added complication of uncertainty. Here the problem is that the insurer does not know the type of customer, but in setting the premium the insurer must take into account that an insurance with a high premium is only attractive to high-risk customers. High premiums have an adverse selection effect: the insurer ends up with high-risk customers only. In the case of wages, it is of course low wages that have the adverse selection effect.

The argument is most easily grasped in the bare bones setting of observationally indistinguishable workers. That is, a firm has no information at all about the productivity of a particular individual. All applicants look alike and a firm's hiring decision is modelled as if it made a random draw from a pool of applicants. Of course, in practice there are differences between the workers. Each has a certain endowment (ability, say) and, crucial to the story, a reservation wage, which is an increasing function of their endowment. Furthermore, the productivity (y) of a worker is also an increasing function of their endowments.

The model is depicted in Figures 22.6(a)–(c). Figure 22.6(a) depicts the joint distribution of the reservation wage and productivity. Consider a firm offering a wage of w_1. This wage is below the reservation of all workers with a productivity greater than $\mathbf{y}(w_1)$. Thus the expected productivity of a worker drawn from the region bounded by w_1 and $\mathbf{y}(w_1)$ would be quite low, $\mathbf{y}(w_1)$ say. At a higher wage, however, w^* say, the firm would attract workers from the much larger region bounded by w^* and $\mathbf{y}(w^*)$. As drawn, this would only exclude the most able workers whose productivity exceeds $\mathbf{y}(w^*)$. Consequently, the expected productivity at w^* would be higher.

Figure 22.6(b) sketches the relationship between the expected productivity and the wage that can be derived from the joint distribution of Figure 22.6(a). The ray from the origin to a point on this function indicates the expected cost per efficiency unit of labour, $w/\mathbf{y}(w)^e$. With a wage of w_1, the slope of this ray is quite large because the expected productivity of a worker is low. The slope of the ray is at its minimum when it is tangent to the $\mathbf{y}(w)^e$ function. Thus, the corresponding wage, w^*, is the wage at which the cost of an efficiency unit of labour is minimized. In other words, w^* is the efficiency wage.

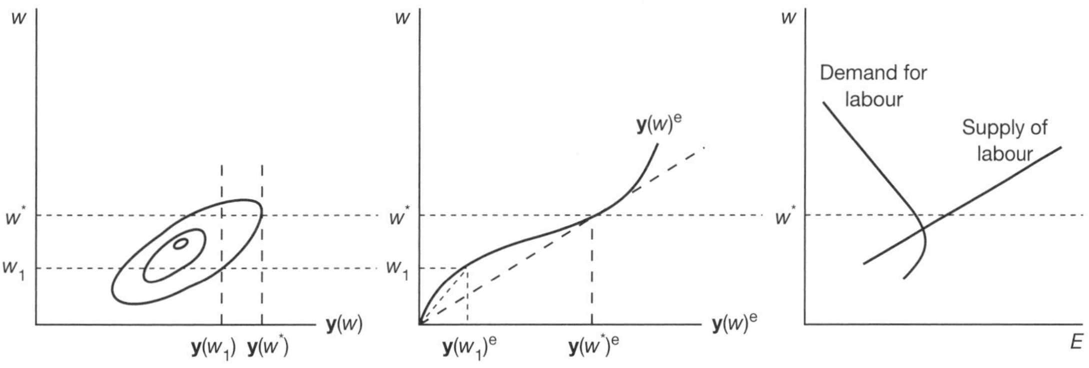

(a) Joint distribution of reservation wages and productivity

(b) Relationship between the wage and expected productivity

(c) Equilibrium in the adverse selection model

Fig 22.6 The adverse selection model.

Figure 22.6(c) brings all this together. It has a rather unusual demand curve which is backward bending. To understand why, we first need to understand the essential property of the efficiency wage w^*. By being the minimum cost of labour in terms of efficiency units, w^* is also the wage at which firms would demand the most efficiency units of labour. But this does not translate into the largest number of workers and, in Figure 22.6(c), demand is expressed in terms of employee rather than efficiency units. Consider what would happen to the demand for workers at a wage lower than w^*. Two effects are at work. First, as the wage is lowered more workers are required to obtain a certain amount of labour services. This effect tends to increase the demand for workers at lower wages. Second, as the wage is lowered below w^*, the cost per efficiency unit increases and firms will demand fewer efficiency units of labour. This would tend to reduce the demand for labour at lower wages. The positively sloped portion of the demand curve is therefore due to the second effect dominating the first. We would expect this to be the case in the region where the $\mathbf{y}(w)$ function is relatively steep. In this region a small drop in the wage gives rise to a relatively large fall in expected productivity and, thus, to a large increase in the cost of efficiency units of labour.

The supply curve drawn in Figure 22.6(c) is more conventional. It is drawn to shown an unemployment equilibrium with supply greater than demand at w^*. This is not a necessary outcome, but the sorting effect may give rise to an unemployment equilibrium. Irrespective of the positions of the curves, however, w^* is an equilibrium wage. Firms have no incentive to lower the wage even though they could obtain the labour they require at lower wages. A lower wage would increase cost by reducing the expected productivity of workers by more than is saved by the lower wage. By construction, w^* is the wage at which the cost of labour services is lowest – an excess supply of workers does not change this.

But even if firms are in equilibrium, the obvious objection is that surely the workers are not. The unemployment is involuntary, those who are unemployed would be willing to work at the equilibrium efficiency wage, and some at an even lower wage. To gain employment, they could offer to work for less (i.e. lower their reservation wages). An incomplete answer to this question is that an individual worker cannot increase their chances by offering to work at a wage below w^*, $w^* - \Delta$ say. By doing so they reveal that their true reservation wage is less than $w^* - \Delta$ and thus their expected productivity is less than $\mathbf{y}(w^* - \Delta)$. But that makes the cost of this worker, per efficiency unit, larger than the firm's existing average cost by efficiency unit – by definition $(w^* - \Delta)/\mathbf{y}(w^* - \Delta)^e > w^*/\mathbf{y}(w^*)^e$. This is an important result with implications for labour market policy. The answer is incomplete, however, because it begs another question. What if all unemployed workers lower their reservation wages? Would this change the joint distribution of reservation wages and productivity on which the efficiency wage is based? So far there has not been an entirely satisfactory answer to this question. The answer seems to depend on where the joint distribution comes from – but this remains a weak link in the model.

The crucial assumption – that the workers' reservation wages are an increasing function of ability – is uncontroversial in the case of a single firm. As one firm increases its wage it becomes attractive to higher-earning, and thus more productive, workers. However, the assumption is more problematic at the aggregate level. When the market wage increases where do these higher-ability individuals come from? Weiss (1980 and 1990) relies on a two-sector model of the economy to answer this question – an industrial (market) sector which pays efficiency wages in order to attract workers from a self-employment sector. Those who do not seek jobs in the industrial sector are the high-ability self-employed. There is some evidence in favour of this assumption and Weiss draws upon studies which have shown that, controlling for other factors, the earnings of the self-employed are significantly higher than for employees. However, data for most countries indicate that self-employed persons earn much less than employees. This does not necessarily refute the Weiss argument – the self-employed may well include a significant number of high-ability individuals even though the average earnings are diluted by an even larger number of individuals from the low-ability range. Perhaps a more significant objection to the adverse selection story comes from what we know about labour supply elasticities. These are highest for individuals who are on the fringe of the labour market and put a high value on non-market time. It is doubtful that these are also the high-ability individuals that the higher wages are supposed to attract.

7 Other explanations for efficiency wages

A number of other explanations have also been put forward to explain the payment of efficiency wages. Among these, the most well known is Akerlof's (1982) gift-exchange model in which he argues that high wages can raise group work norms. The starting point of his analysis was two observations about the situation in a particular firm in which: (i) the minimum performance standard set by the firm was regularly exceeded by a group of workers; and (ii) these workers were paid more than the going rate for the type of work they did. This he thought was inexplicable by reference to received neoclassical theory. Why did the workers produce more than the firm required of them and/or why was it that the firm did not increase standards or lower wages? While inexplicable according to neoclassical theory, Akerlof argued that the behaviour was more readily explained in a standard sociological model. Through the interaction between the workers and the firm both parties develop an attachment or sentiment for each other. In such situations exchange often takes the form of reciprocal gift giving, Christmas presents for example. Thus Akerlof used the term gift exchange to account for the behaviour of the workers and the firm. That is, he viewed the above minimum performance of the workers as a gift to the firm, which the firm reciprocated by paying higher wages. Gift exchange is not fundamentally different from any other form of exchange. There are 'terms of trade', in this case the excess performance given in exchange for the higher wage, but Akerlof argued that the terms in gift exchange, the *quid pro quo*, are established in a somewhat different way. In particular, notions of fairness and regard for the other party play an important role. This notion gives rise to norms, and in this case these relate to what is a fair performance in exchange for additional pay.

Quite apart from the sociological connotations of the gift-exchange argument, the concept is a useful way to think about the wage–effort issue. In most situations workers retain some discretion about the amount of effort they supply. In other words, effort is non-contractible – it cannot be traded through explicit contracts in which the terms of the trade, the extra wage to be paid for extra effort, is determined prior to trading. If this is the case, the exchange of the workers' discretionary effort can only take place through gift exchange, both parties giving something extra in the hope that the terms obtained constitute a Pareto improvement.

There is, however, a very fine distinction between Akerlof's sociological account and a more neoclassical explanation of the same phenomenon. Solow (1989) also argued that the explanation for efficiency wages may be found in social norms. However, as might be expected from a Nobel Laureate, his explanation has a stronger foundation in economic theory. His primary concern is why, if unemployed workers' reservation wages are above the market clearing efficiency wage, is the wage not competed down? The answer given by the shirking model was that firms would not accept offers to work for less because of the averse effect on effort. But do unemployed workers even try to undercut those in work? Causal empiricism would suggest not. Solow's explanation was that the workers and firms are playing an infinitely repeated game. The actions we observe –

workers not underbidding the wage other workers are paid and the firms not cutting wages below that of other firms – may well be an equilibrium. This suggestion derives from the so-called Folk Theorem, which states that in an infinitely repeated game, any combination of actions is the outcome of some subgame perfect equilibrium providing that certain conditions are satisfied. The Folk Theorem tells us that we cannot claim that any particular behaviour arises in equilibrium. Thus, the actions we observe, no underbidding, may be due to workers following what we may call a 'grim' strategy – as long as nobody else underbids they won't do it either, but as soon as one deviates, by bidding less, all other workers offer to work at the reservation wage for ever. The key to this being an equilibrium is the threatened revision to reservation wages for ever. The individual who is unemployed at the above reservation and market clearing wage does not underbid the wage of those employed because it is better to take a chance on finding a job at the existing wage. If they were to underbid, they know that in all future periods all that they will receive is the reservation wage.

This argument should be taken as a metaphor rather than a literal description of the workers' strategies. More realistically, experience and reason lead to the emergence of social norms which sustain a high wage equilibrium. As Solow puts it,

> We do not compete for each other's job by nibbling away at the wage level because we have been taught that it is unfair to do so, or demeaning, or unacceptable, or – perhaps – self-destructive. (Solow, 1989, p. 49)

How such norms come to be established is difficult to say and game theory does not provide an explanation. But, once established, they draw their force from shared values and approbation, and game theory provides a rationale for why the norms remain unchallenged.

8 Synthesis

In all four types of model the efficiency wage is posed as a solution to a contracting problem. In the shirking and the gift-exchange models effort is non-contractible, in the sorting model, the contract cannot be made contingent on productivity and, in the turnover model, the contract cannot prevent a worker from leaving the job. All four approaches can also be regarded as different types of principal–agent model. The principal (the firm) offers agents (workers) a contract to induce the agent to act in closer accordance with the principal's interest. The precise structure, however, differs between models. In the turnover model the contracting problem is due to uncertainty – a worker may quit if a better alternative emerges (i.e. it depends on the state of the world after the parties have entered into a contract). In both the shirking and sorting models uncertainty is absent. Instead, the contracting problem is a result of asymmetric information. The worker knows the effort they provide, but it is only observable to the firm at a cost. Likewise, in the adverse selection model the worker knows their ability but the firm does not.

9 Critique of efficiency wage theory

Returning to the proposition that efficiency wage theory should be seen as a solution to a contracting problem, the obvious question is whether there is a better explanation. The reason for asking this question is reinforced by the fact that, in all cases, the efficiency wage contract is inefficient. The resulting unemployment is involuntary. Potentially, there may be some more ingenious employment contracts which, even if not fully Pareto efficient, are at least 'better' than efficiency wages.

The most widely discussed alternative is that workers pay a bond, or entrance fee, to firms on taking up their employment. This solution is relevant to the discussion of specific training given that the payment of a bond might be a way of overcoming a firm's capital loss when a worker with firm-specific training leaves. The argument is exactly the same in the case of the turnover model, the only difference being that turnover costs encompass more than just training costs. Applied to the shirking model, the bond would be forfeited when a worker is caught shirking and dismissed. The threat of losing the bond substitutes for the threat of becoming unemployed. In this case, unemployment is not required, as a discipline device, and firms have no reason to elevate the wage above the market clearing level.

While theoretically elegant, the fact they rarely, if ever, appear in employment contracts suggests that there are flaws to the bonding solution. One is that workers may have problems in financing a bond in a less than perfect capital market. Additionally, bonds present a moral hazard problem. Firms would have an incentive to claim that workers are shirking and dismiss them, or harass a worker to quit if the bond was posted as a security against quitting. The validity of these objections is difficult to evaluate. Bonds are very common in tenancy contracts and, although sometimes a contentious issue, seem to work well. There are, however, several important differences between a tenancy and an employment relationship. The moral hazard problem, the landlord harassing the tenant to leave or allowing the property to fall into disrepair, is fairly easily circumscribed by explicit contractual provisions which can be enforced at low cost by a third party. This is more difficult to achieve in employment contracts and where effort is a nebulous concept, any agreement about performance is not easily enforced by a third party. Thus, in an employment relationship, the firm's moral hazard problem can only be ensured by self-enforcing arrangements. Lazear (1981) has shown that the firm's concern for its reputation may do the trick. There are other contractual arrangements which are equivalent to bonds which also were discussed in connection with specific training. These include upward-sloping earnings– tenure profiles, which provide for earnings below the marginal product in the early years, and above marginal product in later years. These are, to all intents and purposes, equivalent to bonds, and, in contrast, appear to be in common use. In theory, the moral hazard problem still applies, but Malcolmson (1984) has shown that it can be overcome by pre-commitment by the firm. Thus, a commitment by the firm to a fixed proportion of higher-paying positions, as in a fixed hierarchal structure, is easily verifiable. This makes it difficult for the firm to default on its obligation to pay higher wages to those who have stayed the course.

The relevance of the bonding objection to efficiency wage theories has been subject to extensive discussion in the literature. In the process many claims and counter-claims have been made. Sufficient to say, efficiency wage theory has survived reasonably intact.

The bonding and related alternatives do not apply to the adverse selection explanation for efficiency wages. Instead, the credible alternatives are arrangements which ameliorate the source of the problem, primarily the informational asymmetry. This could be achieved by workers signalling their abilities or firms screening workers (i.e. Spencer's signalling explanation why individuals acquire education). This is one way to overcome the problem, albeit a very costly method. Signalling ability through education might be more inefficient than the unemployment associated with the efficiency wage explanation. However, there may be other lower-cost signals. In turn, firms can screen workers before they are taken on. It is a bit far fetched to suggest that firms have no information at all about individual ability. Education, previous experience, appearance and presentation, and, if used, aptitude and ability tests, can provide a substantial amount of information. However, even though there are a number of ways in which the informational asymmetry can be ameliorated, the residual uncertainty about workers' productivity may still be large enough for the sorting effect of wages to be significant. Whether or not this is the case is largely an empirical matter.

Rather than chip away at the specific explanations put forward, a more eclectic approach may be warranted. Even though each specific explanation may be lacking in some aspect, perhaps efficiency wages still represent the most efficient solution to a range of contractual problems, including incentives for effort, the resolution of adverse selection and disincentives for quitting. Each specific problem may be dealt with more efficiently by some other contractual arrangement, but not all of them together. Such an eclectic approach is akin to the internal labour market construct. The internal labour market theory suggested that the governance structure was the key to the resolution to a range of contractual problems. Our eclectic interpretation of efficiency wage theory argues that the resolution is provided by above market clearing wages.

CASE STUDY 1 Henry Ford's $5 day

In January 1914 Henry Ford initiated a $5 a day wage in his automobile factory in Detroit. This doubled the pay of most of his workers. According to Henry Ford himself, the $5 wage could be classified as an efficiency wage,

> The payment of five dollars a day for eight hours a day was one of the finest cost cutting moves we ever made. (Raff and Summers, 1987)

continues

CASE STUDY 1 continued

The years prior to 1914 had seen dramatic changes to the production of automobiles at Ford. A collection of skilled craftsmen's shops had been transformed into an assembly line that was capable of turning out cars at a hitherto unknown rate. Aligned to this change the composition of the workforce had undergone dramatic changes – from mainly skilled craftsmen to common labourers who could be put on the assembly line straight from the street. The pace of the work was brisk, unpleasant and onerous, and there were signs of dissatisfaction. Turnover was endemic. In 1913, the turnover rate was 370 per cent and absenteeism was running at 10 per cent.

Despite this, Ford had no problems in replacing the workers that left and a range of other evidence suggest that the \$5 a day wage was well above the minimum required to attract workers. For example, in the weeks immediately following the rise, long queues for jobs were all too evident (there were reports of 12,000 men queuing outside the gates). In the absence of a competitive explanation for the wage rise it can only be presumed that Henry Ford's *ex post* justification was indeed the true reason and the subsequent events proved him right. The turnover rate fell to 54 per cent during 1914, productivity increased by anything between 30 and 70 per cent, prices continued their trend decline and profits continued to soar. How was this attained, in view of the fact that the pace of work was already fairly high prior to the introduction of the \$5 day? Raff and Summers suggest a combination of factors: simply turning up the speed, more intensive use of fixed and quasi-fixed factors through better coordination and a smoother flow of work, improved morale, lower turnover costs, more cooperative behaviour and an end to collusion among workers to restrict output. Learning-by-doing effects may also have been important (see Berndt, 1991, pp. 66–67).

This was a very impressive result, although, taking everything into account, the savings from higher productivity, lower turnover, etc., were probably less than the cost of the wage increase.

Source: Raff and Summers (1987).

10 Empirical evidence for efficiency wages

10.1 Stylized facts and efficiency wages

Since efficiency wage theory was developed to provide an explanation of two stylized facts of labour markets – involuntary unemployment and sticky wages – the theory should, by construction, be consistent with these twin facts.

The claim in respect of unemployment has become fairly well accepted. The theory provides a strong argument why involuntary unemployment should persist as an equilibrium phenomenon. It is also broadly consistent with the cyclical variations in unemployment and many other facts about unemployment, for example that it is concentrated among the unskilled.

The claim that efficiency wage theory is compatible with sticky wages is more complicated. First, efficiency wage models are real models which, in themselves, have nothing to say about the behaviour of the values of nominal variables. Thus the sticky wage property refers to real wages, while the more central macroeconomic issue has been the reason for why nominal wages are sticky. Second, the term sticky is a somewhat loose term which can lead to confusion. The Solow condition implies that the efficiency wage is invariant with respect to output, but this implies rigidity of the real wage at the firm or industry level. At the macro level, on the other hand, the efficiency wage may be sticky (i.e. slowly changing) but it is not necessarily rigid. In the shirking model, for example, an inward shift of the aggregate demand curve implies a lower real wage and higher unemployment. The adjustment towards this lower wage may well be sluggish (as argued by Shapiro and Stiglitz, 1984), but it is difficult to make strong claims about this without the aid of a fully specified dynamic macro model. Third, to complicate matters further there is no consensus about the behaviour of real wages over the business cycle. It is, in other words, questionable what the stylized facts that a model should account for really are.

Other stylized facts can also be difficult to reconcile with the theory. Productivity is generally procyclical, i.e. workers work harder when there is more to do but slack off during a recession. The simplest shirking model does not provide an explanation for this. If anything, if real wages did not fall during a recession, it predicts that workers would put in more effort when unemployment is high. Thus productivity should increase in a recession. However, even if this prediction is incompatible with what is generally the case, a number of authors have drawn attention to the fact that this is indeed what happened in the UK during the 1980s. Notwithstanding the high level of unemployment, real wages grew strongly and was accompanied by a massive increase in productivity in manufacturing.

10.2 Testing the theory

The compatibility of a theory with selected stylized facts is not a very powerful test of a theory. This comment applies with particular force to efficiency wage theory which, in its most general form, is virtually tautological. It states that firms may elevate the wage level above its market clearing level because it is profitable for them do so. One would be hard pressed to come up with an alternative explanation – whatever firms do it must be because it is profitable. As we have explained in this chapter there are of course several reasons why it may be profitable to pay high wages. However, it still remains the case that we started from the assumption that the wage level is above the market clearing level, and then put forward reasons why that might be consistent with profit-maximizing behaviour. If the assumption is correct, the argument for efficiency wages is an argument by elimination. In the absence of alternative explanations we conclude that the payment of efficiency wages is the explanation.

For these reasons one would like to see more direct tests of particular efficiency wage theories or an evaluation of the merit of alternative explanations. Such tests are difficult to construct. For example, to test the shirking model, one would like to ascertain whether the wage-effort relationship and the production function combine to sketch out a no shirking constraint which would lead a firm to pay a wage above the reservation level. This presumes that the analyst is able to infer something about effort from observable data. But if the analyst can do this, so can a firm, and then the very reason for paying efficiency wages vanishes. If a firm can infer the effort of its workers, we would expect a contract with an effort contingent wage, not an efficiency wage.

In view of these problems it is not surprising that a fully satisfactory test of efficiency wage theory is yet to be conducted. In the meantime there have been two main approaches to testing efficiency wage theory.

10.2.1 Industry and firm wage differentials

Although efficiency wage theory does not predict that workers with identical characteristics receive different wages it does provide a possible reason for it. To the extent that the cost of monitoring, turnover and the productivity effects of adverse selection differ between firms, the efficiency wage, the wage that minimizes labour cost per efficiency unit, would also vary between firms. If we then observe that firms pay different wages for labour of apparently the same quality the facts are, on the surface, consistent with efficiency wage theory.

Because of the scarcity of wage data at the firm level, most of the empirical research in this field has focused on industry differences in wages. The most prominent contributors have been Krueger and Summer (1988) and Dickens and Katz (1987). The principal technique in these studies is to estimate the proportions of variance in industry pay which are due to: (i) individual characteristics which can be expected to determine earnings (primarily level of education, age and sex, but also factors like marital status, union membership); and (ii) the attributes of the jobs. In the long-run equilibrium of the competitive model only these two sets of factors should have an influence. Once we control for these, there should be no differences in pay between industries.

The researchers mentioned above have, however, found that substantial pay differences remain after they controlled for the first two groups of factors. An example of the type of results obtained is given in Table 22.1. In the case of the USA we see that the standard deviation of log of industry wages is 0.24 whether it is measured from aggregate industry data or individual data. The standard deviation of log of pay is used because of its ease of interpretation. The standard deviation of 0.24 in the average pay simply means that in 65 per cent of industries the average pay is within plus or minus 24 per cent (one standard deviation) of the mean for all industries. Controlling for type (i) and (ii) factors reduces the standard deviation markedly, but the standard deviation in pay across industries remains more than half of what it was.

Table 22.1 Industry wage differentials in the USA and Sweden

Country	Standard deviation of log of average industry wages		
	Aggregate data	Individual data (without controls)	Individual data (with controls)
USA	0.241	0.240	0.140
Sweden	0.081	0.083	0.013

Source: Edin and Zetterberg (1992)

There are at least two facts about industry wage differences which lend support to the efficiency wage explanation. First, the differences are very stable over time, or at least change very slowly. This suggests that the differences we observe at a point in time reflect a long-run equilibrium situation. Second, the same pattern of industry wage differences can be observed in a number of countries. An industry that is high paying in one country is also a high-paying industry in most other countries. Since the technology of production is the same across countries this suggests that industry wage differences are associated with the different technologies used by different industries. The last step in the reasoning is then to argue that the cost of monitoring, turnover, etc., depend on the technology used and thus that industry wage differences reflect differences in the efficiency wage premium. Of course, if the technology itself varies for the same industry across countries, the argument is undermined.

A third fact about industry wage differences is, however, less favourable to the efficiency wage explanation: that is, the positive correlation between the wage premiums in different occupations. In high-pay industries, all workers, irrespective of their occupation, tend to receive high pay. This raises the question why, for example, are secretaries in the high-paying chemical industry paid more than secretaries in the low-paying apparel industry? Differential costs of monitoring or turnover do not seem a plausible answer, at least not in this particular example.

The result from the studies of US industry differentials has not been replicated in studies for other countries. In the case of Sweden, Edin and Zetterberg (1992) report that: (i) industry wage differences are very much smaller than in the USA; and (ii) individual and job attributes account for almost all of the variations in industry wages. After controlling for individual and job attributes, the standard deviation of average industry pay was only 0.013. (meaning that in 95 per cent of industries, the average falls within a 5.2 percentage point range around the overall mean). It might be that very small wage premiums may be sufficient to discourage shirking in Sweden while US workers require a higher premium. But this is stretching the argument too far. The more obvious conclusion is that the Swedish evidence does not provide any support for efficiency wages.

Apart from the lack of conclusive findings compatible with efficiency wage theory, the link between industry wage differentials and efficiency wages has been criticized as being tenuous. Alternative explanations have been considered in the literature but no consensus has been achieved. In view of the large number of alternative explanations for industry wage differentials this is understandable. Groshen (1991) examines a number of alternatives, including sorting by ability, compensating differentials, and random variations due to costly job search. To complicate matters further, there are several variants within each of the main groups. Thus discriminating between efficiency wages and alternative explanations is a difficult task. For that reason more direct tests of efficiency wage theory appear to offer a more promising route. A weak point of the efficiency wage explanation for industry differentials is the assumed link between industries and wage premiums. But precisely what are the characteristics of high-paying industries which give rise to high wages? Murphy and Topel (1990) suggest that research which seeks to answer this question might be more fruitful.

10.2.2 Wage–supervision trade-off

The shirking model of efficiency wages implies that a wage premium is a cost-effective substitute for more intensive supervision. Krueger (1991) found that pay in company-owned and operated fast food outlets was higher than in franchised outlets run by the franchisee. This he argued was consistent with the efficiency wage model – the salaried managers in company-operated outlets had a weaker incentive to provide effective supervision and thus higher pay was necessary to obtain the required effort from the workforce. Three further studies have looked at the relationship between pay and the supervisor/employee ratio (Leonard, 1987; Fitzroy and Kraft, 1988; Groshen and Krueger, 1990). One study found the negative relationship expected by efficiency wage theory, but in the other two there was no significant relationship between pay and supervision intensity. In other studies researchers have looked at the pay of piece rate workers and compared the pay of workers on piece rate and time rates. When workers are paid on piece rate there is no monitoring problem and no reason to pay efficiency wages. However, Brown and Medoff (1989) found that the firm size effect (the tendency for pay to increase with firm size) of piece rate workers was larger than the firm size effects reported in previous studies. Chang and Edin (1994), who compared the industry effect on the pay of workers on piece rates and time rates, also failed to find much evidence in favour of efficiency wage theory.

11 Policy implications

In the shirking model the policy issues are best approached by recognizing that the basic problem is an externality. A single firm, in raising its wage, imposes a negative externality on other firms who then must raise their wages or incur additional monitoring cost to prevent shirking. This externality is also evident from noting that there is a divergence between private and social cost. The private cost of an extra worker is the wage, the social cost is the cost of effort, and, as was shown, in equilibrium the former is higher than the latter. In a partial equilibrium framework, externalities are easily corrected by the appropriate tax or subsidy. In this case, a wage subsidy would do the trick. With reference to Figure 22.2, a wage subsidy would shift the aggregate demand curve to the right but would have no effect on the no shirking constraint. Thus, the two curves would intersect further to the right at a lower level of unemployment. There is of course a limit to how far unemployment can be lowered. If we take it that subsidies are financed by a lump sum tax on profits, the total subsidy is limited by the amount of profits that can be taxed away. It is interesting to note that although this would increase output and employment it is not a Pareto improvement since profits would fall.

Wage subsidies would also reduce unemployment in the adverse selection model. The key point here is that a subsidy would leave the efficiency wage unchanged, while, as in the shirking model, the lower cost of labour would expand employment. In addition Weiss (1990) suggests that the root cause of the problem, the asymmetry of information, might also be mitigated by government intervention which improves information in the labour market. Of course, all developed countries have an extensive system of public and private job matching agencies and it is difficult to see what more could be done.

The possibility of an unemployment equilibrium in the turnover model can also be seen as an externality problem – a single firm setting a higher wage does not take into account the higher turnover cost this imposes on other firms. In theory the solution is straightforward although somewhat far fetched. A tax on quits would shift the cost of turnover curve in Figure 22.4 downwards and lower the upper limit of the equilibrium range. In principle, such a tax could be set at the level at which the upper limit ($w^{\max}$) is equal to the market clearing wage which would guarantee full employment. However, this solution is very much an artefact of the simplicity of the model – there are no benefits from turnover (such as a better match between workers and firms), only a cost. Another, and more realistic, form of intervention is suggested by the model having multiple equilibria. If the current equilibrium wage exceeds the market clearing wage all firms would be quite happy to lower their wage, providing all other firms did likewise. This suggests a role for government as a coordinator of the wage-setting process, to try to push the economy towards a wage level closer to the market clearing level.

12 Summary

The efficiency wage is a wage which minimizes labour cost per efficiency unit and which is higher than the wage firms need to pay to attract a given quantity of labour. There are three main reasons why firms would pay an efficiency wage. In the shirking model firms pay an efficiency wage to ensure that workers provide the labour services they have contracted to exchange. In the turnover model the reason is to lower the cost of labour turnover, and, in the adverse selection model, to be able to hire more productive workers. In all three models the equilibrium efficiency wage may be above the market clearing level. Thus, the payment of efficiency wages may give rise to involuntary unemployment. Since this is inefficient critics have argued that the basic problem can be solved by some other contractual arrangement which does not involve unemployment. For example, in the shirking and turnover models the contracting problem could be resolved by workers posting a bond with their employer.

The empirical evidence for efficiency wage theory is somewhat limited. Direct tests of the theory are not possible. Some studies have argued that persistent differences in pay between industries reflect different efficiency wage premiums. Some other studies have reported a negative association between pay and the intensity of supervision which is consistent with the shirking explanation for efficiency wages, but the evidence on this issue is mixed.

Notwithstanding the lack of solid empirical support, efficiency wage theory has become accepted as a credible additional explanation for involuntary unemployment. It should by no means be regarded as the only or even the primary explanation, to the exclusion of a number of other important reasons, but some of the unemployment could have an efficiency wage explanation.

CASE STUDY 2 Efficiency wages and the firm's product market performance

The payment of efficiency wages implies that the higher than necessary wages must somehow be reflected in improved performance. Normally it is conceived that the improved performance is obtained through higher productivity. However, as pointed out by Konings and Walsh (1994), the improved performance can also result from the generation of higher rents in an imperfectly competitive product market. At the same time, the rents obtained in an imperfectly competitive market may be a reason for paying higher wages. A firm may have to share some of its product market rent with its workers in the form of higher wages.

Since there are several explanations why firms pay high wages it is clearly essential to be able to discriminate between the competing hypotheses. In their paper Konings and Walsh develop a method which discriminates between the efficiency wage explanation and the pure rent-sharing reason.

If the efficiency wage explanation applies, firms which pay efficiency wages should have lower costs. This is true by definition. Unless lower costs were obtained a firm would not have any reason for paying higher wages. But it is not the lower costs *per se* that make it profitable to pay efficiency wages. The firm uses these lower costs to obtain additional rent in the product market. However, only a fraction of this additional rent will accrue to the workers in the form of efficiency wage payments (how the additional rent is obtained is explained below). This follows from the Solow condition: the optimal efficiency wage is independent of product market conditions.

The basic idea can be explained with the aid of the Cournot model. The figure depicts the symmetric equilibrium in a two-firm Cournot model (see Figure 22.7). The Nash equilibrium occurs at the intersection of the respective reac-

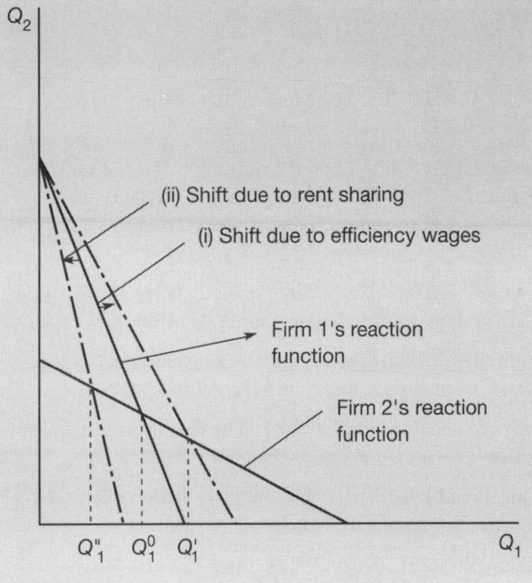

Fig 22.7 How a firm's reaction function and equilibrium output is affected by (i) efficiency wages and (ii) rent sharing in a two-firm Cournot model.

continues

CASE STUDY 2 Continued

tion functions of the two firms. Suppose now that the conditions for the payment of efficiency wages were favourable in Firm 1 but not in Firm 2. By paying higher wages Firm 1 would then have lower costs, its reaction function would pivot outwards and, in equilibrium, it would have the larger market share. If, on the other hand, Firm 1 paid higher wages than Firm 2 because it was forced to share its product market rent with its workers it would have higher costs. The reaction function of Firm 1 would be inside the original reaction function and, in equilibrium, it would have a smaller market share.

The efficiency wage explanation is most likely to apply to firms in which only a small proportion of the workforce are in a union. Conversely, the rent-sharing explanation would be more likely in the case of highly unionized firms. Thus Konings and Walsh divide their sample of firms into two groups, low unionized and high unionized firms. To each sample they fit a simple model where the market share is a function of last period's market share, the level of wages, sales, the difference between the retail and wholesale prices in the industry and a time trend. The estimates from this model provide strong support for their hypothesis. In the low unionized sample wages have a positive coefficient but in the high unionized sample the coefficient on wages is negative. That is, in the low unionized sample, the firms which do pay high wages seem to do so for efficiency wage reasons.

These results provide some direct evidence for the payment of efficiency wages. However, firms which pay high wages do not necessarily do so for the reasons suggested by efficiency wage theory. There are other reasons, such as rent sharing under conditions of imperfect competition, why we may observe high wages in some firms.

Source: Konings and Walsh (1994)

References

Akerlof, G.A. (1970). 'The Market for Lemons'. *Quarterly Journal of Economics*, 84, 488–500.

Akerlof, G.A. (1982). 'Labour Contracts as Partial Gift Exchange'. In G. Akerlof and T. Yellen (eds) (1986). *Efficiency Wage Models of the Labour Markets*. Cambridge: Cambridge University Press.

Akerlof, G. and T. Yellen (1986). *Efficiency Wage Models of the Labour Markets*. Cambridge: Cambridge University Press.

Berndt, E.R. (1991). *The Practice of Econometrics: Classic and Contemporary*. Reading, MA: Addison-Wesley.

Brown, C. and T. Medoff, (1989). 'The Employer Size Wage Effect'. *Journal of Political Economy*, 97, 1027–1059.

Chang, P. and P.A. Edin (1994). 'Industry Wage Differentials, Efficiency Wages and Method of Pay', Mimeo.

Dickens, W. and L. Katz, (1987). 'Inter-industry Wage Differences and Industry Characteristics'. In Lang, K. and S. Leonard (eds) *Unemployment and the Structure of Labour Markets*. New York: Blackwell.

Edin, P. and T. Zetterberg (1992). 'Inter-Industry Wage Differentials Evidence from Sweden and a Comparison with the United States'. *American Economic Review*, 88, 1341–1349.

Fitzroy, F. and K. Kraft (1988). *Efficiency Wages and Supervision in the Firm Test with FRG Microdata*. Draft. December.

Groshen, E. (1991). 'Sources of Intra-Industry Wage Dispersion: How Much Do Employers Matter?'. *Quarterly Journal of Economics*, 106, 869–884.

Groshen, E. and A. Krueger (1990). 'The Structure of Supervision and Pay'. *Industrial and Labour Relations Review*, 43, 134–146.

Konings, J. and P.P. Walsh (1994), 'Evidence of Efficiency Wage Payment in UK Firm Level Panel Data.' *Economic Journal*, 104, (May), 542–555.

Krueger, A. (1991). 'Ownership, Agency and Wages: An Examination Franchising Food Industry'. *Quarterly Journal of Economics*, 106, 75–102.

Krueger, A., and L. Summer (1988). 'Efficiency Wages and the Inter-Industry Wage Structure'. *Econometrica*, 56, 259–293.

Lazear, E. (1981). 'Agency, Earnings, Profiles, Productivity and Hours Restrictions'. *American Economic Review*, 71, 4, 606–620.

Leonard, T. (1987). 'Carrots and Sticks: Pay, Supervision and Turnover'. *Journal of Labour Economics*, 5, S136–S153.

Malcolmson, T. (1984). 'Work Incentives, Hierarchy, and Internal Labour Markets'. *Journal of Political Economy*, 92, 486–507.

Murphy, K., and R. Topel (1990). 'Efficiency Wages Reconsidered: Theory and Evidence'. Chapter 8. In Yoram Weiss and Gideon Fishelson (eds) *Advances in the Theory and Measurement of Unemployment*. New York: St Martin's Press, pp. 204–240.

Raff, M.G. and L.H. Summers (1987). 'Did Henry Ford Pay Efficiency Wages?'. *Journal of Labour Economics*, 5, S57–S86.

Salop, S. (1979). 'A Model of Natural Rate of Unemployment'. *American Economic Review*, 69, 117–125.

Shapiro, C. and Stiglitz, T. (1984). 'Equilibrium Unemployment as a Worker Discipline Device'. *American Economic Review*, 74, June, 433-444.

Solow, R. (1979). 'Another Possible Source of Wage Stickiness'. *Journal of Macroeconomics*, 1, Winter, 79–82.

Solow, R. (1989). *The Labour Market as a Social Institution*. Cambridge, MA: Blackwell.

Stiglitz, T. (1974). 'Incentives and Risk Sharing in Sharecropping'. *Review of Economic Studies*, 41, 219–256.

Stiglitz, J.E. (1985). 'Information and Economic Analysis: A Perspective'. *Economic Journal*, 95, Supplement, 21–41.

Weiss, A. (1980). 'Job Queues and Layoffs in Labour Markets with Flexible Wages'. *Journal of Political Economy*, 88, 526–538.

Weiss, A. (1990). *Efficiency Wages. Models of Unemployment, Layoffs and Wage Dispersion*. Oxford: Clarendon Press.

PART VII Competition, Segmentation, Union Effects, Wages and Earnings

CHAPTER 23

Introduction to competition, segmentation, union effects, wages and earnings

1 Introduction

So far the book has primarily been concerned with the way in which the supply of and demand for labour interact to determine the statics and dynamics of wage and employment outcomes. We have developed the neoclassical framework, including the human capital model, and have also taken a close look at modern approaches to the employment relationship, which alter the predictions of the labour market outcomes that result from the profit-maximizing behaviour of firms and utility maximization of workers, under competitive conditions. In this part of the book, however, we pay regard to the possibility that institutional factors such as unions can have an important influence on labour markets and also explore a quite different view of labour markets from the mainstream approach adopted so far. In particular, we examine the view that labour markets are fragmented because of imperfect information, barriers to mobility, as well as social and institutional influences. This view is best described as 'segmentation theory'.

One of the concepts that is important in the segmentation approach is that of discrimination. Groups that get into 'bad' segments of the labour market are there, at least partly, because of discrimination against them. We, therefore, also look at the economics of labour market discrimination. Having dealt with the issues of discrimination, segmentation and the role of unions, we then progress naturally to the analysis of the determinants of wages and earnings. We argue that in organizing discussion of the structure of earnings it is useful to distinguish between competitive and non-competitive forces. In the chapter on wages and earnings we look at the way that labour economists have analysed empirically the way in which these various forces impact on the structure of wages and earnings.

The book so far has tended to emphasize competitive forces, but this part concentrates more on non-competitive forces. In this chapter, by way of introduction, we discuss some alternative ways of viewing the operation of labour markets and the determination of wage differentials under the headings of 'competitive' and 'non-competitive' theories. This provides a useful backdrop to what follows in Chapters 24 to 26.

2 Competitive and non-competitive theories

2.1 Competitive theories

A good starting point for this discussion is the 'wage competition model' of the labour market. In this model wages are determined competitively by the forces of supply and demand and respond readily to shortages or surpluses of labour in their various markets. Thus the forces of supply and demand interact to determine a structure of wages and earnings that reflect the willingness of labour to supply themselves to the various jobs on offer and the willingness of employers to pay workers for their marginal products. Any deviation of wages from such an equilibrium will cause a movement of labour from jobs where wages are 'too low' to jobs where they are 'too high' causing wages to adjust to their equilibrium level. This model is in accordance with the theory of 'compensating wage differentials' the origin of which lies in Adam Smith's theory that the net advantages of all jobs tend to be equalized by competitive forces. Thus jobs that are dirty or dangerous, for example, or require greater investments in education and training, require higher wages in order to compensate for these disadvantages. This, in turn, is consistent with human capital theory, which focuses specifically on the compensation for the cost of investments in education and training, as outlined in Part V of the book. Under this theory, the structure of earnings is highly dependent on the costs of these investments, including the forgone earnings associated with time spent in education or training.

This set of theories, which are at the heart of the standard competitive view of labour markets, have been the subject of a number of criticisms. First, empirical evidence has shown that similar jobs in different firms are often associated with significantly different wage rates. Second, the persistence of unemployment has cast doubt on the competitive model. Unemployed workers have often found it difficult to price themselves back into jobs. Third, wages have shown a degree of stickiness that appears inconsistent with the wage competition model. There have been various attempts to reconcile these observations with a competitive view of labour markets. We saw some of these in Part VI of the book on the employment relationship. Thus, both the implicit contract and efficiency wage theories, for example, predict wage stickiness and the persistence of unemployment in models that still imply competitive behaviour by firms and workers' labour markets. Efficiency wage theory also has an explanation for different wages for persons in different jobs (i.e. it is more likely that the wage per unit of worker effort tends to be equalized by competitive forces rather than the wage per worker).

Another view is that while the basic competitive model is essentially the appropriate framework for analysing labour markets, institutional forces such as trade unions can distort the operation of labour markets, leading to wage rigidities, unemployment, and a structure of wage differentials that do not accord completely with the predictions of the competitive model.

2.2 Non-competitive theories

The job competition model provides a stark contrast. This is a good starting point for considering non-competitive theories. In the job competition model people enter the labour market with a set of skills and compete for jobs in the form of a queue, on the basis of the cost of training them for the jobs. There are a range of jobs across the economy, each with a wage attached to it, which determines the distribution of earnings. The nature of jobs is essentially technologically determined and the wages attached are based upon established social norms of fairness. Who occupies the jobs then depends to a large extent upon the costs of training employees to perform the jobs.

Social norms are seen as determining the wage structure, rather than competitive forces. Thus, the tendency for labour mobility to respond to wage differentials and cause wages to adjust to balance supply and demand is not a feature of the model. High-paying jobs may have long queues attached to them, but these queues are not thought to bid down the wages. Rather they allow employers to be more 'discriminating' in their choice of who to hire. Such discrimination could be on the basis of objective characteristics such as skill, but the possibility of subjective discrimination on the basis of gender or race, for example, can also be incorporated into this model. The job competition model, therefore, does not see wage stickiness, unemployment, or different wages for similar jobs as a puzzle in the same way as the competitive model.

The idea that labour markets are fragmented, and that certain groups are badly treated, is consistent with the job competition model. Those who believe strongly in such fragmentation and the associated problems of imperfect information, barriers to mobility, social and institutional influences, have often been referred to as 'segmentationists'. One view of segmentation is the dual labour market theory, in which there is a primary and a secondary market. The primary market contains 'good jobs' and is characterized by the prevalence of internal labour markets. The secondary labour market contains 'bad jobs', which tend not to be found in internal labour markets and face unstable demands. This characterization of segmentation has not received strong empirical support and more prevalent descriptions of segmented labour markets involve either 'multiple segments' or a continuous job queue along the lines of the job competition model in which rewards are highly differentiated but no clear segments are distinguished.

3 Conclusion

In this chapter we have sought to provide a brief overview of alternative ways of viewing the labour market. These various 'models' emphasize competitive or non-competitive forces, and social or institutional forces to a greater or lesser extent. This introduction provides a backdrop for the remaining chapters in this part of the book. In Chapter 23 we consider the economics of discrimination and the theory and evidence relating to labour market segmentation. Chapter 24 focuses upon the influence of industrial relations on the labour market, with a special emphasis on the role of unions. Chapter 25 looks at the factors which determine the structure of wages and earnings, paying regard to the distinction between competitive and non-competitive theories that we introduced above.

CHAPTER 24 Discrimination and segmentation

1 Introduction

The approach of this textbook has largely reflected that of mainstream labour economics, which adopts a supply and demand framework and is based largely on the neoclassical paradigm. Within this framework wages are a return for the productivity of labour and the supply of labour responds to the wage incentives that are available. In other words, although markets may not be perfect, and may not always be clear, the approach assumes there is a long-run tendency for the net advantages of alternative job choices to be equalized by competitive forces. However, we have seen how wage stickiness and unemployment have puzzled economists, but that explanations have been found, such as implicit contracts and efficiency wages, that do not fundamentally challenge the basic neoclassical view of the world, in which rational economic agents are optimizing their utility. Even the concept of internal labour markets, which was originally viewed as being a contradiction to the neoclassical paradigm, can be interpreted as a rational response of profit-maximizing firms to transaction costs.

Not all labour economists, however, are satisfied with this orthodox approach. Imperfect information, barriers to mobility, social and institutional influences, they argue, render this essentially competitive model inappropriate. They emphasize the fragmented nature of the labour market and the tendency for certain groups to be badly treated. This view of the labour market is best described as 'segmentation theory'. One of the concepts that is important in the segmentation approach is that of discrimination. Groups that get locked into bad segments of the labour market are there partly, at least, due to discrimination against them. Thus, there is an intimate link between discrimination and segmentation. Before we consider this link, however, we must also recognize that neoclassical economics has made a contribution to the theory of labour market discrimination, following Becker's theory of discrimination. This theory of discrimination is in the orthodox paradigm, and represents a useful starting point for this chapter. As the chapter proceeds, however, we shall see how segmentation theorists consider this orthodoxy to be greatly lacking. We will provide an overview of the alternative approach that has been put forward and consider some of the main empirical evidence that has resulted from research on segmentation and discrimination.

2 Discrimination

2.1 Introduction

Interest in discrimination amongst labour economists has resulted, for example, in research relating to the labour market performance of black people in the USA, and more generally to the position of women in the labour market. Labour market discrimination is said to exist when workers with identical productive capabilities receive different rewards for their attributes because of the population group to which they belong. A distinction is sometimes made between pre- and post-market discrimination. Pre-market discrimination essentially entails inferior access to education and training, while post-market discrimination entails wage, employment and occupation or job discrimination. Wage discrimination means that one population group, say females, are paid less than male workers despite equal productivity, or more generally, that wage differentials are greater than productivity differentials. Employment discrimination is when black people, for example, bear a disproportionate burden of unemployment. Finally, occupational discrimination occurs when females, for example, are restricted from entering certain occupations, and/or are crowded into others, despite equal capabilities between them and males in the jobs in question. This is closely linked with job discrimination.

2.2 Becker's theory of discrimination

The following exposition of Becker's theory of discrimination draws heavily on Joll *et al.*, (1983, Chapter 6). In standard neoclassical theory we assume that firms are profit maximizers. In other words their utility is a function of the level of profit,

$$u = \mathbf{u}(\pi) \qquad (1)$$

and workers' utility is a function of goods and leisure,

$$u = \mathbf{u}(G,L) \qquad (2)$$

Becker introduced discrimination into this model by allowing firms or workers to have a 'taste for discrimination'.

2.2.1 Employer discrimination

If there are two groups of workers, *A* and *B*, and group *B* is discriminated against by employers, then the firm's utility function becomes

$$u = \mathbf{u}(\pi,B) \qquad (3)$$

where *B* is the number of *B* workers employed. The marginal utility of profit is positive, and the marginal utility of employing *B* workers is negative ($u_\pi > 0$, $u_B < 0$).

Thus there is a trade-off between higher profits and higher employment of *B* workers. Figure 24.1 shows how the firm has a set of indifference curves which slope up to the right, when profits are on the vertical axis and the number of *B* workers employed on the horizontal axis. Thus, as firms employ more and more *B* workers, up to a maximum of 100 per cent, so they require more profit to compensate for the associated disutility. The increasing slope of the indifference curves implies that as firms employ more and more *B* workers, so they need greater amounts of compensation in the form of higher profits. This can result from the diminishing marginal utility of profit or the increasing marginal disutility of employing *B* workers, or both. The slope of each indifference curve at any point, which measures the amount of profit that the firm requires to employ one more *B* worker, or $-u_B/u_\pi$, is called Becker's discrimination coefficient. The stronger the discrimination the higher the discrimination coefficient and the steeper the slope of the indifference curves.

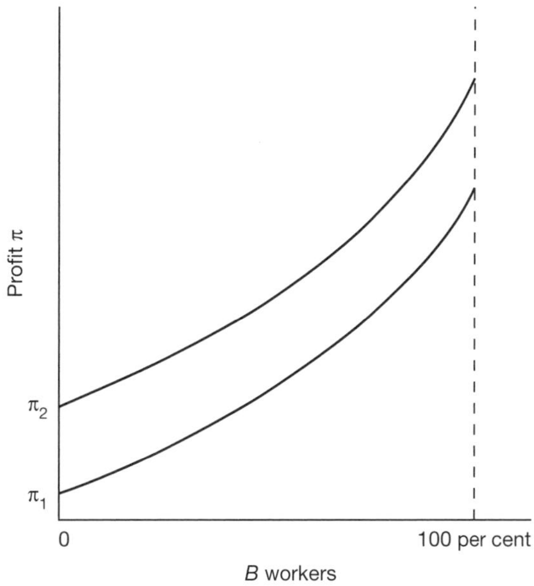

Fig 24.1 Employer discrimination.

The firm seeks to maximize utility subject to the constraints imposed by its demand and production functions. Assuming that *A* and *B* workers are perfect substitutes and that the firm is a price taker then, in the short run, output *Q* is a function of labour, *E*, and the short-run production function (with capital fixed) can be expressed as:

$$Q = \mathbf{Q}(E) = \mathbf{Q}(A + B) \qquad (4)$$

and profits are

$$\Pi = \mathbf{p}Q(A+B) - w_A A - w_B B \qquad (5)$$

where **p** is the product price, and w_A and w_B are the exogenously given wages of *A* and *B* workers respectively.

If $w_A = w_B$ the firm's profit will not vary with the number of *A* and *B* workers employed to produce its profit-maximizing level of output Q^*. The horizontal line *cd* in Figure 24.2 depicts the possible combinations of *A* and *B* that are consistent with such a solution, indicating that profits, Π_0, are earned regardless of the proportion of workers E, who are of type A or B. If all workers are type A then profits are

$$\Pi_{A0} = pQ^* - w_A A \quad (6)$$

If all workers are type B, profits are

$$\Pi_{B0} = pQ^* - w_B B \quad (7)$$

and $\Pi_{A0} = \Pi_{B0}$. Thus the line cd must be horizontal.

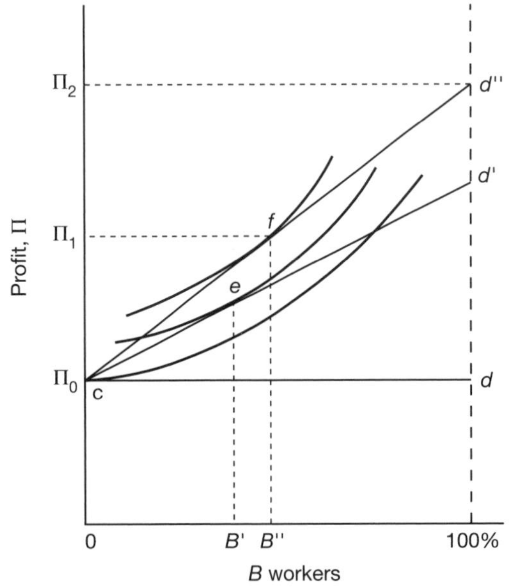

Fig 24.2 Employer discrimination – equilibria under different relative wages.

If, however, the wages of B workers are less than the wages of A workers, $w_B < w_A$, the line which constrains the utility-maximizing solution will be upward sloping such as cd' in Figure 24.2. This indicates that the firm can increase its profits by employing more B workers. The greater the difference between the wages of A and B workers the steeper the slope of this constraint, as in cd''. Given that $w_B < w_A$, the firm can maximize its profits by employing all B workers, and, at the lowest wage of B shown in Figure 24.2, would earn Π_2. If, however, the firm ignored the wage relativities and employed type A people, its profit would be significantly lower, $\Pi_0 > \Pi_2$. A straightforward profit-maximizing company would choose to employ type B in preference to A.

Imagine, however, that the employer associated disutility with the employment of B workers, (i.e. has a taste for discrimination against B workers). Under such circumstances, the firm may not choose that solution. The utility-maximizing solution thus depends upon the firm's taste for discrimination. Figure 24.2 depicts two indifference curves of the firm that has a taste for discrimination against B workers. If the wages of A and B workers are equal, and it faces the constraint cd', it will choose to employ all A workers at the corner solution at point c. If the wages of B workers are less than those of A, such that the constraint it faces is cd, then it chooses the tangency solution at point e, employing the proportion B'. At point e the discrimination coefficient is equal to the slope of the constraint which reflects the relative wages of A and B workers. The firm is trading off possible higher profits against the disutility associated with employing B workers. The firm's demand curve for B workers is expected to be negatively related to the relative wages of the two types of workers. Thus, if w_B falls, then the constraint that the firm faces increases its slope to, say, cd''. The new tangency solution is at point f and the firm employs more B workers, B'', $B'' > B'$, but still earns lower profits, $\Pi_1 < \Pi_0$, than the non-discriminating profit maximizer.

Aggregating across all firms in the relevant labour market we get a market demand curve, $D(B)$, shown in Figure 24.3. There are some non-discriminating employers, which thus provides a demand for B workers, $0B$, even if there is no wage differential between A and B workers. Thereafter demand for B workers requires a wage differential to emerge. The greater the wage differential the more employers that will demand B workers and the more B workers they are likely to be demanding. This produces the market

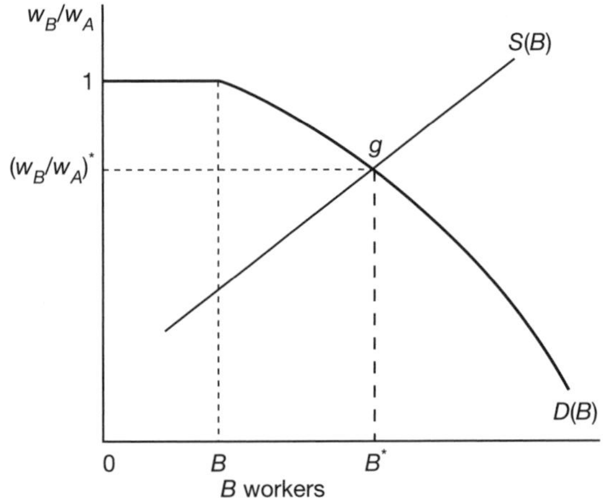

Fig 24.3 Market equilibrium with employer discrimination.

demand curve $D(B)$. If the labour supply of B workers is a normal upward-sloping supply curve, such as $S(B)$, with more B workers supplying their labour as their wage increases, the equilibrium solution is provided by point g. Thus the equilibrium relative wage is $(w_B/w_A)^*$.

Thus, if enough employers have a taste for discrimination, this model elicits pure wage discrimination. Further, an increase in the numbers of discriminating employers or a general rise in the strength of employers' taste for discrimination against B workers would steepen the demand curve and lower B's relative wage, as would an outward shift in the supply of B labour. Thus, utility-maximizing employers with a taste for discrimination are prepared to forgo profits to employ higher proportions of A workers than profit maximization would imply. This raises the question how do such firms survive? In competitive markets we would expect the non-discriminating employers to survive and the discriminators to be forced out of the market. It would appear, therefore, that for such discrimination to persist employers must have freedom to pursue non-profit-maximizing objectives, which implies some degree of imperfect competition.

2.2.2 Worker discrimination

Workers may also have a taste for discrimination. If A workers have a taste for discrimination against B their utility functions include the number of B workers employed:

$$u = \mathbf{u}(G,L,E^B) \tag{8}$$

The marginal utility of goods, G, and of leisure, L, is positive and the marginal utility of the employment of B workers is negative ($u_G > 0$, $u_L > 0$ $u_B < 0$). This produces indifference curves like those in Figure 24.1. Thus workers require higher wages to compensate for higher levels of employment of B workers. The increasing slope of the indifference curves implies that the compensation required for an additional B worker increases with the employment of B workers. This can result from increasing marginal disutility associated from the employment of B workers. The result of this is that if B workers are introduced into the firm, the wage offered to A workers must be higher the greater the proportion of the labour force that is made up by B workers. This produces the conclusion that firms employ either all A workers or all B workers. If A and B workers are perfect substitutes, and the firm is a profit maximizer it will employ an all-B workforce if $w_B < w_A$, and an all-A workforce if $w_A < w_B$. The only situation in which firms might have mixed workforces is if there is an insufficient supply of A or B workers at the going wage.

2.2.3 Customer discrimination

A third source of discrimination in the labour market can arise from amongst customers. If customers prefer to be 'served' by type A rather than B workers, then type B individuals must accept lower wages to become attractive to employers. Again this tends to produce segregated workforces. Firms catering for the discriminatory customers will hire A workers, pay higher wages and charge higher prices than firms that employ B workers.

2.3 Market power models

Becker's model is developed within a competitive framework, and tends to lead to the conclusion that discrimination, especially on the part of employers, is likely to be competed out of existence in the longer term. Some economists, dissatisfied with this approach, have preferred to view discrimination as occurring within a world in which market power enables employers to undertake persistent discrimination and, indeed, in the case of the monopsonistic discrimination model, it turns out to be profitable for the employer. First, we will outline the crowding hypothesis and then proceed to the monopsonistic discrimination model.

2.3.1 Crowding and segregation

The 'crowding model' can be presented in a simple supply and demand framework similar to a normal competitive model. It requires, however, that factors are at play which prevent the operation of competitive market forces to reallocate labour towards their most productive uses. These factors could be social norms and/or a general tendency for employers to discriminate against one or more groups of workers. It also requires the ability for them to sustain this, which implies that they possess significant labour market power. Otherwise we would, again, expect non-discriminating competitive employers to compete this crowding effect way.

Figure 24.4 illustrates this idea in a simple supply and demand framework. Panel (a) represents a labour market (the uncrowded sector) in which

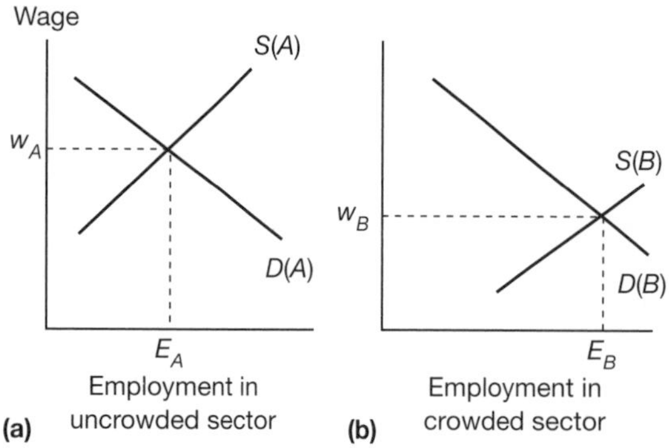

Fig 24.4 Crowding and segregation.

supply is low relative to demand, which produces relatively high wages. Panel (b) represents the crowded sector where supply is large relative to demand, producing relatively low wages. The two markets might be populated by males and females respectively or by whites and blacks. The underlying idea is based on the concept of non-competing groups and is consistent with the idea of labour market duality which we explore later in this chapter. If markets were competitive we would expect persons from the crowded sector to be attracted by the higher wages in the uncrowded sector and for this to compete away the wage difference and to expand employment in the uncrowded sector and to reduce it in the crowded sector. This in turn would increase total output, because the labour attracted into the previously uncrowded sector would produce higher marginal products than when they were located in the crowded sector. Such competitive forces are assumed not to prevail, however, under this crowding hypothesis, and thus discrimination and consequent segregation persists. The theory therefore implies that some barriers are created that prevent the movement of individuals from the crowded to the uncrowded sector. It is also consistent with the idea that individuals are sorted into (two) groups, based on factors other than their productivity, and then allocated between the two markets.

2.3.2 Monopsonistic discrimination

Just as it can be demonstrated that it can be profitable for monopolistic sellers of products to practise price discrimination between different groups of consumers, so it can be demonstrated that it can be profitable for monopsonistic buyers of labour to practise wage discrimination between two different groups of workers. Figure 24.5 presents a diagrammatic exposition of this theory. Panel (a) presents the case of the non-discriminating monopsonist. Setting the marginal wage cost equal to the marginal revenue product produces a profit-maximizing wage and employment outcome of wage w_0 and employment E_0.

Now assume that there are two groups of labour, *A* and *B*, say men and women or whites and blacks, who have different slopes to their supply curves. Group *B* have a steeper labour supply curve, perhaps because they are not as easily mobile as *A*. It is now open to a profit-maximizing employer to practise wage discrimination. Instead of paying wage w_0 for

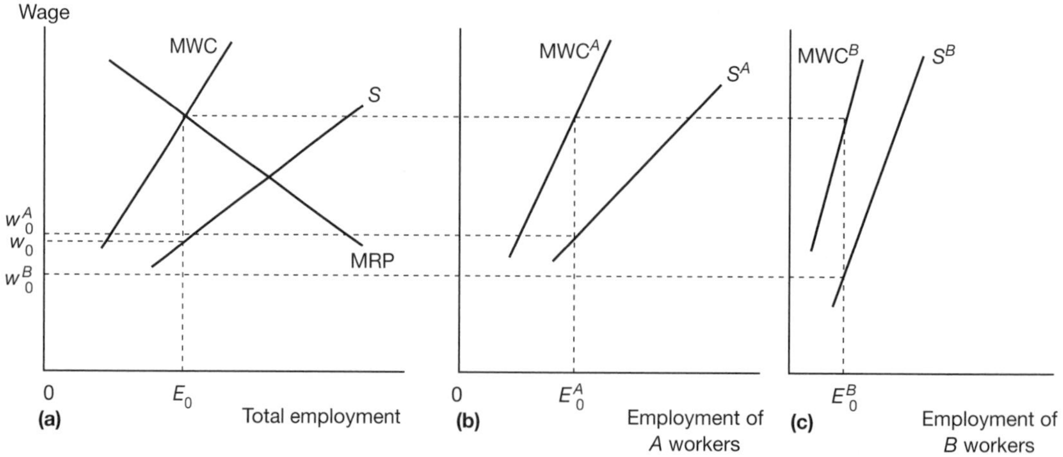

Fig 24.5 Monopsonistic discrimination.

employment E_0 in panel (a) of the figure, they can now employ the same total number of workers, but the composition between the two groups is now different, as are the wages offered. Examination of the three panels of Figure 24.5 shows that the discriminating monopsonist can maintain MWC = MRP overall, by hiring E_0^A of type A workers at a wage w_0^A, along with E_0^B of type *B* employees with a corresponding wage w_0^B. Further exploration of the result reveals that $w_0^A > w_0^B$. By separating the two groups the monopsonist is able to increase profits, at the expense of the *B* workers, despite the fact that the employer has no preference for *A* workers over *B* workers *per se*.

2.4 Statistical discrimination

The theory of 'statistical discrimination' provides another explanation of why rational employers with no taste for discrimination might in practice discriminate in favour of particular groups and against others. Statistical discrimination arises from the problem of imperfect information. A good example in a different market context concerns discrimination against teenage males in vehicle insurance, because, on average, this group represents a higher risk. While there may be particular individuals within this group who are in fact low risk, it is not possible for the insurance company to distinguish them from the high category.

Similarly, in the labour market it may be impossible, or too costly, for employers to obtain sufficient information to obtain an accurate estimate of the productivity of each prospective employee. Thus, they have to rely on the person's characteristics to guide them about their likely productivity. These can include factors such as years of education and qualification levels, but may also include factors such as gender or race. It may be, for example, that, on average, black workers are less productive because they have received inferior schooling to whites, or women in particular jobs may be expected on average to have higher labour turnover, making them less attractive employees. In these circumstances it may prove to be rational for the firm to take account of these characteristics in its hiring decisions, thereby reducing the demand for and, therefore, the wages and employment of particular groups below the levels that would have occurred if they had been given equal treatment with the favoured group.

There may be productivity tests that can be used, such as interviews, aptitude test scores, etc., which may reduce the reliance placed upon such discrimination, but unless such tests are perfect this discrimination can still be rational and affect wage and employment outcomes.

3 Job competition, dual labour markets and segmentation

3.1 Introduction

Economists dissatisfied with orthodox, predominantly competitive, analyses of the labour market, who emphasize labour market fragmentation and the importance of institutional and social influences and the persistence of discrimination, are often labelled as being 'labour market segmentationists'. One approach to labour market segmentation has been that of dual labour market theory, which suggests that there is a primary market with good jobs and a secondary with bad jobs, and little if any mobility between them. Empirical evidence has tended not to support the existence of this simple duality, but segmentation theory has developed in a way that does not rely on duality. In this section, therefore, while we discuss dual labour market theory, we also seek to do justice to the concept of labour market segmentation by discussing the wider body of literature that falls under this heading.

McNabb and Ryan (1990) have pointed out that, historically, labour market segmentation can be traced back to John Stuart Mill and Cairnes, who rejected Adam Smith's representation of the labour market which was basically a competitive model, in favour of the concept of 'non-competing groups' (Mill, 1885; Cairnes 1874), and to the American institutionalists of the 1940s and 1950s who developed the concepts of balkanized and structured labour markets (Dunlop, 1957; Kerr, 1954). The institutionalists emphasized the role of unions in wage determination and the importance of social comparisons, and the concept of structured labour markets, which are governed by rules and procedures. This latter concept was developed by Doeringer and Piore (1971) into the modern concept of internal labour markets, which we have covered in Chapter 19. While a modern mainstream view of internal labour markets is that they are a rational response of optimizing firms in the face of imperfect information, training costs, etc., Doeringer and Piore tended to emphasize the importance of custom and practice and more institutional explanations. Indeed Piore has been a major figure in dual labour market theory, and has emphasized the importance of structured internal labour markets in the primary sector of the dual labour market.

3.2 Job competition model

An important theory of the labour market that helps to underpin the segmentationist approach is the 'job competition model'. Thurow (1975) developed this model of the labour market, in stark contrast to the traditional 'wage competition model' which lies at the centre of mainstream labour economics. In the wage competition model people enter the labour market with a set of skills and compete for jobs on the basis of the wage that they are prepared to accept. In the job competition model, people compete for jobs in terms of their place in a queue, on the basis of the cost of training them for the jobs. On-the-job training is seen as the major form of skill transfer and acquisition, and jobs are viewed as on-the-job training slots. Thus, there is an economy-wide distribution of jobs, each with a wage attached to it, which determines the distribution of earnings. The nature of jobs is essentially technologically determined and the wages attached are based upon established social norms of fairness. Who occupies the jobs then depends considerably upon the costs of training employees to perform the jobs. Thus, there is a distribution of job opportunities which are filled by a screening process whereby employers select workers from a labour queue with the highest-paying jobs given to workers who have the most desired characteristics, which minimize the costs of training them to perform the job in question. The background characteristics that affect the worker's position in the queue include such attributes as education, age, race, socioeconomic background and natural ability. These attributes are thought to be the types of factors that are perceived by employers to influence on-the-job training costs. Not all employers will apply the same weights to all the characteristics. Thus, workers with the same characteristics may receive different wages in different firms. Second, employer discrimination can influence the place of certain groups in the queue.

3.3 Dual labour markets

Piore described labour market duality in the following way:

> the primary market offers jobs which possess several of the following traits: high wages, good working conditions, employment stability and job security, equity and due process in the administration of work rules, and chances for advancement. The ... secondary market has jobs, which, relative to those in the primary sector, are decidedly less attractive. They tend to involve low wages, poor working conditions, considerable variability in employment, harsh and often arbitrary discipline, and little opportunity to advance. The poor are confined to the secondary labour market. (Piore, 1970)

3.3.1 Institutional explanation

Piore emphasized demand side and institutional factors, in contrast to the emphasis on the supply side and individual characteristics in orthodox theory. Nonetheless, secondary jobs tend to filled by groups whose attachment to paid employment is weaker, such as black people, females and youths. Primary jobs tend to be the filled by prime-age white males. Jobs in the primary segment tend to be part of internal labour markets in which pay structures are determined by organizational requirements. Employees tend to be unionized and firms tend to enjoy some degree of monopoly power in their product markets. Product demand tends to be stable and firms undertake large- scale investment. Jobs in the secondary segment tend not to be in internal labour markets as tasks require little general or specific training. Firms tend to face unstable product demand and operate with labour- intensive technologies.

McNabb and Ryan (1990) point out, however, that instability is not the only cause of being in the secondary sector. Declining industries which experience little capital investment may also be the home of secondary labour market jobs. Further, Piore observed that primary and secondary jobs can exist in the same firms. Where production is not technically suited to mass production, especially where the size of market is limited by the customer service requirements, some work tasks remain complex and require high skill, while others may be reduced to a low skill level and form part of the secondary sector.

3.3.2 Radical theory and duality

Radical economists from the USA, such as Reich *et al.* (1973), have put forward a different explanation which involves a 'divide and conquer' strategy by large capitalist firms, as a form of labour control. Previous systems of labour control such as the personalized discipline of 'simple control' and the impersonal machine pacing of 'technical control' proved decreasingly effective as firms became giant corporations and labour tended to become more homogeneous. This homogenization of the labour force posed a potential threat to capitalist power and control of the economy, in the form of worker solidarity in the labour movement. The creation of internal labour markets and their associated job ladders was one of the mechanisms used by capitalists in response to this problem.

> First, it gave workers a sense of vertical mobility as they made their way up the ladder, and was an incentive to workers to work harder... . The other advantage of the job ladder arrangement was that it gave the employers more leverage with which to maintain discipline. The system pitted each worker against all others in rivalry for advancement and undercut any feeling of unity which might develop among them. (Reich *et al.*, 1973, p. 362)

Piece rate schemes to focus workers on their individual work efforts, and paternalistic welfare programmes to tie workers with their employers and weaken their association with the labour movement, were examples of other mechanisms used in this divide and conquer strategy.

3.3.3 An efficiency wage explanation

Some efficiency wage theorists (see Chapter 22) believe that they also have an explanation of labour market duality. The argument is along the following lines. In some firms and industries it would be very costly to monitor workers' productivity. Instead they pay a higher efficiency wage and the employee is aware that they will lose the job if they are found shirking. This threat reduces the monitoring costs that are necessary to induce high work effort and productivity. In other firms and industries, particularly small firms, the employer may choose to pay lower wages and monitor the employee's productivity more closely, because it is cheaper to do so. Thus in primary labour markets firms pay efficiency wages and in secondary labour markets wages are determined more along the lines of conventional labour market theory, and determined by the forces of supply and demand.

3.4 Segmentation and stratification

Partly because of the lack of evidence to support the simple duality version of segmented labour markets, one variant of the segmentation hypothesis includes an upper and lower tier in the primary labour market. In the upper tier are professional and managerial jobs where job changes are quite frequent, as such personnel seek career advancement. In the lower tier of the primary labour market internal labour markets dominate.

McNabb and Ryan (1990) point out that although dualism has dominated the segmentation literature, a number of authors have viewed the labour market in terms of multiple segments (Freedman, 1976; Buchele, 1976) or of a continuous job queue along the lines of Thurow's job competition model which we outlined above. In the latter version job rewards are highly differentiated but no clear segments are distinguished. Based upon Figure 24.6 McNabb and Ryan (1990) suggest that two versions of segmentation can be distinguished and contrasted with the competitive model. Panel (a) represents the competitive model in which competitive forces tend to compress job rewards. Panel (b) represents the Thurow-type version of segmentation where the dualist terminology can still be retained, as when all jobs above an arbitrary frontier are defined as primary and the remainder as secondary. Panel (c) represents the strict dualist position which would imply a bimodal distribution of job rewards.

4 Evidence on discrimination and segmentation

4.1 Discrimination

4.1.1 Wage discrimination

While average earnings of different population groups, say men and women or whites and blacks, for example, may differ substantially, to test whether discrimination is an important cause of this is a difficult task. Some of the difference at least may result from differences in productivity resulting perhaps from differences in education and experience. A common technique for testing this statistically is known as the Oaxaca decomposition method (Oaxaca, 1973). This involves the following steps.

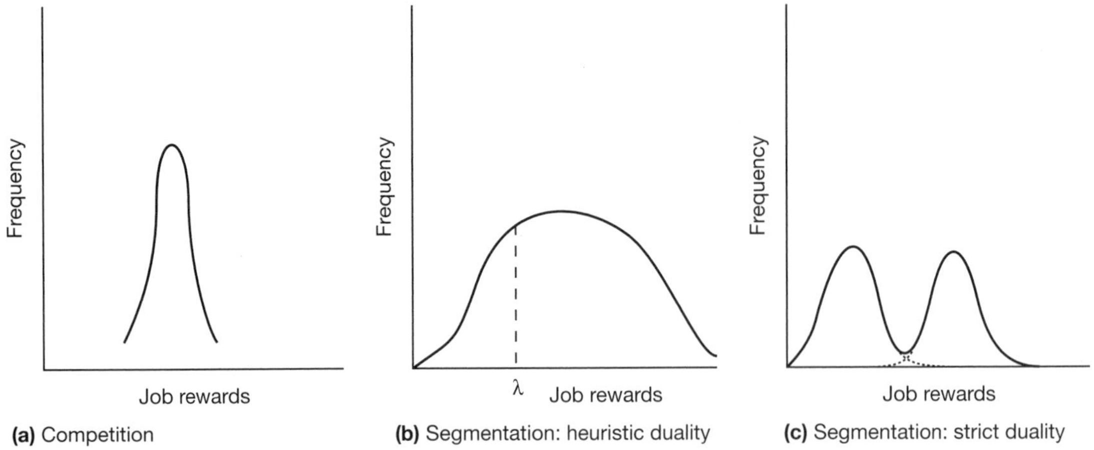

Fig 24.6 Duality and segmentation.

First we estimate an earnings function for women identifying the contribution of the various characteristics of female workers to their earnings. These characteristics normally include such variables as education, experience, hours of work, firm size, industry, etc., but should, in principle, take into account all those factors that can be expected to determine worker productivity and earnings. We then use the estimated 'pay-offs' to women of their various characteristics to estimate the amount that women would earn if they possessed the same stock of productive characteristics as men. Finally we compare the hypothetical earnings of women (if they had the same characteristics as men) with the actual earnings of men. In principle, the difference should be a measure of wage discrimination.

This method can be criticized on the grounds that the earnings functions used do not capture all of the qualities that contribute to productivity differences between, say, men and women. There may be some unmeasurable characteristics and some that are not adequately measured. Thus, it is usually argued that the unexplained wage difference is an upper estimate of the effect of discrimination, and, in principle, at least, it sometimes could be substantially lower.

A review of some of the studies using this or similar methods is presented in Chapter 26, but to give an idea of the findings at this stage, estimates of gender wage discrimination in the USA, for example, have included estimates as high as 66 per cent of the male–female wage differential (Blinder, 1973) and 56 per cent (Corcoran and Duncan, 1979). Segregation studies in Australia have estimated that 78 per cent of the male–female differential is due to discrimination (Chapman and Mulvey, 1990) and using a different methodology, an estimate of around one-third to one-half of the differential (Drago, 1989). A UK study by Zabalza and Arrafat (1985) estimated that about 30 per cent of the gender wage differential was unexplained or due to discrimination. Similar results were obtained by Joshi and Newell (1987).

4.1.2 Segregation

There are various measures of segregation. The index of dissimilarity, for example, varies from zero to 100. It measures the percentage of one group (typically one gender) that would have to change occupations for the two genders to have equal occupational distributions (assuming that there was no change in the occupational distribution of the other gender). Thus an index of zero implies an equal occupational distribution and an index of 100, total segregation. A study in the USA by King (1992) produced an index of 66 per cent for 1970 and 57 per cent in 1988, for gender segregation, suggesting that such segregation was declining.

One problem with measures of segregation is that the use of different measures tends to tell different stories. In an Australian study, for example, Karmel and Maclachlan (1988) show that different indices generate different trends and it is thus unclear whether segregation increased or decreased between 1961 and 1981. Another problem with interpreting these measures, with respect to the issue of identifying the presence and extent of discrimination, is to determine what value the indices would be expected to take if there was no labour market discrimination. There may, for example, be differences in preferences between males and females about job choice which influence the outcomes. No measures have been devised to estimate the proportion of occupational segregation that can be attributed to unequal treatment by employers.

4.2 Segmentation

McNabb and Ryan (1990) point out that it is very difficult to obtain strong tests of the segmentation hypothesis. Sloane *et al.* (1993) identify 16 studies which have attempted to test for the presence of segmentation. They point to the diversity of tests and their conflicting findings. They argue that this results from the 'theoretical obscurity' of labour market segmentation and the difficulty of determining precisely where neoclassical economists and segmentationists part company. Nonetheless there have been some very interesting attempts from a range of angles to shed light on the viability of the segmentation hypothesis. Here we briefly review some of the main empirical findings that have been produced in examining the segmentation hypothesis – in addition, see Case Study 1.

4.2.1 Different earnings for people with similar attributes

The segmentation hypothesis implies that workers of equal quality will receive different rewards dependent upon the segments in which they find themselves. Studies such as that by Osterman (1975) in the USA, and McNabb (1987) in the UK, using earnings functions for different segments of the labour market,

CASE STUDY 1 Labour market segmenation in Aberdeen

Sloane *et al.* (1993) use four different methods of analysis (a simple career/non-career model, cluster analysis, factor analysis and switching regressions) to test for the existence of segmentation in six local labour market areas. These areas were: Aberdeen, Northampton, Swindon, Kirkaldy, Coventry and Rochdale. In general the findings of all the tests pointed to basic 'labour market homogeneity'. That is, analysing the labour market in different segments does not significantly improve the explanation of labour market outcomes. There are, however, one or two caveats. First, the simple career model suggests that rewards were higher in the career than in the non-career sector of the labour market. Second, the switching regressions model was found to be consistent with labour market duality in one of the six local labour markets – that of Aberdeen.

Table 24.1 presents estimates based upon the switching regression analysis of the percentages of persons in Aberdeen, in different groups of the population, who were in the primary sector.

Table 24.1 Switching regression – Aberdeen

Demographic group	Percentage in primary sector
Males	47
Females	43
Married persons	56
Multiple job holders	21
Aged < 30	28
Aged 30–40	60
Aged 40+	48
Whole sample	45

Flatau and Lewis (1993) used a two-stage analysis to investigate the presence of labour market segmentation in Australia. The first part involved principal component analysis to determine the degree of commonality in the set of specified job characteristics thought to affect labour market segmentation. The second part used cluster analysis to assign occupations to particular segments on the basis of these characteristics. Their analysis produced three 'segments' and a number of single-occupation 'outlying clusters'. Table 24.2 lists the occupations in the different 'segments'.

Flatau and Lewis define Segment A as the secondary sector but add that

> Cleaners have very poor scores on every indicator suggesting that it is an occupation clearly in

continues

CASE STUDY 1 continued

Table 24.2 Results of cluster analysis

Segment A Cluster 1	Food tradespersons Stenographers and typists Filing, sorting and copying clerks	Receptionists, telephonists and messengers Sales assistants Tellers, cashiers and ticket salespersons	Miscellaneous salesperson Personal service workers Miscellaneous labourers, related workers
Cluster 2	Amenity horticultural tradespersons	Trades assistants and factory hands	Agricultural labourers and related workers
Segment B Cluster 1	Medical, science and technical officers Engineering and building associates and technicians Miscellaneous para-professionals Metal fitting and machining tradespersons Other metal tradespersons	Building tradespersons Printing tradespersons Vehicle tradespersons Data processing and business machine operators Numerical clerks	Material recording and despatching clerks Miscellaneous clerks Mobile plant operators (except transport) Stationary plant operators Machine operators
Segment C			
Cluster 1	Sales representatives		
Cluster 2	Other teachers and instructors	Registered nurses	
Cluster 3	Natural scientists Miscellaneous professionals	Building professionals and engineers	Business professionals
Cluster 4	Specialist managers		

Source: Flatau and Lewis (1993). Occupations within clusters have been listed according to Australian Standard Classification of Occupations; there are a number of single-occupation outlying clusters.

the 'secondary sector' but at the lowest rung of this segment. It has not clustered with other occupations presumed to lie in the secondary sector ... because it has its own very different characteristics, i.e. job rewards are so low on every indicator. (Flatau and Lewis, 1993, p. 291)

Sources: Sloane *et al.* (1993); Flatau and Lewis (1993)

suggest that persons who are statistically comparable in the secondary segment receive 20 per cent and over 30 per cent, respectively, less than their counterparts in the primary sector. As we saw with the studies of discrimination based upon earnings functions, such studies are always open to the criticism that if unmeasured differences in the quality of the workers in the two segments were accounted for, the differences would disappear.

4.2.2 Returns to human capital investment

Earnings functions have also been used to estimate returns to education in different segments of the labour market. The study by Osterman (1975), for example, found significant returns to schooling and work experience in the primary segment only. This is sometimes referred to as the 'incremental' formulation of segmentation. It has been pointed out, however, that the absence of a return to human capital in the secondary segment is neither necessary nor sufficient for the viability of the segmentation hypothesis (Ryan, 1981). It is not necessary because even if two segments provide returns to education and experience they may pay different levels to workers in the two segments. It is not sufficient because higher returns to experience in one segment may be compensated for by lower starting rates – that is not to deny that lower or non-existent returns to education or experience in the 'secondary sector' could be a feature of segmentation.

4.2.3 Links between product and labour markets

McNabb and Ryan (1990) argue that there is now sufficiently extensive evidence of the link between employer attributes, production technologies and product markets on the one hand, and labour market outcomes on the other, to underline the credibility of many segmentationist propositions. They point to studies such as Beck *et al.* (1978), Baron and Bielby (1980) and Woodward and McNabb (1978) that find associations of both pay and mobility with product market concentration ratios, capital/labour ratios, firm size, and access to government contracts.

4.2.4 Over-representation of disadvantaged groups in secondary segments

Segmentation theory argues that particular groups such as youths, black people, or married females, tend to be over-represented in secondary jobs (i.e. jobs with low rewards). Marsden and Ryan (1986) examined the relationship between the pay of adult males and the employment of youths across manufacturing and mining industries in European Union economies and found a consistent and generally significant negative relationship, thus suggesting that youths tend not to be employed in primary sector industries. As McNabb and Ryan (1990) point out, the negative relationship between adult male pay and the employment share of youths could arise in a competitively determined industry wage structure only if high adult male pay were to reflect high skill levels, with youths as poor substitutes. They point to evidence that adult pay is only weakly correlated with the skill mix across sectors, and argue that a more convincing explanation involves segmentation with wages determined by social and institutional forces and employers faced by relatively high wages employing adult males rather than youths.

4.2.5 Mobility between segments

An important feature of the segmentation hypothesis is that disadvantaged workers in secondary segments are trapped in bad jobs. This is sometimes referred to as the 'confinement' proposition. Tests of the confinement proposition based on the dualist approach to segmentation have typically found quite high rates of mobility across the frontier between the 'primary' and 'secondary' segments, with human capital playing an important role in determining this mobility (Rosenburg, 1977 and 1980; Mayhew and Rosewell, 1979). Schiller (1977), concerned not with movements across an arbitrary frontier, but with travelling a substantial distance along a spectrum of job rewards, also found evidence of quite high mobility. McNabb and Ryan (1990), however, point out that evidence was found of a lower rate of movement across an arbitrary dualist frontier than what would be expected on a random basis, but the result nevertheless weakens support for the segmentation hypothesis. However, they also point out that the studies in question exclude females, for whom segmentation is likely to be a more severe problem than for males. They also suggest that the apparently high mobility rates may result from the failure to control for retirements from, or expansion of, the primary segment, or for changes in the size of the primary segment due to economic expansion. Evidence that downward mobility from primary jobs is lower than upward mobility from secondary jobs (Rosenburg, 1977) is put forward to support this point.

4.2.6 Wage–quit relationship

Another prediction of the segmentation hypothesis is an inverse wage–quit relationship among comparable workers. Those in high-wage, primary-sector jobs are expected to hold on to their advantages, producing a low quit rate. Those in low-wage, secondary-sector jobs are expected to have high quit rates. The main problem in testing this relationship is controlling for labour quality across sectors. Pencavel (1970) undertook such a study and found a highly significant inverse wage–quit relationship, with statistical controls for workforce quality. The range of quit rates, controlling for workforce composition, was from 0.92 to 1.81 per cent per month across industry sectors in the USA.

However, an alternative interpretation of the inverse wage–quit relationship is offered by the competitive model. In the traditional model, it is also expected that low-wage employers will lose labour faster than high-wage employers. This is consistent with the efficient allocation of labour owing to the operation of competitive market forces. McNabb and Ryan (1990) point out, however, that the competitive model also predicts that the wage structure will adapt in the face of mobility. As labour is attracted from low pay to high pay, so supply and demand should tend to bring pay rates together for comparable workers. Thus, combining information about the wage–quit relationship with evidence of persistence of pay differences for comparable workers provides some support for the segmentation hypothesis. Further, it is argued that the workers quitting from low-paid jobs tend to move into other low-paid jobs and only gain access to primary employment when retirement and expansion create vacancies (Ulman, 1965).

4.2.7 Strict duality

In their review of the evidence on segmentation McNabb and Ryan (1990) point out that

> interpretations of the labour market in terms of strict duality (including bimodality) have failed to muster adequate empirical support ... Bimodality is typically found, if at all, only in one of the several dimensions of industrial structure (factors) ... the bimodality in such studies refers to product-market attributes rather than to labour market outcomes ... . The labour-market consequences of bimodal dualism (in studies attempting to establish strict duality) has been limited to differences in earnings or turnover in the two segments ... . No one has established the existence of bimodal duality in pay or turnover parallel to that in industrial characteristics ... . The plain fact is that the links between product and labour markets are too multidimensional and complex for a strict dualist formulation to prove viable (Wallace and Kalleberg, 1981; Hodson and Kaufman, 1982). (McNabb and Ryan, 1990, pp. 166–169).

4.2.8 Summary of evidence on segmentation

As we noted earlier, it is difficult to obtain strong tests of the segmentation hypothesis. For this reason the debate about segmentation remains inconclusive. We can be confident, however, that the labour market cannot be characterized in terms of strict duality. Sufficient evidence has been put forward, however, to lead us to believe that a broader concept of segmentation has something interesting and useful to contribute to our understanding of the operation of labour markets. The evidence is not strong enough to cause mainstream labour economists to lose faith in the value of the neoclassical paradigm. The conventional wisdom is probably that orthodox labour economics can still provide the basic framework of analysis for most issues in labour economics, but that it is important to bear in mind the possibility of segmentation.

5 Conclusions

In this chapter we have examined both theory and evidence concerning labour market discrimination and segmentation. While neoclassical economics has a theory of labour market discrimination, this theory predicts that discrimination will disappear in competitive markets. Even under the orthodox theory, however, discrimination can persist where market power exists in the labour market and can even be profit maximizing in the model of discriminating monopsony. Also imperfect information in the labour market can lead to 'statistical discrimination'. Such statistical discrimination is expected in the job competition model in which wages are quite rigid and determined institutionally, while the allocation of jobs is based upon job queues.

Internal labour markets imply similar employer behaviour as the job competition model predicts, and some proponents of these theories have argued that labour markets tend to be segmented. An extreme form of segmentation is labour market duality. The primary sector in this model includes good jobs within internal labour markets giving rise to relatively high rewards, and bad jobs in the secondary sector which tend to be relatively unskilled, where internal labour markets do not apply. Other explanations of duality include 'radical theories' in which employers divide and rule, and an efficiency wage explanation, which diverges less from mainstream thought.

While there is a lack of evidence to support strict duality, broader definitions of labour market segmentation are more plausible. It is difficult, however, to test rigorously the segmentation hypothesis, and while some evidence has been uncovered that gives some credence to the concept, it has not been strong enough to cause mainstream labour economics to lose confidence. Conventional wisdom is, probably, that mainstream labour economics is an appropriate framework for analysing a range of labour market issues, but that the possibility of some degree of segmentation should be borne in mind.

References

Baron, J.N. and W.T. Bielby (1980). 'Bringing the Firms Back In: Stratification, Segmentation and the Organisation of Work'. *American Sociological Review*, October, 45, 737–765.

Beck, E.M., P.M. Horan, and C.M. Tolbert (1978). 'Stratification in a Dual Economy: A Sectoral Model of Earnings Determination'. *American Sociological Review*, October, 43, 704–720.

Becker, G. (1957). *The Economics of Discrimination*. Chicago, University of Chicago Press (2nd Edition 1971).

Blinder, A.S. (1973). 'Wage Discrimination: Reduced Form and Structural Estimates.' *Journal of Human Resources*, 18, 4, Fall, 436–455.

Buchele, R.K. (1976). 'Jobs and Workers: A Labour Market Segmentation Perspective on the Work Experience of Young Men'. Unpublished PhD Dissertation, Harvard University.

Cairnes, J. (1874). *Some Leading Principles of Political Economy*. London, Macmillan.

Chapman, B.J. and C. Mulvey (1990). 'An Analysis of the Origins of Sex Differences in Australian Wages'. *Journal of Industrial Relations*, 28, 4, 504–520.

Corcoran, M. and G.J. Duncan (1979). 'Work History, Labour Force Attachment, and Earnings Differences between the Races and Sexes', *Journal of Human Resources*, Winter, 3–20.

Drago, R. (1989). 'The Extent of Wage Discrimination in Australia'. *Australian Bulletin of Labour*. 14, 4, 592–609.

Doeringer, P. and M. Piore (1971). *Internal Labour Markets and Manpower Analysis*, Lexington, MA: D.C. Heath.

Dunlop, J.T. (1957). 'The Task of Contemporary Wage Theory'. In G.W. Taylor and F.C. Pearson (eds). *New Concepts in Wage Determination*. New York: McGraw-Hill.

Flatau, P. and P.E.T. Lewis (1993). 'Segmented Labour Markets in Australia'. *Applied Economics*. 25, 285–294.

Freedman, M. (1976). *Labour Markets; Segments and Shelters*. Montclair, NJ: Allanheld, Osmun.

Hodson, R., and R. Kaufman (1982). 'Economic Dualism: A Critical Review'. *American Sociological Review*. December, 47, 6, 727–729.

Joll, C., C. McKenna, R. McNabb and J. Storey (1983). *Developments in Labour Market Analysis*. London: George Allen and Unwin.

Joshi, H. and M.L. Newell (1987). 'Pay Differences Between Men and Women: Longitudinal Evidence From the 1946 Cohort'. *Centre for Economic Policy Research*, Discussion Paper No. 156. London.

Karmel, T. and M. Maclachlan (1988). 'Occupational Sex Segregation – Increasing or Decreasing?'. *Economic Record*, 64, 186, 187–195.

Kerr, C. (1954). 'The Balkanisation of Labour Markets'. In E.W. Bakke (ed.) *Labour Mobility and Economic Opportunity*. Cambridge, MA.: MIT Press.

King, M. C. (1992) 'Occupational Segregation by Race and Sex, 1940–88'. *Monthly Labour Review*, 115, 30–37.

Marsden, D. and P. Ryan (1986). 'Where do Young Workers Work? The Distribution of Youth Employment by Industry in Various European Economies'. *British Journal of Industrial Relations*. March, 24, 1, 83–102.

Mayhew, K. and B. Rosewell (1979). 'Labour Market Segmentation in Britain'. *Oxford Bulletin of Economics and Statistics*. 41, 2, 81–116.

McNabb, R. (1987). 'Testing for Labour Market Segmentation in Britain'. *Manchester School*, September, 55, 3, 257–273.

McNabb, R. and P. Ryan (1990). 'Earnings Determination and Labour Market Duality in Britain'. Paper Presented to Annual Meeting of International Working Group on Labour Market Segmentation, Cambridge.

Mill, J.S. (1885). *Principles of Political Economy*. New York: Appleton.

Oaxaca, R. (1973). 'Male–Female Wage Differentials in Urban Labour Markets'. *International Economic Review*, 14, 693–709.

Osterman, P. (1975). 'An Empirical Study of Labour Market Segmentation'. *Industrial and Labour Relations Review*, July, 28, 508–523

Pencavel, J.H. (1970). 'An Analysis of the Quit Rate in American Manufacturing Industry'. Industrial Relations Research Section. Princeton University, Princeton, NJ.

Piore, M.J. (1970). 'The Dual Labour Market; Theory and Applications'. In R. Barringer and S.H. Beer (eds). *The State and the Poor*. Cambridge, MA: Winthrop.

Reich, M., D.M. Gordon and R.C. Edwards (1973). 'A Theory of Labour Market Segmentation'. *American Economic Review*, 63, 359–365.

Rosenburg, S. (1977). 'The Marxian Reserve Army of Labour and the Dual Labour Market'. *Politics and Society*, 7, 2, 221–228.

Rosenburg, S. (1980). 'Male Occupational Standing and the Dual Labour Market'. *Industrial Relations*. Winter, 19, 1, 34–49.

Ryan, P. (1981). 'Segmentation, Duality and the Internal Labour Market'. In F. Wilkinson (ed.) *Dynamics of Labour Market Segmentation*. New York: Academic Press.

Schiller, B.R. (1977). 'Relative Earnings Mobility in the United States'. *American Economic Review*, December, 67, 5, 926–941.

Sloane, P.J., P.D. Murphy, I. Theodossiou and M. White (1993). 'Labour Market Segmentation: A Local Labour Market Analysis using Alternative Approaches'. *Applied Economics*. 25, 569–581.

Thurow, L. (1975). *Generating Inequality*. New York: Basic Books.

Ulman, L. (1965). 'Labour Mobility and the Industrial Wages Structure in the Post-War United States'. *Quarterly Journal of Economics*. February, 79, 1, 81–95.

Wallace, M. and A. Kalleberg (1981). 'Economic Organisation of Firms and Labour Market Consequences: Towards a Specification of Dual Economic Theory'. In I. Berg (ed.). *Sociological Perspectives on Labour Markets*. New York: Academic Press.

Woodward, N. and R. McNabb (1978). 'Low Pay in British Manufacturing'. *Applied Economics*, 10, 49–60.

Zabalza, A. and J.L. Arrafat (1985). 'The Extent of Sex Discrimination in Britain'. In A. Zabalza and Z. Tzannatos (eds). *Women and Equal Pay: The Effects of Legislation on Female Employment and Wages in Britain*. Cambridge: Cambridge University Press.

CHAPTER 25 Industrial relations, bargaining and the effects of trade unions

1 Introduction

An important institutional feature of the labour market is the organization of a part of the labour force into unions. These are traditionally referred to as 'trade unions' because the early unions (and many contemporary unions as well) were based upon particular crafts or trades. The level of 'unionization' has been declining in many countries in recent years, but still accounts, for example, for over 30 per cent of employees in the UK and over 40 per cent in Australia. In the USA unions do not have such a strong tradition and currently only about 15 per cent of the labour force is unionized.

Part II of the book made little or no reference to the effect of suppliers of labour joining together into trade unions. In our consideration of the interaction of supply and demand in Part IV of the book, we made some references to the presence of trade unions, but not a great deal. For example, in Chapter 13 we considered the effect of monopoly on labour market outcomes. Trade unions are the institution which can create this type of monopoly power in some labour markets, in particular those where 'closed shop' provisions apply. Thus, this part of the book is concerned with outlining how the presence of trade unions impacts on the operation of labour markets, both from a theoretical and empirical perspective.

There is an extensive literature on trade unions and on their impact on the labour market, some of which falls within the field of 'industrial relations', some within the field of 'labour economics' and some on the boundaries between the two. In this book we concentrate primarily on the theory and evidence about trade unions that is most important in contemporary thinking about the economics of the labour market. Nonetheless, to understand the operation and effects of trade unions, it is useful to consider the institutional context within which unions operate.

In Section 2 of this chapter, we present a brief discussion of the different types of industrial relations systems and labour market institutions that exist in various industrialized economies. Section 3 provides a brief description of the origin and structure of trade unions. Section 4 discusses models that seek to explain union membership and variations in the level of unionization. Section 5 introduces 'the bargaining problem' and the principal theoretical solutions that have been proposed. Section 6 considers the theory and evidence of strikes. Section 7 outlines the concept of a union's utility as a function of wages and employment and considers different forms that this function might take. In Section 8 we describe the 'simple monopoly union' and 'right to manage' models. Section 9 discusses the concept of 'efficient bargains' including the 'insider-dominated efficient bargain'. Section 10 reviews that part of labour economics concerned with the empirical analysis of the effects of unions. Finally, in Section 11 we present some conclusions.

2 Industrial relations systems and labour market institutions

Industrial relations systems and labour market institutions vary considerably across countries, with respect to: the degree of centralization or decentralization of wage determination; the importance of unions in the wage determination process; the degree of regulation of wage and employment outcomes. The USA, Canada and Japan, for example, are generally regarded as very decentralized. Austria and Sweden are generally regarded as being more centralized. Further, the latter two have often been referred to as good examples of 'corporatism' in which the 'social partners' of unions, employers and government get together at the 'centre', to achieve consensus about aggregate wage settlements in the light of macroeconomic objectives. Nonetheless, there may still be a certain amount of flexibility at the local level, around these 'centralized norms'. Australia and New Zealand have, for most of this century, had distinctive industrial relations systems in which industrial tribunals or arbitration commissions have played a key role, typically in a quite centralized way, in setting wages and conditions of work, reducing the importance of bargaining in wage setting. New Zealand, however, abandoned this system in the 1980s. So far, Australia has retained the system but sought to decentralize its operation and increase the importance of enterprise bargaining within it.

We will not attempt in this book to develop an extensive analysis of industrial relations systems, but it is useful to bear in mind the sort of differences outlined above, when considering the economics of trade unions and bargaining.

3 Origin and structure of trade unions

The origin of trade unions can be traced back at least to the organization of skilled workers into craft unions in the mid-19th century in the UK. Later in the 19th century, unskilled manual workers began to organize themselves into unions. From that time union membership grew steadily until the 1980s, with the major post-war development being the growth of white collar unionism. Union membership in the UK reached a peak of about 50 per cent of the labour force in the late 1970s, but this has declined substantially during the 1980s and now stands at little over 30 per cent. The union movement in Australia also peaked at around 50 per cent of the labour force, but, although it has declined significantly in recent years, membership has held up more strongly than in the UK, currently remaining at over 40 per cent of the labour force. In the USA, unions developed in a rather different way, reaching a peak of around 25 per cent in the early 1970s, before falling back to about 15 per cent of the labour force.

The historical origin of trade unions is probably best thought of as a response to industrialization which undermined self-employment as the predominant mode of employment. In the industrialized economy workers were organized into unions as a form of protection against possible or real exploitation by employers, and sought to establish acceptable wages and conditions for their members.

There have been a number of classifications or typologies of unions. These include, for example, the distinction between craft, general and industrial unions, and that between 'closed' and 'open unions' (Turner, 1962). These different types of unions imply different types of membership, different sizes, and different objectives. For the purpose of the present chapter, the main thing to bear in mind is that unions are not homogeneous, have different objectives, and use different ways of exerting their influence on labour market outcomes. For example, some craft unions have tended to have a 'closed membership' based upon particular trade qualifications, with the aim of establishing and maintaining substantial wage differentials for their skills, and influencing labour market outcomes through restricting the supply of labour. In contrast some very large unions, whether based upon a particular industry or cutting across a range of industries (such as unions representing a large number of unskilled workers), have sought to affect outcomes more by their strength of numbers and union coverage, affecting the general level of wages rather than wage differentials.

4 Union membership and 'unionization'

4.1 Introduction – a supply and demand model

As noted above, the level of union membership or 'unionization' of the labour force has varied substantially over time and between countries. Before examining the empirical evidence on such variations we outline a well-known model of union membership, developed by Ashenfelter and Pencavel (1969) and Pencavel (1971). This model involves a supply and demand framework for union membership. The demand for union membership by employees is a function of the price of union membership which includes union dues, the cost of time spent on union activities, etc. *Ceteris paribus*, the higher the price, the lower the percentage of employees who will want to be union members. This is represented by $D(T)$ in Figure 25.1. The supply curve reflects the costs of representing workers and is considered to be a normal upward-sloping supply curve, $S(T)$ in Figure 25.1. The equilibrium outcome is the level of unionization T^* and price of union membership $p(T)^*$.

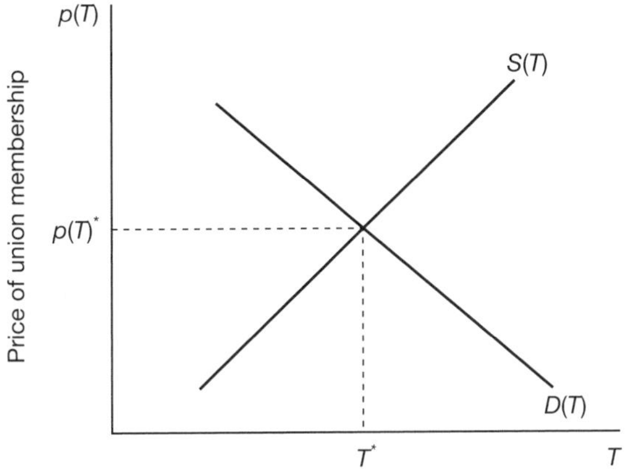

Fig 25.1 Unionization: a supply and demand framework.

If the demand curve shifts to the right, the proportion of persons unionized (or 'union density') increases and the price of union membership also increases. This would happen, for example, if the perceived net benefits from union membership increased or if there was a change in tastes in favour of union membership. If the supply curve shifts to the right, union density increases and the price of union membership falls. This could be caused by labour legislation making it easier for unions to operate effectively or changes in the industrial structure that make it easier to organize the labour force. The decrease in union membership experienced in the UK, Australia, the USA and other countries, in the last 20 years, can be thought of to a greater or lesser extent as associated with leftward shifts in the supply or demand curves or both.

4.2 Empirical evidence on unionization

4.2.1 Introduction

Table 25.1 provides figures for trade union density in each of 18 OECD countries for 1970, 1980 and 1988. It can be seen that there is a great deal of variation across countries and over time. In 1988, for example, union density ranged from 12 per cent in France to 85 per cent in Sweden. Over time union density has declined in Japan, the Netherlands and France, as well as the USA and the UK, while it actually increased over this period in Sweden and Finland

Table 25.1 Union density in OECD countries, 1970, 1980 and 1988 (per cent)

	1970	1980	1988
Canada	31.1	35.1	34.6
USA	n/a	23.0	16.4
Japan	35.1	31.1	26.8
Australia	n/a	49.0	42.0
New Zealand	46.2	55.0	42.1
Austria	59.8	53.8	45.7
Belgium	46.0	56.5	53.0
Denmark	60.0	76.5	73.2
Finland	51.4	69.8	71.3
France	22.3	19.0	12.0
Germany	33.0	37.0	33.8
Ireland	53.1	57.0	52.4
Italy	36.3	49.3	39.6
Netherlands	37.0	35.3	25.0
Norway	50.6	56.9	57.1
Sweden	67.7	80.0	85.3
Switzerland	30.7	30.7	26.0
UK	44.8	50.7	41.5

Source: OECD Trends in Union Membership, *Employment Outlook*, July 1991, pp. 97–120.

4.2.2 Cross-sectional determinants

Bean and Holden (1994) have reviewed the evidence on the cross-sectional determinants of union density and estimated a simple cross-country econometric model. They emphasize the importance of the industrial relations system as a determinant with centralized bargaining having a positive effect on union density, and the importance of the public sector in creating an environment that is conducive to unionism.

More unified union systems are also thought to be an influence on unionization (Visser, 1988) as is the concentration of capital (Stephens, 1979). Wallerstein (1989) concludes from an empirical study of 20 countries that the size of the labour force itself, which represents the potential union membership, is also significant in explaining cross-country variations in union density. It is argued that the negative relationship that is found between union density and 'potential membership' results from the fact that in smaller labour markets unions can achieve higher levels of density more cheaply in terms of recruitment costs, which depend to some extent on the numbers being recruited.

Cross-sectional studies using data about individuals have found some evidence of the effect of personal characteristics such as gender, family responsibility, occupational status and educational attainment (Fiorito and Greer, 1982; Bain and Elias, 1976). More recent studies by Booth (1986) and Deery and de Cieri (1991) have found that job and industry characteristics are the major determinants, swamping the effects of individual characteristics. As Bean and Holden (1994) point out, these studies seem to suggest that characteristics pertaining to the occupations or industries in which employees work appear to affect either the evaluation of the benefits of union membership by individual employees, or the propensity of trade unions to secure their coverage.

4.2.3 Explaining time series variation in union density

Considerable efforts have been made to explain the substantial variations in union density over time. We outlined the simple theoretical model of Ashenfelter and Pencavel (1969) in Section 4.1, which the authors used to underpin their time series econometric model for the USA. They have five explanatory variables in their model: (i) rate of change of prices; (ii) lagged union density; (iii) rate of change of employment; (iv) peak unemployment in preceding trough; (v) strength of the Democratic Party. It was thought that the rate of change of prices would have a positive effect because the higher the inflation rate the more likely it was that workers would wish to protect their real living standards by joining unions. Lagged union density enters the model because of the hypothesis that the higher the level of unionization already achieved the harder it would be to increase it. The rate of change of employment measures the tightening of the labour market. The idea is that employer retaliation to unions is reduced when labour markets tighten, and it is easier and less costly to launch successful union organizing drives. The amount of peak unemployment in the preceding trough is used as a proxy for labours' 'stock of grievances'. The strength of the Democratic Party variable attempts to capture the effects of the political climate and favourable legislation.

The estimated model produced apparently good results and had a big influence on the literature. Subsequent researchers, however, including Moore and Pearce (1976) and Shelfin *et al.* (1981), found evidence of a structural break in the model, in 1937 in the latter case, possibly reflecting the effect of the Wagner Act. The Moore and Pearce (1976) results suggested that the model did not work well in the post-war period.

Bain and Elsheikh (1976) attempt to formulate a model that could work consistently over time and across countries. Their model had the rate of change of union density as the dependent variable and included the following variables: (i) rate of change of prices; (ii) rate of change of money wages; (iii) the unemployment rate; (iv) lagged union density. Rather than a supply and demand framework, the inclusion of these variables was based on the idea that for union membership to grow, workers required both a 'propensity' to join a union and the 'opportunity' to become a member. Thus, rising prices increase the workers' propensity to join, along similar lines to that suggested in the Ashenfelter and Pencavel model. Such inflation may also raise the opportunity to join unions because employers may be more willing to concede worker demands and grant union recognition when increased labour costs can be passed on in the form of higher prices. Rising wages may be attributed by workers to unions and lead to continuing support for unions. The unemployment rate was thought to affect negatively both the propensity and the opportunity to join unions, because of fears of antagonizing employers, and of employer resistance to unions in an environment that gives firms more bargaining strength.

The model was tested for four countries and in general provided support for the effects of economic conditions on union density. It worked particularly well for the UK. It needed to take into account the effects of legislation (i.e. the Wagner Act in the USA), and the special nature of the arbitration system in Australia, which led to the hypothesis that the prices variable would be insignificant, since arbitration tended to adjust wages in line with the cost of living – countering the effect that rising prices pose for workers' living standards. In Sweden the rate of change of money wages was not found to be significant and had the wrong sign. It was argued that the centralized collective bargaining system reduced the 'credit effect' ascribed to unions for wage increases.

Thus, although it has been criticized on various grounds the Bain and Elsheikh model had an important influence on the literature. Richardson (1977), for example, criticized the conceptual framework for lacking a theoretical explanation especially in relation to the 'credit effect' associated with money wage increases. It has also been criticized for not taking into account simultaneous relationships between union membership increases and the other variables in the model. Recent estimates of the model for the four countries in question (Bean and Holden, 1994) have found some continuing empirical support, but have exposed some econometric problems associated with autocorrelation in the USA and Sweden, and structural instability in the same countries.

Modern time series econometric modelling, following Engel and Granger (1987), have used 'error correction mechanisms' and cointegration methods in modelling trade union membership. This involves finding variables that are 'cointegrated' which gives the long-run relationship, and then estimating the 'error correction model' which explores the short-run dynamics. Using this method, Caruth and Schnabel (1990) find a long-run relationship for Germany in which employment, unemployment and real wages have positive effects on membership while the proportions of foreign workers and service workers have negative effects. In contrast, Holden and Thompson (1991) find a negative relationship between density and unemployment for Australia, as does Van Ours (1992) for the Netherlands.

While it is not true for all countries, inspection of Table 25.1 reveals that, for most OECD countries, there was a decline in union density in the 1980s. Bean and Holden (1994) review the evidence on the causes of this decline. Rising unemployment is thought to explain some of the decline and changes in industry structure might explain a further small amount of it in some countries. More unfavourable legislative environments are thought to have been a very important influence. Freeman and Pelletier (1990, p. 156), for example, contend that 'the vast bulk of the decline in union density in the UK is due to the changed legal environment of industry relations'.

5 Bargaining problem

5.1 Introduction

Chapter 13 shows how bilateral monopoly leads to a bargaining problem, in which the monopoly supplier of labour is a union. We saw that the outcome was indeterminate, depending on the relative bargaining strength of employers and unions. These comments suggest that the answer to the indeterminacy problem lies in getting a handle on what 'bargain strength' and 'power' are all about. Much of the literature has taken that route. Thus, in the context of union/employer bargaining, the prime candidates for relative bargaining strength have been the effectiveness of a union (or the union movement as a whole) in representing the workers, and the state of the labour market. These ideas have developed primarily in the context of empirical work on wage determination and the incidence of industrial conflict. While intuitively very plausible, the theoretical underpinnings have not been very strong and theory has taken a different route, by focusing on the pure bargaining problem, but by largely abstracting from the institutional setting in which employer and union bargaining takes place. In the first instance, we review the major developments in the pure theory of bargaining, before linking these theoretical developments with the more applied work in the field.

The bare bones of the bargaining problem has the following structure. In the absence of an agreement, two parties can attain a certain level of utility represented by c, the conflict point, in Figure 25.2 – u_u represents the utility of the union (or union members) and u_e, the corresponding utility of the employer. The conflict point belongs to a larger set, the pay-off space, P, which represents all levels of utility that could be attained if the two parties were to agree (to trade or cooperate) amongst themselves. Classical economic theory can only make one, or possibly two, statements about the nature of an eventual agreement. First, individual rationality demands that both parties must be no worse off as a consequence of an agreement. Thus, the agreement point must lie within the segment ab. Second, it can be argued that an agreement should be Pareto efficient

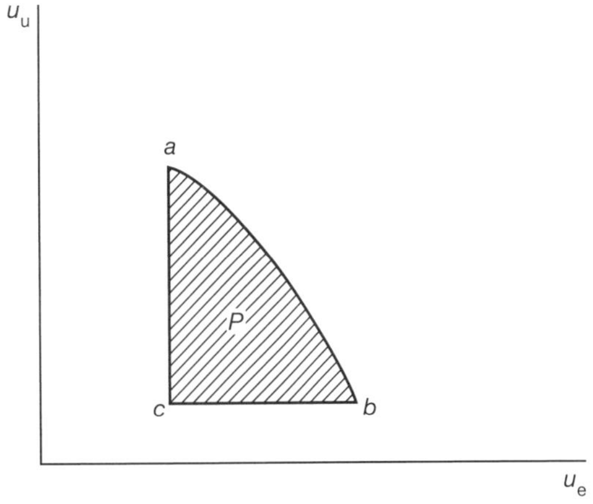

Fig 25.2 The bargaining problem.

(i.e. that the agreement point should lie on the arc *ab*), but we hesitate to say that this is implied by economic theory. This is as far as classical economic theory takes us. It does not tell us how the gains from an agreement are to be divided between the two parties. By 1881, Edgeworth had already stated (rather unambiguously) that, a 'contract without competition is indeterminate', and his view held sway for a very long time.

To make further progress, stronger assumptions have to be imposed. In the following sections we review three approaches to solving the bargaining problem: Hicks' (1936) model, the Nash bargaining solution (1950 and 1951) and Rubinstein's (1982) 'alternating offers' model.

5.2 Hicks' model of union–employer bargaining

Hicks' central assumption was that a trade union will undertake (or seriously threaten to undertake) a strike only if the cost of doing so is less than the cost of accepting a lower wage. The reasoning is that, since there is a large cost in terms of forgone higher wages associated with accepting a lower wage, it would be worth while to engage in a long strike to secure a higher wage. In case of a high wage, the converse applies. Thus, the length of time the union is willing to strike is a declining function of the wage, shown by $\mathbf{t}_u(w)$ in Figure 25.3. Hicks called this function the union resistance curve. The same principle governs the behaviour of the employer. An employer refuses to pay a certain wage if the strike that is likely to result from this refusal costs less than granting that wage. Longer strikes cost the employer more as well, but, to the employer, the higher the wage settlement, the longer the strike it is prepared to endure. Thus, the corresponding function for the employer, $\mathbf{t}_e(w)$ is increasing in w, and referred to as the employer concession curve.

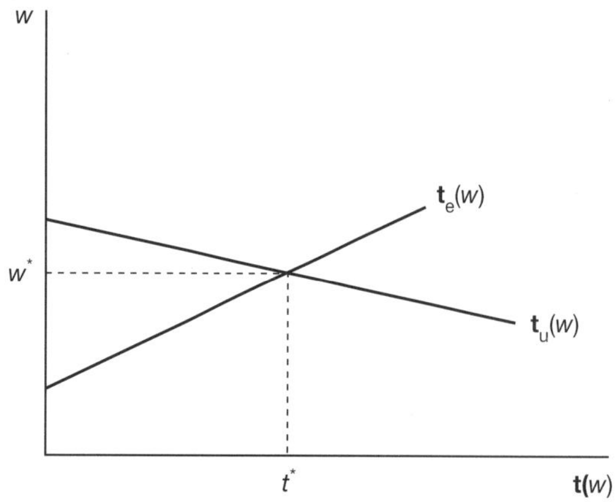

Fig 25.3 Hicks' bargaining model.

The model depicted in Figure 25.3 now becomes transparent. Consider a wage, $\mathbf{t}_u(w) > \mathbf{t}_e(w)$; at this wage the union is willing to engage in a strike which lasts longer than the employer is willing to endure. Clearly, the employer could not refuse to pay this wage. On the other hand, if $\mathbf{t}_u(w) < \mathbf{t}_e(w)$, this is a wage that the union could not refuse, because the employer is willing to put up with a strike longer than the union is prepared to undertake. The solution to Hicks' model is then w^*, at which $\mathbf{t}_u(w) = \mathbf{t}_e(w)$. At this wage, the union is prepared to strike t^* periods in support of a higher wage, but knows that the employer is indifferent between the prospect of a strike of t^* periods and paying w^*. In Hicks' words, w^* is the 'highest wage which skilful negotiation can extract from the employer'. The employer's acceptance of w^* follows by the same reasoning.

Although there is every prospect of a strike, in equilibrium, a settlement occurs without such action when both parties know the other party's $\mathbf{t}(w)$ function. Hicks himself was well aware of (but somewhat uneasy about) this implication. As we shall see, however, subsequent models also have this implication, although Hicks' concern is still relevant. During the past 50 years there have been many critical remarks made about Hicks' model. Pen (1952, p. 25) wrote, 'I fail to see why the intersection [of the resistance and concession curves] determines anything'. Shackle (1957) felt the necessity of reformulating Hicks' model – whilst accepting the logic of the employer's resistance curve, he thought that 'the whole meaning of Professor Hicks' construction is very elusive' (p. 301) and proposed a different construction. However, these critical remarks should not detract from what is a seminal contribution fundamentally influencing further work in this area.

5.3 Nash bargaining solution

The most well-known approach to the bargaining problem is due to Nash (1950 and 1951). It is normally referred to as the Nash bargaining solution, to distinguish it from the equally well-known Nash equilibrium concept which plays such a central role in non-cooperative game theory. The Nash solution is best described with reference to the 'bare bones' bargaining problem. A certain amount is to be divided between two parties. If the size of the pie is unity, one part getting x means that the other receives $1 - x$. If they agree about the division of the given amount, they receive the payoffs $\mathbf{u}_u(x)$ and $\mathbf{u}_e(1 - x)$ respectively. If they do not agree, they receive the conflict amount c, which in utility terms is worth $\mathbf{u}_u(c)$ and $\mathbf{u}_e(c)$ respectively. The situation is again depicted in Figure 25.2 with the union's utility on the vertical axis and the employer's utility on the horizontal axis. Any division such that the respective utilities fall within the utility frontier is feasible.

The Nash solution to this problem is an axiomatic one. He stated a number of properties (axioms) which he thought should characterize the solution, and then discovered that these actually determined a unique solution. But instead of stating axioms and proving that a solution follows, it is more illuminating to follow a different approach. If two reasonable people sit down at a table to split a pie it is plausible that they would seek to maximize a weighted average of the two parties' utilities subject to the feasibility constraint:

$$\text{Max } [a\mathbf{u}_u(x) + b\mathbf{u}_e(1 - x)]\ a + b = 1 \tag{1}$$

That is to say, if they agree, we would expect them to attain a division where the (weighted) average utility is greatest. This is a fairly innocent assumption, but it does not solve the problem. The crucial issue, whose utility is to matter most, remains.

The first-order condition of this maximization problem is

$$a\mathbf{u}'_u(x) = b\mathbf{u}'_e(1 - x) \tag{2}$$

but, to solve this, the ratio of the weights attached to the two parties' utilities a/b has to be specified. One possibility is that

$$a\mathbf{u}_u(x) = b\mathbf{u}_e(1 - x) \tag{3}$$

in which case, both parties receive identical increments in utility when compared with the conflict outcome of zero. Since there is no particular reason why this should be the case, a more general formulation is

$$(1 - k)a\mathbf{u}_u(x) = kb\mathbf{u}_e(1 - x) \tag{4}$$

where $0 < k < 1$. The closer to one k is, the more the balance of power is tilted towards the employer. For that reason, k is often interpreted as an index of relative bargaining power.

Solving for a/b and substituting into the first-order condition yields

$$k\mathbf{u}_e(1 - x)\mathbf{u}'_u(x) = (1 - k)\mathbf{u}_u(x)\mathbf{u}'_e(1 - x) \tag{5}$$

which we recognize as the solution to the maximization problem

$$\text{Max } [\mathbf{u}_u(x)^k\ \mathbf{u}_e(1 - x)^{(1-k)}] \tag{6}$$

The value of x, x^* say, that solves (6) is the Nash solution. This can be confirmed by taking logs and totally differentiating (6), setting the result equal to zero for a maximum and rearranging the resulting expression. One problem remains, however – the value of k. Nash's solution to this was to impose a symmetry requirement that neither party has more power than the other, that is $k = 1/2$. The unique solution is then

$$x^* = \arg\max\ [\mathbf{u}_u(x)\mathbf{u}_e(1 - x)] \tag{7}$$

the product of the two parties' incremental utility, relative to the conflict point (where utility is assumed to be zero).

To get a feeling for the properties of the Nash solution, a few examples are helpful. If the two parties have identical utility functions and (as assumed so far) the same conflict point, the Nash division splits the pie in half. Some more revealing examples are set out in Table 25.2. The first case illustrates what happens when the union has less to lose from a conflict than has the employer. As might be expected, this results in a larger share for the union, but the reason is not that the bargaining power of the union is enhanced by this. It is just the equal division of the previous case in a different guise. With reference to Figure 25.2, the new origin is effectively at the point (1/2, 1/4), and it is the gain relative to this origin that is divided equally. In the second case, the employer has a convex utility function (i.e. is risk averse), while the union is risk neutral. With reference to Figure

Table 25.2 Examples of the Nash solution for different utility functions and conflict points

	$\mathbf{u}_u(x)$	$\mathbf{u}_u(c)$	$\mathbf{u}_e(1-x)$	$\mathbf{u}_e(c)$	x	$1-x$
Different conflict points	1/2	x	$(1-x)$	1/4	5/8	3/8
Employer risk averse	x	0	$(1-x)^{0.5}$	0	2/3	1/3
Different conflict points and employer risk averse	x	1/2	$(1-x)^{0.5}$	1/4	4/5	1/5

25.2, the bargaining frontier becomes steeper as it approaches the horizontal axis. As can be seen the employer's risk aversion costs it dearly in the form of a one-third share. This property is not implausible. Finally, in the third example, the combination of having less to lose and being less risk averse gives the union the lion's share of the pie.

The Nash solution to the bargaining problem is best understood as a prediction of the kind of agreement two parties to a bargain would arrive at if they had to share a given amount. It has become the standard method of predicting the bargaining outcome in economic theory (Binmore *et al.*, 1986). Its application is, however, limited by the axiomatic properties of the solution. This leaves many questions unanswered, in particular, about the kind of bargaining situations the Nash solution is applicable to (see Roth, 1979, for a discussion). Many of the developments in bargaining theory since Nash's seminal papers have been concerned with this issue. This research agenda has been called the 'Nash program' (Binmore and Dasgupta, 1987) – developing explicit strategic models of the negotiation process which are both realistic and sufficiently simple to be amenable to analysis.

5.4 Alternating offers

Foremost among the newer strategic models is Rubinstein's (1982) 'alternating offers' model, which involves an explicit description of the bargaining process. The process is a series of rounds in which the two parties alternate in making offers that the other party can accept or reject. If an offer is rejected, the bargaining moves into the next round in which it is the other party's turn to make an offer and so on. An important assumption, which drives the bargaining process, is that some time elapses between each round and that the parties discount future payoffs (i.e. a given agreement reached in the first round is worth more than the same agreement reached in the second round, etc.).

As an example we use a simplified version of the Rubinstein model, summarized below. In this simplified version there is a final period T. If agreement is not reached at T (or before) both parties receive their conflict payoffs (equal to zero in the example below) as in the discussion of the Nash solution. The main assumptions of the alternating offers bargaining model (Rubinstein, 1982), are as follows:

(i) Actions and Events

- (1) Union claims x_1
- (1') Employer accepts or rejects
- (2) Employer offers x_2
- (2') Union accepts or rejects
- .
- .
- .
- (T) Union claims x_T
- (T') Employer accepts or rejects

(ii) Payoffs (if the union's claim is accepted in round t, $t < T$)

Union share	$\delta_t x_t$
Employer share	$\delta_t (1 - x_t)$

(if the employer's offer is accepted, the shares are reversed), where $\delta = 1/(1 + r)$, where r is the rate of time preference (interest rate).

To solve this model we use the backward induction technique and adopt the simplifying convention that if a party is indifferent between accepting and rejecting an offer they will always accept. This avoids cluttering the argument with non-essential matters.

Suppose then that an agreement has not been reached by period T and it is the union's turn to make a claim. The rejection of the claim by the employer would give rise to a conflict situation in which both parties receive nothing. The union, knowing this, would then claim the whole share for itself. The employer, having nothing to gain by refusing, would then accept according to our convention. The outcome, if the bargaining were to reach period T, is displayed in the last row of Table 25.3. However, the employer anticipating this outcome in period T would offer the unions a share of δ in period $T - 1$. To the union, getting a share δ of a pie that is worth δ^{T-2} is equivalent to getting the whole share of δ^{T-1} in period T. Thus the union would accept δ in period $T - 1$.

To continue with this reasoning, in period $T - 2$ the union would claim a share such that the employer is indifferent between accepting this claim and what it would get if the bargaining were to proceed to the next round. The latter is given by $(1 - \delta)\delta^{T-2}$, so a share of $\delta(1 - \delta)$. By continuing with this line of reasoning we would eventually reach period 1, but as the argument becomes increasingly complex it is best summarized in Table 25.3 using a discount factor of 0.9. In the example it is assumed that there is one round per period, so the discount factor of 0.9 is associated with a rate of time preference of (approximately) 10.1 per cent per period. Clearly the discount factor, which refers to the value of the payoff in

Table 25.3 Outcomes of the alternating offers bargaining model (with a discount factor of 0.9, if the bargaining process were to end in round 1, . . ., *T*)

Round	Union share	Employer share	Total value
1	0.53	0.47	1
.	.	.	.
.	.	.	.
.	.	.	.
$T-2$	0.91	0.09	0.9^{T-3}
$T-1$	0.9	0.1	0.9^{T-2}
T	1	0.0	0.9^{T-1}

round t relative to the value in round $t-1$, will be larger the more rounds there are per period. For example, if the rate of time preference is 10 per cent per year, and there is one second between the rounds, by the rules of continuous compounding, $\delta = 0.999999985$ approximately.

In each round either party would claim/offer a share that is just as acceptable to the other party as it is for that party to delay a settlement to the next round in order to obtain a larger share. Thus, the bargaining process would never reach period T, because in period $T-1$ the employer would offer the union an acceptable deal. But the bargain would not reach period $T-1$ either, for the same reason. Nor would it reach $T-2$ or $T-3$ or $T-(T-1)$. The union would simply claim a share, $1/(1+\delta)$, in period 1, which the employer would accept. The alternating offers model results in instant agreement and the party that can make the first offer gets the larger share.

The result that the union (the first mover in our case) will get a share of $1/(1+\delta)$ is not an artefact of the example we have used to illustrate the model. Rubinstein (1982) proved that this result is a unique perfect equilibrium of an alternating offers bargain even when the number of bargaining periods is infinite. The solution can also be generalized to the case where the discount factors of the two parties are different. The first mover (union in this case) share is then given by

$$x_u = \frac{(1-\delta_e)}{(1-\delta_u\delta_e)} \qquad (8)$$

To see what drives the solution to this model it is instructive to consider the position of the two parties in round 1 of the bargaining process. If the union were to claim a share greater than $1/(1+\delta)$ in the first round the employer would most certainly reject this claim. In doing so, it delays a settlement, but it knows it can do better in round 2, that is by waiting. It is this preparedness to wait which determines the outcome of the bargaining process. When one party makes an offer, the onus is put on the other party. If they want a better deal it is necessary to wait, and they alone can avoid waiting by accepting the offer.

The discount factor reflects this preparedness to wait. If the discount factor is low, the party making the first offer will claim a very large share secure in the knowledge that the other party, not being prepared to wait, will accept. This argument can be taken to its extreme. If the union were to claim 99 per cent of the pie and could credibly commit itself not to consider an alternative offer for the next 100 years, the employer would have little choice but to accept. Rejecting the offer means that the employer would have to wait for the next round!

This extreme case is, of course, atypical. In a particular situation the time between rounds could be very short indeed. If the two parties are sitting at the same table, in principle they could make offers and counter-offers every few seconds. But it is still reasonable to argue that time, and the unwillingness to delay a settlement, is what drives the parties to an agreement. That time matters is perhaps most convincingly put by Cross (1969):

> the passage of time has a cost in terms of both dollars and the sacrifice of utility which stems from the postponement of consumption, and it will be precisely this cost which motivates the whole bargaining process. If it did not matter when the parties agreed, it would not matter whether they agreed at all.

5.5 Experimental evidence

The logic of the Rubinstein model cannot be faulted, but there is a long way from analytical results to valid empirical predications. Models of this type have the advantage that they lend themselves well to experimental study. The testing of economic theories through experiments has become a very fertile area of research, and the Rubinstein model has received particular attention. This literature suggests that the outcomes of alternating offers bargaining is more complex than is suggested by analytical solutions derived through backward induction. One finding from these experimental games is that equity considerations seem to be important. For example, in experiments where the theoretical solution provides for very unequal shares, the player who is 'supposed' to accept a very low share often fails to do so. By not doing so, they will actually end up with less than if they had accepted. A possible explanation for this is that the greed of the first player (the one making the offer) is an affront to what the second player (who can accept or reject) believes is equitable.

6 Bargaining and strikes

6.1 Introduction

A common feature of the models we have discussed is the absence of conflict. Although the threat of a conflict, or delay, is very much in the two parties' minds, the conflict never materializes. Both parties, being rational, and knowing that the other party is rational, can foresee which strategies lead to a conflict, and, since a conflict is costly and manifestly irrational, select a strategy which leads to an agreement. Some economists have criticized the super-rationality implied by the absence of conflicts as an equilibrium phenomenon (Varoufakis, 1991). But there is some merit in this implication. Agreement is the norm in wage bargaining, as in most other forms of bargaining. Although strikes do occur, the proportion of working hours lost due to industrial action is less than 1 per cent in most countries. On the other hand, even though an agreement is the usual outcome, it is seen as important to have a good theoretical explanation of strikes.

A very large number of explanations for strikes have been put forward in the literature. These include the need for unions to maintain sufficient cohesion amongst their members to ensure that the threat of a strike is credible. Going on strike is one way to maintain such cohesion as succinctly captured in the old adage 'weapons grow rusty if unused'. Another well-known model (Ashenfelter and Johnson, 1969) builds a political theory of strikes around the agency problem in unions. While union members are primarily concerned with wages and conditions of employment, union leaders have a wider agenda which includes their own political survival. Even if a strike would not be rational from the members' perspective, their argument was that strikes would still occur to the extent that they bolster the political position of union leaders. Another prominent explanation has a long history and has been developed by a number of economists. Hicks (1936) thought that 'the majority of actual strikes are doubtless the result of faulty negotiation'.

6.2 Strikes due to asymmetric information

The explanations mentioned above, and others, are often very rich in institutional and empirical content and offer considerable insight into how and why strikes occur. The more recent literature, however, has followed the approach taken in the general area of game theory, by relaxing the complete information assumption. In particular, one of the parties, usually the union, is assumed to have incomplete information. It does not know something the firm does, and it is this asymmetry of information which is the root cause of a strike. An extensive analysis of these types of models can be found in Roth (1985).

In incomplete information models a strike is a signalling device. In the simplest case there are two types of firms – the profitable and unprofitable (see Hart, 1989, for an example). The union, not knowing whether a firm is profitable or not, opens the bargaining with a high claim it expects profitable firms to accept. Unprofitable firms will reject this claim. In doing so they are signalling to the union that they are unprofitable. If there were no cost to rejecting the high wage claim all firms would do it. Thus for the rejection to be something more than 'cheap talk', it is usually envisaged that it leads to a strike. The union would then moderate its claim in the next round of bargaining and the unprofitable firms would settle at a lower wage. The reason for a strike in these models is that this is the only way a firm can prove that it is unprofitable.

6.3 Empirical evidence on the determinants of strikes

There is a large literature exploring the determinants of strikes, some of which is based on one or other of the theoretical frameworks discussed above. Many, however, have been more empirically driven and concerned with examining the effects of such variables as establishment, firm size, workforce characteristics, union structures, etc., without a particular theoretical framework.

The conceptual framework that tends to be favoured by modern economists is the asymmetric information approach. This is because outside of this framework the parties to a strike appear to be acting irrationally. Some evidence has been uncovered in support of the asymmetric information model. For example, Tracy (1987) has shown that the incidence and duration of strike activity are higher in firms whose profitability varies widely over time. However, as Booth and Cressey (1990) recognize in their attempt to test such a model on UK establishment-level data, it is very difficult to undertake a strict test of an asymmetric information model and their study, which was based on such an approach, did not produce conclusive results. However, they did report some interesting findings:

1 Strike incidence probability increases with establishment size; however, organization size does not significantly affect the strike probability.

2 Where there is trade union recognition, higher union density is associated with a slightly lower strike incidence probability. Where the union is not recognized, union density has no effect on strike incidence.

3 Certain features of the industrial relations system are associated with increased strike incidence probability. There is a greater probability of a strike in establishments where there are payments by results or job evaluation mechanisms, bargaining at the plant or organization level, and where the establishment is a member of an employers' association.

4 Where the establishment is operating at full capacity, the strike probability is reduced, but where sales are rising or stable the strike probability increases. Since the net effect is positive, the strike incidence is arguably procyclical.

5 The greater the percentage of skilled manual workers at an establishment, the higher the strike probability.

In a paper using Australian data, Dawkins and Wooden (1993) review the results that permeate the extensive international empirical literature. A particularly persistent finding is the establishment size effect mentioned in Booth and Cressey's conclusions. This is indeed repeated in the Dawkins and Wooden (1993) results. Another unsurprisingly common result is that measures of union power, such as union density, are generally found to be significant in strikes models. The Booth and Cressey (1990) study, referred to above, however, emphasizes the importance of union recognition rather than density. Dawkins and Wooden (1993) and Whitfield *et al.* (1994) find a positive relationship with variables designed to identify whether unions have an active presence within the establishment.

7 Union utility as a function of wages and employment

7.1 Introduction

Since the early 1980s, a very important part of the literature on the economics of trade unions has utilized the idea that unions have indifference curves defined over wages and employment. The preference functions which incorporate these indifference curves are then used under a range of assumptions to develop theories about how unions might influence the wage–employment outcomes. The theories will be discussed in Sections 8 and 9 below which draw from a useful review by Creedy and McDonald (1991). In this section we discuss the union's indifference curve.

Figure 25.4 illustrates an example of three such union indifference curve maps. In panel (a) we have

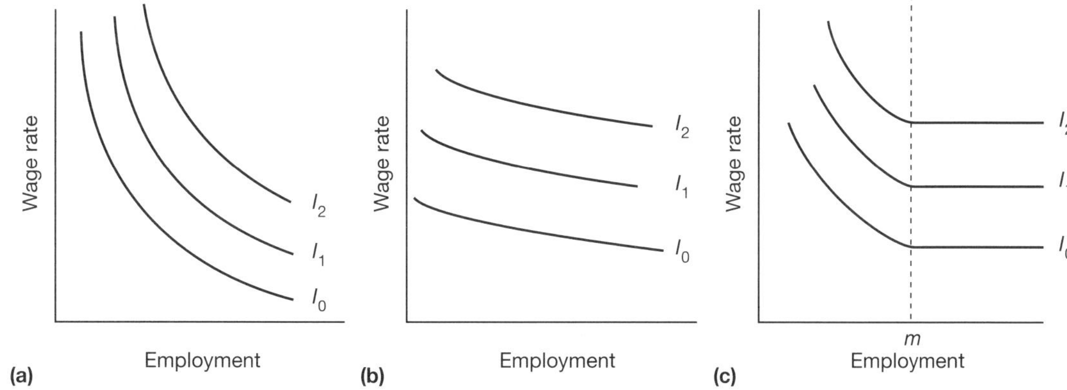

Fig 25.4 Union preferences over wages and employment.

normal downward-sloping convex indifference curves indicating that for the union to remain at the same level of utility after a wage cut, there will have to be an increase in employment. Convexity implies that as wages fall so the rise in employment required to compensate is increasingly large. In panel (b) we also have downward-sloping convex indifference curves, but with a relatively shallow slope. This implies that the union in panel (b) requires greater compensation for a wage cut in the form of increased employment, than the one in panel (a). The panel (b) union is therefore going to be more resistant to allowing wages to be reduced to generate extra employment than the union in panel (a). Panel (c) depicts a union that, above a certain level of employment, m, is not interested in obtaining extra employment at the expense of lower wages. This might, for example, be a 'closed craft union' which would like its existing members to receive employment, but having achieved that objective, can only increase its utility by an increase in the wage.

7.2 Utilitarian union utility function

Oswald (1982) proposed a particular form of the union utility function, known as the utilitarian version, in which union utility is the sum of the utilities of the individual members. This can be written as

$$u = N\mathbf{u}(w) + (M - N)\mathbf{u}(b) \qquad (9)$$

where $\bar{\mathbf{u}}(\ )$ is the utility function of an individual member of the union which has M members, N of whom are employed at wage w. The remaining $M - N$ workers are unemployed and receive unemployment benefit b. Dividing both sides of equation (9) by M we obtain

$$\bar{u} = \frac{N}{M}\mathbf{u}(w) + \frac{M - N}{M}\mathbf{u}(b) \qquad (10)$$

where $\bar{u} = (u/M)$ is utility per worker. Equation (10) represents the expected utility formulation. Utility is a weighted average of the utility derived from employment and from unemployment. The weights, N/M and $(M - N)/M$, are the probability of having a job and probability of being unemployed respectively.

A more general utility function with $\alpha = 0$ as a special case is

$$u = \alpha[N\mathbf{u}(w)] + (1 - \alpha)[(M - N)\mathbf{u}(b)] \qquad (11)$$

where $0 \leq \alpha \leq 1$. The size of α denotes the relative influence on union policy of employed and unemployed workers. The utilitarian formulation implies $\alpha = 0.5$ (i.e. equal weights). The indifference curve of Figure 25.4, panel (c), is one in which α is unity above a certain level of employment.

7.3 Stone–Geary utility function

Another version of the union preference uses the Stoney–Geary function,

$$u = (w - \gamma)^{\theta}(N - \delta)^{1-\theta} \qquad (12)$$

In this function γ and δ denote 'reference values' for wages, w, and employment, N, above which wages and employment are 'supernumerary'. The parameter θ indicates the relative importance attached by the union to supernumerary wages as opposed to supernumerary employment. Thus equation (12) encompasses a number of interesting special cases:

1 In a closed shop, if $\theta = 0.5$ and $\gamma = \delta = 0$, equation (12) becomes wage bill maximization.

2 If $\theta = 0.5$, $\delta = 0$, and γ is the competitive wage, we have Rosen's (1970) rent maximization hypothesis. Thus, unions are conceived of as maximizing union shares of monopoly rents in the form of wages in excess of the wage that would prevail in competitive markets.

Studies by Dertouxos and Pencavel (1980) and Pencavel (1984), based upon the US international typographical union over the period 1945–1965, provided some tentative evidence for the rent maximization hypothesis and some support of kinked indifference curves that tend towards those in Figure 25.4, panel (c).

8 'Monopoly union' and 'right to manage' models

8.1 Simple monopoly union model

The simple monopoly union model involves a situation in which the union is unable to influence employment and employers are unable to control the wage rate. Thus the union 'chooses' the wage and employers set the level of employment. The outcome is shown in Figure 25.5 at point e, producing a wage of w_1 and employment E_1 at the tangency between the

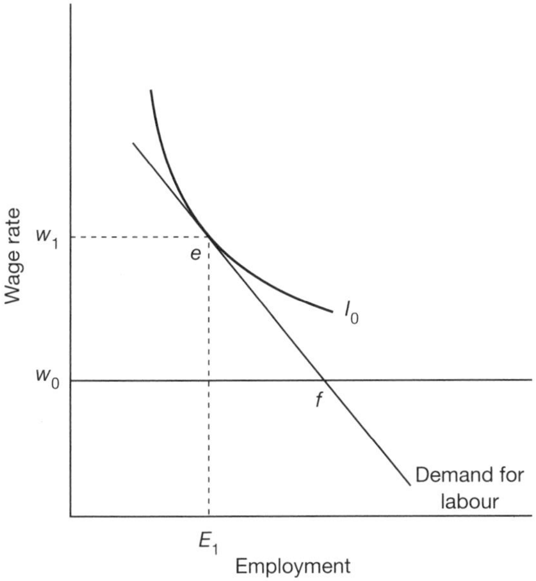

Fig 25.5 The simple monopoly union model and right to manage model.

labour demand curve and the union's indifference curve. The wage rate w_0 in Figure 25.5 represents 'lay-off pay' which is the minimum pay that would be required to entice members to enter employment with the firm. This is a combination of the utility derived by union members from alternative activities (which could include receiving unemployment benefits) and the disutility of work. w_0 is assumed to be a constant which implies that there would be sufficient labour supply at that wage to meet labour demand, if the wage were that low (or effectively a perfectly elastic supply of labour at that wage rate). Thus in the monopoly union model the effect of trade unions is to increase wages above, and reduce employment below, the levels that would be expected without the union. The extent to which they have this effect depends upon the union's utility function and the weights placed upon wages as opposed to employment.

8.2 Right to manage model

In the right to manage model, a monopoly union is retained but faces an employer with bargaining power over wages, and is still constrained by the demand curve. Thus, there is bargaining over wages while the employer controls employment. This has been called the 'right to manage' model by Nickell (1982). The bargaining outcome usually used is the Nash solution (see Section 5.3 above). This solution is subject to the constraint that bargains are on the labour demand curve. The outcome depends upon the relative bargaining power of the firm and the union. When the unions hold all the bargaining strength the outcome is equivalent to that in the simple monopoly union model, at point *e* in Figure 25.5. If the employer holds all the bargaining strength and the union has no power over wages, the wage–employment outcome would be at point *f* in Figure 25.5. Intermediate values for union power result in solutions on the labour demand curve between *e* and *f*.

9 Efficient bargains

9.1 Basic model

The idea of the bargaining contract curve was first put forward by Leontief (1946) and developed by MacDonald and Solow (1981). This is illustrated in Figure 25.6 in which 'efficient bargains' lie on the *GG′* locus of tangency points between union indifference curves and firms' isoprofit curves. Note that the monopoly union equilibrium w_1, derived in the monopoly union model above, is an inefficient bargain. By moving from *e*, one or both parties can gain. By a move, for example, to *h*, the employer obtains a higher level of utility. The ability to achieve such a

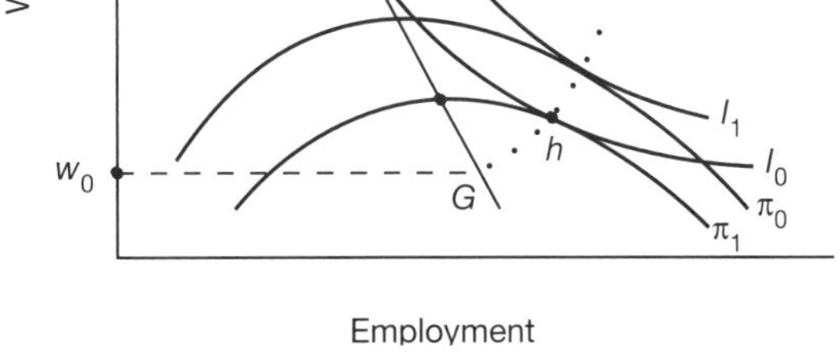

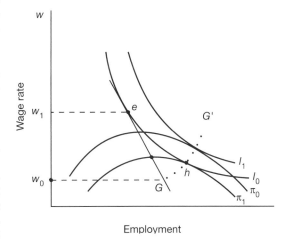

Fig 25.6 Efficient bargain model.

Pareto improvement applies, of course, to any point on the contract curve. The contract curve lies between G at the lowest wages employees will accept, and G', which is the lowest level of profit that employers will accept and remain in business in the long run (i.e. zero abnormal profit). Again the outcome depends on the relative bargaining power of unions and employers.

9.2 Insider-dominated model

In the insider-dominated model of trade union behaviour, the union is only concerned with a sub-group E_0 of the employed, where $\bar{E}$ is total employment. This is illustrated in Figure 25.7. Assuming that the E_0 union members have secure employment, in this situation union indifference curves are horizontal to the right of the vertical line at E_0 because the union gains no extra utility from increasing employment above this level. Tangency between these indifference curves and the employer's isoprofit curves yields the insider-dominated efficient contract, which lies on the labour demand curve. Thus, we have produced a special case where efficient bargains coincide with the labour demand curve, and this results in lower employment than would be the case from efficient bargains where union indifference curves slope downwards.

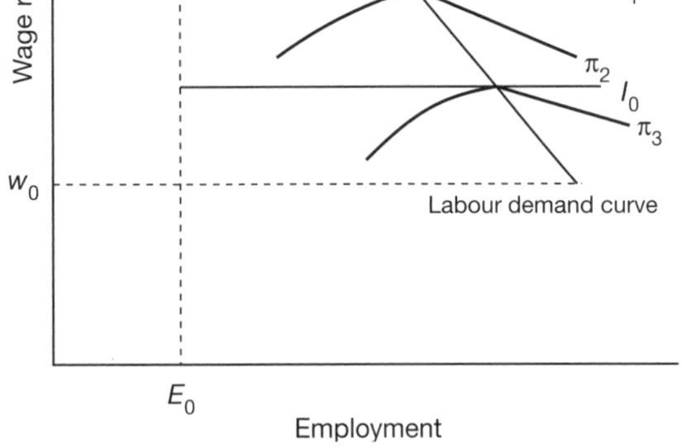

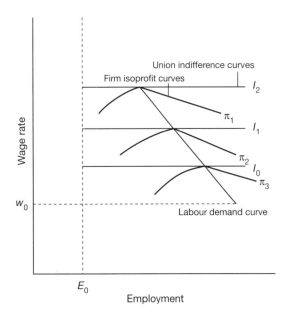

Fig 25.7 The insider-dominated model.

10 Economic effects of trade unions

10.1 Introduction

This section considers the economic impact of trade unions. The longest standing and most extensive part of this literature is concerned with the impact of unions on wages, which is dealt with in more detail in Chapter 26, but here we provide an overview of the research findings for various countries. This leads on naturally to a discussion of the effects on resource allocation of the impact of unions on relative wages. We then outline the 'exit–voice face' of unions as developed by Freeman and Medoff (1984), as opposed to the 'monopoly face'. The exit–voice model suggests that in contrast to the monopoly union effect of unions, union 'voice effects' can lead to increases in productivity. The discussion then considers the empirical evidence about the impact of unions on productivity which has been an important focus for research on the effects of trade unions over the last 10 years. The final four sections discuss the impact of unions on profitability, investment and technological change, labour turnover and employment.

10.2 Trade unions and wages

Chapter 26 outlines in some detail the methods used for estimating the effect of unions on wages, or the union/non-union wage differential, and provides evidence from a range of studies. Here we seek to provide an overview based upon an article by Freeman (1994) which estimates the union/non-union differential for 10 countries using data provided by the International Social Survey Program, and then compares the results with studies from some of the countries in question. The findings shown in Table 25.4 and other similar estimates are derived from earnings functions which seek to control for other influences such as education and experience. While there are important methodological issues that we discuss in Chapter 26, the findings reported in Table 25.4 are broadly consistent with the conventional wisdom and prevailing evidence. Comparison with studies for various countries suggests that the estimates for the UK might be slightly high, rather low for Australia and Germany, and very high for Austria. The most striking evidence, however, is of the high union wage effect in the USA. This is consistent with the results of other studies. This and other studies, reviewed in Chapter 26, therefore suggest that a mark-up of the order of 10 per cent for union members is not uncommon, and for the USA it appears to be substantially higher.

Table 25.4 Coefficients (standard errors) on union dummy variables

	All workers	Manual workers
USA	0.33 (0.05)	0.40 (0.07)
UK	0.14 (0.02)	0.17 (0.04)
Ireland	0.21 (0.03)	0.15 (0.04)
W. Germany	0.10 (0.02)	0.07 (0.03)
Austria	0.14 (0.02)	0.14 (0.03)
Australia	0.03 (0.05)	–0.07 (0.08)
Italy	0.04 (0.03)	0.08 (0.04)
Netherlands	0.09 (0.03)	0.08 (0.03)
Norway	0.03 (0.02)	0.12 (0.04)
Switzerland	0.05 (0.04)	0.12 (0.07)
Median, except USA	0.05	0.12
USA minus median	0.28	0.28

Source: Freeman (1994).
Note: Results are based upon multivariate regressions of log earnings on: years of schooling, experience (age – schooling – 6), years of experience squared, log hours worked, dummy variables for gender, married status, full-time work, and year as well as union status.

10.3 Trade unions and resource allocation

10.3.1 Partial equilibrium framework

The evidence that trade unions have an impact on wages could give rise to some concern about the effect of unions on resource allocation. Rees (1963) provided a way of viewing welfare losses that result from the misallocation of labour. Consider the economy to be divided into two sectors. Demand curves $D(1)$ and $D(2)$ in Figure 25.8 represent the demand curves for labour in the unionized and non-unionized sectors respectively. Assuming the supply of labour to be homogeneous and fixed, it can be represented in total by the vertical S schedule. Aggregating the two demand functions yields an aggregated demand for labour curve *abc*. The intersection of the aggregate demand and supply schedules yields the wage level w^* which would prevail in a competitive market if neither sector were unionized, and employment would

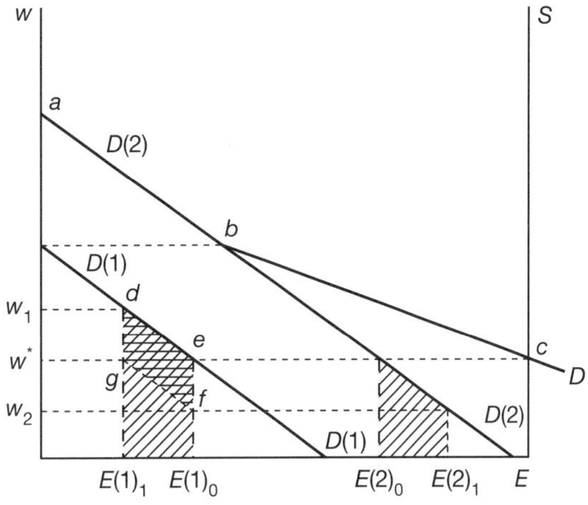

Fig 25.8 Trade unions and resource allocation.

be $E(1)_0$ and $E(2)_0$ in sectors 1 and 2. However, if the effect of unionization is to increase earnings in sector 1 to w_1, the effect would be a reduction in employment in that sector to $E(1)_1$. Assuming that the displaced union labour moves to the non-union sector, the supply of labour in sector 2 increases to $E(2)_1$ and the wage in that sector then falls to w_2. This is the negative spillover effect referred to earlier. Bearing in mind that the demand curves for labour indicate the marginal productivity of labour, then the area under the curves up to the level of employment represents the total product of labour. The output effect can be measured as the difference between the hatched area under $D(1)$ from $E(1)_0$ to $E(1)_1$ and the area under $D(2)$ from $E(2)_0$ to $E(2)_1$. Assuming $D(1)$ and $D(2)$ to be parallel the loss is equal to the hatched area, *defg* in Figure 25.8, and, given the symmetry, this is equal to $(w_1 - w^*)[E(1)_0 - E(1)_1] = (w^* - w_2)[E(1)_0 - E(1)_1]$. Rees has estimated such welfare losses at 0.14 per cent of US GNP, based on earnings in 1957.

Rees conceded that the analysis embodied in Figure 25.8 is very simplistic. For example, labour in the two sectors may be different in quality and the two demand curves need not be perfectly competitive. More important still, however, is that non-union labour markets may be characterized by monopsony on the demand side. In these circumstances it is very difficult to establish the direction of the welfare effect, let alone its magnitude. In particular we have noted that under conditions of monopsony, the monopoly power of a trade union may give rise to an equilibrium wage and employment solution nearer the competitive level than would otherwise prevail (see Chapter 13). It might be added that trade unions may have a positive impact on allocation insofar as they improve the availability of job information and thereby help to reduce frictional unemployment.

10.3.2 Unionization, resource allocation and income distribution in a general equilibrium framework

So far, the economic effect of trade unions has been analysed using a partial equilibrium framework. Johnson and Mieszkowski (1970) examined the effect of unions in a general equilibrium framework based on an application of the geometrical analysis of general equilibrium commonly employed in international trade theory. The model assumes two commodities (*X* and *Y*) and two factors, capital and labour (*K* and *E*). The factors are assumed to be homogeneous and perfectly mobile. Constant returns to scale and perfect competition (aside from the effects of unionization itself) are assumed. On the demand side it is assumed that the preference of the various sections of the community can be treated as an aggregate community preference system, that a reduction in aggregate real income reduces the quantities of both goods demanded, and that a reduction in the relative price of one commodity causes substitution of that commodity for the other in consumption.

Figure 25.9 illustrates the production possibilities open to the economy in an Edgeworth–Bowley box diagram. The quantity of capital available is represented by the vertical sides of the box, the quantity of labour by the horizontal sides. Isoquants are drawn in the box to illustrate levels of production of *X* and *Y*, with origins 0_X and 0_Y respectively. The contract curve passing through point *e* is the locus of tangency points of these isoquant systems. This represents the range of possible outcomes on the members of the union. In Figure 25.9, *X* is assumed to be capital intensive and *Y* labour intensive, such that the contract curve lies south west of the diagonal 0_X0_Y.

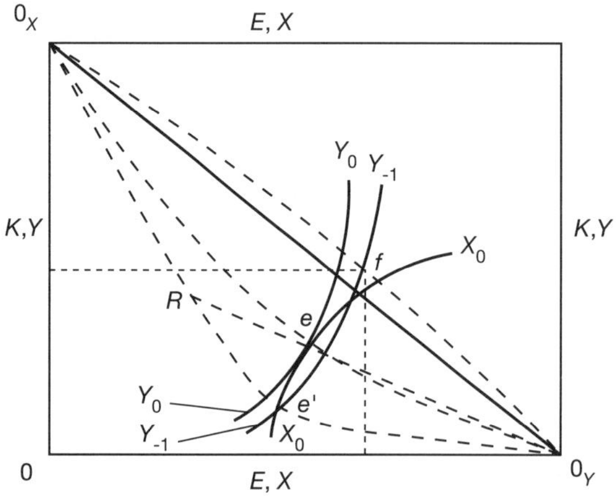

Fig 25.9 Unionization: a general equilibrium analysis.

Johnson and Mieszkowski pointed out that the production possibility curve of the economy can be represented in this box. As the result of assuming constant returns to scale, the quantity of *X* produced at any point on the contract curve *e*, can be measured by the distance along 0_X0_Y from 0_X to the point cut off by the *X* isoquant through *e*. Similarly, the quantity of *Y* produced can be measured by the distance along 0_X0_Y from 0_Y to the point cut off by the *Y* isoquant through *e*. These outputs can be measured in the box with reference to the common origin 0, by dropping perpendiculars to 00_Y and to 00_X. In turn these can be used to plot the production possibility curve which passes through point *f* in Figure 25.9. Point *f* on the production possibility curve corresponds to point *e* on the contract curve.

Unionization is introduced as a fixed proportional excess of wages in the unionized sector over wages in the non-unionized industry. As a result the wage rate (value of the marginal product) in the unionized industry exceeds the wage rate (value of the marginal product) in the non-unionized industry by a certain proportion. In contrast the marginal products of capital in the two industries must still be equal. This is reflected by a movement away from the contract curve resulting from tangency solutions to one in which the slope of the tangent to the isoquant for the unionized industry is steeper than that for the non-unionized industry. Assuming industry *X* (the capital-intensive sector) to be unionized, an equilibrium point *e*′ is created corresponding to an unchanged quantity of *X* produced and a lower output of *Y*. A new contract curve passes through *e*′, such that, at all the points on the curve, the output of one of the goods must be less than it would have been in the absence of unionization, that is unionization makes the allocation of resources less efficient.

In turn the production possibility curve will have shifted in towards the origin 0, except at its extreme points, and it may even have become convex to the origin. The effect of unionization on the costs of production also leads consumers to consume less of *X* and more of *Y* than they would if they were able to choose on the basis of true social opportunity cost which is no longer reflected in relative prices.

Since the price of X (in terms of Y) has risen at point e', unionised labour (in the X industry) is receiving wages with a greater purchasing power in terms of both goods, while non-unionized labour (in the Y industry) is receiving wages with a lower purchasing power in terms of both goods. The earnings of capital, on the other hand, are lower in terms of X and higher in terms of Y. In other words, unionized labour would be better off at e', non-unionized labour worse off, and capitalists might be better or worse off depending on the relative quantities in which they consumed X and Y. Johnson and Mieszkowski point out, however, that production cannot be at e', because the community's real income is lower than it was at e which, by assumption, must result in less consumption of X than at e. Equilibrium must occur with a reallocation of resources towards the production of more Y and less X than at e'. Movement along the new contract from e' towards 0_X must lead to greater capital intensity in both industries, resulting in an increase in the marginal products and wages of labour in both the unionized and non-unionized industries, and a fall in the earnings of capital. Thus the gains of unionized labour, in the final equilibrium, will be larger and the losses of non-unionized labour smaller, than at e', and the capitalists must experience a loss of income by comparison with e'. Johnson and Mieszkowski pointed out that it is even possible that non-unionized labour as well as unionized labour could gain, with the owners of capital bearing the whole or more than the whole gain to unionized labour plus the loss of efficiency in production.

The foregoing analysis applies to the unionization of the capital-intensive X industry. The unionization of the labour-intensive industry changes the conclusions radically. The contract curve and production possibility curves move in the opposite direction to that outlined in Figure 25.9. In these circumstances non-unionized labour must lose while unionized labour may also lose. Capital may be worse off or better off.

The difference between the effect of unionization of the labour-intensive as opposed to unionization of the capital-intensive industry, stems from the fact that unionization is in effect a tax on the labour of the unionized industry, and therefore has the effect of shifting demand away from that industry. If the tax is imposed on the capital-intensive industry, there is a fall in the demand for and price of the services of capital and an increase in the demand for labour, from which both sections of the labour force may gain. If the tax is on the labour-intensive industry, the result is a rise in the demand for capital and a fall in the demand for labour from which both sectors of the labour force may lose. Johnson and Mieszkowski went on to develop a simplified algebraic model and reported empirical estimates which suggest that unionized labour made gains largely at the expense of non-unionized labour.

10.4 Two faces of unions and the 'exit–voice' model

We have been concentrating so far on the effect of unions on wages and their consequent effect on employment and resource allocation. Another issue that has been a strong focus is the effect of unions on productivity. An important contribution to the literature in this area has been made by Freeman and Medoff (1984) who distinguish between the 'two faces of unions'. On the one hand, there is the 'monopoly face' that we have already come across in the monopoly union model. On the other hand, there is the 'collective voice' face, embodied in Freeman and Medoff's own 'exit–voice' model.

10.4.1 Monopoly face

One aspect of the monopoly face that we have already seen is the ability of unions to use their monopoly power to raise their members' wages above the competitive level. By distorting relative factor prices in this way, we have seen that unions can lead to misallocation of labour and as a result reduce national output. Another aspect of the monopoly face is the ability of unions to use their monopoly power to impose non-wage costs on employers, for example in the form of restrictive practices that involve lower work efforts and reduced productivity in the workplace. Thus, except where unions face monopsony power on the other side of the labour market, the monopoly face of unions is seen to be detrimental to the level of productivity and output. A more positive picture of trade unions, however, is painted in the exit–voice model.

10.4.2 Collective voice face

Freeman and Medoff (1994) applied Hirschman's (1970) exit–voice concept, which can apply to a range of economic agents under different circumstances, to the employee–employer relationship. Dissatisfied employees have the choice of exiting the firm, or voicing their complaints, and seeking to have them addressed. Freeman and Medoff argue that the predominant response of non-union labour will be to exit, while the predominant response of unionized labour will be to express their complaints through 'collective voice'. An individual non-union member, they suggest, will be likely to feel vulnerable to employer victimization if they express complaints. Unions, on the other hand, provide protection to their members from such victimization, and thus there is a much greater tendency for complaints to be made to employers, through the collective voice of their unions.

Thus, one of the effects of unions, in this model, is to reduce labour turnover. This is argued to have positive effects on labour productivity and negative effects on labour costs, thus reducing unit costs of production. This is because labour turnover imposes costs on employers in the form of hiring and training costs, and reduced labour productivity from inexperienced employees. Another part of the same story is that employers, faced with lower labour turnover, increase their investment in training the workforce, because they expect to retain their services for longer. In addition to these positive effects on productivity resulting from reduced labour turnover, other positive effects can result from the collective voice mechanism. Improved communication channels between employees and employers, in the form of collective bargaining, grievance and dispute procedures, etc., can result in improvements in productivity resulting from improved information, worker morale, etc. Further, unions can play a role in the monitoring of the performance of their members and reduce interworker rivalry through regulatory procedures such as seniority rules, etc. Thus, the exit–voice model suggests that unionism can improve productivity, and increase the efficiency of firms and the welfare of society as a whole.

10.5 Trade unions and productivity

The theoretical framework for analysing the effect of trade unions on productivity is provided by the production function. Studies have often followed Brown and Medoff (1978) in employing the Cobb–Douglas production function to derive an equation for labour productivity as a function of the capital/labour ratio and union density. If the labour force is divided between a union and non-union sector, the production function can be specified as

$$Y = AK^{\alpha}(E^{n} + cE^{u})^{1-\alpha} \tag{13}$$

where E^n denotes non-union labour and E^u is union labour. This equation can be used to derive the following expression relating labour productivity to union density:

$$\ln(Y/E) \approx \ln A + \alpha \ln (K/E) + (1-\alpha)(c-1)P \tag{14}$$

where $P = E^u/E$ is union density. Thus, where data exist on labour productivity, the capital/labour ratio and union density, equation (14) can be used to estimate the effect of unions on productivity. Studies in the USA based upon this conceptual framework have mixed results but tend to find positive effects on productivity. For reviews of US studies up to 1986 see Freeman and Medoff (1984) and Hirsch and Addison (1986). More recent studies for the USA by Belman (1989) also find positive effects, as do some Japanese papers. Studies in the UK have also had mixed results, but tend to suggest negative effects (for a review of these studies see Metcalf, 1990), as have studies in Australia (Crockett *et al.*, 1993; Drago and Wooden, 1993).

10.6 Trade unions and profitability

We have seen that unions tend to have a positive effect on wages. They may have positive or negative effects on productivity. Their effect on total profits therefore depends upon whether any positive productivity effects outweigh the effect of higher wages. Freeman and Medoff wrote in 1979 that

> unionism may increase productivity in some settings and decrease it in others. If the increase in productivity is greater than the increase in average unit costs due to the union wage effect, then the profit rate will increase; if not the profit rate will fall.

Clarke (1984) showed that the above statement only holds for absolute profits. The effect on the rate of return on capital is more complicated. In particular, the wage effect may cause a substitution towards capital from labour and, thus, reduce the rate of return on capital.

Bearing in mind that unions are sometimes found to reduce productivity, especially in the UK, and given the union wage impact it does not come as a surprise that most research on the effect of unions on profitability finds negative effects. Such UK studies include those by Blanchflower and Oswald (1989) and by Machin and Stewart (1990 and 1994). Studies in the USA and Japan, however, have also found such negative effects (Belman, 1989). Machin and Stewart (1990 and 1994) found that this union effect on the financial performance of the workplace was most pronounced where the firm in question enjoyed a high market share. Their interpretation of this result rests upon unions and firms bargaining over monopoly rents, which are greater the larger is market share. Their result suggests that unions are successful in extracting some of these into their wages. In contrast Clarke (1984) develops a bargaining framework in which unions have their greatest effect on profitability in firms that have low market shares and face a more competitive environment. The intuition of this rests on the hypothesis that, where firms have more monopoly power, they are more able to pass on union wage effects in the form of higher prices without such a large impact on profits. Clarke also finds some empirical support for this with US data.

10.7 Trade unions, technological change and investment

The impact of trade unions on technological change and investment has also received some attention in the literature, linked, in part, with the earlier discussion of workplace productivity and dynamic performance. This has typically been analysed in a conceptual framework in which firms are seeking to maximize their expected net benefits from the technological change or investment. Unions might influence the expected returns because of their perceived opposition to such changes. On the other hand if union voice effects are present they may be reducing labour turnover, resulting in higher training and encouragement of investment in new technology. Other arguments have been put forward to support positive or negative effects and it is an empirical question as to which dominate. Studies in the UK (Latreille, 1992; Machin and Wadwhani, 1991) and in Australia (Drago and Wooden, 1994; Nunes *et al.*, 1993) using similar workplace data (from the *Workplace Industrial Relations Survey*) about process changes suggest quite different effects in the two countries. In the UK union recognition was found to have a positive impact, while in Australia union presence and union density were found to be negatively associated with technological change. One possible reconciliation of these findings is that the changes in the industrial relations environment in the UK in the 1980s reduced the impediments to change in unionized workplaces. In Australia, although there were some changes in the industrial relations environment they were not so radical and thus may not have had such an impact on unionized workplaces.

In contrast to the findings on new technology in the UK workplace, industry-level analyses, tend to find sizeable negative effects of unions on investment in the same period and on research and development. This result was also found in a US study by Hirsch and Link (1987).

10.8 Trade unions and labour turnover

Freeman and Medoff's exit–voice model leads to the hypothesis that unions reduce labour turnover. The extensive empirical investigation generally confirms this suggestion, for example in the USA, UK, Japan and Australia (Kornfeld, 1990; Miller and Mulvey, 1991a, b; and Drago and Wooden 1991). Whether the impact of unions on quits, tenure and thus labour turnover is due to union voice effects, however, is not clear. These models in general do not test that aspect of the Freeman and Medoff theory. Another possible explanation, for example, could relate to the wage benefits associated with jobs held by union members.

10.9 Trade unions and employment

Earlier in this chapter we saw that one way of viewing trade unions was as organizations that tended to raise wages by restricting employment. There have been a limited number of studies of the employment effects of unions, but those available for the USA and UK tend to provide support for a negative employment effect of unions.

11 Conclusions

The industrial relations framework, the nature of the bargaining process and the activities of trade unions can clearly have a significant impact on the operation of labour markets. This is made all the more interesting and important by changes in the extent of unionization over time and differences between countries. We follow up some of these themes in the final part of the book, in particular, looking at the relationship between unions and inflation.

References

Ashenfelter, O. and G.E. Johnson (1969). 'Bargaining Theory, Trade Unions and Industrial Strike Activity'. *American Economic Review*, 59, 35–49.

Ashenfelter, O. and J.H. Pencavel (1969). 'American Trade Union Growth'. *Quarterly Journal of Economics*, 83, 434–448.

Bain, G.S. and P. Elias (1976). 'Trade Union Membership in Great Britain: An Individual Level Analysis'. *British Journal of Industrial Relations*, 23, 71–92.

Bain, G.S. and F. Elsheikh (1976). *Union Growth and the Business Cycle: an Econometric Analysis*. Oxford: Blackwell.

Bean, R. and K. Holden (1994). 'Determinants of Trade Union Membership in OECD Countries: A Survey'. *International Journal of Manpower*, 15, 6, 4–35.

Belman, D. (1989). 'Unions, the Quality of Labor Relations and Firm Performance'. Mimeo. Economic Policy Institute, Washington, DC.

Binmore, K. and P. Dasgupta (1987). *The Economics of Bargaining*. Oxford: Blackwell.

Binmore, K., A. Rubinstein, and A. Wolinsky (1986). 'The Nash Bargaining Solution in Economic Modelling'. *Rand Journal of Economics*, 17, 176–188.

Blanchflower D. and A. Oswald (1989). 'Working Internationally'. In R. Jowell, S. Witherspoon, and L. Brook (eds) *British Social Attitudes: The International Report*, Aldershot: Gower Press.

Booth, A. (1986). 'Estimating the Probability of Trade Union Membership: A Study of Men and Women in Britain'. *Economica*, 53, 41–61.

Booth, A. and R. Cressey (1990). 'Strikes with Asymmetric Information: Theory and Evidence'. *Oxford Bulletin of Economics and Statistics*, 52, 269–291.

Brown, C. and J. Medoff (1978). 'Trade Unions in the Production Process'. *Journal of Political Economy*, 86, 8, 355–378.

Caruth, A. and C. Schnabel (1990). 'Empirical Modelling of Trade Union Growth in Germany, 1956–1986: Traditional *versus* Cointegration and Error Correction Methods'. *Weltwirtschaftliches Archiv*, 126, 326–346.

Clarke, K. (1984). 'Unionisation and Firm Performance: The Impact on Profit, Growth and Productivity'. *American Economic Review*, 74, 5, 893–919.

Creedy, J. and I.M. McDonald (1991). 'Models of Trade Union Behaviour: A Synthesis'. *Economic Record*, 67, 199, 346–359.

Crockett, G., P. Dawkins, P. Miller and C. Mulvey (1993). 'The Impact of Unions on Workplace Productivity in Australia'. *Australian Bulletin of Labour*, 18, 2, 119–141.

Cross, J.G. (1969). *The Economics of Bargaining*. New York: Basic Books.

Dawkins, P. and M. Wooden (1993). 'Understanding Industrial Action in Australian Workplaces'. *The Economics and Labour Relations of Australian Workplaces: Quantitative Approaches*. Australian Centre for Industrial Relations Research and Teaching (ACIRRT).

Deery, A. and H. DeCieri (1991). 'Determinants of Trade Union Membership in Australia'. *British Journal of Industrial Relations*, 29, 59–73.

Dertouzos, J.N. and J.H. Pencavel (1980). 'Wage and Employment Determination Under Trade Unionism: the International Typographical Union'. *Journal of Political Economy*. 89, 1162–1181.

Drago, R. and M. Wooden (1993). 'The Australian Workplace Industrial Relations Survey and Workplace Performance', *Australian Bulletin of Labour*, 18, 2, 119–141.

Drago, R. and M. Wooden (1994). 'Unions, Innovation and Investment: Australian Evidence'. *Applied Economics*, 26, 609–615.

Edgeworth, F.Y. (1891). *Mathematical Psycics*. London: Kegan Paul.

Engel, R. F. and C. W. Granger (1987). 'Cointegration and Error Correction: Representation, Estimation and Testing'. *Econometrica*, 55, 251–276.

Fiorito, J. and C.R. Greer (1982). 'Determinants of US Unionism: Past Research and Future Needs'. *Industrial Relations*, 21, 1–31.

Freeman R.P. (1994). 'Amercian Exceptionalism in the Labour Market: Union–Nonunion Differentials in the United States and other Countries'. In C. Kerr and P. Straddohar (eds) *Labor Economics and Industrial Relations Markets and Institutions*, Cambridge, MA: Harvard University Press.

Freeman, R. and J. Medoff (1984). *What Do Unions Do?* New York: Basic Books.

Freeman, R. and J. Pelletier (1990). 'The Impact of Industrial Relations Legislation on British Union Density'. *British Journal of Industrial Relations*, 28, 141–164.

Hart, O. (1989). 'Bargaining and Strikes'. *Quarterly Journal of Economics*, 104, 26–43.

Hicks, J. (1936). *The Theory of Wages*. New York: Macmillan.

Hirsch, B.T. and A.N. Addison (1986). *The Economic Analysis of Unions*. Boston: Allen and Unwin, Boston.

Hirsch, B.T. and A.N. Link (1987). 'Unions Productivity and Productivity Growth'. *Journal of Labour Research*, 8, 323–332.

Hirschman, A.O. (1970). *Exit, Voice and Loyalty*. Cambridge, MA. Harvard University Press.

Holden, K. and J.L. Thompson (1991). 'Cointegration: An Introductory Survey', *British Review of Economic Issues*, 14, 1–55.

Johnson, H.G. and P. Mieszkowski (1970). 'The Effects of Unionisation on the Distribution of Income: A General Equilibrium Approach'. *Quarterly Journal of Economics*, 84, 547–560.

Kornfeld, R. (1990). 'Effects of Unions on Young Workers in Australia'. Mimeo. Harvard University.

Latreille, P. (1992). 'Unions and the Inter-Establishment Adoption of New Microelectronic Technologies in the British Private Manufacturing Sector'. *Oxford Bulletin of Economics and Statistics*, 54, 1, 31–51.

Leontief, W. (1946). 'The Pure Theory of the Guaranteed Annual Wage Contract'. *Journal of Political Economy*, 56, 76–79.

MacDonald, I.M. and R.M. Solow (1981). 'Wage Bargaining and Employment', *American Economic Review*, 71, 896–908.

Machin, S. and M. Stuart (1990). 'Unions and the Financial Performance of British Private Sector Establishments'. *Journal of Applied Econometrics*, 5, 327–350.

Machin, S. and M. Stuart (1994). 'UK Productivity Growth at the End of the 1980s: Evidence from Establishment Level Data'. Mimeo.

Machin, S. and S. Wadwhani (1991). 'The Effects of Unions on Investment and Innovation: Evidence from the WIRS'. *Economic Journal*, 101, 324–330.

Metcalf, D. (1990). 'Unions, Incomes Policy and Relative Wages in Britain'. *British Journal of Industrial Relations*. XV, 2, 157–175.

Miller, P. and C. Mulvey (1991a). 'Australian Evidence on the Exit/Voice Model of the Labour Market'. *Industrial and Labour Relations Review*, 45, 1, 44–57.

Miller, P. and C. Mulvey (1991b). 'Trade Unions and the Distribution of Paid Overtime'. *Journal of Industrial Relations*, 33, 220–233.

Moore, W.J. and D.F. Pearce (1976). 'Union Growth: a Test of the Ashenfelter–Pencavel Model'. *Industrial Relations*, 15, 242–247.

Nash, J. (1950). 'The Bargaining Problem'. *Econometrica*, 18, 155–162.

Nash, J. (1951). 'Non-cooperative Games'. *Annals of Mathematics*, 54, 286–295.

Nickell, S. (1982). 'A Bargaining Model of the Phillips Curve'. Centre for Labour Economics. Discussion Paper No. 130. London School of Economics.

Nunes, N., G. Crockett, and P. Dawkins (1993). 'The Impact of Competition and Trade Unions on Workplace Reform and Organisational and Technological Change'. *Australian Economic Review*, 2nd Quarter.

OECD (1991). 'Trends in Union Membership'. *Employment Outlook*, July, 97–120.

Oswald, A.J. (1982). 'The Microeconomic Theory of the Trade Union'. *Economic Journal*, 92, 576–595.

Pen, J. (1952). 'A General Theory of Bargaining'. *American Economic Review*, 42, 24, 24–42.

Pencavel, J. (1971). 'The Demand for Union Services: An Exercise'. *Industrial and Labour Relations Review*, 24, 180–190.

Pencavel, J. (1974). 'Relative Wages and Trade Unions in the United Kingdom'. *Economica*, 41, 194–210.

Pencavel, J. (1984). 'The Trade-Off Between Wages and Employment in Trade Union Objectives'. *Quarterly Journal of Economics*, 99, 215–231.

Rees, A. (1963). 'The Effects of Unions on Resource Allocation'. *Journal of Law and Economics*, 6, 69–78.

Richardson, R. (1977). 'Trade-Union Growth'. *British Journal of Industrial Relations*, 15, 279–282.

Rosen, S. (1970). 'Unionism and the Occupational Wage Structure in the United States'. *International Economic Review*, 11, 269–286.

Roth, A. (1979). *Axiomatic Models of Bargaining*. Berlin: Springer-Verlag.

Roth, A. (ed.) (1985). *Bargaining with Incomplete Information*. Cambridge: Cambridge University Press.

Rubinstein, A. (1982). 'Perfect Equilibrium in a Bargaining Model'. *Econometrica*, 50, 97–109.

Shackle, G.S.L. (1957). 'The Nature of the Bargaining Process'. In J.T. Dunlop (ed.) *The Theory of Wage Determination*. London: Macmillan. Reprinted in 1966, pp. 292–314.

Shelfin, N., L. Troy, and C.T. Koeller, (1981). 'Structural Stability in Models of American Trade Union Growth'. *Quarterly Journal of Economics*, 96, 79–88.

Stephens, J.D. (1979). *The Transition from Capitalism to Socialism*. London: Macmillan.

Tracy, J.S. (1987). 'An Empirical Test of an Asymmetric Information Model of Strikes'. *Journal of Labour Economics*, 5, 2, 149–173.

Turner, H.A. (1962). *Trade Union Growth, Structure and Policy*. London: Allen and Unwin.

van Ours, J.C. (1992). 'Union Growth in the Netherlands 1961–1989'. *Applied Economics*, 24, 1059–1066.

Varoufakis, V. (1991). *Rational Conflict*. Oxford: Blackwell.

Visser, J. (1988). 'In Search of Inclusive Unionism: A Comparative Analysis'. Discussion Paper. University of Amsterdam.

Wallerstein, M. (1989). 'Union Organisation in Advanced Industrial Democracies', *American Political Science Review*, 83, 481–501.

Whitfield, K., P. Marginson, and W. Brown (1994). 'Workplace Industrial Relations Under Different Regulatory Systems: A Survey-Based Comparison of Australia and Britain'. *British Journal of Industrial Relations*, 32, 1, 319–338.

CHAPTER 26 Wages and earnings

1 Introduction

Wages and earnings have been a constant source of interest to labour economists since the days of Adam Smith (1776). This chapter draws upon theories developed earlier in the book to discuss the causes of pay differences and changes in the wage structure. In particular it draws upon wages and earnings functions, discussed at length in the context of estimating rates of return to education (see Chapter 16). The aim of the wage equation and earnings function literature is to decompose income into its component parts in the sense that the approach attempts to attribute variations in income across individuals to differences in their education, training (skills), occupation, gender, union membership, etc. The empirical specification is based upon extensions of Mincer's return to education equation. As you will remember from the earlier discussion in Chapter 16, this generally took the form

$$\ln W_i = a + bs_i + cX_i + dX_i^2 + eZ_i + \mu_i \qquad (1)$$

where: W denotes earnings (wages or income); s is a measure of schooling (often the number of years of schooling); X denotes a measure of cumulative experience; Z is a vector of other possible influences (such as age, race, gender, region, etc.); μ is a random error term (reflecting unobserved innate ability and other random influences not accounted for directly); i (=1, ..., n) denotes the ith individual in the sample. We noted in the earlier discussion that, for example, equation (1) might test for the effects of training by the inclusion of a training dummy, T,

$$\ln W = \ln W_0 + \beta s + \gamma X + \delta X^2 + \alpha T + \rho Z + \mu \quad (2)$$

where $T = 1$ if the individual has received training and $T = 0$ otherwise. If earnings are affected by factors such as overtime or unsocial hours payments, these are controlled for by the inclusion of hours of work or shift type as right hand side variables.

In the remainder of this chapter, we explore the application of this approach to establishing the determinants of wages and earnings. Section 2 provides a conceptual framework for considering the influence of competitive and non-competitive forces. Section 3 describes 'competitive' theories and empirical models. Section 4 describes the findings of empirical research on the non-competitive influences on wage differentials. Section 5 considers issues relating to the distribution of earnings. Finally, Section 6 draws the main conclusions of this chapter.

2 Competitive and non-competitive forces

If there was a single, perfectly competitive labour market with all workers capable of performing any job without training, and indifferent between all jobs, there would be one supply of labour curve and one demand curve. These would determine an equilibrium level of employment and wages. In other words every worker would receive the same wage. In the real world, however, it is evident that there is a wide spectrum of wages. The key to understanding the determination of wage differentials and the structure of earnings is to examine the assumptions required to produce a perfect market and one wage level.

First, it is necessary to assume that workers are indifferent between all jobs. In other words, non-pecuniary advantages (or disadvantages) do not make one job more (or less) attractive than another. As Adam Smith (1776) recognized, however, the more dirty or dangerous a job, the less prepared workers are to supply their labour to it at any given wage. Similarly in any given job, workers are generally less prepared to supply their labour at abnormal or unsocial times, such as at night. As Smith pointed out, if all workers viewed the non-pecuniary advantages and disadvantages of jobs similarly, then the various markets for jobs with different non-pecuniary disadvantages would adjust in such a way as to create a structure of wage differentials, such that higher wages just compensate for non-pecuniary disadvantages. The 'net advantages' of all jobs would be equal. Any differences in 'net advantages' would induce labour mobility to restore equality of net advantages.

Second, it is necessary to assume that all workers are capable of performing any job without training. This is clearly unrealistic. Human capital theory shows that education and training are investment activities which are induced when the rate of return is higher than for other, comparable investments. Bearing in mind the direct costs of training and the indirect costs of forgone earnings, skilled labour must receive a wage differential to compensate, the more so the higher the rate at which expected future earnings are discounted.

Non-pecuniary advantages and training do not destroy the perfectly competitive model, but, rather, amend it. Instead of concluding that wages are equal between all workers, and any adjustments occur quickly, we now conclude that in the long run, the present value of expected 'net advantages' is equated in all jobs. Any discrepancies cause movements of labour in the short run where training is not required (or in the long run where it is), to restore equality of this concept of 'net advantages'. However, it is clear that a structure of earnings arises to compensate for non-pecuniary disadvantages and for the costs of training.

The story of wage differentials does not end at this point. Imperfections and other factors conspire to prevent labour markets reaching a point of equality of the present value of lifetime 'net advantages' of all occupations. First, labour is heterogeneous, not only in terms of the amount of training undertaken, but also in terms of aptitudes and abilities before training. Second, labour is often immobile geographically due to family and social ties and to the costs of moving. Third, subjective discrimination may exist on the part of employers, on the basis of social class, sex or race. Fourth, varying degrees of monopoly and/or monopsony power exist in labour markets which can be expected to influence the structure of earnings. All these things compound one another, over and above the effects of the non-pecuniary advantages and disadvantages of different jobs, to give rise to a wide spectrum of wages and earnings.

Bearing all this in mind, the first stage in conceptualizing the way in which the configuration of wages is determined is to regard it as the outcome of the interaction of labour supply and demand, both of which are a function of the wage rate and a range of other factors to do with the characteristics of the labour supplied and demanded and the structure of the market. The nature of these supply and demand functions will be different between the short and long run, with a tendency for competitive forces to be more influential in the long run. If there are, say, m geographical and n occupational groups, there are $q = m.n$ geographical/occupational labour markets. Thus for each geographical/occupational labour market, denoted by subscript j where $j = 1$ to q, there is a labour supply and a labour demand curve:

$$S_j = f_{ij}(X(1)_j, X(2)_j, w_j) \tag{3}$$

$$D_j = g_{ij}(Z(1)_j, Z(2)_j, w_j) \tag{4}$$

where $X(1)_j$ are factors (other than the wage) which determine supply in long-run competitive equilibrium and $X(2)_j$ are factors (other than the wage) which cause supply to deviate from the long-run competitive equilibrium state. Similarly $Z(1)_j$ are factors (other than the wage) which determine demand in long-run competitive equilibrium and $Z(2)_j$ are the factors (other than the wage) which, at any given point in time, cause demand to deviate from long-run competitive equilibrium (though they may disappear in the long run).

$X(1)_j$ are essentially composed of two separate factors. First, there is the human capital endowment required in labour market j. The greater the human capital required the fewer the people willing and able to supply their labour in this market at any given wage. Second, there are the tastes of the suppliers of labour. Assuming heterogeneous tastes, otherwise identical suppliers of labour will be induced to supply their labour at different wage rates and any change in tastes will cause a shift in the supply curve.

$Z(1)_j$ are affected by product demand and the marginal productivity of labour in the long run. This will be influenced by the technology of production which adjusts to relative factor prices in the long run. Of special interest here is that the human capital endowments of the labour force influence its marginal productivity. The higher the relevant skill level of labour, the higher the wage that the employer is willing to pay. Any technological change will cause a shift in the labour demand curve. Assuming that only long-run competitive forces are at play, wages adjust to equal the marginal product of labour in all its uses, and differences in wages reflect a combination of differences in human capital endowments (compensation for human capital investment costs and rents to scarce abilities) and differences in tastes concerning the non-pecuniary advantages/disadvantages of jobs in different markets.

It should be noted that we have not referred to the tastes of employers. Employers may prefer employing workers possessing certain characteristics to others, irrespective of their productivity. This is what Becker referred to as the 'taste for discrimination' (see Chapter 24), and may occur with respect to the race or gender of the individuals supplying labour. However, this would not be possible in long-run competitive equilibrium. Non-discriminating employers would possess a competitive advantage and force discriminators out of the market. Thus, the taste for discrimination is one of the factors that enters the demand function as part of $Z(2)_j$, those factors that cause labour demand to deviate from long-run competitive equilibrium. Other factors include the degree of monopsony power of employers, which may be reduced in the long run, depending upon the extent of entry barriers (or the extent to which markets are contestable).

Labour is at its most mobile in the long run. To the extent that individuals are able and willing to change their occupation or region (subject to investment in human capital) this is allowed for in long-run competitive equilibrium. In the short run, however, extensive sources of immobility may exist. Such sources enter our conceptual framework as part of $X(2)_j$, factors causing labour supply to deviate from long-run competitive equilibrium. For example, to the extent that it takes time to invest in education or training, shortages of skilled labour can cause the wage to rise above the long-run equilibrium level. Geographical mobility is also likely to be lower in the short run due to social and family ties, search costs, etc. Another factor incorporated in $X(2)_j$ is the monopoly power of labour supply in the market. For example, if a union controls the supply of labour to the market in question this may cause a significant deviation in wage (and employment) outcomes from competitive equilibrium (see Chapter 25). The union may choose, for example, to force up wages by restricting labour supply.

This conceptual framework suggests that a wide range of long-run, short-run, competitive and non-competitive factors influence the structure of wage differentials. Long-run competitive forces tend to produce wage differentials that result from differences in the characteristics of those supplying labour whether it be their human capital endowments or their tastes. Demand side forces tend to be more important in the short run because of the time it takes for supply side adjustments to take place. The introduction of non-competitive forces, in particular the market power of employers and unions, also tends to force wages away from long-run competitive equilibrium. Theories of pay differ largely in the extent to which they stress long-run and competitive forces as against short-run and non-competitive forces. Thus we might conveniently divide theories of pay into 'competitive' and 'non-competitive' theories of pay, although the distinction is not always so clear cut in the real world.

3 Competitive theories

3.1 Occupational differentials

It is fairly clear from the earlier discussion that human capital theory makes a significant contribution to theories of pay. In a pure human capital view of the world, wage differentials exist in order to equate the present value of the stream of lifetime earnings of different occupational groups. Thus higher pay for more skilled workers exists to compensate for forgone earnings and direct training costs incurred in human capital investment. Smith notes,

> The improved dexterity of a workman may be considered in the same light as a machine or instrument of trade which facilitates and abridges labour, and which, though it costs a certain expense, repays that expense with a profit. (Smith, 1776 (reprinted 1932), Book II, Vol. 1)

As we noted earlier, it is unrealistic to attribute differences in skill purely to training. Differences in ability, whether innate or developed in childhood before training, allow some people to earn more than others. This is most noticeable where scarce talents exist, for example in the case of sportsmen and women or entertainers. Nevertheless, education and training are important elements in skill development. Given that Chapter 17 has explored the implications of education and training for earnings in some detail, we will not repeat the discussion here. One thing we have not examined, however, is the way in which different education levels, skills and other attributes translate into occupational choice and are, thereby, reflected in occupational earnings differentials.

The theory of occupational choice must take into account the other reasons why wage differentials occur in the long run. Smith (1776) referred to such things as agreeableness, honourableness, trust required, and the constancy of employment. These things are aspects of the non-pecuniary advantages/ disadvantages of particular forms of employment, and underlie the theory of compensating wage differentials outlined above. Again, to quote Smith,

> The whole of the advantages and disadvantages of the different employments of labour and stock must, in the same neighbourhood, be either perfectly equal or continually tending to equality. If in the same neighbourhood there was any employment evidently either more or less advantageous than the rest, so many people would crowd into it in one case, and so many would desert it in the other, that its advantages would soon return to the level of other employments. (Smith, 1776 (reprinted 1932), Book I, Chapter 10)

Empirical interest in occupational wage differentials was stimulated in part by the secular decline that took place in both the UK and the USA during the first two-thirds of the 20th century (Phelps Brown, 1977, pp. 73–75). Such a narrowing might be expected on the basis of human capital theory, given the general expansion of state education. Thus, the resulting decline in the private costs of secondary and higher education reduced the pay differential required to induce investment in education. Similar points can be made with regard to skilled manual workers, as apprenticeships were allowed to commence at a later age and take fewer years. In the USA the narrowing was also encouraged by the cessation of both mass immigration of unskilled workers from Europe and internal migration from farm to city.

These explanations do not, however, appear to explain why the narrowing concentrated in the two short periods of two world wars and their immediate post-war inflations (Phelps Brown and Hopkins, 1955). Reder (1955) argued that the characteristics of workers applying for given jobs vary with the state of the labour market. When there is a scarcity of applicants, employers reduce hiring standards rather than increase wages. Thus workers are promoted from lower grades and the promoted workers are in turn replaced by workers further down the hierarchy. This occurs at all levels except for the least skilled, who cannot be substituted for from below. Some recruitment may be possible from the stock of unemployed, but the scope for this is limited in a tight labour market. Reder argued that it is at this level that wage rates will be increased and thus pay differentials diminish. The question then becomes, why does the reverse not occur on the downswing when the labour market becomes slack? Reder's answer is that a social view is formed of an acceptable minimum wage, and there is resistance to wages falling in the downswing of the cycle. Thus, wages for the unskilled rise in a tight labour market and are sustained in a slack market.

Other institutional explanations have been developed – see Turner (1952) and Routh (1965). Their explanation relies on the role of trade unions and on the evidence that the compression of wage differentials occurred during periods of rapid inflation. If unions negotiate predominantly for absolute wage differentials during inflationary periods the relative differentials decline. Evidence for the UK from the 1960s and 1970s supports this view. It shows how a similar if less dramatic compression of differentials occurred in the UK engineering industry during the period of inflation up to 1976 as shown in Table 26.1.

Table 26.1 Fitters' earnings as a percentage of labourers' earnings

Average weekly earnings in the UK including overtime, both timeworkers and pieceworkers included

Year	Skill* differential	Year	Skill* differential	Skill† differential
1914	165.4	1965	138.2	138.7
1923	138.3	1968	140.2	140.8
1925	138.0	1969	–	142.0
1930	144.2	1970	–	139.2
1935	141.8	1971	–	138.1
1940	148.9	1972	–	136.9
1948	125.4	1973	–	134.1
1951	127.1	1974	–	132.4
1955	129.8	1975	–	131.1
1960	135.1	1976 (est)	–	(127.3)

Sources: * Hart and MacKay (1975)
† ED *Gazette*

More recent data suggest that differentials may no longer be narrowing and a more complex picture is emerging. Certainly the world has been changing significantly, with reductions in the importance of unions, and the growth of multi-skilling and flexibilization. Recent evidence for the UK, based upon changes in rankings over the period 1975–1990, is provided in Table 26.2 (Elias and Gregory, 1994). The authors report that

Table 26.2 Occupations: modal ranking by earnings, 1975–1990

Occupation	Modal ranking, 1975–1990					
	Hourly earnings			Gross pay		
	All	M	F	All	M	F
Corporate managers and administration	3	3	5	2	2	5
Managers/proprietors in agriculture and services	10	11	11	12	12	11
Science and engineering professionals	5	6	4	3	4	3
Health professionals	1	1	2	1	1	1
Education professionals	2	2	1	6	6	2
Other professional occupations	4	4	3	4	5	2,4
Science and engineering associate professionals	7	7	8	8	8	8
Health associate professionals	12	9	10	16	10	10
Other associate professional occupations	6	5	6	5	3	7
Clerical occupations	17	15	14	18	19	15
Secretarial occupations	18	12	12	19,21	13	14
Skilled construction trades	16	18	15	16	17	16
Skilled engineering trades	10,11	13	14	10	10	12
Other skilled trades	16	18	15	16	17	16
Protective service occupations	9	9	9	8	7	6
Personal service occupations	20	20	18	21	20	18
Brokers, buyers and sales representatives	8	8	9	8	7	6
Other sales occupations	22	21	22	22	21	22
Industrial plant and machine operators	15	14	17	14	15	16
Drivers and mobile machine operators	13	17	15, 16	11	14	10, 13
Other occupations in agriculture, forestry and fishing	21	22	21	18	22	21
Other elementary occupations	19	19	19	17	18	19,20

Source: Elias and Gregory (1994)

> For the average employee; and ignoring pay differentials by gender, being employed in the top earning occupation brought hourly earnings around double the overall average, while employment in the lowest-paying occupation brought earnings of 60-65 per cent of the economy wide average, an overall ratio across occupations of around 3.5:1. (Elias and Gregory, 1994, p. 21)

We return to the more recent evidence in the discussion of changes in income distribution in Section 5.

3.2 Hedonic theory

Recent studies have approached the issue of compensating wage differentials by means of the theory of hedonic pricing (an early application in a labour market context was by Welch, 1969). In the simplest model, earnings are a function of the attributes of each worker. These personal characteristics command a uniform price across all markets. Each job has a number of non-wage attributes,

$$z = (z_1, z_2, \ldots, z_n) \tag{5}$$

Each attribute has an implicit value (i.e. its shadow price multiplied by the quantity of the attribute) which, when combined together, produce observed wage differentials. Each supplier of labour has an 'acceptable wage' function,

$$\sigma(z, u^*) \tag{6}$$

which shows the payments a worker must receive to make them indifferent between jobs with different attributes. σ is the acceptance wage and u^* a constant utility index. This function can be represented by a set of indifference curves between the worker's acceptance wage and different non-pecuniary job attributes.

The worker maximizes utility subject to the wage function $w(z)$, which describes the available combinations of w and z when the labour market is in equilibrium. This maximization produces the optimum condition that the marginal rate of substitution between the acceptance wage and each job attribute is equal to its shadow price, or

$$\frac{\partial\sigma}{\partial z} = w'(z) \tag{7}$$

As workers' tastes differ there is a distribution of acceptance wage functions along the market equilibrium wage frontier. From the firm's point of view, job attributes can affect profitability. In the case of inconvenient hours, it can increase profitability due to increased capital utilization. Also the reduction of some unfavourable attributes (e.g. noise of machinery) can impose direct costs on the firm. Following McNabb (1987), the firm's profit function is written

$$\pi = g(E, z) - w(z)E - C(z) \tag{8}$$

where: $g(E,z)$ is the firm's production function; E is the labour input; C is the cost of the job attribute. Firms maximize profits subject to the constraint imposed by the labour market equilibrium function $w(z)$, resulting in an offer function

$$\phi(z,\pi^*) \tag{9}$$

which illustrates the wage offered ϕ, at different levels of the job attribute at given profit levels. This produces a set of isoprofit curves for each firm. Their trade-offs between wages and job attributes vary across firms owing to differences in production technologies and their ability to adjust job characteristics. Optimal hiring occurs when

$$\frac{\partial\phi}{\partial z} = w'(z) \tag{10}$$

for each job attribute.

Long-run competitive equilibrium is represented by a tangency of the offer curve and the $w(z)$ frontier consistent with zero excess profits. In the equilibrium the outcomes for both workers and firms are appropriately matched. McNabb (1987) estimated earnings equations to test this hedonic theory of wages with UK data from the *General Household Survey*. The estimated equation was

$$\ln w = \alpha + \beta z_1 + \gamma z_2 + \mu \tag{11}$$

where: z_1 is a vector of distasteful job attributes; z_2 is a vector of control variables; and μ is a random error term. His results provided some confirmation for the theory, especially for manual employees. On average employees who worked inconvenient hours receive an earnings premium of 5 per cent, other things equal. Workers in jobs with unfavourable or disagreeable working conditions, or whose jobs lack security, received a premium of 2.5 per cent over other workers. The link here between observed wages and the insecurity of employment suggests some proportion of the workforce is willing to accept a greater likelihood of temporary lay-offs in return for higher wages when they are in employment; firms are willing to pay this differential in return for increased flexibility to meet varying or uncertain product demand.

3.3 Skills, choice and selection

In the Welch (1969) model workers are indifferent between jobs in different sectors of the economy. This arises because each of the attributes possessed by the individual is associated with the same price in every sector. Thus, if employers can costlessly repackage these attributes into bundles that form jobs and earnings are the driving motivation in job choice, then individual workers are indifferent with regard to which sector they choose. In practice, the world is not as simple as this. The conditions under which the prices for attributes are identical across sectors are not met in the real world, however, and it seems more likely that individuals exploit their comparative advantage in the choice of jobs (self-selection), reflecting their (measured and unmeasured) heterogeneous skills (Heckman and Sedlacek, 1985).

Individuals choose between two markets (manufacturing and non-manufacturing) and one other state (not in the labour force). Each sector requires a unique sector specific task, t_i. Each individual is endowed with a set of skills, s, that define the amount of the sector-specific tasks that the individual can perform, $t_i(s)$. Thus, their skill endowment defines the amount of the task the individual can do in each sector (i = 1,2). Skills are distributed across the population (s is continuously distributed with density $g(s|\theta)$, where θ is a vector of parameters). Thus, the model is in some sense short run, as skills are invariant, and the skill distribution of the population is fixed. The individual can only enter one sector or state at a given point in time. Thus, firms' demands in each sector are based upon required tasks, represented by 'packages of skills', which cannot be unbundled.

In this world, an individual's wage is dependent on their skills, which, in turn, are mapped to tasks demanded by employers,

$$\ln w_i(s) = \ln \alpha_i + \ln t_i(s) \tag{12}$$

where α_i is a constant for the sector in question. While there are considerable similarities, equation (12) is not a conventional hedonic wage function of the type described above. In this model, the components of s are not priced out individually, only each task, t (which is a bundle of s), is priced. Skills, s, are distributed across the population. Thus, as individuals decide in which sector they are going to work, this defines the skills that flow into each of the two sectors and, thereby, the total supply of the tasks in each sector. Equilibrium in each sector exists if the prices which prevail induce an aggregate supply of tasks to each sector which is consistent with the aggregate demand for such tasks (which depends on the overall technology of the firm and, thereby, the role of non-labour inputs).

In the original 'Roy model', individuals choose between two possible wages,

$$\ln w_1 = \ln \alpha_1 + \mu_1 + \varepsilon_1 \qquad (13)$$

$$\ln w_2 = \ln \alpha_2 + \mu_2 + \varepsilon_2 \qquad (14)$$

In the 'Roy model', the density function for skills, $g(s|\theta)$, and the task functions, $t_i(s)$, are assumed to possess properties such that ($\ln t_1$,$\ln t_2$) is normally distributed with mean (μ_1,μ_2), and (ε_1, ε_2) is a mean zero normal vector. Given that, $w_i = \pi_i t_i$, Heckman and Sedlacek (1985, p. 1083) show that this leads to the expectation that,

$$E(\ln t_1|\ln w_1 > \ln w_2) = \mu_1 + \sigma_1\lambda(c_1) \qquad (15)$$

$$E(\ln t_2|\ln w_2 > \ln w_1) = \mu_2 + \sigma_2\lambda(c_2) \qquad (16)$$

Thus, the expected value of the supply of task 1 to sector 1 is equal to the mean population value of task 1, μ_1, plus a self-selection term, $\sigma_1\lambda(c_1)$, which reflects the relative sizes of the variance and covariance of the distribution of skills and therefore wages across the population.

This leads to the following conclusions. First, if endowments of tasks, $\ln t_1$ and $\ln t_2$, are uncorrelated, self-selection always causes the mean of log task 1 used in sector 1 to exceed the population mean of log task 1, μ_1. Second, the opposite occurs when $\ln t_1$ and $\ln t_2$ are sufficiently positively correlated. Under such circumstances the mean of the log task 1 used in sector 1 falls below the population mean of task 1, μ_1. Third, in the basic 'Roy model' the two sectors are mirror images of one another in the sense that, if the mean of log task 1 used in sector 1 is less than the population mean of log task 1, μ_1, then the mean of log task 2 used in sector 2 exceeds the population mean of log task 2, μ_2. Finally, if individuals did not self-select themselves into the two sectors, but were randomly selected to each of the sectors from the population as a whole, the observed means in each of the two sectors would equal the population means.

In practice, the 'Roy model' is rejected when it is tested on US *Current Population Survey* earnings data, disaggregated into manufacturing and non-manufacturing sectors. Thus, Heckman and Sadlacek (1985, pp. 1090–1091) argue the need for various extensions. First, a more general functional form within which the lognormal distribution (on which the Roy model is based) is nested. The resulting model can produce a Pareto tail to the distribution of wage rates (or tasks), unlike the Roy model, where the tail is thinner than the corresponding Pareto distribution. Second, a more general model in which self-selection can increase inequality both within and between sectors *vis-à-vis* what would have been the case without self-selection (in the Roy model, self-selection reduces within-sector inequality). Third, the extended model includes a third 'sector', which allows for the fact that individuals can choose not to participate in the labour market (the manufacturing and non-manufacturing alternatives are maintained). Fourth, individuals maximize utility (rather than income), which depends on wage rates, employment risk, job status, etc.

The authors estimated both sectoral choice and wage equations which include many of the normal regressors used in earnings functions. The results of the sectoral choice equations indicate that education and work experience both tend to increase participation in the labour market, especially in the non-manufacturing sector. The South dummy was only weakly related to the choice between non-market and manufacturing activities, but more strongly between non-market and non-manufacturing activities. A positive coefficient was found on the (predicted) non-labour income variable. The authors prefer to interpret this as the fact that individuals choose employment in sectors which offer higher sector-specific social benefits (rather than as an indication that leisure is an inferior good). The results of the wage equation indicate that education has a strong positive effect on wage rates, particularly in manufacturing. In addition, wages grow more strongly with experience in manufacturing than in non-manufacturing. The South dummy is insignificant in both cases. The underlying distribution suggests a Pareto tail to wage rates (see Section 5 below) in the non-manufacturing sector, although not in manufacturing.

The results provide considerable insights about the effects of changes in industry structure on wages in each sector and in the economy as a whole, termed an 'aggregation bias' (Heckman and Sedlacek, 1985, pp. 1107–1110). An oil price hike tends to hit manufacturing employment relatively hard and, other things being equal, would tend to depress wages in manufacturing relative to non-manufacturing. In practice, the workers that flow from manufacturing to non-manufacturing turn out to be those at the lower end of the skill spectrum in manufacturing. Thus, their exit raises the average quality of labour remaining within manufacturing, and the wage reduction in manufacturing is therefore lower than would otherwise have been expected. On the other hand, the displaced workers entering non-manufacturing are also at the lower end of the non-manufacturing skill spectrum, reducing the average quality of individuals in this sector and accentuating any decline in real wages.

The results also throw light on the effects of self-selection on the inequality of wage rates (Heckman and Sedlacek, 1985, pp. 1110–1112). Inequality is measured as the variance of the natural logarithm of wages for white males. Thus, the authors compare observed variance in (log) wages with the variance which would have been observed if individuals had been randomly assigned to each of the three sectors. The principal result is that the random assignment of individuals increases the difference between the sectoral means of log wages to 0.317 (from a value of 0.145 in the 'self-selection' economy). In other words, self-selection narrows the differential between sectors. In addition, the results indicate that self-selection lowers the variance of log wages (i.e. the measure of inequality) *vis-à-vis* the case of random selection by 8.3 per cent in non-manufacturing and 9.1 per cent in manufacturing (note that within-sector-variance was always more important than between-sector variance). As for the economy as a whole, self-selection reduces within-sector inequality (i.e. manufacturing and non-manufacturing combined) by 7.4 per cent, between-sector inequality (which was not large anyway) by 83 per cent and overall (i.e. based upon the variance in log wages) by 11.5 per cent (from 0.329 to 0.291).

4 Non-competitive theories

In this section we present some theories of pay that are based on non-competitive views of the world. In particular we consider the theory of labour market segmentation, discrimination and trade unions. Screening and the 'job competition' model would also fall under the heading of non-competitive theories, but, as we noted in Part VI, it is impossible to distinguish the results of this model from those of the traditional human capital model using historical data.

4.1 Segmentation

The theory of labour market segmentation was discussed in Chapter 24. In essence, it is based on the idea that there are important barriers to labour mobility that tend to trap workers into particular segments from which it is difficult to escape. The concept of a dual labour market (or bipartite division) has been important in the literature, although more complex models have been considered (i.e. tripartite division). In dual labour market theory there is a primary and secondary labour market. The primary sector, which contains 'good' jobs with higher average wages and better non-wage provisions, tends to be populated by predominantly male, white, unionized labour forces. The secondary labour market contains 'bad jobs' with low pay and short job durations and tends to be populated by weakly unionized, 'marginal' workers such as immigrants and women. Even if secondary workers gain qualifications, access to the primary market is denied because of entry barriers, a feature which is reinforced by the lack of experience and specific training of the secondary workers. The secondary market is more closely aligned to the wage–competition model and tends to produce a roughly uniform rate of pay. The overall wage structure, as a result, depends on the supply of 'good jobs' (with their hierarchical wage structure) relative to the supply of 'bad jobs' (with a uniform wage rate). We reviewed much of the relevant evidence relating to segmentation in Chapter 24. In this chapter we focus on a paper by Blackaby *et al.* (1994), which analyses wage differentials and is, perhaps, more supportive of a form of dual labour markets than some of the other studies.

Blackaby *et al.* (1994) develop a model in which there are two groups: 'regular' workers, R, associated with jobs in the primary sector, and 'marginal' workers, M, linked to the secondary sector, and thus,

$$\ln W_i^R = X_i\beta_i + \mu_i^R \quad i = 1, \ldots, m \tag{17}$$

$$\ln W_i^M = X_i\gamma_i + \mu_i^M \quad i = m + 1, \ldots, T \tag{18}$$

where the reward attached to a particular characteristic, X, differs between the regular and marginal groups if $\beta \neq \gamma$. Of course, the balance of characteristics will also differ between the two groups. These form the two principal dimensions of segmentation: (i) that individuals with certain types of characteristics (white, male, professional, etc.) are over-represented in one group (regular workers) and there are a disproportionate number of individuals with other characteristics (black, female, non-professional, etc.) in the other group (marginal workers); (ii) that regular workers with the same characteristics as marginal workers (i.e. female workers) have more favourable labour market experiences (lower unemployment probabilities, higher earnings, etc.).

The employed, E, and unemployed, U, groups contain different proportions of regular and marginal workers. Taking the expected values of the earnings functions for the employed and unemployed groups

$$E(\ln W_i^E) = X_i[a\beta + (1 - a)\gamma] = X_i\Pi \quad (19)$$

$$E(\ln W_i^U) = X_i[b\beta + (1 - b)\gamma] = X_i\Omega \quad (20)$$

where: a is the probability of observing a regular worker amongst the employed group and b is the probability of observing a regular worker amongst the unemployed group. As long as such a differential exists, it should be possible to derive this from equations (19) and (20) as $E(W_i^E)$ and $E(W_i^U)$ are both formed as weighted averages of the earnings of regular and marginal workers, where the weights differ between the employed and unemployed groups. Thus, it is possible to demonstrate the relationships between the two components of segmentation and the observed earnings relationships of the employed and unemployed workers,

$$X_i(\Pi - \Omega) = X_i(a - b)(\beta - \gamma) \quad (21)$$

Equation (21) indicates that the size of the differential turns on: (i) the difference in reward for the same characteristic ($\beta - \gamma$); (ii) the difference in probability of appearing in the employed and unemployed groups ($a - b$). Equation (21) is a variant of the methodology developed by Blinder (1973) and Oaxaca (1973) to isolate the effects of discrimination (see Chapter 24).

Blackaby *et al.* (1994) use *Family Expenditure Survey* data for full-time male workers of working age, over the period 1979 to 1986, to estimate the stochastic relationship,

$$W_i^E = X_i\Pi + \epsilon_i^E \quad (22)$$

$$W_i^U = X_i\Omega + \epsilon_i^U \quad (23)$$

where the dependent variable was average hourly earnings and the regressors included: schooling and experience variables; occupation, industry and regional dummies; marital status and non-head of household dummies. They explored the effects of selection into the two groups. The null hypothesis $\Pi = \Omega$ was rejected; according to the authors,

> Our key finding is that the potential earnings of the employed are substantially higher (on average 29.8 per cent over the period 1979–1986) compared to the unemployed. Roughly two-thirds of this difference is due to the unemployed having less favourable characteristics and one-third of this is due to the fact that given characteristics are less well-rewarded. We interpret this finding as being supportive of a dual labour market. (Blackaby *et al.*, 1994)

Edwards (1979) produced a tripartite model, in which the primary labour market is divided into the 'subordinate' primary and 'independent' primary segments. The subordinate primary segment contains most blue collar jobs or what Edwards calls the 'traditional proletariat'. The independent primary segment contains the 'middle layers' or white collar jobs plus some skilled manual jobs. The subordinate primary market is more open, but unions ensure that wages and other conditions are better than in the secondary labour market which contains the 'working poor'. Edwards estimated that 17 per cent of the US labour force are in the secondary labour market, 47 per cent are in the subordinate primary market and 36 per cent in the independent primary market.

4.2 Discrimination, gender and race

4.2.1 Persistence of discrimination

We have seen how discrimination might be built into a competitive model of labour markets (Chapter 24). Under competitive conditions, however, discriminators are forced out of the market in the long run. In the real world, it appears that earnings differences not only exist but also persist over long periods of time. Data for the USA, for example, suggested a ratio of: females to male earnings of 0.62 in 1967 and 0.65 in 1984; black to white earnings of 0.70 in 1967 and 0.76 in 1984 (McConnell and Brue, 1986, Table 11-1, p. 291). In the UK, the *NES Panel Data Set* indicates that women's weekly earnings (including overtime payments, and excluding individuals whose pay was affected by absence) rose from 0.58 of male earnings in 1975 to 0.65 in 1993 (Elias and Gregory, 1994, p. 22).

It is arguable, therefore, that some market imperfection, such as monopsony, is needed to explain persistent discrimination (Berndt, 1991, p. 181). However, according to Ashenfelter (1978) and Nickell (1977), there is no evidence that monopsony power is a significant source of discrimination. For one thing the monopsony argument requires the labour supply of females to be less elastic than for males, which is not consistent with the available empirical evidence; for another it is unlikely to be true in larger conurbations where a number of employers hire from the same local labour market (Berndt, 1991, p. 181). A more likely explanation might arise from monopoly power in the labour market, if for example it could be shown that trade unions lead to segregation of women and racial minorities, or restrict access to apprenticeships (Ashenfelter, 1972). If this is the case, then we would expect to see a reduction in discrimination in countries such as the UK as union power has been reduced. This is clearly consistent with the empirical evidence outlined in the previous paragraph, but many other factors may have been at play. This line of argument leads to less 'orthodox' theories of discrimination which assume that wage structures are determined by social and institutional forces and that minority groups such as women and racial minorities are fitted into the existing wage structure according to social prejudices. 'Unorthodox' theories also argue that discrimination may take the form of cohesive behaviour amongst employers or in some cases employees.

4.2.2 Gender differentials

Using the sort of decomposition method outlined above, Blinder (1973) attributes 34 per cent of the gender differential in the USA to differences in the various characteristics which directly affect their productivity and 66 per cent to discrimination. Other authors suggest that differences in productivity-related characteristics explain 44 per cent of the gap, with 56 per cent attributable to discrimination (Corcoran and Duncan, 1979). The difference in the sample periods is also consistent with the generally accepted findings of a reducing gender differential (Gunderson, 1989). Evidence for the USA suggests gender discrimination is generally larger than race discrimination for two main reasons: the earnings differential is larger for men and women than by race; less of the observed gender differential can be explained by differences in productivity enhancing characteristics (Berndt, 1991, p. 188). There is some evidence that the size of the discrimination effect is reduced as more comprehensive databases become available (i.e. incorporating a wider range of more accurately measured productivity-enhancing characteristics). On the other hand, such findings change the emphasis of the discussion from why women are not paid the same amount for the same productivity-related characteristics to why they do not tend to possess such characteristics in the first place.

UK evidence based on *NES* data indicates some increase in the relative price of female labour over the period 1970–1982 (Sloane, 1990). Further analysis revealed that this was highly concentrated in the period 1974 to 1976, which spans the date at which the equal opportunities legislation came into force in the UK. On the other hand, while male unemployment increased by 97 per cent over this period, female unemployment rose by 296 per cent. It seems that the move towards equality had normal market effects through relative prices and the balance of supply and demand (Sloane, 1990, p. 169). Such changes may have been exacerbated by segmentation. Despite finding some favourable occupational and skill shifts in favour of women. Sloane concludes that

> the overall impression gained from this disaggregated analysis of the NES data is that there is a high degree of sex segregation which has modified little if at all over the period 1970 to 1982. (Sloane, 1990, p. 132)

The empirical evidence, however, suggests that occupational segmentation is not in itself a major determinant of gender differentials (Sloane, 1990, p. 132). The male and female earnings differentials at that time appear to reflect large differences within given occupations rather than the occupational distribution of male and female employees (see Chiplin and Sloane, 1974 and 1976; Sloane, 1990). One explanation is that a disproportionate number of women work in small firms which, according to the Bolton Committee, paid 20 per cent less in earnings than larger firms. This is in keeping with evidence from the USA, where it was found that sex differentials within establishments for workers on similar tasks were much smaller than between groups of establishments (McNulty, 1967).

Further evidence for the UK is presented by Greenhalgh (1980) using data from the *General Household Survey*. Earnings functions were estimated for men and women, disaggregated by marital status. The earnings of single women were only slightly lower than for single men, and single women appeared to have different age-earnings profiles especially with respect to experience. Their earnings differential narrowed between 1971 and 1975 probably due to the Equal Pay Act. Married women had not experienced such an improvement which, Greenhalgh suggested, is because of the high incidence of part-time work, amongst married women, where the Equal Opportunities legislation is less effective.

She found a much greater disparity between married men and married women and that much of the difference in age–earnings profiles is attributable to marriage. There is considerable support for the effect of marriage on women's pay in the literature (for a review see Sloane, 1985, pp. 130–134). The discussion covers issues of limitations on the geographical job search of partners, the effects of raising children, discontinuity of employment and depreciation of human capital during absence from the labour market. A sample of US women aged 30–44, for example, suggested that on average, married women with children spent 62 per cent of their time out of the labour force after leaving school, compared with only 9 per cent for women who had never married (Mincer and Polachek, 1974). Further US evidence suggests that withdrawal from the labour market reduces wages by about 1.5 to 2.0 per cent for each year that the female is absent (Mincer and Ofek, 1982). Two-thirds of the loss can be attributed to skill attrition and one-third to the loss of cumulative experience. Controls for occupation, skill, experience, etc., to some extent encapsulate the effects of marriage, reducing the gender differential from this effect.

In a study upon the *NES Panel Dataset*, Elias and Gregory conclude

> the gender differential in earnings remained fairly constant over the 1980s, with evidence of a rise in the ratio of women's to men's hourly earnings in the early 1990s. Examination of these trends by occupational category shows that there are certain key areas where women have recently made gains relative to men. These are secretarial occupations, protective service occupations and other sales occupations. Surprisingly, an occupational area in which women have made little or no headway in terms of their earnings relative to men is the category corporate managers and administrators.

The last finding, concerning women managers, is of considerable interest, as this is taken as a key indicator of the success of women in overcoming discrimination. The rather negative result on differentials parallels a reversal in the growth of women in senior management positions in the UK in the early 1990s.

4.2.3 Race differentials

There has been very considerable interest in wage differences between racial groups, particularly in the USA. The theoretical considerations surrounding race differentials are very similar to those for gender. If workers of every race, colour or creed were identical in their objective supply characteristics, any differences in wages would be the result of discrimination in the labour market. A number of authors have explored the changes in the differential over time. Again, there appear to be two principal dimensions to this. First, it is clear in the USA that 'blacks' possess less human capital than 'whites' and part of the earnings difference is a reflection of this difference. Thus, in part, discrimination may take the form of differential access to education and training. Second, earnings differences occur between blacks and whites who possess equal human capital.

Bearing these problems in mind, let us consider the US estimates of the non-white/white ratio of earnings that would exist if non-whites (predominantly blacks) had the same productivity-related characteristics such as education, age, etc., as do whites. Work by Blinder (1973) for the USA in 1967 suggested that income for blacks was about 66 per cent of that of whites. Using the type of decomposition discussed above about 60 per cent of the differential could be attributed to differences in endowments, the remainder was the result of racial discrimination. A number of authors have explored the changes in the differential over time. Earlier evidence had suggested a ratio of 0.71 for 1959 and one of 0.79 for 1969, implying that the effect of discrimination is over 20 per cent, but the effect is declining over time. By the mid-1970s one study suggested that the earnings of young, male, black college graduates were roughly equal to those of comparable whites.

Further support for this is given in Freeman (1981), who argues that only about 3 per cent of the average earnings differential between young black and white workers can be attributed to discrimination compared with 22 to 32 per cent for older males, although part of the latter may reflect the mismeasurement of the quality of schooling for the older group. It is not clear, however, whether this intergenerational difference really reflects the better prospects for young blacks or whether they will have poorer career development leaving them increasingly disadvantaged as they grow older. Indeed, other evidence suggests a slowdown or even reversal of this trend in the USA in the 1980s (Smith and Welch, 1989). For a review of other work, see Berndt (1991, pp. 184–187).

McNabb and Psacharopoulos (1981) used data from the *General Household Survey* to examine the sources of differences in earnings between white and black employees in the UK. They found that the major cause of the difference was in the return to education. They also found that unlike white employees, the industry of employment did not affect the earnings of blacks. The reason may be that the earnings of the black group tend to be more uniform, possibly because they were concentrated into a few industries or firms. This interpretation appears consistent with the dual labour market hypothesis.

4.2.4 Union/non-union differential

General issues In Chapter 24 we discussed the economics of trade unions and had a preliminary look at the effect of unions on wages, deferring a more thorough consideration to this part of the book. The empirical problem of estimating the effect of unions on wages or earnings arises because it is not possible to observe what the earnings of a union worker would be if they were not so represented. Even if we could observe two groups of workers, one unionized and the other non-unionized, who were identical in every other respect, interpreting the difference between their wages as the impact of trade unions could be misleading for two reasons. First there is what is known as the spillover effect. An increase in the union wage may lead to an increase in the non-union wage because of the employer's fear of its labour becoming unionized. This is called the 'threat effect'. The wages of non-union labour may also go up in response to union wages in order to retain workers in a tight labour market. However, there can also be a negative spillover effect: the non-union wage may fall in response to a wage increase in the union sector, if the result of the latter is a reduction in demand for union labour and a consequent increase in the supply of non-union labour which drives down the non-union wage. A second problem of interpretation is that the level of unionization and the level of wages may be simultaneously determined rather than the causal relationship being purely from the former to the latter. Indeed it could be that there is a more general reverse causation with more highly paid labour more likely to join a union.

Dummy variable and related methods of estimation The equation which has often formed the basis of estimates of the union/non-union relative wage effect is derived from the manipulation of an identity,

$$w_{ij} = w_{ij}^n + [\log(1 + m_j)]\,\mathrm{DUM}_{ij} \tag{24}$$

where: w_{ij} is the log of the wage of individual i in industry j; w_{ij}^n is the log of an individual's wage who is not in the union and m is the union/non-union differential in industry j; DUM_{ij} is a zero-one variable which indicates whether the individual is a union member or not. Defining w_{ij}^c as the log of the individual's wage in the absence of all unions, and S_{ij} as $w_{ij} - w_{ij}^c$ (i.e. the spillover effect), we have

$$w_{ij} = w_{ij}^c + [\log(1 + m_j)] + DUM_{ij} + S_{ij} \tag{25}$$

Assuming that the wage level in the absence of all unions is a function of the vector of individual characteristics, X_{ij}, such as age, gender, skill, etc.,

$$w_{ij}^c = f(X_{ij}) \tag{26}$$

and the union/non-union differential depends upon the average level of unionization in industry j, such that

$$\log(1 + m_j) = \alpha_0 + \alpha_1\, TU_j \tag{27}$$

and the spillover effect also depends upon the level of unionization,

$$S_{ij} = \beta_0 + \beta_1 TU_j \tag{28}$$

then by substitution we obtain

$$w_{ij} = f(X_{ij}) + a_1 TU_j + a_2 DUM_{ij} + a_3 DUM_{ij} TU_j \tag{29}$$

Note that the autonomous element of the spillover effect, β_0, can never be identified as this would require observations of the economy both with and without unions. However, equation (29) disaggregates the union mark-up into three components: the differential across industries (a_1); the differentials across individuals (a_2); and the effect of industry coverage on the mark-up itself (a_3). Most of the equations tested empirically have been special cases, obtained by placing restrictions on equation (29).

Separate wage equations for union and non-union sectors The use of dummy variables for union membership is not the only and, perhaps, not even the best method of estimating the union/non-union differential. The simple inclusion of a dummy variable for union membership makes the implicit assumption that the rewards to education and experience are the same in the union and non-union sectors when, in practice, there are strong grounds for expecting them to differ (Berndt, 1991, p. 177). In particular, education may be under-rewarded in the union sector where seniority systems are likely to be more prevalent. In addition, unions are believed to flatten the age–earnings profile (with the peak occurring earlier in unionized establishments). As a consequence, the 'standard' procedure which has evolved in the literature has been to estimate separate equations for the two sectors

$$\ln W^u = X\beta^u + \mu^u \quad (30)$$

$$\ln W^n = X\beta^n + \mu^n \quad (31)$$

from which the average differential can be calculated as $\bar{X}(\hat{\beta}^u - \hat{\beta}^n)$ where $\bar{X}$ is the average value of the various characteristics.

A US study by Bloch and Kuskin (1978) uses two principal approaches: (i) a union/non-union dummy; (ii) the estimation of separate earnings functions for the union and non-union sectors. In the second case, however, they use two methods of calculating the differential, one based on the parameter estimates from the union function

$$\overline{\ln W^u} - \overline{\ln W^n} = \beta^u(\overline{X^u} - \overline{X^n}) \quad (32)$$

and the other using the parameter estimates from the non-union function,

$$\overline{\ln W^u} - \overline{\ln W^n} = \beta^u(\overline{X^u} - \overline{X^n}) \quad (33)$$

where $\overline{X^u}$ and $\overline{X^n}$ denote the mean value of the productivity-enhancing characteristics in the union and non-union sectors respectively. Based on a sample of white males, aged 25–64, from the US *Current Population Survey, 1973*, the simple dummy variable approach suggests a mark-up of 16 per cent, while the two-equation method (using the two alternative coefficient weights) produces estimates of 9 and 16 per cent respectively.

Simultaneity and sample selection In most studies of the union mark-up it is assumed that the positive relationship between unionization and wages represents a causal flow from unionization to wages. We noted earlier, however, that higher wages in the union sector may cause unionization. Most authors argue that a failure to account for this simultaneity implies that OLS estimates of the effects of unions on wages are biased upwards. The underlying reasoning is that employers who are forced to pay the higher, union wage tend to try and attract higher quality workers (i.e. with 'better' unobservable characteristics). The use of simultaneous equations models explaining both wages and union membership is tantamount to addressing the issue of selection (i.e. the non-random selection of individuals into the unionized or non-unionized sectors), particularly where micro (individual) data are used. Thus, a second group of models use Mill's ratio (IMR) or 'Heckman correction' techniques. We report briefly upon both below.

Ashenfelter and Johnson (1972) developed a simultaneous equations model in which unionization is also a dependent variable. Labour quality is also a dependent variable (higher wages for union labour may lead employers to employ higher-quality labour). Ashenfelter and Johnson demonstrated with the use of OLS estimates that the traditional single-equation model leads to an upward bias in the estimated union mark-up. They found a union mark-up of 40 per cent in US manufacturing using such a method, compared with a mark-up in the range 0–20 per cent in a model based upon the simultaneous determination of wages, unionization and labour quality, but never significantly different from zero. If anything, their results suggested that unionization did not have a significant effect on wage rates, but that the wage rate had a significant impact on the extent of unionism.

Lee (1978) used a simultaneous equations model with qualitative and limited dependent variables, accounting explicitly for the selection of employees into unions based upon the US *Survey of Economic Opportunity Sample* of 1967. Separate equations were estimated for union and non-union wages. The results confirm that the parameter estimates are often different for the two sectors. In particular education appears to be more highly rewarded in the non-unionized sector. Lee concludes that this may well reflect the operation of seniority rules in the union sector. The results also show that males are better paid than females and whites better paid than blacks (the latter is less clear cut in the unionized sector, although blacks are less likely to be in the unionized sector). The results for these groups are illustrated in Table 26.3.

Table 26.3 Average union/non-union wage differentials by race and gender

	White	Non-white
Male	16.2	28.5
Female	2.8	12.7

The selection equation explicitly deals with the probability that the individual will be in the union. The approach is a simultaneous equations one, as the union/non-union wage differential appears in the selection equation, and turns out to be the most powerful factor determining unionization status. Thus Lee concludes,

> Unionism does have a significant effect in raising wage rates. On the other hand, union membership is determined mainly by wage gains and the selectiveness of employers' employment policy. Unionised firms tend to select highly productive workers. This finding explains why unionised and non-unionised firms coexist in the same product market. Their unit labour costs do not differ by enough to allow the non-unionised firms to drive the unionised firms out. (Lee, 1978, p. 432)

Further discussion of the empirical evidence A well-known US study by Lewis (1963) used time series data for two groups of industries, one highly unionized and the other largely non-unionized. The results have been converted into percentage union/non-union differentials (Mulvey, 1978), and are reproduced in Table 26.4. It is noticeable that the union impact shows considerable variation over time and might broadly speaking be taken as a reflection of the tightness of the labour market (see Layard and Nickell, 1985). In particular the greatest impact was in the slack labour market of the depression when unions resisted wage cuts. Studies by other economists in the USA of particular groups of workers appear to broadly confirm Lewis' findings of a relative wage effect in the region of 20 per cent in the interwar period and of a considerably lower effect during and after the Second World War. In a review of a large numbers of US studies covering the period 1967 to 1979, Lewis (1986) found a range of mark-ups from around 0.07 to 0.22, with an average of about 0.15.

Table 26.4 The union/non-union differential

Period	Estimated difference
1920–1924	17
1925–1929	26
1930–1934	46
1935–1939	22
1940–1944	6
1945–1949	2
1950–1954	12
1955–1958	16

There are few examples of empirical studies of union mark-ups in the UK until the 1970s. Estimates then proliferated, stimulated in part by the availability of the *NES*. Pencavel (1974) estimated that in 1964 union workers in industries which did not engage in a significant degree of plant bargaining had a zero differential, but that workers in industries in which there was a significant amount of plant-level bargaining achieved a differential of about 14 per cent. These estimates would appear to suggest that UK unions affected relative wages to a significantly lower degree than US unions did. On the other hand, in 1964 the market was tight and this may have reduced the union mark-up. There is also some evidence that the spillover effect may be greater in the UK than the USA – see Mulvey (1978, p. 111). At this time, data from the *NES* suggest that about 31 per cent of workers who were not union members were nevertheless covered by collective agreements and therefore paid the 'union wage' implying a potentially substantial 'spillover effect' which could give rise to severe underestimates of the impact of unions when using unionization data. Layard *et al.* (1991, pp. 196–197) also point to the interaction between the product and labour markets. As the extent of unionization increases in a given industry, the potential for customers to buy products produced by non-unionized firms declines, and the own-price elasticity of demand for the unionized product falls. Thus, we would expect to find the wages in both unionized and non-unionized firms positively related to union density.

There have been several subsequent studies of the union mark-up in the UK (e.g. Treble, 1981; Minford, 1983; Stewart, 1983; Blanchflower, 1984). Blanchflower has provided a summary of UK estimates. These are reported in Table 26.5 along with Blanchflower's own results. In common with Ashenfelter's US results, Blanchflower finds that trade unions had the effect of narrowing skill differentials and that the union mark-up for semi-skilled manuals (operatives) was larger in non-manufacturing than manufacturing. Despite the growing sophistication of the models in this area, the range of estimates is wide, as various reviews of this topic have revealed (Freeman and Medoff, 1981; Lewis, 1986). As Blanchflower (1984) points out, the union mark-up estimates in the UK should therefore be regarded as 'preliminary'.

While there is an enormous proliferation of estimates of the union/non-union mark-up in the UK, there are relatively few estimates of how this mark-up has changed with the passage of time. Layard *et al.* (1977), however, provide some estimates, based upon three digit industries in the UK, and updated values are reported in Layard *et al.* (1991, p. 197). They argue that, while not too much emphasis should be placed upon the absolute level of the mark-ups, they should provide some indication of the movement over time.

Table 26.5 Impact of unions on relative wages in the UK: survey of estimates

Study	Date	Observations	Data set	Dependent variable	Differential
Pencavel[a] (1974)	1964	29 production industries	Various	Average hourly earnings of manual workers	0%–14.5%
Mulvey[b] (1976)	1973	77 MLH manufacturing industries	*New Earnings Survey* 1973 Census of Population 1971	Average hourly earnings of manual workers	26%–35%
Mulvey and Foster[c] (1976)	1973	99 occupational groups	*New Earnings Survey* 1973	Mean gross weekly of full-time adult males (manual and non-manual)	22%–36%
Nickell[d] (1977)	1972	121 MLH manufacturing industries	Various	Full-time male and female manual hourly earnings	18%–26%
McNabb and Demery[e] (1978)	1964	See Pencavel (1974)	Various	Average hourly earnings of manual workers	11.6%–16%
Wabe and Leech[f] (1978)	1973	101 MLH manufacturing industries	Various	Average hourly earnings for adult male manual workers	–6%–21.5%
Layard, Metcalf and Nickell[g] (1978)	1973	4300 individuals	*General Household Survey* 1973 *New Earnings Survey* 1973	Hourly wage rates of male (manual and non-manual) workers	25%
Mulvey and Abowd[h] (1980)	1974	26 two-digit industries	*New Earnings Survey* 1974	Average hourly earnings of male manual workers	3.8%–8.1%
Treble[i] (1981)	1973	See Mulvey (1976)	*New Earnings Survey* 1974	Average hourly earnings of adult male manaul workers	8.3%–10%
Minford[k] (1983)	1964–1979	Aggregate time series data	Various	Real average earnings of industries	74%
Geroski and Stewart[l] (1982)	1973	See Mulvey (1976)	*New Earnings Survey* 1973	Average hourly earnings of adult male manual workers	10.5%–16.2%
Stewart[m] (1983a)	1975	5352 full-time manuals in manufacturing	*National Training Survey* 1973	Weekly earnings of full-time male manual workers	7.7%
Nickell and Andrews[n] (1983)	1951–1979	See Layard, Mecalf and Nickell (1978)	*General Household Survey* 1973 *New Earnings Survey* 1973	Hourly wage rate of male manual workers	7%–32%
Blanchflower (1984)	1980	2040 working establishments	*Workplace Industrial Relations Survey*	Gross weekly earnings of manual and non-manual employees	0%–13.8%

Notes: For the detailed footnotes to this table, see the original article, Blanchflower (1984, pp. 312–313)

Table 26.6 shows a rising mark-up through to the early to mid-1980s. The figures suggest that there may have been some lag between the reduction in union power caused by various Acts introduced by the Conservative Government and the impact of unions on wages (Layard *et al.*, 1991, p. 197). Again, consistent with the US results over the period 1920–1958, the recession of the 1980s may have helped to maintain the mark-up, given the stickiness of union wages. However, alternative explanations

Table 26.6 Changes in the union mark-up over time: the UK

Year(s)	Coefficient on union coverage
1956–1959	0.15
1960–1964	0.17
1965–1969	0.19
1970–1974	0.27
1975–1979	0.27
1980–1984	0.32
1985–1987	0.22

exist. First, the switch to management-driven wage setting relating to effort: as effort rises so do wages (p. 198). Second, there is tentative evidence of a link between the removal of restrictive practices and compensatory pay rises, which would be more important in the unionized than the non-unionized sector. Third, there appears to have been a link between unionized firms and technological change during this period that may have allowed scope for pay rises.

As measures of the union/non-union differential have proliferated, authors have turned their attention to the lessons that can be learnt from international comparisons. This appears an interesting issue. We have already noted, for example, that the UK appeared to have a lower union mark-up than the USA. In addition Chapter 25 reported Freeman's (1994) comparative figures based upon a simple dummy variable approach using the 1987–1989 survey files of the *International Social Survey Programme.*

As Freeman points out, these figures have to be treated with some caution given problems of data comparability and the adoption of a simple, dummy variable technique. However, the results not only confirm the US position relative to the UK, but show the USA to be a 'special case' compared with all other countries in the sample. Freeman concludes,

> American exceptionalism in union/non-union differences is found not so much in outcomes influenced by the 'voice' side of the institution but rather on the 'monopoly wage' side. Union wage effects are larger in the United States than elsewhere because of the decentralised wage setting system. This in turn seems to underlie the large positive productivity effect, and the substantial adverse profits effect in the United States. (Freeman, 1994).

5 Distribution of earnings

Another way of analysing the structure of earnings is to rank individuals by the magnitude of their earnings and examine the resulting distribution. We have already touched on this topic indirectly as the earnings functions described above make explicit assumptions about the underlying frequency distribution in choosing a particular empirical specification (such as the semi-log form). However, the distribution is also of special interest to policy makers for both social and economic reasons. They need to know the causes of the observed distribution and the factors that make it change, such as the impact of progressive income taxes and transfer payments. They are often interested in the tails of the distribution, particularly at the lower end, where individuals lie close to or below subsistence levels. We return to this below. The distribution of personal incomes is of course dependent on property incomes as well as labour earnings. As we noted in Part II of the book, the participation decision is influenced by non-labour income (including benefits). Our principal interest here, however, is on earned income. In the first instance we focus on the distribution of earnings in a particular year and, then, we briefly turn to one or two dynamic issues.

5.1 Static distribution

A very detailed study of earnings distribution was undertaken by Lydall (1979), who analysed the 'standard distribution'. This distribution excludes part timers, workers susceptible to unemployment, juveniles and farm workers. The basic shape of the distribution, which is found to be a distribution fairly common across countries, is positively skewed (i.e. the average earnings, W^a, exceed the modal, W^m) and leptokurtic (i.e. hump shaped) *vis-à-vis* a normal distribution (which is, by definition, symmetric). The distinction between the skewed income distribution and the normal distribution is illustrated in Figure 26.1.

The implication is demonstrated using Figure 26.2, which represents a 'Parade of Dwarfs (and a few Giants)', suggested by Pen (1971, p. 59). The idea is that the individual's height is made proportionate to the absolute value of their income. Individuals are then ranked according to their height (income) as they march past, with the lowest income first and the highest income last. The whole parade takes one hour. As the figure relates to all personal income (rather than just earned income), it is possible to observe some negative values as, for example, some self-employed go bankrupt. Putting this possibility to one side, in the first few minutes we see a number of

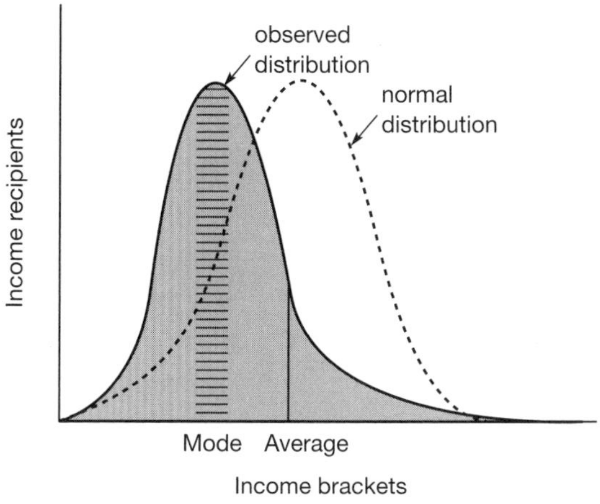

Fig 26.1 The frequency distribution.

very small people. From then on the height of individuals gradually increases, but all these who march past are smaller than the average height of all individuals. Then there is a sudden spurt in height, but it is almost 50 minutes into the parade before the observed height reaches the overall average. After this, height accelerates and in the last 10 minutes of the parade we observe very tall people and, eventually, giants.

Figure 26.3 illustrates the link between incomes and the distribution. The distribution of the top 20 per cent of incomes closely approximates Pareto's 'Law', which states that $N = AY^{-\alpha}$ where A and α are constants and N is the number of incomes above a given income Y. However, the 'Law' was found to be

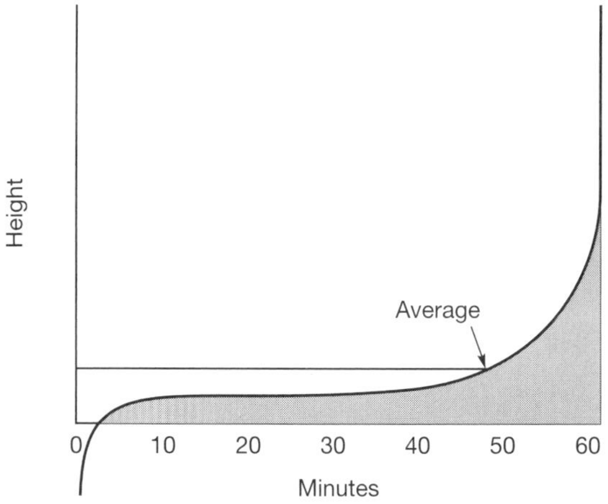

Fig 26.2 A parade.

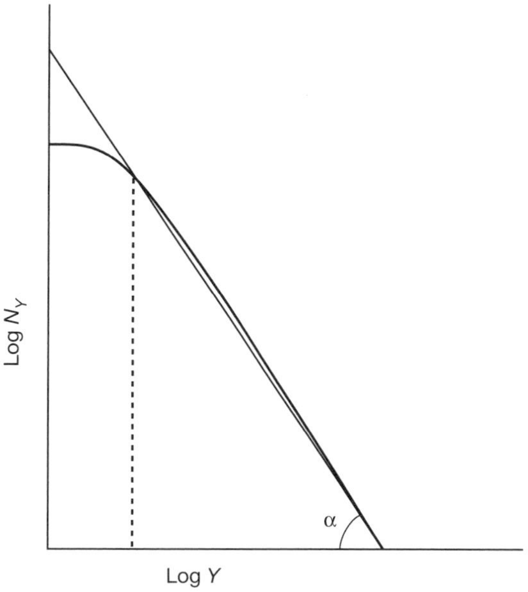

Fig 26.3 Pareto line.

a rather poor description of income distribution amongst the lower-income groups and has undergone substantial revision by Gini and Wilks (Pen, 1971). While the precise form of the distribution is important in ensuring the correct specification of empirical models, students of income distribution often make do with more 'ball-park' figures. A traditional way of describing inequality in incomes is based upon the Lorenz Curvê, as shown in Figure 26.4.

Individuals are ranked according to their absolute incomes and, then, the cumulative percentage of income is plotted against the cumulative percentage of income recipients. The leading diagonal represents complete equality (a 1 per cent increase in recipients is associated with a 1 per cent increase in total income). However, in the real world, given that inequality exists, at the lowest income levels (i.e. close to point *a*), a 1 per cent increase in the number of recipients is associated with a less than 1 per cent rise in total income. Thus the Lorenz Curve is bowed downwards towards point *d*. To the right of point *d* (point *d* is where the slope of the Lorenz Curve is 45°), further additions to the percentage of recipients result in disproporately higher increases in the percentage of income. The Lorenz Curve bends upwards until it meets the 45° line at point *c* (i.e. 100 per cent of recipients account for 100 per cent of total income). The Lorenz Curve is summarized in a simple ratio, the shaded area (*acd*), divided by the

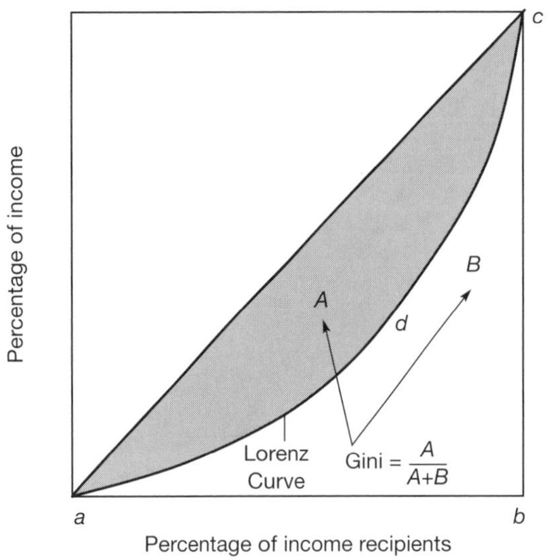

Fig 26.4 Lorenz Curve and Gini coefficient.

area corresponding to complete equality (*abc*); in other words, the Gini coefficient is *acd*/*abc*.

The apparent paradox which many analysts have attempted to confront is that if earnings depend upon productivity as neoclassical labour economics would suggest, when psychological testing suggests a normal distribution of abilities, why is the distribution of earnings skewed and more closely approximated by a lognormal distribution? The explanations that have been offered depend to varying degrees upon an economic analysis of labour markets. Mincer has developed a human capital explanation of the skewed distribution which dates back to Mincer (1979). Put simply, a man's earnings in period *j*, Y_j, are,

$$Y_j = y_j + \sum_{t=0}^{j-1} r_t k_t - W_{ej} \tag{34}$$

where: y_j are the earnings of 'raw uneducated ability'; k_t is the level of investment in education in each period; r_t is the rate of return to that investment; and W_e the earnings forgone in the current period due to education. If r and k are uncorrelated but normally distributed a skewed earnings distribution emerges since they combine multiplicatively. If more able people achieve a higher rate of return to education, investment in more education, where r and k are correlated, further increases the skewness of the earnings distribution.

Lydall's explanation of the distribution is similar but more broadly based. He argues that 'general educated ability' is a mixture of genetic ability, energy or motivation and environmental factors including education – see Lydall (1979). If these elements are normally distributed and independent, but combine multiplicatively, then 'general educated ability' and thus earnings will be positively skewed. Furthermore one of the elements (i.e. education) is itself positively skewed. As far as the Pareto tail is concerned, Lydall uses an institutional explanation based on the hierarchical structure of earnings in the upper echelons of hierarchical institutions.

Tinbergen has explained the skewed distribution statistically in terms of the 'mismatch' between the distribution of job requirements and the distribution of skills and other relevant characteristics of the working population (Tinbergen, 1956). This explanation has the virtue of recognizing the significance of the demand side of the labour market as well as the supply side.

Finally, we note that the paradox of a skewed distribution of income with a normal distribution of abilities might be more apparent than real. It has been pointed out that the nature of the distribution of abilities depends how you test and measure these abilities. It has been argued that

> It is worth noting here that there is very little evidence suggesting that specific forms of ability are normally distributed; with intelligence tests, for example, it is the IQ test scores that are normally distributed by construction and not necessarily the underlying intelligence. (Berndt, 1991, p. 161)

5.2 Changes in the distribution of income

The interwar and early post-war periods appear to have been characterized by declining inequality in the UK and USA. The subsequent post-war trend in inequality for the USA was somewhat less clear, as was the evidence for the UK, at least until the early to mid-1970s (Lydall, 1979, pp. 132–134). The evidence of the more recent period, at least from the mid- to late 1970s (and perhaps even before that), however, is quite different. Murphy and Welch (1993) describe changes in the distribution of income in the USA using the *Current Population Survey* (CPS) (similar evidence emerges from Topel, 1993). They demonstrate for example that for employed men aged 25–54, wage dispersion increased over the period 1963 to 1990, and the rate of growth in dispersion was approximately constant. They show that, from 1963 to 1990, the logarithmic spread between the median and the 75th centile increased by 0.117

(roughly an increase of one-third on its 1963 level) and the corresponding logarithmic spread between the median and the 90th centile grew by 0.168 (about an increase of one-half over its 1963 level).

The authors go on to discuss changes in some of the key relativities in the US economy, using ratios based on 'trimmed geometric means' (i.e. those calculated after excluding information about the upper and lower quartiles of the distributions) (Murphy and Welch, 1993, p. 105). They demonstrate the decreased 'college premium' to newly qualified graduates up to the late 1970s, followed by a sharp rise from 1978 to 1985 and then a reversal in the mid-1980s. As in the UK reversal of rates of return to education, it appears that the downward US pattern of the 1970s was the result of unprecedented numbers of graduates flowing onto the market during that period. No corresponding reversal is seen in the 'all college graduate' figures in the late 1980s (i.e. all ages), reflecting the difficulties faced by college graduates just beginning their careers. The relative earnings of more/less experienced individuals (based on years in the labour market) were higher in 1990 than 1963 for both the college and high school graduate groups, although the pattern over time first showed an increase before falling back somewhat. They argue that these results are both consistent with increased wage dispersion, as wages increased the most amongst higher-wage earners. Nevertheless, evidence of increased equality was found for some relatively disadvantaged groups. Women gained relative to men, with most of the gains concentrated in the 1980s. The mean wage of blacks increased relative to whites, although, in this instance, most of the gains were concentrated in the period prior to 1975.

The papers by Murphy and Welch (1993) and Topel (1993) point to the enormous growth in the inequality of income in the USA with reductions in real income amongst the poorest groups. The same is true for the UK. Figure 26.5 shows a monotonic relationship between the rate of change of real net income (before housing costs) over the period 1979 to 1991, and income at the start of the period (Hutton, 1994). Indeed, according to these figures, the top 5 per cent of income earners in 1979 experienced a rise of over 50 per cent in their income, while the poorest group actually experienced a reduction in real income. It appears that this is close to being a social and economic disaster for individuals at the lower end of the spectrum.

While these factors throw light on the individual distribution of income in the USA, there is also the question of the household distribution (Murphy and Welch, 1993, p. 108). On balance, although marriage rates have dropped, married men tend to earn more than unmarried men. Wage rates for married men

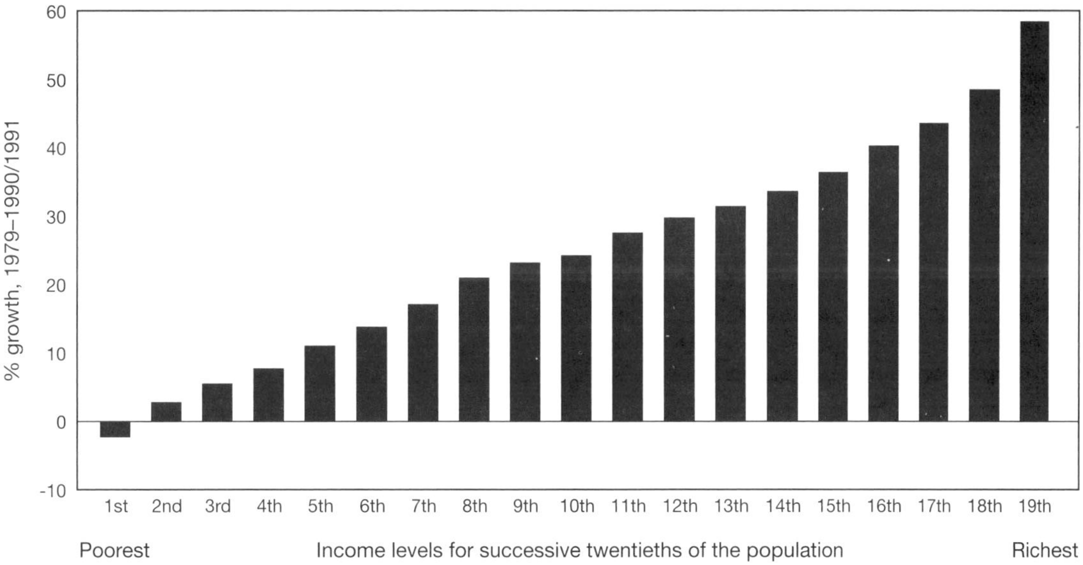

Note: Income is real net income before housing costs

Fig 26.5 Between 1979 and 1991 income growth was greater for better-off income groups.

have been compressed towards the mean (the percentage of married men in the lowest quartile fell from 81 to 53 per cent, while in the top quartile it fell from 94 to 83 per cent). The US results, however, show that the education levels of husbands and wives are positively correlated. It also shows that the negative correlation between female participation and male earnings to be found at the beginning of the period had disappeared by the end of the period. Finally, the authors note that

> In 1963, the working wives of men in the top quarter of the wage distribution earned about 93 per cent as much annually as the wives of men whose wages placed them in the lowest quarter of the distribution. By 1990, the wives of top quartile men averaged 30 per cent more than the wives of men in the first quartile of the distribution. (Murphy and Welch, 1993, p. 108)

The evidence therefore points in the direction of an increasing dispersion of household incomes, as well as increasing inequality of individual income.

5.3 Income mobility and lifetime earnings inequality

The previous sections have largely considered the distribution of income as a static or comparative static phenomenon, focusing on earnings in a particular year or changes in the distribution from year to year. It is easy to demonstrate that the distribution in any one year is important. If your income falls below subsistence level, then, without any other means of support, you will die! On the other hand, such measures can also be misleading insofar as individuals are mobile across the income distribution over their lifetime (Creedy, 1992), consistent with dynamic labour supply theories.

A 'snap-shot' at any one point in time obscures the fact that individuals within the distribution experience quite different trajectories. Indeed, it may be misleading to look at the distribution of income in the sense described above, as the same individuals may not appear in, say, the bottom 5 per cent in each period. What is important, therefore, is to trace the trajectories of different groups over time. It is a world in which individuals who meet certain skill requirements are able to reach the level of the board where the ladders begin and then can experience upward career mobility. However, redundancy causes downward mobility. When redundancy occurs individuals 'lose a lot' (Topel, 1993), particularly those higher up

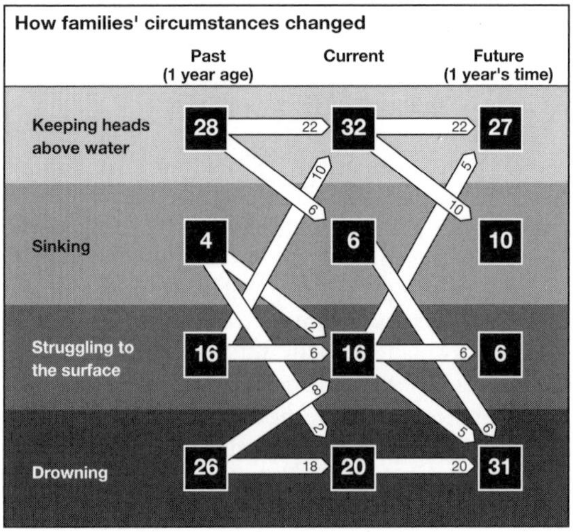

Fig 26.6 How families' circumstances changed.

the distribution, especially where they have experienced long tenure in the job which they lose (i.e. insofar as their human capital becomes irrelevant). Although they bump down, however, in general, they don't fall all the way down the distribution. The key to the distribution is that individuals higher up the spectrum have a much lower probability of being made redundant than those at the bottom. In addition, the duration of unemployment (joblessness) increases at the lower end, which has its own implications for skill attrition and reemployability.

Figure 26.6, reported in Dibben (1994, p. 14), shows the results for 74 low-income families living in inner city areas in London, the West Midlands and Manchester (Kempson, 1994). Sample numbers here are small and the period under consideration is extremely short. From the viewpoint of the present chapter, the important result is simply that there is considerable mobility between groups in both directions (although the principal flows are horizontal, i.e. intra-group). There is an interesting analogy with the game of snakes and ladders, insofar as the way in which the game plays out depends on the number, length, slopes and positions of the snakes and ladders. However, the analogy is not perfect, as some sectors of the board appear to be out of bounds to some players, the properties of the dice appear to change as you move up the board and the design of the board and the properties of the dice appear to change over time.

It is important not to lose sight of the fact that even short-term poverty can be catastrophic for the individual concerned, but persistent poverty is likely to be worse. The evidence of Kempson (1994) is that families develop 'coping strategies' that to some extent allow them to ride out short-term problems. In the longer term, however, these strategies run out and, unless the family can move on to an upward income trajectory, they are no longer able to cope. The persistence of poverty and the magnitude of the associated 'poverty escape rate' are therefore crucial.

Kempson's own data suggest that some proportion of families who were classified as drowning one year previously, nevertheless manage to move on to an upward trajectory. Further data on this is provided in Table 26.7 (Duncan, 1994). Poverty is defined as an income of less than half of the national median level. Persistent poverty involves the family being in this state for three years in a row. The poverty escape rate is defined as the proportion of families that move from just below the poverty line to at least 10 percentage points above it.

The first column of Table 26.7 shows a 'static' picture based on family income in a single year. The results show remarkable differences in poverty rates across countries, with the USA at the top end of the spectrum, with 20 per cent of families falling into this category; Finland and Sweden were at the other end, with only 3 per cent categorized as in poverty. The situation for blacks in the USA is even worse, with 49 per cent in this group.

In practice, however, there is a considerable degree of mobility, at least for most groups within the population. A significant proportion of families in poverty in one year were found to jump up the distribution in the next year. In the USA, for example, 22 per cent of families below the poverty line in one year moved to a point over 10 percentage points above the poverty line in the next year. The corresponding rates for other countries were even higher with Finland recording 47 per cent of families making such a move. Thus, the percentage of families in poverty for at least three years in a row was 14 per cent in the USA, 12 per cent in Canada and around 1 to 2 per cent for all the other countries in the sample. Given that benefits are relatively high for European countries, the author concludes,

> The belief that generous social assistance programmes are a key impediment to economic mobility is not supported by these data. (Duncan, 1994, p. 6)

What is also clear, however, is that the USA and Canada appear to have a persistent poverty problem.

Nevertheless, the point is made that the measures of inequality based upon a single year may give quite different results to those based upon lifeline earnings. Creedy (1992, p. 78), for example, shows that the coefficient of variation of income for the longer-term (T-period) measure, $\eta_{(T)}$, is less than the weighted average of the annual measures η^*. Hence, in a two-period model, for example, $\eta_{(2)}$, the longer-term measure, cannot exceed the highest value of η_1 or η_2, the corresponding annual measures. On the other hand, in principle it can take a value lower, than **any** of the annual measures, although, in practice, empirical evidence suggests it generally falls somewhere between the lowest and highest single-year measures.

For one thing, we know that the age–earnings profile is essentially parabolic in shape and that young people start on low incomes but may borrow against future income, and as income falls away for the older group they may consume out of past savings. The importance of the life-cycle to measures of inequality have been recognized for around a century, since the

Table 26.7 Poverty and poverty escape rates (%)

Country	Single-year poverty rate	Persistent poverty rate	Poverty escape rate
Finland	3	n/a	47
Sweden	3	n/a	45
France	4	2	32
Luxembourg	4	1	29
West Germany	8	2	24
Canada	17	12	23
Netherlands	3	1	23
Ireland	11	n/a	23
USA	20	14	22
USA blacks	49	42	15

pioneering work of Seebohm Rowntree in York in 1899. Rowntree identified 'five alternating periods of want and comparative plenty' in a labourer's life: childhood; early adulthood; having children; working life after children grow up; and old age.

The approach adopted by O'Higgins (1988), therefore, is to disaggregate cross-sectional data from the UK *Family Expenditure Survey* by different types of family unit and to compare relative incomes over time. Ten different types of family unit were distinguished (e.g. one adult aged under 35; married couple with between one and six children all aged under 5, etc.) and comparisons were made with a base group (married couple, with no children, where the female is aged under 35). Observed income is translated into a more consumption or welfare-orientated measure by means of equivalence scales. The equivalence scales are used to account for the fact that, on average, the size of the income unit increases with the income of the unit. Thus, the highest income units may not experience the greatest welfare, an adjustment must be made for the number of adults, number of children and other dependants. The equivalence scales used in this study were: one adult (0.61); two adults (1.0); each subsequent adult (0.61); children aged 0–4 years (0.25); children aged 5–15 (0.40) (O'Higgins, 1988, p. 63). Of course, it is easy to see that these scales will change over time as the relative prices of different commodities change or as the burden of payment for various items shifts between the family and the state.

Comparing across different types of family unit, O'Higgins (1988, p. 67) found striking differences in equivalent income. In particular he noted the 'relatively low levels of economic welfare available to families with children', which were often little more than half the value of that available to younger married couples without children. Some categories of families with children experienced worse living standards than retired households. Comparing data for 1971, 1976 and 1982, the author concludes that there had been downward shifts in the relative position of family units at each stage of the child-rearing cycle. By the late 1970s, 'families with children replaced retired households as the largest occupier of the bottom quintile of economic welfare'.

While this disaggregation throws considerable light on the dynamics of income inequality, it suggests that some measures of lifetime earnings or well-being may be more appropriate than others. A wide range of measures have been reported in the literature, including the present value of lifetime earnings and *ex ante* permanent income. In practice, inequality might be better measured in terms of consumption or, more accurately, potential consumption. Thus, for a given individual or household, based upon some assumptions about their length of life and the interest rate, it is possible to calculate 'an income annuity' which corresponds to some given lifetime wealth constraint. This annuity can be interpreted as the highest, constant value of consumption that can be carried out in each year of the individual's or household's lifetime (Nordhaus, 1973). It is possible to show that the constant annual consumption is a complex function of the time preference rate, the intertemporal elasticity of substitution, the rate of interest and lifetime income.

6 Conclusions

This chapter has attempted to provide a flavour of the empirical work which has focused on wages and earnings. It has demonstrated the way in which the investigations of the effects of various influences, such as race, gender, unions, training, etc., have evolved from the early work on the human capital model. The chapter has organized these diverse influences according to whether they can be viewed as part of the 'competitive model' paradigm or, alternatively, as essentially 'non-competitive' in nature. Many of the resulting models make some implicit assumption about the underlying distribution of income. The chapter therefore ended with a brief review of the work in this area.

References

Ashenfelter, O. (1972). 'Racial Discrimination and Trade Unions'. *Journal of Political Economy*, 80, 435–464.

Ashenfelter, O. (1973). 'Discrimination and Trade Unions'. In O. Ashenfelter and A. Rees (eds) *Discrimination in Labour Markets*. Princeton, NJ: Princeton University Press, pp. 88–112.

Ashenfelter, O. (1978). 'Union Relative Wage Effects: New Evidence and a Survey of their Implications for Wage Inflation'. In R. Stone and W. Peterson (eds) *Econometric Contributions to Public Policy*. London. Macmillan.

Ashenfelter, O. and G.E. Johnson (1972). 'Unionism, Relative Wages and Labour Quality in US Manufacturing Industries'. *International Economic Review*, 13, 3, October, 488–508.

Berndt, E.R. (1991). *The Practice of Econometrics: Classical and Contemporary*. Reading, MA: Addison-Wesley.

Blackaby, D., K. Clark and D. Leslie (1994). 'Dual Labour Markets and the Potential Earnings of the Unemployed'. Discussion Paper. Manchester University. (Forthcoming in *Scottish Journal of Political Economy.*)

Blanchflower, D. (1984). 'Union Relative Wage Effects: A Cross-Section Analysis Using Establishment Data'. *British Journal of Industrial Relations*, XXII, 3, 311–332.

Blinder, A.S. (1973). 'Wage Discrimination: Reduced Form and Structural Estimates'. *Journal of Human Resources*, 18, 4, Fall, 436–455.

Bloch, F.E. and M.S. Kuskin (1978). 'Wage Determination in the Union and Non–Union Sectors'. *Industrial and Labour Relations Review*, 31, 2, January, 183–192.

Chiplin, B. and P.J. Sloane (1974). 'Sexual Discrimination in the Labour Market'. *British Journal of Industrial Relations*, 2, 371–402.

Chiplin, B. and P.J. Sloane (1976). 'Male–Female Earnings Differences: A Further Analysis'. *British Journal of Industrial Relations*, 14, 77–81.

Corcoran, M. and G.J. Duncan (1979). 'Work History, Labour Force Attachment and Earnings: Differences Between the Races and Sexes'. *Journal of Human Resources*, 14, 1, Winter, 3–20.

Creedy, J. (1992). *Income Inequality and the Life Cycle*. Aldershot: Edward Elgar.

Dibben, M. (1994). 'Struggling to Stay Afloat'. *Search*, March 20th, 13–15.

Duncan, G.J. (1994). 'Welfare Can Fuel Upward Mobility'. *ISR Profiles Newsletter*, 18, 2, May, 6.

Edwards, R.C. (1979). *Contested Terrain*. New York: Basic Books.

Elias, P. and M. Gregory (1994). *The Changing Structure of Occupations and Earnings in Great Britain 1975–1990.* Research Series No. 27. May. London: Employment Department.

Freeman, R.B. (1981). 'Black Economic Progress After 1964. Who has Gained and Why?'. In S. Rosen (ed.) *Studies in Labour Economics*. Chicago: Chicago University Press, pp. 247–294.

Freeman, R. (1994). 'American Exceptionalism in the Labour Market: Union/Non–union Differentials in the United States and Other Countries'. In C. Kerr and P. Standohar (eds) *Labor Economics and Industrial Relations Markets and Institutions*. Cambridge, MA: Harvard Univeristy Press.

Freeman, R. and J. Medoff (1981). 'The Impact of Collective Bargaining: Illusion or Reality' In J. Steiber., R. McKersie and D. Mills (eds) *US Industrial Relations 1950–1980: a Critical Assessment*, Wisconsin: IRRA.

Geroski, P. and M. Stewart (1982). 'Trade Union Differentials in the UK: A Strange and Sad Story'. Mimeo, October.

Greenhalgh, C. (1980). 'Male–Female Wage Differentials in Great Britain: is Marriage an Equal Opportunity?'. *Economic Journal*, 90, 360, 651–675.

Gunderson, M. (1989). 'Male–Female Wage Differentials and Policy Responses'. *Journal of Economic Literature*, 27, 1, March, 46–72.

Hart, R.J. and D.I. MacKay (1975). 'Engineering Earnings in Britain 1914–68'. *Journal of the Royal Statistical Society Series A*, 138, 1, 322–350.

Heckman, J.J. and G. Sedlacek (1985). 'Heterogeneity, Aggregation, and Market Wage Functions: An Empirical Model of Self–Selection in the Labour Market'. *Journal of Political Economy*, 93, 6, 1077–1125.

Hutton, W. (1994). 'A Question of Relativity'. *Search*. March 20th, 20–23.

Kempson, E. (1994). *Hard Times? How Poor Families Make Ends Meet*. London: Policy Studies Institute.

Layard, R. and S. Nickell (1985). 'The Causes of British Unemployment'. *National Institute Economic Review*, February, 62–85.

Layard, R., D. Metcalf and S. Nickell (1977). 'The Effect of Collective Bargaining on Relative and Absolute Wages'. *British Journal of Industrial Relations*, 16, 287–302.

Layard, R., S. Nickell and R. Jackman (1991). *Unemployment: Macroeconomic Performance and the Labour Market*. Oxford: Oxford University Press.

Lee, L.F. (1978). 'Unionism and Wage Rates: A Simultaneous Equations Model With Qualitative and Limited Dependent Variables'. *International Economic Review*, 19, 2, June, 415–433.

Lewis, G. (1963). *Unions and Relative Wages in the United States*. Chicago: Chicago University Press.

Lewis, G. (1986). *Union Relative Wage Effects: a Survey*. Chicago: Chicago University Press.

Lydall, H. (1979). *A Theory of Income Distribution*. Oxford: Clarendon Press.

McConnell, C.R. and S. L. Brue (1986). *Contemporary Labour Economics*. New York: McGraw-Hill.

McNabb, R. (1987). 'Testing for Labour Market Segmentation in Britain'. *Manchester School*, Vol, 55, 3, September, 257–273.

McNabb, R. and D. Demery (1978). 'Effects of Demand on Union Relative Wage Effects in the UK'. *British Journal of Industrial Relations*, 16, 303–308.

McNabb, R. and G. Psacharopoulos (1981). 'Further Evidence on the Relevance of the Dual Labour Market Hypothesis for the UK'. *Journal of Human Resources*, 16, 3, 442–448.

Mincer, J. (1979). 'Human Capital and Earnings'. In D. Windham (ed.) *Economic Dimensions of Education*. Reprinted in A.B. Atkinson (ed.) (1980). *Wealth, Income and Inequality*. Oxford: Oxford University Press, pp. 103–128.

Mincer, J. and H. Ofek (1982). 'Interrupted Work Careers: Depreciation and Restoration of Human Capital'. *Journal of Human Resources*, 27, 1, Winter, 3–24.

Mincer, J. and S. Polacheck (1974). 'Family Investment in Human Capital: Earnings of Women'. *Journal of Political Economy*, 82, 2, Part 2, March, S76–S108.

Minford, P. (1983). 'Labour Market Equilibrium in an Open Economy'. *Oxford Economic Papers*, 35, Supplement, 207–244.

Mulvey, C. (1976). 'Collective Agreement and Relative Earnings in UK Manufacturing in 1973'. *Economica*, 43, 419–427.

Mulvey, C. (1978). *The Economic Analysis of Trade Unions*. Oxford: Martin Robertson.

Mulvey, C. and J. Abowd (1980). 'Estimating Union/Non–Union Wage Differentials: A Statistical Issue'. *Economica*, 47, 1, 73–79.

Mulvey, C. and J. Foster (1976). 'Occupational Earnings in the UK and the Effects of Collective Agreements'. *Manchester School*, 44, 258–275.

Murphy, K.M. and F. Welch (1993). 'Inequality and Relative Wages'. *American Economic Association. Papers and Proceedings*, 83, 2, 104–109.

Nickell, S. (1977). 'Trade Unions and the Position of Women in the Industrial Wage Structure'. *British Journal of Industrial Relations*, 15, 2, 192–210.

Nickell, S. and M. Andrews (1983). 'Unions, Real Wages and Employment in Britain, 1951–1979'. *Oxford Economic Papers*, 35, 1, 183–206.

Nordhaus, W. (1973). 'The Effects of Inflation on the Distribution of Economic Welfare'. *Journal of Money, Credit and Banking*, 5, 465–508.

Oaxaca, R. (1973). 'Male–Female Wage Differentials in Urban Labour Markets'. *International Economic Review*, 14, 3, October, 693–709.

O'Higgins, M. (1988). 'Inequality, Social Policy and Income Distribution in the United Kingdom'. In J.P. Jallade (ed.) *The Crisis of Redistribution in European Welfare States*. Stoke-on-Trent: Trentham Books.

Pen, Y. (1971). *Income Distribution*. Harmondsworth: Penguin.

Pencavel, J. (1974). 'Relative Wages and Trade Unions in the United Kingdom'. *Economica*, 41, 194–210.

Phelps Brown, H. (1977). *The Inequality of Pay*. Oxford: Oxford University Press.

Phelps Brown, H. and P. Hopkins (1955). 'Seven Centuries of Building Wages'. *Economica*, New Series, 22, 87. 195–206.

Reder, M.W. (1955). 'The Theory of Occupational Wage Differentials'. *American Economic Review*, 45, 5, December, 833–885.

Routh, G. (1965). *Occupation and Pay in Great Britain, 1906–60*. London: Cambridge. University Press.

Sloane, P.J. (1985). 'Discrimination in the Labour Market'. In D. Carline, C.A. Pissarides, W.S. Siebert and P.J. Sloane (eds) *Labour Economics: Surveys in Economics*. New York: Longman.

Sloane, P.J. (1990). 'Sex Differentials: Structure, Stability and Change'. In M.G. Gregory and A.W. J. Thomson (eds) *A Portrait of Pay, 1970–1982*. Oxford: Clarendon Press, pp. 125–171.

Smith, A. (1776). *An Inquiry into the Nature and Causes of the Wealth of Nations*. New York: Modern Library, Random House. (Reprinted in 1932.)

Smith, J.P. and F.R. Welch (1989). 'Black Economic Progress After Myrdal'. *Journal of Economic Literature*, 27, 2, June, 519–564.

Stewart, M.B. (1983). 'Relative Earnings and Individual Union Membership in the United Kingdom'. *Economica*, New Series, 50, 111–125.

Tinbergen, J. (1956). 'On the Theory of Income Distribution'. *Weltwirtschaftliches Archiv*. [See *Income Distribution*. Amsterdam: North-Holland, 1975.]

Topel, R. (1993). 'What Have We Learnt from Empirical Studies of Unemployment and Turnover?'. *American Economics Association. Papers and Proceedings*, 83, 2, 110–115.

Treble, J.G. (1981). 'A Critique of the Lewis Method for Estimating the Union/Non–union Wage Differential'. University of Hull Research Paper. No. 78. Hull.

Turner, H.A. (1952). 'Trade Unions, Differentials and the Levelling of Wages'. *Manchester School*, 2, 3, 277–282.

Wabe, S. and D. Leech (1978). 'Relative Earnings in UK Manufacturing: A Reconsideration of the Evidence'. *Economic Journal*, 88, 296–313.

Welch, F. (1969). 'Linear Synthesis of Skill Distribution'. *Journal of Human Resources*, 4, 311–327.

PART VIII

Labour Markets and Economic Performance

CHAPTER 27 Introduction to labour market outcomes

1 Introduction

The final part of this book deals with a number of economic outcomes that are directly linked to the manner in which labour markets operate. Many of these issues have a long pedigree in the macroeconomics literature. They include key measures of economic performance, such as the growth of employment, unemployment and the rate of inflation, which often form the centrepiece of political debate. Other outcomes, however, have only begun to emerge with any clarity in more recent years. A particular example is the role of education and training in the creation and maintenance of a skilled and highly qualified labour force that both encourages and ensures successful innovation and sustained economic growth. Taken overall, this is a potentially massive area which we can only begin to touch upon. However, it is natural to round off a labour economics book of this type with some overview about the way in which labour market outcomes impact on the current and longer-term economic performance of the economy. This chapter therefore lays the foundations for the discussion which takes place in Chapters 28 to 30.

Given that unemployment, in particular, is used as a key indicator of the health of the economy, the present chapter provides a taxonomy of labour force states. In other words, we demonstrate that the population can be broken down into its component parts, distinguished by the nature and degrees of attachment to the labour market. In doing so, we provide a definition of unemployment and note the alternative ways in which it can be measured. Section 3 then goes on to discuss empirical evidence of participation, employment and unemployment. It provides both time series information and a comparison across European and OECD countries. Chapter 28 extends the analysis, presenting a number of empirical models that throw some light on the determinants of the incidence and duration of unemployment.

The principal way in which labour market outcomes impact on the economy is via the rate of change of costs and prices. Inflation is another macroeconomic indicator, with significant implications for consumers and producers. The government again uses it as a key touchstone of the performance of the economy. The present chapter picks up on at least two earlier themes. First that wage costs, which are an important component in the price equation, are influenced by productivity. Improvements in labour productivity, for example, intervene to mitigate the impact of wage rises on product prices. Second, that, at any given productivity level, wage increases are inherently inflationary, with potentially important implications for product demand, the balance of payments, output and employment. Again, the present chapter primarily presents some empirical evidence about comparative performance over time and across countries. Chapter 29, however, provides a more analytical treatment exploring and linking together some of the underlying models which appear in the literature. Finally, Chapter 30 brings together some of the main issues addressed in this final part of the book, in a policy context.

2 Labour force status

2.1 Taxonomy of labour force status

Figure 27.1 shows the way in which the population of working age can be divided into those in and those not in the labour force. In turn, the labour force is

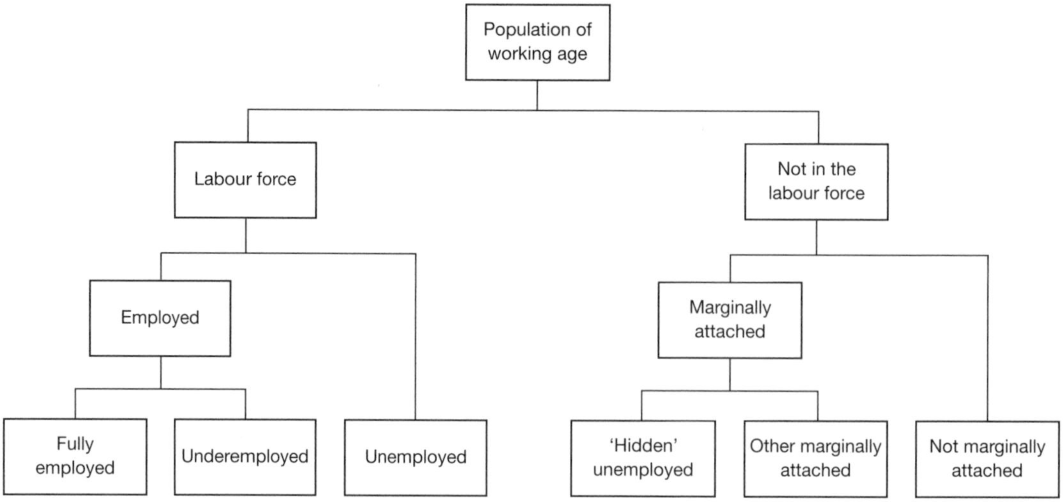

Fig 27.1 Population of working age: economic activity.
Source: ABS Employment, Underemployment and Unemployment 1966–1983. Cat. No. 6246.0

comprised of the employed (including the self-employed), who may or may not be fully utilized (i.e. some may be on short time), and the unemployed. Being unemployed is usually regarded as being willing and able to work, but, although looking, unable to find work – the so-called 'search' definition of unemployment. Most countries use this definition of unemployment. The unemployed are therefore those who are not in work, who are seeking a job, are capable of work and are available to work. Individuals who are not in the labour force are further separated into the marginally attached and the not marginally attached. Marginal attachment is associated with the idea of tenuous and intermittent links with the labour force, and can be illustrated using the sub-set comprised of discouraged workers. These are individuals who are not allocated to the labour force because they are not in employment and are not actively seeking work because they feel that there are no (suitable) jobs available. In effect, this group of individuals perceive that the net returns to search are non-positive. However, they are marginally attached because they would be willing to accept work and are available to start within some defined period (i.e. a month).

Figure 27.2 provides a more detailed breakdown of those who are 'not in employment', and further illustrates the concept of marginality. Only the individuals who follow the single route to the box in the left hand corner of the diagram are part of the labour force (i.e. the unemployed). Those who are looking for work, but are not available to start within some set period, form part of the marginally attached and are excluded from the labour force. The period over which they are not available is quite important because it is set at different levels by different countries and can influence the proportions allocated to the unemployed and marginally attached. All those who are not in employment and not actively looking for work, even though they would like work (as in the case of discouraged workers), are also automatically excluded from the labour force.

2.2 Defining and measuring unemployment

Although at first sight our definition may appear quite straightforward, unemployment continues to pose considerable conceptual and measurement problems. The main problem stems from the fact that the unemployed may also be in receipt of benefits. In the UK, the number of individuals registering as unemployed or, more recently, receiving unemployment benefit has been used as a key economic indicator, even though, historically at least, it has not corresponded closely with the search-based definition outlined above. More recent changes in the claimancy rules in the UK, moving from 'unemployment benefit' to a 'job seeker's allowance', have brought the two further into line. It is important to note, however, that this is only one of a large number of changes of definition and coverage to official 'register-' or 'benefits-based' measures of unemployment, which, on balance, have tended to reduce the recorded rate of unemployment. These changes give rise to major

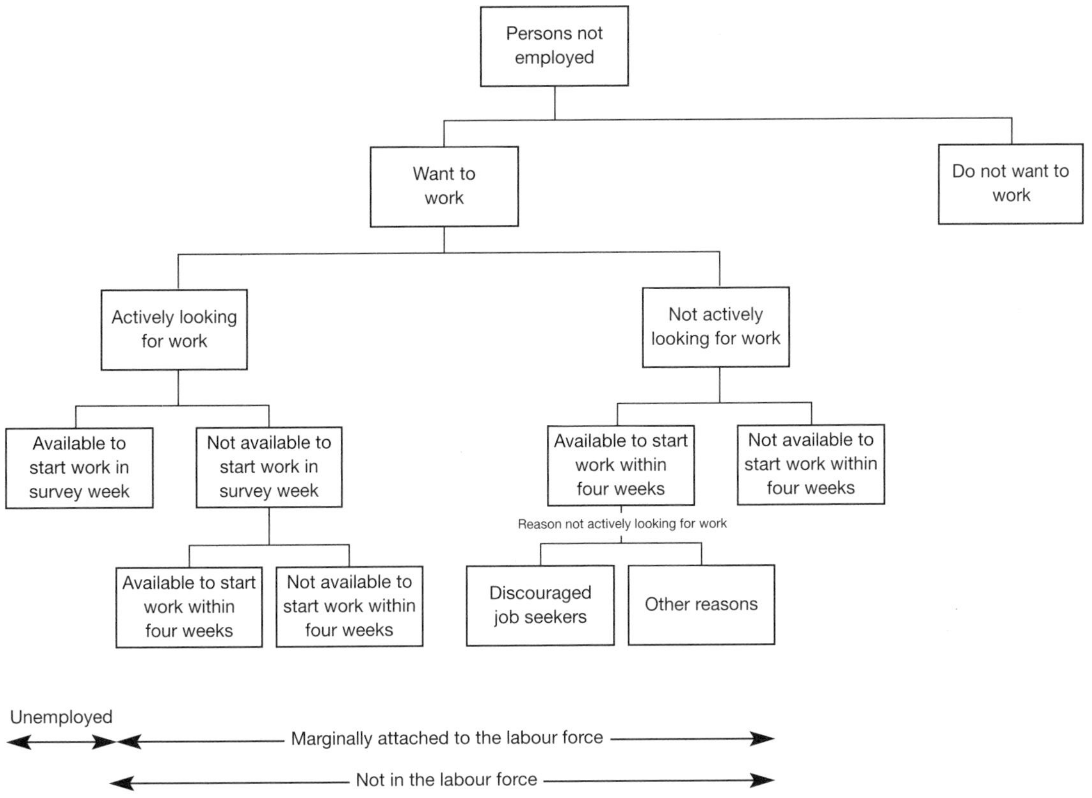

Fig 27.2 Unemployment and marginal attachment.
Source: ABS Employment, Underemployment and Unemployment 1966–1983. Cat No. 6246.0

problems in constructing a consistent time series for use in empirical work.

There are a number of reasons why, for example, the measures based on the administrative data may over- or underestimate the unemployment rate. First, some people claiming benefit are not genuinely willing to work (sometimes referred to as the 'sturdy beggars' or the 'welfare parasites'). The extent of this problem is a politically sensitive issue, giving rise to a wide range of estimates. However, there is tentative evidence to suggest that it is unlikely that this group represents more than 10 per cent of the unemployed stock in the UK. Second, there are the fraudulent claimants who obtain unemployment benefit while at the same time undertaking paid work. Another group included in the registrants and claimants are the 'unemployables', although this is a very difficult group to define. People who are regarded as unemployable at one time may become employable at another when the labour market is tighter. At various times, efforts have been made to move some of this group off the register, redefining them as disabled.

2.3 Hidden unemployment and underemployment

The measurement of unemployment is particularly complicated by the group of individuals who do not register, although they can hardly be classified as employed. There is an element of hidden unemployment in every economy, such as individuals living with families or friends, perhaps helping out in the home or on the farm. They receive an income (perhaps in goods) and may have a marginal product that is close to zero. They may be individuals who are drawn into the economically active stock during periods of relative boom, but return to the unregistered unemployed during recession (i.e. seasonal workers). A second dimension of underemployment concerns individuals who do not use all of the knowledge and skills they possess. This does not automatically imply a waste of resources: skills may be 'free goods' and there may be no demand for the particular skills possessed, or the individual may be more productive in using certain skills than in using others. Hence, underemployment might be defined as a situation where the value of an individual's output is not as large as it could be if skills were more fully or efficiently used.

3 Labour force states

3.1 Participation

3.1.1 Population of working age and the labour force

The size of the labour force in any given country is driven by the population and participation rate. This section provides comparative international data focusing primarily on OECD countries and, in particular, the EU. The EU forms a small proportion of the world's population (345 million people, 6.5 per cent in 1990), but slightly more of the population of working age (around 7 per cent). Australia, despite its large land mass, has only 0.4 per cent of the world's population of working age compared with 5.1 per cent for the USA and 2.7 per cent for Japan (CEC, 1993, Figure M4, p. 61). Thus, the Community is a 'large player' in world markets in terms of its population and developed group of economies. As might be expected the rate of growth of population in the EU has been relatively slow – under 1 per cent per annum over the last 20 years for those of working age, which is below the rates for Japan and the USA. These rates are dwarfed by the rapid and sustained growth of LDCs, which averaged 2 to 3 per cent per annum worldwide, with North African countries at the top end of this range, consistent with links between income and family size. Rates of growth of the population of working age in the EU appear set to slow slightly over the period to 2010 (0.2 per cent per annum, although net inward migration may bolster this somewhat). The projected rate for the USA is also expected to be lower than previously (0.7 per cent per annum) and Japan will exhibit a decline in its population of working age (–0.2 per cent per annum). Rates of growth of population of working age in the developing world, however, are likely to be maintained at a higher level. Australia's population of working age is set to grow at about 1.1 per cent per annum. These developments are 'double edged': on the one hand, faster population growth of working age requires a larger number of job opportunities unless unemployment or non-participation is to rise (with the employed population finding that it is supporting a higher proportion of those not in employment); on the other hand, slower population growth of working age often results in a growing proportion of older individuals (creating problems of providing benefits and facilities).

3.1.2 Participation rate

Participation is positively related to the volume of employment opportunities. On balance, the growth of employment opportunities in the EU has failed to keep pace with the number of people joining the workforce over the last 20 years; not enough new jobs have been created, unemployment has remained high and this has depressed participation rates. It would appear that there is a relatively large pool of 'marginally attached' individuals who are induced onto the market during periods of relative boom and are barely suppressed from appearing during recession (CEC, 1994, p. 59). A number of economists have therefore turned their attention to the greater apparent success of the USA in creating new employment opportunities.

When we compare the USA and EU, in the 1970s they both had similar rates (of about 62–63 per cent of working-age people) and labour force participation (of around 65–66 per cent) (CEC, 1993, pp. 24–25). Between 1973 and 1985 the employment rate in the EU fell to around 57 per cent whereas the USA rose to 67 per cent. This increase in the USA occurred despite the fact that it experienced a rise of about 6 per cent of people of working age. In other words, the USA was able to create sufficient jobs to offset the growth in the population of working age. In the EU 90 per cent of the fall in the employment rate was caused by an increase in unemployment; if anything, the participation rate fell slightly. Over the past 30 years the EU only managed to increase the participation rate significantly from 1985 to 1990 (the participation rate went up by 2 per cent and the employment rate by just over $3\frac{1}{2}$ per cent). The increase in the employment rate was primarily due to people entering the labour market, as only 30 per cent of the additional jobs were filled by people previously unemployed. During this period, however, the USA experienced a rapid rise in jobs created (the employment rate rose by 4 per cent and the participation rate by 3 per cent).

3.1.3 Changes in participation by gender and age

There have been major changes in the participation rates of men and women in different countries (CEC, 1993, pp. 145–170). The trends in the EU appear broadly consistent with the 'added worker' and 'discouraged worker' hypothesis. Relatively high levels of 'hard to move' unemployment appear to have encouraged labour force participation amongst secondary workers, linked to the changing occupational and industry structure, and a shift towards female employment. At the same time, primary workers have been induced to give up job search because of the relatively high rates of unemployment and low level of hiring activity. This is linked to the reduced employment opportunities for males and an increasing tendency for them to move outside the labour force, particularly, though not exclusively, amongst older workers, where some form of early retirement package can be worked out. While women only represented 30 per cent of the working population of the EU in 1960, by 1991 they represented 40 per cent or more. Women's participation rates are, however, lower in the USA and some of the EU Member States. Thus the average conceals wide variations across Member States. The patterns also have to be seen against the major economic, social and cultural changes that occur as some countries develop and grow – see Case Study 1.

The rise in the participation rate of women between 25 and 49 years old shows no sign of slowing down. During the recession of the early 1990s, there was little evidence of a decline in female participation in Western Europe, partly because women were more heavily involved in the service sector, which was somewhat less affected by the downturn. The longer-term increase in the participation of women in Europe can be attributed, in part, to the decline in activity amongst old and young males. It is therefore the increase in the participation of the 25–49 year old age group that has accounted for the main increase in the workforce in the Community during the 1980s.

CASE STUDY 1 Female participation in Spain

Spain is an interesting case, in part because it is one of the less developed countries of the European Union and partly because female participation in Spain remains amongst the lowest of the EU Member States. Nevertheless, Spain's rapid development since joining the EU suggests that we can expect to see more accentuated trends *vis-à-vis* some of the more industrialized EU countries.

Over the past 30 years, Spain has seen virtually no increase in the number of males in the labour force (Greece, Italy and Portugal showed declines), and labour force expansion has come almost entirely from the growth in female participation. Spain is not unique in the shift away from males and towards females, as both the UK and Belgium have experienced falls in the male labour force since 1960; only Germany and the Netherlands have shown some degree of expansion, which can be traced primarily to immigration. However, while all Member States experienced substantial growth in their female workforces, there was a growth of over 50 per cent in Spain and Greece over the 30 years to 1992.

The changing labour force participation in Spain of women aged 25-44 over recent years is shown in Figure 27.3 (Bover and Arelland, 1994, p. 32). A significant part of the increase in female employment in Spain can be traced to the recession of the early 1980s, with the loss of traditional jobs pushing unemployment up to 21 per cent by 1986. Figure 27.4 (CEC, 1994, p. 54) demonstrates that female participation has increased over time for all ages from 20 to 60, although there is some evidence of reductions in the very youngest and oldest age groups.

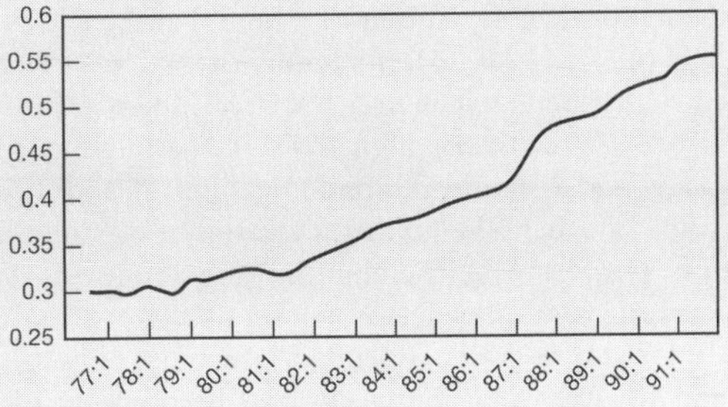

Fig 27.3 Labour force participation, women aged 25–44.

continues

CASE STUDY 1 continued

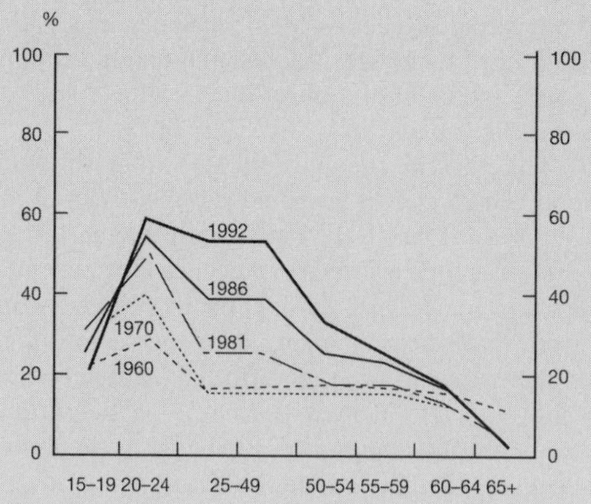

Fig 27.4 Participation rates of Spanish women by age group, 1960–1992.

A further part of the story has been the rapid increases in the qualification levels of females. While only 1.5 per cent of the cohort of women born in 1942–1946 possessed a university degree, this rose to almost 8 per cent for those born between 1957 and 1961. In practice, women's wages grew faster than men's in part because the improvement in female educational levels was greater than for males. The other key related factor is female fertility rates. While the decision to have children and participation in the labour market are jointly determined, the increasing education levels and declining fertility rates of females are entirely consistent with the rapid increases in female participation rates in Spain. Bover and Arelland (1994) conclude

> In this paper we have analyzed the determinants of the formidable increase in the participation of prime age women in the labour market that took place in Spain during the 80s. We conclude that this increase in participation was mainly due to structural factors that shifted female earnings potential, in particular to the increase in university education and the decrease in birth rates, after controlling for their endogeneity. This is important because it implies that the levels of prime age female participation that have been reached and that were never experienced before are here to stay. Even if these levels remained constant in the future, we would expect the total female participation rate to increase due to the replacement of the older cohorts.

Sources: Bover and Arelland (1994); CEC (1994)

3.2 Work patterns

3.2.1 Hours of work

From 1983 and to 1992 average usual weekly hours of work by employees in industry and services went down by about 4 per cent (i.e. around 1½ hours) in the EU as a whole (CEC, 1994a). Hours fell by over 12 per cent in the Netherlands, which may be part of the explanation for its relatively high rise in employment. Germany and Belgium exhibited declines of about 5 per cent. In other EU countries the figure was more modest. However, the examination of average hours can conceal variations across workers. *LFS* evidence for the UK suggests a considerable 'bunching' of hours around 38–40 (usual) per week, but the dominating peak of 40 hours observed in 1983 has disappeared and a greater dispersion of hours now occurs. The UK appears to be something of a special case,

> a large proportion of employees tend to work very similar hours and ... in most parts of the Community a standard working week of a given number of hours is clearly discernible (though in a few Member States, the UK, in particular, this is far from the case). (CEC, 1994a, p. 105).

An exploration of the distribution of hours across countries by gender reveals the very special case of males in the UK, with over 20 per cent in 1983 and nearly 30 per cent in 1992 working more than 48 hours per week. The causes of this are not clear, but long hours are often the result of an attempt to maintain living standards in the face of relatively low pay rates. Female hours are clearly influenced by the prevalence of part-time working, and we turn to that issue in the next section. However, it remains the case that men tend to work longer than women, at least in paid employment.

3.2.2 Part-time working

As noted in Part II of the book, part-time working is primarily undertaken by women; females account for 85 per cent of all part-time employment across the EU and 31 per cent of female employees are in part-time jobs (CEC, 1994, p. 116). In comparison only 4 per cent of men in the EU worked part time in 1992. The pattern of full-time/part-time working over the life-cycle suggests that young females are very similar to males in taking full-time employment, but this falls away dramatically during the main child-bearing years before rising again. This general pattern appears to have changed little over time, at least in the UK. The use of part-time working has been growing primarily in the service sectors (Wilson and Lindley, 1993, p. 21). Indeed, the use of part-time working appears to have declined in the manufacturing sectors in the UK, which may be a reflection of the increased use of shiftworking and the attempt to maintain or increase capital operating hours. While, historically, part-time jobs have been filled by female workers, there are some signs that males are also beginning to accept part-time employment (although they may also be multiple job-holders). In the UK, all of the net increase of 1.2 million in employment between 1980 and 1990 is accounted for by part-time jobs. This trend towards an increased proportion of part- to full-time jobs is generally seen in other EU countries.

In the UK, at least, some commentators argue that the increased importance of part-time working reflects a greater flexibility of the labour market and increased ability of the economy to adjust to changes. Conservative politicians have been heard to argue that individuals are now 'mixing and matching' different part-time jobs to form patterns of employment that are most suitable to their own domestic circumstances. Others continue to see the changes as a mechanism for keeping undertrained and unqualified individuals off the unemployment register, enabling the UK economy to compete in low-technology/low-quality areas, in some cases against less developed economies. We return to this argument in the concluding section below and in Chapter 29.

3.2.3 Shift systems and weekend working

While work patterns appear to be fairly standardized there are in fact a great variety of systems which can be found in European industries (Bosch, 1994; Lehndorff, 1994). The decoupling of hours from capital operating time in Europe has led to many innovative systems, including weekend working, compressed work weeks, standby contracts (particularly covering absenteeism, but also for unplanned machine repair and maintenance). The Japanese rigidity, for example, in their adoption of a two-shift system in car production, with set teams of workers, gives much more control over quality both within shifts and in the transition between shifts. On the other hand, it has important implications for the hours of work of employees, with long annual hours and a lack of flexibility in the length and timing of worker holidays. Most EU countries have worried about the social and physiological effects of 'abnormal' or 'unsocial' hours of work (as reflected in the work of the European Foundation for the Improvement of Living and Working Conditions). On the other hand, some economists have argued strongly for the macroeconomic benefits of increased shiftworking.

By 1992, around 5 per cent of men and 3 per cent of women usually worked nights in the EU (and some 11 per cent of men and 5 per cent of women sometimes worked nights). As we have discussed in earlier chapters, there are important industry and occupation differences in night and shiftworking. Transport and communications, public utilities and certain parts of the chemicals industry are more heavily involved (other areas are also associated with night working, as in key services such as hospitals, police, etc.).

In the early post-war period, some form of weekend working (such as Saturday mornings) was considered the norm, at least for males. By the 1970s or early 1980s, at least in the UK, weekend hours for males, at least in the production industries, were considered to be 'unsocial'. With the growth of both shiftworking and 'flexibilization', this may again have changed, with weekends becoming a more integral part of the 'normal' working week. In 1992 around 20 per cent of male employees in the EU usually worked Saturdays, while almost 50 per cent had jobs which involved some form of Saturday working (i.e. either usual or occasional). The corresponding proportions for women were 25 and 42 per cent respectively. As might be expected, Sunday working was less prevalent. In 1992 only about 8 per cent of male employees usually worked Sundays; the proportion for women was very similar. A further 15 per cent of individuals occasionally worked Sundays (i.e. about 23 per cent had jobs involving some form of either regular or occasional Sunday working). In the early 1990s, the UK passed legislation further relaxing the laws on Sunday trading, which may provide a further stimulus to weekend working. Resistance to change has also diminished in other countries – see Case Study 2.

CASE STUDY 2 Weekend shifts: the French experience

The French weekend shifts are just one of a number of shift systems which have emerged internationally, involving weekend working within the context of traditional shift patterns. France changed its regulations to allow firms to work weekend shifts in 1982 (Butel and Bloch-London, 1992). This was a fairly radical departure under French labour laws, insofar as it removed the right to a day of rest on Sunday. The regulations were further amended in 1991, to allow the weekend shiftworkers to replace normal shift teams during collective holiday periods. The introduction of such systems requires a company agreement or authorization by the labour authorities (following consultation with company delegates). Wages for weekend workers are set at least 50 per cent higher. The most common arrangement involves two 12 hour shifts on Saturday and Sunday.

Firms that adopted weekend shifts tended to be those that experienced steady growth after stagnation or recession. Weekend shifts appeared to be chosen when other forms of flexibility (i.e. longer overtime working) formed an inappropriate response to the firm's production requirements or economic situation. Firms tended to be one of two types: those treating the adoption of weekend shifts as a temporary measure (even if circumstances subsequently prolonged its use) and those adopting it as a long-term pattern. The 'short-term' group saw it as a form of cyclical adjustment (implying that the firm would probably withdraw from the weekend shift agreement when economic circumstances changed). The 'long-term' group adopted it as a conscious strategy related to the optimal utilization of the capital stock.

Weekend shifts generally involved a small team operating only a part of the productive equipment, a feature which characterized all but one of the 12 firms investigated by Butel and Bloch-London (1992) The choice of which activities were undertaken at the weekends was based on factors such as the need to overcome bottlenecks in the existing capital stock, more fully utilize certain pieces of expensive equipment and produce a greater volume of certain key products.

The weekend shifts were organized in one of two ways. In the first group, weekend working was treated as a largely separate and almost independent activity from the remainder of the work week. At the extreme, some of these firms hired exclusively from outside the firm for the weekend shift and imposed contingent contracts (i.e. temporary or casual contracts). Thus, the weekend workforce had little if any experience of the general activities of the firm undertaken in the rest of the week, and training tended to be limited and centred on the work post. In the second group of firms, there was an explicit organizational and social strategy which made the company more likely to anticipate the upheavals resulting from the introduction of weekend shifts. Such companies were more likely to use more experienced and qualified employees and, hence, were more likely to opt for internal recruitment. Participation by employees in the decision to move to Sunday working tended to produce a convergence of the interests of employees and employers.

The economic benefits and costs of the weekend shift strategy were diverse and differed significantly between sectors. Benefits included the ability to meet increased demand from existing plant and machinery. For some companies it allowed an increase in flexibility through the use of contingent contracts, although this was to some extent offset by the need to use more highly experienced and qualified workers in order to make the system a success. The faster depreciation of capital increased firm costs, but needed to be balanced against the ability to replace the capital stock more frequently with more modern machines. In some sectors, continuous working avoided the problems of warming up the machinery, but also posed problems for the timing of planned maintenance activities. From the worker's viewpoint, weekend shifts led to social isolation and marginalization in some circumstances. Butel and Bloch-London (1992) suggest that firms generally underestimated the extent and cost of the organizational adjustment in some instances to weekend shifts. Three of the 12 companies that the authors studied retrospectively decided that weekend shifts were not profitable (one because of maintenance problems, one because of management dysfunctions and one because investment in new capital offered a more profitable alternative). The results also suggest that potential economic benefits were to some extent offset (sometimes outweighed) by the social and organizational costs.

Source: Bosworth, D. (1994).

3.3 Unemployment

3.3.1 Incidence

Unemployment can be viewed as an imbalance between the supply of and demand for labour, where in this instance supply exceeds demand. The growth of unemployment in the UK, but also in a number of other OECD countries, has often placed it at the centre of the macroeconomic debate (Malinvaud, 1993). While unemployment is inherently cyclical, each peak has tended to exceed earlier peaks, although even when employment rises, a lot of this is taken up by those not in the labour force and unemployment rates do not decrease by the same amount. Unemployment rates for European Community countries are shown in Table 27.1. They show higher incidence rates for women than for men across the Community as a whole, although this is not the case for certain countries, such as the UK. In general the rate of unemployment fell from 1985 to 1991. However, it should be noted that 1985 was close to the trough and generally a period of upswing, while 1991 was at the peak or the start of the downturn. It can also be seen that the rates of unemployment differ significantly across countries, with the highest rates in Spain and Ireland, with very low rates in Germany, Portugal and Luxembourg.

3.3.2 Duration

Considerable attention focused on long-term unemployment in the early to mid-1980s, when it became a significant problem in the UK and other EU countries. Across the EU as a whole, the proportion of individuals who were unemployed for more than a year was as high as 52 per cent in 1985. During the late 1980s many countries experienced relatively strong employment growth and the problem of long-term unemployment abated somewhat. Nevertheless, it remains a very significant economic and social problem in many countries. The failure to solve the problem of long-term unemployment has given rise to an extensive empirical literature, which we touch upon in Chapter 28 below.

3.3.3 Consequences

Economists have voiced concern about the potential waste of resources: labour services cannot be stored, and if they are not used in a particular year, the goods that they would have produced are lost for ever. Economists also recognize that unemployment has many economic side-effects. In particular, it disrupts career plans, erodes the stock of human capital and increases the inequality of income (Topel, 1993). In addition, it has broader effects – sociologists and psychologists see unemployment as an event that can adversely affect individuals throughout their lives and

Table 27.1 Unemployment in the European Community

Member State	1985			1991		
	Males	Females	Total	Males	Females	Total
Belgium	7.4	17.8	11.3	4.6	10.6	7.0
Denmark	6.4	9.5	7.8	8.3	10.0	9.1
Germany	5.8	8.5	6.9	3.6	4.8	4.1
Greece	5.7	11.7	7.8	4.8	12.9	7.7
Spain	19.6	25.0	21.3	12.0	23.2	15.9
France	8.5	12.6	10.3	7.2	11.7	9.2
Ireland	17.4	19.1	18.0	15.4	16.6	15.8
Italy	6.4	15.4	9.5	6.8	15.8	10.1
Luxembourg	2.2	4.3	3.0	1.1	2.0	1.5
Netherlands	9.5	12.4	10.5	5.6	10.0	7.3
Portugal	6.8	11.7	8.5	2.6	5.7	3.9
UK	11.8	11.0	11.5	9.4	7.4	8.6
All European Union	9.4	12.9	10.8	7.2	10.9	8.7

Source: Eurostat (1993). *Community Labour Force Survey*. EC give rise to patterns of behaviour detrimental to the whole of society. There is some evidence, for example, that crime rates, as well as suicide and death rates, are linked to unemployment. Politicians also view unemployment as an important influence on electoral success. The social consequences of unemployment depend very much on the duration of unemployment spells. While most spells are short, most of the days lost are the result of a relatively small number of long spells, and long-term unemployment remains an important problem in many countries.

4 Productivity, inflation and growth

4.1 Other aspects of economic performance

While the growth of employment opportunities and the incidence (and duration) of unemployment are key macroeconomic indicators of the state of the economy, there are other measures of economic performance linked directly to the labour market. A number of chapters, for example, pointed to the role of the labour market in determining the level of and changes in the wage rate. What happens to wages potentially has an important bearing on product prices and, thereby, the rate of inflation in the economy. While wage increases tend to be inherently inflationary, other factors are important in determining whether the upward pressures manifest themselves in higher prices. Such factors include changes in profit margins; however, the main influence is productivity. Improvements in labour productivity may reduce employment opportunities at any given level of product demand, but they also offset the effects of wage increases on the wage bill and, thereby, total costs. In this section, we therefore explore both time series and international comparative data on these performance measures.

4.2 Productivity growth

4.2.1 UK productivity growth

The average annual rates of labour productivity growth for the UK over the period 1700 to 1983 suggest that there is not a single estimate of the long-run rate of productivity growth in the economy as a whole, but that it varies from period to period (Lee, 1986). In addition, this long-run perspective appears to reveal significantly faster rates of labour productivity growth for the UK in the period after the Second World War. Of course, early data may be less reliable and the choice of periods is important given that productivity moves procyclically (increasing during the upswing and decreasing – or growing less fast – during the downswing). Thus, the more reliable estimates are calculated peak to peak (or trough to trough). In terms of the post-war period, therefore, the most reliable estimates will be for periods up to 1973 (when cyclical activity in the UK was less marked), 1973 to 1979 and 1979 to 1989. Apart from the relatively rapid rate of labour productivity growth post-war, a review of the literature as such suggests a range of estimates, which vary from cycle to cycle.

Table 27.2 suggests that, post-war, the 'golden age' of productivity growth appears to have been from 1960 to 1973 (rates of over 3.5 per cent per annum were recorded), higher than both the 1950s and the 1970s. The 1970s were a period of 'productivity slowdown', with growth rates up to 2 per cent per annum less than in the 1960s. The rate of productivity growth increased again in the 1980s, although perhaps not to the level found in the 1960s.

Some common features emerge. First, services have experienced lower rates of productivity growth than manufacturing (although there is disagreement about the estimates and whether there was a recovery in the 1980s from the productivity slowdown that took place in services in the 1970s). Second, the estimates for manufacturing are more consistent, suggesting that labour productivity grew by about 4 per cent per annum during the 1960s, with considerable slowdown in the 1970s (when the rate fell to around 1 or 2 per cent per annum), and recovery in the 1980s (i.e. while the rate of productivity growth was low from 1979 to 1981, it increased as the economy recovered). Third,

Table 27.2 Ranges of estimates of aggregate UK labour productivity growth (per cent per annum)

Period	Estimate
1950–1960	2.3
1960–1973	3.5–3.8
1973–1979	1.3–2.1
1979–1988	2.5–2.8

Source: Bosworth *et al.* (1994)

double deflation measures (i.e. the separate deflation of gross output and raw material inputs by their associated price indices – rather than the application of a single deflator to nominal net output) indicate a slower rate of growth of manufacturing productivity from 1979-1989, perhaps 1.5 percentage points lower, because output prices rose relative to input prices, particularly in the years 1984–1986 – largely as a result of the fall in oil prices, not reflected in lower output prices (Stoneman and Francis, 1994). This can be interpreted in two ways: first, that productivity growth was not as high as some estimates suggest; second, that one explanation for the high rate of productivity growth in manufacturing in the 1980s was the relative decline in the prices of raw material and intermediate inputs.

The key question which we take up in Chapter 29 is the extent to which these, sometimes rapid improvements in labour productivity are reflected in overall economic performance. As we will see below, there is little evidence, at least over the period covered by the data, that the UK improved its relative economic position *vis-à-vis* its main industrial competitors. The answers appear to lie in the extent to which improved labour productivity impacts upon increased total factor productivity, reduced unit costs and higher profits. Some hint of the answer is provided in the remainder of this chapter, but we take up the story in more detail in Chapter 29.

4.2.2 Comparative international productivity

Downturns in the business cycle have a habit of concentrating politicians' minds wonderfully. The recession of the early 1990s produced the following response in Europe:

> The present recession has intensified concerns, however, about the Community's ability to compete in world markets with high technology producers in Japan and the US, and with low-tech producers in developing countries. (CEC, 1993, pp. 10–11).

This statement highlights a natural tension in competitiveness between reducing costs and increasing productivity, bearing in mind increases in the quality of products. In the UK the lack of competitiveness of the 1970s, followed by the recession of 1980/1981, produced a policy shift that tended to concentrate on relative UK unit costs; a cost-reducing policy. During the recession in the early 1990s, a number of German commentators called for a greater focus on costs and cost reductions – with some calls for greater flexibility in their domestic labour market.

Given that the rate of labour productivity growth in manufacturing has outstripped the rate of growth of manufacturing output, employment in the manufacturing sector has declined in almost every country. Even in a country such as Germany, while improvements in technology raise real net exports, export prices, the volume of trade and employment in the economy, these are not sufficient to offset the rationalization effects of the new technology. The 'best' results appear to be where new technologies are introduced in a strategic 'export offensive', resulting in lower rates of unemployment growth in the domestic economy (but obviously at the expense of other countries). In some countries, the rate of growth in manufacturing demand has been sufficiently slow to cause the share of manufacturing in total economic output to contract. In some, such as the UK, the changes have been rapid and sustained, leading to major structural change and adjustment in the economy. Of course, labour displaced from the manufacturing sector flows primarily into services, where the measured labour productivity growth is low. This clearly has implications for the level and rate of growth of wages in the service sector.

Thus, in general, the overall level of productivity in the economy, which is a weighted average of primarily the manufacturing and service sectors, declines as the proportion of manufacturing in total economic activity contracts, sometimes termed 'Baumol's Disease'. There is considerable evidence to suggest that technological and organizational changes are now being introduced into certain parts of the service sector (such as banking and finance), with consequent major job losses. It is not clear whether rapid productivity growth in services (unlike manufacturing) can produce compensating increases in demand for output (i.e. through increased competitiveness, higher export performance and reduced import penetration, as services, at least at present, are not so extensively traded internationally).

Table 27.3 sets out information about the rate of growth of real value added per person employed across five key industrial economies, and provides corresponding information for OECD countries as a whole. It can be seen that the UK outperformed the OECD average during the period 1979 to 1988, as well as doing better than it did in the 1970s. The data also suggest that, for this period, the UK did better than France and the USA, and possibly even better

Table 27.3 Growth in real value added per person employed in manufacturing (per cent per annum)

Year	France	Germany	Japan	USA	UK	OECD
1979	4.0	4.1	6.2	–0.8	0.2	2.5
1980	0.4	–	6.3	–2.1	–4.5	–0.5
1981	2.6	0.3	3.2	2.5	4.9	2.6
1982	2.3	0.7	6.2	0.9	6.4	1.8
1983	2.6	4.3	6.0	7.9	9.3	6.1
1984	0.9	3.3	9.1	6.6	6.2	6.3
1985	2.5	3.2	5.9	4.6	3.8	4.3
1986	2.0	–0.8	1.1	1.9	3.4	1.6
1987	2.1	–2.7	8.6	4.6	6.9*	4.1
1988	4.8	3.3	5.9	–	5.2*	3.8
1989	3.4	3.2	–	–	–	2.1
1960–1968	6.8	4.7	11.1	3.2	3.4	4.7
1968–1973	5.8	4.5	9.5	3.5	3.9	4.9
1973–1979	3.7	3.1	5.0	0.9	0.6	2.6
1979–1989	2.4	–	–	–	–	3.2
1960–1989	4.5	–	7.6	2.7	3.1	3.8

Source: *Economic Outlook, Historical Statistics 1960–1989*. Paris: OECD
Notes: – not available; * estimated from CSO data

than West Germany – a development termed the 'Thatcher Miracle'. This apparently surprising result should be balanced against a number of other pieces of information. First, that the UK set off at the beginning of this period at a significantly lower productivity base than its main competitors and, even if it were able to sustain this improvement, it would be a considerable number of years before it overtook them. Second, that the results do not indicate the extent to which they were achieved via the substitution of other inputs for labour and, therefore, not reflected in overall cost savings. Third, the data also reveal that, with the exception of the odd year, Japan outperformed the UK. Fourth, other authors have questioned the measure of productivity used, suggesting that a 'double deflated' measure is superior, which may give less impressive results for the UK.

4.3 Wage costs and inflation

4.3.1 UK wage pressure

Labour costs can play a central role in determining both the level and rate of change of prices; however, as we have shown, labour productivity increases can intervene to reduce their impact on unit costs. The pattern over the period from 1989 onwards is given in Figure 27.5. Pay settlements fell away from over 8 per cent in 1990, as the economy moved into recession. The upward movement in unit labour costs up to this time (caused by rate of pay increases in excess of labour productivity improvements) fell away as pay settlements fell back in recession and as productivity growth recovered from its early recession set-back. We expect such movements to be related to labour market conditions, with periods of relatively high pay settlements linked to 'tight' labour markets. The period since 1991 has been an uncertain one, however, with some commentators arguing that the UK has never really recovered and others that there has been a 'seed change' in the labour market that has banished wage increases as a significant source of inflationary pressure.

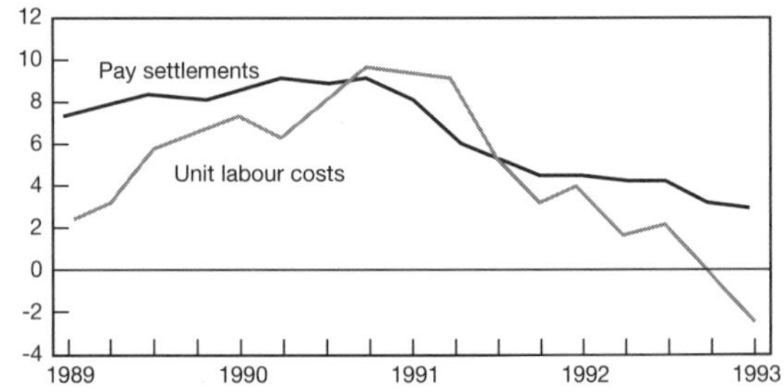

Fig 27.5 Manufacturing pay settlements and unit labour costs (% annual increase).
Source: Dept of Employment/CBI Pay Databank, from a paper by Andrew Sentance.

4.3.2 Comparative international labour costs

Given that the key to job maintenance and creation depends upon comparative international performance, it is important to juxtapose UK labour costs with those of its main competitors. Figure 27.6 presents data on both wages and on-costs within the European Union. On this basis, it appears that, although the UK wage rates are not the lowest in the Union, overall costs are almost the cheapest – nearly half as low as those in Germany. Of course, as we have pointed out, this does not necessarily make unit production costs in the UK lowest. This depends on the extent of substitution towards capital and raw materials and intermediate inputs and total factor productivity. Indeed, as we will argue in subsequent chapters, the low labour costs may be more a reflection of inadequate skills and poor economic performance, rather than a source of reassurance about the UK's dynamism.

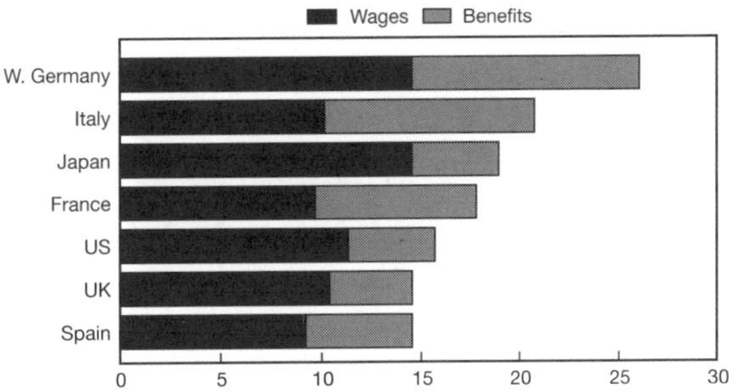

Fig 27.6 Comparative manufacturing labour costs, 1992 (annual average, dollars per hour).
Source: Institute of German Industry, Cologne

4.3.3 Cost competitiveness

One index of competitiveness is, therefore, unit labour costs. These are set out in Figure 27.7, which shows that, if anything, the UK's position deteriorated very slightly over the 1970s. However, the advent of the Conservative administration in 1979 saw a significant change. While at first sight, this might be linked with the introduction of anti-union legislation, the rapidity of the change suggests that it is probably more closely tied to a change in the exchange rate. The subsequent behaviour of normalized unit costs clearly reflects the business cycle, as unemployment rose until the mid-1980s and then fell to the late 1980s, before rising again. While it is quite clear that the period after 1979 is quite different to that of 1963 to 1978, nevertheless, the UK was not very much more competitive in terms of its unit labour costs in 1993 than in 1966.

4.3.4 UK performance and policy

We now turn to the implications of the labour market for UK economic performance. The results are summarized in Figure 27.8. RP shows what UK prices would have been on world markets without the changes in exchange rates. ERI shows the changing value of the £ sterling *vis-à-vis* the UK's main com-

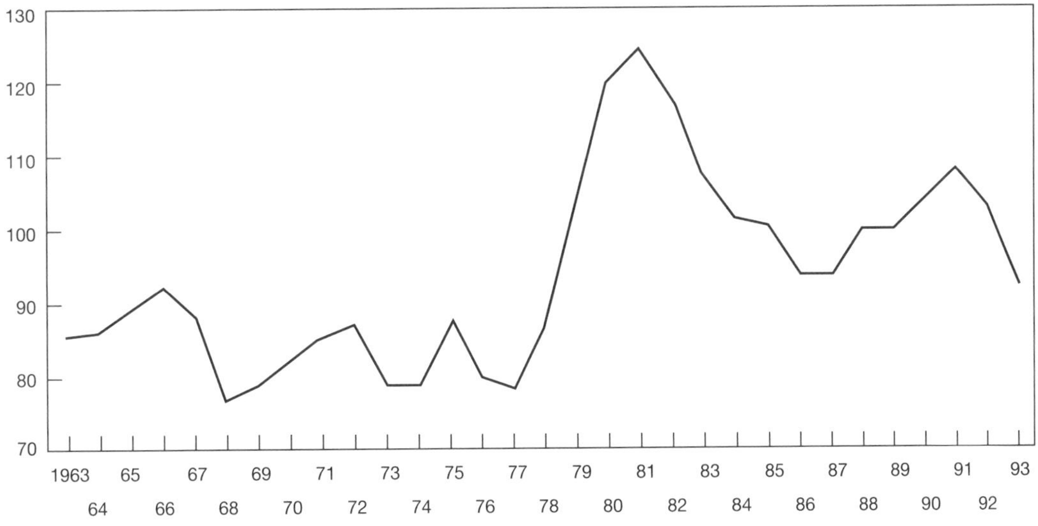

Fig 27.7 UK labour cost competitiveness; IMF index of normalized unit labour costs, 1985 = 100.
Source: IMF/CBI estimates (*)

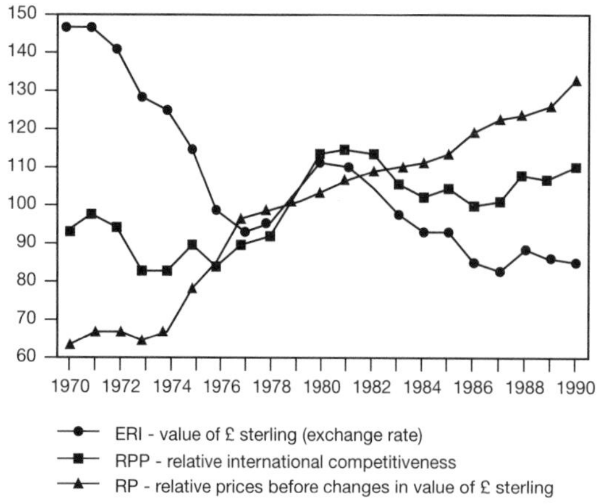

Fig 27.8 UK relative costs, exchange rates and competitiveness.

petitors. Finally, RPP is the exchange-rate-adjusted measure of the price of UK goods on world markets. The picture is very clear: in essence, total factor productivity growth has not been fast enough to overcome increases in input prices and UK competitiveness has been crucially dependent on the devaluation of the £ sterling. In the light of these trends, the UK's departure from the Exchange Rate Mechanism appears an almost foregone conclusion.

5 Conclusions

This chapter has presented a range of times series and comparative international data about a number of key variables that are heavily dependent on labour market outcomes. We now proceed to explore one or two of these from a somewhat more conceptual angle. In particular, Chapter 28 examines the influences on the incidence and duration of unemployment. Chapter 29 explores the inter-relationship between inflation, factor productivity and economic growth. Finally, Chapter 30 examines a number of more general labour market policies designed to improve overall economic performance.

References

Bosch, G. (1994). 'Working Time and Operating Hours in the Japanese Car Industry'. In Anxo *et al.* (eds) *Work Patterns and Capital Operating Time: An International Comparative Study of Work Patterns and Capital Operating Time*. Boston: Kluwer, pp. 339–356.

Bosworth, D. (1994) *Sunday Working: Analysis of an Employer Survey*. Research Series No. 33. London: Employment Department.

Bosworth, D.L., P. A. Stoneman and J. Roe (1994). *Water and Sewerage Industries: General Efficiency and the Potential for Improvement*. Report to Ofwat. Warwick Research Institute. Coventry: Warwick University.

Bover, O. and M. Arellano (1994). *Female Labour Force Participation in the 1980s: the Case of Spain*. Madrid: Banco de España.

Butel and Bloch-London (1992). 'Weekend Shifts in Pursuance of Flexibility'. In M. Ebbing (ed.) *Aspects of Part-Time Working in Different Countries. Arbeitspapier 1992–7*. Arbeitskreis Sozialwissenschaftliche Arbeitsmarktforschung (SAMF). Gelsenkirchen, pp. 117–137.

CEC (1993). *Employment in Europe*. Directorate General. Employment, Industrial Relations and Social Affairs. COM(93)314. Luxembourg.

CEC (1994). *Employment in Europe*. Directorate General. Employment, Industrial Relations and Social Affairs. COM(94)381. Luxembourg.

Lee, C.H. (1986). *The British Economy Since 1700: A Macroeconomic Perspective*. Cambridge: Cambridge University Press.

Lehndorff, S. (1994). 'Working Time and Operating Time in the European Car Industry'. In D. Anxo *et al.* (eds) *Work Patterns and Capital Operating Time: An International Comparative Study*. Boston: Kluwer, pp. 311–338.

Malinvaud, E. (1993). 'Are Macroeconomic Employment Theories Challenged by the Present European Recession?'. Keynote Speech. European Association of Labour Economists. Maastricht.

Stoneman, P. and N. Francis (1994). 'Double Deflation and the Measurement of Output and Productivity in UK Manufacturing 1979–89'. *International Journal of the Economics of Business*, 1, 3, 423–437.

Topel, R. (1993). 'What Have We Learned from Empirical Studies of Unemployment and Turnover?' *American Economics Association. Papers and Proceedings*, 83, 2, 110–115.

Wilson, R.A. and R.M. Lindley (1993). *Review of the Economy and Employment: Occupational Assessment*. Institute for Employment Research. Coventry: University of Warwick.

CHAPTER 28 Unemployment

1 Introduction

This chapter examines a key labour market outcome which is a continuing focus of intense political scrutiny and debate, namely unemployment. The present discussion should be read in combination with a number of earlier chapters. In particular, the supply chapters in Part II dealt with the concept of job search, with the idea that individuals not in employment, but available and looking for work, can be classed as unemployed. Part IV of the book examined labour market outcomes in which imbalances between supply and demand occurred. At that stage, the analysis concentrated primarily on labour shortages, leading on to the subsequent discussion about education, training and human capital. However, we noted the alternative possibility that disequilibrium might involve an excess supply of labour, which would be reflected, in part, in higher unemployment. Finally, Chapter 27 provided some data about the extent and nature of unemployment, outlining changes over time and differences across countries.

The present chapter attempts a somewhat more analytical treatment of the unemployment issue. It demonstrates how time series, cross-sectional and cohort or panel data sets have been analysed to assess the influences on unemployment. In doing so, the discussion concentrates on two related dimensions of the problem: the incidence and the duration of unemployment. Here we return to the questions initially posed in Chapter 27 about the influence of heterogeneity (relating to the different skills and attributes of the unemployed) and the key issue of 'duration dependence' (in other words, having controlled for observed and unobserved heterogeneity, whether the length of the spell of unemployment itself impacts on the probability of leaving that state).

Section 2 considers the potential economic costs of unemployment, although it is recognized that these almost certainly understate the true social costs, including the impacts on psychological well-being and health. Section 3 outlines a taxonomy of unemployment. While it briefly considers the issue of voluntary versus involuntary, its main focus is on a decomposition of unemployment by source, including demand deficiency. Section 4 looks at the incidence of unemployment and reports on a model of the UK economy which explains the major increase in rates which took place between the end of the 1950s and the mid-1980s, producing evidence about the major macroeconomic influences. Section 5 again uses time series data, but this time broken down by length of spell, with a view to analysing the transitions across duration thresholds and out of unemployment. Results are reported for three European countries. Section 6 then outlines the use of survival methods to explain the 'hazard rate' (i.e. the probability of leaving unemployment) and reports on a number of results based upon panel data sets. Finally, Section 7 draws the main conclusions of this chapter.

2 Importance of unemployment

There are several ways of measuring the 'costs of unemployment' or 'recession'. The most obvious method concerns the potential waste of resources: labour services cannot be stored, and if they are not used in a particular year, the goods that they would have produced are lost for ever. Economists also recognize that unemployment has many economic side-effects. In particular, it disrupts career plans, erodes the stock of human capital and increases the inequality of income (Topel, 1993). In addition, however, it has broader effects. Sociologists and psychologists see unemployment as an event that can adversely affect individuals throughout their lives and give rise to patterns of behaviour detrimental to the whole society. There is some evidence, for example, that crime rates, as well as suicide and death rates, are linked to unemployment. Politicians also view unemployment as an important influence on electoral success.

The static output losses can be approximated by the difference between the potential output at full employment, GDP*, and the actual levels of output, GDP (Junanker, 1989). Regressing

$$U = f\left(\frac{\text{GDP} - \text{GDP}^*}{\text{GDP}^*}\right)$$

for each country, the coefficients can be interpreted as the reduction in the rate of growth of output caused by a 1 per cent increase in unemployment. Thus, Table 28.1 shows the percentage losses, where the two columns for each year are based on alternative assumptions about the success of government policy in influencing unemployment. Partial calculations of the costs of unemployment omit the macroeconomic multiplier effects of the income loss associated with the initial increase in unemployment, but, on the other hand, should also reflect the impact on the rate of inflation. However, while static output loss measures are obviously restrictive, they may be 'a good first approximation in assessing the social costs of recession and slack' (Okun, 1981, p. 272).

Table 28.1 Output losses due to unemployment

	1980		1983	
	Low	High	Low	High
West Germany	–	6.7	13.4	20.6
France	6.1	13.3	14.1	21.2
Italy	3.4	6.8	13.5	16.9
UK	3.0	6.5	13.7	17.2

Source: Junanker (1989, p. 278)

The costs of unemployment to the individual of the lost income (minus the value of the increased leisure) increase with the duration of unemployment. While the short-term impact on the individual's income may be cushioned by the consumption of existing financial and physical capital, this is at the expense of reduced levels of wealth. Thus, from society's point of view, the cost of unemployment is directly related to both the numbers out of work and the average length of the uncompleted period of unemployment

An alternative approach to measuring the costs of recession is based on the idea that the cycle exposes agents to risk. Thus, a measure of the associated costs is reflected in how much people would be willing to pay to avoid such risks (Lucas, 1987). This aggregate method introduces a consumption stream that varies randomly around some constant growth path. The size of the random shock is Z_t, such that $Z_t \sim N(0, \sigma_Z^2)$, with a mean value $\exp(\sigma_Z^2/2)$. The individual consumers are allowed to be risk averse, valuing a consumption stream which grows at a constant rate, μ, more highly than one which, on average, grows at the same rate, but it is subject to random shocks. Thus, bearing in mind the need to discount, a consumer will need a higher rate of growth in consumption the larger the random shocks and the greater their risk aversion. Thus, treating the business cycle as a source of random shocks to individuals, it is possible to calculate

> the percentage increase in consumption, uniform across all dates and values of the shocks required to leave the consumer indifferent between consumption instability of σ_Z^2 and a perfectly smoothed consumption path. (Lucas, 1987, pp. 25–26)

Estimates for the UK (based upon quarterly figures for 1955 to 1990) and the USA (data from 1957 to 1990) are shown in Table 28.2. Thus, depending upon the degree of smoothing the estimated costs vary from less than one-tenth of 1 per cent in both the UK and USA, up to 1.23 per cent of GNP in the UK and 2.20 per cent in the USA. Note, however, that the result is dependent on the choice of the utility function, the assumed degree of risk aversion and the choice of Π.

Table 28.2 Business cycle costs calculated as percentage of GNP

Degree of smoothing (Π)		UK	USA
Low Π =	50	0.08	0.07
	1600	0.25	0.29
	2000	0.27	0.31
	50,000	0.59	0.66
Perfect*	∞	1.23	2.20

* Equivalent to being smoothed to a least-squares linear trend

Clark *et al.* (1994) generalize this approach at the individual level, calculating the proportion of consumption employed individuals are willing to undergo in order to face a zero unemployment risk. The authors point out,

> The present measure is not comparable with Lucas 'pure risk' measure .... In contrast to Lucas, the measure is composed of two parts (i) a fall in expected consumption owing to a positive unemployment risk (ii) a premium above this as a result of risk aversion. The present measure therefore is almost bound to reveal a higher recession cost (p. 24)

The results are based upon data from the UK *Family Expenditure Survey* over the period 1979 to 1988. The recession costs for the 'representative household' are set out in Table 28.3. The second column shows the gross cost, while the third column indicates the pure risk cost, which excludes the loss in expected consumption. The element associated with the pure risk cost is simply the difference between the recession cost for the risk-averse and risk-neutral households (which must be zero when no risk aversion is assumed). The final two columns take into account that individuals can to some extent smooth income (i.e. through unemployment 'insurance' they have taken out themselves or through state benefits). Thus, the estimated losses are that much smaller. The final point to note is that the average for the 'representative unit' conceals major variations for different types of household, dependent on region, age, occupation, housing tenure, family composition, etc.

3 Types of unemployment

3.1 Components of unemployment

The economics literature has attempted to distinguish different types of unemployment. They include frictional, structural, seasonal, cyclical and demand-deficient, and technological unemployment. An important, although somewhat independent, theme, with strong political undertones, that has pervaded the literature has been the distinction between voluntary and involuntary unemployment.

Voluntary versus involuntary unemployment Shackleton (1985) focused on this distinction, defining individuals as voluntarily unemployed,

> if they choose not to work rather than take available jobs for which they are qualified, because wages or other working conditions are less attractive than the option of not working.

By the same token he defined involuntary unemployment as existing when,

> individuals cannot obtain work even if they are prepared to accept lower real wages or poorer conditions than similarly qualified workers who are currently in employment.

The reader is referred back to the discussion of the reservation wage in Part II of the book and the connection with implicit contract theory in Part VI.

Frictional unemployment In an economy subject to economic shocks, the free working of the market mechanism demands that some workers will be changing jobs (i.e. away from markets with an excess supply of labour and towards markets with an excess demand). Unless job changes are instantaneous, therefore, there will be a transitory element of the so-called frictionally unemployed. In the longer term, where there are no major economic shocks, frictional unemployment gradually sinks to a less significant level.

Structural unemployment While frictional unemployment, at least in part, represents the work of the market mechanism, structural unemployment is a more fundamental problem arising out of shifts in the balance of demands between products. The UK,

Table 28.3 Business cycle costs for a representative UK household (per cent of consumption)

Degree of risk aversion		Gross recession cost	Net recession cost	Gross recession cost (adjusted)	Net recession cost (adjusted)
Zero	0	3.79	0	3.39	0
	0.5	4.23	0.43	3.73	0.34
	1	4.73	0.94	4.12	0.72
High	2	5.95	2.16	5.03	1.63

for example, has experienced a decline in manufacturing employment, and a rise in the service sector. Major structural changes are inherently associated with a skills loss, as old skills become redundant, and create a need to train or retrain in skills relevant to the expanding area. The lower the degrees of occupational, functional and regional mobility, the greater the problems of structural unemployment for any given change within the economy. Much depends on whether individuals and employers receive the correct indicators to retrain or to move areas, and the speed and extent to which they react.

Seasonal unemployment Seasonal refers to the component of unemployment with a 12 month cycle. It arises partly because of variations in product demand and the timing of labour inputs over the year. An example where demand varies over the year is the tourist industry and an example where the timing of inputs is important is in harvesting agricultural produce. Even where demand for output varies over the year, this may not be transmitted to labour demands if output is (cheaply) storable. Seasonal fluctuations may also reflect the pattern of labour supply, with, for example, students and school leavers seeking unemployment at the end of the academic year.

Demand-deficient and cyclical unemployment Demand-deficient unemployment occurs when the level of aggregate expenditure in the economy is insufficient to provide an adequate number of employment opportunities for those seeking work and, therefore, subsumes cyclical unemployment and certain aspects of seasonal unemployment. Lipsey (1965) argued that demand-deficient unemployment could be defined using the concept of the Phillips curve. Figure 28.1 shows a modified Phillips curve, *PP*, which for the present purposes is assumed to be a stable relationship showing the trade-off between the rate of change in prices and the rate of unemployment – see, however, the discussion in Chapter 29. The curve's shape arises because, as aggregate demand falls, and the economy moves from a low- to a high-pressure situation, increasingly important bottlenecks appear in the markets and prices start rising more rapidly. The extent of demand-deficient unemployment is defined in terms of the policy makers' indifference map. Curves, such as *II*, indicate equal levels of government disutility regarding combinations of unemployment and inflation: curves further from the origin are associated with greater disutility. The lowest level of disutility that the policy maker can achieve by varying the level of aggregate demand is where *II* is tangential to *PP* at point *e*. If the economy is initially at point *f*, with unemployment U_0, then $U_0 - U_1$ denotes the demand-deficient unemployment defined as the unemployment component which can be removed by expansionary policies without decreasing social welfare. Further expansion of demand causes an increase in inflation that reduces societal welfare by a greater amount than the reduction in unemployment adds to welfare. U_1 is therefore formed mainly by structural and frictional unemployment. Other measures, such as increased retraining and mobility allowances, may shift the Phillips curve inward allowing the attainment of a higher level of societal welfare as at point *e*'. The more steeply sloped the *PP* curve, other things being equal, the lower the relative importance of demand-deficient unemployment. At the extreme, a vertical curve such as *P''P''* touches the indifference curve at a corner point, and there is zero demand-deficient unemployment.

Technological unemployment Changes in product technology cause changes in the patterns of consumer expenditure and, in this way, technological change contributes directly to structural imbalance in

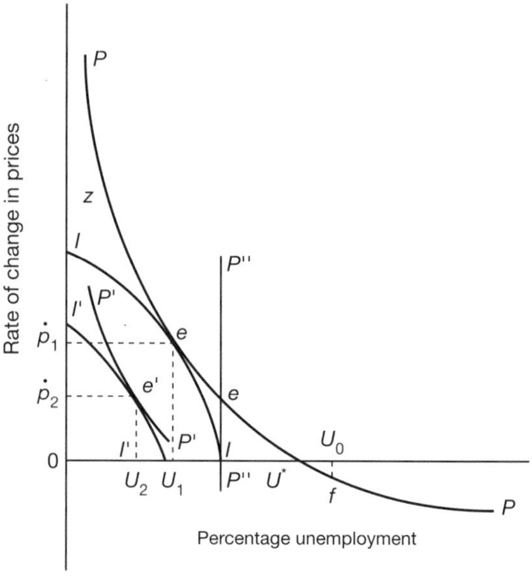

Fig 28.1 Demand-deficient, frictional and structural unemployment.

the economy. The flow of new products may create job opportunities, but Schumpeter's theory of 'creative destruction' describes the way in which one product is overtaken and removed from the market by newer and more advanced products using new technologies and labour skills in their production. Even if there were no changes in product design, process changes can alter the pattern of demands for different sorts of labour, creating jobs for certain skills (i.e. computer operators) and reducing the demand for others (i.e. draughtspeople). Insofar as technological change is exogenously determined (i.e. not induced by labour scarcity and high wages) it may result in productivity growth at a faster rate than the growth in product demand, resulting in technological unemployment.

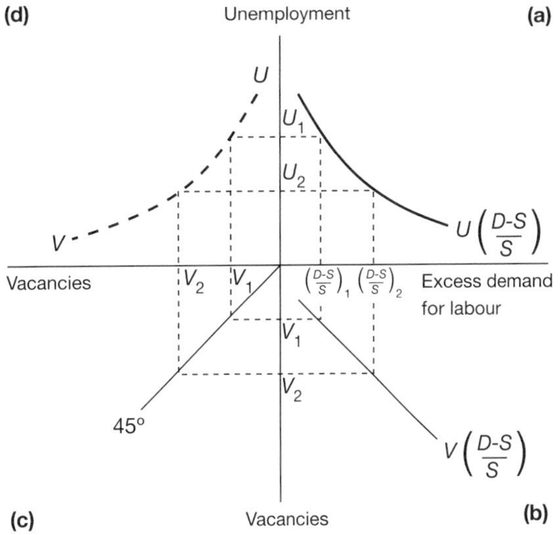

Fig 28.2 UV relationship.

3.2 Beveridge curve: decomposing types of unemployment

The relationship between unemployment and vacancies has a long history in the literature on structural change in the labour market. An apparently stable relationship between these variables was first noticed by Beveridge (1944), and is often called the 'Beveridge curve'. One use of the *UV* curve is as a practical method of dividing unemployment into its various components. The *UV* method uses vacancy (*V*) data alongside unemployment (*U*) data in order to separate unemployment into demand-deficient, frictional and structural components. In turn, the structural component can be divided into three further categories: spatial, occupational and mixed spatial/occupational components. The development of this decomposition is primarily due to Dow and Dicks-Mireaux (1958).

The derivation of the *UV* curve can be explained with reference to Figure 28.2. Quadrants (a) and (b) show unemployment and vacancies depending on the excess demand for labour. Unemployment reflects the excess supply of labour and vacancies the unsatisfied demand for labour. The negative relationship between unemployment and the excess demand for labour is non-linear because there will always be some frictional unemployment. Quadrant (b) shows a simple, positive, linear relationship between the excess demand for labour and vacancies. When excess demand is at $((D - S)/S)_1$ unemployment is U_1 and vacancies take the value V_1. As excess demand increases to $((D - S)/S)_2$ unemployment falls to U_2 and vacancies increase to V_2. With the help of the 45° line in quadrant (c), this produces a negative non-linear relationship between unemployment and vacancies (*UV* in quadrant (d)). Any movement along the *UV* curve reflects a change in excess labour demand. If the unemployment or vacancy functions shift, the *UV* function also shifts. For example, forces leading the unemployed to spend longer searching for jobs (e.g. increased unemployment benefits) would be expected to shift the unemployment function upwards and produce an outward shift in the *UV* curve. Alternatively improved information flows or higher labour mobility would shift the curves inwards. More recently, the *UV* relationship has been derived from a matching framework in which the critical relationship is the matching function, the number of jobs filled per unit of time (Pissarides, 1990). In this case the convex *UV* curve is explained by unemployment being lower when there are more vacancies because the unemployed find jobs more easily.

The way in which the relationship can be used to distinguish between frictional, structural and demand-deficient unemployment is illustrated in Figure 28.3. Demand-deficient unemployment is assumed to be zero where $U = V$ (i.e. on the 45° line), at the level of unemployment U_0. If observed unemployment is at U_1, then $U_1 - U_0$ is taken to be demand deficient in that it can be eliminated by moving down the *UV* curve until unemployment reaches U_0. Thereafter for any further increased

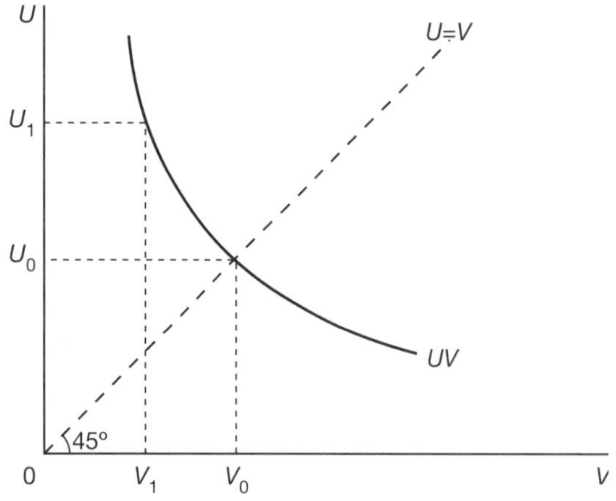

Fig 28.3 Demand-deficient and non-demand-deficient unemployment *UV* method

demand to the right of $U = V$, there are sufficient jobs available for all the unemployed. Below U_0 all unemployment can be regarded as structural or frictional, and can be further decomposed by considering how easily the unemployed can be matched with the available vacancies. While this approach appears both simple and intuitively attractive, the data on unemployment and vacancies for the UK in Figure 28.4 show that the *UV* relationship has not

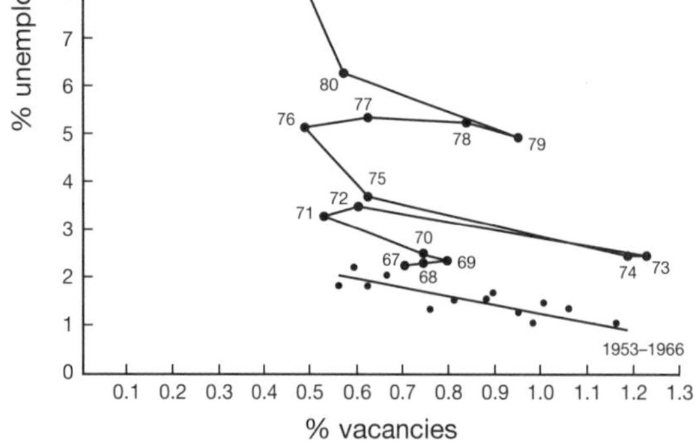

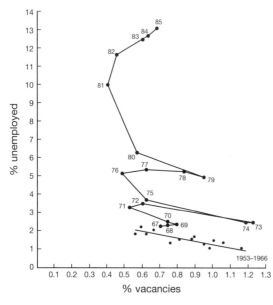

Fig 28.4 Registered unemployed (%) and notified vacancies (%): UK 1953–1985.
Source: Taylor (1986)

been stable over time. A sequence of upward shifts of the relationship occurred in the UK from the mid-1960s. The shift was particularly marked during 1976–1979 and again during 1981–1985. Indeed, the evidence for the 1980s suggests that an expansion of labour demand does not guarantee a reduction in unemployment in the way it did during the first two post-war decades. Some authors suggest that the outward movement of the *UV* curve has been the result of lower job search intensity by the unemployed.

4 Incidence of unemployment

More recent time series work explaining the incidence of unemployment has not entirely lost sight of the conceptual taxonomy outlined above. Certainly issues such as demand deficiency, structural mismatch and technological change are still reflected in the variables which appear in the models. In this section we illustrate this approach using the time series model of the UK economy by Layard and Nickell (1985), which attempts to provide an explanation for variations in the incidence of unemployment, which increased from 2 per cent in the late 1950s/early 1960s to around 13 per cent towards the middle of the 1980s. The model is based upon a strong theoretical framework, to which we cannot hope to do justice in this brief review. However, the heart of the model is a three-equation system which is broadly recursive in nature, explaining: (i) prices (as a mark-up over wages); (ii) wages (as a mark-up over prices); (iii) unemployment (or labour demand). The first two equations allow an exploration of the inflationary mechanism, and the solution for long-run equilibrium of the system of equations produces an estimate of the underlying natural rate of unemployment – see Chapter 29 for a discussion. Here we focus upon the main sources of unemployment.

The long-run solution to the employment equation in the model can be written as

$$\log E = \log K - 0.91 \log(w/p) + 0.32\sigma \qquad (1)$$

where $\log U = \log L - \log E$, and

$$\sigma = \log(p^*/\bar{p}) + 5.07(\mathrm{AD} + \mathrm{AD}_{-1}) + 1.27\mathrm{WT} \qquad (2)$$

The definition of the variables is given in Table 28.4. The way *K* enters equation (1) comes from an assumption about long-run neutrality (Layard and Nickell, 1985, p. 74). Real cost per unit of labour has the anticipated negative impact on labour demand

Table 28.4 Summary of variable definitions in the Layard and Nickell model

Notation	Definitions
E	Employees (males and females)
K	Gross capital stock at 1970 replacement cost
L	Labour force (i.e. employment plus unemployment)
w/p	Real product wage including employer labour taxes
σ	Deviations of aggregate demand from full utilization of resources
$p^*/\bar{p}$	UK international price competitiveness (world/domestic UK prices)
AD	Adjusted public sector deficit as proportion of potential GDP
WT	Deviation of world trade from trend
MM	Index of mismatch reflecting changes in employment structure
$p_m/\bar{p}$	Import to domestic output price
U_p	Union power, represented by the union/non-union mark-up
t_1	Employment taxes borne by firms
IPD	Incomes policy dummy
U	Male unemployed as a percentage of the employed plus unemployed

and aggregate demand has a positive effect. Equation (2) shows that aggregate demand is driven by UK price competitiveness, the state of world demand and the fiscal stance, represented by the strength of domestic government expenditure. Again other restrictions drive the functional form.

Without reporting the real wage equation in detail, it can be used to substitute out w/p from equation (1). Using $\log U = \log L - \log E$, we obtain

$$(U + 0.0637U) = \text{const} - 0.23\sigma + 0.26\text{MM} + 0.18\rho + 0.33(\upsilon \log p_m/\bar{p}) + 0.29\Delta(\upsilon \log p_m/\bar{p}) + 0.060\,U_p + 0.30t_1 - 0.017\text{IPD} \quad (3)$$

where the authors note that $\Delta(\log p_m/\bar{p})$ is retained even in the long run because of the persistence of its trend. The form of the equation is again explained in detail in the original paper. Note, however, that equation (3) now contains many variables that throw some light on the types of unemployment, causes of unemployment and policy issues.

Table 28.5 now sets out the implications for the causes of unemployment. This was undertaken by considering the contribution of each of the variables based upon their mean values in each of the sub-periods, before looking at the changes from one period to the next. Thus, the actual change in unemployment rate was 1.82 percentage points between 1956 and 1966 and 1967 and 1974, 3.01 percentage points between 1967 and 1974 and 1975 and 1979, compared with 7.00 percentage points between 1975 and 1979 and 1980 and 1983. The predicated changes were broadly in line (based on the second of three models reported) with 1.97, 3.45 and 5.72 percentage points. The changing sources of unemployment can now be seen from the interior of the table. While the replacement ratio was positive in the first column, it was very small and negative in the final two columns. The effects of unions were positive throughout, but not enormously important even in the early period (contributing 0.61 percentage points) and even smaller in the final column. Real import prices helped in the early and late periods, but they contributed 0.96 percentage points to the growth of unemployment in the interim. Mismatch played a small positive role at the beginning, which increased throughout the sample period. Demand factors are particularly interesting, because, while they were positive throughout, they became particularly important in the final period when, in effect, the economy moved into quite deep recession – giving support for the hypothesis of increasing demand-deficient unemployment at this time. Finally, the *UV* shift variables showed moderate increases in the level of the unemployment caused by lower search intensity and a higher degree of selectivity exercised by employers.

Table 28.5 Breakdown of the change in the male unemployment rate, 1956–1983

Periods	1956–1966 to 1967–1974	1967–1974 to 1975–1979	1975–1979 to 1980–1983
Benefit replacement ratio (ρ)	0.10	–0.02	–0.02
Unions (U_p)	0.61	0.61	0.40
Real import prices ($p_m/\bar{p}$)	–0.30	0.96	–0.71
Mismatch (MM)	0.19	0.24	0.58
Demand factors (σ)	0.47	0.67	4.49
UV curve shift (*s*)	0.90	0.99	0.98
Total	1.97	3.45	5.72
Actual change	1.82	3.01	7.00

Source: Layard and Nickell (1985).

5 Movements between economic states: transition models

The models that emphasize the transition between economic states refocus the analysis away from the 'stock' of unemployed in any given period, to the underlying flows. This turns out to be extremely important because, while stocks often appear to be stable from one period to the next, this can mask significant flows which largely offset one another – in other words, a large inflow may be counteracted by equivalent outflows. An important illustration of this is that the majority of unemployed are only in that state for a short period, flowing out within six months of entering. We return to this feature in a number of places below. We illustrate the idea of transition models using a study which relies on official time series data, based on administrative records of the numbers registering as unemployed and/or claiming benefit broken down by duration category (Berg and Ours, 1993). It should be added that these data are characterized by a number of problems, including: changes in the definition of unemployment and the stringency with which claimancy rules are applied; the lack of information about the characteristics of the unemployed (hence, giving rise to a major problem of unobserved heterogeneity); which economic state individuals enter on leaving unemployment.

Despite their problems, these data have been used in a comparison of unemployment dynamics and duration dependence in France, the Netherlands, and the UK (Berg and Ours, 1993). Their method attempts to allow for the heterogeneity of the unemployed implicitly by statistical methods, rather than explicitly. The approach uses a mixed proportional hazard (MPH) model, in which calendar time replaces the (unobserved) explanatory variables. The conditional probability that the individual leaves unemployment (i.e. the hazard rate) of duration *v* at time *t* can be written as,

$$\theta(v|t,X) \text{ s.t. } Pr(0 \leq \theta(v|t,X) \leq 1) = 1 \tag{4}$$

where *X* denotes the set of personal characteristics and other influences which impact on the hazard rate. The MPH specification is

$$\theta(v|t,X) = \Psi_1(v).\Psi_2(t)X \tag{5}$$

It is assumed that *X* does not depend on *t* (which, of course, is only a first approximation over the cycle). $\Psi_1(v)$ and $\Psi_2(t)$ represent the duration dependence and the time dependence of the exit rate out of unemployment. The distribution of *X* therefore denotes the distribution of unobserved heterogeneity.

As noted above, one of the main problems with the traditional time series of unemployment duration data concerns the lack of information about the heterogeneity of the unemployed in different duration categories. The authors attempt to avoid this by integrating out the unobserved *X*, which allows it to be replaced by its expected value $E_i(X_i) = \mu_i$ where $i = 1, \ldots, v$. This enables a reasonably straightforward ratio of hazard rates for the first two duration categories to be constructed.

$$\frac{\theta(1|t)}{\theta(0|t)} = \eta_1 \frac{1 - \theta(0|t-1)\,\gamma_1}{1 - \theta(0|t-1)} \tag{6}$$

where $\eta_1 = \Psi_1(1)/\Psi_1(0)$ and $\gamma_1 = \mu_2/\mu_1^2$. The expressions for subsequent duration categories are more complex.

The authors report empirical estimates based upon quarterly data from the end of the 1970s to the early

1990s. In summary, their results suggest the following. First, strong negative duration dependence amongst UK males (i.e. a decline in the exit rate as duration increases); the results for France indicate no strong duration dependence; those for the Netherlands gave an inverse 'U'-shaped duration dependence over the first three quarters. Second, with regard to unobserved heterogeneity, the French and Dutch results indicated a strong role for unobserved heterogeneity, but it did not appear to be statistically important for UK males. While we have used the Berg and Ours (1993) model to illustrate the use of time series duration data, there are clearly important points of debate regarding the approach (i.e. the assumptions underlying the MPH model and the failure to use what other, limited information may be available about the heterogeneity of the different duration groups – such as age in the UK). In the case of the UK, however, the results appear to confirm those of number of other studies including that of Jackman and Layard (1991), which finds strong negative duration dependence and weak evidence of unobserved heterogeneity.

6 Duration of unemployment

6.1 Key issues

The problem of long-term unemployment is made worse by the fact that the longer someone has been without work the harder it becomes to find a new job. In other words, the probability of finding employment declines with the duration of unemployment. This may result from a variety of factors. First, the 'heterogeneity effect' arises from the fact that individuals who enter unemployment vary in their skills, abilities, aptitude, etc., and those with the 'most desirable' qualities leave the register first. Second, the length of the spell of unemployment may itself affect the re-employment probability. This is often termed 'duration dependence'. Pure duration dependence effects, however, become intertwined with unobserved heterogeneity. This is partly caused by demand side factors, for example duration of unemployment is used as a screening device by employers; partly by the supply side, for example individuals' search activity falls away with the duration of search; and partly by a mixture of both, for example skills deteriorate when they are not used.

6.2 Longitudinal data

A proper empirical treatment of durational issues requires longitudinal data. Unemployment studies are often based upon a cohort (or panel) data set, retrospective 'work history' data, or some combination of the two. Examples of such a cohort might be a sample of individuals who enter unemployment during a particular month or reach the minimum school-leaving age during a particular year (i.e. the *Youth Cohort Study*). These individuals are then followed up at successive points in time to collect information about their work (event) histories, including their unemployment and employment experiences. Thus, insofar as some individuals move out of unemployment during the period covered by the various sweeps of the survey, cohort data can provide information about complete duration of unemployment spells, at least for a part of the sample. It is possible therefore to calculate the hazard rate (i.e. the probability of leaving unemployment) for individuals in different duration categories, conditional on age, health, qualifications, family commitments, etc.

Such data sets are often based on information of the type illustrated in Figure 28.5, which shows a random sample of individuals who flow onto the register at time $t = 0$ and are followed up n periods later. This may involve two 'sweeps' of the survey – one at

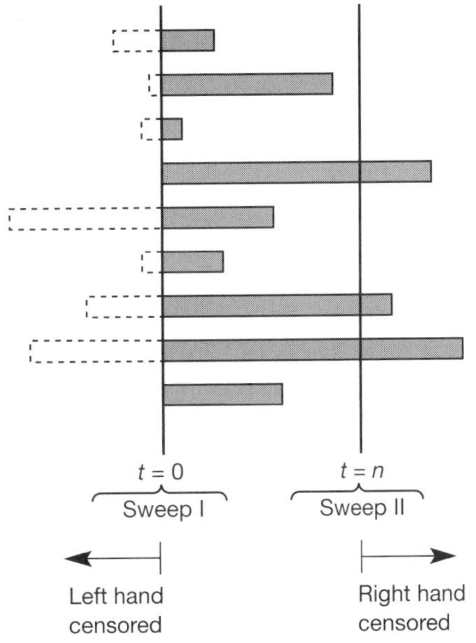

Fig 28.5 Cohort data: unemployment.

$t = 0$ and the second at $t = n$ (it might also be dealt with in a variety of other ways, such as the use of 'administrative' data from the benefit office at $t = 0$ and a single survey at $t = n$, collecting retrospective event history data). Those that return to employment (or change to some other state) are asked at what date this occurred. In general, the data are partially right hand censored, as shown by the group of unemployed with a spell longer than $t = n$. Keifer also notes that

> typically, duration, that is spell lengths, are the dependent variables under study, but it should be kept in mind that these durations are not spells in 'real time' unless the origin is the same for every spell. (Keifer, 1988, p. 650)

Thus, if the sample was drawn from those unemployed at time $t = 0$ (rather than new inflows), then the data are also left hand censored, and further information would have been sought (during the first sweep) about the date at which they became unemployed (see the dashed cases to the left of $t = 0$ in Figure 28.5. Survival techniques have been developed that, where necessary, handle both right and left hand censored data.

6.3 Survival analysis: duration of unemployment

Survival analysis is an extremely useful way of exploring questions about duration, including the length of spell of unemployment or job tenure (Keifer, 1988). Figure 28.6 outlines the cumulative probability distribution, with duration, T, on the horizontal axis and the probability of having left the unemployed stock, $F(t)$, on the vertical axis. We can write this as

$$F(t) = Pr(T < t) \tag{7}$$

Imagine, for example, that we observe a cohort of individuals that flow into unemployment at a given point in time. At the point they flow in, their duration is zero and the proportion having left unemployment, $F(t)$, is also zero. Over time, however, some flow out, leaving the proportion of survivors, $S(t)$. By implication, the survivor function can be written

$$S(t) = 1 - F(t) = Pr(T \geq t) \tag{8}$$

In other words, equation (7) shows the probability that the random variable T (the duration of spell) is less than some length of time t, and equation (8) gives the 'mirror image' probability that it will be greater than or equal to t.

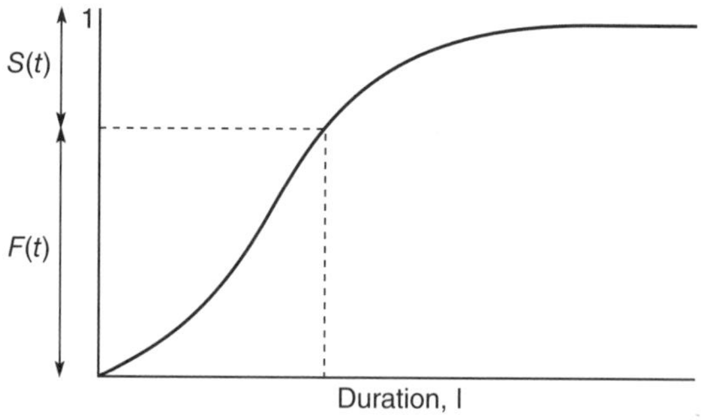

Fig 28.6 Cumulative probability distribution.

The corresponding density function is shown in Figure 28.7,

$$f(t) = dF(t)/dt \tag{9}$$

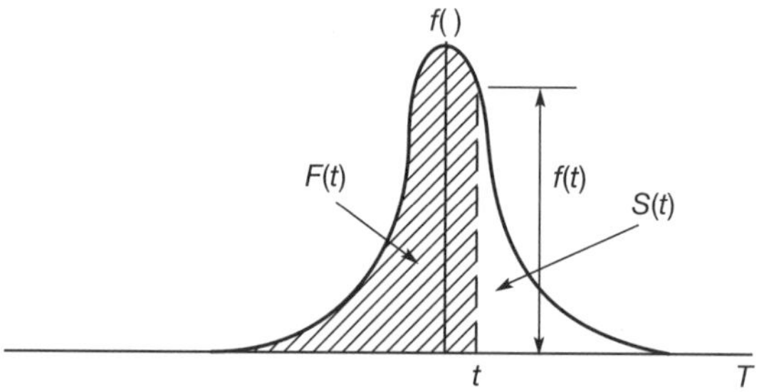

Fig 28.7 Probability density function.

which shows the proportion of the original cohort who leave at time t, conditional on having survived in unemployment up to that time. The 'hazard function' is written as

$$\lambda(t) = f(t)/S(t) \tag{10}$$

where $\lambda(t)$ is the rate at which spells will be completed at duration t, given they last until t (i.e. a conditional probability). Or, to put it another way, it is the proportion of those who survived up to that duration who leave within the period. It can be shown that the hazard function can also be written as

$$\lambda\,(t) = \frac{f(t)}{S(T)} = \frac{dF(t)/dt}{S(t)} = -\frac{dS(t)/dt}{S(t)} = \frac{-d\ln S(t)}{dt} \tag{11}$$

6.4 Duration dependence

The hazard function is a convenient way of defining duration dependence. Duration dependence is positive or negative at time t^* depending on whether the hazard rate (i.e. the probability of exiting) increases or decreases around t^*,

$$d\lambda(t)/dt \gtreqless 0 \text{ at } t = t^* \quad (12)$$

By implication, there is no duration dependence at t^* if $\lambda(t)$ is neither increasing nor decreasing at this point in time.

There appear to be two approaches amongst researchers, who are divided between: (i) specifying a priori the shape of the hazard function (i.e. exponential, Weibull, log-logistic, etc. – see Keifer, 1988, pp. 650–655); and (ii) those who prefer a general specification, which, according to Keifer (1988, p. 655), can contain 'everything and its square'. The exponential form can be written as

$$\lambda(t) = \gamma;\ d\lambda(t)/dt = 0 \quad (13)$$

and it can be seen that the hazard function is constant and reflects no duration dependence. The expected duration from this model is therefore $1/\gamma$. In the Weibull case,

$$\lambda(t) = \gamma\alpha t^{\alpha-1};\ d\lambda(t)/dt = \gamma\alpha(\alpha-1)t^{\alpha-2} \quad (14)$$

which contains the exponential as a special case, $\alpha = 1$. In general, therefore, the function can capture positive, $\alpha > 1$, negative, $\alpha < 1$, and no duration dependence, $\alpha = 1$. If $\alpha < 1$ the expected duration is greater than $1/\gamma$, and, if $\alpha > 1$ the expected duration is less than $1/\gamma$. Finally, the log-logistic form, can be written,

$$\lambda(t) = \frac{\gamma\alpha t^{\alpha-1}}{1 + t^{\alpha}\gamma};\ \frac{d\lambda(t)}{dt} \gtreqless 0 \text{ as } (\alpha - 1) \gtreqless \frac{\alpha\gamma t^{x}}{1 + t^{\alpha}\gamma} \quad (15)$$

and the hazard first rises with duration and then falls if $\alpha > 1$, but the hazard rate falls with duration if $\alpha \leq 1$.

6.5 Empirical results

Thus, we obtain the estimating equation, such as Lancaster's proportional hazard model, in which $\lambda(t)$ takes the Weibull form,

$$\lambda(t;Z) = \lambda(t)\,e^{Z\beta} = \alpha t^{\alpha-1} e^{Z'\beta} \quad (16)$$

and the results suggest that the re-employment probability $\lambda()$ is significantly related to age, unemployment, and the replacement ratio – see Table 28.6. The re-employment probability decreases with the length of time out of work, other things being equal. Further evidence concerning the role of unemployment benefit is given in Case Study 1.

A review of the empirical evidence from panel data sets is provided by Peders and Westergård-Nielsen (1993). After a number of reservations regarding the comparability of the results, they report that: (i) demographic factors have the same direction of influence as in the cross-sectional studies (a 'U'-shaped relationship between unemployment and age when the younger and oldest age groups are both included and a lower escape rate for younger and older workers); women tend to be worse off than men, particularly in their escape rate to a job; married men have shorter spells of unemployment than married women; children adversely affect the labour market position of women, particularly single mothers; there are negative effects of poor health and disability; (ii) higher levels of education generally improved employment prospects, although no clear evidence emerges about the potentially beneficial effects of training; (iii) no clear evidence about the direction of duration dependence (at least, the results differ between countries); (iv) US and UK studies tend to find significant negative effects of unemployment benefit on the escape rate from unemployment (particularly amongst short-term unemployment, less so amongst the long-term unemployed), but not in other European studies where the effects are generally insignificant; (v) post-unemployment wages tend to be lower than pre-unemployment and the evidence suggests that the reservation wage fails with duration.

Table 28.6 Summary of results from Lancaster's model

	Coefficient	Standard error
log AGE	–0.66	0.25
log UNEMP	–0.34	0.18
log REPL.RATIO	–0.41	0.21
α	0.77	0.09

7 Conclusions

This chapter has explored a key economic performance indicator – unemployment. The chapter has shown that even the economic costs of unemployment taken by themselves may be quite high, and these are likely to be only a proportion of the total

CASE STUDY 1 Benefits and duration

The effect of benefits on duration has been a major focus of attention by both economists and politicians. The political debate has surrounded whether high benefit levels have encouraged individuals to remain unemployed, acting as a cause of long-term unemployment. As Narendranathan and Stewart (1993, p. 361) point out, this decomposes into two dimensions: (i) how does the level of income an individual receives while unemployed relative to that in employment affect the probability of leaving employment; (ii) how does the impact of income while unemployed change as the length of spell increases? The second of these is therefore concerned with duration dependence in the benefit effect.

While a number of politicians, particularly those from the right wing, have tended to treat the continuation of unemployment benefit as a form of 'feather bedding', most research, however, has uncovered no such effect. Questionnaire surveys and interviews suggest that the unemployed become increasingly desperate to find work as duration rises, with the majority either willing to 'accept anything at all' or willing to do so 'within limits'. Econometric work reveals that, perhaps with the exception of certain minority groups (i.e. teenagers), the replacements ratio becomes less important and, eventually, insignificant, as a determinant of the hazard rate as the spell grows longer. As an overview, a period of about six months appears to provide the cut-off in terms of a significant role.

As we have noted in the main text, there is an obvious difficulty in disentangling the durational effects of benefits from those of other factors, such as unobserved heterogeneity. Narendranathan and Stewart (1993) take considerable care in investigating these effects applying a variety of statistical techniques that might improve on the traditional proportional hazard model. While the results differ with the form of the model and the estimation technique, the general pattern associated with the coefficient on the benefit variable is both largely consistent and confirms the findings of other studies. Table 28.7 sets out the estimated exit probabilities with respect to unemployment income based upon three alternative models. The general decline in the parameter estimates with duration is apparent in all three models. Only the coefficients up to 12 weeks are significantly different from zero. Where specific allowance is made for omitted heterogeneity the conditional probability of leaving remains significant up to about the 20th week.

Table 28.7 Estimated elasticities of exit probability with respect to unemployment income

Weeks	Extreme value model	Probit model	Logit model
4	–1.210	–1.692	–1.516
5	–0.825	–1.049	–0.937
6	–0.549	–0.625	–0.572
7	–0.347	–0.336	–0.344
8	–0.348	–0.424	–0.362
9	–0.311	–0.372	–0.327
10	–0.521	–0.643	–0.548
11	–0.392	–0.472	–0.432
12	–0.573	–0.708	–0.604
13	0.422	–0.514	0.448
14	–0.016	–0.036	–0.018
15	–0.111	–0.139	–0.117
16	–0.296	–0.341	–0.308

Sources: Narendranathan and Stewart (1993); see also Atkinson and Micklewright (1991). Elasticities calculated at the sample exit proportions

private costs which include psychological and health effects. The social costs may be even greater. The chapter then went on to explore the different types and sources of unemployment. We reported on the results of a detailed time series model of the incidence of unemployment, showing the relative importance of factors such as trade unions, demand deficiency, etc., which varied from period to period. The chapter then turned to the question of transitions from unemployment and, in particular, the influences on the duration of unemployment. This is interesting because long-duration unemployment tends to be a persistent problem associated with high private and social costs. In the next chapter, we extend this analysis to explore the links between unemployment, inflation, unit costs and economic growth.

References

Atkinson, A. and J. Micklewright (1991). 'Unemployment Compensation and Labour Market Transitions: a Critical Review'. *Journal of Economic Literature*. Vol. 29, December, pp. 1679–1727.

Berg, G.J. and J.V. Ours (1993). 'Unemployment Dynamics and Duration Dependence'. Proceedings of Fifth EALE Annual Conference, September 30 – October 3 (subsequently published in *Economic Journal*).

Beveridge, W.H. (1944). *Full Employment in a Free Society*. London: George Allen & Unwin.

Clark, R., D. Leslie and E. Symons (1994). 'The Costs of Recession'. *Economic Journal*. 104, 433, January, 20–36.

Dow, J.C.R. and L.A. Dicks-Mireaux (1958). 'The Excess Demand for Labour: A Study of Conditions in Great Britain'. *Oxford Economic Papers*. 10, 1–33.

Jackman, R. and R. Layard (1991). 'Does Long-Term Unemployment Reduce a Person's Chance of Getting a Job?'. *Economica*. 58, 93–106.

Junanker, R. (1989). 'Unemployment in the European Community: Counting the Costs'. In J. Muysken and C. de Neubourg (eds). *Unemployment in Europe*. London: Macmillan, 269–280.

Keifer, N. M. (1988). 'Economic Duration Data and Hazard Functions'. *Journal of Economic Literature*. Vol. 26, June, 646-679.

Layard, R. and S. Nickell (1985). 'The Causes of British Unemployment'. *National Institute Economic Review*. February, 62–85.

Lipsey, R.G. (1965). 'Structural and Deficient-Demand Unemployment Reconsidered'. In A.M. Ross (ed.) *Employment Policy and the Labour Market*. University of California Press.

Lucas, R.E. (1987). *Models of Business Cycles*. Oxford. Basil Blackwell.

Narendranathan, W. and M. Stewart (1993). 'How Does the Benefit Effect Vary as Unemployment Spells Lengthen?'. *Journal of Applied Economics*. 8, 361–381.

Okun, A. (1981). *Prices and Quantities*. Oxford: Basil Blackwell.

Pedersen, P.J. and N. Westergård-Nielsen (1993). 'Unemployment: A Review of the Evidence from Panel Data'. Session II. Unemployment Duration. Proceedings of the EALE Conference, University of Limburg, Holland.

Pissarides, C.A.(1990). *Equilibrium Unemployment Theory*. Oxford: Blackwell.

Shackleton, J.R. (1985). 'Is the Labour Market Inflexible?' *Royal Bank of Scotland Review*, 147, September, 27–41.

Topel, R.(1993). 'What Have We Learned from Empirical Studies of Unemployment and Turnover?' *American Economics Association. Papers and Proceedings*. 83, 2, 110–115.

CHAPTER 29 Economic performance and the labour market

1 Introduction

This chapter further extends the discussion of labour market outcomes. It brings together a number of other topics which link the labour market with overall economic performance, including wage and price inflation, labour market imbalances (unemployment and skill shortages), productivity and growth. We provided some of the background statistical evidence in Chapter 27. The present chapter focuses on a more analytical treatment of these measures of economic performance.

The first issue therefore concerns the way in which labour market influences spill over into changes in wages and incomes and, thereby, into price inflation. Wages are, after all, a significant proportion of total costs in most areas of industry and commerce. Thus, increases in wage rates can have an important impact on producer costs and prices. Despite its lack of current fashion, we review the Phillips curve which suggests a negative relationship between the rate of change in wages and the level of unemployment. One of the earliest explanations for this relationship was that unemployment was a proxy for the tightness of the labour market, although other, more institutional rationales have also been offered. In the absence of instantaneously clearing labour markets, it seems intuitively plausible that periods of relative surplus might have a depressing effect on wages and prices, and periods of skill shortages will tend to be inflationary. In practice, as we will show, the picture is more complex than this; although, on balance, the evidence provides some support for such a mechanism in the short run, the existence of a long-run trade-off of this type has been the subject of intense debate.

The amount of cost inflation that a firm (or the economy as a whole) can accommodate depends crucially on what is happening to factor productivity. Increased wage rates may be partly offset by factor substitution away from labour, greater worker effort and, in the longer term, induced technological change. In principle, higher wage rates can be accommodated without any inflationary pressure if labour productivity rises by an amount sufficient to compensate. In addition, higher wages may not all be passed on to the consumer in the form of higher prices if, for example, firms accept lower profit margins. However, as we clearly demonstrated in Chapter 27 the UK has singularly failed to translate increased labour productivity into cost and price improvements throughout much of the post-war period. Thus, the UK's competitive position has tended to deteriorate relative to its main industrial competitors, making it heavily reliant on the depreciation of sterling and making its exit from the ERM an almost foregone conclusion. It seems that a long-term improvement to the competitiveness of the UK economy depends crucially not only on sustained productivity growth, but also on the translation of that improvement into relative cost advantage. Here we have come full circle, because such improvements in turn depend on the quality of the UK's workforce and, thereby, on the rate of product and process technological change.

2 Productivity, cost and prices

2.1 Framework for productivity growth

This section demonstrates the close linkages between productivity, costs and inflation. The relationships here are central to understanding the linkages between the labour and product markets which underpin the comparative economic performance outlined in Chapter 27. The main features can be shown using an accounting framework, in which,

$$pY = w_1X_1 + w_2X_2 + \Pi \tag{1}$$

where: p is product price; Y is real output; X_1 and X_2 are the physical amounts of two factors used in production; w_1 and w_2 are the corresponding factor prices; Π is total profit. The product demand curve is downward sloping if there is some degree of monopoly power, $\mathbf{p} = \mathbf{p}(Y)$, and the rate of change of the left hand side of equation (1) can be written as

$$\frac{1}{pY}\frac{\mathrm{d}(pY)}{\mathrm{d}t} = \left(1 + \frac{1}{\xi_p}\right)\left(\frac{1}{Y}\frac{\mathrm{d}Y}{\mathrm{d}t} + \frac{1}{p}\frac{\mathrm{d}p}{\mathrm{d}t}\right) \tag{2}$$

where $\xi_p = (\partial p/\partial Y)(Y/p)$ is a measure of the own-price elasticity of demand (for simplicity, we assume ξ_p is constant). The corresponding expression for the right hand side appears as

$$\frac{1}{pY}\frac{\mathrm{d}(w_1X_1 + w_2X_2 + \Pi)}{\mathrm{d}t} = \frac{w_1X_1}{pY}\left(\frac{1}{w_1}\frac{\mathrm{d}w_1}{\mathrm{d}t} + \frac{1}{X_1}\frac{\mathrm{d}X_1}{\mathrm{d}t}\right)$$
$$+ \frac{w_2X_2}{pY}\left(\frac{1}{w_2}\frac{\mathrm{d}w_2}{\mathrm{d}t} + \frac{1}{X_2}\frac{\mathrm{d}X_2}{\mathrm{d}t}\right) + \frac{\Pi}{pY}\left(\frac{1}{\Pi}\frac{\mathrm{d}\Pi}{\mathrm{d}t}\right) \tag{3}$$

Thus, setting equation (2) equal to (3) and rearranging, we obtain

$$\left(\frac{\Pi}{pY}\right)\left(\frac{1}{\Pi}\frac{\mathrm{d}\Pi}{\mathrm{d}t}\right) = \sum_{i=1}^{2}\left(\frac{w_iX_i}{pY}\right)\left\{\left(\frac{1}{p}\frac{\mathrm{d}p}{\mathrm{d}t} - \frac{1}{w_i}\frac{\mathrm{d}w_i}{\mathrm{d}t}\right) + \left[\left(1 + \frac{1}{\xi_p}\right)\frac{1}{Y}\frac{\mathrm{d}Y}{\mathrm{d}t} - \frac{1}{X_i}\frac{\mathrm{d}X_i}{\mathrm{d}t}\right]\right\} + \left(\frac{\Pi}{pY}\right)\left[\frac{1}{p}\frac{\mathrm{d}p}{\mathrm{d}t} + \left(1 + \frac{1}{\xi_p}\right)\frac{1}{Y}\frac{\mathrm{d}Y}{\mathrm{d}t}\right] \tag{4}$$

and examination of equation (4) shows that the rate of change in profit is driven by: (i) a relative price component for each factor

$$\left(\frac{1}{p}\frac{\mathrm{d}p}{\mathrm{d}t} - \frac{1}{w_i}\frac{\mathrm{d}w_i}{\mathrm{d}t}\right)$$

such that, if product price rises more quickly than factor prices, this has a positive impact on profitability; (ii) a real component

$$\left[\left(1 + \frac{1}{\xi_p}\right)\frac{1}{Y}\frac{\mathrm{d}Y}{\mathrm{d}t} - \frac{1}{X_i}\frac{\mathrm{d}X_i}{\mathrm{d}t}\right]$$

such that increases in output which outstrip those of inputs used in production give rise to higher productivity and profits; (iii) the final term requires interpreting with some care as, in general, p and Y are not independent (and, in general, ξ_p is not constant), but, where the firm is able to raise prices at a rate that is not matched by proportional decreases in demand and output, then profitability rises.

We can think of traditional measures of productivity change as being the difference between the rate of growth in profits with and without changes in real input per unit of output (see Chapter 10):

$$\frac{1}{A}\frac{\mathrm{d}A}{\mathrm{d}t} = \frac{\Pi}{pY}\left(\frac{1}{\Pi}\frac{\mathrm{d}\Pi}{\mathrm{d}t} - \frac{1}{\Pi}\frac{\mathrm{d}\Pi'}{\mathrm{d}t}\right) = \sum_{i=1}^{n}\frac{w_iX_i}{pY}\left[\left(1 + \frac{1}{\xi_p}\right)\frac{1}{Y}\frac{\mathrm{d}Y}{\mathrm{d}t} - \frac{1}{X_i}\frac{\mathrm{d}X_i}{\mathrm{d}t}\right] \tag{5}$$

It is possible to derive an almost identical expression based upon a Cobb–Douglas production function, where $(1/A)(\mathrm{d}A/\mathrm{d}t)$ denotes total factor productivity growth. The equation can be simplified in the normal manner found in the productivity and growth accounting literatures. By assuming perfect competition in the product market, then $\xi_p = -\infty$ and $(1 + 1/\xi_p) = 1$ and we derive the standard result that the rate of productivity growth is equal to the difference in the rate of growth between output and input(s). At first sight the term in profits looks peculiar, but we can think of Π/pY as normal profits, and the first term in brackets would be zero under perfect competition; but the second term reflects the negative impact on the profits of the competitive firm if it fails to adopt the factor-saving change.

Note, however, that equation (4) has more to say than this. If firms, for example, have no real control over wages, their natural instinct is to put up prices (or increase labour productivity), in order to maintain profit performance. While this clearly has macroeconomic consequences, a failure to do so may have implications for firm survival and for investment in dynamic activities.

2.2 Multi-factor productivity and total factor growth

The general picture, at least of manufacturing therefore, is one of rapid post-war productivity growth, particularly in the 1960s and 1980s. However, as equation (4) demonstrates, an analysis based upon labour productivity alone can be misleading as other forces are at work, including changes in other factor productivities. The point we make here is that higher labour productivity may be the result of shifts around the production isoquant, associated with lower productivity of other factors. Thus, insofar as higher labour productivity involves, say, greater investment, firms' costs are not reduced as much as first appears. In a three-factor, Cobb–Douglas production function the change in output can be written as

$$\frac{1}{Y}\frac{dY}{dt} = \frac{1}{A}\frac{dA}{dt} + \alpha\frac{1}{K}\frac{dK}{dt} + \beta\frac{1}{E}\cdot\frac{dE}{dt} + \gamma\frac{1}{F}\frac{dF}{dt} \qquad (6)$$

where: K is capital; E is employment; and F raw materials, fuels and intermediate goods; by implication, A is the growth in output not accounted for by changes in the volume of factor inputs. In fact equation (6) is a three-input version of equation (5); where factor prices (w_i) are constant and reflect marginal productivities, there is perfect competition and constant returns (i.e. factor remunerations completely account for total revenue).

We noted in Chapter 27 that, while the UK appeared to have significant rates of labour productivity growth (at least in certain sectors, such as manufacturing), this may have been the result of a substitution towards other factors, and not reflected by commensurate falls in unit costs. The importance of this for the UK is illustrated in a paper by Mahoney and Oulten (1990), which estimated productivity growth rates for around 130 individual sectors in UK manufacturing for the period from 1954 to 1986. The authors use a gross output formulation of the production function that explicitly includes raw material and intermediate inputs, F. The production function is log-linear and perfect competition is assumed. The work has been carefully undertaken to allow for different types of labour and hours worked, and also takes considerable care over estimates of the capital inputs.

Table 29.1 provides a summary of the results, giving averages across the sectors. The estimated labour productivity growth in manufacturing of 3 per cent during the 1980s is similar to figures reported by other authors. The well-documented productivity slowdown of the 1970s is clear. In addition, however, the figures demonstrate the considerable growth in raw materials and intermediate inputs per employee. The data can be used to show that material inputs have been growing faster than output throughout the period, reflecting changes in sub-contracting patterns in UK industry and the movement towards a more component-assembly type of production, linked to the internationalization of trade. The principal implication is that the growth in output per head has been partly driven by the strong susbstitution towards capital and intermediate inputs. While there are probably strong economic grounds for such substitution, the potential gains from the growth of labour productivity are to some extent offset by the increased use of other inputs.

Table 29.1 Productivity growth in UK manufacturing (per cent per annum)

Period	*Y/L*	*K/L*	*F/L*
1963–1968	5.04	5.22	5.70
1968–1973	4.89	5.09	5.60
1973–1979	1.97	4.38	4.41
1979–1986	3.91	5.88	4.89

Source: Mahoney and Oulton (1990)

Table 29.2 reviews the data in a slightly different form, indicating three main sources of labour productivity growth reported by Mahoney and Oulton (1990). The first involves a substitution away from labour and towards capital, which accounts for less than one percentage point of the growth of labour productivity in every sub-period. The second concerns the growth of raw materials and intermediate inputs, which account for the bulk of the improvement, of the order of 2.9 percentage points out of 3.9 per cent growth in gross output per employee in the period 1979 to 1986. The residual effect of technological change and other factors not accounted for explicitly above is quite large in the period 1963 1973, but, on balance, negative in the subsequent period taken as a whole. Again the main conclusion is that the growth in UK output per head has been associated with strong substitution towards capital and intermediate inputs, implying that some of the potential gains from the growth of labour productivity are offset by the increased use of other inputs.

Lynde and Richmond (1993) adopt a similar approach, but based on a net output measure (which, by definition, does not allow them to look at the role

Table 29.2 Sources of labour productivity growth (per cent per annum)

Period	Growth of *Y/L*	Due to growth of:		
		K/L	*F/L*	Residual
1963–1968	5.04	0.87	3.14	1.03
1968–1973	4.89	0.84	2.83	1.21
1973–1979	1.97	0.63	2.59	–1.25
1979–1986	3.91	0.79	2.92	0.20

Notes: UK manufacturing sector, based on cross-industry averages.
Source: Mahoney and Oulton (1990)

of raw materials and intermediate goods). Table 29.3 presents data on labour productivity growth rates and the estimated contributions of private, *PK*, and public capital, *GK*. In addition, they attempt to decompose the residual contributions. The estimates for the 1980s show that the major part of the growth in labour productivity can be attributed to scale economies, changes in raw material prices (relative to the price of output) and technological change, *B*. Increases in public and private capital per employee do not seem particularly important. However, material and intermediate input prices (relative to output prices) fell throughout the 1980s at an annual average rate of 2.5 per cent, with a significant impact on their double deflated value-added measure. The residual, *B*, is still the major determinant of labour productivity growth over the period from 1966 to 1972 (which, in terms of rates of growth of labour productivity, is similar to the 1980s), although imperfect competition had a greater negative effect in this period and public capital had a positive rather than negative effect. Again material prices (relative to output) fell between 1966 and 1972 at a faster rate than during the 1980s. Thus, there is a significant difference between the 1970s and the other two periods because, in the former, material prices (relative to output prices) rose, whereas, in the latter two periods, they fell.

This suggests that we should obtain a clearer picture of the effects on improved competitiveness from changes in total factor productivity than from partial measures, where total input is defined as a weighted total of labour, capital, etc., and its rate of change is shown by $(1/A)(\mathrm{d}A/\mathrm{d}t)$ in equations (5) and (6). Table 29.4 presents estimates reported in Crafts (1992). Again, these results are indicative of the importance

Table 29.3 Average annual rates of manufacturing productivity growth 1966–1990 (per cent per annum)

	Period:		
	1966II–1972IV	1973I–1979IV	1980I–1990II
Growth rate of *Y*/*L*	3.86	1.25	3.97
Contribution of:			
PK/*L*	0.52	0.34	0.74
GK/*L*	0.60	0.27	–0.13
A	–1.91	–0.47	–0.36
B	4.65	1.11	3.72

Notes: *A* is a partial accounting for imperfect competition, *B* is the rest of the 'residual'
Source: Lynde and Richmond (1993).

of factor susbstitution away from labour. Thus, cost reductions are muted by the extent to which physical labour savings are offset by increases in consumption for other factor inputs at going input prices. In addition, clearly, the effect on unit costs is going to depend in what happens to factor prices themselves.

Table 29.4 Rate of growth of total factor productivity (per cent per annum)

Period	Estimate	Period	Estimate
1913–1950	0.35	1960–1973	2.2
1950–1973	1.27	1973–1979	0.5
1973–1987	0.82	1979–1988	1.9

Source: Crafts (1992), based on Maddison (1991) and Kendrick (1990)

3 Inflation and the labour market

3.1 Wage costs and inflation

Labour costs can play a central role in determining both the level and rate of change of prices. The pattern over the period from 1989 was presented in Chapter 27. In traditional classical and neoclassical theory full employment was assured by equilibrating market forces and inflation was essentially a monetary phenomenon. Confronted with evidence of large-scale unemployment Keynesian economists postulated that there could be substantial demand-deficient unemployment. Against this background, Phillips' (1958) empirical investigation of the relationship between wage inflation and unemployment gave rise to the view that the level of unemployment could be reduced by demand management, although there may be inflationary consequences.

Phillips used UK data for the period 1861 to 1957 to demonstrate a non-linear relationship between the rate of change of money wage rates, $\dot{w}$, and the rate of unemployment, *U*, of the type shown in Figure 29.1. This relationship suggested a trade-off between $\dot{w}$ and *U*, such that, if the rate of productivity growth was equal to 2 per cent, an equal rate of wage inflation was consistent with zero price inflation. This position could be achieved by manipulating unemployment to the appropriate level, which, according to the Phillips curve, was of the order of $2\frac{1}{2}$ per cent. At lower levels of unemployment price inflation

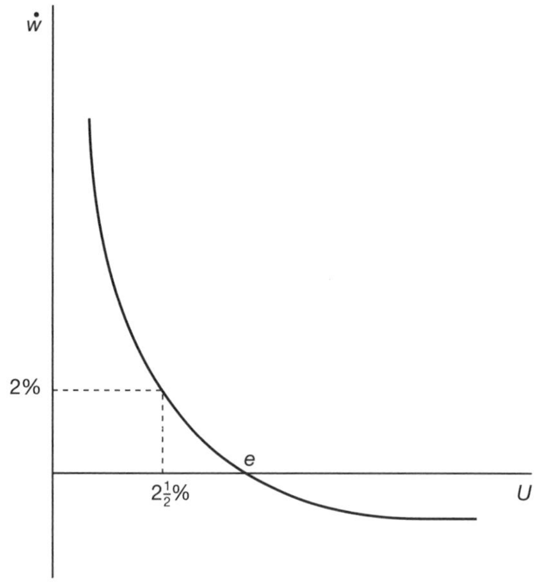

Fig 29.1 Phillips curve.

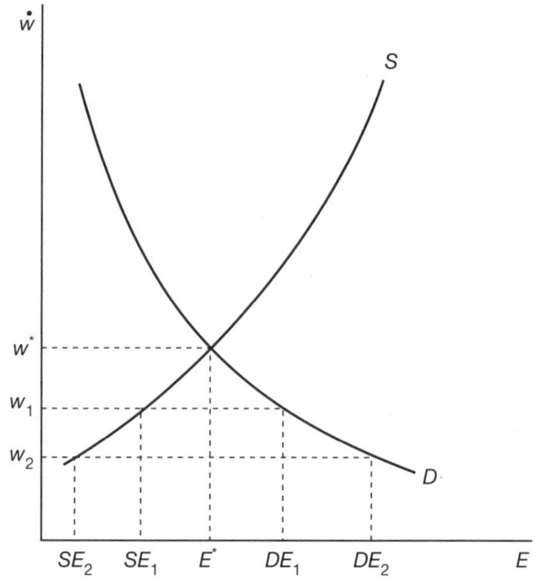

Fig 29.2 Excess demand and the wage rate.

would occur. Thus, we can think of this as a 'natural rate' of unemployment.

It should be said that, in the context of the Phillips curve literature, however, it is more appropriate to refer to the 'non-accelerating inflation rate of unemployment' (NAIRU) than to the 'natural rate'. The concept of the natural rate is sometimes considered to be associated with Walrasian equilibrium and thus has strong neoclassical underpinnings. The NAIRU, however, is simply that rate which is consistent with a stable rate of inflation. Nevertheless, it can be seen that there are close links between the Phillips curve literature (and its derivatives) and the unemployment literature.

3.2 Excess demand explanation

A theoretical explanation for this relationship was developed by Lipsey (1960) in which the rate of change of wages, $\dot{w}$, was argued to be a function of the level of excess demand for labour. This assumes that, where excess demand exists in the labour market, wages increase. Figure 29.2 shows that, at the wage rate w_1, excess demand for labour $(DE_1 - SE_1)/SE_1$ exists and wages increase towards w^*. At wage rate w_2 excess demand is even greater $(DE_2 - SE_2)/SE_2$, and wages have a tendency to increase towards their equilibrium value by an even greater proportion. Thus, the greater is the excess demand for labour, the faster money wages adjust upwards,

$$\dot{w} = f\left(\frac{DE - SE}{SE}\right) \tag{7}$$

Thus at a level of employment E^* in Figure 29.2, unemployment is purely 'frictional', resulting from movement between jobs (corresponding with point e in Figure 29.1). At wage rates below w^* excess demand for labour is higher and movement between jobs is quicker, resulting in lower unemployment. However, it is impossible that it could be reduced below zero, so that excess demand approaches infinity as U approaches zero. At wage rates above w^*, there is excess supply and unemployment is higher. Thus, the relationship between excess demand and unemployment is written as

$$U = g\left(\frac{DE - SE}{SE}\right) \tag{8}$$

and substitution of equation (8) into (7) produces a relationship between $\dot{w}$ and U essentially the same as the Phillips curve.

While the shape of the excess demand/unemployment relationship is crucial in determining the shape of the Phillips curve, we should perhaps say a few more words about equation (7), which represents the wage adjustment curve. Keynesian economists would argue that different rates of adjustment apply depending on the point of the business cycle: with a faster rate of wage adjustment under conditions of excess demand and a slower rate under excess supply (in the extreme, with no downward money wage movement). In the case of a homogeneous aggregate labour market, this simply means that the Phillips curve in Figure 29.1 becomes even more shallowly sloped to the right of point *e*. This asymmetry between downward and upward flexibility of wages is an important feature is the generation of inflationary spirals.

Where we are dealing with an aggregate of a set of heterogeneous labour markets, the existence of different rates of upward and downward wage adjustment has implications for the position of the curve itself even if, on balance, excess supply of labour in one set of markets is equal to excess demand in the remaining markets (Barro and Grossman, 1975). In this case, the more rapid rate of wage increase in the markets with excess demand outweighs wage decreases in the markets with excess supply. This implies that a rate of wage change equal to zero in the economy as a whole occurs at a slightly lower level of aggregate demand than in the homogeneous market case. In other words, the Phillips curve is essentially the same shape, but lies somewhat further to the right. It can be shown that the asymmetric wage response in heterogeneous labour markets generates counter-clockwise movements about the aggregate Phillips curve which correspond to the empirical observations of Phillips.

3.3 Bargaining and union explanations

An alternative view of the underpinnings of the Phillips curve is that it reflects the relative power of workers and firms such as the models of the Phillips curve based upon Johnston's bargaining model. These suggest that the rate of change of real wages are related to the: (i) rate of change of the employer's estimate of the union's real claim; (ii) real profit per employee; (iii) capital/labour ratio (which determines the equilibrium real wage); (iv) union militancy; and (v) level of unemployment, U. Thus, the empirical work in this area has increasingly focused on the role of unions in pushing up wages and stimulating inflation.

The original Phillips relationship suggested that the government could choose a point along a stable trade-off between inflation and unemployment. In the late 1960s and early 1970s, however, observations relating to $\dot{w}$ and U were seen to be lying further and further away from the origin. One explanation was that trade unions were showing increasing militancy and using their bargaining power to push up wages faster than they would otherwise go. In an economy where some workers are unionized and others are not, the general level of wages can be considered as a weighted average of union and non-union wages:

$$w = \alpha w_1 + (1 - \alpha)w_2;\ 0 < \alpha < 1 \qquad (9)$$

where: w, w_1 and w_2 are the overall average, the union and the non-union wage rates respectively; and α is the proportion of the labour force earning union wages $0 \leq \alpha \leq 1$. If the union/non-union differential equals m then

$$w_1 = w_2(1 + m) \qquad (10)$$

where $m \geq 0$. Substituting equation (10) into (9) and rearranging gives

$$w = w_2(1 + \alpha m) \qquad (11)$$

The implications for wage inflation are obtained by differentiating equation (11) with respect to time,

$$\dot{w} = \dot{w}_2 + \frac{m}{(1 + \alpha m)}\frac{d\alpha}{dt} + \frac{\alpha}{(1 + \alpha m)}\frac{dm}{dt} \qquad (12)$$

where the dot over a variable indicates a rate of change over time. Equation (12) suggests that there are at least three channels by which the unions influence wage inflation: $dm/dt > 0$, implies the union/non-union differential is increasing; $d\alpha/dt > 0$ means the percentage of the labour force receiving union wages is increasing; the union may cause $\dot{w}_2 > 0$ if the spillover effect is positive, resulting in the non-union wage increasing over time.

Various studies have focused on one or more aspects of equation (12). One of the best known and most controversial was by Hines (1964) who argued that 'trade union pushfulness' could be proxied by the rate of change of unionization, $\dot{T}U$. This variable is basically a proxy for $d\alpha/dt$, above. However, the argument was not that if $\dot{T}U > 0$ then more people would be paid the union wage (thus increasing the average level of wages), but that

> when unions are being aggressive they simultaneously increase their membership and bid up the wage rate. When a union puts in a wage claim it seeks immediately before and during the period of negotiation to increase its bargaining power by increasing the proportion of the labour force over which it has direct control. (Hines, 1964)

Thus, the rate of unionization, $\dot{T}U$, is a measure of 'trade union pushfulness' and Hines regressed $\dot{w}$ against $\dot{T}U$ using UK data for three sub-periods: 1895–1912; 1921–1938; and 1949–1961. He found a particularly strong correlation for the inter-war period and the coefficient on $\dot{T}U$ was highly significant for both the inter-war and the post-Second-World-War periods. Given the subject matter and the apparent strength of the results, it is not surprising that Hines' study gave rise to a considerable amount of interest and controversy. However, there was increasing criticism of the methodology and, in particular, the use of $\dot{T}U$ as a proxy for trade union pushfulness (Purdy and Zis, 1974).

Ashenfelter (1978) in the USA and Mulvey and Gregory (1977) in the UK estimated the combined effect of the increase in union/non-union differential and the increase in union density on average wages. Mulvey and Gregory claim also to have taken into account the spillover effect because their data are based on union wage coverage rather than unionization. Ashenfelter estimated the union impact (excluding the spillover effect) on wages in the USA as a 1.2 per cent increase between 1967 and 1973 out of a total wage inflation of 44 per cent. Mulvey and Gregory suggested an effect of 9.9 per cent out of a total wage inflation of 70 per cent, in the same time period. Mulvey and Gregory's estimates could reasonably be regarded as the total impact of unions on wages if there was no spillover effect onto the wages of 'uncovered' workers. The authors therefore came to the conclusion that trade unions could not be regarded as a major cause of inflation.

More recent estimates provided by Layard and Nickell (1985) also use the union mark-up as a measure of union power in the explanation of average wages. The authors find a positive role in both the short-run price and wage equations, as well as the long-run wage/price mark-up equation. The long-run coefficient suggests that a 1 per cent increase in the union/non-union mark-up produces a 0.07 per cent rise in the real wage.

On balance these results suggest that, if unions play a significant role, it works through a large spillover effect onto uncovered workers. It is difficult to observe the magnitude of such an effect, but if it exists, there should be a significant correlation between the rate of change of wages of covered and of uncovered workers. While such a test has not been undertaken for covered and uncovered workers, Flanagan found no significant influence of union wages on non-union wages in a study of US manufacturing covering the period 1969-1975. Mulvey (1978) pointed out that since the union/non-union differential based on coverage statistics as estimated by Layard and others varied between 15 per cent and 36 per cent in the period 1961–1975, it would appear that union and non-union wages have not changed in close harmony over time. The average mark-ups reported in Layard *et al.* (1991) vary from 0.15 in 1956–1959 to 0.32 in 1980–1984. However, such arguments are based on very indirect evidence which cannot be regarded as very satisfactory. Consequently, while the literature about trade unions and wage inflation based on the manipulation of identities has made an important contribution to the debate, it would be wrong to assume the issue is resolved.

It might be added that there is another way in which trade unions can affect the level of real wages which is picked up by such analysis. We have noted that an increase in union wages might be expected to lead to a certain amount of unemployment of union labour (and even possibly of non-union labour depending on the nature of the threat effect). If, however, the government places a high priority on keeping unemployment down and uses demand management to maintain employment levels, the effect of unions on wages may not lead to the unemployment that would result without government intervention. If trade unions are confident about the authorities reacting in this way they could formulate wage demands with relatively little concern about employment consequences. The resultant expansion of demand by the government fuels the inflation and facilitates faster wage increases than would otherwise result. While government compliance is required, it might be naïve to assert that under such circumstances the government is the sole cause of inflation, with trade unions not affecting the process. UK experience in the 1960s and earlier 1970s can be viewed in this light, although not in more recent years, when governments have been less willing to comply and show a greater concern for controlling demand by use of monetary policy.

3.4 Expectations augmented Phillips curve and the NAIRU

An alternative approach to the explanation of increasing levels of wage inflation associated with given levels of unemployment can be traced to the 'expectations augmented Phillips curve'. Here, the supply of and demand for labour are a function of real wages, not money wages, in keeping with the neoclassical model. Equation (13) shows the revised expression, where $\dot{W}$ is the rate of change in real wages:

$$\dot{W} = h(U) \quad (13)$$

However, the rate of change of real wages is equal to the rate of change of money wages minus the rate of inflation, $\dot{W} = \dot{w} - \dot{p}$,

$$\dot{w} = h(U) + \dot{p} \quad (14)$$

Two further modifications to the equation are required. First, wage claims are generally decided in advance, at a time when the rate of inflation is not known. The wage change therefore depends on the expected rate of inflation, $\dot{p}_e$, rather than $\dot{p}$. Second, there is a question mark over the extent to which wages adjust to changes in the rate of inflation. This can be accommodated by including a parameter, γ, on the price term, $0 \le \gamma \le 1$.

$$\dot{w} = k(U, \dot{p}_e) = m(U) + \gamma \dot{p}_e \quad (15)$$

where $\gamma = 0$ is the case of complete money illusion and $\gamma = 1$ is the opposite extreme of no money illusion. For the moment, we continue on the assumption of $\gamma = 1$, and the wage increase that clears the labour market depends upon what the price level is expected to be.

Figure 29.3 illustrates the implications for the Phillips curve. Now, there is one Phillips curve for each expected inflation rate. If $\dot{p}_e = 0$, and the rate of growth productivity of labour is 2 per cent, then, according to Friedman (1968), U_N is the natural level of unemployment. Only at the natural level of unemployment are expected price increases realized and the labour market in equilibrium. If the government attempts to reduce unemployment to U_1, as long as $\dot{p}_e = 0$, in the short run, some extra workers will be employed who expect the 4 per cent increase in money wages to give them 4 per cent higher real wages. However, with only 2 per cent productivity growth, 4 per cent wage inflation gives 2 per cent price inflation and, when expectations adjust, if the same level of unemployment, U_1, is to be maintained, $\dot{w}$ must become 6 per cent. Thus, a second Phillips curve emerges with $\dot{p}_e = 2$ per cent. However, wage increases of 6 per cent further fuel inflation, causing ever increasing prices as long as the government attempts to maintain unemployment artificially below the natural level. If, however, the government allows unemployment to return to the natural level U_N, the labour market returns to a stable equilibrium, but at a higher rate of inflation than the economy started from. Whichever Phillips curve the economy is on, a stable equilibrium exists at the unemployment level U_N.

According to Friedman, the long-run Phillips curve is vertical at the natural level of unemployment and, in the long run, there is no scope for the government to manipulate aggregate demand to reduce unemployment below this level. A point on this vertical curve is consistent with a 'non-accelerating inflation rate of unemployment' (NAIRU). This vertical long-run Phillips curve requires the labour market to respond fully to expectations (i.e. $\gamma = 1$). It has been argued, however, that with partial adjustment the coefficient lies between 0 and 1. In this case the expectation augmented Phillips curve becomes less than vertical (such as case *a* in Figure 29.3, lying between the two extremes of no adjustment to expectations (case *b*) and full adjustment (case *c*)). The case for partial adjustment in the real world had been argued on the basis of the nature of wage negotiations which occur infrequently.

It is possible to demonstrate that where price expectations adjust adaptively a negative relationship emerges between the change in unemployment and the change in the rate of inflation in the short run,

$$\frac{dU_t}{dt} = \frac{(1-\lambda)}{m'(U_t)} \frac{d\dot{p}_t}{dt} \quad (16)$$

where λ, $0 \le \lambda \le 1$, represents the speed with which expectations are adjusted, with $\lambda = 0$ meaning no

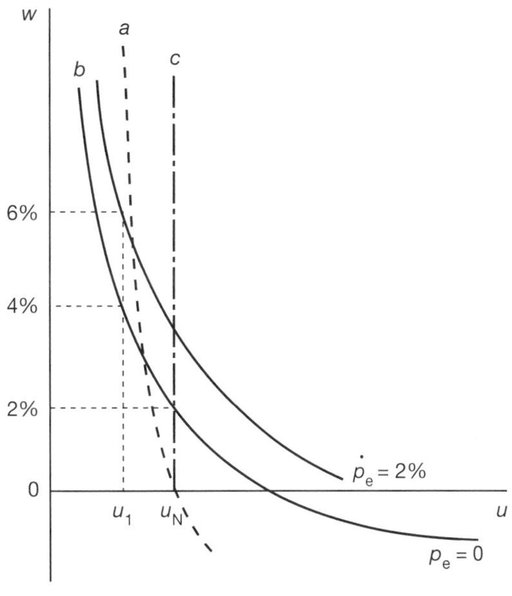

Fig 29.3 Full employment and the natural rate of unemployment

adjustment within the period and $\lambda = 1$ corresponding to complete adjustment. This negative relationship disappears in the long run (see Appendix 1). In the case of rational expectations individuals anticipate the actual change in price although with a random error. In this case,

$$m(U_t) = \mu_t \qquad (17)$$

where μ is the random error, and no negative trade-off emerges either in the short or long run (again see Appendix 1).

Estimates based on a pooled time series–cross-section regression for 19 OECD countries for the period from 1956 to 1985 yield

$$\frac{\mathrm{d}p_{it}}{\mathrm{d}t} = a_i + b_{it} - \underset{(4.5)}{0.32}U_{it} - \underset{(3.0)}{0.48}\frac{\mathrm{d}U_{it}}{\mathrm{d}t} \qquad (18)$$

where i denotes the ith country (Nickell, 1991). Thus, if the assumed adaptive expectations mechanism does not itself adjust in the face of systematic government policies the result suggests it is possible to use unemployment as a mechanism for controlling inflation. Nickell reports that there is both a well-defined trade-off and evidence of hysteresis.

3.5 Changes in the NAIRU over time and differences across countries

Empirical evidence began to emerge during the 1980s, confirming the intuitive belief that the natural rate had been shifting outwards over time. At the heart of the Layard and Nickell (1985) model of the UK economy are three equations (essentially determining employment, prices and wages), which, when solved in long-run equilibrium, yield estimates of the natural rate. Table 29.5 reproduces the results obtained, which are based on the assumption that average unemployment was at the natural rate in the period 1955 to 1966. The table reports estimates based upon two alternative model specifications. The key result, however, is that the rate of unemployment consistent with non-accelerating inflation shifted outwards in the UK from just below 2 per cent in 1955–1966 to around 11 per cent in 1980–1983.

Estimates of the natural rate have also been constructed for OECD countries (Layard *et al,* 1991, p. 436), and are reported in Table 29.6. The differences between Tables 29.5 and 29.6 for the UK are, in part, caused by different models and by the fact that the averages relate to different time periods. The results are not very reassuring, with the UK ranked 13th from the top (out of 19) in 1960–1968, 15th in 1969–1979 and 16th in 1980–1988. This suggests that the UK has a long-term endemic unemployment problem that requires a seed change in government policy.

Since the influence of demand factors has tended to be thought of in terms of movement along the *UV* curve and short-run Phillips curves or movements up the long-run vertical trade-off, upward movements in the NAIRU have tended to be regarded as determined by supply side factors and as reflecting an increase in voluntary unemployment.

Thus, most of the policy debate has surrounded 'supply side' issues. In particular, it has been suggested that the natural rate is positively related to: (i) the rate of increase in labour supply when the demand for labour curve is given; (ii) increases in unemployment benefit, which reduce the (potential) employees' acceptance probability at a given level of wage; (iii) increases in tax rates that have reduced the propensity to work at any given gross wage; (iv) the effects of unions in raising wages above the market clearing level (Knight, 1987, pp. 259–291). Outward shifts in the NAIRU have also been linked with 'hys-

Table 29.5 Estimates of the 'natural' rate of unemployment (males percentages)

	1955–1966	1967–1974	1975–1979	1980–1983
Table 4, model 1				
'Natural' unemployment rate	1.96	4.12	7.80	10.72
Actual unemployment rate	1.96	3.78	6.79	13.79
Table 4, model 2				
'Natural' unemployment rate	1.96	4.03	8.61	11.20
Actual unemployment rate	1.96	3.78	6.79	13.79

Source: Layard and Nickell (1985)

Table 29.6 Estimates of the 'natural' rate and the unemployment–inflation trade-off

	Actual unemployment, U			Equilibrium unemployment, U^*		
	1960–1968	1969–1979	1980–1988	1960–1968	1969–1979	1980–1988
Belgium	2.34	4.53	11.07	3.77	4.82	7.04
Denmark	1.98	3.64	8.56	2.19	4.64	7.30
France	1.69	3.65	8.98	1.76	3.88	7.81
Germany	0.71	2.13	6 .07	0.47	1.87	4.04
Ireland	4.99	6.72	14.12	6.08	9.13	13.09
Italy	3.82	4.37	6.87	4.31	4.94	5.42
Netherlands	1.16	3.67	9.89	1.52	4.28	7.27
Spain	2.43	4.12	17.74	4.55	9.73	14.95
UK	2.63	4.30	10.32	2.55	5.15	7.92
Australia	2.17	3.66	7.67	2.35	4.01	6.10
New Zealand	0.18	0.58	4.18	0.43	1.96	3.91
Canada	4.73	6.44	9.48	5.46	7.01	8.14
USA	4.74	5.85	7.38	5.01	5.97	6.36
Japan	1.36	1.61	2.51	1.59	1.82	2.14
Austria	1.61	1.32	3.14	0.94	0.48	2.95
Finland	1.84	3.48	5.01	1.40	2.61	4.65
Norway	2.00	1.75	2.51	2.13	2.22	2.50
Sweden	1.32	1.65	2.21	1.64	1.93	2.36
Switzerland	0.11	0.52	1.87	0.09	0.83	1.44

Source: Layard *et al.* (1991)

teresis' effects; unemployment becomes persistent when demand deficiency is sustained. The so-called natural rate U_N increases if the rate of unemployment in the previous time period exceed's that period's natural rate. One plausible explanation for this is that the skills of the unemployed tend to depreciate the longer they are unemployed (an alternative explanation is that employers use the duration of unemployment as an indicator of unobserved characteristics of individuals). As a consequence the *UV* curve shifts out because of the increasing number of long-term unemployed who become less 'employable' as their skills depreciate. Some doubt has been cast on this view, however, in an empirical paper using unemployment flows data in the UK (Pissarides, 1986). This paper suggests that the shift towards long-term unemployment that has taken place is not a cause of the rise in unemployment. Rather, the shift towards long-term unemployment and the rise in unemployment are both a consequence of a general decline in the rate at which unemployed workers of all durations leave unemployment. In the remainder of this chapter, however, we relate the rising natural rate to both the effects of duration on skills and more general changes in the skill level of the economy.

4 Labour, competitiveness and growth

4.1 Introduction

In the remainder of this chapter we attempt to make clearer the very direct links which exist between the labour market, unemployment, inflation and growth. To do this we need to take a longer-term view. While the focus of government policy is often short run, it should be clear from what we have said already that the UK's problems (and perhaps the emerging employment difficulties in Europe) are longer term in nature. The growth in the NAIRU from the 1950s to 1980s is indicative of this. The rise has occurred against a background of slowly rising real earnings, with the UK slipping down the international rankings of living standards. The UK's policy response, at least in recent years, has been to focus more heavily on the control of inflation, while at the same time making the labour market increasingly flexible, in an attempt to absorb larger numbers of individuals without further increases in unemployment. While both strategies have points in their favour, they seem to be born out of the need to cope with adverse trends, rather than protective policies to generate growth and more rapid improvements in future income and wealth. To understand both the problem and some alternative solutions, we need to consider some of the new developments in growth theory.

4.2 Nature of the problem

While it may not be immediately obvious what growth theory has to do with labour economics, the two are inextricably intertwined. For one thing, the rate of growth of output determines future levels of income and employment (and under certain circumstances the size of the future population). It is clear that the rate of growth is, in part, determined by the rate of growth in the labour force. The growth accounting literature demonstrates that labour is an input into the production process and the more labour a country has, in principle, the more it can produce. There are clearly exceptions to this rule. As Malthus would have pointed out, in the lowest income per head countries, the marginal product of labour falls close to zero and it cannot be raised without the injection of new capital stock. In such countries, as the labour force grows, income per head is forced down. In addition, given that such countries are often highly dependent on agriculture, they are susceptible to sudden climatic changes and other natural disasters.

Given that the rate of labour productivity growth in manufacturing has outstripped the rate of growth for manufacturing output, employment in the manufacturing sector has declined in almost every country. Even in a country such as Germany, improvements in technology raise real net exports, export prices, the volume of trade and employment in the economy, but not to a sufficient extent to offset the rationalization effects of the new technology. The 'best' results appear to be where new technologies are introduced in a strategic 'export offensive', resulting in lower rates of unemployment growth in the domestic economy (but obviously at the expense of other countries). With one or two exceptions, therefore, most countries have experienced declines in the volume of employment in manufacturing and, in some, such as the UK, the changes have been rapid and sustained, leading to major structural changes and adjustments in the economy. Of course, labour displaced from the manufacturing sector flows over primarily into services, where historically at least, measured labour productivity growth is lower; this has implications for the level and rate of growth of wages in the service sector. Thus, in general, the overall level of productivity in the economy, which is a weighted average of primarily the manufacturing and service sectors, declines as the proportion of manufacturing in total economic activity contracts – sometimes termed 'Baumol's disease'. More problematically evidence is emerging that similar technological and organizational changes are now being introduced into certain parts of the service sector (such as banking and finance), with consequent major job losses.

The picture is consistent with an inward-shifting demand curve for labour in manufacturing, offset by some outward shift in the demand for services. The structural changes have been enormous, and a considerable part of the stock of specific skills and even some general skills, as individuals have not only moved between firms but also changed sectors, have been lost. At the same time the (potential) labour supply has been shifting outwards, driven particularly by female participation. The overall consequence of these changes is that competition for lower paid jobs has become intense in the service sector, stimulated by increased labour market flexibility. Thus, wage rates at this end of the market are low, leading to a less clear-cut distinction in the relative advantages of employment, unemployment and marginal attachment. Income distribution has become more unequal.

There seems to be a growing realization that a longer-term solution requires the generation and maintenance of a more skilled workforce, linked to higher rates of technological change:

> The present recession has intensified concerns, however, about the Community's ability to compete in world markets with high technology producers, in Japan and the US, and with low-tech producers in developing countries. (CEC, 1993, pp. 10–11)

There seem to be a number of dimensions to this argument, which we explore in more detail in subsequent sections of this chapter. The first argument is linked to traditional neoclassical theory: more skilled and educated individuals tend to be paid more. The second relates to the new growth theories: that there are spillover effects of investment in education and training. The third is that a more skilled and educated workforce increases the extent and success of innovatory activity. We expand this final theme to consider product innovation and the provision of an attractive location for production activities of foreign multinational companies.

This statement highlights a natural tension in competitiveness between reducing costs and increasing product quality. In the UK the lack of competitiveness of the 1970s, followed by the recession of 1980–1981, produced a policy shift that tended to concentrate on relative UK unit costs, a cost-reducing policy. During the latest recession, a number of German commentators have been calling for a greater focus on cost and cost reductions.

CASE STUDY 1 Role of formal education in growth

Jorgenson and Fraumeni (1992) focus on the role of education and report results separately for the education and non-education (i.e. business and government) sectors of the economy. The first column of data in Table 29.7 reports on the various rates of growth in the non-education sector. Over the period 1948 to 1986 as a whole, for example, value added increased at an average rate of 3.3 per cent per annum. The corresponding rates of input growth were 3.3 per cent for capital and 1.6 per cent for labour respectively. The next three rows of the first column disaggregate this growth according to its source (i.e. capital, 1.3 per cent per annum, labour, 1.0 per cent per annum, and increases in factor productivity, 1.0 per cent per annum – which in combination produce the 3.3 per cent per annum growth noted above). The results therefore indicate that the growth of capital is more important than the growth of labour in the non-educational sector, accounting for almost 40 per cent of overall growth compared with only 29 per cent attributable to labour. Productivity growth accounted for a not insubstantial 31 per cent of the growth of value added over this period.

The final set of rows in the table decompose the contributions of both capital and labour inputs into their quality and quantity components. Thus, in the non-educational sector, only 15 per cent of the 1.32 per cent per annum that the growth of capital makes to output growth can be attributed to improvements in the quality of the capital stock (by implication, 85 per cent can be attributed to the physical growth in the stock of given quality). In the case of labour, however, the relative contribution of quality is quite different. Of the just under 1 per cent per annum overall contribution of labour to economic growth, 24 per cent can be attributed to improvements in the quality of labour, compared with 76 per cent to the quantity of labour.

Given that the education sector only forms about 7 per cent of the national product, it is not surprising to find that the direct contribution of the education sector to economic growth is quite small (as contributions are weighted by their relative importance in overall production). The

Table 29.7 Sources of economic growth in the USA, 1948–1986

Variable	Non-educational sector	Educational sector	Total economy
Value added	0.0329	0.0255	0.0293
Capital input	0.0334	0.0382	0.0335
Labour input	0.0160	0.0247	0.0220
Intermediate input		0.0679	
Contribution of capital input	0.0131	0.0001	0.0065
Contribution of labour input	0.0096	0.0244	0.0179
Contribution of intermediate input		0.0007	
Rate of productivity growth	0.0102	0.0003	0.0050
Contribution of capital quality	0.0019	0.0000	0.0010
Contribution of capital stock	0.0111	0.0001	0.0055
Contribution of labour quality	0.0023	0.0034	0.0075
Contribution of hours worked	0.0073	0.0209	0.0104

Source: Jorgenson and Fraumeni (1992, Tables 1 and 3)

continues

CASE STUDY 1 continued

education sector is, however, of considerable interest in its own right and the second column in the table provides evidence of the contributions of capital, labour and intermediate inputs to the gross output of the sector. In the way that the Jorgenson and Fraumeni model is estimated, the output of the educational sector is a measure of the economy's investment in education. Over the whole of the period, 1948 to 1986, this grows at 2.6 per cent per annum. The capital input grows at 3.8 per cent, labour at 2.5 per cent and intermediate inputs at 6.8 per cent per annum.

In contrast to the non-educational sector, the principal source of growth of output in the sector is the growth in the labour input. According to Jorgenson and Fraumeni (1992, p. S.61), the combined contribution of capital, intermediate inputs and productivity only accounts for one-tenth of the contribution of the labour input. Of course, there are enormous problems in measuring the quality and quantity of both inputs and outputs in the sector (not only human capital inputs, but also computers – for a discussion of the issues see, for example, Denison, 1989)

The final column of Table 29.7 presents the overall set of growth accounting results which include both the educational and non-educational sectors. In these results, the rate of growth of value added is 2.9 per cent per annum over the period as a whole, somewhat lower than for the non-educational sector alone. Thus, the addition of the educational sector reduces the overall rate of growth of the US economy. All this is saying is that the education sector has grown somewhat more slowly than the non-educational (business and government) sector. Overall capital input now grows at 3.4 per cent and labour at 2.2 per cent per annum. The contribution of capital is just under 0.7 per cent per year, compared with labour's contribution of 1.8 per cent; the remaining productivity component is now significantly smaller at 0.5 per cent per annum. Labour can be seen to account for about 61 per cent of the overall growth of the economy, of which about 42 per cent arises because of an improvement in labour quality.

Of course, these results give rise to some interesting questions about the manner in which a model of this type can capture the dynamic contribution of education. We return to this in subsequent sections.

Source: Jorgenson and Fraumeni (1992)

4.3 Growth accounting, human capital and the residual factor

In a pioneering paper, Solow (1957) used a functional form similar to equation (6) above to examine what proportion of output growth could be attributed to the growth in capital and labour. The rate of growth of output was argued to be a function of the rate of growth of capital and the rate of growth of labour. The rate of growth in output is decomposed into its constituent parts by weighting the growth in each input by its (relative) factor share (e.g. some measure of its importance in costs or production) and subtracting each from output growth. The proportion of output growth that cannot be attributed to these two factors was termed the 'residual factor', which a number of commentators at the time associated with technological change. In practice, Solow found that only about one-seventh of output growth could be attributed to the growth in capital and labour and, thus, six-sevenths was associated with other unobserved factors, including technological change. This finding was consistent with a number of other studies around that time that emphasized productivity improvements as the predominant source of economic growth. This finding stimulated a great deal of work in the 1960s on the residual factor, including the influence of technology (which, it was argued, could not be observed directly).

Part of this work continued to use and further refine the growth accounting framework. The 'second generation' of growth accounting models not only allowed for the substitution between capital stock and labour (person hours), they also included substitution between different types of person hours worked and different types of capital stock. In other words the later models allowed for the heterogeneity (and, thereby, to some degree, the quality) of the inputs. The later, more detailed growth accounting work of the mid-1960s and early 1970s appeared to indicate a much smaller role for the 'residual factor' and, therefore, for technological change (e.g. Jorgenson and Griliches, 1967). These new models effectively 'chipped away' at the residual by allowing for the different 'qualities' of the inputs explicitly within the accounting procedure. For example, in place of 'manpower' (weighted by its factor share –

based on, say, the average wage), the new models separated unqualified, qualified and highly qualified persons, each weighted in the growth accounting procedure accordingly. Indeed, the level of detail at which this 'accounting' takes place is startling. In terms of the labour input, for example, Jorgenson and Fraumeni report

> Hours worked for each sex are cross-classified by individual year of age and individual year of education for a total of 2196 different types of hours worked. Each type of hours worked is weighted by the corresponding wage rate. (Jorgenson and Fraumeni, 1992a, p. S.58).

Different types and ages of capital are dealt with in a similar manner – see Case Study 1.

Thus, the difference between the results of the first- and second-generation growth accounting models is analytically important and, indeed, useful. Again, we can use Jorgenson and Fraumeni to illustrate the point:

> We define growth rates of capital and labour quality as the differences between growth rates of input measures that take substitution into account and measures that ignore substitution. Increases in capital quality reflect the substitution of more highly productive capital goods for those that are less productive. This substitution process requires investment in tangible assets or nonhuman capital. Similarly, growth in labour quality results from the substitution of more effective for less effective workers. (1992a, p. S.58)

Bearing in mind that there may still be a residual factor in the second-generation models, although it is likely to be much smaller in magnitude, technological change and quality change have become irretrievably intertwined. The growth accounting procedure imposes the underlying production function on the data. Thus, changes in the mix of labour from less qualified to more qualified produces a movement around the underlying production function by definition, rather than a shift of the function. In practice, it is not clear that this is really the case. Nevertheless, the relative importance of quality versus quantity of inputs in the process of growth is of considerable interest in its own right (bearing in mind any question marks over the assumed form of the production function). In addition, we have a particular interest in the role of labour quality within this process. If the tenants of human capital theory are correct,

> Substituting more for less effective workers increases output per worker. More highly educated or better trained people are more productive than less educated or poorly trained people. However, education and training are costly, so that substitution of people with more education and training requires investment in human capital. (Jorgenson and Fraumeni, 1992a, p. S52)

Human capital theory suggests that this will be the case, insofar as more highly qualified individuals are more highly paid than less qualified individuals, and this payment is the outcome of market forces remunerating them for their higher productivity.

The addition of an educational sector is clearly an important first step in the understanding of the contribution of education to growth of the economy. It also has the spinoff of providing estimates of human wealth. The Jorgenson and Fraumeni income-based estimates of the output of the education sector, which have the advantage of being based on the standard human capital approach, exceed Kendrick's estimates by a factor of 10. Nevertheless, the estimates of the stock of human wealth and the contribution of education are still likely to be underestimated. For one thing, the formal education sector is only a part of the total of human resource development that occurs within the economy. For another, despite the move to capture future income streams, it is not at all clear that the relatively simple technology is able to capture the true dynamics of the contribution of education.

4.4 Endogeneity, increasing returns and externalities

It seems unsatisfactory that economic growth should be so crucially dependent upon disembodied technological change. While not denying the possibility of such a mechanism, students would be more comfortable if there was something endogenous to the model driving growth. In addition, the standard neoclassical model gives rise to a result which is not observed in practice – that all national economies with access to the same technology converge on the same rate of productivity growth in the long term. The so-called 'new growth theories' start by questioning the convergence proposition, arguing that the growth rate itself should be endogenous to the model and potentially different between countries (Solow, 1991, p. 398). They also generally include some form of externality or spillover effect, which can be traced back to earlier work on the returns to R&D (Griliches, 1992). The 'new growth theories' have turned to human capital accumulation as an explanation, as opposed to R&D. The focus on human capital is not a problem; we have already demonstrated the close links between invention and human capital development. However, these theories, typified by the work of Romer (1986, 1987 and 1990) and Lucas (1988), are still in their infancy, based on fairly heroic assumptions in order to make the mathematics tractable. Inevitably, students interested in the complexities of technological change are invariably disappointed, but the theories are thought provoking and generally impose more logic and rigour in the treatment of intertemporal issues.

At the heart of the Romer (1986) model is the assumption that human capital exhibits increasing marginal productivity. As Solow (1991, p. 399) notes, this makes a large difference. In particular, it results in a model in which the growth rate can increase for ever, although it has an upper limit. It also allows the possibility of a low-level equilibrium trap, which is useful in explaining the failure of some less developed economies. More importantly, however, it allows small differences in starting conditions to cause divergences in performance over time. Likewise, it is possible for policies applied 'mid-course' to influence the subsequent growth path. Again, these characteristics are important if growth models are to be useful in explaining real-world phenomena.

Solow (1991, p. 400) points out that increasing returns to scale are important to consistency at different values within the model. Households are assumed to maximize some discounted sum of current and future utility. The technology of production can be written as

$$Y = \mathbf{f}(h, H, X) \tag{19}$$

where X denotes capital, raw materials and any other input, which are given and invariant over time, and can effectively be dropped from the problem. In addition, h represents the firm's current stock of human capital, while H is the overall stock in the economy. Note it is assumed that $H = Nh$ where there are N identical firms. It is important to note the role played by H in the model. H carries the externality. It occurs because, while every firm knows about H and takes into account its effects on their own production, no individual firm has a significant influence on H. As far as the firm is concerned, therefore, the production function, $\mathbf{f}(\;)$, is homogeneous of degree 1, which is consistent with competitive equilibrium (i.e. the firm acts as a price-taking competitor). As far as the economy as a whole is concerned, however, the production function, $\mathbf{f}(h,H,X)$, exhibits increasing returns to scale across all inputs. In other words, once the externality associated with the aggregate stock of human capital is taken into account, there is increasing marginal productivity.

Human capital generation follows the normal route adopted by the dynamic labour supply literature (see Part II of the book),

$$\mathrm{d}h/\mathrm{d}t = \mathbf{g}(I, h) \tag{20}$$

where $I = Y - C$ is the forgone consumption (i.e. income, Y, minus consumption, C) at time t, invested in human capital generation. It can be thought of as equivalent to expenditure on R&D. Note that the benefits do not dissipate at the end of the individual's lifetime. The generation process depends on the initial human capital endowment. If $\mathbf{g}(\;)$ is assumed to be homogeneous of degree 1, then

$$\dot{h}/h = \mathbf{g}(I/h) \tag{21}$$

As Solow (1991, p. 401) points out, this is a 'dreadfully mechanical model of the research process'. The model imposes some other constraints, for example, to ensure that it does not pay to postpone consumption on too large a scale or for too long.

The competitive equilibrium cannot be efficient because of the externality, which ensures that there is underinvestment in human capital. The main point, however, is that the model generates unbounded growth in Y, C, h and H without the need to assume exogenous technological progress. The lack of an upper bound allows growth rates to increase over time, for economies to grow at different rates, and for shocks and policy interventions to result in sustained differences in economic performance.

4.5 Labour and comparative economic performance

An increasing number of empirical studies have focused on the link between education, skills and comparative economic performance. As we have demonstrated in earlier chapters, in a sense, all of the human capital literature is based on the hypothesis that an increase in qualifications raises productivity and incomes (i.e. is a source of economic growth). Developments in the growth accounting literature have increasingly focused on the role of quality, including human capital, in this process, showing that a significant proportion of the 'residual factor' can be accounted for by substitution from lower- to higher-quality inputs. Finally, the 'new growth theories' attempt to endogenize the factors leading to growth, with a special focus on human capital and, to a lesser extent, R&D. All of these developments certainly take the study of the role of labour in the right direction, but, to date, fail to reflect fully the richness of the evidence emerging which links human capital with growth and comparative economic performance.

The demand for factors of production depends on the demand for the UK's products, which is determined by their quality and cost. Quality is driven by product invention and by the skills of the workforce and its managers (i.e. via systems of quality management and decisions taken about the dynamic investment of the firm). Per unit costs are driven by process improvement, input productivity levels and rates of factor remuneration (of course, remuneration and productivity are themselves related in a variety of ways). In general, higher-technology/higher-quality products require a more highly qualified and skilled workforce. This is sufficient to define, at least in broad terms, what a country has to do to maintain or improve its international competitive performance: (i) produce goods and services to quality levels and at costs that at least match those of overseas competitors; (ii) introduce new products and services at a rate and of a specification at least equal to those of overseas competitors.

The discussion suggests a virtuous circle of successful product invention resulting in: knowledge and skills on which future inventions are built; 'rents' which can be used to fund further R&D and product invention. In addition, consumer demand for the new products feeds through in terms of employment opportunities in production. One of the most efficient ways of employment creation is via export-led (import-saving) new technologies. We demonstrated in earlier sections that the UK only remained as competitive as it did on world markets by devaluing sterling and other evidence suggests that the balance of its exports has been changing, with a falling share of the world's high-technology exports. Again, the USA and UK (as well as some other European countries) show a distinct pattern to the Pacific Rim countries. The evidence suggests therefore that the UK has failed to introduce new products at a rate and of a specification at least equal to a number of its key overseas competitors.

A large number of studies by the National Institute for Economic Social Research (NIESR) clearly demonstrate that the productivity gaps between the UK and other countries are closely linked to differences in education, training and labour force skills. Amongst other things, their results highlighted inadequacies in the quality of UK schooling, and the interaction between schooling and the training system, as a comparison of UK and Dutch establishments revealed:

> The higher skill levels found throughout the Dutch engineering industry primarily reflect that country's widespread provision of full-time courses of education and training. As elsewhere, trainees completing full-time courses of vocational schooling still need to undergo programmes of structured on-the-job training when they first enter employment. However, the relatively high attainment of students at junior and intermediate technical schools in the Netherlands give Dutch employers a considerable head start over their British counterparts in terms of the trainability of their workforce, both as entrants to the labour market and subsequently as adult workers who may need retraining and updating. In this context Dutch employers are able to carry out training to given standards more quickly and cost effectively than is possible in Britain, and in many cases they are able to set their training standards much higher than is feasible for their British counterparts.
> (Mason and Van Ark, 1994)

The principal thrust of their work, however, has demonstrated the significant UK deficit at intermediate skill levels. In one study, for example, about 53 per cent of the gap between UK and German manufacturing industries was attributed to the lower skill levels of the UK workforce. Similarly, the greater training of hotel managers was an important factor in explaining the higher productivity of German than UK hotels. The story is broadly the same across other sectors and in comparisons with other industrialized countries. More recently, however, they have turned their attention to the very highest qualification levels, such as PhDs, and found similar deficiencies in the UK. This case-study evidence is generally so consistent and pervasive that it seems difficult to dispute, but it is also in line with a variety of large-scale survey and econometric evidence on this topic. The *Skill Needs in Britain* data, based upon a government-funded survey of over 4000 establishments, examine both the extent and consequences of skill shortages in the UK. These indicate that the establishments most likely to report skill gaps and skill shortages are those which undertake the least dynamic investments, such as the introduction of new product and process technologies, but most importantly, those with the greatest skill problems do least in terms of training their workforces.

For many years, although less so now as services have become increasingly internationally traded, many commentators viewed manufacturing as the engine of growth in advanced, industrialized economies. It is perhaps not surprising therefore that there has been considerable interest in the UK's continuing relative economic decline in manufacturing.

Many authors have pointed to the failure to train sufficient numbers of engineers and to employ them in positions of sufficiently high responsibility. Finniston (1980) was the latest of a long line of government inquiries in the UK that date back to the middle of the 19th century. The underlying idea is that a higher quantity and quality of engineers would improve economic performance and increase demand for their skills (a kind of 'Says' Law' in which supply creates its own demand). In practice it is not clear that increases in the supply of engineers have been easily accommodated by the labour market or that the purported benefits have emerged. A number of explanations have been offered, including short termism on the part of the City and a lack of skills and qualifications amongst existing managers. An international study of the perceptions of managers about the quality of their colleagues in other countries placed UK managers low on the list compared with their US, Japanese and German counterparts (IRIC, 1994).

One important aspect of this is that individuals with different levels and types of qualifications appear to have different approaches to problem solving. First, more highly qualified individuals appear to take a longer-term view. Second, faced by some economic shock which increases competition, an engineer might seek, for example, a 'quality-increasing' solution, while an accountant or finance person might consider a 'cost-reducing solution'. What seems to be emerging is the importance of qualifications at the highest levels in companies. There is tentative evidence that qualified scientists and engineers are involved not only in the successful introduction of new technologies, but also in the successful management of companies. The clearest evidence, however, is that companies managed by qualified individuals (whatever the qualification) are more innovative and successful than those managed by unqualified individuals. It has been shown elsewhere that it is possible to have two kinds of equilibria (i.e. a high technology, high skill, high value added and a low technology, low skill and low value added). While both routes can be equally viable in the short run, the low-technology route is a dead-end in the long run.

There is strong evidence that, over much of the post-war period, the UK failed to produce internationally traded goods of a price and quality which were competitive with other industrialized countries. While labour productivity growth has often been strong in the UK, this was achieved through factor substitution and a further proportion of the gains were lost through higher factor costs. At the same time, the throughput of new products has declined, with increased reliance on foreign-owned multinational companies with production facilities based in the UK. The net effect has been a major loss of jobs in the manufacturing sector. Displaced workers have found their skills largely redundant and many of them have gravitated to less skilled jobs in the service sector. The movement of individuals into services has only been accommodated by the 'flexibilization' of the labour market, including the growth of part-time working and self-employment. This has been a further influence on the growing inequality of income. There is some support for the view that the low skilled in the UK and USA are increasingly competing with the low skilled of LDCs. As an increasing part of the service sector becomes affected by IT and internationally traded, further job losses are likely to accrue and it is not clear how the labour market will cope.

5 Conclusions

The period after the Second World War has been one of remarkable technological changes. Of these, the development of microelectronics and information technology has perhaps been the most radical and pervasive, with, to date, the most significant labour market implications. We have already demonstrated, for example, that the post-war period has seen more rapid and consistent productivity improvements in the UK than almost any other period for which quantitative records are available. We have shown how the differential rates of productivity growth in the manufacturing and service sectors have modified the structure of employment within the industrialized economies. In fact, those economies in which the organizational structure was most conducive to technological change, such as Germany and Japan, experienced more rapid growth in their manufacturing sectors, which, despite rapid rates of productivity growth, helped to protect employment levels within these sectors. This greater success can be attributed in part to their earlier introduction of process technologies, raising their productivity and competitiveness, but also to the higher rate of flow of new product technologies. In many ways we have painted a picture of the UK as a reactive, rather than a proactive, economy. The productivity changes have been forced upon the UK economy. Historically, at least, the lack of skills at all levels of the hierarchy has made this inevitable. The restructuring has been painful and, if anything, skill depleting as individuals were made redundant from manufacturing and moved into unemployment and/or across to service sector jobs. The scale of the change has been accommodated by government policies to encourage 'flexibilization', with part-time, temporary and self-employment. It is not clear how the labour market is going to cope as increasing parts of the service sector become internationally traded and the pool of 'jobs-of-last-resort' dry up. The realization of the importance of education and training and their links with research and development has come late in the UK and it is not clear that the current policies are adequate to halt the slide, let alone reverse it.

Appendix 1 Adaptive and rational expectations

This raises the question about the way in which expectations may be formed and the importance of this mechanism for the wage inflation/unemployment outcome.

In the adaptive expectations approach, expectations were assumed to be adjusted in the light of past errors. $E(\dot{p})_{t-1}$ is defined as the rate of inflation that, at time t–1, was expected to prevail during period t. A simple Koyck adjustment mechanism appears as

$$E(\dot{p})_t - E(\dot{p})_{t-1} = \Lambda[(\dot{p})_t - E(\dot{p})_{t-1}] \qquad \text{(A.1)}$$

where: Λ denotes the speed at which expectations are adjusted, $0 \le \Lambda \le 1$. $\Lambda = 1$ indicates that complete adjustment takes place within the period, while $\Lambda = 0$ implies that no adjustment at all takes place within the period. Keeping $E(\dot{p})_t$ on the left hand side, and collecting the remaining variables on the right hand side,

$$E(\dot{p})_t = E(\dot{p})_{t-1} + \Lambda[(\dot{p})_t - E(\dot{p})_{t-1}] \qquad \text{(A.2)}$$

In other words, the expectation at time t (relating to inflation at time $t + 1$) is equal to the expectation at time $t - 1$ plus some adjustment for the difference between the expected and actual values in that period. If, however, the rate of adjustment remains constant over time, we could equally write an expression for $E(\dot{p})_{t-1}$ in terms of $\dot{p}_{t-1}$ and $E(\dot{p})_{t-2}$. Continued substitution into equation (A.2) yields

$$E(\dot{p})_t = \Lambda\sum_{x=0}^{X}(1 - \Lambda)^x\dot{p}_{t-x} \qquad \text{(A.3)}$$

It is possible to use this expression to examine the short-run Phillips curve, based on the adaptive expectations approach. If it is assumed that prices are a constant mark-up over wages, it is possible to rewrite the expectation augmented Phillips curve (see equation (15) in the main text) as

$$\dot{p}_t = \mathbf{m}(U_t) + E(\dot{p})_t \qquad \text{(A.4)}$$

Substituting for $E(\ )$ from equation (A.3) and rearranging terms, it is possible to show that

$$\mathbf{m}(U)_t = (1 - \Lambda)\dot{p}_t - (1 - \Lambda)\dot{p}_{t-1} + (1 - \Lambda)\mathbf{m}(U_{t-1}) \qquad \text{(A.5)}$$

Bearing in mind that lagged values (i.e. $\dot{p}_{t-1}$ cannot alter, differentiating with respect to time yields

$$\frac{dU_t}{dt} = \frac{(1 - \Lambda)}{\mathbf{m}'(U_t)}\frac{d\dot{p}_t}{dt} \qquad \text{(A.6)}$$

where: $\mathbf{m}'(\ )$ is the derivative of $\mathbf{m}(\ )$ with respect to U. As $\mathbf{m}'(\ )$ is negative and $(1 - \Lambda)$ is positive, $dU/dt < 0$ and the short-run expectations augmented Phillips curve has a negative slope.

A negative relationship does not emerge in long-run equilibrium. Assume that the rate of inflation settles to a steady rate, $\dot{p}_0$, in the long run and, thus, $\dot{p}_t = \dot{p}_{t-1} = \dot{p}_0$ holds for all subsequent t. The first two terms on the right hand side of equation (A.5) cancel and

$$\mathbf{m}(U_t) = (1 - \Lambda)\mathbf{m}(U_{t-1}) \qquad \text{(A.7)}$$

Given stability of the underlying adjustment mechanism, equation (A.7) applies to all time periods, and we can write

$$\mathbf{m}(U_{t+1}) = (1 - \Lambda)\mathbf{m}(U_t) = (1 - \Lambda)^2\mathbf{m}(U_{t-1}) \qquad \text{(A.8)}$$

If this process is continued sufficiently far into the future, $(1 - \Lambda)$ raised to the corresponding power approaches zero, for $\Lambda < 1$. Thus, there is no long-run trade-off between the rate of change in wages and the rate of unemployment; in other words, the long-run expectations augmented Phillips curve is vertical. With adaptive adjustment mechanisms, individuals make the same direction of error in each period and the errors are serially correlated. If this is the case, we would expect individuals to learn from their mistakes and, at worst, move off a slow adjustment path to a fast one. The outcome is somewhat more complex in the case of multiple heterogeneous labour markets, giving rise to the possibility of endogenously generated inflationary spirals around a vertical long-run relationship (Barro and Grossman, 1975).

A different result emerges if expectations are rational, rather than adaptive. This approach assumes that individuals make full use of all of the information available to them when reaching a decision about the dependent variable. In this case, the expected value of a variable depends on current and past values of independent variables, and not on the lagged values of the dependent variable. This does not mean that individuals have complete or perfect information and, by implication, they may make a mistake in their estimate. However, when expectations are formed rationally, any error, μ, is random (i.e. serially uncorrelated, with mean of zero). If expectations are rational, then

$$\dot{p}_t = E(\dot{p})_t + \mu_t \tag{A.9}$$

The implications of this for the Phillips curve can be observed by rearranging equation (A.9) in terms of $E(\dot{p})_t$ and substituting the resulting expression into equation (A.4),

$$\mathbf{m}(U_t) = \mu_t \tag{A.10}$$

In other words, in the case of rational expectations, there is neither a short- nor a long-run trade-off between the rate of change in money wages (or prices) and the rate of unemployment. The deviation from the natural rate of unemployment is simply a random error, μ_t.

Source: Levačić and Rebmann (1982)

References

Ashenfelter, O. (1976). 'Union Relative Wage Effects: New Evidence and a Survey of Their Implications for Wage Inflation'. In R. Stone and W. Peterson (eds) *Econometric Contributions to Public Policy*. New York: St Martins Press.

Barro, R.J. and H.I. Grossman (1975). *Money, Employment and Inflation*. Cambridge: Cambridge University Press.

CEC (1993). *Employment in Europe*. Directorate-General. Employment, Industrial Relations and Social Affairs. Luxembourg.

Crafts, N. (1992). 'Productivity Growth Reconsidered'. *Economic Policy*, October, 387–414.

Denison, E.F. (1989). *Estimates of Productivity Change by Industry: an Evaluation and an Alternative*. Washington DC: Brookings Institute.

Finniston, Sir M. (Chair) (1980). *Engineering Britain's Future*. Cmnd 7794. London: HMSO.

Friedman, M. (1968). 'The Role of Monetary Policy'. *American Economic Review*, 58, 1–17.

Griliches, Z. (1992). 'The Search for R&D Spillovers'. *Scandinavian Journal of Economics*, 94, Supplement, 29–47.

Hines, A. (1964). 'Wage Inflation in the United Kingdom, 1893–1961'. *Review of Economic Studies*, 31, 221–251.

Institute for Research into International Competitiveness (1994). *How Others See Us Competitively*. IRIC, Curtin University, Perth.

Jorgenson, D.W. and B.M. Fraumeni (1992). 'Investment in Education and US Economic Growth'. *Scandinavian Journal of Economics*, 94, Supplement, 51–70.

Jorgenson, D.W. and Z. Griliches (1967). 'The Explanation of Productivity Change'. *Review of Economic Studies*, 34, 3, 249–283.

Kendrick, J. (1990). *International Comparisons of Productivity Trends and Levels*. Discussion Paper No. 9002. George Washington University.

Knight, K.G. (1987). *Unemployment: an Economic Analysis*. London: Croom Helm.

Layard, R. and S. Nickell (1985). 'The Causes of British Unemployment'. *National Institute Economic Review*, February, 62–85.

Layard, R., S. Nickell and R. Jackman (1991). *Unemployment: Macroeconomic Performance and the Labour Market*. Oxford: Oxford University Press.

Levačić, R. and A. Rebmann (1982). *Macroeconomics: an Introduction to Keynesian and Neoclassical Controversies*. Second edition, London: Macmillan.

Lipsey, R.G. (1960). 'The Relationship Between Unemployment and the Rate of Change of Money Wage Rates in the United Kingdom, 1862–1957: a Further Analysis'. *Economica*, New Series 27, 1–31.

Lucas, R.E. (1988). 'On the Mechanics of Economic Development'. *Journal of Monetary Economics*. 22, 3-42.

Lynde, C. and J. Richmond (1993). 'Public Capital and Long-run Costs in UK Manaufacturing'. *Economic Journal*, 103, 419, 880–893.

Maddison, A. (1991). *Dynamic Forces in Capitalist Development*. Oxford: Oxford University Press.

Mahoney, M. and N. Oulten (1990). *Growth of Multifactor Productivity in British Industry, 1954–1986*. Discussion Paper 182. London: NIESR.

Mason, G. and B. Van Ark (1994). 'Vocational Training and Productivity Performance: an Anglo-Dutch

Comparison'. In R. McNabb, and K. Whitfield (eds) *The Market for Training: International Perspectives, Methodology and Policy*. Aldershot: Avebury, pp. 335–335.

Mulvey, C. (1978). *The Economic Analysis of Trade Unions*. Oxford: Martin Robertson.

Mulvey, C. and M. Gregory (1977). 'The Hines Wage Inflation Model'. *Manchester School*, 45, March.

Nickell, S. (1991). 'Unemployment: A survey'. In A.J. Oswald (ed.) *Surveys in Economics*. Vol. 1. Royal Economics Society. Oxford: Blackwell, pp. 136–185.

Phillips, A.W. (1958). 'The Relationship Between Unemployment and the Rate of Change in Money Wage Rates in the United Kingdom, 1861–1957'. *Economica*, New Series, 25, 283–299.

Pissarides, C.A. (1986). 'Unemployment and Vacancies in Britain'. *Economic Policy*, 3, 499–559.

Purdy, D. and G. Zis (1974). 'Trade Unions and Wage Inflation in the United Kingdom: A Reappraisal'. In D. Laidler, and D. Purdy (eds) *Inflation and Labour Markets*. Manchester: Manchester University Press.

Romer, P.M. (1986). 'Increasing Returns and Long-Run Growth'. *Journal of Political Economy*, 94, 1002–1037.

Romer, P.M. (1987). 'Growth Based on Increasing Returns to Specialisation'. *American Economic Review, Papers and Proceedings*, **77**, 56–72.

Romer, P.M. (1990). 'Endogenous Technical Change'. *Journal of Political Economy*, 98, Part II, 71–102.

Solow, R.M. (1957). 'Technical Change and the Aggregate Production Function'. *Review of Economics and Statistics*, 39, 312–320.

Solow, R. (1991). 'Growth Theory'. In D. Greenaway, M. Bleaney and I.M.T. Stewart (eds) *Companion to Contemporary Economic Thought*. London: Routledge, pp. 393–415.

CHAPTER 30 Labour market policies and outcomes

1 Introduction

This final chapter of the book takes a more policy-orientated perspective. In doing so, it briefly reviews some of the more important of the policy issues raised in earlier chapters. We do not, however, attempt to write about current unemployment or tax rates, for these figures would be well out of date by the time the book is published. It therefore takes a more broad-brush approach, looking at some lessons of the past in the context of the longer-term trends and problems associated with labour markets that still need to be resolved. These broader and longer-term issues, rather than policy minutiae, also have a wider international interest. We begin with an international perspective, based upon OECD experiences, before turning to the case of the UK.

2 International context

The OECD has promoted the idea of 'active manpower policies' at least since the early 1960s (OECD, 1990, p. 13). The term 'active' was 'borrowed' from the Swedish policies of the 1950s, which were themselves a reaction to policies based upon wage restraint. The Swedish concept was one which, in principle, allowed for selective interventions on both the demand and supply sides, but leaving the wage-setting process alone. This reduced the role of wage adjustment in market clearing, allowing the trade unions scope for 'solidaristic wage policy' and the pursuit of reduced wage differentials. The term 'manpower' was borrowed from the North American policies of the early 1960s. Manpower policies were essentially a response to a 'creeping unemployment' which appeared unresponsive to traditional monetary and fiscal policies.

The OECD established the Manpower and Social Affairs Committee in 1961 with the aim of encouraging active labour market policies amongst Member States. Whilst the emphasis of the programme of work has varied over time, at least three continuing themes have emerged:

> to develop human resources and adjust manpower resources to structural changes with a view to fostering economic growth; to improve both employability of and opportunities for disadvantaged groups, and thus contribute to social equity; to improve the trade-off between inflation and unemployment by stabilising employment during the cyclical downswing and by removing labour market bottlenecks during the upswing. (OECD, 1990, p. 11)

A flavour of the OECD's evolving programme of work can be found in a series of key recommendations and declarations outlined in OECD (1990, p. 11).

In reporting on the policy situation as it had emerged by the late 1980s, OECD (1990, p. 19) makes a distinction between changes in the regulatory framework of the labour market and labour market programmes. The deregulation of the labour market has been a particularly important policy theme in a number of OECD countries, not least the UK – we return to this in more detail below. More broadly, however, OECD see the challenge as being two-fold:

> (i) Sufficient labour market flexibility will have to be achieved within a socially acceptable regulatory framework. Thus, necessary regulations must not stifle innovation and change but prevent an undue burden of adjustment falling on individuals or particular groups. ... this can best be achieved by internal and external labour

> market flexibility coexisting and playing a complementary role. (ii) Public expenditure on labour market programmes will have to be reoriented to maximise cost-effectiveness. ... priorities should be switched from 'passive' to 'active' measures, in other words, that policy should be changed from a static concept of income support and protection to a dynamic and future oriented one of 'investing in people'. (OECD, 1990, pp. 19–20)

Comparative international information about the relative expenditures on different types of labour market programmes for OECD countries shows that public expenditure on labour market programmes as a percentage of GDP varies widely, from as little as 0.16 per cent in Turkey to 5.71 per cent in Denmark (OECD, 1990, pp. 52–53). Within these extremes, Japan shows a relatively low value of 0.52 compared to 2.87 in France. Clearly, the percentage reflects a wide variety of factors, including the level of development of each country, the degree to which each has a labour market problem and the priority that the government in question attaches to that problem. Again the ratios of 'active' labour market measures versus 'income maintenance' measures vary significantly. Amongst the countries distinguished, the lowest ratio is 0.23 for Australia and the highest is 0.46 in France. However, France, Germany, the UK and USA ratios do not differ enormously, ranging from 0.39 (USA) to 0.46 (France).

OECD (1990, pp. 8–10) outlined three areas of the (then) current concern in the labour market: (i) the reduction in the number of young people; (ii) the impact of new technologies increasing the skill intensity of jobs, requiring skilled, versatile workers undertaking training and retraining throughout their working lives; (iii) restructuring and the need to counter long-term unemployment. To this end, OECD discusses three main areas of policy: (i) 'mobilizing labour supply' – involving active measures such as training, placement and rehabilitation programmes for the unemployed, the inactive and those on welfare, in order to give greater equality of opportunity and to break dependency cycles; (ii) 'developing employment-related skills' – reducing the size of emerging skill gaps, by developing new relationships with the education system and reinforcing the key role of the private sector in human resource development; (iii) 'promoting a spirit of active search' – providing a sufficient range of efficient job-seekers' services for both individuals and firms, emphasizing the career development of individuals and forward-looking human resource management in firms.

3 Labour market policies in the UK

3.1 General macro policies

The early post-war view was that governments needed to intervene in the economy in order to achieve 'full employment'. This view was based upon Keynesian theory and embodied, for example, in the famous UK White Paper on Employment Policy published in 1945. Broadly speaking, this represented the conventional wisdom in the UK at least until the late 1960s and perhaps, with increasing unease, until the late 1970s. Under this approach, the role of government was generally considered to be one of managing the level of aggregate demand using fiscal policy, broadly speaking – counteracting recessions by general reflation and booms by deflationary measures.

The 1970s were a period of policy flux and change. There was growing evidence of the UK's lack of success *vis-à-vis* its main industrial competitors, for example in terms of the growth of income; it was a period of considerable tension and dispute with a union movement that had grown in size, power and militancy; there were important trade and budgetary problems; in addition, the old mechanisms for controlling the economy simply appeared to give rise to high levels of inflation. It is not surprising, therefore, that the late 1970s and early 1980s saw a seed change both in the political climate and in the development of alternative theoretical models, in the form of 'Monetarism' and the 'New Classical Economics'. Broadly speaking the result was an increased scepticism about the ability of government successfully to intervene, at least in a direct and fairly general way – a change which has radically changed the prevailing ideas about government policy with regard to employment.

More recently, therefore, direct government intervention, where it has been used at all, has more often taken the form of 'selective employment measures' rather than general reflation or deflation. In practice, this appears to have meant that there have been times when the government might have successfully intervened in the more traditional way – we saw, for example, in Chapter 29, that there was a significant level of demand deficiency in the economy in the early 1980s. Nevertheless, as a result of the shift in policy, there have been a large number of more targeted 'labour market programmes', as well as important changes in the regulatory framework.

These programmes can be regarded as having at least three objectives: (i) to reduce the overall level of unemployment; (ii) to overcome imperfections in the workings of the labour market, particularly related to training; and (iii) to enhance the long-term prospects of participants to produce a fair distribution of employment and training opportunities across the population. It is possible to see that the UK has broadly followed the OECD pattern outlined above, involving: changes in the regulatory framework alongside the use of labour market programmes; a shift from 'passive' to active labour market policies.

It is not clear that the policy shift from broad, macro measures to selective employment measures has, so far, produced the desired results. The control of the economy via monetary policy seemed no more capable of delivering sustained growth than Keynesian policies, at least in the hands of politicians with a four-year time horizon dictated by election needs. As we have discussed at various stages during the book, the UK economy became increasingly cyclical. Periods of strong growth were interspersed with reversals, some of which led to extremely damaging negative periods of growth. The effects on skill shortages and inflation on the one hand, and unemployment on the other, were fairly transparent – the effect of the massive structural change in the economy, which undermined the relevance of hard-earned skills and the associated training infrastructure, was less obvious, but, in retrospect, no less important. Both the human capital theory (Part V) and the 'new growth theories' (Part VIII) appear to be telling the same story – there are increasing returns to education and training, which are not picked up in the individual decision process, causing the privately determined level of investment to be less than the social optimum. It is not clear that TECS, LECS or any of the other institutional changes seem likely to act as a sufficiently comprehensive infrastructure, delivering the required level and quality of training.

3.2 Wage and employment subsidies

Historically, wage subsidies have represented an important part of selective employment policies. At different times, various governments have experimented with most forms of wage or employment subsidy. While it is probably fair to say that current UK governments would reject most, if not all, of the following measures, it is nevertheless important to report the lessons learnt.

The three principal forms are general, recruitment and marginal subsidies. General subsidies effectively apply to all the employed and, therefore, such schemes provide substantial 'windfall gains' to employers. As the funds are spread very thinly a relatively small number of unemployed gain jobs and the benefits of reduced unemployment are small relative to the overall size of the subsidy. Recruitment subsidies apply to the wages of newly hired workers and there is an incentive for firms to increase their labour turnover to continue receiving the subsidy, rather than create extra employment. Marginal subsidies are payments based upon changes to the stock of employed persons and apply only to the cost of those hired above a given base level of employment. It is generally considered that marginal wage subsidies are, in theory, superior to other forms of subsidies.

On the face of it, the policy of marginal wage subsidies appears to have considerable potential, particularly where labour demand is highly responsive to wage changes. However, a major problem arises when establishing the 'displacement' and other, 'general equilibrium' effects of such policies. While firms may be induced to employ extra labour (of particular types when the marginal wage subsidies are targeted at particular groups, e.g. youth), these may lead to reductions in employment elsewhere. Unless aggregate demand rises at least by as much as the extra output produced by the subsidized workers, employment will decline elsewhere. In other words, subsidized firms gain a competitive advantage over the non-subsidized which leads to lay-offs (or reductions in new hires). In an open economy the effects may be at the expense of overseas workers (rather than domestic), and wage subsidies become equivalent to export subsidies. In addition, some proportion of wage subsidies accrue as 'windfall gains' to employers, insofar as firms receive subsidies for labour they would have hired anyway – representing a deadweight welfare loss. Research into the size of displacement and windfall effects of wage subsidy schemes have typically led to the conclusion that they are quite large. For example, a government evaluation of the UK Youth Employment Subsidy estimated windfall gains of around 75 per cent and net employment gains of little more than 10 per cent.

The Temporary Short Time Working Scheme, which replaced the Temporary Employment Subsidy, represented an alternative approach to reducing unemployment – that of cutting labour supply. Whereas the TES averted redundancies by subsidizing firms to keep workers on to produce output, the

TSTWS averted redundancies by subsidizing firms not to produce output. Policies of this kind, which tend to subsidize leisure rather than work, are sometimes referred to as 'worksharing' and, within the broad range of such policies, are early retirement, increased annual leave and sabbaticals. It is sometimes argued that unsubsidized reduced working time can help to reduce unemployment, but the case for this is hard to prove. Reduced working hours without commensurate reductions in pay lead to increased hourly labour costs and increased unit production costs, with offsetting reductions in labour demand. Whether working time reductions with commensurate reductions in pay can be exogenously imposed on unwilling workers is doubtful.

An alternative employment policy is public sector job creation, which effectively involves a 100 per cent employment subsidy. Such programmes are sometimes used, for example, as a source of employment for the most disadvantaged section of the labour force. Sheltered employment of the disabled has some of the characteristics of this type of job creation. However, subject to one or two special cases, most European countries have tended to shy away from direct job creation over recent decades for a number of reasons: the policy is relatively expensive compared with subsidies; jobs tend to be temporary; they do not integrate workers into the labour market; and they are not an efficient way of producing public sector output.

It can be seen that there are considerable doubts surrounding the efficiency arguments for selective employment measures of the type discussed in this section. There was a general recognition that, at best, they were a short-term, stop-gap measure and were certainly not a source of long-term employment creation. The principal case for such measures appears to hinge on equity grounds. That is, they can be used to improve the welfare of those most disadvantaged in the labour force.

3.3 Policies to reduce wage pressure

The first rationale was the 'wage theorem' view, arising from the work of Keynes. Measurement in the *General Theory* was done in terms of variables measured in 'wage units' which Keynes intended (most of the time) as being in 'real' terms. This leads to the implication that a rise in money wages would be accompanied by an equiproportional rise in prices (and in the money supply) – the so-called 'wage theorem'. Keynes characterized the issue of the determination of money wages as a 'political rather than an economic problem', a view developed by Kalecki, Robinson and Worswick who argued that interunion rivalry makes it impossible for the lesson that higher wages means higher prices to be learned by the actors, and encourages an inflationary spiral. According to this view a wage policy is required and its successful formulation requires a degree of centralization of union bargaining. Essentially, the costs of pursuing an inflationary spiral must somehow be endogenized to the actors.

The discovery of the Phillips curve seemed for a while to deal a severe blow to the wage theorem view. Keynesians were heartened by the discovery which seemed to fill a missing box in the Keynesian system and to endogenize the money wage. A stable, steeply sloped Phillips curve dispenses with the need for an incomes policy because moderate demand management policies can then bring about jointly 'acceptable' levels of inflation and unemployment. Notwithstanding, incomes policies were pursued by practical politicians, and their role was defended by economists by reference to the Phillips curve! Lipsey and Parkin (1970), for example, argued that incomes policy shifted and swivelled the Phillips curve in such a way as to reduce wage inflation at low levels of unemployment (but to increase it at higher levels of unemployment!). With the discovery of the instability of the Phillips curve in the late 1960s and 1970s there was a reassertion of the 'wage theorem' and renewed enthusiasm for incomes policy on that basis.

However, alongside the reassertion of the 'wage theorem' came the alternative, augmented Phillips curve literature, in which the position of the short-run Phillips curve depends on inflationary expectations. As Chapter 29 above demonstrated, under these circumstances, if money illusion is absent, there is a 'natural rate' of unemployment which is compatible with any steady rate of inflation, with no long-run trade-off between inflation and unemployment. However, the case for incomes policy can still be made if the formation of inflationary expectations is sensitive to such a policy. If an incomes policy can reduce inflationary expectations, then the cost of an inflation control programme in terms of lost output and employment can be reduced, especially if the short-run Phillips curve has a shallow slope. Artis argued that a specific form of incomes policy suggested by the expectational argument is that of *indexation*:

> The rationale is that an offer of indexation can 'buy out' the incubus of unduly high inflation expectations (such as

> would be generated by adaptive expectations in a period of accelerating inflation), and so reduce the employment and output cost of an inflation control programme. (Artis, 1981, p. 12)

If expectations are rational and if it is rational to take the view that incomes policy will be unsuccessful, however, the case for incomes policy is obviously greatly weakened.

Another rationale for incomes policy based on the augmented Phillips curve is one which is directed at reducing the NAIRU. It has been argued that union power has raised the NAIRU and incomes policy could be an instrument for reversing this. Artis concludes, however, that

> The chances of incomes policy being successful in such an endeavour are not obviously large, for what seems to be at stake is a willingness to see incomes policy as a means of reducing the power of unions to raise real wages and so to reduce employment. If unions are to be involved in the implementation of the policy, the employment costs of their actions must be internalised to them, and it is not clear how this is to be achieved. (Artis, 1981, p. 14)

Layard, writing at about the same time as Artis, stressed this aspect of incomes policy, and went on to claim that only a permanent incomes policy can substantially reduce the NAIRU. To do this he proposed an incomes policy that works by incentive rather than by regulation, specifically a tax on wage increases, or 'tax-based incomes policies'.

Support for incomes policy can also be found in the 'real wage resistance hypothesis' which suggests that nominal wage inflation is the outcome of a process in which unions endeavour to secure a path of *real* after-tax wages. Nominal wages respond positively to a rise in actual and expected inflation and to a rise in the actual or expected 'tax'. In this view a permanent reduction in inflationary pressure can occur only if incomes policy or unemployment experience induces a long-lasting reduction in aspiration real wages or an increase in the capacity of the economy to deliver higher real wages. Of special concern here is that the incomes policy may have a perverse effect by encouraging an increase in real wage aspirations on the removal of the policy. If, however, incomes policy can have a long-term 'educating effect' it can be viewed as an alternative to a permanently higher unemployment level. The real wage hypothesis also suggests a role for fiscal policy in inflation control. Changes in the tax ratio may be offered to reduce inflationary pressure.

The distributional aspects of incomes policy are also important. First, incomes policy often has an effect on wage differentials. Second, those who argue for incomes policy as a method of reducing the NAIRU aim to reduce real wages, which raises a distributional issue between capitalists and the employed, and the employed and the unemployed.

Incomes policies also influence productivity and efficiency. In this sense, while incomes policies distort resource allocation, particularly through its effects on the labour market, there may be some countervailing gains in productivity.

Many Western economies have employed incomes policies from time to time during the post-war period. Even the USA, which is generally viewed as one of the more extreme free market economies, experimented over the period 1962 to 1971, culminating in the wage freeze of 1971. The UK had a statutory incomes policy (1966 to 1970 and 1972 to 1974), compulsory policies (1975 to 1977) and a whole series of voluntary policies (1948 to 1950, 1961 to 1962 and 1977 to 1979). Evidence about their success is mixed. While there is some evidence that they have been beneficial in some economies, the general view is that, in the UK, they were, at best, a temporary measure. As we saw in Chapter 27, UK policy has headed in quite a different direction since the Thatcher Government of 1979, with reduced union power and reductions in unionization, and the removal of the Wages Councils. Successive Conservative governments have encouraged competition both in product markets (with deregulation, privatization and the reduction and removal of trade barriers) and labour markets (with increased part-time, temporary, casual and self-employment). The Conservative governments have also been keen to reduce the magnitude of non-wage labour costs ('on-costs'). On the other hand, the reduction in union power, amongst other things, has allowed the UK government to keep tight control over the growth of incomes in the public sector.

3.4 Human capital: education and training

We dealt with many of the education and training issues and programmes in Part V and earlier chapters from this, Part VIII of the book. The pervasive case study evidence that accumulated, mainly from the work of the National Institute for Economic and Social Research, pointed to a training failure – primarily, though not exclusively, at the intermediate skill level. We have followed this up to show how skill gaps and shortages have crucial consequences for successful innovation and the long-term performance of the economy. There have been some major question marks over UK policy in this area.

As an overview, it seems that the early training schemes were characterized by a number of significant problems. They appeared to be more a response to the political problem of, first, youth unemployment and, second, a more general growth in long-term unemployment. The early schemes were heavily criticized for their lack of any real training component. These initial policy interventions did little to stay or reverse the deterioration of the training infrastructure in the private sector. The apprentice system continued to decay, despite the attempt to prop it up using the Youth Training Scheme to fund the first year or two of training. The Industry Training Boards, which the funding firms claimed had been undermined by cross-sector poaching, were allowed to wither and then die. They were eventually replaced, around 1990–1991, by Training and Enterprise Councils and Local Enterprise Companies, which, being locally based, were likely to overcome some of the mobility issues. However, the tripartite governance and (outside of key government programmes – which TECS and LECS provide) largely voluntary nature of these institutions have not resulted in a major stimulus to training.

The attempts to open up access to both further and higher education have certainly dramatically increased staying-on rates in recent years. After some débâcles with the introduction of a National Curriculum – and the turmoil and unease that this caused in the education system – the policy of introducing General National Vocational Qualifications, coupled with the attempt to introduce a more rational and harmonized system of post-school further educational vocational qualifications (i.e. through the National Council for Vocational Qualifications), has met, at least in principle, with more favourable reactions. While there are clearly some advances compared with the 1980s, worries remain over the general issue of the maintenance and increase of standards of education and training in the UK (especially with increased throughput and little, if any, real increase in resource). There is also a question mark over what is a largely supply side policy, concerning where these more qualified individuals are going to find employment. We saw in Chapters 16 and 17 that the major expansion of higher education from the mid-1960s significantly reduced the returns to education. From what we have already said, increased supply may, up to a point, create its own demand – Says' Law; however, a more balanced set of policies may be required. We return to this issue below.

3.5 Labour market regulation, institutions and flexibility

One of the clear lessons of international comparisons is that there are distinct differences in the way in which labour markets operate in different countries. These differences arise from the historical evolution of each country, bearing in mind its culture, politics and institutions. It has long been recognized that such cultural, social and economic differences make it impossible simply to transplant the methods and policies of one economy into another. It is not possible, for example, directly to remould UK manufacturing organization, management and technology identically on the 'Japanese model' (even insofar as some 'typical' model exists). On the other hand, it is possible for one economy to learn from another and transplant suitably modified systems.

Over the past decades, all European countries have introduced institutional changes with a view to improving their labour market and, thereby, their macro performance. To varying degrees, these changes have had the aim of increased labour market flexibility:

> Governments and employers' organisations then turned their attention to the labour market, where they saw inbuilt factors of rigidity (e.g. restrictive working practices, job demarcation, fixed working hours, labour costs, lack of education and training) resulting in economic stumbling blocks which had to be removed to regain a competitive advantage, to re-establish profit margins, to stimulate growth and thereby to create new jobs. (Sarfati and Kobrin, 1988, p. 1)

Sarfati and Kobrin, writing in an international context, see 1984 as something of a watershed in this development. Prior to 1984, they argue, increased flexibility was simply seen as a mechanism for limiting the growth of unemployment during a period of major restructuring. After 1984, however, although containment of unemployment remained a significant issue, the emphasis changed to one of improvements in productivity, work patterns organization and the internal social environment within the company (Sarfati and Kobrin, 1988, p. 2). While the broader issues were likely to have emerged anyway, they were almost certainly stimulated by the economic growth that took place in the second half of the 1980s, moving unemployment further down the policy agenda.

There are a variety of dimensions of flexibility highlighted in the literature, including a number already touched upon in this and earlier chapters. These include: (i) Pay – the greater flexibility of wages, with the reduction of indexation, more decentralized and individual bargaining and, as a consequence, more diversified pay rates, which are more performance related. (ii) Employment contracts – the reduction in the 'traditional' full-time, permanent contracts, and the growth in: temporary, casual and part-time working; sub-contracting and self-employment. (iii) Working time – the movement away from a standard five day 40 hour working week, towards reduced hours of work; greater flexibility of hours; differences between hours contracted and worked and between hours paid and worked; decoupling of employee hours and capital operating time; growth in shiftworking; increases in unsocial times of work. (iv) Work organization – the movement away from single-skilled, demarcated jobs, towards: multi-skilling; team working; quality chains; continuous or lifelong training.

While the pressures for such change may have been widespread internationally, this movement appears to have taken place more quickly and is therefore significantly more advanced in the UK than many of its European partners. A succession of Conservative governments in the UK, for example, has been instrumental in introducing a sequence of institutional changes with a view to increased flexibility and liberalization. Some of these have not been aimed specifically at the labour market, such as the privatization of previously nationalized industries. Nevertheless, these have resulted in important labour market consequences (such as the impact on productivity and employment, as well as the concentration on core commercial activities and sub-contracting). Other changes have been more specifically targeted at the labour market. This is perhaps epitomized by the changes in trade union legislation which, in fact, began prior to the Thatcher Government of 1979. However, there are innumerable other examples, including: the erosion and eventual removal of the Wages Council; the removal of protection for women and young workers from night working; the negotiation of an opt-out clause from the Social Chapter; the passing of the Sunday Trading Bill, which allows small shops to open all day on Sundays and the larger retailers to open for a maximum of six hours; reductions in factory legislation.

The UK approach over the last few decades appears to be more consistent with ensuring 'flexibility in the labour market' as opposed to 'the flexibility of the workforce'. An example of this, which we discussed earlier in Part VIII, was the freeing up of external labour markets in the UK, such that, as a firm's skill needs changed over time, it could, at relatively low cost, remove those workers with redundant skills and hire new employees with appropriate skills; on the other hand, a German or Japanese company would be more likely to look to the flexibility of its existing workforce, coupled with additional training, without resort to the external labour market. Again, this appears to place a greater onus on some form of external infrastructure for training in the UK – which may not exist, at least in a form which is adequate to meet the additional strains placed upon it.

It seems that 'flexibilization' of the labour market is a policy response which allows the adopting economy to adjust to major structural changes, enabling a higher proportion of individuals to find some form of employment. The evidence from the UK is that this occurs through their transfer into relatively low-skilled/low-technology jobs, historically, at least, located in the service sector. There is probably some element of truth in arguing that the flexibilization of the labour market in the UK has lead it more in the direction of being a low-skilled/low-technology economy, while other countries have attempted to move in exactly the opposite direction – towards the high-skilled/high-technology end of the spectrum. The coexistence of the two types of economy is reconciled through the quality of products they offer, the prices paid and relative incomes received. These two types of economy have quite different trajectories – the former being a 'dead-end' and the latter 'open ended'. We have already pointed to the increasing inequality of incomes in the UK, mirroring US experience. There is growing evidence that the market for the lower-skilled jobs is in excess supply, a situation which the growing international trade in services can only make more acute unless the UK proves more competitive in these product areas than occurred in manufacturing.

Finally, we return to the theme we developed at the beginning of this sub-section – we clearly do learn from our international competitors. This learning process has been greatly aided by the location of foreign, particularly Japanese, multinationals' productive capacity in the UK. It is important to acknowledge that part of the reason for this can be traced to the relatively high skilled labour that can be found in abundance in some localities, relatively low labour costs, a lack of restrictions and a high degree of flexibility. The combination of an educated and qualified workforce, enabling and encouraging the diffusion of other countries' technologies, has provèd a successful, if limited, strategy – one that has proved even more successful in other countries, such as Singapore. However, it is a limited strategy, with some worrying aspects. The indications are that foreign multinational companies which come to the UK may find the government subsidies, availability of greenfield sites and access to European markets, amongst other things, equally important. Indeed, a number of surveys have suggested that the amount of training such companies do generally exceeds their UK domestic counterparts. While there is nothing wrong with the strategy *per se*, it perhaps leaves the UK over-reliant on foreign sources of technology, know-how and investment – which becomes more uncertain if (or when) UK income levels begin to approach those to be found in the foreign investor's home base. Our earlier discussion in the book suggested that long-term job opportunities in the UK would be improved by an increased flow of indigenous new products, on which an export offensive could be based.

References

Artis, M. (1981). 'Incomes Policies: Some Rationales'. In J.L. Fallick and R.F. Elliot (eds) *Incomes Policies, Inflation and Relative Pay*. London: George Allen and Unwin, pp. 6–22.

Lipsey, R.G. and J.M. Parkin (1970). 'Incomes Policy: A Reappraisal'. *Economica*, May.

OECD (1990). *Labour Market Policies for the 1990s*. Paris: OECD.

Sarfati, H. and C. Kobrin (eds) (1988). *Labour Market Flexibility: a Comparative Anthology*. Aldershot: Gower Press.

Index